IN A PURE MUSLIM LAND

ISLAMIC CIVILIZATION

AND MUSLIM NETWORKS

Carl W. Ernst and Bruce B. Lawrence, editors

Highlighting themes with historical as well as contemporary significance, Islamic Civilization and Muslim Networks features works that explore Islamic societies and Muslim peoples from a fresh perspective, drawing on new interpretive frameworks or theoretical strategies in a variety of disciplines. Special emphasis is given to systems of exchange that have promoted the creation and development of Islamic identities—cultural, religious, or geopolitical. The series spans all periods and regions of Islamic civilization.

A complete list of titles published in this series appears at the end of the book.

In a Pure Muslim Land

SHIʿISM BETWEEN PAKISTAN AND THE MIDDLE EAST

Simon Wolfgang Fuchs

THE UNIVERSITY OF NORTH CAROLINA PRESS *Chapel Hill*

Manufactured in the United States of America
Set in Huronia by Tseng Information Systems, Inc.

The University of North Carolina Press has been a
member of the Green Press Initiative since 2003.

Cover illustration: Shiʿi posters in Lahore, Pakistan, 2013.
Photograph by Simon Wolfgang Fuchs.

Library of Congress Cataloging-in-Publication Data
Names: Fuchs, Simon Wolfgang, 1982– author.
Title: In a pure Muslim land : Shiʿism between Pakistan and
the Middle East / Simon Wolfgang Fuchs.
Description: Chapel Hill : The University of North Carolina
Press, [2019] | Series: Islamic civilization and Muslim networks
Identifiers: LCCN 2018045750| ISBN 9781469649788 (cloth : alk. paper) |
ISBN 9781469649795 (pbk : alk. paper) | ISBN 9781469649801 (ebook)
Subjects: LCSH: Shiʿah—Pakistan. | Islam—Pakistan. | Shiʿah—Middle
East. | Islam—Middle East.
Classification: LCC BP192.7.P18 F83 2019 | DDC 297.8/2095491—dc23
LC record available at https://lccn.loc.gov/2018045750

A substantial part of the argument in chapter 4 was first developed
in Simon Wolfgang Fuchs, "Third Wave Shiʿism: Sayyid ʿArif Husain
al-Husaini and the Islamic Revolution in Pakistan," *Journal of the
Royal Asiatic Society* 24, no. 3 (2014): 493–510.

For Andreas and Alexander, who kept their promises

CONTENTS

Acknowledgments ix

Abbreviations xiii

Note on Transliteration xv

Introduction: Alternative Centers of Shiʿi Islam 1

1 All-Indian Shiʿism, Colonial Modernity, and the Challenge of Pakistan 16

2 Theology, Sectarianism, and the Limits of Reform: *The Making of Shiʿism in the Land of the Pure* 53

3 Projections and Receptions of Religious Authority: *Grand Ayatollahs and Pakistan's Shiʿi "Periphery"* 95

4 Khomeini's Perplexed Pakistani Men: *Importing and Debating the Iranian Revolution since 1979* 119

5 Longing for the State: *Dialectics of the Local and the Transnational in Sunni-Shiʿi Sectarianism* 152

Conclusion: South Asia, the Middle East, and Muslim Transnationalism 186

Glossary 193

Notes 199

Bibliography 275

Index 335

ILLUSTRATIONS

MAPS

South Asia and the Middle East xviii

Pakistan xix

FIGURES

The Qatalgah complex in Skardu 11

Detail of a Muharram procession in Islamabad, 2013 65

Library of the Sultan al-Madaris madrasa in Sargodha 78

Photo shop in Najaf, Iraq 103

Cover of the journal *al-Muntazar*, 20 February 1972 116

ACKNOWLEDGMENTS

Thankfully, transnational scholarship is no lonely, solely text-focused affair. While dusty rooms, ink-stained fingers, and crumbling pages are the bread and butter of such an endeavor, I was fortunate to receive the help of countless institutions and individuals. In Pakistan, I am especially grateful to the late Sayyid ʿArif Husayn Naqvi, who welcomed me into his stunning private library, which stands as a testimony to his dedication in cataloging the intellectual heritage of the subcontinent's Shiʿi community. During the early days of research Zill-i-Hasnayn gave his full endorsement to all my shy requests for scanning Shiʿi journals in the Punjab Public Library. Later on, ʿAzraʾ ʿUsman, the library's new director, was equally supportive of my project. Sayyid Riyaz Husayn Najafi, principal of the Jamiʿat al-Muntazar in Lahore, did not hesitate to grant me the permission to freely explore the seminary's book stacks. Muhammad Husayn Akbar, principal of the Idarah-i Minhaj al-Husayn in Lahore, provided me with liberal access to the many treasures housed in the school. Irshad Nasir, former editor of the journal *al-ʿArif*, personally retrieved for me all of its issues, along with those of its predecessor, *Rah-i ʿAmal*. Saqib Akbar was always generous with telephone numbers and arranging contacts in Karachi, Lahore, and Qum. Muhammad Husayn Najafi Dhakko was not only willing to squeeze an interview into his tight scholarly schedule but also allowed me to utilize the library of the Sultan al-Madaris madrasa in Sargodha. The late Sayyid Muhammad Saqalayn Kazimi and the wide collection of Shiʿi reformist works available in his Islamic Book Centre in Islamabad were essential for the project.

I am greatly indebted to the conversations I had with Hameed Haroon, Sayyid ʿAli Hasan Naqvi, Dr. Muhammad Hasan Rizvi, Professor Zahid ʿAli Zahidi, Sayyid Zamir Akhtar Naqvi, and Dr. ʿAqil Musa in Karachi. Muhammad Hasan Jaʿfari, Shaykh Ahmad Nuri, and Taqi Akhundzadah were generous with their time in Skardu, as were Murtaza Pooya in Islamabad and Sayyid Nisar ʿAli al-Husayni al-Tirmizi and Dr. Suheyl Umar in Lahore. Sayyid ʿAbbas Rizvi of the Iranian Cultural Center in Lahore granted me the permission to browse the shelves there, and Hamid ʿAli, senior librarian of the Oriental Section in the Punjab

University Library, was exceptionally helpful in making Shiʿi journals and printed works available to me.

In India, I enjoyed working with the staff of the Nehru Memorial Library, the Aligarh University Library, and the Iranian Cultural Centre New Delhi. I am grateful to Razak Khan and Professor ʿAziz al-Din Husayn, who made my trip to Rampur and its splendid Raza Library incredibly rewarding. Ali and Amir Khan of Mahmudabad provided a thrilling afternoon at the library of the Mahmudabad estate.

In the United Kingdom, I have incurred debts to Mirza Hasan Pooya, Hasan Riza Ghadiri, Robert Gleave, Jan-Peter Hartung, and Morgan Clarke. Justin Jones and Ali Usman Qasmi gave my research a boost early on by inviting me to present at the conference "Shiʿa Islam in Modern South Asia: An Interdisciplinary Perspective," which was held at Royal Holloway in September 2011. I would like to express a special word of gratitude to Faisal Devji for providing constant encouragement along the way.

My research trip to Iran was kindly and professionally facilitated by Hidayat Yusifi of Mofid University. In Qum, I benefited tremendously from the activities of the Markaz-i Ihyaʾ-i Asar-i Barr-i Saghir and especially Sayyid Saghir ʿAbbas Naqvi, who provided me with digital copies of many late colonial Shiʿi works produced in India. The more contemporary holdings of Qum's Urdu library Kitabkhanah-i ʿAllamah Iqbal Lahori, which were made accessible to me by its director, Muhammad Hasan Sharifi, served as a very useful complement. The Library of Grand Ayatollah Husayn Burujirdi was a treasure trove for Pakistani Shiʿi journals.

Shaykh ʿAli Najafi was instrumental in making my journey to Iraq possible. I am grateful for our conversations in Najaf and for arranging a meeting with his father, Grand Ayatollah Bashir Husayn Najafi, who took the time to answer all my questions about transnational Shiʿism. It was a distinct pleasure to work in Najaf's libraries, most of all in the Maktabat al-Imam al-Hakim, especially thanks to the hospitality of Sayyid Jawad al-Hakim.

These extensive research trips between the United States, Europe, the Middle East, and South Asia were possible only through the unwavering generosity of various funding bodies. Princeton University and its Department of Near Eastern Studies have supported this project in an unconditional manner and over many years. I am particularly grateful for a Whiting Fellowship and indebted to the Princeton Institute for International and Regional Studies (PIIRS) for multiple grants. I also would like to thank the Deutsche Morgenländische Gesellschaft for a research stipend. Gonville and Caius College in Cambridge proved to be a very conducive environment that helped me to further develop the manuscript during a research fellowship.

But sitting in front of a digital and physical heap of texts in Urdu, Arabic, and Persian alone would not have equipped me with the necessary encouragement and the intellectual tools to imagine, commence, and finally craft this monograph. The input, guidance, and criticism of colleagues and friends fills the following pages. Muhammad Qasim Zaman kept pushing me to engage those issues, time periods, and geographical locations which I initially preferred to avoid. He provided gentle challenges whenever I was bent on taking a shortcut. In hindsight, I regard those chapters and parts which took me beyond the familiar and the accessible as the most rewarding and convincing contributions of this monograph. My project has also gained tremendously from the scholarly exchanges with Mirjam Künkler. Her collaboration with Morgan Clark of the University of Oxford led to two very productive meetings dealing with the topic "Traditional Authority and Transnational Religious Networks in Contemporary Shīʿī Islam." This forum enabled me to discuss my work with Sabrina Mervin, Chiara Formichi, Elvire Corboz, Edith Szanto, Katie Manbachi, Philip Bruckmayr, Mara Leichtman, Andrew Newman, and Roy Motahedeh. Likewise, I am very much indebted to Andreas Rieck, who was willing to share with me his manuscript (not yet published) on Pakistan's Shiʿi minority. Rieck's truly pioneering research informed my own choices and approaches and made the project as a whole much more feasible. I am grateful for the support I have received from Rainer Brunner, Werner Ende, Naveeda Khan, and the late Mariam Abou Zahab, as well as Christophe Jaffrelot, who repeatedly gave me the opportunity to present my findings in Paris. Working with Elaine Maisner and everyone at UNC Press has been a truly rewarding, professional, and all-around enjoyable experience.

Finally, there are too many dear friends and family members to mention. They welcomed me under their roofs—often for very extended stays—during my sojourns between the United States and South Asia. They helped me stay grounded, opened their ears and hearts, hiked the Alps with me, let me borrow their bikes, spoke wisdom, sat with me around the campfire, shared treats in various beer gardens, and kept me up-to-date in terms of vinyl and fiction. You know who you are and how you and your children continuously enrich my life. And of course, a thank-you beyond words to Maria for all these years.

ABBREVIATIONS

AISC	All India Shiʿa Conference
AISPC	All India Shiʿa Political Conference
APSC	All Pakistan Shiʿa Conference
ISO	Imamia Students Organisation
ITHS	Idarah-i Tahaffuz-i Huquq-i Shiʿa (Organization for the Protection of Shiʿi Rights)
JI	Jamaʿat-i Islami (Islamic Society; an Islamist party)
JUH	Jamʿiyyat al-ʿUlamaʾ-i Hind (Organization of the Religious Scholars of India, primarily a Deobandi organization)
JUI	Jamʿiyyat al-ʿUlamaʾ-i Islam (Organization of the Religious Scholars of Islam, primarily a Deobandi organization)
ML	Muslim League
PPP	Pakistan People's Party
SSP	Sipah-i Sahabah-i Pakistan (Army of the Companions of the Prophet)
TI	Tahrik-i Istiqlal (Independence Movement)
TNFJ	Tahrik-i Nifaz-i Fiqh-i Jaʿfariyya (Movement for the Implementation of Jaʿfari Law)
UP	United Provinces, today called Uttar Pradesh (state in northern India)

NOTE ON TRANSLITERATION

For the sake of readability, this book adopts a simplified form of transliteration in the main text. Only *ʿayn* and hamza are kept as diacritical markers. Terms in Urdu, Persian, and Arabic are italicized on first occurence. If they appear more than four times in the text, they are romanized therafter. For the notes and bibliography, I follow mostly the transliteration guidelines established by the *International Journal of Middle East Studies* (*IJMES*) for Arabic and Persian words. In order to transliterate Urdu texts, I applied the *IJMES* rules suggested for Persian. Retroflex consonants particular to Urdu (ٹ, ڈ, ڑ) are transliterated with one dot underneath (ṭ, ḍ, ṛ), instead of two dots as recommended, for example, by the Library of Congress system of romanization. Even though this gives rise to a certain ambiguity (the letters ط and ٹ are both rendered as ṭ and the [Arabic] transliteration for ض [ḍ] is identical to the transliteration for the Urdu letter ڈ), I am confident that the potential confusion is kept to a minimum. Similarly, and in order to make the transliteration not too burdensome, I have decided against transliterating the letter خ as <u>kh</u> (as in Persian *khūd*, "self"), which is supposed to clearly distinguish it from the aspirated Urdu form کھ (as in *khānā*, "food"). Both letters are transliterated simply as *kh*, and it is hoped that the specialist should have no trouble telling them apart in the specific contexts in which they appear. The letter چ is given as *c* (as in *cashm*, "eye") in order to separate it from the aspirated form *ch* (as in Urdu *chat*, "roof").

I transliterate vowels in Persian and Arabic words as a, *i*, *u*/ā, ī, *ū* and reserve e and o/ō for constructions specific to Urdu, such as *ke liye* (for) or the postposition *kō*, which denotes a direct object. Nasal vowels are rendered as ṉ following the vowel in question (as in *gāʾōṉ*, "village").

Persian and South Asian Muslim names are transliterated as they are pronounced in Persian and Urdu, e.g., Ṣanāʾullāh instead of Thanāʾullāh or Abū al-Fażl instead of Abū al-Faḍl. For major and well-known figures like Khomeini, Muhammad Ali Jinnah, or Zia ul-Haq I use the established Anglicized spelling of their names, but I fully transliterate the names of less famous figures. The same rule applies to the names of cities and places. Established Arabic religious and legal terms are spelled in the common Arabic transliteration (e.g., *madhhab*, instead of *maẕhab*). When an Urdu religious work has an Arabic title (a very common phenomenon), this title is transliterated following the *IJMES* rules pertaining to Arabic. The final hamza in the word *ʿulamā* (religious scholars) is usually omitted when the word appears alone but otherwise written out (e.g., *ʿUlamāʾ-i Islām*). English terms used in Urdu are not transliterated but written in their common, English spelling.

IN A PURE MUSLIM LAND

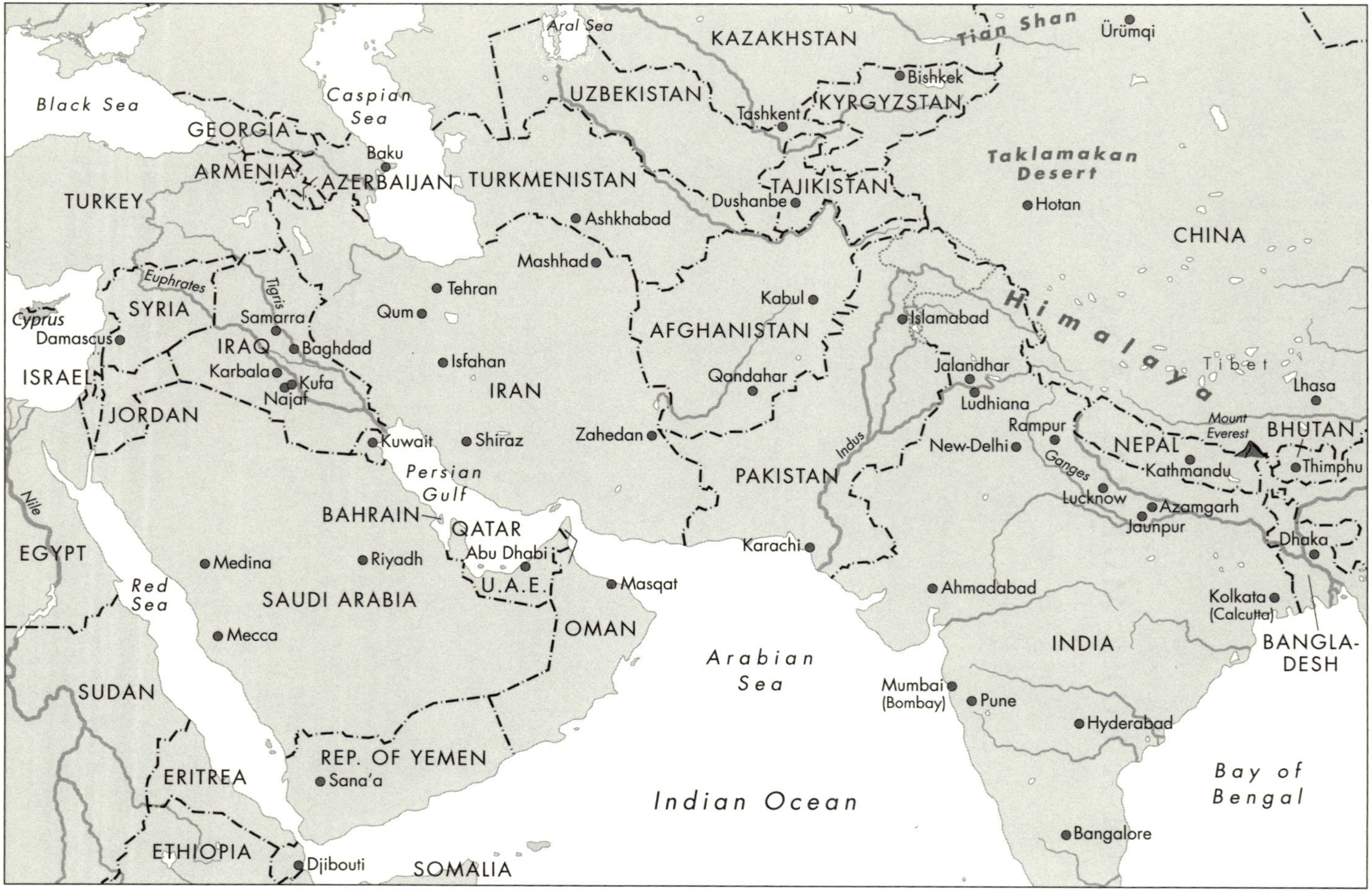

South Asia and the Middle East. © Peter Palm.

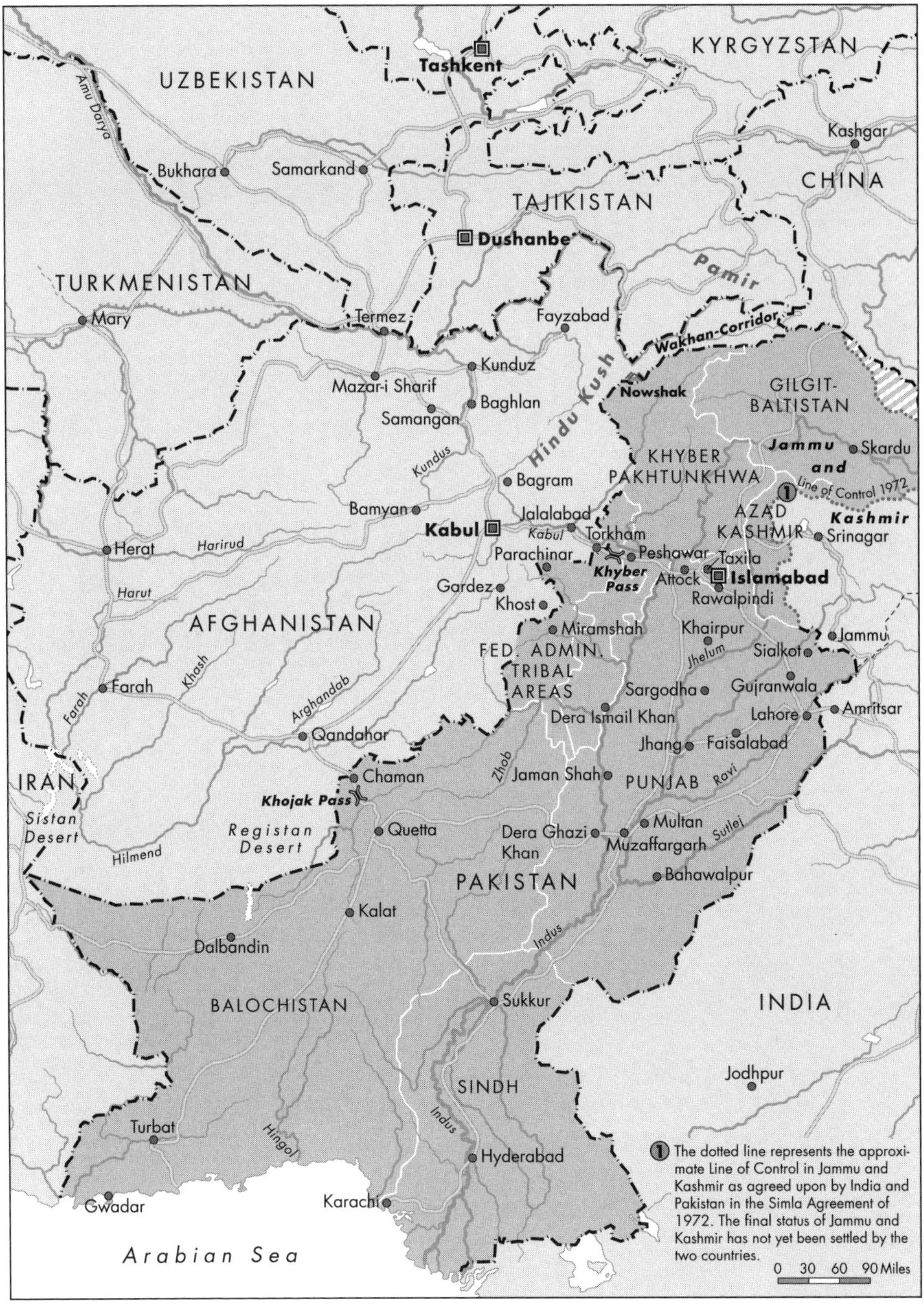

Pakistan. © Peter Palm.

INTRODUCTION

Alternative Centers of Shiʿi Islam

In the early twentieth century, the region that today makes up the Pakistani Punjab formed a veritable Shiʿi "periphery."[1] Looking back on his youth around the years of World War I, the Shiʿi preacher Sayyid Muhammad ʿArif Multani recalled in 1929 how he had been unable to locate even a single Shiʿi religious school (madrasa) near his hometown of Multan. Disappointed, he tossed aside any hope for further formal religious training. His father, however, offered him two crucial pieces of advice: first, he encouraged his son to enroll in a Sunni school instead. Pious dissimulation (*taqiyya*) was permissible in such a context. Muhammad ʿArif should apply this Shiʿi principle and model his praying and fasting on the Sunni way. He was also supposed to stay clear of any polemical debate that might reveal his true allegiance. Second, if his son ever fell into serious doubt about Shiʿi teachings, he should not hesitate to hasten to the holy city of Najaf in Iraq. At this global seat of Shiʿi learning, he would be able to study both Sunni and Shiʿi books and would come to realize who possessed the truth.

Muhammad ʿArif heeded his father's advice and enrolled in a local Sunni seminary in 1916. And here, according to his report, endless tribulations began. All his Sunni teachers knew about his family background and criticized him on a daily basis for clinging to such a despicable interpretation of Islam. They berated him and Shiʿis in general for denigrating the Companions of the Prophet Muhammad and for bowing during their processions in front of horses and mock graves of their Imams.[2] The employees of the madrasa where he studied threatened to expel Muhammad ʿArif if they ever found him praying in the Shiʿi way. Even switching institutions proved to be of no avail for the Shiʿi student. A letter from his former principal arrived only three days after his admission to a new school and disclosed his Shiʿi faith. Muhammad ʿArif kept his head down and endured the taunts until the school year was over and he finally obtained his diploma. His Sunni teachers felt vindicated and victorious. They were pleased that their Shiʿi student now publicly disassociated himself from his coreligionists. Yet Muhammad ʿArif could not bear it any longer. While his classmates moved on to the famous reformist seminary of Deoband, he knew that he had to seek out a purely Shiʿi environment.[3] Even though he felt not yet ready for the journey to Najaf, a remedy for his religious crisis was available in the subcontinent, too. Muhammad ʿArif made all the necessary arrangements and set out for the prestigious Nazimiyya seminary in Lucknow, then India's leading center of Shiʿi learning.[4] Writing from there, he lauded efforts under way to improve the bleak educational situation in the Punjab in general and in his hometown in particular. Already in 1925, the Shiʿi Bab al-ʿUlum school in Multan had opened its gates.[5] Over the next decades—and especially after the founding of Pakistan in 1947—the expansion of Shiʿi education accelerated significantly and put an end to the earlier marginality. In 2004, there existed 374 Shiʿi schools for male students and 84 for female students in Pakistan, with 218 and 55 respectively in the Punjab province alone.[6]

This book is concerned with the fundamental transformations of Shiʿi thought and conceptions of religious authority that occurred in tandem with the expansion of Shiʿi religious educational institutions in colonial India and Pakistan. Several of the issues that were salient for Sayyid Muhammad ʿArif Multani also guide my inquiry in the following chapters, which draw on fifteen months of archival fieldwork and interviews conducted in Pakistan, India, Iran, Iraq, and the UK. My research explores the implications of Shiʿi Islam in Pakistan being relegated to the periphery of the Shiʿi world in scholarship and often also in self-perception, even though the country is home to the second-largest Shiʿi community worldwide; only Iran has more Shiʿis. Francis Robinson has noted the general paradox that Shiʿis in South Asia have been "both highly visible but in scholarly terms largely invisible."[7] In Pakistan, a nation of more than 207 million people, Shiʿis constitute around 15 percent of the population and thus number more than 30 million individuals.[8] In the colonial period, Lucknow was a major Shiʿi center in its own right, one that produced generations of religious scholars qualified to exercise independent legal reasoning (*ijtihad*).[9] So far, however, the rich writings of Pakistani Shiʿis in Urdu have not been utilized to illuminate questions of religious authority, the relationship between Islam and modernity, or sectarianism. Instead, existing anthropological accounts tend to focus primarily on the variety of meanings Pakistani Shiʿis attribute to their religious rituals.[10] Contributions in the field of sociology have studied the shifting nature of Sunni-Shiʿi tensions and the impact of the Iranian Revolution in the country. These scholarly works have not considered, however, how these far-reaching developments are reflected and debated in textual sources produced by the Shiʿi community and their Sunni opponents.[11] While there is an excellent monograph on the historically troubled relationship between Shiʿi communal organizations and the Pakistani state,[12] the internal struggle over Shiʿi orthodoxy in Pakistan and its ties to the Middle East has received scant attention.[13]

Given this state of the field, I pay close attention to the impact of transnational flows of thought and transnational religious authority, which is a hallmark component of Twelver Shiʿism in the modern period. This book explores how the connections, interactions, and exchanges between South Asia and the Middle East have waxed and waned during the twentieth and twenty-first centuries. What consequences does it have for local religious authority in Pakistan that the most senior Shiʿi scholars, the *marajiʿ al-taqlid* (sing. *marjiʿ*, Source[s] of Emulation) do not reside in the subcontinent but instead in the shrine cities of the Middle East?[14] Through what networks are these grand ayatollahs and the preeminent Shiʿi seminaries connected to Pakistan? What sort of spaces have local South Asian religious scholars (*ʿulama*, sing. *ʿalim*) carved out for themselves? These questions touch on the ways in which religious ideas travel between the two regions and how they become adapted, contested, and reinterpreted in the process. Consequently, the book is also interested in how the Iranian Revolution of 1979 was perceived in Pakistan and how its impact has played out over the last decades. A further major concern of this study, and one which also comes to the fore in Sayyid Muhammad ʿArif's educational experience discussed over the previous pages, is the evolving nature of Sunni-Shiʿi sectarianism in both colonial India and Pakistan. How have arguments of exclusion changed over the course of time and what role has the Pakistani state played in this context? What is the transnational dimension of such polemics?

KEY ARGUMENTS: SECTARIANISM, TRANSNATIONAL CONNECTIONS, AND LOCAL AUTHORITY

Throughout the book, I make several innovative key arguments that relate to these dimensions of Shiʿi Islam in late colonial India and independent Pakistan. In the context of sectarianism, I hold that the interplay of Pakistan as a homeland for the Muslims of the Indian subcontinent and the Iranian Revolution fundamentally altered the thrust of Sunni-Shiʿi polemics. Building on recent revisionist scholarship on the conceptualization and envisioning of Pakistan, I show how the specter of sectarianism and the possibility of the creation of an exclusively Sunni state were perceived as deeply unsettling by Shiʿis in the 1940s.[15] This ideologically charged nation-state opened up unprecedented ways to imagine Islam and majority-minority relations. After the partition of India, both reformist and traditionalist Shiʿi scholars attempted to contain this dangerous potential. They strove to find common ground with the Sunnis by either emphasizing a law-based redefinition of Shiʿi identity or by propagating a Sufi-Shiʿi synthesis anchored in the subcontinent's Islamic scholarly and mystical tradition. Yet the downfall of the Shah in 1979 and the establishment of an Islamic Republic in Iran under the leadership of Shiʿi ʿulama brought the alternative and diametrically opposed Sunni Pakistani and Shiʿi Iranian visions of a modern Islamic state into sharp relief. This development led sectarian Deobandi actors in Pakistan to frame Shiʿi Islam as an inherent political problem for their vision of creating a model Islamic polity with a claim to global leadership. In a country whose name can be translated as "Land of the Pure," Shiʿis became denounced as a blemish. According to this view, they had no belonging and deserved no part in envisioning Pakistan's future.

As far as transnational Shiʿism is concerned, I question trends in the wider literature on modern Islam to either emphasize the wholesale adoption of specific models—imported from the "core lands"—in the "periphery," or, in stark contrast, to point to instances of contestations and outright rejection of the international dimension in various local Muslim contexts.[16] My point is that both approaches are unhelpful in understanding the complex negotiations of closeness and distance which are playing out for Pakistan's Shiʿis and Sunnis in their relationships to the Middle East. In order to appreciate these dynamics, it is necessary to tap hitherto unused sources. These allow me to investigate how local actors employ the Islamic scholarly tradition in their arguments, how they tie their claims to centers of scholarship, and how they vow to faithfully uphold such central authority only to subtly rework arguments emanating from there.[17] Ideas, after all, never travel unimpeded.[18] In this context, I regard an observation by Terje Østebø as highly illuminating. Østebø has formulated a concept of *impetus* and *response* with regard to the transnational flow of Salafi ideas. This method pays "attention to the strategies applied by such actors in appropriating and localising the *impetus*, and [. . .] entails an enterprise which integrates the factors and conditions, both local and translocal, relevant for its appropriation within the particular locality. Such an approach implies that the processes of change should be seen as embodied through situated actors, it recognises the active participation of such actors and the creativity of human agency in transmitting and appropriating outside influences."[19]

Throughout this book I show the substantially interrelated character of transnational *impetus* and domestic *response* for the Shiʿi community. Such dynamics manifested themselves inter alia in the ways both reformist scholars and their traditionalist, esoteric-minded opponents since the 1960s have called on authoritative voices in Iran and Iraq to bolster their own diverging interpretations of Shiʿi cosmology. Another example can be adduced in the form of the intensive debates over the emergence of a new and universal Source of Emulation in the 1970s. These provided local Pakistani ʿulama with an opportunity to substantially redefine the authority such a supreme scholar would hold.[20]

It is important to note that transnational ties always incorporate translation, too. Pakistani ʿulama acted as brokers between texts written in Arabic and Persian and the vernacular medium of Urdu.[21] This intermediary position enabled them to develop almost two personalities, as I show, among other examples, in the case of the anti-Shiʿi Salafi scholar Ihsan Ilahi Zahir.[22] He wrote most of his major works in Arabic but was also prolific in Urdu, a language his Saudi sponsors were neither able nor interested to understand. This catering to various audiences proved a useful strategy when Shiʿi scholars referred to the Islamic scholarly tradition of the subcontinent. In premodern India, Qur'anic commentaries, works of Islamic law, and Sufi tracts were usually composed in Persian (and less often in Arabic). These texts hence qualify as foreign territory to the modern Pakistani reader, too. By claiming to merely provide a summary and faithful translation of the original text into Urdu, Shiʿi and Sunni ʿulama had another instrument at their disposal to speak seemingly authoritatively about certain issues while in fact adapting and modifying their sources. Religious scholars also frequently invoked their (imagined) influential standing in the wider Muslim world, which endowed them with additional legitimacy back home.[23]

Intimately connected to these transnational ties is the assertion of local religious authority vis-à-vis the centers of scholarship and learning. The clerics utilized their own spiritual capital accumulated through long years spent studying and teaching in Iran and Iraq.[24] It made it possible for them to take on the role as respected spokespersons for the shrine cities and to even critically discuss "aberrations" as they saw them in the Middle East. Shiʿi ʿulama underlined the past intellectual glories of the Indian subcontinent, which let them speak on an equal footing with Iranians and Iraqis. At the same time, they sought to retroactively claim for themselves ownership over the promise of Pakistan as a gift to the world that would enable Islam to come into its own. This meant propagating unique and self-confident Shiʿi visions of a pure Muslim land. I discuss instances of religious scholars seizing opportunities for the local dispensation of legal opinions after the death of a leading Middle Eastern marjiʿ. In the context of Pakistani perceptions of the Iranian Revolution, I document accounts of political leadership exerted by Pakistani scholars that set them on a level equal to Khomeini. Pakistani ʿulama at times even rebuked the Iranians for having strayed from their own revolutionary path, which made it necessary that Pakistan's Shiʿis rectify this unfortunate situation. Such a self-conception extends to sectarian Sunni scholars as well, who claimed that they were the first worldwide to have woken up to the danger of Shiʿi proselytization and exporting of the Iranian Revolution. These sectarian actors also advanced a unique understanding of how the Qurʾan confirmed the exalted position of the Prophet Muhammad's Companions (*sahaba*). Similarly, a shared Sunni-Shiʿi trait of perceived South Asian superiority manifests itself in the frequently extolled spiritual gifts and esoteric insights available to Pakistani scholars. These blessings were even incorporated by staunch Salafis who otherwise reject mystical conceptions of authority.

THE TRANSNATIONAL STUDY OF IDEAS

The main focus of this book is on religious ideas and their transnational transformation instead of on Shiʿi organizations and their conflictual relationship with the Pakistani state. The latter aspects have already been studied in depth by Andreas Rieck.[25] Tracing transnational intellectual debates, as my study does, has its own pitfalls. It is necessary to demonstrate the relevance of the voices unearthed and the thickness of the connections proclaimed.[26] Since Shiʿi Islam in Pakistan is still a very embryonic field with most of the protagonists who appear on the subsequent pages neither known to the specialist nor to the interested reader alike, I had to be selective by necessity. Some choices of authors and periodicals have also been dictated by the availability of sources, as I discuss in more detail below. Yet I have tried to present convincing rationales for the inclusion of individual scholars, journals, and viewpoints in the following chapters. I generally provide biographical data for the authors discussed, often in the endnotes in order not to render the main text too burdensome, and attempt to demonstrate their standing and authority within the Shiʿi community.[27] The same holds true for my investigation of transnational connections, which I approach with an eye toward instances of palpable and significant influence.[28] I rely on Shiʿi biographical dictionaries and other secondary sources from Pakistan, India, Iran, and Iraq, as well as on interviews and conversations in all of these countries. This does not mean that my selection necessarily agrees with the views of my interlocutors. The often-repeated statement, for example, that the reformist author Muhammad Husayn Najafi Dhakko, who plays a prominent role in chapter 2, lacks a following and does not exert any influence in Pakistan and beyond prompted me to include him all the more. The other side of this coin—and surely also a danger of transnational intellectual history—is the tendency in the field to focus on elite discourses.[29] I hope to have remedied this concern in part by also incorporating a wide range of perspectives expressed by those Shiʿis who are not part of the clerical establishment or who are, at times, dismissed by their more established colleagues as impostors and "extremists" outside the fold of Islam (*ghulat*, sing. *ghali*). I have also relied extensively on anthropological studies on Islam in Pakistan. At the end of the day, through my focus on texts, videos, and interviews I can offer a careful, informed, and problem-driven though by no means comprehensive account of the Pakistani Shiʿi landscape.

A remark may be appropriate regarding my practice of operating with terms like the "Islamic scholarly tradition" or even the "message" of the Iranian Revolution.[30] When I use these terms, I try to stay clear of "airy and thin" comparisons between concrete Pakistani examples, on the one hand, and only abstract, idealized generalities or an essentialization of discourses emerging from Iran and Iraq, on the other.[31] Instead, my goal is to put into conversation concrete texts and specific messages. Being mindful of unequal positions of authority and power, I attempt to explore how arguments and those who voice them become reshaped during their travel between the Middle East and South Asia.[32] In order to do so, I try to forge a connection between scholarship produced on the history of both regions and Islamic studies.[33]

DEFINING CONCEPTS

Before providing an overview of the individual chapters of the book, I briefly spell out how I use the terms "religious authority," "transnational Shiʿism," and "sectarianism." I discuss the first two topics, religious authority and transnational Shiʿism, together because both are to a large degree intertwined.

Scholars have noted the difficulty of pinning down clear and fixed attributes of religious authority in an Islamic context. One suggestion is to consider it as a relational concept that rests on "recognition and acquiescence" and is of an intrinsic contingent quality.[34] The ʿulama are themselves not a homogeneous group but divided into different schools of law, theological camps, and sects. Being a religious scholar can mean primary expertise in the traditions of the Prophet Muhammad (hadith) and Islamic law (*fiqh*), but also in history, grammar, or literature.[35] What unites them within this diversity is "a combination of their intellectual *formation*, their *vocation*, and, crucially, their *orientation*, viz., a certain sense of continuity with the Islamic tradition."[36] Over the course of Islamic history, they seldom had a comprehensive or institutionalized monopoly in the religious sphere but were challenged by popular preachers, Sufis, philosophers, and at times the state.[37] Conceptions of orthodoxy, enshrined as they were in social practices and institutions, and the drawing of boundaries nevertheless emerged but it was usually up to the ruler's discretion whether he saw it feasible to enforce certain legal rulings.[38] Orthodoxy in an Islamic context should hence be understood as "the exercise of power through the production of knowledge in interpretive institutions, in book publishing, and in local communities that remain connected to the larger Muslim world through specific means of communication."[39] In the twentieth century, the ʿulama met with new challenges in the shape of nation-states that encroached on their former prerogatives in the spheres of education and the formulation of Islamic law.[40] Additionally, modernist thinkers, Islamists, and Salafis, who advocated a radical revisiting of the Islamic scholarly tradition or circumvented it altogether for unmediated access to Qur'an and hadith, presented themselves as more suitable spokespersons for Islam.[41]

In a Shiʿi context, these processes have seemingly taken a different form. It has been observed that in the modern period religious autodidacts and *petits intellectuels* have managed to make far fewer inroads into the domain of the religious scholars than has happened among the Sunnis.[42] One explanation for such a comparatively more comprehensive role for the Shiʿi ʿulama has to do with their ability to gradually appropriate prerogatives of the Imams since the time of the Twelfth Imam's definitive Occultation in 329/941 and the consequent inaccessibility of these divine guides to the Shiʿi community.[43] The literature supporting this view emphasizes that modern Shiʿi Islam is distinguished from Sunni Islam by the fact that it "has a clergy that is hierarchically organized."[44] This relative lack of nonclerical competitors does not mean, however, that modern and contemporary Shiʿi religious scholars have been insulated from popular pressures on their authority.[45] Chapters 1, 2, and 3 discuss in more detail how the influence of Shiʿi religious scholars has developed since the mid-nineteenth century and, at the same time, how it has become a site of contestation in late colonial India and Pakistan.

Important in this context is the *transnational* character of Shiʿi religious authority. Each of the *marajiʿ* in the centers seeks to project his "influence as far away as possible in the transnational geography of Shiʿism. The scope of his reach to believers at a distant horizon is a de facto mark of his authority. Given that most followers will never lay eyes on him, he nevertheless needs to symbolise his presence among them."[46] Transnational Shiʿi Islam, if viewed from the periphery, is thus always a mediated form of authority. With a supreme religious scholar in the distance, who usually also seeks to emphasize his political independence from his (temporary or, more often, long-term) host country, a grand ayatollah is by definition not engaged directly with local affairs abroad.[47] Instead, he is the proponent of a shariʿa discourse that is difficult for any particular state to dam. In its independence it "leaks out from between the fingers, a sort of 'neo-calligraphic not-state,' or 'anti-state.'"[48] The task of connecting to local communities is delegated to a marjiʿ's representatives (*wukala'*, sing. *wakil*), and at times his sons, which opens up many spaces for local reformulations of religious authority.[49] These reflections also underline what a fundamental break with Shiʿi structures of authority the Iranian Revolution really was. After 1979, Shiʿi transnationalism suddenly became tied to a specific state and its government. It was no longer executed within the modest surroundings of a marjiʿ's office in Najaf, Qum, or Mashhad. Strictly speaking, one could argue that transnational Shiʿism proper begins with the Iranian Revolution. Before this pivotal event, Shiʿi discourses play out between nations but transcend them at the same time and thus display a more global flavor.[50]

The last concept to consider is sectarianism. I operate with a broad definition of sectarianism that includes both texts such as religious polemics, declarations of unbelief, calls for ostracization, pleas to the state to intervene, as well as actions which can take the forms of religious violence, public rituals, or demonstrations. Resting on a bedrock of established theological differences, the process of "minoritization," which portrays a certain group as religiously deviant, morally degenerate, and politically dangerous, requires the existence of certain social and political conditions.[51] In case these are ripe, "identity entrepreneurs" can find fertile ground to emphasize collective identities of both their own sectarian group and their respective opponents.[52] The affiliation to one particular Sunni or Shiʿi sect should neither be seen as an exclusive identification but rather as one "particular cluster of narratives [. . .] in which human beings find themselves emplotted." Human beings shape and are shaped by these narratives of belonging, which can be sustained by institutions, become more refined over time, or even disappear.[53] This observation brings me to a further point: sectarianism as a tool of analysis always runs the risk of reinscribing monolithic blocks, such as a unified Sunni front against the Shiʿis, and vice versa. Yet, as the following chapters demonstrate, discourses seemingly directed against an out-group may target equally (or primarily) certain actors, concepts, or groups that do not qualify as "the other" but are squarely located within the respective broader Sunni or Shiʿi spectrum.[54] Last, my working definition of sectarianism proposed explicitly avoids being drawn into or engaging with Weberian distinctions of "church" and "sect" because these do not hold much analytical value for both Sunni or Shiʿi Islam.[55]

SOURCES AND GEOGRAPHICAL SCOPE

I rely primarily on sources that have not been utilized by scholars so far and which are to a large extent unavailable in Western libraries. These consist of periodicals, monographs, pamphlets, collections of speeches, and video recordings of lectures in Urdu. I pay special attention to Indian and Pakistani Shiʿi journals as well as to the *Proceedings of the All India Shiʿa Conference* for the pre-Partition period.[56] Interviews with Shiʿi scholars and activists, which I conducted in Pakistan, Iran, Iraq, and the UK, inform many of the questions this study raises. Even though issues of gender come up in several chapters of this book, the structure of religious authority within the Shiʿi community, the focus of my work, and practical concerns of access all have as a consequence an almost exclusively male-centered story.[57] I supplement this material with primary and secondary sources in Arabic and Persian for comparative purposes. Even though I make use of British archival records for the colonial period, my arguments are mostly built on texts produced by Shiʿi actors themselves. This choice has to do with the often-onesided ways in which India's religious traditions as well as their leaders and groups are portrayed in these official documents. If religious issues are mentioned at all, these records are mostly concerned with "outbreaks or threatened outbreaks of violence owing to the desecration of religious symbols—proofs in the colonial view [. . .] of the essential religiosity, irrationality and fanaticism of the local people, ingredients that would ensure a return to anarchy if ever the controlling hand of the colonial power were to be withdrawn."[58]

Given the political climate in Pakistan during the time that my research took place and the difficulty of gaining access to state institutions, I have not attempted to incorporate unpublished archival government records from the post-1947 period. The country's instability also prevented me from visiting places such as Quetta, Peshawar, or the Tribal Areas, which have a significant Shiʿi presence, too.[59] I am confident, however, that this lacuna should not be too detrimental to the book as a whole. Its main geographical focus lies on Pakistan's Sindh and Punjab provinces. The numerically largest Shiʿi populations are concentrated in these two regions and the most admired popular preachers reside there. The main Shiʿi seminaries are located in Lahore, Islamabad, Karachi, Multan, and the smaller towns of the Punjab. The Karakorum areas of Gilgit and Baltistan, which have been labeled as a "stronghold

The Qatalgah complex in Skardu comprises a mosque, cemetery, and imambargah *for Shiʿi mourning sessions. It underlines the importance of Shiʿi Islam in Pakistan's remote Gilgit-Baltistan autonomous territory, from where many of the leading scholars in the lowlands hail. Photograph by the author.*

of Shiʿa orthodoxy," make an appearance insofar as many of the ʿulama who later became influential in the "lowlands" were born in this mountainous region. Bangladesh, which formed Pakistan's eastern wing from 1947 until 1971, only has a Shiʿi population of about 1 percent. It is not only on these grounds of relevance, though, that the country is excluded from the present study.[60] Scholars have also pointed out the local and linguistic distinctiveness which Bengali imagination of Pakistan took in the 1940s as well as after the creation of the new Muslim homeland in South Asia.[61] With regard to the late colonial period, my geographical focus is on North India.[62]

PLAN OF THE BOOK

This study consists of five chapters that follow a roughly chronological order. Even though the individual chapters are distinct in their thematic focus, each of them discusses the key themes of sectarianism, transnational connections, and local religious authority.

The first chapter, "All-Indian Shiʿism, Colonial Modernity, and the Challenge of Pakistan," explores the late colonial milieu with its opposing discourses of communalism and nationalism that also left a deep impact on Shiʿi community formation. Yet I argue against the claim that this led Shiʿis to conceptualize themselves as adhering to a "freestanding" religion. Instead, India's Shiʿis, in dynamics that bear a certain semblance to how Hindu *bhadralok* rentiers in Bengal attempted to claim superiority over (nominally) Hindu tribes and castes, tended to emphasize their higher spiritual level in contrast to the common (Sunni) Muslims. Nevertheless, once the Muslim League (ML) adopted the creation of Pakistan as its goal, influential Shiʿi voices expressed deep and increasing skepticism toward the founding of a state that claimed to form an inclusive homeland for all Muslims of the subcontinent. Shiʿi authors, intellectuals, and ʿulama referred to widespread Sunni-Shiʿi riots during the 1930s in Lucknow as an ominous foreshadowing of what Pakistan might entail for their community. They pointed out calls by Deobandi ʿulama and ML members to implement an Islamic system in Pakistan built exclusively on Hanafi interpretation of Islamic law (fiqh). Shiʿis feared, in other words, the potentially oppressive nature of a "Land of the Pure." This chapter also demonstrates the substantial links that connected South Asian Shiʿis to major events in the Middle East like the 1926 destruction of the Jannat al-Baqiʿ cemetery, which is located in the city of Medina in the Hejaz and in which four of the twelve Shiʿi Imams lie buried. In noting these connections, I position myself against scholarship that has emphasized how local concerns overshadowed all other orientations for India's Shiʿis during this time period. Finally, I also show that Lucknow's *mujtahids* were far from secure in their leadership position of the Shiʿi community (*qaum*). The modernist-minded All India Shiʿa Conference (AISC), whose proceedings are studied here for the first time in a comprehensive manner, was engaged in an open confrontation with Lucknow's ʿulama. Its members viewed these mujtahids as hopelessly out of touch with the challenges of the time and regarded the AISC as a more appropriate vehicle of communal leadership.

The second chapter, titled "Theology, Sectarianism, and the Limits of Reform: The Making of Shiʿism in the Land of the Pure," investigates the first decades after the founding of Pakistan in 1947. Shiʿi immigrants from North India became pitted against a local Punjabi trend of reformist Shiʿi teaching that maintained close ties with the leading seminaries in Iraq. Young scholars accused the immigrants of being wolves in ʿulama clothes who held dangerous "extremist" views and subscribed to "superstitious" rituals. In documenting these exchanges, I take issue with a notable bias in studies on modern Shiʿi thought, namely the tendency of scholars to adopt a decidedly modernist perspective that dismisses traditionalist thinkers as dubious "populist" actors who bend religion to their own benefit. Instead, I make the case that the traditionalists defended a coherent and transcendent vision of God that built on important impulses from Ismaʿili cosmology and implied a radically contrasting conception of religious authority. Pakistan, in their view, was a pure Muslim land blessed by the Shiʿi Imams that had no need for the jurists' legal sophistry. This chapter pays attention to the various local and transnational dimensions of these debates because both sides attempted to marshal positions held by Iranian and Iraqi scholars in support of their particular views. Khomeini's writings play a particularly important role in this regard. I also argue that both reformist agendas and their traditionalist refutations were driven by the hope of reaching a rapprochement with the Sunnis. While reformist ʿulama suggested discontinuing "offensive" Shiʿi rituals and rethinking the events of Karbala as a political struggle, traditionalist scholars propagated a Sufi-Shiʿi synthesis and universal access to the Hidden Imam.

In the third chapter, "Projections and Receptions of Religious Authority: Grand Ayatollahs and Pakistan's Shiʿi 'Periphery,'" I investigate the arguments exchanged about a lay believer's obligation to emulate a high-ranking scholar in his daily conduct (*taqlid*). My findings question the view of Pakistan as a mere Shiʿi "backwater," where even fundamental religious concepts have not yet taken root, by focusing on the intensive discussions on the subject in the twentieth century. Instead, I argue that Pakistan should be understood as a veritable center of religious vitality in its own right. In particular, I explore how the leading grand ayatollahs, residing mostly in Najaf and Qum, attempted to influence the debate about who should be recognized in Pakistan as the preeminent global scholar and how these claims to authority were received and reinterpreted in the country. I illuminate the crucial moments of succession after the death of one widely accepted and revered marjiʿ, the Iraqi scholar Sayyid Muhsin al-Hakim (d. 1970). His demise played into the hands of the decidedly internationally minded Iranian jurist Sayyid Muhammad Kazim Shariʿatmadari (d. 1986). The latter was the founding director of the Institute of Islamic Preaching in Qum which took translation into various Islamicate languages, among them Urdu, very seriously. This accessibility, in combination with a remarkable campaign by his students, ensured that Shariʿatmadari had acquired the largest following of any marjiʿ in Pakistan by the mid-1970s. This chapter also demonstrates the creativity jurists in the "periphery" can display when arguing about the "centers" by showing how local Shiʿi ʿulama bolstered their own authority. In particular, I explore instances of one Pakistani scholar redefining the religious hierarchy. He played up his role as an "exclusive" representative of a leading scholar, implying that he was acting as the "representative of the representative of the Imam" (*na'ib-i na'ib-i imam*) in Pakistan. Additionally, in my close reading of three Shiʿi journals of the early 1970s, I document various instances of local scholars stepping into the void of leadership during the times of uncertainty when a universally accepted marjiʿ had not yet been recognized. This case study is intended as a contribution to the underdeveloped field of how a Source of Emulation is made and "emerges" in the twentieth and twenty-first centuries.

The Iranian Revolution of 1979 is a further outside factor that looms particularly large in Pakistan, and I discuss it in chapter 4, "Khomeini's Perplexed Pakistani Men: Importing and Debating the Iranian Revolution since 1979." Existing scholarship has hardly considered the ways in which the revolutionary message was relayed to Pakistan and received in the country. I argue that during the early months and years after the political change in Iran, Pakistani Shiʿi ʿulama remained primarily occupied with domestic events. Even ardent supporters of Khomeini were not sure what his authority should mean for them outside of Iran. A lack of both available literature and direct contacts with the neighboring country led these religious scholars to make sense of the revolution in familiar South Asian terms like nonviolence or the concept of the "renewer of religion" (*mujaddid*). Additionally, Pakistan's Shiʿis at that time were engaged in their own political mobilization against the military dictator Zia ul-Haq (d. 1988). While the Iranian Revolution constituted an important "background noise" to these efforts, Shiʿi leaders drew more prominently on their community's own past experiences of activism and made deliberate efforts to appear independent of Khomeini. A second step in the reception can be discerned with the rise of the young cleric Sayyid ʿArif Husayn al-Husayni (d. 1988) to the helm of Pakistan's most influential Shiʿi organization at the time, the Movement for the Implementation of Jaʿfari Law, in 1984. Husayni, who had studied briefly in Iran, clearly and consistently drew on the hallmark themes of the Iranian Revolution. In doing so, however, he was often forced to bend aspects of the revolutionary message, like Muslim unity or the leadership of the clerics, to his Pakistani context. I also pay attention to the unprecedented embrace of Iranian ideas that is anchored in contemporary Lahore. This last group is represented by the influential cleric Sayyid Javad Naqvi who spent nearly his entire adult life in Iran. Naqvi goes to great lengths in promoting the Iranian concept of the direct rule of a cleric (*vilayat-i faqih*) as a viable, desirable option for Pakistan that could help to realize its potentials as a pure Muslim land. He even criticizes the Iranians for not doing enough to export their revolution; a role—

so much is implied—which he aims to fulfill himself.[63] I contend that these three stages of reception are united by Pakistani attempts to reap benefits and gain authority from their close connection to revolutionary Iran, while at the same time making sure to tightly control the message that is distributed to the Shiʿi public.

The fifth and final chapter, "Longing for the State: Dialectics of the Local and the Transnational in Shiʿi-Sunni Sectarianism," studies the changing discourses of sectarianism since the 1970s. During this decade, anti-Shiʿi rhetoric was the prerogative of Ahl-i Hadis scholars with close ties to Saudi Arabia. The polemics of the famous agitator Ihsan Ilahi Zahir (d. 1987) were centered on doctrinal points. Zahir especially castigated the Shiʿis for their belief in the "alteration" of the Qurʾan (*tahrif*). I contend, however, that for the ʿulama of Pakistan's most virulent anti-Shiʿi group, the Sipah-i Sahabah-i Pakistan (Army of the Companions of the Prophet; SSP), the Iranian Revolution constituted a threatening attempt at world domination and subversion of the fundamentals of Islamic politics. In highlighting this aspect of sectarianism in Pakistan, I challenge conventional accounts that portray anti-Shiʿi speeches, publications, and violence as directly caused by economic grievances and merely imported from Saudi Arabia. Even though these Deobandi scholars—in the vein of Zahir—still highlighted doctrinal incompatibilities between "real" and Shiʿi Islam, the Shiʿis were now primarily framed as a political problem: they blocked Pakistan from being molded into its true form: namely, that of a Sunni state with aspirations to global leadership. Public manifestations of Shiʿism had to be erased, so that the country could finally adhere to a pure version of Islam. Scholars affiliated with the SSP provided a unique rereading of the Qurʾan and the Muslim tradition of the subcontinent and beyond to raise the clout of the sahaba. But in formulating their answer to Khomeini, these sectarian Sunni ʿulama attempted to reclaim the caliphate as a divinely sanctioned office that strikingly resembled and transcended Iran's model of government. The Shiʿis, in turn, either continued to call for a proper Islamic revolution in order to do away with these ills of sectarianism or tried to influence public opinion against the SSP. The latter, they claimed, subverted the very foundations on which the God-given polity of Pakistan had been established.

CHAPTER ONE

All-Indian Shiʿism, Colonial Modernity, and the Challenge of Pakistan

The annual meeting of 1940 was an exception for the All India Shiʿa Conference (AISC). Since its foundation in 1907, delegates had usually met in North Indian cities of substantial size, such as Calcutta, Lucknow, or Lahore. For the 1940 session, though, organizers around the Shiʿi notable Navab Nisar ʿAlikhan Qizilbash (d. 1944),[1] had set their eyes on uncharted territory. They had decided to gather that fall in the small *qasba* of Dokoha in the Punjab, a settlement of predominantly Shiʿi Sayyids located outside of the city of Jalandhar.[2] The preparation committee was bent on staging a splendid affair and relied mostly on the largess of the Qizilbashes and another, even more affluent Shiʿi landholding family of North India, the Mahmudabads.[3] Accordingly, they erected an entire new, if only temporary, city of tents and canopies next to a pond outside of Dokoha, covering approximately five hectares and guarded by an imposing concrete gate.[4] The distance between the entrance and the main canopy was lined with colorful electrical lights,[5] visible not only to conference attendees but even to railway passengers traveling at night on the Jalandhar-Ludhiana line.[6] The flag of the AISC proudly flew at a height of forty feet. It depicted against a green background Imam ʿAli's famous sword Dhu 'l-fiqar along with a stylized sun, representing the Prophet Muhammad as the "sun of the message" (*shams al-risala*), and emitting twelve rays that stood for the twelve Shiʿi Imams.[7] The stage of the conference offered seating space for five hundred delegates who would enjoy precious carpets under their feet. The area below them could accommodate two thousand visitors, who would find themselves surrounded by flags and banners of the 128 Shiʿi voluntary organizations affiliated with the AISC.[8] The gathering was also an opportunity to showcase the activities of the Conference: its daily newspaper, *Sarfaraz*—named after its former president Navab Sarfaraz Husayn[9]—was represented by a tent. The Shiʿi orphanage in Lucknow had its own showroom where one could buy handicrafts produced by orphans fostered there.

With all these preparations in place, disaster struck. The night before the grand opening of the Dokoha session, strong winds and rain lashed the camp. The small pond turned into an unexpected menace. The bamboo structures of the canopy snapped and many of the colorful lights were smashed. While roughly three hundred men of the *qasba* were at hand to clear up the most serious mishaps early the next morning, the meeting had lost some of its elaborate luster. And the next disappointment was not far off when it became clear that far fewer participants than expected would come to attend.[10] The organizers tried to make sense of this poor showing, blaming a lack of propaganda activities, the decision to schedule the convocation on a workday, and the inclement weather, which had rendered traveling difficult.

Far more serious, though, were two other reasons cited by the general secretary of the Reception Committee, the pleader Sayyid Tajir Husayn.[11] He pointed to the infamous *tabarra* agitation in Lucknow of 1938–39, one of the most significant instances of Sunni-Shiʿi sectarianism during the colonial period.[12] In the aftermath of these events, Punjabi Shiʿis had turned their backs on the AISC and refused to come to Dokoha, accusing the organization of inactivity during this episode of united Shiʿi struggle. According to Tajir Husayn, Punjab's Shiʿis regarded the gathering as a waste of their time. The Punjabis had also supposedly taken steps to no longer extend invitations for processions and mourning ceremonies to any of those ʿulama and *zakir*s (popular preachers) who had not wholeheartedly participated in the "battlefront of Lucknow" (*mahaz-i Lakhnauʾ*). Another major problem that drove down attendance at the 1940 conference was, according to its general secretary, the lack of participation by any ʿulama and mujtahids of repute.[13] Such an open display of Shiʿi disunity came at a most unfortunate time for the AISC. As the organization saw it, the Shiʿi community was in dire need of a representative organization in order to forestall a brewing danger. Only a couple of months earlier, in March 1940, the Muslim League had passed its Lahore Resolution. This document called for the establishment of "autonomous and sovereign" units in the northwestern and eastern zones of India, meaning separate states in areas with a Muslim majority.[14] Speakers at the AISC meeting found the prospect of Pakistan deeply troubling. They did not shy away from denouncing it as an oppressive vision of a Sunni Islamic state that would target Hindus, Sikhs, and Shiʿi Muslims alike.[15]

This vivid account of the 1940 AISC session leads right into the turbulent late colonial period, which is the temporal frame of this chapter. My goal is to explore questions of religious authority, Shiʿi identity, and sectarianism through three specific lenses. First, I map how the internal tensions between the ʿulama and Western-educated Shiʿis played out within the AISC and beyond. Second, I am interested in how Indian Shiʿis in the late colonial period positioned themselves vis-à-vis Sunni Islam. Such a concern with sectarian identity is intimately connected to the increasingly exclusive and purist vision of Pakistan as formulated by the ML and ʿulama affiliated with it. Third, I explore the international dimensions of Shiʿi thought during the last decades of British rule and investigate to what extent Indian Shiʿis were in conversation with events and Shiʿi scholarship beyond the subcontinent. In examining these three aspects, I draw extensively on the *Annual Proceedings* of the AISC, which have not yet been sufficiently studied.[16]

My discussion makes several major interventions with regard to existing scholarship. One contribution of this chapter is my suggestion to rethink the authority enjoyed by leading Shiʿi ʿulama in the first half of the twentieth century. Scholars have hinted at conflicts between modern educated activists and Lucknow's clerics but have attributed challenges to the standing of the mujtahids primarily to external shocks like the Khilafat movement or sectarian strife. I argue that such a view falls into the trap of reinscribing the colonial gaze on religious developments in the subcontinent and fails to explore how and why this rift developed. The Proceedings of the All India Shiʿa Conference in particular grant us a unique window into these internal Shiʿi deliberations, involving personalities from all over North India. As chapters 2 and 3 explore in more detail, the modernist critics set the tone for challenging the authority of the jurists by attacking their general uneducated backwardness as well as the concept of taqlid, the obligation of a lay Shiʿi to follow the authoritative legal rulings of a senior scholar. This contestation partially explains the energetic efforts by Shiʿi ʿulama after the partition of British India to finally establish the duty of taqlid in the midst of the Pakistani Shiʿi community. Assaults on the authority of Lucknow's mujtahids lead me to a related problem in the existing literature, namely its almost exclusive focus on this city as *the* center of Shiʿi Islam in North India. Lucknow undoubtedly was home to the most impressive architectural Shiʿi structures in the subcontinent, which it had inherited from its Navabi past.[17] It was regarded as the seat of India's leading Shiʿi Usuli scholars and boasted the most advanced Shiʿi religious seminaries.[18] Nevertheless, it is problematic to let the city's Shiʿi sphere speak with such an almost exclusive voice during the first half of the twentieth century. Instead, I suggest that the Punjab constitutes a new and exciting frontier for the future study of South Asian Shiʿi Islam.[19]

Second, I take issue in this chapter with the notion of Shiʿism developing as a "freestanding religion" during this time period. In my view, the Shiʿis of late colonial India were primarily concerned with presenting their practices and beliefs as a faithful expression of the "original," "essential," and "pure" nature of Islam. While they did not necessarily exclude the Sunnis from the fold of religion, they styled themselves as a spiritual elite that transcended the views held by the "common Muslims" (*ʿamm musalman*).

On a related point, my research also calls into question the supposedly ecumenical character of the Pakistan movement, which, according to such an understanding, easily appealed to Sunnis and Shiʿis alike. Instead, I give voice to the deep Shiʿi skepticism regarding the potentially oppressive and Sunni-dominated future Muslim homeland, concerns that have often been swept aside in the existing literature.[20] As the debate in the 1940s about the increasingly religious character of Pakistan heated up, Shiʿis expressed fear that a state built on "pure Islam" might be an entity that could not tolerate difference. As I show in chapter 5, this debate over the meaning and the implications of Pakistan was taken up again in the 1980 and 1990s when anti-Shiʿi sectarianism became an increasingly pervasive phenomenon in Pakistan. While fleshing out these continuities, I also hope to demonstrate that we encounter a variety of "sectarianisms" in the context of the colonial period and later in Pakistan. Sectarian discourses remained far from stagnant but were crucially shaped through the impact of the Iranian Revolution.[21]

A final topic I revisit in this chapter is the notion that before Partition Shiʿis in the subcontinent were almost exclusively focused on Indian concerns because these overwhelmed and drowned out attention paid to the Middle East. My goal is instead to bring back the crucial importance of transnational connections and to emphasize the strong and substantial ties which bound the Shiʿis of the subcontinent to events in Iran, Iraq, and the Arabian Peninsula.

As the following pages show, contestations of religious authority, sectarianism, and transnational concerns do not form entirely discrete issues but are to a large extent interrelated. Before discussing these topics, I briefly engage questions of community formation and the sectarian situation in colonial Lucknow in order to set the scene for the following discussion in this chapter.

LATE COLONIAL INDIA: SHIʿI ISLAM AND THE FORCES OF SECTARIANISM, NATIONALISM, AND COMMUNALISM

The last decades of colonial rule in the Indian subcontinent gave rise to an unprecedented "publicness" of debates over "Muslim self-definition" that played out in newspapers, processions, mass meetings, and elections.[22] Associations on a local, provincial, and national level promoted socioreligious reform and devised new models of educational institutions that combined training in modern sciences with the emphasis to "utilize them according to the will of the Almighty."[23] Graduates of these institutions formed new generations of Western-educated Muslims who staffed the bureaucracy of the colonial state and administered the subcontinent's princely states.[24] Contradictory universalizing and particularizing conceptions of Islam were on offer and performed in poetry or religious processions.[25] Notions of communalist arguments competed in the public arena with diverging visions of Indian society that emphasized nationalism as the only "forward-looking, progressive, 'modern' way" out of this downward spiral of increasing compartmentalization.[26] Appeals to nationalist sentiments did not necessarily require, however, that Indians should give up their particular religious identities and opt for secularist worldviews. Most prominently, the Khilafat movement was able to channel a seemingly exclusively Muslim cause, namely preserving the temporal power of the Ottoman sultan because it was crucial for fulfilling his spiritual role as "Caliph of Islam," into a pan-Indian rallying cry espoused by Gandhi.[27] The latter conceived of the Khilafat movement primarily as an anti-British issue. For Gandhi, it was a means "to bring the Muslims into the nationalist movement, and a big boost to his plans to reorganize and redirect the Congress into a mass movement."[28] Deobandi ʿulama affiliated with the Congress attempted to make the case for "united nationalism" (*mutahhida qaumiyyat*) in India. To do so, they stressed that a nation was not constituted by ties of faith. Religious solidarity was rather the basis of a religious community (*milla*) and in this regard Indian Muslims were not distinct because they were part of the universal Muslim community. This argument was meant to enable the Muslims of the subcontinent to live together with their Hindu neighbors as constituting one qaum.[29] Examining deliberations in the Indian Legislative Assembly surrounding potential persecution for insulting the beliefs of another religion, Neeti Nair has also suggested that "competitive, obdurate and relentless" communalism did not rule the day in the late 1920.[30]

Shiʿi organizations did not stay on the sidelines of this confusing thicket of communalism, nationalism, and pragmatism but waded right into it. The Shiʿis of colonial India "adapted entirely to the national currents of community-based activism and pressure-group petitioning that characterized public life in the era of elite nationalism."[31] The All India Shiʿa Conference with its claim to nationwide representation, its flag, its past history of founding a Shiʿi college, and its focus on defending Shiʿi rights appears to fall squarely into the camp of communalist expressions.[32] This is also the way how the colonial officials perceived the organization, emphasizing that "we do not want to have to recognise yet another minority body; Shias must sink their fortunes with the Sunnis and be treated as 'Moslems.'"[33] Yet the conference also contained members with decidedly nationalist attitudes, as its political arm, the All India Shiʿa Political Conference (AISPC), demonstrated.[34] It had probably been founded as an effort to promote a powerful Shiʿi voice within discussions in the late 1920s regarding India's constitutional future.[35] Sayyid Vazir Hasan (1872–1947), a former chief judge at the High Court in Lucknow who had once played an important role in the Muslim League (ML) before being expelled, presided over the AISPC session in Lucknow on 11 October 1937.[36] In his speech, he deplored that "communalism raised its head at every step that was taken or intended to be taken on the march to the goal of freedom by the Congress or any group of Indian Nationalists."[37] This accusation was especially aimed at the ML, which in the view of the conference "did not represent the entire Muslims of India." The AISPC held that "the rights of the Shia minority were always crushed by the League," which had also manifested itself in Lucknow, where the League had supposedly stirred sectarian animosity against the Shiʿis.[38]

This statement ties in with the vignette of the 1940 AISC meeting, offered at the beginning of this chapter. It underscores the specter of sectarianism that haunted individual Shiʿi authors and organizations like the AISC and points to the deeper level of intra-Muslim frictions during this time period.[39] The Shiʿis as a double minority were not only forced to choose between the Muslim League and the Congress.[40] They also had to define their relationship with the Sunni majority and, at the same time, answer the question of who could speak authoritatively for their grievances. It is interesting to note in this context the paths not taken by South Asian Shiʿis during the 1930s and 1940s. Various fascist-inspired movements with their "politics of self-expression" that was "based on a *will to power*, but one that had already half-realized its own impossibility" did not catch on with Shiʿi intellectuals and activists during the late colonial period.[41] Nor did they develop a conception of Islamism that was comparable to the ideology of the Jamaʿat-i Islami (Islamic Society) founded by Abu 'l-Aʿla Maududi (d. 1979).[42] Shiʿi experiments with Islamist thought would have to wait until 1979, as chapter 4 discusses in more detail. Instead, I would argue the AISC was a secular attempt to salvage some of the glories of former Shiʿi sovereignty in India that had been swept away by the colonial state. The unwillingness of Lucknow's leading mujtahids to throw in their lot with the AISC has to be seen in the light of a rise of new contenders to the claim of Shiʿi leadership during this time period. Both Western-educated activists and "progressive" ʿulama, who challenged their peers to catch up with modern realities, devised a new style and substance of leadership and presented themselves as "part journalist, part orator, part holy man."[43]

Since many of my arguments below refer to the tabarra agitation of Lucknow in the late 1930s, it is necessary to also briefly review this particular instance of Sunni-Shiʿi sectarianism, which has attracted significant scholarly interest.[44] Lucknow had already witnessed a parting of ways between Sunni and Shiʿi Muharram processions in 1906. This came as a result of the Shiʿis complaining to the British authorities that their solemn commemoration of Husayn's death had been turned into a "carnival" by Sunni participants. But assigning the Sunnis their own burial ground for their *taʿziyas* only exacerbated the situation.[45] The latter began to utilize this separate space in order to recite praises for all four Caliphs as "equal comrades" (*caryar*).[46] The Shiʿis reacted by publicly cursing the first three Caliphs Abu Bakr (d. 634), ʿUmar (d. 644), and ʿUthman (d. 656). They were led by a new generation of vernacular zakirs, who harnessed the potentials of the emerging public sphere and "performed with vernacular fluency and frequent subversion and audacity."[47] Several observers have interpreted this split as an instance of reconciling "the observance of the murder of Husain with more orthodox Islam" and of drawing boundaries for both the Sunni and Shiʿi community.[48] Such an interpretation has been rejected recently on the grounds that it would "insinuate to some degree the internal homogeneity of Shiʿa and Sunni communities, suggesting the coordinated efforts of ʿulama, preachers and patrons on each side and giving little differentiation among them."[49]

The British authorities responded to widespread unrest by enforcing a ban on praising the Companions of the Prophet (*madh-i sahabah*). The resolve to uphold this restriction became increasingly tested from the early 1930s onward by the efforts of the polemicist ʿAbd al-Shakur, who had already been involved in the events of 1906. ʿAbd al-Shakur's attempts to shift devotion from the Shiʿi Imams toward the Sunni Caliphs foreshadowed some of the discourses later employed by the anti-Shiʿi group Sipah-i Sahabah in post-Partition Pakistan.[50] The situation came to a head when in 1938 the Allsop Committee, which had been charged with studying the issue, recommended to keep the ban in place.[51] The Deobandi Jamʿiyyat al-ʿUlamaʾ-i Hind (JUH) received support from the Punjab-based Majlis-i Ahrar organization, and together they launched a broad civil disobedience campaign.[52] The Indian National Congress government, which was in power between 1937 and 1939 in the United Provinces, tried to defuse the tensions. Amid a deteriorating situation of riots and clashes, it gave permission on 31 March 1939 for a Sunni *madh-i sahabah* procession to be taken out on 2 May, the Prophet's birthday (known as *barah vafat* in Urdu).[53] While the decision was supposedly made to retain the JUH and the Ahrar in the Congress camp while weakening the ML, "the vehemence of Shia reactions took everybody by surprise."[54] Thousands of Shiʿi volunteers from all over northern India made their way to Lucknow, and up to fourteen thousand Shiʿis courted arrest during the first four months of the agitation alone.[55] A Sunni eyewitness—Codhri Niʿmatullah, an advocate and member of the United Provinces (UP) Council of State—described the situation on 24 June 1939 thus:[56]

> Those who do not reside in Lucknow cannot have an adequate idea of how the movement manifests itself. It is not merely the case of a Jatha [a gang or a mob] pronouncing Tabarra, coming out of Imambara Asifia and being arrested. The claim that it is of a nonviolent character cannot stand the slightest examination. Tabarra begins from the time when the Jatha is arrested and is lodged in the lorry which takes them to Jail. In transit on the public road Tabarra continues in loud chorus in the hearing of everyone who happens to be on the route. When the Tabarra prisoners are transferred to other districts the railway platform is a scene of Tabarra chorus all the time that the prisoners are waiting for their train, particularly, at the sight of any one suspected to be a Sunni. Once my own presence at the railway platform provoked a most vociferous Tabarra. At night Tabarra is pronounced, through gramophone loud speakers from the topmost roof of many Shia houses so that all the Sunni neighbours may hear it. Tabarra is found to be written on the doors and walls of Sunni houses. Even the bed sheets provided for the Shia prisoners are found to have Tabarra written on them. Very often Tabarra is pronounced not in the conventional form but the names of the three Caliphs and the Prophet's favourite wife are associated with the filthiest abuses. The only sense in which such movements can be declared nonviolent is that Tabarra is mostly pronounced under the protection of the police who see to it that no violence is resorted to by the Sunni hearers.[57]

Among the startling features of this tabarra agitation were not only its organized character and its appeal that stretched over all of north India. The event is also significant because it cut across boundaries of neighborhood, family, class, and political persuasion. Many Shiʿi ʿulama were among those arrested, as were landlords, members of the former royal family of Awadh, and politicians.[58]

COMPETING CLAIMS TO SHIʿI AUTHORITY

It is not surprising that this spectacular manifestation of Sunni-Shiʿi strife has attracted the sustained interest of scholars. One of the most sophisticated analyses of the sectarian scene in Lucknow and its implications for internal Shiʿi debates has been provided by Justin Jones. In his reading, it was external shocks such as the tabarra agitation and the earlier Shiʿi grappling with the Khilafat movement that provided the space for individuals and organizations to challenge the consolidated authority of Lucknow's mujtahids. A case in point is the Shiʿi ML politician Sayyid Riza ʿAli (1882–1949), who protested a joint fatwa by the three mujtahids Nasir Husayn (1867–1942), Sayyid Aqa Hasan (1860–1929), and Muhammad Baqir Rizvi (1868–1928).[59] In May 1920 these religious scholars had called on Shiʿis not to engage with the question of the caliphate.[60] Conferring this title to anyone other than the first Shiʿi Imam, ʿAli b. Abi Talib, implied that such a person would "thereby be totally excluded from the pale of Shiʿism." Sayyid Riza ʿAli ridiculed this declaration and pointed out the "complete estrangement" that had come to pass between Lucknow's leading ʿulama and the Indian Shiʿis. In his Urdu autobiography that was published in December 1943, Sayyid Riza ʿAli later elaborated further on his modernist anticlerical convictions. He wrote that "the business [*muʿamalah*] of religion [*mazhab*] is only a business between the Creator and the created." No one else had the right to assume an intermediary position, since such a view was contrary to the teachings of Islam. He shared this conviction, as he claimed, with the Ahl-i Hadis.[61] Mirza Muhammad Rahim Bulbula, a rather obscure Shiʿi preacher from Baku who had arrived in India in 1917, put additional pressure on the clerical leadership. He founded an *anjuman* to investigate the rumored bombing of Najaf by the British in 1920 and to "harmonize Shiʿa concerns with the wider Khilafat movement." Eventually, the Shiʿi mujtahids came around and voiced support for the anti-British Khilafat cause. Jones notes with surprise how "a number of activists and anjumans only recently apparent in public life managed to trump the networks of magnates, institutions and ʿulama that had for some decades represented the public face of Shiʿism. [. . .] After some thirty years of high public visibility and uncontested guardianship of vested authority, the mujtahids were reduced by the strength of this new political populism to making concessions to existing public opinion in a bid to maintain their profile."[62] Jones identifies a similar dynamic playing out eighteen years later during the tabarra agitation. When the mujtahid Muhammad Nasir (1895–1966) ordered the Shiʿis to halt these public denunciations, an anjuman from Lucknow, the Tanzim al-Muʾminin, publicly opposed this move: "It was a bold gesture against a scholar who was by this time one of the country's most elevated religious authorities and, one may speculate, something that would have been anathema a couple of decades earlier."[63]

I would caution against such a reading, however, as it places too much stress on certain external shocks and singles out instances of sectarianism as the primary avenue to renegotiate religious authority within the Shiʿi community.[64] Jones's focus leaves him with the problem that an assumed accumulated, unassailable standing of Lucknow's leading scholars suddenly got challenged as if out of nowhere. Even more serious, however, is that this account does not question the basic narrative as it emerges from the colonial archive. The British authorities only became involved and developed interest in such exclusively internal Shiʿi debates when they were related to disturbances of the public order.[65] Regaining control of the situation required that the colonial administration identified the participants in such contestations, yet the analysis left behind in the Raj's archive only provides us with a snapshot of crisis, not with a sense for how the debate evolved over time.[66] The Proceedings of the All India Shiʿa Conference, by contrast, show in detail how its modernist members since the 1920s increasingly defied the claimed leadership role of Lucknow's clerical elite. These barristers, bureaucrats, and landowners presented themselves as the true and progressive center of Shiʿi Islam in late colonial India.

How did the AISC come to adopt this role? Scholars have noted that the organization had originally been founded in 1907 as an attempt to reconcile "the old religious and aristocratic establishment with the new class of Shia professionals" or even as "yet another vehicle for maintaining the newly established role of the senior clerical families of Lucknow as visible social activists and speakers."[67] The organization vowed during its founding session, which was attended by nearly one thousand delegates, to safeguard the moral, social, economic, and religious needs of the Shiʿis through means that were not in conflict with the shariʿa. It also emphasized in the adopted charter its willingness to work toward unity among the community's members and to cooperate with other Islamic sects and also followers of other religions.[68] Yet it is problematic to deduce from these stated goals that Lucknow's mujtahids "jealously guarded the role of president [. . .] until at least the early 1920s,"[69] after which they "gradually lost interest."[70] The statement that for at least the first thirteen years the office of AISC president was only held by senior clerics from Lucknow is factually incorrect.[71] Instead there was a growing influence of notables like the ruler of the princely state of Rampur (president in 1912), landlords from the UP, politicians, and civil servants who presided over most of the AISC meetings. In 1935, Sayyid Muhammad

Mahdi, a notable and lawyer from Patna, presided over the annual meeting. For 1936 and 1937, it was the raja of Mahmudabad, Muhammad Amir Ahmad Khan (d. 1973). In 1937, the Shiʿi politician and lawyer Sir Sayyid Riza ʿAli was president and in 1940 the younger brother of Mahmudabad, Amir Haydar Khan, held this office.[72] But a more nuanced explanation of an "alternating" leadership between ʿulama and notables is misleading, too. Only one mujtahid from Lucknow served as president of the AISC after 1911, namely Sayyid Ibn-i Hasan (d. 1949), who took over this position for the 1924 session in Fayzabad.[73] Lahore was more prominently represented than Lucknow with the mujtahid Sayyid ʿAli Haʾiri[74] acting as the elected president in 1914 and Sayyid Hashmat ʿAli (d. 1935) occupying this role in the years 1923 and 1932.[75] The remaining sessions were chaired by dignitaries, landlords, and Shiʿi politicians. The ʿulama and their authority, in other words, had been pushed to the sidelines.

Relations between the AISC and the clerical leadership in fact had already become strained prior to the organization's Multan session in 1921. Najm al-Hasan (1862–1938), a preeminent mujtahid, director of the Madrasah-i Nasiriyya in Lucknow, and former president of the AISC, spelled out in a letter the reasons for his conspicuous absence from the Multan convocation.[76] According to him, the AISC's original goal had been to spread awareness of the rulings of the shariʿa and to rectify unsuitable and wrong phenomena in society. Yet its envisioned setup as a pan-Indian body, designed to accord with the changing times, had obviously backfired because it had given rise to the idea that the opinions of the ʿulama and "of other people of the Shiʿi community" could be treated as equally valid (*ʿulamaʾ-i mazhab aur digar afrad-i qaum ki raʾe musavi haysiyyat men shumar ki jaʾe*). Even worse, the attitude prevalent within the AISC had reached the level that every suggestion made by the religious scholars was rejected out of hand as impractical (*na qabil-i ʿamal*) and even turned into an object of ridicule (*istihza o tasakhkhur*). Najm al-Hasan saw only one way to reestablish his relations with the organization: the AISC had to make sure that it corrected all resolutions and amended any individual behavior that was in conflict with the shariʿa. Only by professing its reliance on the ʿulama could a relationship of trust once again come into being.[77]

This letter and the open criticism by its religious leaders was a blow for the All India Shiʿa Conference. The delegates denied in their response to Najm al-Hasan any wrongdoing or mockery of the ʿulama and argued that the presidents of the conference had always been elected by the mujtahids.[78] In his presidential address, the landlord Navab Muzaffar ʿAli Khan of Jhansath near Muzaffarnagar (UP) underlined that it was "a serious mistake" to think that the ʿulama had no say over mundane matters. It was the pride of the Shiʿis to follow their religious scholars in affairs relating both to this world and the next. Unfortunately, the ʿulama themselves had deprived the people of a special blessing, namely to act as AISC president and dispense their guidance in this way.[79] The conference nevertheless tried to mend fences by nominating a delegation that was supposed to travel to Lucknow in order to sort out its differences with the mujtahids.[80]

Yet the jurists were not willing to meet with these envoys.[81] Instead a potential—if far-reaching—compromise was suggested in 1924 by the Lucknow-based ʿalim Sayyid Abu ʾl-Hasan (1881–1937), who encouraged the AISC delegates to accept a supervisory council.[82] Unfortunately, no records exist of the scholars' internal deliberations but it is tempting to speculate that this proposal was influenced by the heated debates surrounding the public role of the Shiʿi clergy and "*shariʿa*-based constitutionalism" (*mashrutah-i mashruʿah*) in Iran during the Constitutional Revolution in the first decade of the twentieth century. Article 2 of the Supplementary Fundamental Law, passed in October 1907, had given a council of mujtahids the power to "reject, repudiate, wholly or in part, any proposal which is at variance with the sacred law of Islam. In such matters the decision of this committee of *ulema* shall be followed and obeyed, and this article shall continue unchanged until the appearance of His Holiness the Proof of the Age [i.e., the twelfth, Hidden Imam]."[83]

The situation in India under colonialism and in the context of being a minority was obviously very different: Abu ʾl-Hasan stated that the ʿulama had no inclination to get involved with the administrative aspects of the AISC, play a role in politics, or gain any "worldly honor" (*dunyavi ʿizzat*).[84] Yet they also rejected being treated as ordinary participants. The religious scholars saw their role as analogous to the colonial government, which adopted a policy of control and supervision over the AISC (*nazir nigarani*) to make sure that it did not adopt positions that were in conflict with the Indian secular law (*khilaf varzi-yi qanun-i government*). The ʿulama were charged with a different kind of oversight on behest of the "divine kingdom" (*saltanat-i ilahiyyah*). Their task was to guarantee compliance with God's law (*qanun-i ilahi*).[85] Abu ʾl-Hasan explained that the proposed supervisory committee of mujtahids would scrutinize the provisionary agenda ahead of each AISC meeting as well as the published proceedings afterward in order to determine whether all resolutions adopted complied with the shariʿa. This body was supposed to be self-regulating, since only senior scholars would know who was qualified for the task.[86] The mujtahids, he claimed, recognized that there were certain administrative areas, like acting as the conference's president or electing a secretary, that formed a neutral space from the perspective of the shariʿa. The Shiʿi qaum was not bound in obedience to the Prophet and the Imams regarding such matters. Hence, following the rulings of the ʿulama was not required in this context.[87] Generally speaking, however, the shariʿa's reach was universal. It also encompassed areas like trade or government and clearly touched on the topic of internal unity (*ittihad*), which was so important to the AISC. In this context, Sayyid Abu 'l-Hasan identified a happy division of labor between the ʿulama and the modern educated conference members: while the jurists lacked knowledge about how to spur progress (*taraqqi*) for the Shiʿis, the activists of the AISC were equally ignorant (*jahil*) as to whether their course of action was in compliance with the divine law. Once the ʿulama had evaluated the ideas proposed by the modernists and issued a verdict, obedience became mandatory.[88]

The proposal to set up such a *majlis-i nazarat* reportedly found full support from the AISC, which even modified its constitution accordingly. The wording included a passage stating that if there was a disagreement among the mujtahids regarding the shariʿa compatibility of a particular resolution, the AISC would choose the safe path and withdraw this proposal altogether.[89] The project was off to a promising start: Sayyid Abu 'l-Hasan and Sayyid Ibn-i Hasan, both present in Fayzabad, agreed to participate right away. The AISC proposed to include ten other leading scholars.[90] Yet the Supervisory Council only made a brief appearance the following year during the annual meeting in Patna and did not leave any additional traces in the pages of subsequent AISC proceedings.[91]

I would argue that the failure of the Supervisory Council is a direct outcome of efforts by the AISC to further curtail the influence of the mujtahids and to expand the boundaries of the neutral shariʿa space which Abu 'l-Hasan had identified. In 1924, the same year the conference seemingly enthusiastically embraced the *majlis-i nazarat*, it decided to revoke the privilege of Lucknow's mujtahids to elect the AISC president. The organization justified this move as attempting to actually *strengthen* the influence of the ʿulama, since the existing rule had unfairly privileged senior jurists based in Lucknow, thus excluding their colleagues from the Punjab. A more important argument in the eyes of the delegates, however, was that a president elected by the qaum would be able to fulfill his role with much more self-confidence due to this popular backing (*is ko tamam qaum-i shiʿah ne sadarat ka ahl samjha he*).[92] Speeches in the following years repeatedly emphasized a level playing field for all members of the AISC. Everyone could participate with "equal communal rights" (*musavi huquq-i qaum*), be they a "*taʿalluqdar*, a *navab*, a *raʾis*, a *faqir*, a *mujtahid*, or an *ʿalim-i din*."[93] The head of the organizing committee for the 1925 session in Bombay, the businessman Mirza Hashim Isfahani, attempted to claim more room to maneuver for the AISC by arguing that participation in its activities did not fall under the purview of taqlid.[94] According to him, unlike Christianity or Hinduism, Islam was not a religion that would restrict the affairs of religion (*umur-i din*) to a particular group. Rather, every individual Muslim who was knowledgeable about the necessities of his faith could carry them out. Isfahani here echoes notions of Islamic modernism in India that usually have been attributed to Sayyid Ahmad Khan, namely the conception of a new, morally responsible citizen for whom there could be no ancient authority of a "fixed code with ready-made solutions to his problems."[95] Shiʿi Islam, Isfahani held, would take this conviction one step further: in the view of this sect everyone could be a mujtahid for himself (*har shakhs apni zat ke liye khud mujtahid ban sakta he*). For anyone without religious knowledge, the condition of taqlid of course still applied, but this did not entail that Shiʿis would be limited to one particular jurist. Rather, whoever an individual believer acknowledged as the most learned would do. This freedom of choice applied to less well-known (*ghayr maʿruf*) mujtahids as well. Even though Isfahani did not promote any particular alternative to the leadership in Lucknow, he complained in a not-so-subtle manner that the city's senior jurists did not seem to have had the opportunity to truly engage with pressing "worldly, societal, and educational concerns."[96] These were bold words, especially because in 1925 some high-ranking ʿulama from Lucknow were still in attendance at the Bombay session.[97]

The following years only increased this antagonism: in 1928, the AISC president and landlord Navab Mir Fazl ʿAlikhan of Bigan Pali in Madras spoke of nothing less than "war and destruction" (*jang o barbadi*) between the Shiʿi ʿulama and the modern educated strata. Not only India was held in the grips of this conflict between the two camps. It played out in similar forms in the entire Islamic world. The ʿulama were still caught up in the "darkness of conservatism and ignorance" (*qadamat o jahalat ki tariki*). Their modernist opponents, by contrast, rejected the imperial, outward supremacy of Europe but accepted her intellectual and spiritual dominance (*maʿnavi istilaʾ*) and regarded it as their salvation (*najat*). European superiority had led to dramatic changes in many countries. It had transformed existing forms of education and questioned existing ideas. In ʿAlikhan's view, though, the ʿulama ignored these developments and perceived the educated class as the element most corruptive for religion (*sab se zaʾid fasid ʿunsur*). This attitude had led the modern-minded to turn away from Islam altogether because they had begun to perceive Muhammad's message as an obstacle to progress. The only solution would be that the Shiʿi ʿulama in India should, like their peers in Iran, awake and become familiar with new sciences, technologies, and ways of life.[98] The politician Sayyid Riza ʿAli made a similar, if less openly hostile, point. He remembered that back in 1910, while had been attending the AISC for the first time, the question of whether only mujtahids could become its president was hotly debated.[99] He had always supported the notion of human equality (*musavat bayn al-afrad*) and expressed his satisfaction that this issue was now settled once and for all. The AISC members—and not the religious scholars—were striving for the betterment of the Shiʿi community so that it could play its appropriate role in India's national life (*mulki zindagi*).[100] Therefore, a reinterpretation even of taqlid was appropriate: in 1936, the head of the organizing committee proclaimed that resolutions adopted by the AISC were binding on every Shiʿi (*har fard-i Shiʿah ke liye vajib al-ʿamal hoti hen*).[101] In light of such statements, the Punjabi scholar Hashmat ʿAli had already in 1932 remarked that the relations between the ʿulama and the modern educated were damaged beyond repair.[102]

The absence of leading mujtahids from the mid-1920s onward was a problem that the AISC could not simply ignore. The poor attendance at the 1940s session, discussed in the beginning of this chapter, was only the most palpable manifestation of the strained relations. Honorary General Secretary Sayyid Kalb-i ʿAbbas (1891–1974) pointed out the dilemma that the organization faced in a speech he delivered in December 1936 in Lucknow.[103] Sayyid Kalb-i ʿAbbas recalled how during the preparations for the previous annual meeting he had approached a clean-shaven fellow Shiʿi, hoping to entice him to become a member of the organization. The potential recruit rebuffed him, however, citing the lack of ʿulama involvement. As long as Sayyid Nasir Husayn did not give him permission, the man insisted, he could not participate in the AISC.[104] A couple of days later, Sayyid Kalb-i ʿAbbas came across the same individual while he was deeply engaged in the classic race board game Pachisi.[105] The honorary general secretary could not refrain from asking whether the mujtahid had also explicitly condoned such a reprehensible activity. Driving home the lesson of this anecdote, Sayyid Kalb-i ʿAbbas implored the delegates assembled in Lucknow not to provide a pretext to their opponents. They should make it clear that the doors of the AISC were open to everyone and that all of its resolutions fell within the boundaries of the shariʿa. It was crucial to once again reach out to the ʿulama, even if some were convinced by now that such efforts had proven to be futile.[106]

A more promising path than chasing after Lucknow's mujtahids, however, seemed to be the cultivation of ties with alternative ʿulama, namely scholars who were more inclined toward the goals of the organization and saw the pressing need for working toward the reform (*islah*) of the Shiʿi community.[107] Most vocal among this group was Sayyid Ibn-i Hasan Jarcavi (1904–73), who had benefited from the novel educational opportunities in the subcontinent. After receiving his initial religious training from his father, grandfather, and Shiʿi madrasas in Lucknow, Jarcavi studied at the Oriental College in Rampur. He earned a bachelor's degree from Aligarh in 1923, followed by an MA from the Islamia College in Lahore and subsequent advanced degrees in Arabic and Persian from the Oriental College Lahore.[108] In the 1920s and 1930s, the young scholar's fame spread in northwestern India due to his extensive speaking engagements in Sindh, Punjab, and Delhi. He taught from 1930 until 1938 at the Jamia Millia in Delhi[109] and from 1938 until Partition served the raja of Mahmudabad in various functions, inter alia as tutor to his son.[110] Speaking in front of the AISC delegates, Jarcavi declared it unwise to close one's eyes in the face of the religious, civilizational, and economic transformations that lay ahead for the subcontinent.[111] The Shiʿis as a community had negligently shunned useful occupations like agriculture and trade. Instead, they had given too much weight to securing government and office jobs, thereby willingly surrendering themselves to enslavement by capitalists (*sarmayah daran ki ghulami*).[112] In order to simultaneously turn around the socioeconomic fate of the Shiʿi qaum and stem a tide of irreligiosity within it, Jarcavi challenged the ʿulama to support female education, reform religious customs, and familiarize themselves with the "new sciences" (*ʿulum-i jadidah*):[113] "The era of rhetorical or poetical reasoning has come to an end. Today is the time of proofs and demonstrations which are based on philosophy and logic. Therefore, I want this conference to convey to the ʿulama and preachers that they should reconsider their way of preaching. Along with mentioning the virtues and afflictions [of the *ahl al-bayt*] they should also pay attention to the reform of practices [*islah-i rusum*], of morals, and of behavior."[114]

Jarcavi openly spoke out against Lucknow. In his view, merely being part of the city's leading clerical family, known as *khandan-i ijtihad* (the family of ijtihad), or having spent time in Iraq was insufficient to qualify that person for the level of independent legal reasoning.[115]

I would argue that such provocations and accusations of backwardness could not be ignored by India's leading Shiʿi jurists. Jarcavi presented himself as a cutting-edge ʿalim who was familiar with continental philosophy and socialist thought.[116] He corresponded with Gandhi, pointing out to him that the conventional portrayal of the Prophet Muhammad as a military commander was wrong. The Prophet had never engaged in unprovoked war but had, at times, been forced to use violence in order to defend religion. Had Muhammad lived today, he would have surely relied on the League of Nations, international courts, and peace conferences to deal with his opponents. Likewise, ʿAli had only taken up the sword to protect the inhabitants of his "Ashram" (*apne ashram walon ki hifazat ke liye*). He was a man who promoted social justice and the equality of women and taught the same message that had been spread by Lenin, Marx, and Tolstoy. All the Shiʿi Imams, Jarcavi continued, had followed the ideology of passive resistance, bodily labor, and hostility toward capital (*ʿadam tashaddud Passive Resistence* [*sic*] *khamush muqabalah, muzduranah zindagi aur nafrat-i sarmayah*).[117] Husayn's personal example was not meant for the Shiʿis alone but shone for the whole world.[118] Such a reading of Shiʿi Islam puts into perspective arguments in the secondary literature about Sayyid ʿAli Naqi Naqvi's (d. 1988) "revolutionary" and unprecedented Husaynology as spelled out in his influential work *Shahid-i insaniyyat* (The martyr of [or for] humanity), published in 1940.[119] Naqvi was a member of the *khandan-i ijtihad* and South Asia's leading Shiʿi scholar in the twentieth century. He had portrayed Husayn as a decidedly this-worldly "embodiment of an ethical ideal common to all religions," engaged in a struggle against injustice.[120] Yet it seems that many of his thoughts had already been formulated by Jarcavi. I would thus argue that Sayyid ʿAli Naqi Naqvi strove with this book to regain the initiative for the mujtahids who had been challenged by this junior scholar affiliated with the AISC. To put it differently, his reconceptualization of Husayn's role should be understood foremost as a defensive posture.

Unconventionally educated ʿulama were not the only ones who sought to limit the clerical authority of Lucknow. Such an intention was also voiced by a group that has barely been researched, namely Shiʿi *sajjada nashins*, the successors of famous Sufi saints. Tahir Kamran and Amir Shahid have found that colonial gazetteers of the late nineteenth century noted a rise of Shiʿi Islam in some districts of the Punjab, most notably Jhang. According to these reports, a primary cause for this swelling of Shiʿi ranks came through the conversion of formerly Sunni Sayyid families.[121] These dynamics warrant much more attention, especially in the context of the question whether a significant portion of those "converts" might in fact have been secretly practicing Shiʿi Islam for quite some time. This is not to say that we should fall into the trap of projecting backward an exclusively conflictual conception of Sunni-Shiʿi relations or to assume that religious identification as either Sunni or Shiʿi was necessarily clear-cut. Yet, it might be equally problematic to describe Punjab's religious landscape prior to the nineteenth century as "syncretist." Farina Mir has instead suggested that there were several areas of converging, "shared piety" that manifested themselves inter alia through the veneration of saints.[122] Be that as it may, contemporaneous Shiʿi publications at least make the case that British rule enabled the Shiʿi population in the Punjab and elsewhere to abandon their long-held practice of pious dissimulation (taqiyya) and to confess their faith openly.[123] Even though it is thus not possible at present to gauge the precise dynamics regarding the "official" conversion of figures of mystical authority to Shiʿi Islam, it is remarkable that Lucknow's mujtahids felt their primacy questioned from a Sufi-Shiʿi angle. Such a perspective was presented during the 1923 AISC session in Jhang by the head of the organization committee, Pir Sayyid Muhammad Ghaus Shah (d. 1970).[124] The *pir* was the *sajjada nashin* of Shah Ismaʿil Bukhari (d. 1446 or 47/850), who is buried in Chiniot.[125] In his speech, he put those Shiʿi ʿulama who had come to Jhang on a seemingly equal footing with the saints buried in the city and its surroundings. He compared these towering figures of the past, whom he also addressed as ʿulama, with a "torch of guidance" and a "beacon of brightness" for everyone lost in darkness. The saints had been able to draw from "God's repository of hidden realities" (*malik al-mulk ke khazanah-i ghayb se*) both the "esoteric light" (*nur-i batin*) and the "exoteric affluence" (*sarvat-i zahiri*).[126] In the present, their *sajjada nashins* kept this mission alive, which made it possible for the delegates who had assembled in Jhang to benefit from these "holy spirits" (*arvah-i muqaddasah*). The AISC members could address the saints with their prayers and concerns; at the same time, the ʿulama present could give advice on how to cling to the straight path.[127] With this speech, Pir Sayyid Muhammad Ghaus Shah attempted to shift the Shiʿi center of the subcontinent away from Lucknow. This city with its seminaries was nothing more than a recent upstart in comparison to the Punjab's ancient spiritual landscape.[128] This intimate connection with a pure Shiʿi geography will resurface again in intra-Shiʿi polemical debates in chapter 2.

Before moving on I briefly return to the tabarra agitation and discuss how the All India Shiʿa Conference struggled to defend its claimed leadership during these turbulent months. As we have seen, the senior mujtahids did not hesitate to commit themselves to this cause. A pamphlet written by the Honorary Secretary of Sayyid ʿAli Naqi Naqvi's Imamia Mission consequently credited the events with reestablishing trust between the ʿulama and the Shiʿi qaum because the former had proven that they too were people of action.[129] Lucknow had regained its standing through the tabarra agitation, it had been turned into the pole (*qutb*) around which the entire Indian Shiʿi world (*hindustan ka ʿalam-i shiʿiyyat*) circled.[130] The city's jails, which had been the site of intensive deliberation by the "prisoners of tabarra," should be regarded as the real, representative All India Shiʿa Conference. Previous pan-Indian gatherings had only encompassed few people, and by no means every stratum had been represented there.[131] Not surprisingly, the AISC did not accept this negative portrayal of its activities. Rather, it drew a different lesson from the intra-Muslim conflict in Lucknow. The raja of Mahmudabad's younger brother Amir Haydar Khan deplored the lack of a palpable organization or leadership during the turmoil in Lucknow. Instead, the whole affair had played out as an amalgam of particular initiatives that were all striving for their own particular goal. No movement could be successful this way, especially because the present time was the era of "organized social forces" (*ijtimaʿi taqaton*). The Shiʿi qaum and its existing communal organizations had no other choice but to rally behind one (collective) leader and delegate all their powers to him (*apne tamam ikhtiyarat ek qaʾid ko tafviz kar dete hen*). This was a role that should ideally be filled by the AISC.[132]

THE FREESTANDING RELIGION OF SHIʿI ISLAM?

What deeper impact did such instances of colonial sectarianism have on the self-fashioning of India's Shiʿi community? Justin Jones has criticized earlier scholarship that focused primarily on the "generic" Muslim presentation of (elite) Shiʿis, who tried to do away with all distinctively Shiʿi markers.[133] He has argued that Shiʿi writers and orators in the late colonial period reframed Shiʿism as its own freestanding, "independent religious community": "Indeed, the whole language of 'sect' and 'school' that modern literature often applies to Shiʿism looks somewhat misleading, in view of the demands of many Shiʿa for the full communal legitimacy and group parity that would abrogate this assumed Muslim minority status. Shiʿism was gradually articulated as historically, legally and ritualistically separate from other South Asian Islamic traditions; it was distinct not on individual points of tenet, text or custom, but as an explicit religious system itself."[134] Undoubtedly, the notion of a total separation was voiced repeatedly in the context of the AISC when passing resolutions on the necessity of independent religious instruction for Shiʿi students. The organization demanded that Lahore's Islamia College hire a Shiʿi professor in order to develop a separate syllabus of religious instruction for students adhering to this faith. It was not possible for the Shiʿi students to continue attending religious instruction that was taught from the Sunni point of view, because Sunnis "were in their fundamentals of religion and religious beliefs totally different."[135] At the same time, the conference proceedings emphasized the AISC's commitment to render Shiʿism into a "solid pillar" and a "strong and valued part" of the house of Islam.[136]

These two positions are not mutually exclusive, however. I argue that many Shiʿi Indian writings from the late colonial period do not support the notion of Shiʿi Islam being turned into its own, independent, and "freestanding" religion. Speaking of an "explicit religious system" strikes me as anachronistic when describing religious thought in a time period during which Shiʿi thinkers had not yet developed their own approaches toward Islamist understandings of Islam.[137] Instead, Shiʿi authors strove to demonstrate that their interpretation of Islamic history and belief should be regarded as the original, unadulterated version of the faith.[138] Consequently, they were eager to present themselves as a spiritual elite vis-à-vis the general (Sunni) Muslim public. Joya Chatterji has observed a similar strategy among the Hindu landed elite (*bhadralok*) of Bengal. The latter claimed from the 1930s onward that they stood at the apex of a cultural pyramid that supposedly even encompassed "nominally Hindu castes and tribes on the margins of polite society."[139] In the Shiʿi context, such an approach comes to the fore in a tract on the caliphate by ʿAllamah Hindi, a scholar from the *khandan-i ijtihad* who had strong ties with Iraq.[140] He makes the case that the Shiʿis could only accept hadiths handed down through ʿAli and his descendants. All other paths of transmission had to be regarded as expressions of an inauthentic, self-made (*khud sakhtah*) version of Islam.[141] The Prophet and the Imams had been interested not in empire (*mulk dari*) and world domination (*jahan bani*) but in the purification of the soul, the cultivation of humanity, and spiritual development.[142] By contrast, the Companions of the Prophet and the first Caliphs (with the exception of ʿAli) had cared only for conquest (*mulk giri*). Such mundane motivations still propelled the Sunnis of his day, as ʿAllamah Hindi argued. They subjected God's religion to the shaky and whimsical consensus of the community (*ijmaʿ*) and thus submitted religion to the inadmissible workings of democracy.[143] Ibn-i Hasan Jarcavi adduced similar points in his letter to Gandhi, mentioned earlier. He argued that the Imams had denied all worldly power offered to them because they held that their "kingdom is not of this world, we are rulers of spiritual matters" (*hamari saltanat maddi dunya ki nahin ham ruhaniyyat ke badshah hen*).[144] Additionally, what set the Shiʿis apart was their insistence on independent legal reasoning (ijtihad). This approach let them appear as following a truly modern version of Islam that was not bound by stale taqlid or confined to any particular school of Islam.[145] Such an argument is reflected in, for example, the writings of the Amroha-based scholar Sayyid Shafiq Hasan (d. 1920). In his work *Asl al-usul* (The principle of principles) he attempted to establish the polarity of *tawalla* and tabarra as the heart of religion. In a thinly veiled critique of the four established Sunni schools of law, Hasan argued that if one encountered four people with diverging views, it was impossible to claim that they could all be equally valid opinions within the boundaries of the same *maslak*. Truth could not be plural.[146] This perspective was at times even taken by Shiʿi authors, to the point of reading the Qurʾanic verse 36:4 "on the straight path" (*ʿala siratin mustaqimin*) as "ʿAli is the straight path" (*ʿAli siratun mustaqimun*).[147]

One possible explanation for why Shiʿis in undivided India merely insisted on defending the pure version of Islam instead of promoting the self-conception of belonging to an independent religion is that they were not recognized by the British as an autonomous *madhhab*. This stands in sharp contrast to what happened under the auspices of the French mandate in Lebanon. There this recognition and the establishment of a separate Shiʿi Jaʿfari court in 1926 was not only an unprecedented innovation but also marked "a turning point in the trajectory of the Lebanese Shiʿa toward sectarian modernity, in which newly bureaucratized and standardized norms of legal procedure institutionally bound the Shiʿa to the state."[148] This "sectarianization from above" went hand in hand with an active reception of this novel institution from below. Ordinary Shiʿis were eager to bring their cases to their "own" court, since they perceived it as an empowering way to claim individual and communal rights. For Lebanese Shiʿis, the Jaʿfari court opened nothing less than entirely new pathways through which they could oppose "corrupt 'feudal' leaders and clientelist networks of patronage and power."[149]

Whatever might have been the precise cause for Shiʿi self-fashioning in India, such an attitude of superiority made it very difficult for the Shiʿis to embrace Sunni initiatives of reconciliation and rapprochement that aimed at leveling the Islamic playing field. Efforts in this regard had been undertaken, for example, by the Ahl-i Hadis scholar Sanaʾullah Amritsari (d. 1948), who had tried to ease Sunni-Shiʿi tensions in Lahore after the Shiʿi profession of faith had supposedly appeared there inscribed in the bark of a tree.[150] The crude Arabic signs visible on the stem comprised the universal Muslim profession that there is no god but God and that Muhammad was his messenger. Crucially, however, the explicitly Shiʿi statement that ʿAli was God's appointee (*wasi*) and friend/viceregent (*wali*) could reportedly be seen as well.[151] Sanaʾullah Amritsari picked up on the events of Lahore in sermons and in his own journal, claiming that both Sunnis and Shiʿis would accept ʿAli as the *wasi*. While for the latter he was the "appointee in the caliphate" (*wasi bi-khilafa*), the former regarded him as "appointee in love" (*wasi bi-muhabba*). According to Amritsari, in granting this miracle God had avoided taking sides and declaring openly which view He prioritized in order to unite Sunnis and Shiʿis in their fight against the unbelievers (*kuffar*).[152] Similarly, the high-ranking Congress politician Abul Kalam Azad tried to minimize

Sunni-Shiʿi animosity by emphasizing that both groups agreed on the need to obey the Imam. They differed only on the method of choosing him.[153]

The Shiʿis did not catch on to such harmonizing strategies that aimed at papering over the profound differences of opinion between the two sects. One author detailed in a book written in either 1939 or 1940 the qualitative difference that existed between the Shiʿis and the "common Muslims" (*ʿamm musalman*). Due to the constant persecution and mistreatment by the Sunni majority the Shiʿis had been refined in the same way that the pressure a mountain range applied on carbon generated brilliant diamonds.[154] The Shiʿis had more love for each other and for the *ahl al-bayt* (the Prophet's wife and the Imams) than the ordinary adherents of Islam did. They freely disposed of their wealth for the cause of religion. Their understanding of the truths of Qur'an and hadith outstripped by far Sunni capabilities.[155]

The special traits of the Shiʿi qaum were underlined by other arguments as well. These extended from their above-average levels of literacy to the education and intelligence of their women. Hooseinbhoy Lalljee, a politician affiliated with the AISC, remarked that in India literacy was significantly less common than in Europe and that Muslims in general underperformed in this regard. Among the Shiʿis, however, "there are more than seventy-five per cent literates which is a percentage as great as to be found anywhere in the world and while the Shia community has produced and has also at present some of the greatest leaders in politics professions [*sic*], commerce and industry as well as in Zamindari and other walks of life that they should remain suppressed is not only not in the interest of India but is also a sacrifice of the cause of humanity and no such example can be found in any part of the world."[156] A further fascinating example for such constructions of superiority is the fictional work *Jauhar-i Qur'an* (The essence of the Qur'an), in which a literate Shiʿi wife debates and defeats her well-trained Deobandi husband.[157] Hidayat Khatun (literally: Lady Guidance), the main character of the book, grew up in a mixed Sunni-Shiʿi family in Hyderabad (Deccan). Her grandfather on her Sunni mother's side feared that she might tilt toward the religion of her Shiʿi father who had come to the Deccan from Lucknow. In order to forestall this possibility, Hidayat's grandfather hired an anti-Shiʿi polemicist (*munazir*) to oversee the young girl's education and to teach her the Qur'an, Arabic, and polemical literature. The *maulvi* suggested naming the girl Lady Guidance as she might even be able to direct her father toward the "religion of truth" (*mazhab-i haqq*).[158] Yet this elaborate plan came to naught. Hidayat was eager to learn but increasingly became interested in Shiʿi Islam. The last hope was her husband Rukn al-Din, who had studied at Deoband and Rampur. Hidayat's grandfather had full confidence in his abilities and saw no reason to be worried: "How difficult can it be after all to turn a woman into a Sunni?"[159] When husband and wife started debating taqiyya, the role of the ahl al-bayt, the integrity of the Qur'an, or the physicality of God, it quickly became clear that Hidayat would be a tough interlocutor. She was entirely at home in the Sunni scholarly tradition, quick to advance rational arguments, and could deftly navigate the couple's book shelves to underline her arguments with specific quotations.[160] Finally, Rukn al-Din invited three hundred educated Sunnis and explained to them how his wife had invalidated all his arguments. He publicly declared his conversion to Shiʿi Islam, which caused widespread consternation, since neither activists of the Arya Samaj nor Christian missionaries had been able to overcome this talented ʿalim in the past.[161]

CONCEPTUALIZING PAKISTAN

According to most of the secondary literature, however, manifestations of intense Shiʿi-Sunni rivalry as spelled out in a work like *Jauhar-i Qur'an* were nothing more than a tempest in a teapot. Once the Muslims of India had set their sights on the creation of Pakistan, differences took a back seat, to the extent that "both Shias and Sunnis buried their hatchets, hitched their fortunes to the Muslim League bandwagon and undertook their long trek toward the promised 'dar al-Islam' (land of Islam)."[162] Such an evaluation ties in with the consensus that the ML took a decidedly nonsectarian stance.[163] League members like the Bengali surgeon and politician Sir Hasan Suhravardi (1884–1946) predicted the demise of all Sunni-Shiʿi tensions in the future because this "unfortunate schism is now dying out." He expressed his satisfaction that "these small differences have with the expansion of liberal education disappeared in Islamic countries and are fast disappearing in India."[164] Scholars also emphasize the prominent role played by Shiʿis like Jinnah himself.[165] Other influential Shiʿis in the ML were the raja of Mahmudabad, who acted as the League's treasurer and headed the All India Muslim Students Federation; the Shiʿi lawyer Ismaʿil Ibrahim Cundrigar (1897–1960), who became head of the Bombay Provincial Muslim League in 1937 and served as Pakistan's prime minister for two months in 1957; and the Bengali business magnate Mirza Abu 'l-Hasan Isfahani (1902–75).[166] Isfahani, for example, expressed the ML line that the "salvation of the Muslim nation in this vast-subcontinent of India lies in its unity." If divided, "the Muslims will be crushed and the Shias, who constitute a very small minority among them, will suffer greatly." In his view, most of his coreligionists had come around to accepting the League as the only representative organization, which was "the reason why the majority of the Shias and the most prominent of their leaders are active Muslim Leaguers."[167] Muhammad Ali Jinnah publicly expressed his disapproval of the AISC and its political arm. In a letter to Sayyid ʿAli Zahir dated 31 August 1944, Jinnah was of the opinion that Shiʿis who organized outside the ML umbrella were "under some sort of misapprehension." His party stood for "justice and fair play," and there was "no need for the Shias to think that they will not be justly treated by the All India Muslim League."[168]

Faisal Devji has challenged this dominant portrayal of Sunni-Shiʿi dynamics during the last years of the still-unified subcontinent, arguing that we should pay attention to how even within the ML Shiʿi leaders strove to draw attention to Shiʿi concerns in the face of Sunni dominance: "And in this sense the minority protection sought by the League's Shia leaders had to do with their fear of a Sunni majority as much as a Hindu one, something that has been neglected in a historiography marked both by the Muslim League's 'ecumenism' in conceiving of a unified Muslim community, and, to be charitable about it, the inadvertent sectarianism of ignoring its internal difficulties in the name of this unity."[169]

Such problematic trends in the historiography even manifest themselves in works entirely geared toward providing the reader with the full breadth of pre-Partition Muslim debates about Pakistan. Venkat Dhulipala in his contribution deems it sufficient to devote only 12 pages out of 530 to Shiʿi reactions to this envisioned homeland.[170] Moreover, his discussion focuses almost exclusively on the raja of Mahmudabad, even though Dhulipala criticizes existing scholarship precisely for a too-narrow focus on Jinnah and the ML elite while neglecting other voices, such as the ʿulama.[171] Dhulipala comes to the conclusion that after some initial hesitation there was notable "enthusiasm" among the Shiʿis for the idea of Pakistan, starting in 1945: "A new feature of Moharram *alams* [standards] and *tazias* [replicas of the Imams' tombs] that year was the prominence of the Pakistan map in front of every group of processions and the mounting of ML flags on elephants. The usual Moharram slogan *Ya Ali* was replaced by the ML war cry '*le ke rahenge Pakistan*' [we will seize Pakistan]."[172]

This account of a smooth Shiʿi acceptance of the concept of Pakistan is unconvincing in light of documented instances of anti-Shiʿi rhetoric and behavior by crucial supporters of the Muslim League. At the forefront were ʿulama affiliated with the Jamʿiyyat al-ʿUlamaʾ-i Islam (JUI), which had been founded as a breakaway faction of the organization Jamʿiyyat al-ʿUlamaʾ-i Hind (JUH) and countered the latter's critique of Pakistan. In order to achieve Pakistan, these religious scholars attacked the concept of "united nationalism" and argued that devout Muslims should throw in their lot with the nonpracticing, grave sinners (*fasiqs*) of the League.[173]

A case in point for my argument is Shabbir Ahmad ʿUsmani (1885–1949), who "provided the JUI with its ideological moorings," "campaigned vigorously for the ML through the length and breadth of India," and later took a crucial role in shaping Pakistan's Islamic identity.[174] ʿUsmani was the "most highly placed ʿalim in the ruling hierarchy" and had "direct access to the Prime Minister" of the new country. He played a crucial role in the adoption of the Objectives Resolution and also convened a World Muslim Conference before his death in 1949.[175] A fellow scholar from Amritsar had asked ʿUsmani in November 1945, during the run-up to the December general Indian elections, how it was at all possible to support the ML and even term the party "a ship of salvation for the Muslims"—a quotation Urdu newspapers were attributing to ʿUsmani.[176] Even though ʿUsmani's correspondent did not raise the Shiʿi connotations of the term, *safinah-i najat* is a curious choice, since it is used by Shiʿis as an appellation for the Imams, who are thus compared in their function to Noah's Ark.[177] In his reply, ʿUsmani only qualified his use of the term: he had meant to convey, he said, that at present the Muslim League was "the boat of salvation for the communal and political independence of the Muslims" (*musalmanon ke qaumi o siyasi istiqlal ke liye safinah-i najat*). The Deobandi scholar relied on the reasoning of the early Hanafi authority Muhammad b. al-Hasan al-Shaybani (d. 187/803 or 189/805).[178] Al-Shaybani had allowed Muslims to cooperate with the early Muslim sect of the Kharijites if their common fight was against the polytheists (*mushrikun*) and for the sake of "manifesting Islam" (*izhar-i Islam*).[179] According to ʿUsmani, al-Shaybani had arrived at this reasoning even though there was no other sect about which so many "unequivocal texts" (*nusus-i sariha*) existed which condemned them and predicted divine punishment similar to that which overtook the pre-Islamic peoples of ʿAd and Thamud. Consequently, and as an *argumentum a fortiori*, for the time being the Shiʿis as a "false sect" (*firqah-i batila*) could be relied on.[180]

Another founding member of the JUI and ML supporter, Maulana Zafar Ahmad ʿUsmani (d. 1974), published a similar fatwa a couple of weeks later in the League's daily, *al-Manshur*.[181] Both ʿUsmanis thus adopted a much more decidedly anti-Shiʿi stance than their mentor, Ashraf ʿAli Thanavi (d. 1943), who in 1939 had used the same analogical reasoning to justify the cooperation of the ʿulama with the (nonobservant) ML leaders. Not only had Thanavi hastened to add that the ML leaders "were certainly not as debased as the *Khawarij*," he also had nowhere singled out Jinnah as a Shiʿi.[182] The openly sectarian stance of these scholars also implied that the JUI was not even considering including Shiʿi ʿulama in their ranks.[183]

It is probably also not too far off the mark to interpret statements which Shabbir Ahmad ʿUsmani made in January 1946 in front of members of the Punjab chapter of the JUI in this way, too. The ʿalim cautioned that Pakistan would not simply be welcoming all sorts of Muslims. Rather, it was necessary that the new homeland's inhabitants worked toward cleansing their "morals, deeds, thoughts, and emotions" (*akhlaq, aʿmal, khayalat aur jazbat*). This task of living up to the challenge of inhabiting the "Land of the Pure" would of course continue even after the establishment of Pakistan, because building a truly Islamic society was an arduous, gradual process.[184] In addition, ʿUsmani relied in an election flyer on the Qur'anic version of the Golden Calf story in order to buttress the urgent need for intra-Muslim unity. In ʿUsmani's retelling, Aaron justified his lack of action to stop idolatry with the argument that he had feared a splintering of the qaum to an even greater extent.[185] A Shiʿi reader of this ML pamphlet might have wondered what such a reasoning would imply once the pressing need for closing ranks had worn off and Pakistan had been achieved.

This ties in with another major concern for the Shiʿis, namely statements about the future design of the Muslim homeland and, most importantly, on what sources of fiqh it should draw. The Muslim League–affiliated Deobandi scholar Maulana Sayyid Nazir al-Haqq was quoted in the press on 3 November 1945 with the ruling that according to the Prophet "only those who followed the path of the Rightly Guided Caliphs were on the right path, whereas all other groups, parties or sects would be 'a work of Satan.'"[186] Local ML leaders were busy calling for Pakistan's constitution to be based not only on the Qur'an but to be a true reflection of the *hukumat-i ilahiyyah*, the "divine government" of the first four Caliphs.[187] Especially in the 1945–46 elections, the League decided to rely on many pirs and local Sunni scholars, who formulated their own messages by "fanning communal passions at the base."[188] Shabir Ahmad ʿUsmani tried to dampen enthusiasm by pointing out that initially the expectations could not be higher than simply having a "just government" (*hukumat-i ʿadilah*) in place. He did not deny, however, that a "rightly guided caliphate" (*khilafat-i rashidah*) and a "purely Qur'anic and Islamic government" (*khalis qur'ani aur Islami hukumat*) were Pakistan's ultimate goals.[189] At the appropriate time, the *ahl-i hall o ʿaqd* (the people of loosing and binding) would determine the constitutional and institutional nature of Pakistan. For him, the "people of loosing and binding" were most likely the ʿulama.[190]

In the shadow of these Sunni claims, Fazil Muraj, a Bombay-based Shiʿi member of the ML, reported to Jinnah on 19 September 1945 that his attempts at building support among the Shiʿis in the city had been made extremely difficult by certain "influential Muslim League personalities." At their behest "in the Municipal Urdu schools in Bombay a new *Kalima* introducing the names of the four Caliphs was made compulsory for the children of all the sections of Islam. It was at the representation made by a deputation of the Shias that the then Mayor, Mr. Nagindas Master, had it discontinued."[191]

All of this did not necessarily mean that India's Shiʿis were free from grievances regarding the Congress, too. As we have seen above, the tabarra agitation loomed large for the community. They blamed the Congress for both encouraging the Ahrar to become fully involved in the dispute and also for giving free rein to Deobandi scholars affiliated with it.[192] Drawing for his reasoning on Shaykh Ahmad Sirhindi (d. 1034/1624), Sayyid Husayn Ahmad Madani had proclaimed that the public praise of the sahaba should be seen as a "distinct mark of the Sunnis" (*shiʿar-i ahl-i sunnat*). Its public character, in particular, had the advantage of revealing whether someone held wrong beliefs and whether "his heart was sick and his inner life despicable" (*dilash mariz va batinash khabis*). Muslims were obliged to openly confess what distinguished them from the kuffar.[193] Praising the Companions of the Prophet became particularly mandatory if such wrong ideas like ʿAli's supposed status as the Prophet's rightful successor were advocated in imambaras and mosques. Attributing wrong, baseless, and contemptible events (*ghalat aur chute ihanat amiz vaqiʿat*) to the sahaba, who were a source of guidance to humanity as a whole, might as a final consequence lead ordinary Sunnis astray.[194] Several decades earlier and in the context of the Non-Cooperation movement, Madani still had urged Sunnis to abstain from confrontations with the Shiʿis in order to forge a joint front against the colonial government. His intervention in Lucknow was thus a clear "reversal of his earlier role."[195]

But soon, and especially after the Muslim League had passed its Lahore Resolution on 23 March 1940, the attainment of Pakistan became the more pressing issue. Doubts about the future state even affected the surroundings of the raja of Mahmudabad, one of the main Shiʿi backers of the League and the Pakistan movement. In March 1940, his younger brother Amir Haydar Khan wrote to Jinnah, requesting safeguards for the Shiʿis in terms of their representation in elected bodies. He also asked for guarantees that freedom of beliefs and customs would be protected in Pakistan and that Shiʿis would be exempted from potential future laws that were built on Hanafi interpretations of fiqh. If these concerns were adequately addressed, the Shiʿis "could whole-heartedly support the struggle for Pakistan."[196] In his reply, which was not made public until 1946, Jinnah criticized Amir Haydar Khan for "still working in the direction which is not likely to benefit the Shias." In his view, "the one thing alone that matters is that we are all Mussalmans." Jinnah did not offer any safeguards but once again underlined the importance of "fair play" and "justice" for the Shiʿis. He expressed his openness, however, to grant Shiʿis the control over Shiʿi pious endowments (*auqaf*, sg. *waqf*). Jinnah also tried to alleviate Amir Haydar Khan's fears of Sunni domination by stating that if a law was passed according to Hanafi fiqh, "the special principles of Shia Shariat must also be taken into consideration."[197]

The All India Shiʿa Conference embarked on a more public path in voicing its reservations regarding Pakistan. Its journal *Sarfaraz* referred to speeches by the Muslim League member and president of the Punjab Muslim Students Federation Bashir Ahmad (1893–1971), delivered to the All India Muslims Students Association and in the context of the annual meeting of the Anjuman-i Himayat-i Islam in Lahore. Ahmad had stated repeatedly that Pakistan was about spreading a version of Islam that was based on the Qur'an and the example of both the Prophet and the sahaba.[198] The editorial explained its goal of drawing attention to such examples to open the eyes of India's Shiʿis: "If our life will be limited to protest and sacrifice [*ihtijaj aur qurbani*], what sort of need do we have for Pakistan? A united Hindustan is way better for us, because the Hindus do not mind if we proclaim that ʿAli was the immediate successor of the Prophet [*khilafa bi-la fasl*] or engage in mourning rites."

The journal urged its readers not to accept the argument that Bashir Ahmad had only expressed his personal opinion. Pakistan, too, had originated as the idea of an individual.[199] Yet, the conception of a political system based on the sahaba will most likely "spread like a forest fire." Its pull will become unstoppable. *Sarfaraz* contended that it had supported the ML at first, when Jinnah had taken over as its leader and put the organization on "progressive tracks" (*taraqqi pasandanah raston par*). It still deemed the League necessary to stave off Hindu "extremism" (*taʿassub*). Yet, as far as Pakistan was concerned, they could only lend support to the scheme if it was intended to clearly protect freedom of religion and culture (*mazhab o tamaddun ki azadi*) along with the Shiʿis' political rights. There was no military dictator in the vein of Mustafa Kemal Atatürk or Reza Shah Pahlavi of Iran on the horizon who would solve the problem by imposing on the Sunnis "free thinking" (*azad khayal*) and acceptance of the Shiʿis. Without such coercion, of which Jinnah supposedly was not capable, sectarianism would be openly on display.[200] An example of this issue was a book published by a Sunni barrister in Lahore who used "inappropriate" language about ʿAli.[201] *Sarfaraz* accused the Sunni press in the Punjab of not rallying against this work because it was written by a nominal (*nam nihad*) Sunni Muslim. If this is already true, the paper's editor asked, how will it be in a future Pakistan? "Won't there be a system of government and society which is exclusively built on the Sunni point of view?"[202]

This sort of reasoning is also reflected in speeches made during the All Parties Shiʿa Conference, an initiative spearheaded by the All India Shiʿa Political Party. It attracted around eight hundred delegates, among them many representatives of Shiʿi anjumans, and convened in October 1945 in Lucknow and in the following December in Pune.[203] Sayyid Akhtar Husayn Shaʾiq, the joint secretary of the Punjab Shiʿa Political Conference, flatly denied any rosy picture of Shiʿi-Sunni unity in the Punjab. Such an impression had been given by the prominent Shiʿi ML member Raja Ghazanfar ʿAli Khan (1895–1963), who had described sectarian relations in the province as "excellent":[204] "Let the Shia Muslim Leaguers in the Punjab say that there was no Shia-Sunni conflict in that province! They are great men, they move in high and influential circles and as such they might have been receiving such information. But those who represent the middle and lower classes can well realise the opposite. It is a fact that the Sunni majority in the Muslim League is out to crush the Shias completely in our province. We are no doubt tolerant but there is a limit for everything."[205] Hooseinbhoy Lalljee (1886–1971), a Bombay businessman and president of the All Parties Shiʿa Conference, put it in even starker terms.[206] In a meeting with the British Parliamentary Delegation that toured India in January and February 1946, he described the League as "fascist body" and accused it of employing methods similar to Hitler's Germany. The AIML aimed to "crush all opposition and capture power to establish the government of a Sunni Junta, by a Sunni Junta and for a Sunni Junta," for example by exclusively enforcing Hanafi law.[207] Lucknow's Tanzim al-Muʾminin echoed this view to the delegation members. It claimed that "the Shias fear that with the establishment of Pakistan, the Sunni majority will get ample opportunity to persecute the Shia minority in every possible way as had been their tradition for the last 1300 years."[208]

On 25 October 1945 the Shiʿi lawyer, journalist, and AISPC activist Jaʿfar Husayn used a private letter to Fazil Muraj, the Shiʿi Muslim Leaguer in Bombay, to convey a "frank expression" of his views:[209]

> I am a Shia first and a Muslim afterwards. I do not believe in any abstract conception of Islam. We are either Sunnis or Shias. In my very well-considered opinion there lives not one person in this country who is a Musalman pure and simple—neither a Shia nor a Sunni. I may remind you of the famous *Hadis* of our holy Prophet when he said "Musalmans

will stand divided after me in 72 sections and only one out of these 72 will get salvation." This *Hadis* clearly shows that out of these 72 sections that exist today only one represents true Islam and according to our belief and faith we are that one section. I rest my arguments on this *Hadis* and I emphatically say that we represent true Islam and if we are doomed Islam is doomed. Now let me say that the religious, economic, political and social rights of the Shias have never been so much endangered in the country as they are now—not at the hands of the Hindus or the Congress but at the hands of your Muslim League and your Quaid-i-Azam Mr Jinnah.

Husayn continued that he saw on a daily basis "atrocities of the worst kind" being perpetrated by the ML. He pointed out that Shiʿis in Bihar had to suffer under the League, that Shiʿis had been fired from the Customs Department in Calcutta by ML officials, and that the battle for the protection of Shiʿi mourning processions (*taʿziyadari*) in the Punjab was waged against Sunni League Muslims. He also dismissed oral assurances Jinnah had given to the Shiʿis about the protection of their rights in a future Pakistan:

> What is the value of oral assurances in the body politic of today's world? We have seen the oral assurances given by Hitler, Mussolini, Chamberlain, Stalin and Churchill. What can be the value of these oral assurances when we see before our own eyes that long-standing conventions such as the one that existed in Lucknow for the last thirty-five years in favour of the Shias was broken with the help of the Muslim League, by the Sunnis, during the last Municipal Board elections. We have lost all faith in oral promises and even conventions. Nothing short of statutory safeguards can satisfy us. I really fail to understand if Mr. Jinnah is honest in his profession and he does not want to befool the Shias. Why should he not agree to statutory safeguards for this important minority community in India?[210]

A meeting of Shiʿi ʿulama in Lucknow had already in July 1945 declared the League to be "almost entirely a Sunni organisation," cooperation with which was "highly undesirable from religious [*sic*] point of view. We feel confident that all Shia Muslims will action [*sic*] this advice."[211] The picture painted in this way of Sunnis scheming to uproot everything Shiʿis held dear does not diverge substantially from the warnings issued by the Bengali Hindu Mahasabha leader Shyama Prasad Mukherjee (d. 1953) in 1946 about the ML. He wrote in a private note that if Bengal became part of Pakistan and Hindus would hence be forced to live under Muslim domination, "[this] means an end of Bengali Hindu culture. In order to placate a set of converts from low caste Hindus to Islam, very ancient Hindu culture will be sacrificed."[212]

Bleak views of this kind were not shared by all prominent Shiʿis to the same degree nor was the acrimonious public nature of the debate condoned by everyone. The raja of Mahmudabad and Ibn-i Hasan Jarcavi both supported Jinnah in his election campaign against Lalljee. Jarcavi even agreed to act as one of two religious scholars chosen by Jinnah to elucidate the "Islamic ideology" (*islami nazariyyah*) underpinning the demand for Pakistan during a meeting with the Cabinet Mission—and the other ʿalim selected was none other than Shabbir Ahmad ʿUsmani.[213] At the same time, however, Amir Ahmad Khan hoped to privately convince Jinnah to include a Shiʿi ʿalim among the League representatives for the Constituent Assembly of India.[214] The raja of Mahmudabad never migrated to Pakistan and later pointed darkly to the "general sense of gloom and despondency that pervaded the two newly created states; instead of the joy and expectancy which should have been ours after these years of struggle there were only premonitions of impending conflicts and a promise of future struggle."[215] Jarcavi only made his way to the new country in 1951 after originally claiming that his task was now to provide Shiʿi education in India.[216] Shiʿis in the Punjab were wavering until the last minute between the Muslim League and the Unionist Party, repeatedly shifting their allegiances. Some leaders of the Punjab Shiʿa Political Conference, among them Navab Muzaffar ʿAli Khan Qizilbash had in 1944 declared safeguards offered by Jinnah during a private meeting in Lahore as sufficient to mitigate their concerns about the ML. This announcement led to a strong backlash within the organization, causing Qizilbash to revert to a hardline stance against the League when he served as minister for revenue in Malik Khizr Hayat Tivanah's Congress-Panthic-Unionist government that emerged from the February 1946 elections in the Punjab. After the resignation of the Unionist premier in March 1947, however, Qizilbash's "main concern seems to have become mending fences with the League, which he would later join without much difficulties."[217] What all of this means, however, is that Shiʿis were precisely not jumping on the ML bandwagon but found themselves overtaken by the sheer pace of events. The entrenched power of the Unionist party suddenly was "disintegrating like a mud fort in a monsoon."[218]

That the Muslim League managed to obtain power in the Punjab so quickly and unexpectedly had to do with its weak position in the province. The changing of sides by several leading families, many of them also acting as *sajjada nashins* in the countryside, set an avalanche in motion.[219] Influential pirs raised "personal identification with Pakistan to a level that transcended politics," with the pir of Golrah Sharif warning his *murid*, Prime Minister Malik Khizr Hayat Tivanah, "not to separate himself from the Islamic movement lest he become 'fuel for the fires of Hell.'"[220] When in March 1947 no new government could be formed and the Punjab came under governor's rule, it set the stage for "Punjab's own midsummer nightmare," namely methodically planned acts of killing, arson, and sabotage committed by members of the Hindu, Sikh, and Muslim communities. Cities like Rawalpindi, Lahore, and Amritsar were all affected.[221] The violence and massive migration of people crowded out all other concerns for Sunnis and Shiʿis alike in the spring and summer of 1947.

THE SALIENCE OF TRANSNATIONAL CONNECTIONS

Before closing this chapter, I take a brief look at arguments about the predominance of Indian concerns in Shiʿi thought during the late colonial period. Gail Minault holds that the reaction of the Khilafatists in the face of Turkey's decision to abolish the caliphate demonstrated the movement's "totally Indian character."[222] Justin Jones has come to a similar conclusion, namely that Shiʿi associational life in colonial India displayed an "apparent lack of extensive direct engagement with issues affecting the Shiʿa in the wider world." In his view, the AISC had merely passed "tokenistic resolutions expressing 'concern' over events in Persia and Iraq"; there were "no substantial reactions" to events like the Constitutional Revolution in Iran or the damage done to the shrine of Imam Riza in Mashhad. This lack of concern for transnational Shiʿi issues could be attributed to the "contemporaneous development in the Urdu ecumene of a *qaumi* construction of Shi'ism, one which emphasized the autonomy of 'Indian' manifestations of religion, and, by extension of its politics, from the wider world."[223]

The evidence presented in this chapter runs counter to such an evaluation. Shiʿi ʿulama displayed a keen interest in an Iranian-style supervisory council. In fact, the idea had such a wide appeal that Ashraf ʿAli Thanavi attempted to persuade Jinnah to install a similar but surely Sunni-dominated body within the hierarchy of the ML.[224] Functionaries of the AISC expressed their high regard for the modernization policies of both Atatürk and Reza Pahlavi. Still reeling from how the colonial state had undermined the position held by the Shiʿi aristocracy in North India, they saw these models applied beyond the subcontinent perhaps also as successful alternatives for a future "secular" and independent Indian state.[225] I thus suggest that it is impossible to disentangle the transnational dimension from Shiʿi self-understanding during the late colonial period. I discuss the complex interactions with the centers of Shiʿi learning and religious veneration in Iran and Iraq more fully in the following chapters, but here I point to M. Naeem Qureshi's useful corrective to the assumption that the Khilafat movement was confined to the subcontinent. Instead, Qureshi has written, "pan-Islam, even though it proved chimerical in the end, played a central role in mobilizing Indian Muslims for mass politics and in so doing contributed decisively to the development of Muslim nationalism in the long run."[226]

One major concern for the Shiʿis in the period under discussion was undoubtedly the (second) destruction of the Jannat al-Baqiʿ cemetery of Medina in April 1926 at the hands of ʿAbd al-ʿAziz b. ʿAbd al-Rahman Al Saʿud's (d. 1928) warriors. No less than four Shiʿi Imams lie buried in this first and oldest Muslim graveyard.[227] Ibn-i Hasan Jarcavi was active as a preacher in the Punjab during this time and is credited with having gathered around forty thousand people in Multan to protest the devastation of this holy site.[228] He denounced Ibn Saʿud (as he was known to the British and in South Asia) as a new Yazid and called on the subcontinent's "Wahhabis" to convey his message to their supposed chief patron, mocking his capabilities in the face of South Asian devotion: "Look around how many replicas [*shabihen*] of Husayn's tomb exist in the world. After destroying the Jannat al-Baqiʿ, you will see that we will not just be able to construct one or two [graves] but instead reproduce the cemetery thousands of times. A cemetery's bricks and plaster might tumble down but are you not aware that in the hearts of hundreds of thousands of Muslims a tomb for Fatima has been erected?"[229]

Jarcavi cautioned his listeners not to take up swords and set out for the Hejaz in order to fight the "savages from Najd." Instead, he advised, they should use their economic weapons and refuse to go on hajj, thus depriving Ibn Saʿud of an important source of income.[230] Ibn-i Hasan Jarcavi also urged those in the audience to get involved with the Anjuman-i Tahaffuz-i Maʾasir-i Mutabarrakah (Association for the Protection of the Blessed Memorials). This association had been founded from within the AISC in 1926 and saw itself as a propaganda tool against the Wahhabi threat. The association approached Indian and Iraqi mujtahids for fatwas against Ibn Saʿud, which it later combined and published, and composed Persian appeals that were launched in Iranian newspapers in Mashhad and Tehran.[231] It sent thousands of letters every year to other Shiʿi organizations and individuals, used the forum of *majalis* (mourning sessions) to spread awareness about the situation in the Arabian peninsula, and organized a yearly "Day of Grief" in many localities of India and in Iraq.[232] Additionally, the annual proceedings of the All India Shiʿa Conference carried a speech the mujtahid Sayyid Muhammad (Miran Sahib) had delivered at a Hejaz Conference in Delhi on 14 April 1933. This lecture demonstrates Shiʿi efforts to build a united and transsectarian front against the "clouds of misguidance" (*zalalat ke badil*) that had positioned themselves in front of the "sun of Islam."[233] Sayyid Muhammad cast the Wahhabis as a common enemy who labeled both Hanafi Muslims and Shiʿis as unbelievers and regarded their life and property as licit.[234] No other forum for Muslims was as important in order to facilitate "love and solidarity" than their "international gathering" (*majlis-i bayn al-aqvam*) and "annual convention" (*salanah ijlas*), namely the hajj.[235] Sayyid Muhammad called for a "rain of blood" to fall on the Hejaz and to destroy the Saudi kingdom.[236] This could be achieved by sending out delegations across India, who were to unite the existing Muslim organizations, collect funds, and recruit an army of volunteers.[237]

These are by no means the only indications for the importance of concerns beyond the subcontinent. The younger brother of the raja of Mahmudabad, Amir Haydar Khan, commented in 1940 on the international character of anti-Shiʿi propaganda. Publishing houses in both Egypt and the Hejaz attacked Shiʿi accounts of the events surrounding Karbala and dismissed their hadith collections as fabricated. He recommended answering these insults by turning Shiʿi mourning sessions into a "well-structured propaganda" (*munazzam propaganda*) and to observe "military discipline" (*fauji tanzim*) during the community's processions.[238] The AISC—in line with many other Indian organizations of the time—also set up its own paramilitary force, the Rizakaran-i Jannat al-Baqiʿ. Besides publicly denouncing the Saudis, their purpose was to act as marshals at AISC convocations and other events.[239] Also, as we have seen, the modernists held up Iran and Turkey as symbols of progress and as examples to which India's Shiʿis should aspire.[240] Sayyid Riza ʿAli, for example, criticized the discrepancy between widespread admiration for the reforms of Reza Shah and Atatürk, on the one hand, and the lack of willingness to implement universal education, Islamic and national equality (*islami ya mulki musavat*), or proper support for the poor, on the other. He singled out the two men, calling each of them a great "warrior" (*ghazi*) in both their military and civilian capabilities. While the Shiʿis in the subcontinent, given their situation as colonial subjects, could not make use of insights derived from the leaders' battlefield tactics, both statesmen surely had lessons to teach regarding the successes they had achieved in peacetime.[241] The rulers of Iran and Turkey had to be credited especially for their attempts to restore "Islam's pure roots that had become polluted over the course of hundreds of years." If only the Sunnis had paid attention to Turkey's "impartial policy" (*ghayr mutaʿassib policy*) and if the Shiʿis had been aware of the "current trends in religious ideas" (*maujudah mazhabi khayalat ki ravish*) in Iran, the whole *madh-i sahabah* and tabarra trouble in Lucknow would not have come to pass.[242]

Finally, it is also necessary to mention the intrinsically international experience of the ʿulama during this period. The next chapters explore how the dynamics of studying in the shrine cities of Iran and Iraq later played out in Pakistan. Increasing emphasis by the jurists on the significance of these centers of Shiʿi learning did not forestall the possibility of carving out independent, local spaces of authority for those who made such claims—quite the contrary. Shiʿi scholars positioned themselves as gatekeepers and brokers of ideas flowing from the Middle East to South Asia and reworked these in the process. Even though the late colonial period offered an increasing array of alternative educational venues, Lucknow an important one among them, all senior ʿulama active during the decades under consideration had at least spent some years in the Middle East, as can be gleaned from the biographical data provided in the endnotes throughout this chapter. ʿAllamah Hindi used his own frequent travels between the two regions to encourage young Indians to go abroad. He supported an initiative by the AISC to send South Asian students to Iran on a yearly basis in order to learn "oriental sciences" (*ʿulum-i mashriqi*) and Persian. ʿAllamah Hindi pointed out that they would thus follow in the footsteps of Sayyid Dildar ʿAli Nasirabadi. By this time Iran had become the "center of knowledge" for young Indian Shiʿis.[243]

CONCLUSION

In this chapter, I have offered several reinterpretations of Shiʿi Islam in the late colonial period. In my view, the religious authority of Lucknow's leading mujtahids was by no means challenged only during the flare-up of high-profile sectarian tensions in the subcontinent. Instead, beginning in the 1920s the All India Shiʿa Conference attempted to aggressively position itself as a modernist alternative to clerical leadership. The AISC emphasized that it was far more attuned to the educational and economic needs of India's Shiʿis than the bookish mujtahids were. By absorbing and integrating such pressing concerns into their intellectual edifice, younger religious scholars like Sayyid ʿAli Naqi Naqvi were able to reclaim some relevance for the Usuli leadership. Contestations over religious authority came into the open even more forcefully following the establishment of Pakistan. The new state's lacking of a center of learning and scholarship comparable to Lucknow opened up new avenues for esoteric interpretations of the Shiʿi message, as chapter 2 discusses in detail.

In addition, I hold that Sunni-Shiʿi sectarianism during these decades has to be understood as a phenomenon operating on several levels. Even in the midst of a general rise of communal consciousness, Shiʿis did not perceive themselves as divorced from their Sunni coreligionists but rather framed their interpretation of Islam as both more sophisticated and more faithful to Muhammad's original message. At the same time, they were keenly aware of the potentially sinister implications of Pakistan, a state that in the mid-1940s became increasingly charged with exclusivist religious language that attempted to weed out "impure elements."

Debating all these complex questions did not entail that India's Shiʿis lost sight of the wider concerns of the Islamic and Shiʿi world. Instead they displayed a clear awareness of the international scene and interpreted their particular local environment through a transnational prism. Many questions of course remain to be answered in future research. One of the problems is that we do not have precise figures as to whether the threat of a Sunni-dominated Pakistan significantly impeded Shiʿi migration to the new state. I have suggested that the large scale of Partition violence against Muslims in places like the Punjab might have rendered such considerations a rather mute question. But we can at least point to the fact that many influential Shiʿis, among them ʿulama and landlords, stayed behind in the United Provinces or only migrated to Pakistan with a significant delay.[244]

Initially, the alarmist positions on Pakistan were given ample ammunition. The Muslim League in June 1947 nominated an exclusively Sunni committee of seven experts to advise Pakistan's Constitutional Assembly on the implementation of the shariʿa.[245] The Jamiʿat al-ʿUlamaʾ-i Islam in January 1948 passed a resolution which demanded that the government appointed a "leading ʿālim to the office of Shaikh al-Islām, with appropriate ministerial and executive powers over the qādīs throughout the country."[246] The Lahore daily *Ihsan* in November 1948 during Muharram called on the Shiʿis to give up their "irrational" beliefs in the Imams and urged them to speak and behave only as "Muslims" in Pakistan.[247] In early 1950, about fifteen hundred Shiʿis were arrested for defying a ban on a procession in Naroval.[248] But the biggest fears expressed during the pre-Partition period did not materialize. This may well have had to do with the death of Shabbir Ahmad ʿUsmani in December 1949. Other Deobandi scholars, such as Ihtisham al-Haqq Thanavi (1915–80), followed a more inclusive line. As we will see in chapter 5, Thanavi had convened an ʿulama gathering in 1951 that also included Shiʿi scholars. The meeting passed a resolution that spelled out twenty-two principles of an Islamic state, including a clause that enshrined the right for each "established Islamic sect" to be bound by its particular interpretation of Islamic law. Shiʿi scholars eagerly embraced this initiative and happily made common cause with their Sunni colleagues in their demands to declare the Ahmadis a non-Muslim minority.[249] They hoped to show themselves as falling within the

Islamic mainstream and as participating in defining the new country's still fluid Islamic identity that had been conceived as a promise for the renewal of Islam on a worldwide scale.[250] Yet, as the next chapter demonstrates, Sunni-Shiʿi tensions remained a major issue in internal Shiʿi debates over the next decades, and they were never far from the minds of reformist and traditionalist ʿulama alike. Furthermore, the Iranian Revolution of 1979 once again forcefully pushed the Shiʿis out of the fragile post-Partition Islamic consensus and labeled them as an element that should have no say in elaborating the religious character of Pakistan.

CHAPTER TWO

Theology, Sectarianism, and the Limits of Reform

THE MAKING OF SHIʿISM IN THE LAND OF THE PURE

If ʿAli had no comprehensive authority, then say
what is the point of turban, cloak, and gown?
— Sayyid ʿIrfan Haydar ʿAbidi, *Tamancah bar rukhsar-i munkir-i vilayat-i ʿAli*

Who dares to say that the nightingale's song remains
unanswered when, behind the curtain of their petals,
the hearts of hundred thousand roses were slit open?
— Muhammad Husayn al-Najafi Dhakko, *Islah al-rusum al-zahira*

The Pakistani pilgrims did not realize how privileged they were to set their feet on Iraqi soil. When the five-busload strong group arrived in the country in late October 1973, they could hardly have predicted that only two years later Saddam Hussein's government would clamp down on visas issued to foreign Shiʿis. Visits to the shrine cities of Karbala, Samarra, and Najaf in pursuit of education or religious tourism became nearly impossible after 1975.[1] The Pakistanis were also completely unaware of the hidden authority exercised by one of the three religious scholars who were traveling with them, viewing him as merely responsible for overseeing and facilitating proper visitation to the holy sites (*ziyarat*). Indeed, Muhammad Hasnayn al-Sabiqi had nothing particularly remarkable about him at the time. He was twenty-seven years old, had received six years of religious education at the Madrasat Sultan al-Madaris in Khairpur,[2] and had taught in various religious schools in the country over the last ten years. All in all, this was a quite common trajectory for an aspiring young scholar. Only a couple of months earlier al-Sabiqi had arrived in Najaf to pursue higher religious education.[3] And he revealed his true qualities on the following Thursday night, 1 November

1973, during a visit to the shrine of the Eleventh Shiʿi Imam Hasan al-ʿAskari (d. 260/873) in Samarra.[4] Al-Sabiqi led a majlis right next to the enclosure around the Imam's tomb, focusing with great emotional vigor on Hasan al-ʿAskari's many afflictions in life. In the midst of his speech, one female pilgrim from ʿAlipur in the district of Muzaffargarh suddenly became drenched in sweat despite the cold weather. She started to shake in an uncontrollable manner, wept loudly, and collapsed. Once the woman regained her consciousness, she told the stunned crowd how her gaze had strayed from al-Sabiqi toward the tomb's enclosure. There she suddenly had seen an exalted personality (*buzurg shakhsiyyat*) reciting the Qur'an. The stranger addressed her directly, ordering the pilgrim to look away from him but to pay attention to the ʿalim's speech. After this admonition, he promptly vanished from her sight. When her fellow pilgrims realized the implications of this experience, they started a great commotion. All the signs pointed to the fact that the apparition had been none other than the son of Hasan al-ʿAskari, the Twelfth, Hidden Imam himself. According to the account in which this particular incident is mentioned, the story still enjoyed widespread currency in the 1990s among pilgrims from the districts of Bahawalpur, Multan and Vihari. The encounter was also attested by two other scholars who were present in Samarra that night along with al-Sabiqi, Sayyid Aqa ʿAli Husayn Qummi and Sayyid Bashir Husayn Shirazi.[5] Hence, there could be no doubt that the Mahdi himself not only approved of al-Sabiqi's exalted conceptions of Shiʿi doctrine but also that he personally affirmed the ʿalim's scholarly achievements.[6]

For al-Sabiqi's supporters, this cosmological blessing at one of the most significant shrines of Shiʿi imagination was later interpreted as a crucial endorsement.[7] In the heated intra-Shiʿi struggle over proper orthodoxy and belief in Pakistan, which is the focus of this chapter, al-Sabiqi wholeheartedly stood on the side of truth against falsehood. Regardless of the accuracy of this claim, he was definitely among the most active Pakistani scholars who agitated over the course of several decades against efforts to reform and "rationalize" the community's beliefs and customs.[8] Al-Sabiqi saw himself as a protector of the simple believers who instinctively shunned the authority of those ʿulama whom they perceived as misguided usurpers: while claiming to be reformists, these scholars in reality conspired to attack the exalted status of the Imams.[9]

The incident in Samarra, then, lends itself to the interpretation of being the expression of a strategy to obtain a competitive edge in the contested arena of "marketplace" Shiʿism, where religious authority even for the most senior ʿulama is highly contingent on being able to "monopolize the academic and nonacademic spheres by having the largest constituency of emulators and agents."[10] Scholars over the last years have attributed increasing value to conceptualizing religious actors as operating in ways analogous to the logic of economic exchanges. Nile Green has made the case for applying the language of religious firms and the production of religious goods to the scholarly treatment of "traditionalist" and "reformist" arguments. In his view, this approach "gives life to the category of Islam as a ritual and discursive mine of deployable resources used for specific industrial or collective purposes rather than as a set of static 'traditions' that once founded are passively handed down until they become 'reformed' in a decisive 'modern' epoch."[11] Studying the Islamicate environment of Bombay at the turn of the previous century, Green found that customary, miracle-focused forms of Sufi Islam managed to find a rather easy fit with the disruptive, uprooting conditions of capitalist modernity: "For many Muslims, a world with no helper other than a distant Allah was a lonely world indeed. With their shrines and lodges near the cotton mills of Bombay and the plantations of Natal, the charismatic shaykhs who form the focus of *Bombay Islam* were infinitely closer to their client than a faceless and absent God."[12]

Al-Sabiqi portrays himself as such a traditionalist religious leader who is fully attuned to both the emotional and intellectual needs especially of a lay Shiʿi audience. He appears as a successful religious entrepreneur, not unlike those young Shiʿi scholars and preachers in late colonial India, described by Justin Jones, who were challenging the authority of the established mujtahids through "an increasingly expressive and contentious tone of public preaching" and the "diversification of popular practice" in order to "secure for themselves a role in an increasingly crowded religious marketplace."[13] Consequently, Andreas Rieck has labeled al-Sabiqi and other anti-reform-minded scholars and preachers as a "populist" camp that is well versed in utilizing emotionally charged majalis to further their agenda.[14]

I would argue, however, that such a framing of the conflict as a replay of the eternal battle between sincere, "high," orthodox, and rational Shiʿism against "extremist" and "superstitious" popular beliefs promoted for ulterior motives, pinning "sagacious and far-sighted *ʿulamāʾ*" against propagandists of "not genuine Shiite beliefs" reflects most of all academic bias in favor of reformist discourses.[15] Such an attitude is even palpable in Sabrina Mervin's magisterial study of Shiʿi reformism in Lebanon. Describing mourning sessions in contemporary Damascus that are organized in the example set out by the important Shiʿi reformist ʿalim Muhsin al-Amin (d. 1952), Mervin mentions that she witnessed during a visit in 1994 how the participants were engaging in intensive weeping "without, however, exaggerating during the mortification. The sessions in al-Kharab took place in a sober manner."[16] Husayn

ʿArif Naqvi is more explicit in his evaluation of al-Sabiqi's scholarship, which he dismisses—along with that of other traditionalists—as weak and consisting of baseless heterodox propaganda.[17] Similarly, Andreas Rieck classifies the polemical responses of scholars in Pakistan to reformist publications as a "gross overreaction" that demonstrated the "low level to which the internal dispute among a section of Pakistani Shias had sunk."[18] Ali Rahnema takes such criticism a step further in a recent study that aims at establishing the existence of an "ideology" which had been developed in his view by the seventeenth-century editor of the famous collection of Shiʿi traditions *Bihar al-Anwar*, Muhammad Baqir al-Majlisi (d. 1110/1698). The latter, according to Rahnema, managed through a "mass brain-wash" to create an "unquestioning and fatalistic community" among Shiʿi believers in Iran.[19] Rahnema defines Majlesism as "an anti-rational and pro-superstition school of thought [which was] fostered and promoted as state ideology."[20] These core components of "Majlesism" are supposedly alive and well in Iran today.[21]

Problematic and relevant for our purpose is that Ali Rahnema simply adopts the criticism that was formulated by the reformist Iranian thinker ʿAli Shariʿati (d. 1977) and that targets "Safavi Shiʿism" in general and al-Majlisi in particular.[22] Shariʿati termed such interpretations of Shiʿi Islam as "socially and politically reactionary, despotic, repressive, exploiting and bankrupt," and charged them with "religious ignorance, misrepresentation, falsification, fabrication and superstition."[23] Such one-sided views on reform and its proponents are not exclusive to Shiʿi studies, however. In the Sunni context, Indira Falk Gesink has made comparable observations. Tracing debates revolving around proposed reforms for Egypt's al-Azhar University in the late nineteenth and early twentieth centuries, she holds that the existing literature has paid disproportionate attention to the Arabic journals and newspapers owned by a "relatively small coterie of intellectuals" who favored the European modernizing project. Their views "passed down into the canon of authoritative Orientalist works on Islamic intellectual and social history, while the views of their opponents were set aside."[24] This unfavorable view of traditionalist authors who rejected reform and their dismissal as half-baked intellectuals and self-interested manipulators has led to a lack of scholarly interest in their responses to reformist arguments.[25] Justin Jones has consequently argued that "academic assessments of sectarianism need to take greater account of discordances among the Shiʿa (and, equally, among Sunni communities) subsisting underneath the impression of binary Shiʿa-Sunni conflict."[26]

The perception of a Pakistani battle between an enlightened, sober understanding of Shiʿi Islam and various unreasonable deviations from it also does not pay sufficient attention to how deeply various "traditionalist" authors have come to be influenced by reformist ideas and the pressure which these create. Once arguments about proper orthodoxy and reform are released into the open and are thus no longer confined to intimate and close-knit scholarly circles, even those who are opposed to any changes to doctrines and practices cannot afford any longer to simply ignore these challenges. Instead, they have to engage the questions at hand.[27] Oskar Verkaaik noted such dynamics in his study on the Sindhi separatist movement, which attempted to define Sufism as the quintessential tradition of South Asian Islam. As a consequence, "Sufism ceased to be merely a religious practice and became an object of intellectual activity."[28] Katherine Ewing has made a similar point regarding the responses by Sufi masters toward reformist discourses in Pakistan:

> Nearly every pīr I talked to was very sensitive to the parameters that Islam imposes on their practice, a sensitivity that can be attributed to reformist pressure. One pīr, for example, read me a statement of principles of Islam that he had carefully crafted in anticipation of my question about his practice as a pīr. [. . .] The principles of Islam, though presented by this pīr as the timeless Law laid out in the Quran and in the practice of the Prophet (sunnat), were in many respects the outcome of reformist objectifications, manifested in the practice of even those who are resistant to antipīr ideologies.[29]

For the colonial period, Dietrich Reetz has shown that it was important for the Barelvis, too, to be perceived as reformers. Ahmad Riza Khan Barelvi (d. 1921) and his followers defended a conception of reform that put taqlid and adherence to the sunna of the Prophet center stage and attacked their opponents as innovators (*bidʿatis*). While emphasizing the correct character of the ways in which the Barelvi movement venerated the Prophet and viewed the spiritual power of saints, they spoke out against practices like musical performances at certain rituals or the participation of women since these would go against the shariʿa. Furthermore, Ahmad Riza Khan preferred to be perceived as a scholar first and a Sufi second. He underlined his claim to be counted among the ranks of the ʿulama by editing hadith collections and issuing written legal rulings.[30]

This chapter explores some implications of these observations for Pakistani Shiʿis in more detail below. At this point I will say only that al-Sabiqi, the guide of the Pakistani pilgrims, shared an important trait with his reformist opponents. He had studied in Najaf, too, and was eager to refer to the licenses (*ijazat*) he had received from leading ayatollahs of the time, which designated him as their representative (*wakil*) in Pakistan.[31] It is significant in this context that the Mahdi in Samarra was explicitly concerned with emphasizing al-Sabiqi's scholarly standing. The following chapter, on debates revolving around taqlid in particular, elaborates on the issue of transnational Shiʿi religious leadership based outside Pakistan's borders. Here I will emphasize the profound impact that being cut off from Lucknow and the seminary's decline had on Pakistan's Shiʿis. These developments put an end to the possibility of producing a new generation of mujtahids indigenous to the Indian subcontinent. Consequently, even for traditionalist scholars the attention shifted to the centers of Shiʿi learning in the Middle East. While ʿAli Naqi Naqvi's legal opinions at times were included in their reasoning, Iranians and Iraqis were now called on as key witnesses to establish opinions opposed to reform. To put it differently: traditionalist scholars, too, had to refer to the leading grand ayatollahs and to acknowledge their authority. This phenomenon shows once again the difficulty of clearly distinguishing between supposedly "popular" and "high" forms of Shiʿi Islam, especially also since the monographs produced by traditionalist scholars, brimming with complicated theological debates, were hardly written with only a lay audience in mind. In cases when these scholars referred to the life-worlds of their audiences, it was a distinctive middle-class idiom they used. Sayyid Jaʿfar al-Zaman Naqvi Bukhari, whom I discuss at the end of this chapter, likened the appropriate conduct of the Shiʿi believers during the time of the Occultation to the behavior of a public servant who was actively awaiting and preparing for his "auditing team." The appearance of the Mahdi was "judgment day and audit day" (*hisab ka din he, audit ka din he*) and it was of utmost importance that one's "personal records" (*aʿmal ke kaghazat*) should be in order on that occasion.[32]

In this chapter I make two major arguments regarding debates over Shiʿi religious reform since the inception of Pakistan in 1947. First, these debates revolving around reform are also about radically diverging conceptions of theology that, in turn, condition different visions of religious authority. Both reformists and "traditionalists" (for a lack of a better term) exchanged blows over the nature of God's unicity (*tauhid*) and the human ability to comprehend such matters. The traditionalists made the case for an utterly transcendent vision of God that required the Imams to take on an essential intermediary function. This had significant ramifications for the role of the ʿulama. It brought into sharp relief efforts by the reformists to foreground clerical authority based on the emulation of leading jurists (taqlid) and their opponents' denial of any role for human leadership during the time of the Twelfth Imam's Occultation. I would argue against the perception that among South

Asian Shiʿis in the twentieth century there was "a tangible trend toward emphasizing the humanity of the Imams, demystifying their significance and hence presenting them as worthy temporal guides."[33] As it will become clear below, those scholars in Pakistan who dared to advocate such ideas and thereby "humanize" the Imams have faced (and continue to face) very hostile reactions from within their own community. The reformists have experienced marginalization instead of being part of a successful, tangible, or even sweeping trend. Their traditionalist opponents, by contrast, have emerged victorious. They felt emboldened to propagate their esoteric vision of Shiʿi Islam and of Pakistan as a pure Muslim land under the protection of and in direct contact with the Infallibles.

Second, the question of whether Shiʿi praxis and beliefs are in need of reform is always tied up with the persistent and constantly worsening problem of sectarianism. Calls for internal change are motivated to a large extent by the question of how one can remain Shiʿi in an increasingly hostile environment and, at the same time, devise a way toward intra-Muslim unity and a rapprochement with the Sunnis. "Traditionalist" scholars who reacted to reformist initiatives often shared the concern of sectarianism. Yet they presented divergent conceptions of *how* Muslim unity could be achieved and gave its conceptualization a particular spin. This argument goes against the position taken by Andreas Rieck, who holds that "those preachers and *zākirs* who propagated exaggerated notions about the *ahl al-bait* had also a large share in widening the gulf between Shias and Sunnis in Pakistan," since they attempted to "safeguard Shia religious identity in Pakistan at all cost."[34] The sources examined in this chapter provide us with a significantly different picture. This surely also has to do with the fact that Shiʿis could no longer count on the (relative) aloofness of the colonial British government, which after taking over from the East India Company had tried to portray itself as a "transcendent arbiter in a country divided along religious lines."[35] In my view, the traditionalist scholars had the advantage of being able to rather easily subvert the plausibility of reformist arguments by placing the proponents of reform in the same category as their sectarian Sunni opponents, whom they were quick to label as extremists and bent on destroying Shiʿi Islam. The traditionalists seized on the overlap between many of the critiques of religious rituals and beliefs voiced by Shiʿi reformists and sectarian Sunni ʿulama alike. Reformist discourses faced further limitations in the form of a "dilemma" for Shiʿi clerics, namely that speaking out against popular customs might entail "losing control over the uneducated masses of their community."[36] Taken together, then, I argue that not only the reformists deserve being credited with the double concern for propagating pure tauhid and caring deeply for the unity of the Muslims.[37] Rather, these topics are of equal concern for those who are staunchly opposed to reform.[38]

In the remainder of this chapter, I lay out the Shiʿi landscape after Partition. This is followed by an investigation of the thought of two of Pakistan's most committed reformist Shiʿi scholars. They also offer a window onto the changes to reformist discourses brought about by the Iranian Revolution. The last major section of this chapter then analyzes in detail the traditionalist backlash these two ʿulama provoked.

PARTITION AND THE REFORMIST-TRADITIONALIST DIVIDE

The debate over religious reform in Pakistan is intimately connected with the experience of Partition and the shake-up of religious authority and institutions that this shift entailed. Sayyid Husayn ʿArif Naqvi has connected controversies among preachers and ʿulama in Pakistan with the rise of Shaykhism in the new state, a school of speculative theology that he portrays primarily as a "foreign," Indian import accepted by few scholars native to the area that later became Pakistan.[39] Shaykhi theology within Twelver Shiʿism goes back to Shaykh Ahmad al-Ahsaʾi (1753–1826) and emerged as a distinctive school after the Shiʿi ʿalim Muhammad-Taqi Baraghani (d. 1847) proclaimed *takfir* of al-Ahsaʾi for denying the return of the physical body at the time of the resurrection.[40] The third master of the school, Muhammad Karim Khan Kirmani (d. 1870), developed an idea al-Ahsaʾi had only alluded to. He supplemented the first three pillars of the Shiʿi profession of faith, namely God's unicity (tauhid), the mission of the prophets (*nubuwwa*), and the mission of the Imams (*imama*), along with a fourth. This "fourth pillar" (*al-rukn al-rabiʿ*) was meant to denote the true Shiʿis, "those initiated into the Imams' esoteric teachings, the most worthy of whom are in spiritual relation with the Hidden Imam."[41] The existence of this spiritual elite is necessary because without it "all humanity would lose the transcendental meaning of its being and sink into the darkness of impious ignorance."[42] Such teachings—and Karim Khan's efforts to establish his own supreme religious authority—antagonized the leading Shiʿi scholars in Iran and Iraq, since their raison d'être was challenged and their "understanding of the true faith" labeled as "shallow and incomplete."[43]

Since there was no serious institution of higher Shiʿi learning in Pakistan at the time of Partition, nearly all influential scholars who emigrated to the newborn country had received their training in Lucknow. There Shaykhi leanings supposedly had managed to flourish, despite the opposition of the leading scholars teaching in the seminaries.[44] The precise mechanism of the early transmission of Shaykhi ideas to Pakistan warrants further investigation,[45] however, especially because Juan Cole has argued that the Usuli ʿulama of Awadh had managed to stamp out what they perceived to be a heresy in the 1830s. The Usuli approach to religion and law triumphed over the esoteric charismatic approach of the Shaykhis, perhaps "because Awadh bureaucrats and tax-farmers, many of them intellectually formed by the rationalist Niẓāmī method of the Farangī Maḥall, could better appreciate the rational-legal techniques of the mujtahids."[46] It also has to be noted that the name "Shaykhi" can be easily (mis)used as a derogatory term to slander opponents who are more inclined to the inherent esoteric potential of Shiʿism and should thus be viewed with caution. What emerges from the existing secondary literature, however, is that the esoterically minded migrants (*muhajir*s) who arrived from those parts of the subcontinent that became integrated into the Republic of India did not encounter any real doctrinal opposition due to the relative "unsophistication" of local Shiʿis in Pakistan. They also managed to introduce hitherto unknown practices and slogans into processions in Sindh and Punjab.[47] Sayyid ʿAli Naqi Naqvi mentions, for example, that the custom of walking over a fire while beating one's breast during mourning ceremonies had been current in Burma, Madras, the Deccan, and Lucknow before being taken up in Lahore after Partition.[48] Scholars residing within the boundaries of what is today Pakistan were rather late to establish bonds with eminent mujtahids in Iraq or to set up an infrastructure of Shiʿi madrasas and seminaries.[49] None of Lucknow's leading scholars discussed in the previous chapter migrated to the new Muslim homeland. In this context it is remarkable that we can see a clear dividing line between a local, Punjab-based reformist trend in the mold of Sayyid ʿAli Haʾiri and Sayyid Hashmat ʿAli rising up against the new immigrants who were predominantly born in towns that are part of the present-day Indian state of Uttar Pradesh (UP).[50] This becomes clearer if we compare the basic biographical data of some of Pakistan's most outspoken traditionalist scholars—some of whom will be discussed in more detail below—with that of their reformist counterparts. None of those figures who attacked reformist ideas after Pakistan came into being hailed from the new country's territory:

Muhammad Bashir Ansari (1901–73), born in Shikarpur (UP)
Mirza Yusuf Husayn (1901–88), born in Lucknow (UP)
Muhammad Ismaʿil (1901–76), born in Sultanpur Ludhiyan
(today Indian Punjab)

Sayyid Zamir al-Hasan Rizvi (1916–93), born in Azamgarh (UP)
ʿAli Hasnayn Shiftah (1924–91), born in Jaunpur (UP)

By contrast, the reformists, who are in most cases slightly younger, were predominantly born in the (later) Pakistani part of the Punjab:

Muhammad Husayn al-Najafi Dhakko, born 1932 in Sargodha, Punjab
Mufti Jaʿfar Husayn (1914–83), born in Gujranwala, Punjab
Sayyid Muhammad Yar Shah Najafi (1915–90), born close to ʿAlipur, Punjab (Muzaffargarh District)
Sayyid Gulab ʿAli Shah Naqvi (1915–92), born in Pindi Gheb, Punjab (Attock District)
Husayn Bakhsh Jara (1920–90), born in Jara, close to Dera Ismaʿil Khan, today located in the Khyber Pakthunkhwa province of Pakistan
Sayfullah Jaʿfari (1925–80), born in Ludhiana in the Indian Punjab
Akhtar ʿAbbas (1925–99), born near Kut Addu in the Muzaffargarh district, Punjab[51]

The Punjab, therefore, seems to once again demonstrate its potential as an especially fertile ground for reformist thought. Kenneth Jones has singled out as an explanation the diversity of religious communities in the province, which "led to a greater number of socio-religious movements than in any other region of South Asia."[52] Its character as a "region in turmoil" filled with "aggressive religious competition" facilitated before Partition the export of attitudes, strategies, and organizations predominant in this specific locale to other parts of British India.[53] The Shiʿi case implies that such a role continued for the Punjab well into the era of Pakistan's independence.

The first tensions between advocates for Shiʿi religious reform and their opponents can be dated within the first two decades post-Partition. Journals from the 1950s and early 1960s are full of complaints that not enough action was taken to establish communal life similar to India.[54] An editorial in the Lahore-based journal *Asad*, which usually did not distinguish itself through reformist proclivities, revealed on 10 May 1959 the "bitter truth" of the Shiʿi qaum's total indifference toward spreading the "education and sciences of the Al-i Muhammad." This situation persisted even though founding educational institutions was of the "utmost necessity" to ward off a double threat.[55] The truth of Shiʿi Islam was under assault not only from the quarter of the so-called "educated" classes, who made fun of religion but also from the "sovereigns of the pulpit" (*tajdar-i minbar*), namely the popular preachers. Due to a severe lack of "exalted clerical leadership," these zakirs deepened the "slavery of the common people" on a daily basis. In countering these threats, only one school, the Dar al-ʿUlum Muhammadiyya in Sargodha, could so far be designated as an unmitigated success. It was not only supported by the two leading Shiʿi organizations of the time, the All Pakistan Shiʿa Conference (APSC, the successor to the AISC) and the Organization for the Protection of Shiʿi Rights (Idarah-i Tahaffuz-i Huquq-i Shiʿa, ITHS), but also amply assisted by prominent Shiʿi doctors and lawyers.[56] The journal praised the comparatively small Makhzan al-ʿUlum Jaʿfariyya in Multan as an example of how a madrasa could be run even without relying on an endowment bequeathed by an influential landholder. Instead, this institution depended solely on small contributions in the form of *zakat, khums,* and donations.[57] Given these calls on the Shiʿi community to increase their financial support for their educational institutions, it is fitting, then, that the first major controversy revolved around the issue of khums. This debate was initiated by Muhammad Ismaʿil, a convert to Shiʿi Islam who had been brought up in an Ahl-i Hadis family. He later attended Deobandi madrasas and became known in the Shiʿi community as *muballigh-i aʿzam* (The Greatest Preacher) due to his rhetorical prowess. Ismaʿil led the charge against using khums for religious schools.[58] In a series of articles published in his journal, *Sadaqat,* he argued that this religious tax was the exclusive right of needy sayyids.[59]

Gradually, however the focus of debates over reform shifted to questions concerning Shiʿi rituals in general and the practices connected with majalis in particular. The early reformist figure Husayn Bakhsh Jara (d. 1990),[60] for example, claimed in his book *Lumʿat al-Anwar fi ʿaqaʾid al-abrar* (The glow of lights in the creeds of the pious), that "those people who occupy the *minbar* are in their outward appearance, actions, and character far removed from religion." This led to the "constant rise of the smoke of anti-religiosity" (*dini dushmani ka dhuan*). The popular preachers would consider the propagation of "true Islam" (*kalimah-i haqq*) as the "death knell to their business." They had consequently managed to turn away the common people from any serious and mainstream teachings. It was a waste of time to reason with them since they openly took pride in immoral behavior and regarded the minbar as giving them access to "the arena of a luxurious life style" (*ʿayyashi ka akharah*).[61] From there it was only a small step until more fundamental concerns of Shiʿi theology took center stage because widely diverging views on what should be considered orthodox Shiʿism underpinned this battle over rituals.[62] The intensification of these debates overlapped with the return of young Shiʿi scholars in the 1960s from Najaf. Pakistani ʿulama in general had been eager to catch up and take advantage of the intrinsically international Shiʿi experience of learning, flocking in large numbers to Iraq's prominent scholars.[63] The 1960s were arguably the heyday of Shiʿi religious students rushing to the shrine cities of Mesopotamia, followed by a steep decline in the 1970s, caused by the Iraqi government's stricter visa policies, as already discussed.[64] The reformist voices of the 1960s attacked "superstitious" rituals and accused their colleagues, who had been exclusively trained in the subcontinent, of deifying the ahl al-bayt, the members of Muhammad's household. This chapter now turns to the most influential proponent of such reform.

Muhammad Husayn Najafi Dhakko and the Struggle for Shiʿi Identity

Muhammad Husayn al-Najafi Dhakko (b. 1933) had studied in Najaf from 1954 until 1960 with leading Shiʿi grand ayatollahs such as Muhsin al-Hakim, Sayyid Muhammad Shahrudi, and Aqa Buzurg Tehrani (d. 1970).[65] On his return to Pakistan, he served as the principal of the already mentioned Dar al-ʿUlum Muhammadiyya in Sargodha (founded in 1949), then the most influential Shiʿi religious seminary in Pakistan.[66] Dhakko's concerns initially revolved around what he considered "objectionable" customs that had crept into Shiʿi mourning ceremonies. He criticized the prevalence of melodies and songs adapted from Bollywood movies, the scheduling of majalis that overlapped with the obligatory daily prayers, and the fact that clean-shaven preachers spoke from Husayn's pulpit.[67] The reformist scholar expressed his indignation at undue veneration of Zuljanah, the white horse representing Husayn's steed that is taken out during *ʿazadari* processions in the subcontinent.[68] Dhakko lamented that children would walk underneath the horse or feed it grains while consuming the leftovers, implying that such contact with the horse would entail a blessing. He ridiculed those who tied pieces of paper with requests to Zuljanah as if it would carry them directly to the Hidden Imam.[69]

These issues were of grave concern since they pointed to a much deeper problem, namely that Muslims in today's Pakistan were still the cultural slaves of the (former) Hindu majority and their British colonial masters.[70] They had developed a habit of clinging to harmful customs that had shaped their consciences, an addiction that was extremely difficult to break.[71] It did not help, in Dhakko's view, that his coreligionists were under the control of evil scholars (*ʿulamaʾ-i suʾ*) who were interested only in worshipping their own bellies. They sold Islam to the highest bidder and turned majalis into a for-profit business.[72] These fraudulent ʿulama and preachers had taken over Islam's blessed garden. Like pests, they prevented the growth of its roses and sweet-smelling plants, which were the expression of its original religious form.[73] Because the common people lacked a moral compass, however, they were not able to distinguish the true scholars from the false.[74] According to

Bloody mourning processions such as this one in Islamabad give high visibility to Shiʿi Islam in Pakistan. They are also a major site of internal contestations about proper theological beliefs and orthopraxy. Photograph by Myra Iqbal.

Dhakko, these tricksters had never made any effort to "render the future of the Shiʿis in Pakistan brilliant and luminous" by establishing a religious infrastructure for the community through the opening of madrasas and training teachers and prayer leaders. Instead, they had regarded the Shiʿis of the country as a "highly valued prize [*sone ki ciriya*] which they have clutched with both hands" and established a front against the ʿulama.[75]

Even in his earliest writings, however, Dhakko made clear that his reformist project aimed at more than only removing reprehensible customs, because creed (*ʿaqida*) and action (*ʿamal*) were intimately intertwined.[76] A milestone in this respect was the translation of Ibn Babawayh al-Saduq's (d. 991) influential work *Risalat al-Iʿtiqadat*) Epistle on the principles of faith) into Urdu, along with a substantial commentary by Dhakko.[77] With this book, the ʿalim laid the ground for a controversy that was still continuing more than three decades later. He "presented his own views on 'correct beliefs' about the Shiʿi Imams and other subjects in a categorical manner" and directly attacked well-established scholars such as Muhammad Bashir Ansari and Muhammad Ismaʿil, accusing them of deliberately twisting the truth.[78] Dhakko held that in the beginning the message of ʿaqida had been utterly pure and also instantly comprehensible for everyone, whether "a fool or a wise man, a rural camel-driver or an urban philosopher, man or woman, young or old."[79] The essence of this original ʿaqida was tauhid, Islam's "pinnacle of distinction" (*turrah-i imtiyaz*), which the reformist scholar, interestingly, defined in very controversial terms. The unforgivable sin of *shirk* (polytheism) was committed by a Muslim who infringed on God's two supreme privileges, namely to acknowledge His right to absolute lordship (*rububiyya*) and His right to being the exclusive addressee of worship (*uluhiyya*). This implied that the fire of hell awaited those who either credited anyone besides God with creating life and providing sustenance (*shirk-i rububi*) or worshipped and prayed to anyone besides Him (*shirk-i uluhi*).[80] Anyone who regarded ʿAli as *khaliq* (creator) was a kafir and outside the fold of Islam.[81] In advancing this argument, Dhakko's position is difficult indeed to distinguish from the reflections of Ibn ʿAbd al-Wahhab (d. 1206/1792), who made this so-called double tauhid a centerpiece of his thought. In doing so, he went beyond Ibn Taymiyya's (d. 728/1328) deliberations on the subject by emphasizing that confessing God's unicity with one's heart and tongue is not enough to render someone a Muslim. Even the early Muslim apostates (*ahl al-ridda*) and the polytheists (*mushrikun*) during the time of the Prophet had confessed outwardly that God alone provided the means of subsistence, had the power over life and death, and ruled the seven heavens and the two worlds. In Ibn ʿAbd al-Wahhab's conception of tauhid it was devotional acts exclusively directed toward God, like a human being only invoking God, only fearing Him, and only worshipping Him, that confirmed the profession of faith and became crucial in distinguishing between Muslims and kuffar.[82] Dhakko thus differs in his explicit usage from the important modernist Iraqi Shiʿi ʿalim Muhammad Rida al-Muzaffar (d. 1963). Al-Muzaffar adduced in his *al-ʿAqaʾid al-imamiyya* (Beliefs of the Twelver Shiʿis) the terms *tauhid al-dhat* (unicity of the essence), *tauhid al-sifat* (unicity of the attributes), and *tauhid al-ʿibada* (unicity of worship), without, however, relying on the terms *uluhiyya* or *rububiyya*. The Iraqi also stayed clear of any criticism of Shiʿi mourning ceremonies or visiting of graves. He did not attempt to establish boundaries of appropriate behavior but simply remarked that these actions were to be counted among "the pious lawful deeds" (*al-aʿmal al-saliha al-sharʿiyya*).[83]

The pejorative designation "Wahhabi" has, of course, a long and colorful polemical history in South Asia and beyond.[84] Given these findings, however, a more nuanced approach might be more appropriate than the "ridiculous term," as Andreas Rieck puts it, of "'Wahhabi Shias'" that Dhakko's opponents used for him and his supporters.[85] At any rate, Dhakko used his understanding of correct tauhid to undercut the idea that the prophets and Imams had any independent information pertaining to the unseen world.[86] He argued not only that they were totally dependent on God for any knowledge (*ʿilm*) they possessed but also that no form of esoteric knowledge (*ʿilm-i ghayb*) per se existed.[87] Instead, God had made known to all believers that truly hidden and unknowable phenomena associated with the end of the world, such as the scales to weigh people's deeds (*mizan*), the resurrection, and paradise, were all real.[88] That prophets received revelation (*wahy*) and the Imams inspiration (*ilham*) did not render them qualitatively different from other human beings. *Wahy* was not part of the prophets' essence (*dhati*). Rather, all of them had at one point in their lives existed without this additional quality, as demonstrated by Qur'an 42:52: "Even so We have revealed to thee a Spirit of Our bidding. Thou knewest not what the Book was, nor belief; but We made it a light, whereby We guide whom We will of Our servants. And thou, surely thou shalt guide unto a straight path."[89]

Consequently, the Imams did not differ intrinsically from other human beings.[90] They were not made out of light and did not exist with God before creation. Dhakko held that all references in the Shiʿi tradition which described the Imams as *nurani* (consisting of light) should be understood only in a metaphorical sense (*min bab al-majaz*). He adduced a hadith, attributed to the Sixth Shiʿi Imam, Jaʿfar al-Sadiq (d. 148/765), and taken from al-Kulayni's *Kafi*, in which God explained that before creation He brought into being only the spirit (*ruh*) of Muhammad and ʿAli, which the philosophers have termed the First Intellect (*al-ʿaql al-awwal*). While human beings had to concede that they were not able to completely penetrate this truth, *nur* probably referred to the guidance offered by the Imams in the midst of the darkness of *shirk* and their acting as God's repository of knowledge.[91] The Qur'an, the words of the Imams themselves, Islamic history, and the demands of the original human condition (*fitra*) all excluded the possibility that these "holy personalities" would have descended directly from heaven. Only Adam and Eve had no parents, and only Jesus was born without a father, but whoever doubted a regular human birth for the Imams was a "denier of the Qur'an and completely devoid of faith."[92] The Imams also did not command any extraordinary powers that would give them authority over life and death or enable them to provide sustenance to human beings. If God had delegated these exclusive prerogatives to them, this would be a serious attack on the Islamic doctrine of tauhid.[93]

It was thus inconceivable that the *maʿsumin* (Infallibles) would act as independent intermediary authorities between God and the believers. Dhakko only conceded a very limited role for a *maʿsum* to act as an intermediary (*wasilah*). He argued that God would bestow favors on the people due to the blessing (*baraka*) of the Imams. Crucially, though, they had no active role in this themselves.[94] Dhakko hence rejected an understanding of *vilayat-i takvini* that attributed powers to the Imams qua their function (*wazifah*) or which came necessarily in conjunction with their office (*farz-i mansib*).[95] All hadiths that seemed to confirm a cosmological role for the Imams were unreliable.[96] Only because these holy personalities were human, too, they could act as God's proof (*hujjat*) toward us. If they had capabilities beyond our comprehension, we would not be able to appreciate their perfect obedience to God, exemplified by their praying in biting cold, fasting in scorching heat, and bearing all sorts of challenging afflictions with exemplary patience.[97] To be sure, Dhakko was careful to add that his mission to disenchant the Imams had limits. They might share our humanity but there were still levels of distinction even within one species (*jins*). Compared to the Prophet, for example, "we are a stone but he is a diamond. We are a flint stone but he is a philosopher's stone [*paras*]. We are a particle but he is the sun. We are foolish but he is wise. We are imperfect but is perfect. He is human but the embodied spirit [*ruh-i mujassam*], he is a body but a body infused with spirit [*jism-i murawwah*]."[98]

Building on these claims, Dhakko tried to create an alternative Shiʿi identity that was not focused on a deeply emotional veneration of the Imams but rather had its basis in a specific approach toward Islamic law, which, he reasoned, would constitute a far lesser obstacle to Sunni-Shiʿi unity. The true greatness of the ahl al-bayt lay in the important function they played in the "system of the shariʿa," namely as "heads and chiefs" of the court that clarified the specifications of the divine law. Only through them did the believers have a grasp of the categories of permissible (halal) and forbidden (haram).[99] What was specifically Shiʿi in this context, Dhakko said, was that Shiʿis in their legal reasoning avoided relying on analogy (*qiyas*) or *al-maslaha al-mursala* (the unattested benefit without a clear indication in Qur'an or hadith).[100] Such approaches would only lead to unlawful innovations (*bidaʿ*), which even in a worldly context were illegal since no Pakistani had the right, for example, to introduce his own currency. These innovations constituted an open rebellion against God and would imply that Islam as a religion was not complete (*din-i Islam mukammal nahin he*).[101] Instead, Shiʿis relied only on the Qur'an and on hadiths transmitted from the Imams.[102]

This narrow view of what it means to be Shiʿi goes very much against the traditionalists who identify other factors, such as the cosmological position of the Imams, the acknowledgment of their superhuman powers, and the reliance on their capabilities to provide help to their adherents, as summarizing Shiʿi identity. Dhakko was aware of the implications of his uncompromising stance. He actively tried to accommodate Shiʿi sensibilities by arguing, for instance, that the Shiʿi way of praying with open hands reflected the Prophet's original custom.[103] He condoned the Shiʿi usage of the phrase *Ya ʿAli madad* (Help, oh ʿAli!) if those who uttered these words did not use it instead of the proper Islamic greeting *al-salam ʿalaykum* and meant no more than asking ʿAli to implore God on their behalf for assistance. ʿAli and the other Imams only "caused God to give" (*dilvana*) but did not provide themselves.[104] Similarly, the ʿalim criticized the Sunni practice of performing additional prayers (*tarawih*) during the nights of Ramadan as *bidʿa*.[105] The same applied to turning *ʿashura* into a day of celebration.[106] Dhakko also conceded that there had been a tampering with the call to prayer: right from the beginning it had contained the words "hasten to the best of works" (*hayya ʿala khayr al-ʿamal*). It was the second Caliph ʿUmar who replaced this phrase with "Prayer is better than sleep" (*al-salat khayr min al-naum*). In this decision he was driven by his own whims and thus acted against God's clear ruling (*hukm*).[107] While Dhakko in this context defined the Shiʿi version of the *adhan* as the original Islamic one, he did not take the same position with regard to the significantly more important Shiʿi addendum "ashhadu anna ʿAliyyan wali Allah" (I confess that ʿAli is the friend/viceregent of God). The latter was in his view an innovation dating back to the Buyid dynasty.[108] In his argumentation, Dhakko's position is clearly informed by the stance taken by al-Saduq, who likewise rejected the third *shahada* as a fabrication.[109]

Dhakko's motivation was similar to the controversial Iraqi scholar Muhammad b. Muhammad Mahdi al-Khalisi (d. 1963). Both men aimed at suppressing the third shahada in the *adhan* in order to make room for Sunni-Shiʿi rapprochement.[110] Yet it proved difficult for the Pakistani to back up his ruling with references to scholars active closer to his own time period, because the pendulum had swung back forcefully toward condoning the third shahada since at least the Safavid period.[111] Dhakko was eager to make the sweeping case that if we considered the opinions of the "most learned ʿulama and greatest *fuqaha*'," they would all declare the third shahada impermissible. He told his readers he was sorry that he could at this point only provide a brief summary, but that more information was surely available on request. Yet those rulings by prominent scholars such as Muhsin al-Hakim or Sayyid ʿAbdullah al-Shirazi (d. 1984)[112] that Dhakko was able to mention did not outlaw the third shahada. They only refused to make it mandatory and to treat it as an integral part of the *adhan*.[113] Studying the positions held by the most prominent Shiʿi ʿulama regarding this question in the 1960s, Werner Ende thus argued that nearly all leading figures of the time, including Muhsin al-Hakim, opined that the third shahada "was not only a recommended act, but also the cornerstone (*rukn*) or secret (*sirr*) of the true faith, the perfection (*kamal*) of religion, the symbol (*ramz*) of Shiʿism and its distinguishing mark (*shiʿar*) which must not be abandoned."[114] Muhammad al-Khalisi lost the battle over the same question in the context of Iraq, Lebanon, and elsewhere because his opinions were challenged by a generation of former students of grand ayatollahs such as Muhsin al-Hakim, Sayyid Husayn Burujirdi (d. 1961), Abu 'l-Qasim al-Khu'i (d. 1992), and others who defended the use of the third shahada.[115] Consequently, the practice was transformed from the status of unlawful innovation (*bidʿa*) to a "recommended act (*mustahabb*) and, moreover, the symbol of Shiʿism and the esoteric mystery of the faith."[116]

But Dhakko did not pin his hopes of a rapprochement only on the *adhan*. In the 2000s, he also expected to attain Shiʿi-Sunni unity by attaching Shiʿi political power to an already-existing, very concrete "coalition of the willing." This Islamist alliance called Majlis-i Mutahhidah ʿAmal (United Working Committee), comprised Barelvi, Deobandi, and Ahl-i Hadis parties led by ʿulama. It only excluded scholars affiliated with the SSP, which had victimized Dhakko in the past. He accused the latter of having attacked and burned his library in the 1980s in response to a polemical work he had published. In the 2004 interview, Dhakko opposed a new imprint of this "proof-based and logical" book, arguing that he was now striving toward unity and unanimity (*vahdat va yiganigi va yikdili*) among Muslims and did not want to provide any pretext for the Sipah-i Sahabah to attack the Shiʿis.[117] Dhakko did not specify his precise role in the process of joining the Majlis-i Mutahhidah ʿAmal, simply stating in an interview that "we formed it" (*tashkil dadahim*).[118] He was more explicit, however, that for this project to succeed, it was necessary to go beyond all those "excesses" that made the Shiʿi madhhab appear unreasonable. Undue veneration of Zuljanah, for example, was prone to disgrace Shiʿi Islam in the eyes of others. It provided the "enemies of the Household of the Prophet" with a pretext for regarding the community as "worshippers of the horse and *taʿziya*" (*ghora aur taʿziyah parast qaum*). By citing Ahmad Riza Barelvi, Dhakko underlined the shared Shiʿi-Barelvi rejection of performing rites associated with *ziyarat* at mock graves that were supposed to represent the shrines of the Imams.[119] As we have already seen, Dhakko did not restrain himself when excoriating practices associated with current majalis, which in his view could often be mistaken for either pub brawls or other forms of bawdy entertainment that had led the majority of the population to turn away from seeking any sober "scientific presentation" in such venues.[120] In order to rectify this situation, those who organized majalis should transcend any personal preferences and tastes. They should strive only for the goal of educating their audience about the purpose (*maqsad*) of Husayn. Meritorious and upright speakers should be selected to talk about how the Third Shiʿi Imam had sacrificed himself to unmask Yazid's plan to destroy Islam (and thus humanity) by removing God's clear standard of demarcating between right and wrong.[121] By speaking of Husayn as *shahid-i insaniyyat* (the martyr of/for humanity), Dhakko attempted to connect his reading with the example of Sayyid ʿAli Naqi Naqvi.[122]

At the same time, Dhakko was deeply concerned with preserving the authority of the ʿulama. The standing of the clerics was not only undermined by the fact that the opponents of reform resorted to unacceptable ad hominem attacks against him and spread hatred toward the ʿulama in general.[123] Dhakko also took serious issue with their argument that taqlid was forbidden in the "fundamentals of religion" (*usul al-din*). This interpretation was absurd, he claimed. How could the simple believers be bound in affairs relating to the minor branches of the law (*furuʿ*) but be at liberty to form their own interpretations in the much weightier matters related to theology? The true meaning of the principle adduced was that in issues concerning creed any taqlid without proof was impermissible.[124] Higher criteria of certainty applied, too, which were fulfilled only by hadiths that were *mutawatir* (documented through multiple chains of transmission) and Qur'anic verses that did not belong to the ambiguous verses (*mutashabihat*). Emulating the ʿulama was hence of utmost necessity in the area of *usul al-din* as well; otherwise the madhhab would be turned into a "plaything or a nose of wax" (*mum ki nak*), something that could be twisted and shaped at will according to one's caprices.[125] The influence of the ʿulama was threatened from another angle, too: Shiʿis claimed that they could hand over their zakat and khums directly to needy sayyids without channeling this money through the religious scholars.[126]

Dhakko saw himself in line with earlier reformist ʿulama, especially the Lebanese "great reformer" Muhsin Amin al-ʿAmili. Al-ʿAmili's opponents had branded him an "enemy of ʿazadari who was worse than the Umayyad army" simply because he had called for giving up certain flagellation practices and removing "fabricated" traditions from the majalis.[127] Dhakko suggested that the subcontinent had always been especially prone to undermining reformist efforts, a phenomenon experienced even by scholars residing in the centers of Shiʿi learning, such as Husayn b. Muhammad Taqi al-Nuri al-Tabarsi (d. 1902). His book *al-Luʾluʾ wa-l-marjan fi adab ahl al-minbar* (The pearls and the corals regarding the appropriate behavior of the people of the minbar) was supposedly labeled as misguided among Shiʿis in India.[128] Al-Nuri al-Tabarsi had offered in his work an early positivist-rationalist critique of the classic majlis manual, *Rawdat al-shuhadaʾ* by Kamal al-Din Husayn b. ʿAli al-Waʿiz al-Kashifi (d. 910/1504–5). Among others, the important revolutionary Iranian scholar Murtaza Mutahhari (d. 1979) relied on "al-Nuri's critique of *Rowẓat al-shohadā* in a series of lectures on the distortions [*taḥrīfāt*] that have infiltrated the literary and ritual-devotional commemorations of Karbala. Motahhari extols Hajji al-Nuri's trenchant critique of the *rowẓeh-khwāns* for telling lies, being ignorant of true history, and being greedy for fame and fortune."[129] A similar push back against reformist literature had affected the towering Indian mujtahid Sayyid ʿAli Naqi Naqvi. His library had been set on fire because he challenged the narrative of the unbearable thirst that Husayn and his company had allegedly suffered during the tragic events of Karbala.[130]

In the context of Pakistan, Dhakko perceived himself as the victim of a Shaykhi smear campaign. He felt obliged to disclose the "bitter and hidden truth" that his opponents only pretended to be Shiʿis but were in reality beyond the pale due to their promotion of Shaykhi doctrines.[131] Besides establishing these shared trajectories of reform, the reformist scholar also frequently emphasized his credentials and the special favors God had bestowed on him.[132] He clearly regarded himself as a superior religious scholar with immense mental capabilities, and he claimed that his books had never been refuted.[133] Dhakko was not shy to dismiss his opponents as mere *maulvis*, *malangs* (antinomian, wandering dervishes), and popular preachers who were skilled only in the art of *rauzah khani*.[134] In an interview with the Iranian journal *Hauzah*, he boasted that he had astonished everyone during his studies in Najaf by finishing the second level of the cycle of religious education at the seminaries, comprising the "surfaces of jurisprudence" (*sutuh al-fiqh*) and the "upper surfaces" (*al-sutuh al-ʿulya*), within only one year.[135] Harnessing these qualifications, Dhakko made the case that only an ʿalim who commanded knowledge of seventy thousand hadiths in Arabic had the right to approach the sayings of the Prophet and the Imams in an unmediated manner.[136] Such an elitist attitude was also on display in a letter he wrote in the late fall of 1969. Negotiators had tried to broker an agreement between Dhakko and his opponents. The reformist laid out stringent conditions for such a meeting to take place, which in any case was only the second-best option to submitting the disagreement of the two sides to the leading marajiʿ of the day and abiding by their decision. Dhakko expressed in this letter his rejection of any public form of intra-Shiʿi *munazara*, since such an occasion would only play into the hands of the Shiʿis' enemies. He suggested instead a private meeting in which he would face all his opponents and their supporters alone with the goal of issuing a shared statement at the end. Moreover, this debate should be an elite conversation held in either Arabic or Persian without any participation of the common people.[137]

Sayyid ʿAli Sharaf al-Din Musavi ʿAliabadi and the Politicization of Karbala

Dhakko's reformist and not openly political thought stands in marked contrast to scholars who were indebted to and politicized by the Iranian Revolution. Chapter 4 explores in detail Pakistani Shiʿi interpretations discussions of Khomeini's role and the meaning of vilayat-i faqih in the local South Asian context.[138] Yet the Iranian influence on reformist attempts that strove to alter the discussion on rituals and theology in order to achieve *taqrib* (rapprochement) is palpable as well. It comes to the fore, for example, in the writings of Sayyid Sharaf al-Din Musavi ʿAliabadi (b. 1942), who hailed originally from the village of ʿAliabad in Baltistan and received advanced religious training in Najaf and later Qum and Mashhad.[139] After his return to Pakistan, he was active in the pro-Iranian Imamia Students Organisation (ISO), serving on the group's Advisory Council and contributing to the ISO journal, *Rah-i ʿAmal*.[140]

Advancing a rationalist reading of the events of Karbala, Sayyid ʿAli Sharaf al-Din Musavi argued that Husayn had declared war on superstitions and won a lasting victory for logic and reason.[141] If most people held a different view, this was because the tragedy of *ʿashura* did not simply speak for itself. The events required interpretation in the same way as an entire research institute in Iran was devoted to making sense of the precise meaning of Imam Khomeini's words, even though all of his speeches were available on audio- or videotapes. No similar record existed for Karbala, which had caused all sorts of conflicting interpretations to spring up in its aftermath. Some people claimed that Husayn's uprising was due to an internal family conflict; others attributed an esoteric meaning to it (*ghaybi tafsir*) or held that Husayn rose up against Yazid in order to take over the caliphate and win power for himself.[142] But if we took into account that Husayn operated always within the four walls of the Qur'an, we would realize that Husayn's main goal was political: namely, to establish an Islamic system.[143] His uprising was directed against the (worldly) injustice and evil of Yazid that threatened to sound the death knell for Islam.[144] The Third Imam never advocated the conceptualization of the imamate as an office with a cosmological reach.[145] Rather, he backed up his decidedly worldly opposition to Yazid with Qur'anic verses in the vein of "And do not obey one whose heart We have made heedless of Our remembrance and who follows his desire and whose affair is ever [in] neglect" (Q18:28).[146] Husayn took up arms only after carefully considering his options and being assured of the support of the Kufans, because commanding right and forbidding wrong always required a position of strength and power.[147]

Taken together, this implied that ʿazadari should be more than an act of worship or an occasion for weeping. Instead, Shiʿi rituals should give expression to the essentially political basis of the events at Karbala.[148] This focus on the political aspects of Husayn's uprising allowed Musavi to rethink Shiʿi majalis as a space that aimed less at fostering Shiʿi identity than at creating intra-Muslim unity. He argued that nothing should be said or done at such a meeting that would stir up the anger of any other Islamic sect, such as cursing the first three Caliphs. Behavior in this vein would be utterly opposed to the "spirit, philosophy, and wisdom" of ʿazadari and was the hallmark of those who supported either the *khawarij* or Muʿawiya (*shiʿah-i khavarij o Muʿaviyah*).[149] It was not the Sunnis that were the enemies of the ahl al-bayt but rather those people who fought and mocked the Prophet, the kuffar and *mushrikun*, like the Jews and the Christians.[150]

According to Musavi, the problem in Pakistan today was, however, that there existed two groups of Shiʿis in the country. He termed those the *shiʿah-i haydar-i karrar* (Shiʿa of the Constantly Attacking Lion [ʿAli]) and the *shiʿah-i isnaʿashariyya* (Twelver Shiʿa), respectively. It was only the latter who clung to the same confession of faith like all other Muslims, built their lives on Qur'an and sunna, and regarded self-made laws and ideas that entered their religion as *kufr* and *shirk*.[151] The *shiʿah-i haydar-i karrar*, on the other hand, despised reason (*ʿaql*), which formed the basis of all Shiʿi *ʿaqida*, and pretended that in religion certain things could not be comprehended by *ʿaql* alone.[152] Musavi accused these mistaken Shiʿis of following an entirely different religion, one with a deficient understanding of tauhid. He criticized the *shiʿah-i haydar-i karrar* for arguing that the Prophet was in need of ʿAli and for promoting *matam* instead of fasting, and breast-beating instead of the prescribed prayers.[153] Musavi also denied their claim that the Qur'an was a deeply esoteric piece of writing that required the Imams' exegesis by pointing out the mismatch between 77,701 words and 6,236 *ayas* of the Qur'an and only 3,352 hadiths transmitted from the Imams that were concerned with Qur'anic exegesis.[154] The reformist scholar explained that turning the Imams into deliverers of worldly needs was a typical strategy to lure people away from God. The wrong Shiʿis were guilty of this approach because they declared that someone who was not able take care of all their material needs did not deserve to be called their *maula* (master). It was this exact ruse that the communists relied on, challenging hungry, thirsty, and unclothed children to ask their God to provide. If the help the poor requested did not materialize, the communists urged them to call on "Lenin and Stalin" instead—and suddenly the gates of plenty opened for them and they received food and clothing. Likewise, contemporary nongovernmental organizations used this mechanism to woo needy Shiʿis away from proper belief. These organizations fostered their dependence through the delivery of "packets of biscuits out of the sky" (*asman se biscuit ke dibbon*) and by providing medical services for their wives and children. With the syringe offered for treatment, they drew religion out of the people (*jis ke zariʿe un se din ko khenc lengi*).[155] While Dhakko was trying to straddle the fine line between, on the one hand, acknowledging that the spirits of the Imams had been created out of light, and, on the other, rejecting the view that this feature meant that they were superhuman or took part in *vilayat-i takvini*, Musavi dismissed such ideas altogether. For him, *nur* was nothing special, since both heaven and earth were filled with God's light and the term should only be understood as a synonym for belief and guidance.[156]

For Musavi, ʿaqida problems in contemporary Pakistan had been long in the making and did not originate in the country itself. Rather, even the Shiʿi ʿulama in Iran and Iraq had neglected their duties.[157] Faced with rising Wahhabi and Salafi tendencies, they had preferred cooperation with worldly rulers and had accepted that ʿazadari was turned into a "mere custom" (*mahz rasm*) in order to protect religion as a whole—or so they thought.[158] This had to do with the ʿulama not trusting their own abilities. To them, religion resembled an ugly girl who was hard to marry off. Hence, the ʿulama were reluctant to impose any obligation on the groom's family (meaning the ordinary believers) because these might turn their backs on them.[159] Musavi chastised his fellow scholars for capitulating in front of the common people. The ignorant masses could not claim to possess more or deeper love for the ahl al-bayt, because the quality of love was directly linked to one's level of knowledge.[160] Musavi had two pieces of advice for the ʿulama: First, they should speak up like him and not be afraid of being called Wahhabi, since the latter were (hypocritical) Muslims, too.[161] Second, the scholars should revamp religious education and equip their students with appropriate *tabligh* skills so they could tackle the spread of reprehensible customs that painted the Shiʿi madhhab in a ridiculous light.[162] Currently, the graduates from religious schools were as useless as a sixth finger, because they acquired knowledge that was only applicable within the four walls of their madrasa. How was this supposed to be medicine for the pains of society (*muʿashare ke kaysi* [*sic*] *dard ki dava hen*)?[163] Yet Musavi was not entirely pessimistic about the prospects of religious Shiʿi reform in Pakistan. Writing in May 1995, he saw arising an unprecedented opportunity for reform that should be seized. While similar calls had been utterly unsuccessful in the past, now Iran's Supreme Leader, Ayatollah Khamenei, had issued a clear verdict delineating the acceptable limits of *ʿashura* customs. This provided the ʿulama with a unique opportunity to publicly present their thoughts (*un afkar o khayalat ko minassah-i shuhud par ane ka mauqaʿ nasib hua*), backed up by the authority of Iran's religious hierarchy.[164] This way, Musavi thought, both the purity of Shiʿi teachings and that of their public manifestations could be restored. He was wrong, however, to assume that the long-standing controversy over reform could be solved simply by decree.[165]

THE TRADITIONALIST REACTION

The opponents of those reforms advocated by Dhakko and Musavi did not remain silent.[166] Making fun of Dhakko for playing up his Punjabi credentials as a "local" (*maqami*) scholar in order to win over the "common people" was among the tamer attacks his *muhajir* opponents launched against him. For example, they pointed out his defective use of Urdu grammar,[167] and on a more serious note they accused him of having denigrated the ahl al-bayt and thus destroyed the Shiʿi ʿaqida, which had remained unified for fourteen hundred years. Once the Mahdi reappeared, they promised, he would do away with people like him through the sword.[168] They saw him as a narrow-minded, fanatic Shiʿi-Wahhabi and a reductionist *qishri ʿalim*, a scholar who was only concerned with the exoteric aspects (literally: the husk) of religious teaching.[169] Some opponents consequently suggested a total social boycott of Dhakko, denouncing him as a *nasibi*, an enemy of the Prophet's household, or called on the Shiʿis to collectively curse him.[170] Dhakko, they argued, had received guidance but was stubborn in denying the virtues of the Prophet and the Al-i Muhammad in general and the third shahada as well as ʿazadari in particular. It was thus incumbent on Pakistan's Shiʿis to follow the example of the Prophet and his house and initiate a divine judgment in the form of a mutual imprecation (*mubahala*) against Dhakko.[171] The reformist was appropriately termed the "Father of Ignorance" (Abu Jahl), thus referring at the same time to an influential Meccan opponent of the Prophet, and a "Najdi pig" (*khinzir-i najdi*).[172] Through such initiatives, his enemies collectively managed to create a climate in which Dhakko's students were afraid to reveal their ties to him, fearing that the connection would prevent them from finding employment.[173] The sad state of Dhakko's (rather grandiosely named) school Sultan al-Madaris in Sargodha underlines the difficulty his reformist agenda had run into. Similarly, Sayyid ʿAli Sharaf al-Din Musavi complained that even moderate figures such as scholars associated with Islamabad's leading seminar Jamiʿat al-Kauthar declared from the pulpit that he had become a Sunni.[174]

God's Incomprehensible Transcendence

As I have demonstrated, Dhakko dismissed all attacks against himself as efforts by cynical popular preachers to protect their lucrative sinecures. But what becomes obvious in the various texts responding to his call for reform is that the arguments of Dhakko's opponents were fueled by serious theological differences. The traditionalists set out to defend the conception of an entirely transcendent God that clearly informed their understanding of tauhid. In their view, no unmediated, direct connection was possible between the Creator and human beings. Such a conviction comes to the fore in the writings of Muhammad Bashir Ansari (d. 1983). Ansari was born in 1901, obtained a *mumtaz al-afazil* degree from Lucknow's celebrated Madrasah-i Nazimiyyah, and for three years took courses on comparative religion at the Madrasat al-Waʿizin in the city.[175] He spent the 1930s as a Shiʿi missionary in the area that later became Pakistan and is credited with large-scale conversions during public debates (*munazarat*) with Sunni opponents. After the foundation of Pakistan, he pushed for the establishment of an All Pakistan Shiʿa Conference (APSC) as a successor to the AISC.[176] Over the next de-

The sad state of the library in the Sultan al-Madaris madrasa, Muhammad Husayn Najafi Dhakko's seminary in Sargodha, speaks to the difficulties and intense opposition advocates of Shiʿi reform have faced in Pakistan. Photograph by the author.

cades, he exchanged letters with pro-Shaykhi figures in Pakistan in which he praised the subtlety of Shaykh Ahmad Ahsaʾi's religious reasoning. Ansari argued that it was perfectly in line with the thought of established Shiʿi figures like Muhammad Baqir Majlisi while publicly denying any leanings toward the Shaykhi school.[177] When these letters were leaked, Ansari attempted to distance himself from the Shaykhis, claiming that "no books had been available to him to study Shaikhiya doctrine thoroughly."[178]

His publications, however, speak a very different language: Ansari wrote in a refutation of Dhakko's works that God's unicity was beyond human comprehension and that it was not possible for Him to directly establish contact between His divine essence and His creation (*khudavand-i ʿalam apni makhluq tak bi-zat-i khud nahin pahunc sakta tha*). The realms of the servant and the master were two discrete and entirely separate entities, one spiritual (*ruhani*), the other one filled with matter (*maddiyyat*).[179] It was only through the Imams acting as transmitters (*vasilah*) that we could obtain an accessible form of tauhid. The maʿsumin, who were themselves manifestations of God's attributes, conveyed knowledge about God's essence to us.[180] Consequently, it did not make much sense to attribute titles like *mushkilkusha* (the remover of difficulties) or *hajat rava* (the granter of wishes) directly to God, as some ʿulama argued.[181] Even though the Prophet and his descendants appeared to us in human form, they were nothing less than God's first creation (*avval-i makhluq*) and had direct, unmediated access to God's knowledge.[182] Their relationship with God was not based on compulsion (*jabr*), because this would entail that their conduct could not be called praiseworthy. Rather, the maʿsumin were acting with the full authority (*ikhtiyari haysiyyat*) that God had granted them. This meant that they themselves commanded supernatural abilities such as talking with animals or raising people from the dead.[183] They spoke while still in the womb and confessed the shahada right after birth. Everyone who was born the same night as them thus automatically became a believer (*muʾmin*). God Himself had crafted their physical features, and they were born without an umbilical cord. The bodies of these holy personalities glowed in the dark, they were able to simultaneously view what was in front and what was behind them, and their sweat was fragrant. No mosquito would ever bite them and no birds would sing while seated above them. They did not cast a shadow, did not grow old, and did not leave footprints in soft soil.[184] These creational (*takvini*) powers implied not only that these holy personalities could split the moon at will but also that the proper categories of allowed and forbidden (*halal o haram*) should be taken from their example.[185] Another prominent traditionalist critic of Dhakko, the influential preacher and former member of the Council of Islamic Ideology Sayyid ʿIrfan Haydar ʿAbidi (d. 1998), put it in similar terms.[186] Even though God had created heaven and earth, the trees and stones greeted not Him but Muhammad when the Prophet passed by them.[187] While God's essence was hidden (*makhfi zat us ki*), it became manifest through the Prophet and his kin who rightly guided the creation. God surely gave the victory, but it was ʿAli who won it at Khaybar, at Khandaq, and when conquering Mecca.[188] Consequently, there was nothing wrong in turning to the Imams to ask for help. The traditionalists denied that any kufr would be involved in such an act, since God himself had elevated the Imams to the level of being rulers (*hakim o raʿi*).[189]

Bashir Ansari could point out several instances when he himself had experienced the ability of the Imams to act as *mushkilkusha*. One time his son Zulfiqar ʿAli had fallen ill with gout, and no treatment proved effective. Zulfiqar could no longer move his legs and was edging closer and closer to a permanent disability. Ansari locked the boy up in the family's own mourning hall (*ʿazakhanah*), which contained a model of Husayn's tomb and a replica of ʿAbbas's standard. While Zulfiqar was imploring his *maula* to heal him, all members of the household were engaging in breast-beating and mourning outside. Suddenly the door opened and Zulfiqar slowly emerged from the hall, walking on his own legs. The whole *ʿazakhanah* was filled with fragrance, and several days later the boy had completely recovered. In another instance, Ansari's two sons Muzaffar ʿAbbas and Ghalib ʿAli were riding a truck not far away from Taxila when their vehicle was frontally hit by another loaded truck and driven off the mountain road. Before losing consciousness, both boys shouted, "Ya ʿAli madad!" When locals approached the scene of the accident, Muzaffar and Ghalib were lying on the ground, wounded but alive. Their truck was totally twisted from the impact. Yet the two boys had somehow been ejected from their seat behind the driver "through an opening which was not big enough for even a cat to escape." Finally, Bashir Ansari himself was diagnosed with a tumor in his throat, four inches long and three inches wide, which rendered eating, drinking, and breathing extremely difficult. Doctors at several hospitals were unsure what to do. When Ansari finally went to a clinic in Hyderabad (Sindh) that boasted specialists trained in the United States, Germany, and the United Kingdom, they wanted to commence the surgery right away. Ansari was hesitant, however. He preferred to consult with his family first and embarked on the long journey back home to Taxila, ignoring his doctors' advice. His relatives at once started a program of *matam* and recitations. Ansari had a dream that night and was told to shed tears for Husayn and to apply earth from Karbala (*khak-i shifa*) to his tumor. Within a couple of days, the swelling became soft and receded. This miracle was also confirmed later by one of the surgeons of the hospital in Hyderabad, who was himself a Shiʿi.[190]

In general, Imami theologians have affirmed the possibility of non-prophetic miracles. Yet they argued that such miracles must fulfill the purpose of verifying the Imam's claim to the imamate. In Ansari's case, this condition does not seem to have been met because the "definition excludes the possibility of non-prophetic miracles which are not preceded by a claim and which serve simply to honour their receiver."[191] What is remarkable, however, is that Ansari's arguments are in line with Shaykhi (and earlier Ismaʿili) cosmology, which opted for an absolute transcendence of God, a pure being that remained "undescribed to the point that its undescription cannot be described."[192] This divine entity was beyond existence, yet it brought into being in an incomprehensible mode of creation (*ibdaʿ*) the First Intelligence, which was perfect and eternal and stood on top of a great chain of cause and effect.[193] The First Intelligence was also conceptualized as God's created will (*mashiʾa*), which originated ex nihilo to preserve God's unicity uncompromised, because attributing a (changing) will directly to God was seen as problematic in this regard. According to al-Ahsaʾi this *mashiʾa* constituted the proper object of theology. It was this external, itself created will of God which set the process of creation into motion and to which everything would return on the Last Day. Al-Ahsaʾi's successor Sayyid Kazim Rashti (d. 1844) used the term *haqiqa muhammadiyya* (the Muhammadan reality) to single out the specific location where the will or act of God manifested itself in the world (*mahall al-mashiʾa, al-infiʿal*).[194] It seems to me that the Pakistani traditionalist religious scholars and preachers under discussion deliberately tapped into these sophisticated metaphysical speculations and suggested an identity between the maʿsumin and the First Intellect, or the *mashiʾa*.[195] At times they went even further than al-Ahsaʾi, who had been careful to point out that the Imams were the personalized command (*amr*) and action (*fiʿl*) of God but had no will of their own. In al-Ahsaʾi's understanding, they should be thought of as God's "passive tools."[196] The indebtedness of the Pakistanis to the complicated Shaykhi cosmology is also demonstrated by their focus on names and their insistence on the third shahada, because the "truth of Islam is a name" (*haqiqat-i Islam nam he*).[197] This could be seen as another expression of the traditionalists' strategy to identify the Imams with God's first creation and even the name "Allah" itself. For al-Ahsaʾi God's real name did not consist of vowels and consonants and was hidden from human comprehension. Rather, "Allah" was a designation that referred to His manifestation in the world of intelligibles.[198]

Redefinitions of Religious Authority

These metaphysical debates had clear ramifications for models of religious authority as well. The traditionalists argued that true religious knowledge was dependent on acknowledging the cosmological positions of the Imams. Promoting them only as worldly rulers and human beings was not enough, because non-Muslims also could experience the holy personalities in this way. The concepts of *nubuwwa, imama, risala, khilafa,* and *wilaya* were all esoteric ranks (*batini maratib*) that could be perceived only with the eyes of the heart.[199] If the sincere believer accepted the Imams as rulers of the universe, he might experience that his heart was thoroughly cleansed and the darkness of the veil being lifted (*aur tariki ke parde hat jate hen*),[200] leading to a higher level of faith (*iman*).[201] This purification of the heart was necessary in order to comprehend the deeper meaning of certain mysterious hadiths.[202] Safdar Husayn Dogar pointed to a conversation between Jaʿfar al-Sadiq and his disciple Zurarah b. Aʿyan. In this encounter the Sixth Imam had likened himself to the mysterious figure of al-Khidr, whom the Islamic tradition identified with the servant of God mentioned in Qur'an 18:59–81. Al-Khidr accepted Moses as a traveling companion and ordered him to remain silent while he committed seemingly outrageous acts like destroying a ship or killing a boy, the profound wisdom of which he only explained later.[203] Zurarah complained about a large number of hadiths which Jaʿfar al-Sadiq had conveyed to him but which he found troubling, to the extent that he felt the urge to destroy and burn his notes containing them. In his answer, the Imam explained that Zurarah's reaction was not unprecedented. The angels had likewise failed to fully comprehend Adam's *fadaʾil*.[204]

By contrast, those who regarded the Imams only as human beings analogous to themselves would only learn from them, the traditionalists argued, but their hearts would not be illuminated by Gnostic knowledge (*maʿrifat*). Ansari thus advocated for a different hierarchy of ʿulama. He ranked the *ʿulamaʾ-i ʿamal* (the scholars of outward practice), who focused on khums, the alms tax, purity, and pollution, as inferior to the scholars of the gnosis (*ʿulamaʾ-i maʿrifat*), who attained the way of truth.[205] Dhakko and his group should acknowledge that all their knowledge and ijtihad were defective. Their entire teaching was confused because they focused on curtailing the virtues and qualities of the Imams even though the latter were limitless beings (*hazrat aʾimmah-i tahirin ki zavat-i muqaddasah ki hadd nahin hoti*).[206] These actions reflected the arrogance of the scholars who adopted grandiose titles like *hujjat al-Islam* ("Proof of Islam") but in reality betrayed simple folk and inflicted damage on Islam.[207] That someone had reached the level of ijtihad was by no means a guarantee that this person could be trusted. All religious scholars, Shiʿis not excluded, had at times sold their turbans to the highest bidder and been eager to endorse fatwas approving of Husayn's killing.[208] Even Qum and Najaf were no longer immune to the spread of reprehensible forms of ʿaqida by scholars who had used their material capabilities and political influence to seize the centers of Shiʿi learning (*marakiz par qabzah kar liya*).[209] The traditionalists adduced the examples of controversial reformists like Musa al-Musawi,[210] Abu 'l-Fazl b. Riza al-Burqaʿi (d. 1991),[211] and, most important, Muhammad b. Mahdi al-Khalisi. They believed that al-Khalisi had been Dhakko's teacher (which he was at pains to deny) and hence labeled the reformist Pakistani scholar the "Khalisi of the present age" (*Khalisi-yi ʿasr*).[212] It was especially due to al-Khalisi's supposedly evil influence that the Shiʿi qaum could no longer distinguish between a true and a "fake" (*jaʿli*) mujtahid.[213] This problem also affected some Pakistani students who pursued higher religious education abroad. They had developed a liking for the "pomp and show" put on by the modernist (*jiddat pasand*) ʿulama, who promoted religious innovations in line with the zeitgeist. Such a strategy was amply reflected in the title (and substance) of al-Khalisi's main fiqh work, *Ihyaʾ al-shariʿa* (Revival of the shariʿa).[214]

Given Dhakko's clear lack of *batini* insights, Ansari advised him to restrict himself to fiqh questions and the *furuʿ* of religion and to be content with discussing khums, zakat, and issues related to the female period and childbirth. He should not try to exert any authority in the context of *kalam* and *ʿaqaʾid*, because this would go beyond his limited capabilities.[215] Even though Dhakko had spent a long time in Iraq, he clearly had not experienced the "spiritual emanations and blessings" (*ruhani fuyuz o barakat*) emerging from ʿAli's shrine, because he had neglected to pay any attention to the *batin*. Dhakko had only claimed his portions of bread from the public kitchen (*langar*) of the "Gate to the City of Knowledge"; he had not made use of ʿAli's Qurʾanic exegesis (*taʾvil*).[216] Yet Ansari's most dangerous weapon in the context of Pakistan was to accuse Dhakko and other reformers of violating the principle of the finality of Muhammad's prophethood (*khatm al-nubuwwat*). Such an attack brought Dhakko dangerously close to the Ahmadis, who through a constitutional amendment had been officially declared non-Muslims in Pakistan in 1974 for upholding the possibility of continued prophecy after Muhammad.[217] Ansari argued that the efforts of the reformers to downgrade the Prophet and the Imams meant eliminating the divide between their exalted position and the mere human. This implied that if an ordinary human being were to try hard enough to study law and obtain the level of ijtihad, he could actually reach a stage equal to that of these holy personalities.[218]

Mainstreaming Esoteric Knowledge

The traditionalist ʿulama did not deem it sufficient, however, only to attack Dhakko and other reformers personally or simply to end the discussion by claiming higher spiritual insights. They clearly reacted to the debate initiated by the reformists and were anxious to demonstrate that their cosmological readings of the Imams were perfectly in line with the mainstream of Shiʿi thought. These scholars argued that they defended the same *ʿaqaʾid* that had been core beliefs for hundreds of years and had been held by millions of Shiʿi ʿulama, saints, philosophers, hadith-transmitters, and mujtahids.[219] Dhakko's response of indiscriminately throwing around the Shaykhi label to dismiss essential Shiʿi beliefs was simplistic at best.[220] It constituted a corruption of the truth clothed in the language of reform, as Qur'an 2:11 emphasized.[221]

In order to situate themselves within the Shiʿi mainstream, the traditionalists pursued two main strategies. First, they played up their scholarly credentials by referring to the *ijazat* they had received from prominent scholars and attempted to argue that Khomeini's view in particular was perfectly in line with their approach. Second, they seized on the veneration of both Sunni and Shiʿi scholars for the Prophet Muhammad and tacitly extended the agreement about his unique standing as God's Messenger to the Imams.

Al-Sabiqi, for example, relied on Dhakko's discussion of the authority exerted by a jurist who met all of the preconditions during the time of the Occultation (*faqih jamiʿ al-sharaʾit*). Such a scholar was entitled to fill the position of *hakim al-sharʿ*, denoting a jurist "who is well-qualified to decide on legal matters and supervise the affairs of Muslims in the area of Shariʿa."[222] Al-Sabiqi concurred that such a *faqih* was tasked by God to establish the *hudud* and discretionary punishments (*taʿzirat*), to command right and forbid wrong, and to act as the caretaker for orphans' property. He then emphasized that eleven ayatollahs and grand ayatollahs, among them Sayyid Abu 'l-Qasim al-Khuʾi (d. 1992), Sayyid Muhammad Baqir al-Sadr (d. 1980), and Sayyid Muhammad Kazim Shariʿatmadari (d. 1986) had appointed him as their *wakil* and delegated the above-mentioned functions to him.[223] Bashir Ansari could claim similar endorsements from, among others, the grand ayatollahs Muhammad Husayn Kashif al-Ghita (d. 1953) and Sayyid Shihab al-Din Marʿashi Najafi (d. 1990).[224] These leading scholars in the Shiʿi centers clearly contradicted Dhakko's views, al-Sabiqi claimed. Al-Khuʾi had stated, for example, that the prophets and Imams were not impaired by the slightest defect during their lifespan. The grand ayatollah ʿAbd al-Aʿla Musavi Sabzavari (d. 1993) was quoted to the effect that the connection the Infallibles had with God and His emanation was of a superhuman quality (*kharij az nauʿ-i bashar ast*).[225] The traditionalists could refer to eighteen modern marajiʿ

who had condoned not only the creation of the Imams from light but also their guardianship over creation (*vilayat-i takvini*).[226] In these lists, the leading Shaykhi scholar of the school's Tabrizi branch, Mirza Hasan al-Ha'iri al-Ihqaqi (1900–2003), also shows up frequently, labeled as both grand ayatollah and reformer (*muslih*).[227] This is not too surprising, since the Tabrizis had adopted a much less controversial outlook than their rival Kirmani branch. They did not condone the concept of the fourth pillar and, in general, had given themselves the image of rather orthodox mujtahids who accepted the concept of taqlid.[228] But the traditionalists' biggest trump card was Khomeini himself, who had affirmed in his work *Hukumat-i Islami* (*Islamic Government*) that the spiritual state of the Imams

> is a universal divine vice regency [*khilafat-i kulli-yi ilahi*] that is sometimes mentioned by the Imams. It is a vice regency pertaining to the whole of creation [*khilafati ast takvini*], by virtue of which all the atoms in the universe humble themselves before the holder of authority [*vali al-amr*]. It is one of the essential beliefs [*zaruriyyat*] of our Shiʿi school that no one can attain the spiritual status of the Imams, not even the cherubim or the prophets. In fact, according to the traditions that have been handed down to us, the Most Noble Messenger and the Imams existed before the creation of the world in the form of lights situated beneath the divine throne; they were superior to other men [*az baqiyyah-i mardum imtiyaz dashte and*] even in the sperm from which they grow and in their physical composition.[229]

This implied that the "Khalisi group" was guilty of raising the voice of discord. These people baselessly labeled the ordinary Shiʿis, who were thoroughly rooted in the officially condoned orthodoxy, as ignorant and extremist.[230]

The traditionalist authors came to their seemingly strong consensus of Shiʿi authorities partly by relying on quotes that referred primarily to the Prophet. They seized on these discussions and quietly extended them to encompass all the maʿsumin. ʿIrfan ʿAbidi, for example, took ʿAli Naqi Naqvi's affirmation that the Prophet had access to "knowledge of the unknown" (*ʿilm-i ghayb*) to argue that the Imams too were blessed with this ability.[231] ʿAli Hasnayn Shiftah attempted to dismantle Dhakko's position that there was no rational counterargument to the possibility of the Imams losing their infallibility. Dhakko had opined that this doctrine simply had to be accepted on the authority of the divine law and the tradition of the Shiʿi school. In his response, Shiftah marshaled evidence from the famous theologian Jamal al-Din Hasan b. Yusuf, called al-ʿAllama al-Hilli (d. 726/1325), who had argued that if the Prophet was not maʿsum, then the people could not trust him. Al-

Hilli had indeed taken this stance in reaction to the Muʿtazili position, which rested on the principle of mutual cancellation (*ihbat*). The Muʿtazilis held that punishment for minor sins was canceled out by praiseworthy actions exceeding it; they intended to thereby make room for minor sins committed by prophets and at the same time exonerate them from any blame connected with such lapses. Since al-Hilli, like al-Sharif al-Murtada (d. 436/1044) before him, rejected this mechanism of *ihbat*, he could not allow that prophets committed *any* sin because this would entail blame, punishment, and compromising their status.[232] Al-Hilli does not provide a discussion of the Imams in this context, but al-Shiftah makes it appear that he did, claiming that the Iraqi theologian had demonstrated "in a rational way" that both the Prophet and the Imams needed to be infallible and that this position was not merely a "school opinion" (*mazhabi ʿaqidah*), as Dhakko had claimed.[233] Similarly, al-Sabiqi adduced the Iranian scholar and philosopher Muhammad Husayn Tabataba'i (1904–81) and his commentary on the Qur'an *al-Mizan fi tafsir al-Qur'an* (*The Scale in the Interpretation of the Qur'an*).[234] Tabataba'i explained that a prophet should be regarded as such even before he started receiving any revelation (*wahy*), because he was equipped from his birth with the special ability to do so. Al-Sabiqi takes it for granted that Tabataba'i's reasoning applied to the Imams as well.[235] Such a strategy also informs Safdar Husayn Dogar's attempt to draw on leading marajiʿ in order to make the uncontroversial point that Shiʿi Islam recognized five *usul-i din*, among them the imamate. Yet Dogar then proceeds to fill out the particular meaning of the imamate by relying on far more obscure and esoteric figures.[236]

Moving even beyond the confines of their own school, traditionalist authors also sought to appropriate Sunni scholars in their endeavor to establish the orthodox character of their thought. An obvious choice for them was Muhammad b. ʿAbd al-Karim al-Shahrastani (d. 458/1153), an author whom the Sunni tradition remembers predominantly as a Shafiʿi jurist and Ashʿari theologian. He is most famous for his heresiography *al-Milal wa-l-nihal*.[237] While al-Shahrastani discussed Ismaʿili cosmology in detail in this work as a seemingly neutral and disinterested observer, he revealed in some of his other writings that he himself subscribed to the distinction between the unintelligible world of God (*ʿalam al-amr*) and our sensual world (*ʿalam al-khalq*). The latter emanated from the First Intellect and hence originated only in a secondary manner through God.[238] Al-Sabiqi utilized especially al-Shahrastani's discussion of prophethood that was presented in *al-Milal* in the form of a supposed munazara during the time of Abraham between a group of Sabeans and an assembly of monotheists (*hunafa'*) opposing them. These monotheists argued that the prophets occupied the "first stage of all stages of existence."[239] Their being was superior to that of ordinary humans in terms of "disposition and capability" (*mizajan wa-istiʿdadan*) and went beyond usual angelic qualities as far as "reception and performance" (*qubulan wa-adaʾan*) were concerned.[240] While al-Shahrastani's thought was a synthesis of Ashʿari, Avicennian, and Ismaʿili concepts,[241] al-Sabiqi called on him as a witness to present a universal ʿaqida that was supposedly shared by Sunnis and Shiʿis alike.[242] Al-Sabiqi also found an ally in the eminent Sunni thinker Abu Hamid Muhammad b. Muhammad al-Ghazali (d. 505/1111), from whom he could adduce quotes that prophets were outwardly human while set apart by their capability to receive revelations. Their intellect resembled the First Intellect, and their souls bore some similarity to the Celestial Soul (*al-nafs al-falakiyya*).[243] In addition, statements on the qualitative difference between prophets and ordinary humans could be gathered from a wide range of Sunni authors, including Husayn b. Masʿud al-Baghawi (d. 516/1122), the Qadi ʿIyad (d. 544/1149), and Muhammad Husayn Mubin Hanafi Farangi Mahalli (d. 1125/1810 or 1811).[244]

Reaching for a Higher Dimension of Rapprochement

These efforts to demarcate a universal Islamic orthodoxy had further implications. The scholars attacked by Dhakko and Sharaf al-Din Musavi also advocated their own versions of a rapprochement with the Sunnis. In doing so, they chose different pathways than the reformists who had argued for an end to controversial practices and beliefs that emphasized a distinct Shiʿi identity.[245] By far the most popular taqrib strategy championed by the traditionalists was to argue for the existence of a Sufi-Shiʿi synthesis. The *muballigh-i aʿzam* Muhammad Ismaʿil had been a particularly loud—if unlikely—voice in this regard. In 1962 he founded his own school, the Dars-i Al-i Muhammad in Faysalabad, with the purpose of training Shiʿi preachers; he also ran his own publishing house.[246] At first glance he seemed to fit the picture of an uncompromising sectarian hothead. For instance, he held public munazaras with Sunnis even one year before his death and openly celebrated his adherence to the Shaykhi school. During the twelfth annual convention of his madrasa on 30–31 August 1975, Ismaʿil unveiled "a huge poster figuring, among other things, words of praise for Shaikh Ahmad Ahsaʾi and his successor S. Kazim Rashti." He also declared his allegiance to the founders of the Shaykhiyya.[247]

Muhammad Ismaʿil clearly emphasized the spiritual and charismatic authority (*walaya*) of the Imams and held that their interpretation of Islam was decisive because they were nothing less than the talking book (*kitab-i natiq*).[248] Yet the "Greatest Preacher" was careful to broaden the appeal of such a message by relying on eminent Sufis from the subcontinent who had written about the concept, even though they had mostly utilized the related (but confusingly in Arabic script identically written) term *wilaya*. The semantic ambiguity of the two terms pertains to both the Shiʿi and the Sufi context. Walaya in Shiʿi thought represented a "principle of spiritual charisma" and denoted "a profound spiritual connection and ontological affinity" between the Imams and their followers.[249] Wilaya, on the other hand, meant "un état d'intimité" with God, to the extent of extinguishing oneself in Him, and might thus be translated as "sainthood."[250] For Sufis, the two terms are no less "semantic fraternal twins that coexist symbiotically," each relying on the other for its meaning. For them, however, Walaya refers to the Shaykh's authority over his followers, whereas wilaya captures the relation of love between the Shaykh and God.[251]

Drawing on this ambiguity, Muhammad Ismaʿil quoted at length from the Indian Naqshbandi Shaykh Ahmad Sirhindi (d. 1034/1624), whose collected letters, the *Maktubat-i Imam-i Rabbani*, had been widely influential in their time, spreading Naqshbandi-Mujaddidi teachings throughout the entire eastern Islamic world.[252] Sirhindi had initially been very hostile to the Shiʿis, penning in his pre-Sufi period a work titled *Risalah dar radd-i rawafiz* (Epistle on the refutation of the rejectionists). In this epistle Sirhindi had argued that anyone who baselessly accused another human being of kufr and enmity to God would himself be subjected to this curse. The *takfir* that the Shiʿis were guilty of with regard to the first three Caliphs would therefore fall back on no one but the Shiʿis themselves.[253] But Yohanan Friedman has argued that Sirhindi later came to mitigate this hostility. In his reading, Sirhindi during the Sufi part of his life conceded a "special spiritual task" to the Twelve Shiʿi Imams and endorsed ʿAli's wilaya.[254] Sirhindi termed ʿAli the leader of those who traveled on the way of sainthood and claimed that the fourth Caliph had held this position even in his preexistence, before he came into this world at the time of Muhammad (*qabl az nashaʾ-i unsuri*). Every participant in the journey along the way of sainthood received the divine blessing (*fayz*) through ʿAli's meditation (*tawassut o haylulat*). After the latter's death, this task of meditation was given to Hasan and Husayn and, later, to the other Shiʿi Imams.[255] These statements do not imply, however, that Sirhindi came to adopt a full-fledged Shiʿi version of wilaya/walaya. Rather, the seventeenth-century Sufi thinker, who—unlike his spiritual teacher, Muhammad Baqi bi'llah Dihlavi (d. 1012/1603)—did not distinguish between these two terms, connected wilaya specifically to the saints who have completed the mystical journey and hence reached the state of "closeness" to or "intimacy" with God (*qurb*). This closeness set them apart from the masses and turned them into an elite (*khawass*) with God.[256] Muhammad Isma'il nevertheless papered over the remaining differences and forcefully made the case for enough common Sufi-Shi'i ground with regard to the slippery term wilaya/walaya.[257] To him, the concept demonstrated the existence of a shared Muslim 'aqida that accepted the Imams' authority. He consequently called on those Sunnis and Shi'is who held the proper creed of believing in the Twelve Imams and the saints (*khush 'aqidah shi'ah sunni barah imam aur auliya'-i kiram ke manane wale*) to unite against the Wahhabi denial of wilaya/walaya.[258]

A related strategy by traditionalist authors was to emphasize the essential overlap, exchange, and peaceful coexistence between Sunni and Shi'i forms of Islam in Pakistan and to single out certain unwelcome Deobandi attempts at rocking the boat. (See chapter 1 for a discussion of comparable initiatives in the late colonial period). Safdar Husayn Dogar remarked that every day, all over Pakistan, hundreds of majalis were held. If it was true that at these venues insulting remarks were regularly made about the first three Caliphs or the Companions, as 'Ali Sharaf al-Din Musavi claimed, then "every house in the country would already resonate with Shi'i-Sunni fighting." The two sects would no longer intermarry or attend each other's funerals—all of which precisely did not take place. Instead, at least in the Punjab, Sunnis frequented Shi'i mourning sessions and, at times, even took part in 'azadari. Demanding from Shi'is to reform their ways in order to qualify as proper Muslims had been the essence of the propaganda of the virulently anti-Shi'i group Sipah-i Sahabah-i Pakistan (SSP). Since their founding in 1985, they had been talking up phenomena that simply did not exist in society. When the SSP activists realized their failure to stoke the flames of sectarian discord, they had planted Sharaf al-Din Musavi as a "hidden enemy" (literally, a snake in the sleeve; *asatin ka sanp*) to render their evil work successful after all.[259] Similarly, al-Sabiqi accused Dhakko of trying to break the strong and ancient Shi'i-Barelvi alliance (*shi'iyon aur barelviyon ka qadim ittihad*). He felt obliged to issue an apology to his Barelvi brothers that a "so-called" Shi'i mujtahid was using such filthy language and leveling accusations of polytheism that were aimed at them too.[260] Both Shi'is and Barelvis cherished majalis in Muharram and in conjunction with the Prophet's birthday. Both acknowledged that Muhammad was created out of light, that he was blessed with knowledge of the unseen, and that he continued to have a spiritual, active presence in this world (*hazir o nazir*).[261] Dhakko's goal, by contrast, was only to please the Deobandis. This was reflected in his reliance on authors adhering to that school. Al-Sabiqi especially took issue with Dhakko for appropriating arguments from Ashraf 'Ali Thanavi's (d. 1943) book *Islah al-rusum* (Reform of customs) in order to buttress his criticism of the custom of holding a recitation encompassing the entire Qur'an during a single Ramadan evening (*shabinah*).[262] This proved that Dhakko in reality conspired to promote taqlid of the Deobandis, not obedience to the Imams and emulation of the marajiʿ.[263] That Dhakko's controversial reformist publication from the 1990s even shared the same title with Thanavi's work demonstrated beyond any doubt that his agenda was entirely built on Deobandi fatwas that were merely given a superficial Shiʿi labeling.[264] This could also be gathered from the way the "anti-Shiʿi centers" (*shiʿah dushman marakiz*) were celebrating the publication of Dhakko's latest book. According to al-Sabiqi, he had received more than five hundred letters and telephone calls urging him to write a reply to this work, since there was the imminent danger that the forces hostile to Shiʿi Islam might make use of its arguments in courts and parliaments as a "reference and proof text" (*havalah aur dastavez ke taur par*) against the Shiʿis.[265]

Finally, I briefly consider a manifestation of traditionalist Shiʿi thought that strives to make a case for taqrib by focusing nearly exclusively on the Hidden Imam. These ideas were promoted by Sayyid Muhammad Jaʿfar al-Zaman (d. 2002), a man who allegedly never enjoyed any formal schooling but was educated by his father Sayyid Talib Husayn Shah Naqvi Najafi, "a spiritualist of higher status."[266] Sayyid Muhammad Jaʿfar al-Zaman assumed the role of a Shiʿi pir and used to hold nightly sessions in the Punjabi village of Jaman Shah that attracted a couple of hundred followers every night.[267] Among them were a good number of educated professionals, who not only helped al-Zaman set up his own website as early as 2001 but also provided editorial assistance with the publication of his final work, *The Last Great Reformer of the World*, which he wrote in English.[268] Jaʿfar al-Zaman criticized those Shiʿi reformers who attempted to deceive the Shiʿi masses by turning their religion into a neatly delineated "package" that was supposedly in line with an "enlightened" (*rushan khayali*) understanding of religion.[269] Yet this reformist system was also devoid of any specific Shiʿi elements like ʿazadari, the Shiʿi *adhan*, or conceptions of the Imams' *fadaʾil* in order to achieve an intra-Muslim unity that was based solely on the understanding of a shared revealed book, *qibla*, Prophet, and God.[270] Al-Zaman, by contrast, advanced a divergent proposal for real, feasible unity that went beyond such allegedly impoverished initiatives.[271] He argued that all religions were expecting a true, comprehensive reformer and savior who would appear at the end of time, a figure whom both Shiʿis and Sunnis identified as the Mahdi. It was only when the Mahdi's face was revealed and, consequently, God's very own omnipotent countenance (*Allah ʿazz o jall ka jabruti cihrah*) became known, that weak human beings could expect to fully comprehend God.[272]

Al-Zaman insisted that it was not up to us to try to expedite the process of the Twelfth Imam's reappearance. In a thinly veiled critique of Iran he wrote that including any mortal person in the Mahdi's government was nothing else than undue haste (*jaldbazi*) and an action that would certainly provoke God's wrath.[273] In another instance of the adoption of reformist vocabulary by traditionalist authors, however, he was eager to underline that the waiting period, properly understood, was supposed to be filled with "exemplary action and not idleness": "The waiting that we are stressing is actually a revolutionary school of thought which has no provision for leisure or easy life. It is the name of the life of a soldier or a commando. Many Traditions say that one who waits is like a soldier fighting in the field."[274]

Like other traditionalist authors, Ja'far al-Zaman rejected claims by the 'ulama, whom he called "religious monopolists" (*mazhabi ijarah dar*) and accused of abusing scripture for their own ends, to be the representatives of the Hidden Imam during his Occultation.[275] Following the commands of a *maulvi*, who was himself a created being, was not compatible with God's greatness.[276] In fact, al-Zaman limited and delineated the 'ulama's role even further than other antireformist writers studied in this chapter. In his view, the only acceptable task for the religious scholars could be to teach the people the traditional Shi'i prayers to hasten the appearance of the Mahdi and to exhort them to seek direct contact with him.[277] During the time of Occultation, there was no obligation more important for the 'ulama than to "safely deliver the seekers of truth and sincerity to the Imam of the Age's palace of guidance."[278] Therefore the 'ulama should make sure that the Hidden Imam took center stage in all their majalis and sermons, that they included the prayer for the Mahdi's speedy return even in the obligatory daily prayers, and that they organized nightly vigils during which the believers should plead for the appearance of the Twelfth Imam. Likewise, the religious scholars were obliged to instill in the people an urge to meet the Hidden Imam in both dreams and awakened states of mind, and to provide them with the appropriate tools to facilitate such a visitation.[279]

Muhammad Ja'far al-Zaman discussed various rigorous spiritual exercises an individual had to undergo before he or she could approach the Lord of the Age (*sahib al-zaman*). For example, the seeker had to follow a strict diet based only on vegetables and fruit. He should put on a loose cotton dress that he himself had washed and that no one else was allowed to touch. The believer should avoid sexual intercourse, refrain from any immoral behavior, and seclude himself from society for at least one week.[280] This possibility was open to everyone, regardless of his or her religion because no guidance existed in the world anyway during the time of the Twelfth Imam's Occultation. Jaʿfar al-Zaman advised his followers to attempt to establish contact with the Mahdi in such a state of ritual purity at midnight on a Thursday. After calling on the Hidden Imam with the Arabic invocation "Ya hadi nawwir qalbi bi-hidayatika" (Oh guide, enlighten my heart through your guidance) 313 times, the believer should pray using the following words:[281]

> You please guide me. I present my religious matters, faith and worldly affairs before you. I present the blank paper of my mind. Presently I have neither any religion nor belief.[282] From today onward my religion and belief will be that, [*sic*] which you imprint on this blank paper. I make a covenant with your exalted self that I shall obey your orders. The belief given by you will be my religion. I will consider things allowed by you as lawful and not allowed as prohibited. I offer my assistance (though you need it not) of every kind. Kindly include my name in your assistants and servants. I proffer my life, possessions and honour to your exalted self. You have complete authority of spending the same as you please or wherever you like. [. . .]
>
> Now I present my last request that if you don't assure me of your entity and presence and don't guide me in the fields of my religion, beliefs, do's and don'ts, then I will plainly tell my Creator, when he will question me about my sins that [*sic*]: Your representative did not guide me despite my request. So there is no fault on my part. Kindly ask your representative about my sins.[283]

If the Mahdi did not appear to the seeker within the first week of seclusion, the former should wait for another week before issuing an ultimatum to his savior through the following demand: "I shall wait for your guidance till the next Friday. If it is not received till then, I will never return to you and will believe that your exalted self is not present in this world."[284] If contact with the Hidden Imam was established, the believer should remain silent about it and treasure it as a personal gift regarding which dissimulation (taqiyya) was obligatory. This held especially true if the Mahdi had given the believer any sort of command or granted him or her a particular revelation. Such a private message should not be divulged publicly. Other people might after all not be able to handle its implications or understand it properly because every individual was different with regard to capability and rational faculty (*har shakhs ka zarf o ʿaql juda juda he, is liye is ke liye sadir hone wale ahkam bhi juda juda hon ge*).[285]

Jaʿfar al-Zaman might at first glance be perceived as thus "democratizing" the Shiʿi experience, and indeed his theories go beyond the accessibility most Shiʿi jurists had conceded to the Imam during the *ghayba* period. Muhammad b. al-Hasan al-Tusi (d. 459 or 460/1066–7) had argued, for example, that the Imam could at times influence a meeting of jurists who were trying to reach a consensus (*ijmaʿ*) on a certain question and—unbeknownst to those who participated—steer the decision in the right direction. But Shaykh Murtada al-Ansari (d. 1262/1864), along with leading Imami jurists, had denied even this limited role because it was simply not possible for the Imam to reveal the truth while being in Occultation.[286] For the Shaykhis, an encounter with the Hidden Imam required nothing less than a "'technique' initiatique secrète" that was the exclusive knowledge of a spiritual elite (*khassat mawalih*).[287] In the twentieth century, cautionary voices remained dominant as well. The Iranian Revolution clearly occurred against the backdrop of high-running expectation about the return of the Hidden Imam.[288] Yet Khomeini (unlike the Shah who played up divine favors bestowed upon him) was always careful to emphasize that he had no special connection with the Mahdi.[289] He suggested instead that the Iranian nation as a collective entity might benefit from a favored status with God as long as Iranians relied on Him and trusted in Him.[290] It was only during the presidency of Mahmud Ahmadinejad (2005–13) that more permissive attitudes toward potential communication with the Mahdi surfaced. Ahmadinejad himself, in fact, is notorious for such claims. The politician found himself in the midst of controversy by suggesting that he had enjoyed contact with the Hidden Imam, among other occasions during the United Nations General Assembly meeting in September 2005, a claim that was ridiculed by many Shiʿi scholars in Iran.[291] Even ʿulama like Muhammad Misbah Yazdi, who actively tried to create a "theoretical space for positing that a cleric such as himself and those whom he approved of were also acting according to the will and demand of the Hidden Imam," did not subscribe to the opinion that the Mahdi could be forced to appear.[292] While the Hidden Imam was of course at liberty to show himself wherever he saw fit, Shiʿi guidebooks usually stipulated that ritual seclusion should be sought at special places like the Sahla mosque in Najaf, ʿAli's mosque in Kufa, the shrine of Husayn in Karbala, or the mosque of Jamkaran near Qum.[293]

Al-Zaman breaks with this tradition of primacy attributed to Shiʿi places in the Middle East suitable to facilitate an audience with the Lord of the Age. According to him, a rural Punjabi setting was in no way less suitable to witness a visitation. Yet it seems that it is not just dynamics of "democratizing" and "localizing" access to the Hidden Imam that are at play in his writings. While undoubtedly reducing the ʿulama to mere handmaidens of a mystical encounter with the Mahdi, Jaʿfar al-Zaman still retains the role of a pir for his followers. We can safely assume that his admonition not to publicly discuss encounters with the Hidden Imam enshrines his own prerogative (or that of his successor) to interpret for his followers the implications of the particular command received.

CONCLUSION

In this chapter, I have argued that Shiʿi religious reformers in Pakistan such as Muhammad Husayn Najafi Dhakko and Sayyid ʿAli Sharaf al-Din Musavi face a dilemma. Their calls to "purify" Shiʿi Islam by abandoning supposedly superstitious rituals and beliefs in order to achieve a rapprochement with the Sunni majority bear an eerie resemblance to anti-Shiʿi polemics advanced by groups such as the Sipah-i Sahabah. At the same time, Dhakko's focus on a legal-based reinterpretation of Shiʿi identity or Musavi's political reading of Karbala did not gain much traction among Shiʿi believers in the country.

This does not mean, however, that their writings did not deeply reshape the discourse about proper Shiʿism in Pakistan. The traditionalist opponents of Dhakko and Musavi—themselves a diverse group, to be sure—reacted to the challenges of reform by foregrounding theological, Shaykhi-inspired arguments about an utterly transcendent God. This focus on the esoteric aspects of the faith not only enabled them to reconceptualize the precise meaning of tauhid but also made it possible to distinguish between the initiated ʿulama, who could comprehend the subtleties of the faith, and the scholars of mere ritual. It was not enough for these scholars to make esoteric arguments and to emphasize the direct engagement of the Imams with the "Land of the Pure," however. Instead they were keen on demonstrating that their theological views not only fit squarely into the Shiʿi mainstream and were indeed held by most senior scholars in the centers of learning and scholarship but also that Sunni authors, when properly read, would condone their views. This strategy for obtaining an aura of respectability also ties in with alternative solutions advanced by these traditionalists to overcome sectarianism either by suggesting a Sufi-Shiʿi synthesis revolving around the ambiguous term walaya/wilaya or by turning the Mahdi into a universal figure who could be approached by adherents of all faiths.

CHAPTER THREE

Projections and Receptions of Religious Authority

GRAND AYATOLLAHS AND PAKISTAN'S SHIʿI "PERIPHERY"

ʿAqil Musa did not hide his feelings about my suggested research on this hot Karachi morning. I had come to see him in the office of his publishing house, located in the city's Soldier Bazaar. With the Imam Khomeini Library close by and surrounded by a multitude of Shiʿi bookshops, *husayniyyas*, and businesses specializing in selling banners, flagellation chains, and various other accessories used during Muharram, it appeared to be an appropriate location to discuss Shiʿi thought in Pakistan.[1] Also, I was curious to hear about Musa's unique perspective: a trained medical doctor, he had made a career change in the wake of the Iranian Revolution. After long years of religious studies in Qum, he was now wearing clerical garb and acted as the principal of the Jamiʿah-i Imamiyyah, one of the most prestigious institutions of Shiʿi learning in Pakistan.[2] But Musa showed no patience with his fellow countrymen and dismissed the idea of studying their religious output: "What do you expect? People have nothing to eat, they fight for their survival. You should not be surprised that religious publications from Pakistan are only of inferior quality."[3] If I was serious about studying Shiʿism, I should instead focus on the foundational texts available in both Arabic and Persian. Similarly, there was, in his view, no benefit to be gained from scrutinizing the speeches delivered by Sayyid ʿArif Husayn al-Husayni, Pakistan's main Shiʿi leader of the 1980s, whose views feature prominently in chapter 4. The way al-Husayni presented the concept of vilayat-i faqih (Guardianship of the Jurist) was identical with Khomeini's vision and merely a faithful translation into Urdu of ideas developed by the Iranian revolutionary.

This anecdote underlines Pakistan's supposed (and acutely self-perceived) status as a Shiʿi backwater with nothing to offer to the centers of the Shiʿi world. Rather, as Musa was eager to emphasize, Pakistani Shiʿis have been and still are merely on the receiving end of knowledge production, which naturally takes place in Iran and Iraq. This Middle East–centered view is shared by those who reject the Iranian model. In a conversation I had in Najaf with Shaykh ʿAli Najafi, son of the South Asian–born Source of Emulation Bashir Husayn al-Najafi (discussed further below), he restricted the religiously relevant, foundational texts to Arabic publications alone. In his view, Persian is only good for political readings of Islam, which he rejects.[4]

My goal in this chapter is to interrogate these claims. I argue that the vocal acknowledgment of transnational authority in general and the embrace of the seemingly rigid system of emulation in particular does by no means render local agency obsolete. Most Pakistani clerics do not dispute the towering position of the grand ayatollahs. But they are successful in developing subtle but far-reaching ways how to mitigate their influence. This is a delicate balancing act, as I show below. Not surprisingly, therefore, many Pakistani Shiʿi ʿulama share and actively promote Musa's bleak view about their own peripheral status. They point to the lack of established educational institutions that are comparable to the pre-Partition role exerted by Lucknow's seminaries, which produced generations of senior mujtahids.[5] Iranian publications are often not even willing to concede this point. Instead, they express deep skepticism about the "scientific" standing of Lucknow as a (historical) *hauza* (major Shʿi seminary) in its own right. The city's seminaries are criticized for not subscribing to a proper Usuli stance on Shiʿism. Instead of focusing on ijtihad and taqlid, the argument goes, Lucknow restricted itself to emphasizing the virtues (*fadaʾil*) and afflictions (*masaʾib*) of the ahl al-bayt and the importance of the imamate.[6] This generally dismissive attitude is not an invention of the twentieth and twenty-first centuries, to be sure. One of the first Indian scholars to pursue advanced religious training in Najaf, Sayyid Dildar ʿAli Nasirabadi (d. 1820), fought an uphill battle during his stay in Iraq. Because of his background, he was not taken seriously as a scholar. His fellow students at the time "found the very thought of an Indian mujtahid absurd, given that only three scholars of the shrine cities were recognized exemplars."[7]

Partition certainly did not help to alter this entrenched perception. As the two previous chapters show, in 1947 Pakistan had only two functioning and rather basic Shiʿi seminaries, located in the Punjab towns of Multan and Sargodha.[8] Despite sustained efforts to establish new schools and upgrade the level of education, the most advanced cycle of traditional, Shiʿi religious learning, known as *dars-i kharij* (lit: "external studies"), is not yet offered in the country.[9] In this final, third cycle of hauza training, no textbooks are used and the students are expected to have mastered the basic works of fiqh and *usul al-fiqh* in order to explore major areas of Islamic law at the level of "pure disputation."[10] One consequence of this lamented lack of educational sophistication is that not one single *marjiʿ al-taqlid* (Source of Emulation) resides in Pakistan today.[11] This is all the more intriguing because South Asian scholars are amply represented in Iran and Iraq. Even among Najaf's current four main grand ayatollahs there is one mujtahid from the subcontinent, Bashir Husayn Najafi.[12] He was born in 1942 in the city of Jalandhar in today's Indian Punjab before moving with his family to Lahore in 1948. Najafi attended the Jamiʿat al-Muntazar seminary and traveled to Najaf in 1965 where he completed the highest cycle of Shiʿi learning and devoted himself to teaching and writing.[13] Surprisingly, though, Bashir Husayn Najafi has never returned to Pakistan nor embarked on any initiatives to strengthen the seminary system in South Asia more broadly. Instead he extols the unrivaled position of Najaf as a hauza and actively works toward bolstering it.[14] Najafi's representatives regularly hold competitions for Shiʿi madrasa students in India. Out of about 2,000 participants every year, 150 to 200 are invited to move to Najaf in order to continue their religious education there, supported by a stipend.[15]

Such clear notions of center and periphery and the dependence of South Asian Shiʿis on Najaf and Qum for their religious guidance come to the fore in the available secondary literature as well. Juan Cole has categorized the rising Usuli influence in North India among Shiʿis since the early 1800s as a direct import from the shrine cities of Iraq. This new "ideology" fiercely attacked local, gentleman-like Shiʿi scholars, who in their literalist Akhbari proclivities (which, to be sure, were the result of earlier connections to the Middle East) "resembled Pentecostalist ministers, who rejected priesthood and whose training emphasized scriptural knowledge, eschewing rationalist theology."[16] The indigenous "egalitarian religious structure" was thus challenged and ultimately transformed by a highly hierarchical form of the faith. During the nineteenth century, a class of religious specialists took shape and Shiʿis "moved from a group in which lay-clerical differences were slight to one in which a vast chasm separated the chief mujtahid from a humble Shiʿi artisan."[17] That either foreign-born or Iraq-educated scholars were the driving force behind sweeping changes like the introduction of communal Friday prayers points to the centrality of the Shiʿi heartlands. Yet Cole also alerts us to the complex interactions between the Middle East and the subcontinent once a genuine Indian religious hierarchy was firmly in place. Whereas the "lower ranks of mujtahids" showed no hesitation in accepting even controversial juridical decisions made by the leading Iraqi marjiʿ of the age,

Lucknow's "top mujtahids" never felt obliged to modify their rulings when they differed in their legal reasoning.[18]

Justin Jones has expanded on these demonstrations of scholarly independence. Criticizing Cole, he suggests that we should move away "from the idea of an 'Indo-Persian milieu'" and the assumption that modern religious developments in Shiʿis Islam could "only be discussed with primary reference to globalization and the enhancement of ties to the Iraqi-Persian heartland."[19] Jones's study attempts instead to chart the emergence of self-consciously "Hindustani" forms of Shiʿism with their own religious leadership and inventories of practice. The lively public sphere of the time, which was populated by various Shiʿi organizations (anjumans), constitutes for him a prime example for such local manifestations of the faith. The founding of these societies was almost exclusively inspired by rival efforts at socioreligious reform within India, namely the opening of colleges, hospitals, and orphanages by Hindu, Sunni, and Christian groups, rather than being dependent on developments in Najaf.[20] Similarly, Jones credits the leading Indian Shiʿi ʿulama of the 1920s with holding political positions that diverged significantly from those of their peers in the Middle East. In taking their stance against the Khilafat movement of 1919–24, these jurists differed from Arab and Persian mujtahids who advocated "pan-Islamic politics during these same months as the best defense against the Anglo-French occupation of Muslim territories."[21] The establishment of specifically Indian seminaries confirms in Jones's view that South Asian Shiʿism since the late nineteenth century has shed the "cultural, religious and psychological leadership located in the wider Perso-Arab world" for a "meaningful and semi-autonomous role" within the Shiʿi international.[22]

If one turns to scholarly appraisals of transnational ties since the inception of Pakistan in 1947, the emerging picture is hardly any clearer. There is no agreement in the literature regarding the importance of relations with the Shiʿi heartlands. Accounts on the marajiʿ, their influence, and the importance of taqlid in Pakistan take two very distinct, antithetical shapes. On the one hand, scholars argue for the continued predominance of international ties that manifested themselves under the towering leadership of Muhsin al-Hakim in the 1960s. Probably born in Najaf in 1889, al-Hakim had reached the level of ijtihad in 1919. Gradually his public presence grew, and he began leading the Friday prayers at Najaf's al-Hindi mosque in 1920 and the evening prayers at the shrine of Imam ʿAli from 1936. After the death of Sayyid Husayn Burujirdi in 1961, al-Hakim achieved a status of *marjiʿiyya* that might be categorized as being a *primus inter pares*.[23] It has been argued that after al-Hakim's demise in 1970 most Pakistanis accepted Abu

ʾl-Qasim al-Khuʾi (d. 1992) as their marjiʿ.[24] Al-Khuʾi made a name for himself as "Teacher of the Hauza" and "supervised hundreds of students while thousands of clerics are considered his indirect students."[25] Vali Nasr holds that the decision for Khuʾi must have limited the revolutionary influence of Khomeini and the appeal of the Iranian conception of vilayat-i faqih in the subcontinent more broadly. He writes that in the late 1980s South Asian Shiʿis addressed al-Khuʾi with the same lofty titles Iran used for Khomeini. Pakistani and Indian Shiʿis regarded Khomeini only as a leader in political matters, whereas in religious questions they were followers of al-Khuʾi, who also received most of their khums.[26] Other students of Pakistani Shiʿis, such as Nikki R. Keddie, have dismissed such a view altogether, arguing that the concept of marjiʿiyya is not meaningful in the context of Pakistan:

> Although Pakistani Shīʿah say that they (like Iranian Shīʿah) follow the guidance of a "source of imitation" (*marjaʿ*) or leading clerics (Khomeini and Khūʾī of Iran and Iraq were the two alternatives named to me in 1985–86), I found none who could mention an actual issue or occasion on which they had followed such clerical guidance. The real if often hidden issue for the Shīʿīs of Pakistan is not doctrinal, but the need for a non-Sunnī destination for the payment of religious taxes, since for Shīʿīs these are owed to the *ʿulamāʾ* as representatives of the Hidden Imām.[27]

Conducting research on Pakistani Shiʿis seventeen years after Keddie's fieldwork, David Pinault made similar observations in 2002. Many of the Shiʿis he interviewed "seemed altogether unfamiliar even with the concept of the *marjaʿ*."[28]

These interventions sit well with other recent anthropological studies of religious reasoning in Pakistan. Magnus Marsden and Naveeda Khan have emphasized local resistance to uniform Islamizing trends. They have hinted at a certain striving and aspirational tendencies by common believers to explore their faith with a critical eye (and even skepticism) toward religious authority exerted by both the jurists and the state.[29] While this chapter attempts neither to solve the general puzzle of religious literacy among Pakistani Shiʿis nor to decisively answer the question about the "quality" of influence the ʿulama enjoy in the country, I suggest that internal Shiʿi debates over taqlid can yield fresh insights into the construction of religious authority by "indigenous" scholars. I am especially interested in exploring how allegiances to a particular grand ayatollah are formed and what the affirmation of his marjiʿiyya means for lower-level Pakistani scholars and lay authors affiliated with these high-ranking jurists. My research—building on the argument made in chapter 1 about the salience of concerns beyond the subcontinent—emphasizes the crucial importance of transnational ties well before the Iranian Revolution of 1979. Rather than confining their debates to South Asian issues without any references to the heartlands, Pakistani scholars follow the opposite strategy by extensively claiming the center's support for their particular views, as I demonstrated at length in chapter 2. I argue, however, that the supreme position of a specific marjiʿ, even if he is explicitly endorsed as the towering ʿalim of the age, does not necessarily limit the claims to religious authority that local ʿulama make. By referring to a distant scholar, his representatives can rely on his prestige to boost their own position or, during the interim period when a new, universally accepted marjiʿ has not yet emerged, might step in as legal experts themselves to fill the void. Pakistani religious scholars and thinkers thus skillfully exploited these potentials of their peripheral status in order to claim a position of influence and central religious vitality in the wider Shiʿi world.

If one considers the criteria which are seen as the sine qua non for an ʿalim to have reached the status of a "Source of Emulation," Pakistani debates do not usually diverge from singling out supreme learning (*aʿlamiyya*) and piety (*taqwa*) as decisive.[30] Yet a conclusive evaluation and comparison of these characteristics, especially if the layperson (*muqallid*) is confronted with a group of (nearly) equally qualified candidates, might at times prove elusive. Even fellow scholars may shy away from endorsing any explicit ranking of those ayatollahs. The remainder of this chapter shows that in such circumstances secondary criteria like accessibility suddenly take center stage in elevating a particular ʿalim's standing among his peers. In the context of the Shiʿi periphery, a jurist's outreach and active interest in the Shiʿi world beyond Iran and the Arab lands can play an equally crucial role, too. The prerogative of local Pakistani scholars in making this choice on behalf of the common people is thereby seen as rather unproblematic, at least as far as the religious specialists under discussion are concerned. By presenting themselves as the "people of experience" (*ahl al-khibra*), they take an elitist approach which attempts to limit the agency that an individual believer theoretically enjoys in choosing his or her "Source of Emulation."[31]

In order to substantiate my claims, throughout this chapter I rely primarily on Pakistani Shiʿi journals. This material makes it possible to trace shifting debates and diverging opinions, unlike, for example, monographs, which at times smooth over such occurrences and thus sanitize the historical picture.[32] In particular, I consult the fortnightly *al-Hujjat* published in the northern Pakistani city of Peshawar under the auspices of Mirza Safdar Husayn al-Mashhadi (d. 1980).[33] I also pay attention to *Payam-i ʿAmal*, the journal of the Pakistani branch of Sayyid ʿAli Naqi Naqvi's Imamia Mission with its headquarters being based in Lucknow. Published from Lahore, *Payam-i ʿAmal* was Pakistan's most widely distributed Shiʿi monthly at the time. Finally, I rely on *al-Muntazar*, the fortnightly magazine of the Jamiʿat al-Muntazar in Lahore, Pakistan's leading Shiʿi seminary since the late 1960s.[34] These periodicals have only been little studied, most likely due to the difficulty of obtaining access.[35] None of the mentioned magazines for the time period under consideration are available in any Western library; I had to assemble copies of them from holdings at the Punjab Public Library in Lahore and the libraries of the Idarah-i Minhaj al-Husayn in Jauhar Town/Lahore, the Madrasah-i Sultan al-Madaris in Sargodha (Punjab), the Jamiʿat al-Muntazar in Model Town/Lahore, Grand Ayatollah Burujirdi in Qum, and Sayyid Muhsin al-Hakim in Najaf. Even though the Center for Research Libraries (CRL) in Chicago features *Payam-i ʿAmal* in its holdings, issues are available only from 1976 onward.

In the following, I discuss the period roughly from 1962 until 1976, thus covering the years when Muhsin al-Hakim had attained the position of a nearly universally accepted global marjiʿ. Al-Hakim is credited with a deep personal interest in Pakistan that was kindled by the experiment of Pakistan as a newly founded Muslim state with a large Shiʿi population and his frequent encounters with Pakistani students in Najaf. Even before 1962 al-Hakim sent representatives to Pakistan and was very supportive of establishing new religious schools in the country.[36] I pay attention to the ways his status as the most learned scholar is affirmed and discussed. I also look into the ensuing uncertainty in the period following his death in 1970 when the question who could fill the void was heatedly debated and answered in widely diverging ways in the Pakistani journals under discussion. The political background of Pakistan during this decade also enters into the picture, most notably in the shape of the ill-fated war with India in 1965 and the return to democracy in the early 1970s after military rule under the generals Ayub Khan and Yahya Khan. The rise of socialist politics, with its call for land reform—which is tied to the campaigning of Zulfiqar Ali Bhutto—left its traces in Shiʿi writings as well. While evidence of controversies about taqlid during the lifetime of the influential marjiʿ Sayyid Husayn Burujirdi (d. 1961) remains elusive,[37] the discussion in the 1980s and 1990s became increasingly overshadowed by the Iranian Revolution, which is the topic of the next chapter. Before turning to Pakistani debates, however, it is necessary both to delineate the crystallization of modern Shiʿi reflections on the role exerted by the "Sources of Emulation" and to take a look at the processes through which these scholars attained their comprehensive position of authority.

THE EMERGENCE OF GLOBAL MARAJIʿ IN THE MODERN PERIOD

Already a century after what the Shiʿis describe as the beginning of the "Greater Occultation" in 329/941, Shiʿi treatises of jurisprudence "speak familiarly of *taqlīd*." While originally discussed in the context of obtaining fatwas from a mufti, by the time of al-Muhaqqiq al-Hilli (d. 676/1277) "*taqlīd* had become the corollary of *ijtihād*" and was increasingly justified by arguments of reason and prophetic precedent.[38] With a transfer of accountability at the root of the concept, the (living) mujtahid relieves the lay believer (the muqallid, the one who emulates) of the responsibility for the correctness of his religious actions. The ʿalim exerts his own powers of ijtihad to the best of his ability in order to determine the character and extent of these divinely prescribed duties.[39] Usuli scholars remain deeply aware of their own limitations during this process. Certainty of religious reasoning that becomes fully identical with God's intentions (*waqiʿ*) will most likely not be achieved during the absence of the Hidden Imam. The mujtahid provides merely a reasoned supposition (*zann*).[40] The necessity of emulating a living mujtahid is usually justified with the argument that there must always be a scholar available to interpret the law according to changing circumstances.[41] In the premodern period, local mujtahids dispensed their legal guidance to lay Shiʿis. The latter were expected to determine whether a scholar qualified for the task in light of their interactions with him and the testimony of reliable witnesses regarding his rank.[42]

In contrast to these dynamics, the emergence of one towering (and spatially far removed) scholar, the most learned mujtahid, is a distinctly modern phenomenon, one facilitated by innovations in transport and communications that rendered a comparatively remote place like Najaf increasingly more accessible to the global Shiʿi community.[43] Scholars have noted that these new possibilities for outreach coincided with the pressing need felt by the Shiʿi establishment to close ranks against challenges posed by the Shaykhi and Babi movements.[44] This transformation of authority is manifested by the rise of the ultimate Shiʿi mujtahid and "sole *marjaʿ al-taqlid* for the Shiʿi world" Murtaza Ansari (d. 1864).[45] Sayyid Muhammad Hasan Najafi (d. 1266/1850), who nominated Ansari shortly before his death as the supreme exemplar after him, had already started the practice of sending delegates to far-flung Shiʿi locales in order to collect the Imam's share of the khums.[46] Ansaris's exalted position and the funds that came with it enabled him to train a substantial number of students who after his death formed the "largest group of competing leaders."[47] He also reworked the procedu-

This photo shop near the shrine of Imam ʿAli in Najaf, Iraq, displays portraits of leading contemporary and deceased Sources of Emulation in January 2013. Photograph by the author.

ral principles of *usul al-fiqh* and even allowed mujtahids to make legal rulings on cases regarding which they had doubts.[48] This contribution "enabled mujtahids to extend the area of law to any matter where there was even a possibility and not just a probability of being in accordance with the Imam's guidance. It thus enabled them to broaden the jurisdiction of their own profession into wider spheres of human activity, thereby further advancing the professionalization of the ʿulamaʾ."[49]

Even more ambitious, Ansari also sought to formalize a new system of religious leadership over which the "most learned *mujtahid* presided." He argued that emulation was a religious duty without which no religious act could be regarded as valid. Ansari delineated an informal hierarchy in which junior mujtahids should only be emulated if their rulings were identical with those of the supreme marjiʿ.[50] Such processes of consolidation were also helped by the rise of printing, which made it possible for jurists to distribute to their followers a legal compendium designed for use by lay Shiʿis, known as *risala ʿamaliyya* (lit. practical treatise).[51] These compendia, while rarely offering "real novelties in legal research," nevertheless made the opinions of one's chosen mujtahid immediately accessible.[52] It was also during the course of the nineteenth and twentieth centuries that titles of Shiʿi scholars marking their rank, such as Hujjat al-Islam (Proof of Islam), ayatollah (Sign of God), or grand ayatollah, were used for the first time and rapidly gained currency.[53] Scholars in the twentieth century added their own suggestions for a more regularized system that would overcome the perceived deficiencies of the unstructured way in which a new marjiʿ emerges and later administers his authority. The Iraqi scholar Muhammad Baqir al-Sadr (killed in 1980), for example, advocated the idea of an "office" of the marjiʿiyya that would not only prevent a particular jurist from making "arbitrary decisions" but would also guarantee continuity and an institutional memory in the transition from one marjiʿ to the next. In al-Sadr's suggested arrangement, the representatives would form "sociopolitical branches" of the marjiʿiyya.[54] Yet despite such attempts by Ansari and other scholars, the process of emergence of one dominating marjiʿ remains until today a "quite ill-defined mix of scholarly and social credentials acquired in Shiʿi seminaries."[55] This holds true for Pakistan as well. The quality of an individual ʿalim's scholarship, his reputation for piety and justice, as well as his intensive studies with a former marjiʿ are all important, as are his ethnic background, connections to business leaders and the merchant community, and networks of patronage that involve his former students.[56] If these building blocks that make up a successful bid for the marjiʿiyya play out on several levels, the same applies to the constituencies that are relevant for accepting a particular scholar in this role. The choice of the muqallids, the opinions of junior scholars who have an intimate acquaintance with the contenders, or the leading grand ayatollahs who recognize one scholar from among themselves as the *aʿlam* might ultimately tip the balance in this very amorphous process of emergence.[57] This chapter, then, also contributes to the scanty literature on the negotiations of religious authority underlying the choosing of a marjiʿ in the wider Shiʿi world in general and in the context of Pakistan in particular.

EMBRACING THE MOST LEARNED AT ARM'S LENGTH: THE CASE OF AL-HUJJAT

The first case study deals with the writings of Mirza Safdar Husayn Mashhadi (d. 1980), who is counted among the leading Pakistani Shiʿi ʿulama of the twentieth century.[58] Born in Bombay in 1901, he received most of his education in Lucknow, initially from his grandfather. After the latter's death, Mashhadi also studied with the mujtahid Sayyid Muhammad Baqir (1868–1928) before switching to Qum.[59] Ayatollah Sayyid Abu 'l-Hasan Isfahani (d. 1946) finally sent him to Peshawar, where Mashhadi later acted as a representative for both Muhsin al-Hakim and Khomeini. His biographers credit him with a very outspoken, uncompromising attitude. Such a fearless proclivity for controversy gained him notoriety for harshly criticizing the moon sightings announced by Radio Pakistan. Mashhadi frequently objected to the "official" dating of Ramadan and the major holidays of *ʿid al-fitr* (Feast of Breaking the Fast) and *ʿid al-adha* (Feast of the Sacrifice) as inaccurate.[60] Unlike other scholars, he did not regard the establishment of a school as his main goal; rather, he embarked on several projects to reform the affairs of his coreligionists in Pakistan. His most enduring legacy in this regard was probably the fortnightly *al-Hujjat*.

In a long series of articles published in this journal in the early 1960s, Mashhadi expounded on his view that in every age only one overarching Shiʿi mujtahid existed. This scholar was not merely a particularly brilliant jurist but also a leader who held far-reaching spiritual power (*ruhani quvvat*). He should be seen as a ruler without a crown. Since this supreme scholar was seated on the "throne of deputyship of the Hidden Imam," he exercised authority over the Shiʿi believers (*riyasat-i millat o mazhab apne hath men lete hen*). He even took on the position of the "silent Imam" (*imam-i samit*).[61] Even though the leading marjiʿ would insist that he was not protected from sin (maʿsum), in reality his lifestyle approached this ideal. A scholar of such a standing would be in a position to crush all base desires and comply fully with the requirements of the shariʿa.[62] These special abilities did not deny the existence of other great mujtahids in the Shiʿi heartlands. But only the leading figure had his flag flying all over the world and commanded a truly global presence. He functioned as the general marjiʿ, and emulating him was necessary. This obligation extended to a certain degree even to his fellow ayatollahs: whoever did not recognize the most learned as such had invalidated his own possible claim to emulation.[63]

Mashhadi did not stop at simply promoting Muhsin al-Hakim's unquestionable superiority. He was also careful to underline his own rank as al-Hakim's representative in Pakistan. Mashhadi built his argument on a critique of those (contemporary) Iranian and Iraqi scholars who did not accept the credentials of the great Indian mujtahids of the past, thereby forgetting the more appropriate attitude of their ancestors. The "supreme learnedness" (*aʿlamiyya*) of Sayyid Aqa Murtaza Kashmiri (1852–1905), for example, had been widely acknowledged in Iraq, but he had stayed aloof from the marjiʿiyya (*marjiʿiyyat se kanarah kash*) by his own free choice.[64] Similarly, even though the Iraqis had recognized the towering position of Mashhadi's own teacher Sayyid Muhammad Baqir, who was also known as Baqir al-

ʿUlum, this scholar did not step forward to claim his deserved global leadership role out of "piety."[65] Having thus made the case that South Asian ethnicity was no hindrance to scholarly excellence, Mashhadi pointed out the hierarchy that flowed from the mujtahid of the age. His appointed representatives were themselves leaders of the Shiʿis (*qaʾid-i mazhab*). They not only collected the khums but also spread education and prepared the way for the application of the shariʿa. The mujtahids of a particular region who did not serve as representatives of the *marjiʿ-i ʿamm* recognized the authority of those who did. Below them in rank we find scholars who had not (yet) reached the rank of ijtihad, which obliged them to restrict their activities to preaching (*tabligh*). One rung farther down the ladder, Mashhadi located people whom the ʿulama could trust in transmitting legal questions. The lowest level in this pyramid was occupied by popular preachers (zakirs), who were indispensable for the holding of majalis and whose influence I discussed in the previous chapter.[66] For Mashhadi, this elaborate hierarchy, which hinges on the centrality of a single Source of Emulation, was so well established and entrenched that it constituted a cause of envy for other Islamic schools of law. It also rendered impermissible any Shiʿi attempts to elect additional or alternative religious and community leaders. The existence of representatives nominated by the center entailed that Shiʿis had no business engaging in factionalism and splintering (*anjuman sazi aur party bazi*).[67] Consequently, Mashhadi was highly critical of Shiʿi participation in democratic politics in Pakistan, which he linked to the ad hoc meeting after the Prophet's death that deprived ʿAli of his rightful role as Caliph (*saqifaʾi usul*).[68]

In his writings Mashhadi thus adopted a tone similar to that of Lucknow's mujtahids of the late colonial period. For him, Shiʿi organizations such as the APSC and the Organization for the Safeguarding of Shiʿa Rights (Idarah-i Tahaffuz-i Huquq-i Shiʿah) had lost sight of their original goal of serving religion through their various activities.[69] Instead, they played the political game out of desire for office and in clear imitation of the British.[70] Since Muhsin al-Hakim formed a link in a chain that reached back to the Imams themselves and had to be considered designated by God (*mansus min Allah*), the Shiʿi community did not have any right to independently designate representatives of the Imam.[71] Rather, the believers had to obey the "deputy of the deputy of the Imam" (*naʾib-i naʾib-i imam*), who consequently partook with his role in a divine arch of authority. Individual scholars, each in his specific local context, exerted such a role of a "particular Imam" (*imam-i khass*).[72] Given this emphasis, it is not surprising that *al-Hujjat* made a conscious effort to portray Mashhadi as al-Hakim's supreme and singular representative in Pakistan. The journal repeatedly referred to personal communications between the two scholars, as in the case of Muhsin al-Hakim arguing against women's right to vote. Reprinting a letter al-Hakim had sent to the Tehran-based scholar Ayatollah Muhammad Bihbahani (d. 1963),[73] *al-Hujjat* noted that Mashhadi had received his personal copy directly from the marjiʿ's office in Najaf.[74] No reference was made to other individuals or organizations who acted as al-Hakim's representatives in Pakistan or who had the right to collect his khums. The Imamia Mission, for example, was deliberately ignored in *al-Hujjat*, even though from the early 1960s the organization openly displayed a letter with Muhsin al-Hakim's seal on the last page of their journal. Al-Hakim had granted them the privilege of collecting khums in his name and of using one hundred thousand rupees each year for the missionary efforts of the organization.[75] Readers would also look in vain for an acknowledgment of Sayyid Gulab ʿAli Shah (1914–92), who served as al-Hakim's first representative in Pakistan at that time. His letter of nomination dated back to 1949.[76] This selective depiction of al-Hakim's activities in and connections to Pakistan may be illustrated with an article from May 1967 which argued against the perception of a lack of able, reformist-minded *fuqahaʾ* in the country. To prove the opposite, the editorial listed prominent scholars for each province of Pakistan but emphasized Mashhadi's countrywide standing and his unique position as the sole representative (*vakil o numayandah*) of Muhsin al-Hakim in order to distinguish and exalt him among his peers.[77] Similarly, a contribution from 1961 credited Mashhadi with having taken the initiative of distributing the unabridged Persian version of al-Hakim's *risala ʿamaliyya* in Pakistan.[78]

Beyond underlining this special status gained from speaking on the behalf of the general marjiʿ (*marjiʿ-i ʿamm*), Mashhadi also hinted at circumstances when the knowledge of local scholars could take precedence over that of the mujtahid of the age. Several articles in the journal described the moon sighting as a task that scholars in faraway Najaf or Qum were not able to carry out for believers in Pakistan. Since the opinion of the former did not attain the rank of a real proof, ʿulama and *fuqahaʾ* based in South Asia had to step in.[79] It was only through their crucial intermediary position that the masses were able to carry out taqlid of the most learned at all.[80] From such a view, it was only a short step to attempts at gaining independence from Najaf altogether. In 1966, Sayyid Muhammad ʿAli al-Hakim, a son in law of Muhsin al-Hakim, stayed in Pakistan for several months to instruct the local believers in basic ritual obligations of which they were supposedly ignorant.[81] While the editorial of *al-Hujjat* lauded his efforts as "eye-opening," it remarked that the old model of scholarly importation was not sustainable in the long run—if only because Iraqis would find it difficult to live in a South Asian setting, forced to consume spicy food.[82] Instead of continuing to bang on the door of Najaf with the urgent plea to send scholars, Pakistanis should take advantage of studying in the holy city in order to become self-sufficient in terms of *ʿilm*.[83]

Interestingly, this position was taken even further after the death of al-Hakim in June 1970. In the following months, two tendencies appear in the articles of *al-Hujjat*. For one, Mashhadi was furious about the campaigns waged by various groups that aimed at positioning their favorite candidate as the new supreme marjiʿ. These people did not shy away from running newspaper ads that featured pictures of their preferred ʿalim or putting up posters all over Pakistan's cities. As Mashhadi saw it, such initiatives instilled in the masses the wrong notion that the common people would have a role to play in the process of discernment and decision-making.[84] In reality, this prerogative was entirely fulfilled by "God's hand" and the Hidden Imam without need for popular participation or anything that might resemble an election. The mujtahid of the age would eventually emerge through the deliberations of the scholars. Regrettably, today religion and politics had been turned into a total mess (*ab mazhab aur siyasat ki khichri ban gayi he*). Many of those who displayed such eagerness to throw their hats into the ring were—according to the opinion of Mashhadi—only on par with al-Hakim's muqallids.[85]

Despite this clear-cut rejection of promotion campaigns, *al-Hujjat* during this time period attempted to claim increased authority for Pakistani scholarship (as defined by the journal). Even though the quest for a supreme marjiʿ continued for the time being, several contributions in the monthly advocated that taqlid might also be possible at the hands of local jurists, be they based in Bombay or Karachi.[86] This did not, however, include, those ʿulama who were active in the political arena because such polluting activities rendered them unacceptable for emulation.[87] While otherwise choosing any mujtahid was permissible, the most righteous (*aslah al-mujtahidin*) ought to be preferred.[88] More striking, however, were attempts by Mashhadi to put a new spin on taqlid, thus effectively loosening the close ties of the concept with Najaf. The shrine city and its ʿulama were no longer considered to be essential for emulation, even though Najaf's leadership and centrality in the field of knowledge (*Najaf ke dar al-ʿilm ki qiyadat aur markaziyyat*) had to be upheld at all costs. This emphasis led the journal to suggest a possible bifurcation of the two aspects, dissociating taqlid from this acknowledgment of centrality.[89] *Al-Hujjat* repeatedly published lists of all living scholars who might be able to carry out the task of preserving the unity of the Shiʿi world without indicating the journal's preference.[90] Instead of committing himself to a new marjiʿ, Mashhadi in the early 1970s openly became a legal authority in his own right, issuing fatwas and answering legal questions in *al-Hujjat*.

In taking on this position, he occasionally backed up his arguments with references to the opinions of Muhsin al-Hakim or other "central" (*markazi*) ʿulama like Abu ʾl-Qasim al-Khuʾi.

This was the case, for example, with the burning question of socialism. The impressive economic growth under Ayub Khan, manifested by an increase of manufacturing by 17 percent between 1960 and 1965, was built on a deliberate policy of "functional inequality." The state and foreign donors poured resources into West Pakistan's industrial sector, which was expected to propel the entire country onto a plane of development, while letting wages stagnate and neglecting investments in the field of agriculture. East Pakistanis in particular felt exploited, but there was a general popular perception of intensifying inequality, which led to strikes and labor unrest.[91] Building on these tensions, the Bengali politician and leader of the National Awami Party (NAP), ʿAbd al-Hamid Khan Bhashani (d. 1976), who was also known as "The Red Mawlana," suggested that "Islamic Socialism" could bring the country back on track.[92] Bhashani was less of an avid reader of communist theory; rather, he found himself frequently "sharing the same platform and making the same demands on the state as Communists and leftist workers." He was able to draw in Marxists as his spiritual followers (*murids*) because of the particular pledge of allegiance (*bayʿa*) demanded by him. Its formula referred not only to God and the Prophet but also to socialism as the "one path to the freedom of all people from all forms of oppression."[93] In West Pakistan, the issue came to the fore in the run-up to the first national elections since independence in 1970.[94] A couple of days into his 1970 election campaign, Zulfikar Ali Bhutto of the Pakistan People's Party (PPP) began to invoke the notion of "Islamic socialism" as well. The party's election manifesto noted that the ultimate goal of its policy "is the attainment of a classless society, which is possible only through socialism in our time. This means true equality of the citizens, fraternity under the rule of democracy in an order based on economic and social justice. These aims followed from the political and social ethics of Islam. The party thus strives to put in practice the noble ideals of the Muslim faith."[95]

After the PPP success in the election, a directive dating from 3 January 1972 put the country's twenty largest corporations under direct state control.[96] Labor laws passed under Bhutto provided workers with rights "previously unheard of in Pakistan's labour history," including social security benefits, pension, and increased management by workers.[97] Promises were given to remove the "remaining vestiges of feudalism," even though the realities of land reform fell short of this radical goal.[98]

Regardless of the effectiveness of these measures, Sunni and Shiʿi ʿulama alike were deeply worried about this changing climate. One hundred thirteen scholars from all schools and sects had already issued a fatwa on 24 February 1970, "ruling socialism as apostasy and co-operation with socialists as *haram* in the light of Islam."[99] While *al-Hujjat* frequently printed articles condemning socialism as un-Islamic, the exile of al-Hakim's son Mahdi al-Hakim in Pakistan from spring 1970 to fall 1971 was perceived as boosting Mashhadi's position. In a fatwa for a Shiʿi from Rawalpindi, Mahdi al-Hakim referred to the rejection of communism by his father.[100] This document was quickly seized on by the journal to demonstrate that Mashhadi's position was perfectly in line with the center, whereas those who argued differently could be dismissed disparagingly as a "bunch of political conspirators" (*cand siyasi gath jor karne vale*).[101] One exception to this general picture was a short note, published in March 1972, which declared Muhammad Kazim Shariʿatmadari the "universal Source of Emulation" (*marjiʿ-i ʿamm*), who granted *al-Hujjat* the privilege of collecting yearly khums of up to two thousand rupees in his name, this decision was quickly reversed. An editorial in August 1972 declared that so far no leading scholar had emerged and that the decision should thus be considered suspended (*taʿviqandakhtah*).[102] The journal seems to have stuck to this line while persistently pushing the scholarly credentials of Mashhadi: later issues addressed him as nothing less than *faqih-i Pakistan* or even ayatollah.[103]

The fine line Mashhadi was treading between the authority of the shrine cities and his own claims did not go unnoticed by the audience. A letter to the periodical, already published in July 1962, criticized *al-Hujjat* for almost exclusively featuring its patron while not providing a similar platform for other scholars. It should not be the goal, the anonymous reader wrote, to turn every Pakistani into a follower of the particular ʿaqida advanced by the magazine. In fact, some damage had already been done: articles published in *al-Hujjat* had led some people to declare that they would follow not Muhsin al-Hakim but Safdar Husayn Mashhadi.[104]

PAYAM-I ʿAMAL AND LOCAL AUTHORITY BETWEEN PAKISTAN, INDIA, AND THE MIDDLE EAST

A striking phenomenon similar to what we have seen playing out in the pages of *al-Hujjat* occurred in the case of the magazine *Payam-i ʿAmal*. This journal was published by the Imamia Mission in Lahore. It served as the Pakistani branch of an organization bearing the same name that had been established in 1932 in Lucknow by Sayyid ʿAli Naqi Naqvi (d. 1988), arguably India's most influential, most widely published and quoted Shiʿi scholar of the twentieth century. Belonging to Lucknow's famed *khandan-i ijtihad*, he is "commonly said today to have been the final great mujtahid of South Asia."[105] Naqvi was deeply troubled by how the onslaught of modernity had affected his fellow Muslims, fearing that religion might be pushed to the sidelines.[106] He blamed rising unbelief as the source of every kind of intellectual, social, and cultural corruption and combated empirical outlooks on the world.[107] The tremendous progress of science had in his view led to a dangerous new epistemological arrogance displayed by the secular educated strata of society, whose hearts were covered with unprecedented "coatings of doubt."[108] In order to counter this state of affairs, Naqvi strove to present to the Shiʿi public an image of Imam Husayn that emphasized "worldly agency rather than intercessionary powers, and a message of temporal action that meant he was a figure to be emulated rather than merely commemorated."[109] In a conscious decision, after 1937 Sayyid ʿAli Naqi Naqvi abandoned his former scholarly audience, with its seminary-style commentaries in Arabic or Persian, to direct himself exclusively to Urdu-speaking Shiʿis. The founding of his organization and its fervent publishing activities were meant to provide the necessary tools to demonstrate the indispensability of religion for social reform and a healthy society.[110]

Payam-i ʿAmal, in turn, clearly betrayed Naqvi's influence. The journal regularly published articles and excerpts from longer works by the Indian mujtahid, ranging from his *tafsir* and extensive reflections on the Shiʿi Imams to discussions of the status of women in Islam. Additionally, *Payam-i ʿAmal* advertised a broad range of Naqvi's numerous books.[111] Yet even though Naqvi was constantly referred to as the *mujtahid-i ʿasr* (mujtahid of the age), *Payam-i ʿAmal* provided hardly any space for the dissemination of his legal decisions.[112] In this context, Muhsin al-Hakim clearly took the front seat. He was hailed as the supreme marjiʿ, the worthiest deputy of the Imams, and the scholar displaying the highest morals.[113] The journal published a separate Urdu translation of his *risala ʿamaliyya* and prominently featured al-Hakim's legal rulings.[114] After al-Hakim's demise, however, and unlike after the death of Burujirdi, *Payam-i ʿAmal* was careful not to endorse one specific candidate. Back in 1961, the Imamia Mission had sent out three telling letters of condolence. The first of these had been addressed to Burujirdi's son, the second to Muhsin al-Hakim, and the third to the shah of Iran.[115] In 1970, by contrast, the journal even kept featuring a letter written by Muhsin al-Hakim, who had granted the Imamia Mission the right to collect and use khums in his name in December 1962, placed prominently on its back page. The magazine continued this practice more than twelve months after the Iraqi scholar had passed away.[116]

In the early 1970s, *Payam-i ʿAmal* kept sending mixed signals as far as the designation of the *aʿlam* was concerned. An article from October 1970, written by Safdar Husayn Najafi (d. 1989), principal of the Jamiʿat al-Muntazar in Lahore and later one of the most important popularizers of the revolutionary Iranian message in Pakistan, claimed that the majority of Shiʿis in Iran, Iraq, India, and Pakistan would all be followers of Khomeini.[117] Likewise, he hailed Khomeini in a different piece as the greatest scholar in Najaf, the fortress of Islam.[118] The same issue also carried legal response by Ayatollah Sayyid Mahmud al-Husayni al-Shahrudi (d. 1974) on issues of the modern banking system.[119] In September 1971, *Payam-i ʿAmal* printed the affirmative answers both Khomeini and Khuʾi had provided in response to an inquiry whether the new office building of the Imamia Mission could have a mosque on its second floor and a hall for majalis and shops on the first floor.[120] A photo series in March 1973 included portraits of al-Shahrudi, ʿAli Naqi Naqvi, Muhammad Kazim Shariʿatmadari, and Mahdi al-Hakim (the latter depicted while visiting a book exhibition organized by the Imamia Mission).[121] Finally, a piece in June 1976 identified Khomeini, Khuʾi, and Shariʿatmadari as the three most widely followed marajiʿ in Pakistan.[122]

In a development that seems to parallel the trend playing out in the case of *al-Hujjat*, the death of Muhsin al-Hakim and the lack of a scholarly consensus about his successor opened up even more space for local South Asian ʿulama. An article in December 1971 pointed out that among 2,000 historical marajiʿ, no less than 108 had achieved a particularly influential status (*markaziyyat*). Among this select group, scholars who hailed from the subcontinent had in no way been less prominently represented than ʿulama from Iran and Iraq.[123] Even more remarkable, however, was the rise of Sayyid Muhammad Jaʿfar Zaydi (d. 1980) as a legal authority in *Payam-i ʿAmal*. Besides serving as the journal's patron (*sarparast*), he had been active all his life as a Friday preacher (*khatib*). Having received no advanced training in his native India, he did not qualify as a mujtahid and was thus much less eligible than Sayyid ʿAli Naqi Naqvi.[124] Nevertheless, he had already provided legal opinions on two occasions shortly before Muhsin al-Hakim's death, though he had been careful at that time to limit the scope of his own authority. Asked about whether performing Friday prayer behind a prayer leader of doubtful morals was permissible, Zaydi pointed out that his goal in answering this question was merely to provide legal information. If he were to touch on controversial issues (*ikhtilafi masaʾil*), he implored any muqallid reader to refer the problem at hand to his or her specific marjiʿ.[125] Such a cautious approach was no longer discernible only a couple of months later. By the end of 1970, Zaydi's name, amply embellished by the title "Pride of the Theologians" (*fakhr al-mutakallimin*), appeared regularly and on equal footing with the leading *fuqaha'* of the age under the rubric "Shariʿa Questions and Their Answers" (*Masa'il-i sharʿiyyah aur un ke javabat*). Zaydi gave legal rulings on how to perform the ritual prayers while traveling and regarding the purity of kitchenware touched by Christians.[126] He also frequently clarified questions on Islamic history.[127]

PUSHING AHEAD: SHARIʿATMADARI AND THE JOURNAL *AL-MUNTAZAR*

Payam-i ʿAmal and *al-Hujjat* both provide a window onto the complex and rather chaotic negotiations of transnational and local Shiʿi religious authority between the Middle East and South Asia. The dynamics at play in the third Pakistani Shiʿi journal under discussion diverge substantially from the first two case studies, at least if one considers the post-Muhsin al-Hakim period. During the lifetime of the Najaf-based scholar, *al-Muntazar* largely resembled the other publications in its treatment of al-Hakim's marjiʿiyya. It hailed his towering role while also making room for the contributions by local Pakistani scholars. The journal promoted al-Hakim's superiority by answering legal questions in light of his rulings and addressed him as "the most knowledgeable of the age" (*aʿlam-i dauran*) or the "undisputed leader of the Shiʿi world."[128] In a highly successful initiative, readers were encouraged to order free copies of al-Hakim's main legal treatise in Urdu translation and were only charged the postage. The publication was announced on 5 June, and by 20 August all available copies had been claimed.[129] A special "Muhsin al-Hakim Number" extolled the late scholar for being both the most influential promoter of the "sciences of Muhammad's household" and a fearless warrior in the path of God.[130] Al-Hakim's biographer Sayyid Murtaza Husayn (d. 1987) also pointed out the Iraqi scholar's remarkable devotion to internal Pakistani affairs.[131] Al-Hakim had stood at the side of the country in its 1965 war with India. The conflict, which ultimately proved militarily inconclusive, centered predominantly on Kashmir; its Indian-held areas were infiltrated by roughly five thousand Pakistani troops in August as part of Operation Gibraltar but also witnessed substantial tank battles along the border in the Punjab and aerial warfare.[132] During these critical times, al-Hakim had declared that he prayed for Pakistan's victory, which he likened to a victory for Islam itself (*Islam ki fath*).[133] In an earlier letter to the military ruler Ayub Khan, al-Hakim had expressed his strong condemnation of the acts of sectarian violence that had erupted in the Sindhi village of Theri in 1963, claiming the lives of 118 Shiʿis.[134] An *imambargah* had been set on fire amid a general upsurge of violence against Shiʿi processions that was, according to Andreas Rieck, stoked by renewed anti-Shiʿi propaganda in the wake of the lifting of martial law in June 1962.[135] Besides these involvements in Pakistan affairs, the marjiʿ had also been at the forefront of supporting religious schools in Pakistan.[136]

Similar intimate, transnational connections proved decisive for the selection of al-Hakim's successor, as I demonstrate below. Yet we also have to briefly consider the curious phenomenon that *al-Muntazar* at times acted consciously against the universal status of al-Hakim by emphasizing the juridical competence of Pakistani scholars in a way that resembles both *al-Hujjat* and *Payam-i ʿAmal*. This tension became apparent in early 1965, shortly after Husayn Bakhsh Jara, whom we have already encountered in the previous chapter, had taken over as principal of the Jamiʿat al-Muntazar. In the following months, Jara was called upon to answer legal questions ranging from the validity of a marriage concluded without consent to problems of inheritance.[137] Whereas Muhsin al-Hakim's rulings printed in *al-Muntazar* never reflected a real case but consisted merely of translations from his legal treatise,[138] Jara aimed at demonstrating his familiarity with the actual issues facing Pakistani Shiʿis. For example, the 20 June 1965 issue of *al-Muntazar* featured a query from Khushab about a traveler who embarked on a lawful journey and hence performed a shortened version of the ritual prayer (*namaz-i qasr*). At some point the traveler was overcome by an impermissible desire (*na jaʾiz gharz*), thus perverting the original purpose of his travels. How would this affect the prescribed length of the prayer? Jara answered that it was no longer permissible for such a person to shorten his prayers. He illustrated his ruling with a visitor who had come to the city of Lahore on some acceptable religious or worldly business, only to give in to the temptation of frequenting a cinema. By linking the abstract and general question of proper Muslim conduct on a journey to a real issue that inhabitants of Punjab's countryside might face, Husayn Bakhsh Jara showcased an attentiveness to practical concerns of everyday life that no distant authority in Iraq could possibly match.[139]

Such rather open claims to local leadership were undoubtedly the exception in *al-Muntazar*. The journal usually went to great lengths in substantiating the superiority of the marajiʿ who resided in the Shiʿi heartlands. Yet this did not mean that Pakistani scholars should necessarily be excluded from transnational debates on leadership. *Al-Muntazar*, in contrast to the two other journals we have discussed, clearly did not feel obliged to wait for any consensus forming in the shrine cities after the demise of Muhsin al-Hakim. In fact, the magazine did not display any qualms about endorsing the marjiʿiyya of Muhammad Kazim Shariʿatmadari in July 1970, exactly one month after the journal had celebrated al-Hakim's legacy in a special issue.[140] A long article by Akhtar ʿAbbas portrayed the Ayatollah's life, underlining the well-rounded personality of this towering figure. Importantly for an audience that might feel threatened by a rise of socialist politics in Pakistan, ʿAbbas hailed Shariʿatmadari's indispensable service in reviving the fortunes of the hauza in Tabriz and keeping the flame of science (*ʿilm*) burning when the Russians occupied the scholar's native Azerbaijan province during (and in the wake of) the Second World War.[141] After Shariʿatmadari had moved to Qum, his penetrating insights were soon recognized by Burujirdi, who used to deliberate challenging legal questions with him, frequently modifying his initial opinion in light of Shariʿatmadari's input.[142] It was during his relentless efforts aimed at the development of the hauza in Qum that his status as a global Source of Emulation had emerged. Consequently, ʿAbbas articulated similar expectations for the advancement of religious training in Pakistan: "It is our hope that you will assume the patronage of Pakistan's religious schools for ʿulama and preachers, hence establishing in the country a basis for the appropriate progress of the Shiʿi school of law."[143]

Yet Shariʿatmadari's single most pertinent achievement, the one that truly crowned his exalted position among his peers, was—according to Akhtar ʿAbbas—his leading role in the founding and running of the mission-focused Dar al-Tabligh-i Islami (House of Islamic Preaching) in Qum. Through it the ayatollah had created an "asset" (*sarmayah*) for the entire Shiʿi world.[144] Such an evaluation by Akhtar ʿAbbas and his unmitigated favoring of Shariʿatmadari is not surprising, given that the former principal of the Jamiʿat al-Muntazar wrote his lines in Qum, where he acted as the head of the Dar al-Tabligh's Urdu section.[145] As a result, this article, which was supposed to demonstrate Shariʿatmadari's *aʿlamiyya*, paid much closer attention to the institution's language classes in Urdu, its vast library, the education of preachers, and the newly established printing press.[146] Given all these achievements, ʿAbbas concluded, along with Shariʿatmadari's insightful initiatives and his acceptance as a marjiʿ by most believers in Iran, it would only take a short while before the overwhelming majority of Pakistani Shiʿis submitted to his "spiritual leadership" (*qiyadat-i ruhani*) and handed over their khums to him.[147] Other prominent voices in *al-Muntazar* echoed ʿAbbas's view. Sayyid Muhammad Yar Najafi, principal of the Bab al-ʿUlum in Multan, endorsed Shariʿatmadari as a much-needed great leader. Moreover, he addressed him as the "father of the Shiʿi community" in the vein of al-Hakim who was especially suited to be recognized as the supreme marjiʿ due to his focus on education.[148] Sayyid Muhammad Dihlavi (d. 1971), the leading Shiʿi political leader of the day,

In 1970 the journal al-Muntazar, *published from Lahore, pushed ahead with promoting Grand Ayatollah Muhammad Kazim Shariʿatmadari as the leading* marjiʿ al-taqlid. *This issue from 20 February 1972 depicts the scholar on the top left corner. Photograph by the author.*

conceded in a joint letter with a group of eight other prominent Shiʿi ʿulama that the highest-ranking mujtahids of the time all occupied nearly the same rank in terms of knowledge and piety.[149] Yet it was Shariʿatmadari's religious activities (*dini khidmat*) in Qum that would lead them to choose him for taqlid in questions of God's law.[150]

Al-Muntazar, following in the footsteps of its earlier policies with regard to Muhsin al-Hakim, not only offered free copies of Shariʿatmadari's *risala ʿamaliyya* but also dismissed attempts at promoting alternative candidates in the next months.[151] If such names were floated, they had to be seen as advanced by self-interested media people, politicians, or some low-level scholars. Their announcements lacked any authority, both legally and rationally speaking (*sharʿan o ʿaqlan*). By contrast, the *ahl al-khibra* in Pakistan all agreed on Shariʿatmadari.[152] Denying rumors that the whole of India would follow Khomeini, one scholar also brought further practical aspects into consideration: even though Najaf had been the religious center in the past, upholding this rank was no longer feasible due to the deteriorating political situation in Iraq. Shariʿatmadari's greater accessibility in Qum was thus turned into a further argument in favor of his towering role.[153] The Dar al-Tabligh continued to feature centrally in the construction of the new marjiʿ's authority, underlined, for example, by the coverage of Mahdi al-Hakim's visit to the institution, during which he applauded its global outreach.[154] When a delegation sent by Shariʿatmadari toured Pakistan in 1971, they deplored the lack of missionary activities in the country. Reiterating the Ayatollah's determination to revamp the religious educational sector in Pakistan, the delegation acknowledged neither the existence of Sayyid ʿAli Naqi Naqvi's Imamia Mission nor its offerings of training courses for *muballighs*.[155]

CONCLUSION

In this chapter, I have paid attention to the various ways in which the authority of the marajiʿ is affirmed, appropriated, and challenged in the context of Pakistan. I have argued that even the outspoken acknowledgment of a "Source of Emulation" might not diminish but rather enhance the scholarly standing of indigenous ʿulama and the marjiʿ's representatives. They manage to carve out their niches of specialized, localized knowledge that caters to the needs of Shiʿi believers in the "Land of the Pure." The period of uncertainty after the death of one supreme jurist and before the emergence of a new towering figure can open additional avenues for "backwater" scholars, as the cases of both Safdar Husayn Mashhadi and *Payam-i ʿAmal* demonstrate, to claim authority and a central religious position. Finally, the embrace of Shariʿatmadari by leading Pakistani ʿulama was intimately tied to the importance he devoted to his international prestige and the contacts he had fostered with Shiʿis in regions beyond the Middle East. He promoted and supported translations of his works into Urdu and was the first among the marajiʿ to open an office in Pakistan.[156]

These findings are in line with Michael Fischer's observations. He noticed that in the mid-1970s Shariʿatmadari, thanks to the activities of the Dar al-Tabligh, "was perhaps the *marjiʿ* best known to non-Persians."[157] Interestingly, Fischer qualifies this claim by arguing that during a visit to Lucknow only the top leadership of the Shiʿi colleges could name a living marjiʿ al-taqlid to him. Given the intensive debate we have witnessed in Pakistan's Shiʿi journals, I question the validity of applying this view to Pakistan. As we have seen, these discussions on the necessity of emulation involved ʿulama and lay Shiʿis alike and were geared toward positioning certain religious scholars at the pinnacle of authority. Whenever a journal offered its readership copies of a *risala ʿamaliyya,* the demand far outstripped the supply of these legal works. Fischer's statement even seems to be questionable as far as India as concerned. Given the unsettled nature of the question, it could well be the case that those Shiʿi ʿulama Fischer interacted with in the mid-1970s were simply reluctant to take sides in a conversation with a non-Shiʿi foreigner. Be that as it may, Pakistan's Shiʿis might not have waged the debate over taqlid in the way the physician-turned-ʿalim ʿAqil Musa would have appreciated—but they were hardly silent about the question. Neither mere pawns of transnational forces nor exclusively focused on the South Asian aspects of their religion, Pakistani Shiʿis displayed a remarkable creativity in rethinking their relations with the shrine cities of the Middle East.

CHAPTER FOUR

Khomeini's Perplexed Pakistani Men

IMPORTING AND DEBATING THE IRANIAN REVOLUTION SINCE 1979

> "Why are you silent?" Irfan was gazing steadily at him. "Silence." Afzal, placing a finger on his lips, signaled Irfan to be silent. "I think we will see a sign." "A sign? What sign can there be now?" Irfan said with bitterness and despair. "Fellow, signs always come at just these times, when all around— " he paused in the middle of his speech. Then he said in a whisper, "This is the time for a sign."
> — Intizar Husayn, *Basti* (1979)

It was the journey of a lifetime for Sayyid Muhammad Qamar Zaydi. His travels to revolutionary Iran in late April 1979 deeply impressed the junior Shiʿi scholar. The Baluch city of Zahedan, which he had experienced as a hotbed of crime during a previous stay in 1963, had been transformed within a matter of weeks. Signs of a virtuous society were palpable even in this provincial setting: women donned the *cadur*, the city's walls were plastered with slogans against America, Russia, and Israel, and, greatest wonder of all, the traffic flowed in a self-regulating manner. Policemen were neither visible on the streets nor required. This did not mean, of course, that authority was absent. Zaydi noted the ubiquitous nature of Khomeini's portrait; even Sikh traders displayed it in their shops. And he himself longed for nothing more than to encounter the Iranian leader face to face.[1] Zaydi had published a biography of Khomeini several months earlier and had finally set out from Karachi as part of a delegation with three Shiʿi scholars who later asked him to prepare a travelogue of their adventures.[2] The group was moved by the various acts of kindness and respect ordinary Iranians showed toward them as religious scholars.[3] They marveled at the lighthearted attitude of Mashhad's inhabitants, who only a couple of months earlier had endured bullets and death.[4] The travel companions were delighted that nakedness, decadence, and love for illegitimate activities—trademarks of Tehran under the Shah—had all but vanished.[5] Every single Iranian ʿalim they encountered was not only well informed politically but also diligently carried out his religious obligations.[6] Iran had clearly transformed itself into a pure Muslim land.

This realized utopia contrasted favorably with the situation back home. In Pakistan, a propaganda war of rumor-mongering and slander (*afvah tarashi o buhtan tarazi*) was being waged against revolutionary Iran, even by certain coreligionists. These misled Shiʿis thereby repeated the evil precedent of first declaring allegiance to ʿAli only to be drawn by the desires of their bellies to the table of Muʿawiya (*dastarkhvan-i Muʿaviyah*).[7] One of his fellow Shiʿis whom Qamar Zaydi might have had in mind was the communist author Sayyid Sibt-i Hasan (d. 1986). The latter early on deplored that the Islamic Revolution was far from a revolution in the Marxist sense of the word, since it had not done away with oppression.[8] Instead, the authoritarian regime of the Shah had been replaced with an *ayatucracy* that featured the same sort of personality cult, now directed toward Khomeini.[9] Sayyid Sibti-i Hasan specifically criticized the ayatollah for his declaration that the Iranians "had not sacrificed their sons for the sake of cheap bread." In his view this cynical statement was an expression of the disdain the new rulers displayed in the face of the masses' plight (*dukh dard*).[10] Such a negative attitude toward revolutionary Iran and a general insincerity regarding the Islamization of society was, in Sayyid Muhammad Qamar Zaydi's view, even more systemic to Pakistan's political system. This was what caused the delegation to reject repeated requests by the Pakistani embassy in Tehran for a meeting. Qamar Zaydi explained that he and his fellow travelers were aware of the "hypocritical disposition [*munafiqanah mizaj*] of many of our countrymen who would have used such a meeting only to make up stories."[11] In Pakistan, the author pointed out, the establishment of an Islamic system of government under the military rule of General Zia ul-Haq (r. 1979–88) was fraught with difficulties. While the Islamization of Pakistan's criminal law, for example, had triggered a passionate debate with many publicly criticizing such steps, Qamar Zaydi emphasized the (perceived) unanimity in Iran's public discourse. In Khomeini's realm the citizens understood that any *suspension* of divinely prescribed punishments would constitute *zulm* (injustice), not their application. Simply pardoning evildoers only appeared to be a superior choice, while in fact such a step destroyed the system of justice. Consequently, even those Iranians who were convicted and sentenced realized their guilt. As the guests from Pakistan one evening witnessed in their hotel room, the culprits happily confessed to their crimes on television and condoned their own punishments as a necessary step on the path of redemption.[12]

This travel account adds to our understanding of the Iranian Revolution as a major watershed for modern Shiʿi thought. Overnight the political change in the neighboring country endowed Pakistan's Shiʿis with nothing less than a sudden but ultimately illusory claim to the leadership of Islamism.[13] Initially, both Sunnis and Shiʿis around the Middle East and South Asia were drawn into the excitement. They wanted to get a firsthand account of the unprecedented experiment of Islamically transforming a powerful, quickly industrializing state. Tufayl Muhammad, amir of the Jamaʿat-i Islami (JI) since 1972 and successor to Maududi, received special permission to fly into Tehran's Mehrabad Airport on 22 March 1979. Muhammad wrote in a recollection of this trip about the simplicity and down-to-earth attitude of the officials he met. He could not forget the dignified behavior of those Iranians he observed at the capital's vast Bihisht-i Zahraʾ cemetery. They had lost their relatives during the revolution, yet Muhammad did not witness any tears, only hands lifted in supplication. The air was full of the word of God and greetings addressed to the Imams (*durud o salam*)—indeed a powerful spiritual sight (*ruh parvar manzar*).[14] In an audience with Khomeini, the cleric's profound vision of the future made a deep impression on him.[15] Ibrahim Yazdi, at that time Iran's deputy prime minister, personally took care of his Pakistani guests and entertained them in his house. He and Tufayl Muhammad discussed the revolution and the worldwide Islamic movement late into the night, an experience the latter described as a conversation not of tongues, but of hearts (*hamare dil baten karte rahen*): "We felt like members of the same family, travelers in the same caravan, wayfarers to the same destination who were transporting their provisions to the same place."[16] Tufayl Muhammad's enthusiasm in narrating his encounters is particularly noteworthy because Vali Nasr describes him as General Zia ul-Haq's "most ardent supporter among the Jamʿat's leaders." The JI provided Zia with crucial backing for his plans to execute Zulfiqar Ali Bhutto, the deposed prime minister, and to suppress any remaining opposition from the Pakistan People's Party (PPP). The close personal connection between Zia ul-Haq and Tufayl Muhammad even survived the falling-out between the JI and the Martial Law Administration when the military ruler backed away from his promise to grant the JI a privileged role in devising the country's Islamization.[17] Although Zia ul-Haq's enthusiasm for the toppling of the Shah never quite reached Tufayl's level, he made sure not to antagonize Iran. During the war with Iraq, the port of Karachi became a major back door for Iranian imports of commodities and Chinese military hardware. Pakistan provided its western neighbor with wheat, sugar, and textiles and also intensified nuclear cooperation during the 1980s.[18]

Zia ul-Haq followed such a pragmatic approach even if the universally "Islamic," ecumenical credentials of the Iranian Revolution quickly faded and the systemic change took on a less inclusive, sectarian character.[19] The next chapter looks at how 1979 reshaped and intensified earlier instances of Sunni-Shiʿi tensions. Nevertheless, for Pakistan's Shiʿis the spell of 1979 proved lasting, as the existing literature emphasizes: "As a consequence of the Iranian Revolution and the resultant Shiʿi religiopolitical activism, Shiʿism in Pakistan became more centralised, more clericalist, more Iranianised, and more integrated with the international Shiʿi community. The revolution especially reinforced the emotional and religious bonds of Pakistani Shiʿah with Iran and its religiocultural centres."[20]

The precise influences of the "Iranian moment" are, however, far more often assumed than actually established. How are we to understand the local manifestations of the "esprit de Qom," which in Sabrina Mervin's view is not only "a revolutionary spirit, but also a certain concept of Islamic modernity which all can adapt and apply after returning to their own societies"?[21] Studying the aftermath of 1979 and its consequences for Shiʿi clerics and organizations in the Gulf states of Bahrain, Kuwait, and Saudi Arabia, Laurence Louër holds that "the domestic political structures were more important than Iranian efforts in shaping the various modalities of the Islamic Revolution's impact." The political change was essentially a "passage to political violence," even though "this violence had different meanings and was perpetrated to achieve different aims."[22] While her book makes a strong case for the increasing "autonomization" of political groups that once formally pledged allegiance to Iran and their skepticism toward or outright rejection of vilayat-i faqih, Louër is not very interested in the *content* of the revolutionary message, its modifications, or the critique of its opponents. For her, ideas in general and the debate over the rule of the jurisprudent in particular are "first and foremost the expression of a competition for religious and political power."[23] Similarly, Roschanack Shaery-Eisenlohr paints a nuanced picture of contestation in her rich anthropological study of Lebanese Shiʿism. Hezbollah, she argues, was eager to limit aspects of the revolutionary package that put them "too obviously in a junior position" vis-à-vis Iran by, among other things, rejecting Arabic-speaking preachers sent from Iran to Lebanon.[24] Hezbollah members "consider some activities to be authentic Islam, while rejecting other Iranian *marjaʿ* and government activities and labeling them as Iranian rather than authentically Islamic."[25]

Mariam Abou Zahab is among the few authors who hint at the complexity of this process of translation and resistance in the context of South Asia. According to her, nearly four thousand students received scholarships from the Iranian government immediately after the revolution to spend between six months and a year in religious institutions in Iran, mostly in Qum. On returning to Pakistan, they toured the Punjabi countryside and the Northern Areas, today known as the Gilgit-Baltistan autonomous territory. The students showed films on the oppression of the Shah's regime and the success of the revolution: "They criticised the traditional *ulama* and their links to Iraq and accused them of being apolitical, quietist and opposed to the leadership of Ayatollah Khomeini. Although the traditional clergy welcomed the revolution because it had replaced a secular anti-*ulama* monarchy with a government of the *ulama*, it was opposed to Khomeini's revolutionary rhetoric and saw the students' activism as a threat to its own authority."[26]

Building on Abou Zahab's insights, in this chapter I take a closer look at the different stages of reception the Iranian Revolution underwent in Pakistan. The first stage covers the initial months and years after the downfall of the Shah. Pakistan's Shiʿis were rather late in establishing contacts with the Iranian clerical leadership. Even though they strove to rectify this situation, during this first wave of reception from 1979 to 1984 they remained primarily occupied with domestic events. The Iranian Revolution constituted an important (and energizing) "background noise" to their own conflicts with the Pakistani state. The transformation of their Shiʿi neighbor could not be ignored, but even ardent supporters of Khomeini were not entirely sure what the latter's authority should mean for them outside Iran. Bound by their own local context, they struggled to make sense of such thorny issues as the guardianship of the jurist (vilayat-i faqih) and their minority situation. Additionally, most ʿulama at this time had received their education not in Qum or Mashhad but in either Najaf or pre-Partition Lucknow. Hence, they did not have a real "insider perspective" on Iran's domestic developments; rather, they tried to grasp the consequences of the revolution in familiar South Asian terms like nonviolence or the concept of the "renewer of religion" (mujaddid).

A second stage of reception can be discerned with the rise of the young Pashto-speaking cleric Sayyid ʿArif Husayn al-Husayni to the helm of Pakistan's most influential Shiʿi organization, the Tahrik-i Nifaz-i Fiqh-i Jaʿfariyya (Movement for the Implementation of Jaʿfari Law; TNFJ), in 1984. Husayni, who had studied briefly in Iran, clearly and consistently drew on the hallmark themes of the Iranian Revolution in the way Sabrina Mervin describes them, as a flexible, easily applicable doctrine. Yet in doing so he was often forced to bend aspects of the revolutionary message, such as Muslim unity or the leadership of the clerics, to his Pakistani context. Turning Pakistan into an equally pure Muslim land that could rival Iran required substantial compromises and, first of all, a closing of ranks among the country's Shiʿi population.

Finally, I briefly turn to a full-fledged and—at least in Pakistan—unprecedented embrace of the Iranian project that is anchored in present-day Lahore. This phase of importing the Iranian Revolution is represented by the influential cleric Sayyid Javad Naqvi, who has spent nearly his entire adult life in Iran. In 2009, he returned to his native country after twenty-six years in Qum and now runs a sprawling new madrasa in Punjab's capital that bears the name Jamiʿat al-ʿUrwa al-Wuthqa (Firmest Bond University).[27] Naqvi fully appropriates Iranian rhetoric, domestic politics, and aesthetics in the design of his websites, layout of his magazines, and even the style of clothing his followers wear. He also goes to unprecedented lengths in promoting vilayat-i faqih as a viable, desirable option for Pakistan and criticizes the Iranians for not doing enough for the export of the revolution, a role—so much is implied—he will need to fill.

In each of these three periods there are complex negotiations of closeness and distance which, in turn, are influenced by the length of time Pakistani ʿulama had direct exposure to post-1979 Iran. By emphasizing personal and robust ties to their revolutionary neighbor, Pakistani clerics could hope to siphon off some of Khomeini's luster for themselves, thereby boosting their own positions of authority. Yet they also felt the need to control the import of Iran's messages and adjust them to the needs of their society. This is not to say that such reluctance or opposition always comes to the fore in an obvious manner but to emphasize that even seemingly universal ideas never travel unimpeded across borders; rather, they are reshaped and modified along the way. Such transformations can occur without those who participate in the processes acknowledging their own altering role. Even though the Iranians tried hard to present the values and implications of their revolution as world-embracing and self-evident, its specific local origin was not lost on Pakistani observers. They brought their own commitments and views to the revolutionary table.

This becomes clearer when we return for a moment to Qamar Zaydi's travelogue. Despite his bleak evaluation of the status of true Islam in Pakistan, it was essential for him to underline abiding, time-tested strengths of South Asian piety that could not be undone by current practical weaknesses. Pakistan was a Shiʿi powerhouse, a pure Shiʿi land, even if its splendor had been temporarily overgrown. Specifically, Zaydi emphasized the profound learning and unique spiritual gifts of Pakistan's Shiʿi ʿulama. Due to these qualities, the Iranians supposedly singled them out among many other Shiʿi representatives and decided to treat them as their equals. The mystery of the delegation's approved Iranian visa, for example, was solved when Qamar Zaydi unexpectedly reconnected with an Iranian cleric he had once interacted with in Karachi. Qamar Zaydi at first had difficulties in recognizing the former exile who had constituted his single physical tie (*zahiri rabitah*) to the Iranian Revolution. This personal connection had been disrupted once the man known to him in Karachi as Aqa-yi Taqva returned to his native country shortly after the success of the upheaval.[28] In Qum the Iranian ʿalim no longer wore Pakistani clothes, and he also had changed his name.[29] Shaykh Ibrahim, as he introduced himself, now worked for the office of Ayatollah Husayn ʿAli Muntaziri (d. 2009), which served as a sort of screening station to determine whether visitors were important enough to meet Khomeini himself.[30] In their process of catching up, Qamar Zaydi mentioned that his group's visa—according to the Iranian embassy—had been personally approved by Khomeini. He speculated that the speedy processing must have had to do with a congratulatory telegram they had sent to the Iranian leader in response to the successful referendum in favor of an Islamic Republic. Shaykh Ibrahim was dumbfounded. Since Khomeini had received no less than seventy thousand such messages, he attributed the delegation's unlikely access to nothing less than the extraordinary religious devotion of Ibn-i Hasan, the delegation's leader.[31] Khomeini's special favors for the Pakistani delegates did not stop here: while Shaykh Ibrahim was making some inquiries behind the scenes, they came across a fifty-member-strong Kenyan delegation, a mission from Libya that included the country's prime minister, and a group from Bangladesh. For over a month, all three of them had tried in vain to obtain an audience with Khomeini.[32] Things played out differently for the Pakistanis, who were granted this coveted favor barely three days after they had set foot in Qum.[33] Likewise, the travelogue leaves no doubt about the unmatched language skills of the South Asian ʿulama. While they were waiting outside Khomeini's office for their meeting to commence, the delegation from Karachi was approached by clerics from Bahrain. The Arabs attempted to strike up a conversation in very poor Urdu, only to be greeted by Ibn-i Hasan's flawless Arabic. Even Khomeini audibly showed his appreciation for the "superior" (*bihtarin*) Persian that distinguished Ibn-i Hasan's introductory speech, commenting on it with the phrase "you have excelled" (*ahsant*).[34] Finally, during the Ayatollah's lecture, it was Qamar Zaydi himself who could not hold back his desire to express admiration for Khomeini's moving remarks. He loudly exclaimed, "Subhan Allah" (Praise be to God), a "sentence that is common in our country to express astonishment while Arabs and Persians use different words." Khomeini acknowledged this heartfelt demonstration of piety with a smile. The ayatollah glanced directly at the Pakistani, went on talking, and overran the set time limit for the meeting by more than an hour, thereby rendering the reception the longest that he had ever granted to a foreign delegation. Not surprisingly, this unusual audience, Qamar Zaydi reports, went viral and became the talk of the town with newspapers, radio stations, Iranian television, and even the BBC covering the episode.[35]

THE FIRST YEARS: LATE CONTACT AND SOUTH ASIAN CONCERNS

Before switching to the immediate Pakistani reaction to the Iranian Revolution and further exploring the processes of its appropriation, I will first provide some background on the domestic political mobilization among Pakistani Shiʿi ʿulama and activists. In conjunction with the discussion of Shiʿi reform in the previous chapter, this helps to put the later changes and their implications in perspective and enables a deeper understanding of the prevalence of local, specifically Pakistani concerns.

The Character of Shiʿi Activism before 1979

During Pakistan's first three decades as a new state, the chances of political organization along religious, Shiʿi lines seemed to be a rather remote possibility. Compared to their coreligionists in Lebanon or Iraq, for example, Pakistan's Shiʿi minority hardly qualified as being counted among the oppressed of the earth.[36] As I briefly discussed in the conclusion of chapter 1, initial fears about Pakistan embracing an exclusive Sunni interpretation of Islam did not materialize to the extent that the alarmist voices in the pre-Partition period had predicted. The Shiʿi community was prominently represented among the dominant landholders, the military, the local and federal bureaucracy, as well as in the industrial and entrepreneurial elite. Each successive Pakistani government included Shiʿi ministers.[37] This relative influence has led some observers to conclude that despite occasional riots during the month of Muharram, most Shiʿis did not feel discriminated against.[38] Mariam Abou Zahab holds that Shiʿi organizations were in general "apolitical and concerned with rituals and the organization of Muharram processions only."[39] Andreas Rieck complicates this picture in his close study of intra-Shiʿi rivalries. He points to the mid-1960s as a period of organizational change which highlighted serious Shiʿi grievances that had nevertheless existed beneath the harmonious surface. The influential ʿalim Sayyid Muhammad Dihlavi (1899–1971) managed to bring together 250 Shiʿi ʿulama at a convention in Karachi in 1964 and later established Shiʿa Mutalabat

Committees (Shiʿa Demands Committees) throughout the country.[40] Dihlavi and his movement called for full freedom and protection for self-flagellation (ʿazadari), separate religious instruction in public schools, and the administration of Shiʿi *auqaf* (religious endowments) by Shiʿis only.[41] Faced with repeated delaying tactics and bans on public speaking, they issued an ultimatum to the Pakistani government in July 1967 to accept their "apolitical, religious and constitutional demands" within three months.[42] When finally some fifteen thousand Shiʿis gathered in Rawalpindi after the expiration of the deadline to discuss strategy for the suggested civil disobedience campaign, the Ayub Khan government acceded to their demands, only a couple of days before its own downfall.[43] Given this ʿulama-led campaign, it is sensible to agree with Andreas Rieck's evaluation that "the new wave of Shia mobilization" in Pakistan following the Iranian Revolution and Zia ul-Haq's Islamization policy "drew on long experiences from the 1950s and 1960s."[44] Dihlavi's role, who had received his entire Shiʿi education in India, is important here. In the light of his activism Abou Zahab's argument, widely shared by Iranian authors, about the apolitical and solely ritual-focused outlook of Shiʿi scholars before the Iranian Revolution, needs to be qualified.[45] Such a claim is especially problematic when intended to cover the whole of Pakistan. In the Northern Areas, for example, the lack of local political representation in the precolonial, colonial, and postcolonial period "has helped the Shiʿa *ʿulamāʾ* a lot to win positions of influence within the local society, apparently unmatched in any other part of Pakistan."[46] This is not to say, however, that debates on reform did not play an equally important, divisive role, as chapter 2 showed. A genuine reconciliation between the feuding camps never took place, as these cleavages haunted the new Shiʿi organizations founded after the Iranian Revolution.[47] This especially came to the fore in the mid-1980s under the leadership of Sayyid ʿArif Husayn al-Husayni, to which we will turn after we have considered the decade's early years.

Reading Iran through the South Asian Looking Glass: Gandhi, Renewal, and Political Activism

The news of domestic troubles for the Shah reached Pakistani Shiʿis while they were already living in a heated atmosphere. Even though they surely knew of Khomeini as a rising star on the ʿulama firmament,[48] they had no direct connection with him until January 1979, when the Iranian cleric still resided in Paris. This lack of direct access extended even to groups such as Pakistan's Imamia Students Organisation (ISO), which distinguished itself as one of Iran's most faithful ideological allies in the course of the 1980s.[49] As late as October 1978, the ISO's journal *Rah-i ʿAmal* (The way of action) did not carry any original material on Khomeini. Rather, it reprinted an Urdu translation of an interview conducted originally on 6 May of that year by the French daily *Le Monde*.[50] In February 1978, when the Iranian emperor came to Pakistan on a state visit, the ISO had already put up posters reading "We do not welcome the murdering Shah." Most Pakistanis, however, found themselves confused by these accusations relating to events they had never heard of. Not until 18 November 1978 did Pakistan witness its first anti-Shah demonstration, when students in Lahore took to the streets.[51] The ISO's sister movement, the Imamia Organisation (IO), which catered to academics after their graduation, issued a press release that day, condemning the Shah's "satanic and yazidic actions" (*shaytani aur yazidi harakaten*).[52] The students were accompanied by Sayyid Safdar Husayn Najafi (d. 1989) and Murtaza Husayn Najafi (d. 1987), who were among the most outspoken, prorevolutionary senior clerics of their time. They frequently attended annual conventions of the ISO and contributed to its magazine.[53] When in January 1979 Safdar Husayn Najafi traveled to Paris, a large crowd of students gathered at the airport in Lahore to see him off, shouting the Iranian slogan "Our movement is Husayn-like, our leader is Khomeini." Yet Khomeini himself seems to have been unaware of his proclaimed leadership role in South Asia. The Pakistani ʿulama who reached his headquarters in Paris were just another anonymous delegation. No preparations had been made for a meeting, and no one had been informed about their arrival or interceded on their behalf.[54]

It is not surprising, therefore, that during these first months, when the literature in Urdu on the upheaval in Iran and its domestic or global implications was scarce, South Asian ʿulama tried to make sense of the events in terms that were familiar to their audience. Murtaza Husayn, for example, emphasized the nonviolent character of the Iranian Revolution in a way that inevitably reminded his South Asian readers of Gandhi. He was thus continuing an earlier Indian Shiʿi tradition, which had tried to relate the Mahatma's approach to the events of Karbala. This is reflected, for example in "ʿAli Naqi's Husainology, which endlessly stressed themes of devotion to peace and self-sacrifice, and a Gandhian model of *satyagraha*."[55] To describe Husayn's struggle with Yazid, Sayyid Ibn-i Hasan Jarcavi, the preacher who tried to present himself as a more up-to-date alternative to Lucknow, also explicitly used the concept devised by the Mahatma that roughly translates as "truth force."[56] Listing the most striking features of the political change in Iran, Murtaza Husayn transcended both these earlier examples. He underlined that the protesters, on Khomeini's orders, remained unarmed (*ghayr musallah*) and willingly sacrificed themselves in the face of state-initiated aggression. They never fell into any of the traps the military had set up. The armed forces had tried repeatedly to provoke a violent response (*ʿavvam ko ishtiʿal dilati thi keh un ki taraf se hamlah ho*) through constant and merciless attacks carried out with cannons and tanks. This steadfastness was even more remarkable in Husayn's view, as the Shah was backed by all the existing empires of the time: the United States, the British, the Russians, and the "Jews." Khomeini stunned the world with his decision to rely on noncooperation and strikes. When he ordered the petrochemical industry shut after the Black Friday massacre of 8 September 1978, everyone in Iran followed suit. The strike spread to electricity providers, waterworks, and the railways. Colleges and universities closed their doors, as did the banking sector, the Ministry of Trade, and the Ministry of Finance. Even the office of the prime minister and the feared intelligence service, the SAVAK, reportedly stopped operating.[57] Khomeini achieved all of this despite lacking any official position. He was not the leader of any party or organization and held no political office. This did not prevent the ʿulama, youth, and women from proclaiming that there was no party besides the party of God (*hizb Allah*) and that their only leader was Khomeini.[58]

Sayyid Murtaza Husayn finished this account according to the preface of his book on 28 July 1980. Here he presented Khomeini as a superior, Muslim Gandhi who had achieved the impossible and taken on a seemingly invincible opponent. Whereas the Indian was only the Mahatma, the "Great Soul," the Iranian's name denoted nothing less than God's spirit, Ruh Allah. Like Khomeini, Gandhi had celebrated his personal independence, which manifested itself in his refusal to become a member of the Indian National Congress. The Indian regarded noncooperation as an important tool to bring the British colonial government to its knees, as this tactic withdrew the crucial "support it receives from good people."[59] Both Gandhi and Khomeini displayed no naïveté about the dire consequences of their struggle, as Murtaza Husayn clearly discerned. When faced with increasingly brutal repression on the part of the regime, the cleric still called on the Iranian people to "broaden its struggle against the Shah with all its strength and to bring down his harmful, disastrous regime." He called the martyrs of the uprising "an eternal source of pride." These men and women would proclaim that "truth may triumph over tanks, machine guns, and the armies of Satan," and show "how the word of truth may obliterate falsehood."[60] Similarly, Gandhi cherished the suffering that the violence produced: "By separating dying from killing and prizing the former as a noble deed, he was doing nothing more than retrieving sovereignty from the state and generalizing it as a quality vested in individuals."[61] Nonviolence, in other words, was not meant to provide some alternative to violence, but instead "to appropriate it and, as the

Mahatma himself often said, to sublimate it."[62] What Murtaza Husayn deliberately overlooks in his portrayal, however, is that Khomeini never expressed any strong, public commitment to nonviolence. He only made comments opposed to an armed struggle against the Shah in private, pointing out that the time was not yet ripe.[63] Gandhi, however, considered it as a cornerstone of his thought, which should not remain a mere ideal but should rather be extended to a national and international level.[64]

It is similarly striking that the influential Pakistani Shiʿi ʿalim Safdar Husayn Najafi, in a book on the fundamentals of Islamic government that he wrote in the fall of 1979, decided to address Khomeini as the mujaddid of the fifteenth Islamic century. To some extent, the author remains faithful to established Shiʿi views on the authority of the ʿulama. Safdar Husayn Najafi argues that man is not himself able to discern his goal (*maqsad*) in life. Instead, he has to rely on an infallible guide, the Imam.[65] The religious scholars, of course, acted as the successors of these luminaries, who were in their divinely prescribed, delegated role distinguished from the common people to the same degree as the earth was separated from the sky (*ʿamm ʿibadat guzar logon aur ʿulamaʾ o fuqahaʾ men zamin o asman ka farq he*).[66] Grafted onto this reasoning are typical Islamist arguments and bits of Khomeini's theory of government with which Safdar Husayn Najafi was clearly familiar. He adduced, for example, an interpretation of Qur'an 5:44 that followed the Egyptian Muslim Brother Sayyid Qutb's reading of this verse, namely that those who do not rule according to what God has revealed should be killed.[67] As far as the qualifications for a ruler were concerned, Safdar Husayn Najafi adopted Khomeini's two criteria of "knowledge of the law" (*ʿilm bih qanun*) and "justice" (*ʿadalat*). Safdar Husayn Najafi stated that if an ʿalim could be found who encompassed these qualities and would form a government, it was incumbent on the people to obey him.[68] Such conclusions were not supported by classical Shiʿi thought, which does not entertain the idea that the ʿulama are called on to rule. Quite to the contrary, the medieval Shiʿi Qur'an commentators al-Tusi (d. 459 or 460/1066 or 1067), al-Tabrisi (d. 548/1154), and Muqaddas Ardabili (d. 993/1585) all asserted that "those in authority (*ulu ʾl-amr*) are neither the secular rulers (amirs), nor the ʿulama—neither of whom is immune from error and sin—but rather the infallible (maʿsum) Imams, ʿAli and his eleven descendants."[69]

Khomeini had delivered his lectures on the topic in 1970 while residing in Najaf and hence in a purely theoretical setting. Safdar Husayn Najafi, however, could draw on several months of experience with the new Islamic Republic in Iran while writing his book.[70] He was keen to downplay the republican aspects of the new Iranian state. Such an attempt comes to light in his discussion of the Assembly of Experts, which was charged with reviewing the rather liberal draft of the Iranian constitution that had already been approved by the cabinet, the Revolutionary Council, and Khomeini himself. Safdar Husayn Najafi emphasized that non-ʿulama had only a very limited role in this process.[71] These laymen lacked the expertise to evaluate whether a certain stipulation was in agreement with the shariʿa. Their task over the summer and fall of 1979 was merely to arrange and adjust Islam's truth, as determined by the ʿulama, to the novel way (*nayi tiknik*) of a constitution, to mold it into this new form.[72] Safdar Husayn Najafi thus echoed Khomeini, who had made it clear in his message to the assembly on the occasion of its inauguration in August 1979 that "determining whether [principles laid down in the constitution are] are or are not in conformity with Islamic requirements is exclusively reserved for the revered jurists who, thanks to God, form a particular group in this assembly."[73] Similarly, Khomeini had only solicited the people's decision in a referendum on whether they supported the establishment of an Islamic Republic in order to win over their hearts (*ta'lif-i qulub*), not to ask for their irrelevant opinion.[74] In Pakistan, however, not even such a limited role could be granted to the masses, since they had not gone through the same process of education, led by the ʿulama. Comparable to the rhetoric employed in the pre-Partition period, Safdar Husayn Najafi stated that the common (Sunni) believers were steeped in blind imitation (taqlid), which only granted the founders of their four schools of law the right to engage in independent legal reasoning (ijtihad).[75] Similarly, Murtaza Husayn lamented the lack of education among Pakistan's Shiʿis. He recalled that when a delegation sent by Muhsin al-Hakim visited Pakistan, the Iraqis quickly realized that the country was not void of personalities who called themselves *ʿallamah* (most learned) or ʿalim but that it lacked knowledge (*ʿilm*) and libraries.[76] Quoting Iqbal's line about the proponents of the school system stifling any form of fresh inquiry (*gala to ghont diya ahl-i madrasah ne tera*) and hence being responsible for the afflictions that Muslims faced worldwide, Safdar Husayn Najafi made a bold and polemical proposal.[77] Given that it would take the Sunnis nearly twenty to twenty-five years to once again groom a scholar capable of legal opinions geared to the needs of the time, why not ask Khomeini to send a mujtahid to Pakistan who could sort out the thorny social, political, and economic questions of turning the country into a truly Islamic state? This way Pakistan's citizens would no longer have to rely on those non-mujtahids and non-ʿulama who currently implemented so-called Islamic laws.[78] In advancing such a claim, Safdar Husayn Najafi here skillfully exploits for his purpose the fact that most Deobandi scholars and institutions until today refrain from labeling their often quite substantial reinterpretation of Islamic law as ijtihad proper.[79] More broadly, this revolutionary Shiʿi intervention also made clear that Sunni thinking about the state is in fact not sufficiently political. Though not subservient to the rulers, it still has to operate within the boundaries of the sacred law. Only a Shiʿi model of Guardianship of the Jurisprudent is truly able to break free from these shackles and to establish sovereignty appropriate for a "Land of the Pure."[80]

Earlier in his book on the principles of an Islamic government, Safdar Husayn Najafi strove to portray Khomeini as a personality that transcended any particular sectarian affiliation by labeling him the renewer (mujaddid) of the fifteenth Islamic century, which, quite conveniently, began on 21 November 1979. Ella Landau-Tasseron points out that this designation, based on a hadith reported in Abu Daʾud's *Sunan* that "God will send to his community at the turn of every century someone [. . .] who will restore religion," did not constitute a major concept in medieval Islamic thought but "was rather an honorific title bestowed on individuals over the ages."[81] It gained a certain prominence in Shafiʿi circles in Baghdad and Cairo but had its real breakthrough only in the later medieval and early modern period in South Asia, helped by the fact that its criteria of eligibility proved easily adjustable to the needs of the time.[82] Shaykh Ahmad Sirhindi (d. 1624/1034), for example, is widely known as *mujaddid-i alf-i sani* (the renewer of the second millennium) and was praised for his mystical insights, his audacity in proclaiming the truth to tyrannical rulers, and his miracles.[83] By contrast, Shah Wali Allah (d. 1176/1762)—the renewer of the twelfth century, as he is termed in South Asia—lived through circumstances very different from those of Sirhindi, who had experienced Mughal rule at its pinnacle. Shah Wali Allah's surroundings were marked by Sunni decline and the political rise of groups like the Shiʿis or the Sikhs. These developments made him interested in curricular reforms for the training of ʿulama, the "pruning of the *sharīʿa* from spurious traditions and deductions by analogy," and "proper" rules for Qurʾanic exegesis.[84] In the twentieth century, the debate remained very lively in Indian Muslim literature. Claims were made on behalf of several religious thinkers. Ghulam Ahmad, the eponym of the Ahmadiyya, himself entered the fray and argued that he was the mujaddid of the fourteenth Islamic century, specifically tasked to counter the ascendance of Christianity in colonial India.[85] Sayyid Abu 'l-Aʿla Maududi held that the pre-Islamic age of ignorance (*jahiliyya*) had made such a resurgence in the modern period that an "ideal renewer" (*mujaddid-i kamil*) would be needed to establish the caliphate after the Prophetic model.[86] While it was still unusual for a Shiʿi ʿalim to adopt such a clearly Sunni-leaning idea, given the flexibility of the concept Safdar

Husayn Najafi could nevertheless comfortably devise a new set of reasons Khomeini deserved this title.[87] He wrote that the Iranian was fighting on behalf of the oppressed masses (*mazlum ʿavamm*) and had delivered defeats to both the United States and the Soviet Union, thereby demonstrating the invincible power of truth. Khomeini had shown that Islam as a religion was distinguished by its broad horizon and was concerned with both practical and theoretical issues. These feats had turned him into a leader who transcended both Iranian and Shiʿi confinement and was, like Imam Husayn, a model for the whole world.[88] In this statement, an echo of ʿAli Naqi Naqvi's work *Shahid-i insaniyyat* is once again discernible, which speaks to the book's influence on the subcontinent's Shiʿi sphere during the twentieth century.

Safdar Husayn Najafi's insistence on Khomeini's identity as *the* renewer is curious, since this idea was not part and parcel of the Iranian revolutionary message. The influential scholar, ideologue, and trailblazer of the Islamic upheaval Murtaza Mutahhari (assassinated in May 1979) had dismissed the hadith because it was not reported in any of the authoritative Shiʿi collections.[89] Even the Sunnis themselves, he contended, could not agree on the precise identity of these supposed renewers and hence debated whether they were scholars, rulers, or Sufis. The object of renewal was contested as well, with suggestions ranging from the fundamentals of religion to legal rulings or matters of creed. Mutahhari argued that the Shiʿis had a comprehensive, superior understanding of *islah* (reform) based on their belief in the reappearance of the Twelfth Imam as the Mahdi. To rid society of unlawful innovations (*mubarazah kardan ba bidʿatha*) was a task to which every individual was called, not just a certain reformer every hundred, two hundred, or five hundred years.[90]

Safdar Husayn Najafi followed a similar South Asian path in regard to his conception of the role of women in society. Revolutionary Iran no doubt tried to discourage female employment and cut back on rights women had enjoyed under the Shah, such as access to divorce. The new government emphasized their position as mothers and educators of children and enforced clothing restrictions.[91] Yet Khomeini also regularly extolled the highly visible role women had played during the overthrow of the old order and lauded their position in reforming society at large.[92] The state initially tried to uphold the image of the Prophet's daughter Fatima and his granddaughter Zaynab as revolutionaries at extraordinary times. Both women had, once peace was restored, reverted to their household duties, and so should Iran's contemporary female revolutionaries. Official statements tried to discourage "the average traditional women from drawing larger and more general lessons from their revolutionary experience."[93] The outbreak of the Iran-Iraq War in September

1980 prolonged this supposed temporary phase. Women were suddenly required to substitute for men who were fighting at the front. As a direct consequence, the female workforce in Iran's ministries reached its former prerevolutionary levels in the mid-1980s.[94] Additionally, the Iranian state in 1985 facilitated the opening of a full-fledged women's religious seminary named Jamiʿat al-Zahra', which was meant to train female *mujtahidas*.[95] Safdar Husayn Najafi did not display any such ambiguities about the role of women in society or even religious leadership. As he wrote in an article in 1980, female seclusion (*pardah*) was one of the few issues on which Muslims of all sects and backgrounds were in agreement. If one considered the history of Islam, even nonobservant Muslims like Yazid b. Muʿawiya (d. 64/683) scrupulously followed this principle. Yazid denied the basic foundations of religion and the prophethood of Muhammad, but he too sent away the people at his court if one of his *cadur*-clothed wives wanted to have a private conversation with him.[96] Quoting Qur'an 33:32–33, Safdar Husayn Najafi made the uncompromising case that women should not leave their houses before their deaths. This position, he (wrongly) suggested, was supported by Khomeini, from whom he then adduced several rulings dealing with *pardah*. None of Khomeini's fatwas, however, was intended to confine women to their homes. Instead, the Iranian leader obliged women to cover themselves in front of men to whom they were not closely related (*na mahram*) and condemned the female use of nail polish, since it rendered proper ablution impossible.[97]

As far as political activism was concerned, the initial impact of the Islamic Revolution was also mitigated by certain prevalent Pakistani concerns. Under the leadership of Mufti Jaʿfar Husayn (d. 1983), the Tahrik-i Nifaz-i Fiqh-i Jaʿfariyyah seems to have continued to operate according to the time-honored strategy of confronting the state to secure Shiʿi rights without any obvious Iranian ideological input.[98] Mufti Jaʿfar's approach manifested itself in a forceful Shiʿi backlash in June 1980 after the government had announced its determination to deduct zakat (obligatory Islamic charity payment) from all bank accounts held by Pakistani Muslims. The Shiʿis, due to far-reaching legal differences in this regard, vehemently opposed these plans.[99] The ISO provided enthusiastic organizational support for ensuing protests across the country, which openly defied the ban on public gatherings under martial law. The organization prided itself that its activists had spread word of the upcoming convention in every Pakistani village. They had also printed one hundred thousand posters, which they put up nationwide and even attached to trains.[100] These demonstrations engulfing the entire country culminated in a two-day siege of Islamabad's government district by Shiʿis from all over Pakistan on 5 July 1980. Faced with such strong Shiʿi protests, the Zia regime finally capitulated.[101] The events of that day led to the so-called Islamabad Agreement, according to which the Shiʿis were free to administer internal affairs in keeping with their law. This success later became a point of reference for the movement when the unfulfilled promises of the agreement were held up to criticize Zia. Shiʿi leaders repeatedly referred to this success, as can be gathered, for example, from issues of the journal *Rizakar* throughout the 1980s. Even Khomeinist ʿulama like Sayyid ʿArif al-Husayni saw themselves very much as heirs to this confrontational legacy, which at times even overshadowed their commitment to the specific, transnational slogans of the Iranian Revolution. Pakistani publications from this time emphasize the impressive authority that Jaʿfar Husayn could wield, which rendered him almost equal to Khomeini. When the masses descended onto Islamabad, their slogans proclaimed Mufti Jaʿfar as their only guide.[102] In the midst of all the excitement surrounding him, the Pakistani scholar remained entirely in control of the ecstatic crowd: his verbal admonishment caused the people to stay behind while only he and a group of ʿulama marched toward the Ministry of Religious Affairs. No riots broke out when a tear gas canister killed Muhammad Husayn Shad from Shorkot, turning him into the first martyr of the Movement for the Implementation of Jaʿfari Law. The crowd even remained calm during the funeral prayers, organized by the ISO. At this point the organization had plenty of experience in ensuring discipline when calling people to prayer in an emotionally charged atmosphere. From 1979 onward, the ISO had gradually begun to make congregational prayer a regular feature of processions during Muharram and on other occasions.[103] When the protesters later surrounded the Pakistan Civil Secretariat in a successful bid to seal it off, Mufti Jaʿfar's word was enough to ensure disciplined behavior. Despite the absence of police or military personnel, no one entered the unlocked gate. They all behaved as the "civilized" (*muhazzab*) people that the scholar had described to the media before the commencement of the convention. With him as leader, the people were "honey-bees, not mosquitoes" (*shahd ki makhiyan thin, barsati makhiyan nahin thin*).[104]

Mufti Jaʿfar did not only stand his ground as an independent religious scholar and political activist inside Pakistan. When traveling to Iran in May 1981, he rejected all offers from the neighboring country to cover his expenses and those of his twenty-two companions by pointing out that Iran was engaged in a war and should not be burdened with such additional responsibilities.[105] After they had met Khomeini, Mufti Jaʿfar faced the Iranian press. Journalists of the newspapers *Kayhan International, Pars, Jihad,* and *Shahid* were eager to know why the revolutionary efforts of Pakistani Shiʿis had as yet come to naught. They also inquired about the real purpose of his trip to Iran and whether it would be possible to compare the Pakistani government to the rule of Shah Reza Pahlavi. Instead of stoking the flames of confrontation, Mufti Jaʿfar diligently drew his interlocutors' attention to the guarantees the Shiʿis had been able to extract from the government. He and his fellow delegates had come to Iran primarily as pilgrims to visit the shrine of Imam Riza in Mashhad, to express their condolences for the martyrs of Iran's revolution and the current war with Iraq, and to thank the Iranians for all the support they had provided for his movement. Mufti Jaʿfar deflected any critique of the Pakistani government. When a journalist brought up a comment by Khomeini, who had criticized Zia ul-Haq for extending his personal power under the smokescreen of Islam, Mufti Jaʿfar only remarked that he had also "felt certain disagreements between the governments of Pakistan and Iran" (*hukumat-i Pakistan aur hukumat-i Iran men kuch ikhtilaf mahsus kiya he*). He expressed hope that these could be resolved on his return to his native country.[106] Some have attributed this nonconfrontational tone to Mufti Jaʿfar Husayn's lack of leadership skills, his "apolitical" stance, and his desire not to undo the achievements of the Islamabad Accord.[107] It is equally tempting, however, to speculate that the reluctance to lash out against the Pakistani government might have also had to do with efforts to finally establish a hauza in Pakistan that year. The plan, pushed by Safdar Husayn Najafi at the Jamiʿat al-Muntazar, was to import a senior mujtahid who could teach *dars-i kharij*. The Iranian scholar Hasan Tahiri Khurramabadi was selected for the job by Khomeini and sent to Pakistan. Due to obstruction by the local authorities, however, his teaching career did not extend beyond two short stays of three and two months each.[108]

The ISO was only seemingly less confused about how to relate to the Iranian Revolution. No doubt, in the early 1980s they frequently and faithfully echoed Iranian viewpoints by denouncing, for example, those Pakistani clerics who were opposed to politicizing the hajj.[109] Before the revolution the group published panegyric poetry praising Khomeini, and in 1979 they called on Pakistanis to close ranks and follow him.[110] They admired the Iranian leader's comprehensive vision for the implementation of policies pleasing to God on the individual and societal levels, whereas other countries only pursued programs aimed at material welfare (*maddi falah*).[111] Yet the ISO activists were also still in a process of determining their own priorities and loyalties. They had no desire to repeat the example of revolutionary Iran, Kuwait, Bahrain, and Lebanon by commencing an armed uprising in their home country. Even though these politicized Shiʿi youths acknowledged that the path to the liberation of Jerusalem led through Najaf and Karbala, thus embracing one of the most important Iranian slogans during the war with

Iraq, they defined their role as denouncing the present Pakistani system in a theoretical, ideological manner (*nazariya'i taur par*).[112] They praised Qum as a religious center only to emphasize in 1984 that Pakistan should have its own hauza too. If the Shah's oppression taught one thing, it was that more than only one serious, major seminary should exist in order to minimize the risk that it could fall prey to an evil regime.[113] In addition, the ISO regularly celebrated its own founding day of 22 May 1972, dating to an era long before any revolutionary excitement was palpable in Iran. The organization declared this day to have been the first step "on the journey toward the Islamic revolution" and held essay competitions to elaborate on this matter.[114]

SAYYID ʿARIF HUSAYN AL-HUSAYNI AND THE HEYDAY OF ACTIVISM IN THE 1980S

This multifaceted, disorderly choir of voices changed remarkably in the mid-1980s, when Sayyid ʿArif Husayn al-Husayni (d. 1988) rose to the helm of the TNFJ. He has been described as being "probably the most ardent admirer of Khomeini among Pakistan's Shia 'ulamā' of his generation and status."[115] Scholars have also argued that "probably single-handedly, ʿArif al-Hussaini internationalised Pakistan's Shiʿi clergy."[116] Mariam Abou Zahab credits him with intensifying the "qomization" of the "ulama-class" with regard to the "rationalization"[117] and "politicization" of rituals, which now focused on the oppression committed by the enemy of the Shiʿis at home and abroad.[118] Iranian publications likewise extol him for spreading the idea of the Iranian Revolution under the leadership of Imam Khomeini, thereby finally breaking the monopoly of influence that wealthy landholders and nonpolitical, conservative circles had enjoyed over the Shiʿi community.[119]

It may be that Sayyid ʿArif Husayn al-Husayni's status as an outsider fostered his unlikely career. Born into a humble, nonscholarly background in late 1946,[120] he grew up close to Parachinar, the capital of the Kurram agency in Northwest Pakistan's tribal areas. He received his initial religious training locally. In 1967 he traveled to Najaf, where he spent six years studying. Ayatollah Asadullah Madani (d. 1981), one of Khomeini's strongest supporters in Najaf, introduced al-Husayni to the Iranian scholar.[121] Al-Husayni's biographers credit him with a very activist stance toward the Iraqi authorities. After traveling to Kufa to pay a solidarity visit to Muhammad Baqir al-Sadr (d. 1980), who had just been put under house arrest, al-Husayni reportedly attacked a group of policemen who were busy abusing Shiʿi students.[122] He also continued sending protest telegrams to the Shah.[123] This outspoken attitude most likely cut his stay in Iraq short: in 1973 he was either deported from

Iraq or left the country voluntarily in order to get married.[124] Officials confiscated an appointment letter as Khomeini's representative (*wakil*) in Pakistan when al-Husayni tried to enter the country from Iran.[125] Al-Husayni only stayed there for a couple of months before continuing his studies at Qum. Once again, he was at the forefront of the fight against the Shah, encouraging fellow Pakistani students to join protests.[126] Abou Zahab holds that he intended to remain in Qum for longer but was "sent back to Pakistan in 1977 with a mission to mobilise the community on the pattern of what Imam Musa Sadr had done in Lebanon."[127] Other accounts argue that he was expelled from Iran after refusing to sign a document not to mingle with revolutionary clerics.[128] Back in Pakistan, al-Husayni earned his first credentials as a community leader in Parachinar in 1980 when he led popular protests after attacks on Shiʿi Muharram processions and was consequently imprisoned for twenty-two days.[129] Despite these activities, he was still largely unknown when the TNFJ convention in February 1984 unexpectedly elected him as leader due to his "energy, courage, political acumen and religious learning."[130]

The broad acknowledgment of al-Husayni's crucial leadership role within the Shiʿi community during the 1980s has so far not been supplemented with a more detailed study of his thought.[131] To be sure, al-Husayni as a busy leader with a very active political life never seems to have found the time to put down his thoughts in writing. For instance, he himself referred to a treatise he had planned to author in order to counter allegations that Shiʿis believed in the corruption of the Qurʾanic text (tahrif). In the end, his busy schedule had required him to delegate these plans.[132] This lacuna can be filled in, however. Al-Husayni gave numerous speeches and interviews throughout his career in both Urdu and Persian, and after his death they were transcribed from recordings.[133] Many of these also include question-and-answer sessions that offer a sense of how the audience reacted to his declarations.[134] Below, I supplement this material with information from various detailed biographical dictionaries of Pakistani Shiʿi scholars, al-Husayni's "official" biography published by the al-ʿArif Academy in Lahore, and issues of the Pakistani Shiʿi weekly *Rizakar* (*The Volunteer*).[135]

I argue that al-Husayni at times sat quite uncomfortably between the two camps of Pakistani Shiʿis that I discussed in chapter 2. His positions definitely harked back to some of the concerns of the reformist camp and were in many respects in line with (the early manifestations) of Sayyid Sharaf al-Din Musavi's thought. Yet Musavi, as a junior scholar in the 1980s, was definitely less influential than reformists in the vein of Muhammad Husayn al-Najafi Dhakko, whom al-Husayni criticized for embracing a too narrow and overly apolitical Shiʿi outlook. At the same time, al-Husayni faced serious opposition from more traditionalist-minded ʿulama. This group had broken away from the TNFJ and on 21 May 1985 had concluded a separate agreement with the government on the legalization of ʿazadari processions.[136] Naqvi points out the Shaykhi leanings of this group, to which al-Husayni also repeatedly referred when emphasizing his disagreement with their leader, Sayyid Hamid ʿAli Shah Musavi, regarding attributing extensive powers to the Imams.[137] The Shiʿi community was obviously quite confused by this open display of conflict. As a consequence, al-Husayni was frequently called on to prove that he was not a self-made fraud.[138] Given this challenge, and in order to make his case as the proper representative of the community, al-Husayni crisscrossed Pakistan, delivering sermons in Urdu as well as in his native Pashto in a hitherto unknown "revolutionary way" (*bah surat-i inqilabi*).[139]

A bloody police crackdown seems to have finally given the decisive impetus that turned al-Husayni into a "real" leader. One year earlier, an article in *Rah-i ʿAmal* had criticized the lack of revolutionary fervor in Pakistan, where people had been reluctant to "fully commit themselves" to the worldwide movement Khomeini had started.[140] Yet when on 5 July 1985 in Quetta thirteen demonstrators died and hundreds were imprisoned while demanding the implementation of the Islamabad Agreement of 1980, al-Husayni had finally found a cause to rally the Shiʿi qaum behind him.[141] In 1987, al-Husayni announced that the TNFJ would transform itself into a political party, demanding that each recognized madhhab should be governed by its own interpretation of Qurʾan and sunna. In addition, Pakistan's various Islamic schools of thought should be given representation in the Council of Islamic Ideology, and a "Popular Islamic Army" should be created to help reduce the distance between the military and the people. Muhammad Qasim Zaman suggests that these demands probably disquieted the Sunnis, since they could imply that "Islam should mean different things to different people, their call to a popular army stoked fear of Shiʿi sectarianism and freedom of religion would mean freedom to curse."[142] But al-Husayni had no time left to prove himself in the arena of party politics. His assassination in Peshawar on 5 August 1988, in close conjunction with Zia ul-Haq's death and the end of the Iran-Iraq War just some days later, arguably marked "the end of the short heyday of political radicalism among Shias in Pakistan."[143]

Localizing the Iranian Revolution

How did this new "revolutionary way," which distinguished him from the other scholars discussed above, manifest itself in al-Husayni's rhetoric? The following discussion is structured according to hallmark themes of Iran's attempted export of the revolution (*sudur-i inqilab*), discussing (a) calls for Muslim unity, (b) the centrality of Imam Khomeini and Iran, (c) authority of the ʿulama and religious awakening, and (d) political activism. This categorization is intended to help determine what efforts al-Husayni exerted in trying to adjust the broader Iranian framework to his specific Pakistani context. I argue that such an adaptation definitely took place. It is true that al-Husayni's language was at first glance a very faithful rendering of Iran's revolutionary rhetoric. If one reads his speeches and interviews closely, however, it becomes clear that he too felt compelled to modify the universalist message. This was due to the heated internal Shiʿi debates and the specific Pakistani legacy of political activism and confrontation with the government.

The Call for Muslim Unity

One of the major topics of revolutionary Iranian discourse revolved around the call for taqrib, an attempt at rapprochement with the Sunnis. Such a closing of ranks seemed essential for Khomeini's goal of establishing an ideal, global Islamic system. This new order should encompass the entire Muslim *umma* and be modeled on the example of Iran, which represented the "pure Muhammadan Islam" (*islam-i nab-i muhammadi*). To be sure, the world's Muslims were weak, at odds with each other, and affected by moral corruption. But revolutionary Iran emphasized that she did not hold Sunni Islam per se responsible for preventing Muslim unity; rather, she blamed the conspiring superpowers. In order to show her willingness to come to terms with Sunnis in practical ways, Iran banned hostile sectarian publications after the revolution, along with the public cursing of the first three Caliphs (*sabb va laʿn*) or the celebration of the murder of the second Caliph ʿUmar (d. 644) (*ʿUmar kushan*). Additionally, Khomeini ruled that Shiʿis should end their habit of praying separately from Sunnis during the hajj.[144]

This theme of taqrib ran dominantly through nearly all of Sayyid ʿArif Husayn al-Husayni's speeches and took on an importance similar to Sayyid Sharaf al-Din Musavi's revolutionary discourse. Al-Husayni's attempts at drawing Sunnis and Shiʿis together were clearly situated in the context of sectarian violence and conflict. Underlining that rapprochement with the Sunnis was no mere theoretical consideration, al-Husayni repeatedly referred to his personal working relationships even with Deobandi and Ahl-i Hadis scholars. At one point al-Husayni approached his fellow Pashto speaker Maulana Fazl al-Rahman of the Jamʿiyyat-i ʿUlamaʾ-i Islam and suggested the formation a united party to advocate the Islamic revolution. At a discussion forum organized by the newspaper *Jang*, the TNFJ leader yielded his time to none other than the virulently anti-Shiʿi author and speaker Ihsan Ilahi Zahir to enable him to continue his critique of the government's proposed Shariat Bill.[145]

He was at pains to convince the Sunnis that the two madhhabs were not enemies. Rather, they both faced a common opponent: polytheism (*shirk*) and unbelief (kufr), along with global imperialism, which threatened the whole Islamic world irrespective of its sectarian affiliation. Especially in the early 1980s, after these powers had failed to turn back the clock in Iran and Lebanon, they were aiming at Pakistan.[146] If his organization called for the establishment of an Islamic system in Pakistan, they advocated not sectarianism (*firqah variyyat*) but instead striving for a system in which all individual creeds were respected.[147] Al-Husayni turned the famous (if contested) hadith "Disagreement among my community is a blessing" (*ikhtilaf ummati rahma*) on its head when he argued that disagreements among Muslims had to be regarded as the soldiers of Satan (*shaytan ke junud*).[148] Every single statement that harmed the umma and benefited the superpowers had to be rejected.[149] The revolutionary scholar also tried to connect his discourse with pioneering taqrib efforts of the nineteenth and twentieth centuries by mentioning the "early heroes" Jamal al-Din al-Afghani (d. 1897), Muhammad ʿAbduh (d. 1905), and Mahmud Shaltut (d. 1963).[150] He called on all Muslims to form one line in prayer and prostration before God, not before the East or the West.[151] Shiʿis should attend the mosque closest to their home, be it Sunni or Shiʿi, for Friday prayers.[152]

The antagonistic context of Pakistan entered the frame in a rather one-sided way: even though al-Husayni also called on the Shiʿis not to insult the Sunnis for their particular prayers during the month of Ramadan (*tarawih*), the latter were supposed to accept ʿazadari as a custom prescribed by God (*shaʿaʾir-i Allah*).[153] Moreover, al-Husayni insisted that sunna was of course not restricted to the deeds and sayings of the Prophet but included the Shiʿi Imams as well.[154] The last question in particular has usually, along with other decisive differences in the field of law and theology, been avoided in official ecumenical Iranian discourse and seriously calls into doubt the feasibility of sectarian harmony.[155] Al-Husayni obviously felt forced to lay emphasis on these Shiʿi particularities because his internal opponents accused him of denigrating the ahl al-bayt. In the run-up to the TNFJ-led "Qur'an and Sunna Conference" on 6 July 1987 in Lahore, they organized a rival "Qur'an and Ahl al-Bayt Conference," demanded that the government revoked the permission for al-Husayni's event, and carried out a bomb attack on the city's railway station to scare away prospective participants.[156]

The Centrality of Imam Khomeini and the Iranian Example

Even while stretching out her hands to the Sunnis, Iran always emphasized the centrality of its supreme leader (*rahbar*). Khomeini and his successor, Khamenei, were hailed as being nearly infallible (*qarib-i maʿsum*) and addressed as ruler of the world's Muslims (*vali-yi amr-i muslimin-i jahan*).[157] Al-Husayni's ecumenism faced the same limitations when he praised Khomeini as being the only personality able to break the dominance of the United States and the Soviet Union, which planned on splintering the Muslim world.[158] The fundamentally different, altruistic Iranian approach, according to al-Husayni, was on display in Afghanistan, where the Islamic Republic was the only outside player to provide disinterested help for the sake of Islam.[159] In the same way that the Muslim umma had only one Kaʿba, it needed to rally around one single leader (*yeki rahbar-i vahidi*).[160] Putting it even more starkly, al-Husayni insisted that no Islamic movement (*harakat-i islami*) which did not acknowledge Iran's centrality (*markaziyyat*) could be accepted as authentically Islamic.[161] This overarching importance of Iran and her leader might also have to do with the special access to assistance from the unseen world (*ghaybi madad*) with which Khomeini was blessed in al-Husayni's view.[162] After extolling the Shiʿi Imams with the customary eulogies, the leaders of the TNFJ addressed Khomeini with distinct but similar-sounding phrases, such as the Destroyer of Unbelief (*kufr shikan*), the Pounder of East and West (*kubandah-i sharq o gharb*), and the Heir of ʿAli (*waris-i ʿAli*). They thus conveyed a connection to the audience that went beyond Khomeini being only the rightful representative of the Hidden Imam (*na'ib-i bar haqq-i imam-i zaman*).[163] Given the Iranian leader's superior insights, an Islamic revolution modeled after the example of Iran was the only thinkable solution for Pakistan's woes, even though Sayyid ʿArif Husayn al-Husayni constantly denied that his organization had a violent upheaval in mind.[164] On the other hand, al-Husayni rarely explained how he aimed to achieve this lofty goal, nor did he elaborate his position on the meaning of vilayat-i faqih in the context of Pakistan, preferring instead to oppose the government. In an interview with the English-language newspaper *The Muslim* he tried hard to evade the question of whether he preferred elections over revolution in Pakistan. Similarly, he was at pains to restrict the applicability of the Iranian model to Pakistan's economic sphere.[165] He and the Tahrik would support any real Islamic system worldwide; it was a mere coincidence that Iran was a Shiʿi country.[166]

Awakening and the Leadership Role of the ʿUlama

In general the political model of vilayat-i faqih also meant a new, central role for the ʿulama in Iranian society, a topic of the utmost importance to al-Husayni.[167] In the early 1980s, religious scholars still faced stiff competition from popular preachers (zakirs) who exerted firm control over Shiʿi mourning sessions (majalis).[168] This particular Pakistani challenge found its way into al-Husayni's arguments when he repeatedly called on his audience to accept ʿulama leadership, lamenting at the same time that many parts of the country were still devoid of their presence.[169] While the rank of marjiʿ al-taqlid was reserved exclusively for Khomeini, lower-ranking scholars in Pakistan could still provide true guidance. They played a crucial role, for example, in identifying the substantial amount of weak hadith material in the Shiʿi compendia, which among other things promoted the transmigration of souls (*tanasukh*) and displayed influences of erroneous Christian and Jewish interpretations.[170]

It was the ʿulama in general—not a lone mujaddid—whom al-Husayni expected to prepare the way for the fundamental reform of fellow Shiʿis and Pakistan at large and to facilitate an Iranian-style awakening (*bidari*).[171] In his view, "before each revolution, a mental revolution is necessary. If our thinking is not overturned, we remain in ignorant sleep while being faced with conspiracies."[172] On another occasion al-Husayni compared an awakened society with a house full of lights and its residents alert, giving intruders no chance to break in and steal.[173] Awakening also meant preparing Pakistani Muslims to accept the idea of a Muslim world government (*hukumat-i jahani-yi Islami*), a concept that was to be spread by cultural work, books, and conferences.[174]

Emphasizing the need for *bidari*, al-Husayni explicitly criticized nonpolitical reformists and traditionalists alike. He clearly distanced himself from Dhakko as an authority when he argued that the reform project for which this ʿalim stood was useless: the extreme exoteric approach (*qishri gari*) of his group neglected to pay attention to the authentic Islamic teachings and did not provide any solution to burning questions like Kashmir or Palestine.[175] Their apolitical stance clearly betrayed their self-identification as reformers: rather, they should be called reactionaries (*irtijaʿiyun*). Contrary to what these people argued, the Qurʾan was not only a book of law and education, but contained guidance in the fields of politics, society, and economy as well.[176] Since politics was a part of religion, it was impossible for a believer to close his eyes in front of events unfolding both in his own country and on the international level.[177] The idea that scholars had no role to play in the political realm, should only sit in the mosques, lead prayers, and discuss questions revolving around the legal implications of menstruation, was a deliberate lie spread by imperialism (*samraj*).[178] The contrast between al-Husayni and other reformist voices appears even starker because, according to the former, the demands of the Shiʿi movement had clearly evolved by 1987: the TNFJ was no longer calling only for a narrow implementation of Shiʿi law, but rather for an Islamic system (*islami nizam*) and an Islamic government.[179]

The traditionalists were of course on an equally wrong path. Such people only spoke according to the wishes of the people, focused on narrow sectarian issues, and did not elucidate what the Qurʾan and the ahl al-bayt demanded from them.[180] While promoting ʿazadari, they forgot that the real purpose of *ʿashura* was not the performance of certain rituals. In its essence, commemorating Imam Husayn meant striving to reform the umma and uniting all downtrodden people (*mustazʿafin*).[181] "If I myself am bound by the chains of flagellation (*zanjir*), how can I set others free?" asked Sayyid ʿArif Husayn al-Husayni.[182] In making such controversial statements, the leader of the TNFJ drew on the authority of the third Shiʿi Imam himself, quoting al-Husayn's proclamation during the battle of Karbala: "I did not go into battle out of impertinence or vanity, nor because I am an evil-doer or morally corrupt, but rather to demand the reform of my grandfather's *umma*."[183] If the popular preachers, despite their importance for the Shiʿi community in Pakistan, refrained from educating the people, they betrayed the "pulpit of the martyr for the whole of humanity" (*shahid-i insaniyyat ke minbar*).[184] The last reference is notable, since al-Husayni thus attempted to broaden the appeal of his message and to link revolutionary Iranian discourse to the leading Indian Shiʿi authority of the twentieth century, Sayyid ʿAli Naqi Naqvi. Far from politicizing Karbala, ʿAli Naqi Naqvi emphasized in his famous book *Shahid-i insaniyyat*, which was originally published in 1940 and has demonstrated its impact repeatedly in the course of the previous chapters, the universal attributes and the unique display of morals surrounding al-Husayn's martyrdom to which people of all faiths could relate.[185]

Reflecting another concern of the Iranian Revolution, a developing one as I have argued earlier, al-Husayni repeatedly conceded a much more comprehensive role to women than many Sunni Islamists or his fellow Shiʿi Safdar Husayn Najafi. He applauded the contributions by female activists in Iran after the revolution who, without neglecting their modesty, played a crucial role in reconstructing and advancing their country, including as members of parliament. According to al-Husayni, women could even dispense religious guidance, provided that they had attained the qualification of independent legal reasoning (ijtihad).[186] Pakistan should follow this model and finally recognize the neglected half of its population as full, respected members of society.[187] The TNFJ leader's awakening project also reflected elements of the Shiʿi heritage that stretched beyond the Iranian Revolution insofar as he emphasized the role of reason and philosophy for believers: if a human being did not develop his rational faculties, perfection was not attainable.[188]

Political Activism

Finally, the endeavor to close ranks among Muslims implied that revolutionary Iran lashed out against the "global arrogance" (*istikbar-i jahani*). Khomeini branded the United States the main enemy of all the deprived and oppressed people in the world, telling his followers it needed to be brought to its knees.[189] Islam offered a third path that was allied with neither the East nor the West.[190] Rhetoric against Saudi Arabia was part and parcel of this view, since Saudi princes were seen as morally degenerate, hypocritical rulers who obeyed their American masters rather than God.[191] Important in this regard was a speech al-Husayni delivered in the aftermath of Muharram 1984, following large-scale attacks on Shiʿis in Karachi, including arson directed at a mosque and dozens of houses in the Liaqatabad area.[192] Here al-Husayni adopted a much more internationalized view of Pakistani's situation that went beyond Mufti Jaʿfar Husayn's predominantly local approach to Shiʿi grievances. Al-Husayni declared that the Shiʿis were aware that "those Wahhabis, who wrap themselves in the mantle of Islam" were behind all these conspiracies. There could be no doubt that Pakistan's Shiʿis were being betrayed by their own government, which made common cause with the Saudis.[193] The latter were free to construct schools in Peshawar and to run a so-called Islamic University in Islamabad that was not worthy of this title, since it accepted neither Shiʿi students nor Shiʿi teachers and was only set up to spread hatred among Muslims.[194] These issues served as examples for al-Husayni of the unchecked spread of deviant ideas (*afkar-i munharif*) and a corrupted version of Islam that was subservient to the United States.[195] Even more deplorable, however, was Saudi Arabia's anti-Shiʿi propaganda in Mecca and Medina and the severe restrictions the country placed on pilgrimage for Shiʿis.[196] These great crimes subjected the Saudis to God's curse (*khuda ki laʿnat*).[197]

Saudi Arabia thus constituted al-Husayni's main "far enemy" with substantial leverage in Pakistan.[198] Such a view, I hold, downplayed the important local Deobandi dynamics of sectarianism, which I discuss in the subsequent chapter. Yet al-Husayni's political activism was more frequently directed against the government of his own country, thereby drawing on and expanding a long-standing Shiʿi theme. Al-Husayni constantly denied that Pakistan under Zia ul-Haq deserved in any way to be termed an Islamic Republic, given that the country was not only allied with the United States but also characterized by widespread exploitation, immodesty, and a general disregard for Islam.[199] The political system itself was immoral (*fasid*) and wrong (*ghalat*) because Western laws and culture dominated.[200] The government which had come to power in the name of religion was, in al-Husayni's view, nothing more than a disgrace for Islam (*Islam ko bad nam kar rahe hen*).[201]

It is interesting to note that al-Husayni remained extremely steady in his anti-Saudi and antigovernment rhetoric, even in the years between 1983 and 1987 when Khomeini deliberately toned down any attacks on the Kingdom due to the Iran-Iraq War. The Islamic Republic and Saudi Arabia even reached a sort of compromise as far as limited Iranian demonstrations in Mecca during the hajj were concerned.[202] Sayyid ʿArif Husayn al-Husayni was obviously unimpressed and continued to explicitly identify Wahhabism as the primary enemy of Shiʿis worldwide. Al-Husayni and Iran were likewise at odds with regard to the scholar's native country as the Iranian government actively reached out to Pakistan, eager to establish good relations with its neighbors and refraining from any criticism in public.[203] The leader of the TNFJ actively resisted these diplomatic overtures. His anti-Zia stance went as far as not welcoming Ali Khamenei, then Iran's president, at the airport when he made a state visit to Pakistan in January 1986. While al-Husayni justified his decision by pointing out that he intended not to lend the slightest legitimacy to Zia ul-Haq, Khamenei reportedly strongly disapproved of his "radicalism."[204]

RAISING THE BANNER OF WILAYA IN PRESENT-DAY PAKISTAN: SAYYID JAVAD NAQVI

It has become apparent that Sayyid ʿArif Husayn al-Husayni remained reluctant to even mention the loaded term vilayat-i faqih in any of his speeches and interviews. He was active on various propaganda fronts and promoted select aspects of the revolutionary package against his opponents. In the midst of these struggles he must either have preferred a cautionary approach or deemed the rule of a jurist irrelevant for Pakistan's Shiʿis, given their minority situation. The last ʿalim I am about to discuss in this chapter does not feel deterred by any such constraints. Rather, Sayyid Javad Naqvi adopted the concept of the Guardianship of the Jurisprudent as the central building block of his thought, rendering it an axis around which nearly all his public announcements revolve. In doing so, his well-crafted omnipresence conveys the impression of a man on the rise. His posters, which usually advertise events at his seminary, dominate the Shiʿi areas of Pakistan's cities. He has opened bookstores in Lahore, Islamabad, and Karachi that exclusively distribute his works and has embarked on an aggressive distribution campaign to other Shiʿi outlets as well. In August 2012, I witnessed how the tiny Shiʿi bookshop Imamiyyah Kutubkhanah in Skardu received a free delivery of Naqvi's latest imprint. The dispatch from Lahore contained so many volumes that the owner visibly had trouble storing all these beautifully bound copies. Naqvi's use of the Internet and social media in terms of both variety of content and production quality dwarfs the efforts of every other Shiʿi ʿalim in Pakistan.[205] One possible explanation for the palpable qualitative shift in rhetoric from the height of revolutionary fervor in the 1980s to present-day Lahore must have to do with Naqvi's uniquely Iran-centered career that distinguishes him from both members of the old guard like Safdar Husayn Najafi and the following generation of which Sayyid ʿArif Husayn al-Husayni is a representative. Unlike them, Naqvi spent nearly his entire adult life in Iran.

Born in Pakistan's Punjab province, he graduated from a high school in Islamabad in 1979 and was immediately thrown into the revolutionary frenzy of the period. In an interview Sayyid Javad Naqvi described impatiently sitting next to his brother as he attempted to tune in to the BBC reporting on Iran to get an update on the latest developments. Naqvi remembers these months as a time when even Sunni ʿulama publicly praised Khomeini and put him on a level with the four Rightly Guided Caliphs (*kih imam bah khilafat-i rashidah rasidah ast*). That crucial summer, Naqvi embarked on a short trip to Pakistan's revolutionary neighbor and later enrolled in a Shiʿi seminary in Islamabad for the initial stages of his religious training. In 1983, he proceeded to Qum, where he first studied and later taught in the city's institutions of higher learning.[206] After his return to Pakistan in 2009, he established his own seminary in the outskirts of Lahore; it became fully operational in 2010.[207] In a way the seminary's name, Jamiʿat al-ʿUrwa al-Wuthqa, already points to Naqvi's goal for his native country: on the one hand, he cleverly exploits the fact that this Qur'anic quote carries nonsectarian connotations because it brings to mind the journal of the same name published by the early hero of Pan-Islam, Jamal al-Din al-Afghani.[208] The term *al-ʿurwa al-wuthqa* also recalls an influential fiqh work with the same name by Sayyid Muhammad Kazim Yazdi (d. 1919), who is credited with clearly defining the notion of *aʿlamiyya* and the obligatory character of taqlid.[209] More important, however, Naqvi repeatedly emphasizes that for him "the most firm bond" is nothing less than ʿAli's wilaya as the Imam, which ties in with his hope that the model of vilayat-i faqih should spread over the entire globe.[210] Even though Naqvi is a member of the relatively recently formed Shiʿi party Majlis-i Vahdat-i Muslimin (Council of Muslim Unity),[211] he is first of all a scholar and has "retreated" to religion, as Laurence Louër describes non-politically-active ʿulama in her book.[212] Yet it is precisely the field of religious thought, free from any "practical" (or rather immediate) involvement with the entanglements of messy politics, where the argument of an increasing autonomization from Iran runs into some complications.

For one, Naqvi is unique among his Pakistani peers in his interest in the domestic affairs of Iran, which form a constant part of his lectures. He was very outspoken against the Green Movement, for example, which he condemned as a foreign conspiracy.[213] In commenting on the 2013 Iranian presidential elections, Naqvi explained in a speech that the votes for the ultimately successful presidential candidate Hasan Ruhani should be understood as a display of faith in the system of vilayat-i faqih because the voters gave preference to the only clerical candidate running for the office.[214] Naqvi also used this opportunity in front of his predominantly young audience to denounce Ruhani's potential but by then already-disqualified contender, Ali Akbar Hashemi Rafsanjani (d. 2017).[215] For Naqvi, this clerical veteran of Iranian politics was nothing more than a power-hungry individual who did not have the slightest reverence for Shiʿism, Islam, or the Guardianship of the Jurisprudent. His only conviction was that of being a staunch nationalist (*Iran parast*) who due to his realpolitik leanings deserved the title "Ayatollah Churchill."[216] But Muhammad Khatami, the former reformist president, was identified as the most substantial threat the Islamic Republic had faced since 1979. In Naqvi's view, the "liberal" Khatami gave precedence to personal freedom over religion (*din*) and did not even intervene when speeches were made against the marajiʿ or Imam Husayn himself on the campus of Tehran University.[217] Naqvi acts in these and many more instances of domestic commentary as a faithful supporter of Iran's leader Khamenei and constantly warns against threats—to Iran, not to Pakistan—that stem from the country's internal and external opponents.

Naqvi's dominant topic, however, is the need to teach Pakistani society the true meaning of wilaya. In contrast to the reformists discussed in chapter 2, this ʿalim is in no way opposed to acknowledging the cosmological dimensions of *vilayat-i takvini*. Rather, in extolling the exalted role of the Imams, Naqvi gains room, in turn, to claim (political) authority for the religious scholars during the Hidden Imam's Occultation. In this context, Naqvi is much more outspoken than al-Husayni when attacking the popular preachers. These people are for him nothing more than "illiterates sitting on the pulpits" who conceal the true ramification of wilaya as the cornerstone of religious thought: "If you want to know about Imamat [*sic*] then don't go and ask those who don't even know if Imamat in Arabic is written with 'Alif' or

'Ain.'"[218] These Shiʿi preachers were part of a broader South Asian problem, namely the prevalence of Sufi ideas, which led the Shiʿis to conceptualize their Imams as analogous to a pir. They were regarded as mere holy personalities whose support is sought in prayer, but they were not granted any authority (*ikhtiyar*) over the lives of the believers.[219] This was a fundamental misunderstanding of their role, Naqvi emphasized, since God had delegated to them the government over his creation. This right to rule, in turn, flowed from the Imams to their chosen delegates, the ʿulama.[220] Since Khomeini had unearthed "the buried Wilayat" and established it in Iran, commands emanating from the country's leader took on a mandatory nature for every human being.[221] Yet Pakistan's Shiʿis had no conception of wilaya as a system that also exposed the serious deficiencies of their political activism since 1947. They had always come to terms with the ruling, corrupt political forces, as long as these parties would permit them to celebrate their rituals in public. Pakistan's Shiʿis implored the authorities to stop sectarian killings instead of being bold enough to advance their rightful claim of acting as the country's protector.[222] Even Mufti Jaʿfar Husayn's efforts with the TNFJ were nothing more than a first step in the direction of forming a true Shiʿi identity.[223] The Tahrik's focus had been helpful in convincing the community that they indeed had a fiqh on their own.[224] Javad Naqvi wholeheartedly lauded this preliminary achievement. He made it clear, however, that the true significance of Shiʿi law was that it contained particular approaches toward government and the political system as a whole, all based on wilaya.[225] If this comprehensive system was not implemented, the Shiʿis should "under no circumstances" ally themselves with any other form of government.[226]

Naqvi does not see any practical constraints for his minority sect that would prevent them from aspiring to the leadership of Pakistan. For him, the Lebanese group Hezbollah had shown the way. In Lebanon, the Shiʿis were neither a numerical majority nor in control of the government, but their self-confident attitude and courageous advancement of the system of vilayat-i faqih had endowed them with a dominating role (*imamat*) in their local context. Sunnis and Christians too had to accept this.[227] Unfortunately, however, Pakistanis could never count on Iran for real support in their struggle. The golden opportunity for exporting the revolution in the early 1980s was missed due to the war Iran fought with Iraq. Blunders by Iranian officials who had the wrong mind-set (*tafakkur-i ghalat*) and displayed only a lukewarm commitment to exporting the revolution added to this failure.[228] Iranian interest in globalizing the revolution further decreased after Khomeini's death in 1989, when suddenly, according to Naqvi, a normalization of ties with other countries was pursued, leading to, among other things, the establishment of the Ministry of Foreign Affairs.[229] In this regard, Naqvi mentions the comments of a former ambassador of Iran to Pakistan who criticized the Pakistanis for putting up posters of Khomeini and Khamenei everywhere. In the words of the diplomat, the revolution was an internal, Iranian affair and had no relevance for South Asia.[230] Needless to say, this sad state of affairs and misconception of the revolution were never intended by Khomeini. Naqvi sees a special closeness the Iranian leader felt for Pakistan in a declaration Khomeini made after the death of Sayyid ʿArif Husayn al-Husayni, calling him his "true son" (*farzand-i haqiqi*).[231] Among the volumes of letters and speeches by Khomeini, Naqvi claims, this personal address stands in an exalted row along with three other short historic texts, including Khomeini's testament. If a reader only familiarized himself with these four writings, he would have encountered the essence of the *rahbar*'s thought.[232] The Jamiʿat al-ʿUrwa al-Wuthqa, then, was ready to finally realize Khomeini's wish and achieve the rooting of the true message of the revolution in Pakistan. Under Naqvi's guidance, the seminary's syllabus covered the entirety of the true Islamic ideology (*nazariyyah*) and was designed to groom a new generation (*nasl*) of Shiʿis who were proud of the imamate and ready to lead the Pakistani nation (qaum) and the worldwide community of Muslims (umma).[233] These young men would tap into the country's unrivaled potential and passion.[234] They would take Pakistan out of its current status of servitude to outside powers and put an end to poverty, terrorism, and deprivation.[235]

CONCLUSION

These last observations on Sayyid Javad Naqvi's conceptualization of the Islamic Revolution once again demonstrate the fascinating tensions between closeness and distance that has already permeated the travelogue that captured the spirit of 1979. Taken together with Sayyid ʿArif Husayn al-Husayni's adaptation of and at times resistance to vilayat-i faqih and various other themes emanating from Iran, the thought of these two men underlines the limits of the control that the Iranians could hope to exert over the Pakistani propagators of their mission.[236] Yet neither al-Husayni nor Javad Naqvi ever opted for a clear-cut "autonomization," the breaking of ties with Iran, because their authority directly depended on being Khomeini's *wakil* or on having studied for decades at the hauza in Qum. Rather, like the ʿulama of an older generation who had been educated in Najaf (see chapters 2 and 3), al-Husayni and Javad Naqvi strove to carve out a niche for themselves as indigenous translators of the revolution, a task no Iranian ʿalim could ever hope to achieve. In so doing, the supposed universal and rational reformulation of Islam was interpreted for Pakistan in ways that remained intimately tied to the requirements of the time and the realities of personal exposure to the neighboring country.

In this chapter I have demonstrated how South Asian concepts and successful locally driven political campaigns and protests shaped the view from Pakistan toward Iran in the first months and years after the revolution. Mufti Jaʿfar Husayn was not willing to relinquish Pakistani leadership over his activism against Zia ul-Haq's military regime. Sayyid Murtaza Husayn and Sayyid Safdar Husayn Najafi tried to comprehend the Iranian upheaval on Gandhian terms or through the concept of the mujaddid. The ensuing mid-1980s witnessed both the height of Shiʿi activism as well as the realization that neither the idea of rapprochement with the Sunnis nor the reform of rituals could be sold easily to a Shiʿi public that remained influenced by traditionalist scholars and popular preachers. Finally, being a follower of Khomeini in today's Lahore means both learning from Lebanon and an attempt at presenting Pakistan as a potential corrective to a revolutionary neighbor that has deviated from its radical path and has become caught up in conventional politics. Sayyid Javad Naqvi, then, also promoted his own Shiʿi vision of Pakistan as a future pure Muslim land suspended in a process of "striving" toward perfection. His native country was called to nothing less than a global mission for the salvation of Islam. Seen from this perspective, arguments about an "Iranization" of Pakistan's Shiʿis and their ʿulama are not wrong—but they disguise the fact that this revolutionary coating has glimmered in many different shades over the course of the four decades since the downfall of the Shah.

CHAPTER FIVE

Longing for the State

DIALECTICS OF THE LOCAL AND THE TRANSNATIONAL IN SUNNI-SHIʿI SECTARIANISM

Ho halqah-i yaran to barisham ki tarah narm.
Razm-i haqq o batil ho to fulad he muʾmin.
When among his friends, he is soft as raw silk.
But on the battlefield of truth and falsehood,
the believer turns into a man of Damascene steel.
— Muhammad Iqbal, "The Believer (In the World)"

When the young Pakistani student Ihsan Ilahi Zahir arrived at the recently opened Islamic University of Medina in 1963, he soon realized that the grass was not always greener on the Saudi Arabian side of the fence.[1] The reason for Zahir's unease was not so much his academic performance, which according to both Pakistani and Saudi sources was flawless.[2] Rather, he quickly noticed that many of the professors who were supposed to teach classes on comparative religion and (heretical) sects within Islam (*adyan o firaq*) lacked a thorough grounding in the subject at hand. The matter was of especially grave concern in his view when it came to lectures on the Ahmadi movement. Zahir recalled that his teachers had to cut their talks short after offering only superficial remarks on this group, undoubtedly due to their inability to tap into the extensive literature on the subject in Urdu. Eventually, he himself, as the only student from Pakistan present at this time at the Islamic University, had to intervene in order to set the record straight. Zahir began writing op-eds in Arabic newspapers, moved on to lectures on the Ahmadis, and finally was encouraged by his professors to compile his thoughts into a book. Navigating the market of academic publishing with such a sought-after topic was a mere formality. The editor of the publishing house that took the project under its wings had only one request. Would it be possible, he asked, for Zahir to appear on the cover with the designation "Graduate of the Islamic University of Medina"? Such a label would definitely boost the sales. Zahir, still far from graduation, hesitated. He consulted with the university's vice chancellor, ʿAbd al-ʿAziz b. Baz (d. 1999), who would later become Saudi Arabia's grand mufti and was in those early years the institution's de facto leader.[3] Ibn Baz took the matter to the university's governing board, which unexpectedly gave its blessing to this unusual move, highlighting the importance they attributed to the book. Yet Zahir was not completely put at ease. What would happen, he inquired, if he failed his final exams, with a publication out that pretended otherwise? Ibn Baz waved this concern aside: if things really turned out that way, they might as well close down the entire university.[4]

Zahir's study on the Ahmadis, *Al-Qadiyaniyyah: Dirasat wa-tahlil* (*Qadiyaniat: An Analytical Survey*), was published in 1967. All his fears proved to be unfounded: he graduated from the Islamic University in 1968 with first-class honors.[5] What renders this episode highly significant, however, is that Zahir later amply fulfilled the hopes of his Saudi patrons. He continued his polemical vision and over the next decades published fourteen books, most of which focused on the Shiʿis and which drew a wide audience. Bernard Haykel has argued that "perhaps no single scholar has been more influential in aggravating Sunni-Shiʿa tensions and violence in the South Asian context than Ihsan Ilahi Zahir."[6] In evaluating Zahir's influence, however, scholars have mostly viewed him through precisely this Saudi lens, pointing out his strong ties with publishers, ʿulama, and the ruling family in the Kingdom. Zahir not only composed nearly all his works in Arabic but also received privileged treatment after being wounded in a bomb attack on a rally he was addressing in Lahore in the spring of 1987.[7] Crown Prince Fahd immediately dispatched a private plane to transfer Zahir to the Military Hospital in Riyadh. After his death, Ibn Baz personally led the funeral prayers in the Saudi capital before Zahir was laid to rest in a grave close to the Prophet's Mosque in Medina.[8]

These links are doubtless important, but they have tended to obfuscate Zahir's Pakistani personality. So far only his output in Arabic has received any attention (which has been minimal), and he is usually discussed as a mere Saudi client.[9] His op-eds, journal articles, and speeches in Urdu have gone completely unnoticed. Even more problematic is that a substantial number of scholars view the case of Ihsan Ilahi Zahir as the paradigm for how anti-Shiʿi sectarianism made headway in Pakistan more broadly. As a scholar trained in the Ahl-i Hadis tradition, Zahir of course belonged to a school of thought that over time had come to develop close affinities with Wahhabi and Salafi interpretations of Islam.[10] The towering Ahl-i Hadis scholar Sana'ullah Amritsari (d. 1948), while applauding Wahhabi activism against polytheism (*shirk*) and unlawful innovations (*bidaʿ*), had initially still lumped the (Hanbali) Wahhabis together with the Deobandis as being stuck in the idea of the madhhab. His opinion shifted only in the wake of the Khilafat Movement, when he increasingly identified the Saudi ruler ʿAbd al-ʿAziz Al Saʿud (r. 1932–53) as an opponent of the British. After Partition, this process of convergence gained even more traction, a development to which Zahir's religious opinions amply testify.[11] Some, however, have attempted to explain even the emergence of the virulently anti-Shiʿi group of the Sipah-i Sahabah-i Pakistan (Army of the Companions of the Prophet; hereafter SSP),[12] which has succeeded Zahir in dominating the Pakistani sectarian scene since the late 1980s, by simply pointing out that it too has received Saudi funding.[13] In order to benefit from the Kingdom's largess, this argument goes, also the Deoband-affiliated scholars of the SSP were only too willing to overlook points of disagreement with the Wahhabis and were thus turned into propagators of hatred and, worse, violence.[14] Equally prominent in the literature is a second argument, one that portrays these sectarian Sunni ʿulama first of all as a group of underdogs who resorted to sectarianism "to stake out their own claim to power and wealth-satiating appetites for power, status and wealth that Islamization had whetted but left unsatiated."[15] Others hold that "for many Sunni extremists becoming involved in sectarian politics of violence was good for business, money, and power."[16] This push for influence, scholars have claimed, coincided with the emergence of economic and political grievances among Sunni rural (and recently urbanized) populations, who saw sectarianism as a way to counter the dominance of large landholders who identified as Shiʿi.[17]

These interventions are important insofar as they alert us to the fact that Pakistan's sectarian violence is not primarily the eruption of some fossilized, primordial, or eternal grievances between Sunnis and Shiʿis. Studying the situation in Lebanon, Ussama Makdisi has drawn scholarly attention to instances of the deliberate production of animosity between Islamic groups. Makdisi has argued that the concept of sectarianism "as an idea and as a practice belongs to the realm of the modern" and is intimately tied to the emergence of the nation-state.[18] Indeed, when studying the issue in a particular context, it appears crucial to identify those political and societal actors that push an agenda of "sectarianization" in order to reach certain goals such as "deflecting demands for political change and perpetuating their power."[19] The problem with many of the existing explanations of the situation in Pakistan, however, is that they rely on a very selective reading of the literature produced by the sectarian groups themselves. Only the SSP's founder, Haqq

Navaz Jhangvi (d. 1990), has received significant attention. Scholars have frequently used a limited number of biographical accounts produced by the movement to make sweeping conclusions about the wider phenomenon in Pakistan. Questionable statistics and lack of clear definitions aggravate this issue, leading to conclusions such as that among 2,500 madrasas in the Punjab, "750 were classed as aggressively sectarian," without any attempt to unpack such questionable statements.[20] The lack of interest in the textual manifestation of sectarian tendencies could also have to do with a biased view toward religious polemics more generally. Supposedly, "little new has been added to the centuries-old grievances and accusations of Sunnis against Shias (and vice-versa) by the SSP and like-minded organisations" in the course of these exchanges.[21] Similarly, Rainer Brunner has remarked that "Shiite refutations brought just as little new as the Sunni polemical tirades that they in turn caused, whose number increased exponentially after the Islamic Revolution of 1979. Whereas the authors of the latter [. . .] make every effort to outdo even [. . .] [the most] spiteful tone, from the former come apologetics that are no less persistent, in which standardized rejoinders are leveled at trite Sunni accusations."[22]

While I do not advocate a monocausal explanation for the rise of sectarianism and religious violence, I deem it important to take a closer look at the intellectual production of sectarian actors in Pakistan. Doing so, I propose, gives us a much clearer idea of what is at stake. In particular, I argue that the scholars discussed below do not see themselves as merely carrying out Saudi Arabia's bidding.[23] Unlike the Middle East, where in the recent past virulent and violent tracts against the Shiʿis have been written almost exclusively by Salafi-inspired groups, local actors steeped in the Deobandi tradition and scholarship in Urdu are at the forefront of such debates in South Asia.[24] Similar to the way Javad Naqvi claimed for himself the mantle of the Iranian Revolution (see chapter 4), we also get a sense of Pakistani actors berating other scholars in the Middle East for having woken up too late to the threat of Shiʿism. My argument, then, also relates to debates over the influx of a "foreign" Islam during the years of the Afghan jihad and supports those observations that have questioned the impact of Arab actors both in the fighting and in the context of the dissemination of ideas. Vahid Brown and Don Rassler, for example, have emphasized the predominance of the Deobandi Haqqani network in recruiting Arab volunteers and turning them from *muhajirs* (emigrants) into *mujahids* (holy warriors). Moreover, they have demonstrated that Jalal al-Din Haqqani's framing of jihad in Afghanistan as an individual duty (*fard ʿayn*) preceded ʿAbdullah ʿAzzam's famous 1984 fatwa by four years.[25]

More important, however, this chapter emphasizes that ʿulama active in the SSP seem to be less motivated by economic grievances and missed opportunities than by an Islamist-like fixation on the state.[26] Even though the SSP followed in the footsteps of Ihsan Ilahi Zahir in highlighting doctrinal incompatibilities between "real" and Shiʿi Islam, the Shiʿis were now mostly framed as blocking Pakistan from being molded into its true form, namely a Sunni entity with a claim to global leadership. The Iranian Revolution constituted a clear and marked watershed that pushed aside an Ahl-i Hadis focus on proper creed (ʿaqida). Shiʿi denunciations of the Companions remained a pressing concern, but no longer simply because they were unacceptable from a religious perspective. Rather, the scholars of the SSP located them within a perceived broader Iranian project of world domination and subversion of the fundamentals of Islamic politics. These debates were also informed by internal Sunni sectarian discourses that reflect attempts to discredit potential rivals like—maybe not so paradoxically—the Islamists in determining the future course of the state. By denouncing (and simultaneously drawing on) the example of the Islamic Republic of Iran and calling for the reinstatement of a divinely ordained and creatively reinterpreted office of the caliphate, the Sipah-i Sahabah also demonstrated a dialectical relationship with the Iranian Revolution. Their call for a new Sunni world order differed markedly from a more mainstream reaction to the revolution on the part of other Sunni ʿulama who were wary of allocating unlimited power and authority over and above the law to an individual resembling Khomeini. Muhammad Qasim Zaman has argued that the doctrine of vilayat-i faqih was precisely what most Sunni ʿulama perceived as highly dangerous, for "in the guise of upholding Islam the state might make it subservient to its own goals and ultimately absorb it within itself."[27] Wael Hallaq has added that it "is this 'guise,' representing no more than a thin veneer, that marks the superficial difference between a self-declared secular state and a self-declared Islamic state."[28] Such supreme power of government is amply reflected in a famous letter that Khomeini sent to Ali Khamenei on 6 January 1988. In this letter Khomeini argued that there could be circumstances when "the interests of the Islamic country" even outweighed clear stipulations of the shariʿa. Consequently, these injunctions could be set aside.[29] Pakistani sectarian actors were less scared than other Sunni groups by the far-reaching implications of this new conception of sovereignty; rather, as I will show below, they embraced them. Finally, this chapter also touches on the important, albeit ambiguous, links that Pakistani sectarian discourses had with the wider Muslim world. It forms thus the flip side to my previous discussion of internal Shiʿi negotiations over the impact and appropriation of the Iranian Revolution.

In the following, I briefly discuss both the extent of the sectarian landscape in Pakistan and scholarly approaches that try to make sense of the phenomenon of at times violent enmity between the various branches of Islam. I then outline Ihsan Ilahi Zahir's understanding of the Shiʿi problem and contrast his polemical writings with the politicized way leading scholars of the Sipah-i Sahabah have responded to the same question. While the latter have relied on many of the same arguments popularized by Zahir, they have drawn vastly different conclusions, namely that the Shiʿis are a problem for the Pakistani state. This section of the chapter also illuminates the modes of religious reasoning on which the SSP embarked in order to justify the need for the specific political entity they envisioned. A final section discusses Shiʿi reactions to these evolving discourses which also, crucially, have centered on the state.

PAKISTAN'S SECTARIAN LANDSCAPE

As this book's introduction makes clear, I draw on a broad definition of sectarianism that includes both texts and actions. The previous chapters on the late colonial period, contestations over reform, and the reception of the Iranian Revolution have demonstrated that discourses seemingly directed against an out-group might target equally (or primarily) certain actors, concepts, or groups that do not qualify as "the other" but are squarely located within the broader Sunni or Shiʿi spectrum, respectively. My goal is to document comparable dynamics in this chapter. While the discussion focuses primarily on discourses and ideas, it has to be emphasized that these do not remain in the realm of the theoretical. Rather, most of the protagonists discussed below have at some point or other been imprisoned by the Pakistani authorities. All of them have met a violent death. Their positions, expressed during sermons or rallies or on various Facebook pages, reverberate in the form of very palpable acts of violence. Consequently, Pakistan's Shiʿi citizens face a very grim reality. Innocent civilians like the Hazarah community in Quetta[30] or residents of the Kurram Tribal Agency can feel virtually under siege.[31] Shiʿi lawyers,[32] doctors,[33] university professors, and other well-educated members of the community are routinely targeted.[34] The various episodes of carnage seem to blend into each other when yet another instance from Gilgit or Balochistan is reported during which militants, usually dressed in Pakistani army fatigues, order a bus to stop and its passengers to disembark. The militants then check ID cards. If a certain name alone does not give away the traveler's identity as a Shiʿi, the gunmen ask their victim to lift his shirt so they can look for the scars that result from Shiʿi mourning ceremonies.[35] Reports of the execution are met with strikes by Shiʿi traders, "long marches" to Islamabad, and demonstrations involving the burning of tires. Yet the 1990s, the main focus of this chapter, present us with a picture that is perhaps equally grim but definitely less one-sided. Tallying official (and thus likely incomplete) data, Andreas Rieck estimates that between 1990 and 1997, 208 Sunnis and 289 Shiʿis lost their lives during a total of 1,112 sectarian incidents in Pakistan's Punjab province alone.[36] What this means is that Shiʿis were (and are?) perpetrators too, even though barely anything is known about the violent offshoots of successor organizations to the TNFJ besides the names of their leaders.[37]

Especially this veil of secrecy surrounding many of the sectarian organizations has tempted scholars to speculate about the real, hidden motives for their activism, publications, and, ultimately, violence. Taking a different path and following Faisal Devji, I reaffirm in this chapter the importance of the study of ideas because "however 'material' they might be, interests are the most transient of things. Ideas invariably exceed them and are the great survivors of history, living beyond the political conjunctures within which they were produced, to shape new futures."[38] Devji problematizes the narrow focus on "criminological" history, which aims at retrospectively assigning blame by "providing a blow-by-blow account of what 'actually' happened in a merely belated fashion" instead of laying bare forms of argumentation and lines of reasoning that both transcend and survive such intentionality to decisively impact the process of history.[39]

It is precisely such a focus on interests that dominates the literature on sectarianism in the Islamic context, in Pakistan and beyond. Toby Matthiesen, for example, attributes sectarianism in the states of the Persian Gulf to "sectarian identity entrepreneurs" who use this discourse to foster their personal aims.[40] While I agree that "political sectarianism [. . .] only arises under certain conditions," I do not share his view that an analysis of the mere "doctrinal" aspects of these discourses are not also worthy of our attention.[41] As far as Pakistan is concerned, the emergence of increasing tensions and violence between Sunnis and Shiʿis is frequently connected with the specific situation in the Punjabi city of Jhang, where sectarian violence was sparked by "the struggle for political power between the traditional feudal families who are primarily Shia and rural-based and the emergent middle-class which is largely Deobandi or Ahl-i-Hadith and urban-based."[42] The rise of this middle class, several authors hold, was fueled by the labor migration to the Gulf states of rural Pakistanis who became urbanized after returning to their native country. The recorded figures behind these movements are no doubt impressive: since the mid-1970s, more than 4.59 million Pakistanis have left the country to take up work elsewhere, mainly in the Middle East. While the 1990s witnessed a sharp decline in temporary employment options abroad, this trend was reversed by the mid-2000s. In 2008, approximately 430,000 workers went abroad, sending home remittances of more than $7 billion, an amount that rose to $14.9 billion in 2013.[43] These large-scale socioeconomic transformations might indeed have spurred the search for new anchors of identity to which sectarian organizations responded. It is possible that these groups provided an outlet for a frustrated middle class that saw its aspirations hindered by Shiʿi figures who blocked their social climbing.[44]

So far, however, we do not have the data to back up such arguments either for Jhang or other areas of Pakistan more broadly. Quite to the contrary, surveys demonstrate that households who send migrants to the Gulf not only report a significant improvement of their economic situation but also find that their social status has risen.[45] Claims of Pakistani labor migrants bringing back "a redefined religious identity that was militantly Sunni and regarded Shiʿis as 'the other'" are problematic: few if any studies have looked into manifestations of religious change that can be connected with labor migration.[46] More rigorous anthropological accounts are a major desideratum in this context because the existing literature treats the effects of exposure to the Gulf states rather schematically. This is captured by the following quote, taken from a study on two villages in northern Punjab: "In other words, from the migrant's point of view, a long absence does not change his relationship with his background. His cultural identity is deep-rooted enough not to be disturbed by the social environment of the receiving countries, especially when they are Arabic [*sic*]. The common Pakistani does not consider the Arabic [*sic*] society to be as intellectually and culturally developed as the Pakistani society and consequently does not have any desire at all to establish himself there."[47] One exception to this trend is Attiya Ahmad, who in her work on conversion to Islam among female domestic workers in Kuwait has emphasized that "becoming Muslim" is a gradual process that often has its origins in the close interaction of these women with their employers. Ahmad's Indian and Nepalese interlocutors usually started attending classes of Islamic proselytizing (*daʿwa*) after these personal interactions had instilled in them a deeper interest in Islam. In her account, *daʿwa* classes focus mostly on piety, the main ritual obligations in Islam, and advice of how (if at all) to convey the newfound faith to families back home.[48] Other scholars have pointed out that Pakistani migrants are often neither exposed to nor particularly attracted to their host societies in the Gulf.[49] A final problem is that economic analysis is applied rather haphazardly. The Sipah-i Sahabah is credited with appealing simultaneously to the "Sunni middle-classes," the "urban bourgeoisie," the "lower middle-classes," "businessmen," "traders," a "rising commercial class," the "bazaar merchants," "transporters," "shopkeepers," "industrialists," "peasants," the "working-class," "returned workers from the Gulf," the "urban-poor," the "semi-educated, unemployed urban youth," "new migrants," and "artisan migrants."[50]

The key to making sense of the virulent and violent animosities between Sunnis and Shiʿis since the 1980s, I suggest, has to be located within the realm of the political instead. These decades brought contending, grand visions of how to establish an Islamic state on the national and international level into stark relief. Active and not necessarily sectarian engagement with politics has been of course the hallmark of many ʿulama in Pakistan since 1947.[51] In doing so, they have engaged—along with various parties, the courts, the modernists, progressive writers, military dictators, and so on—in a broad process of "striving."[52] As Naveeda Khan has observed, this effort is grounded in Pakistan's suspension in a permanent incomplete form since its inception. The country's founders emphasized the sheer unprecedentedness of their vision. For example, Muhammad Ali Jinnah, Pakistan's first governor general, explicitly made no distinction between the British or the Mughal rulers of the past, labeling them all as "imperialists."[53] Instead, Jinnah wanted the creation of an entirely new, social contract–based entity without any connection to the colonial state: "To envision the country's partition and freedom as an inheritance from the Raj, thought Jinnah, reduced this unprecedented event to a mere squabbling after the spoils of empire while at the same time denying the break with history that a social contract implied."[54]

This idealist conception deliberately chose to ignore how many bureaucratic practices, laws, and the system of justice were largely inherited from the colonial legacy, "in some cases intact in their original form, and in most cases molded in the colonial mode and ethos, even if promulgated after independence."[55] Consequently, Pakistan was set on its path guided by "an Islam with an open future and tendency toward experimentation."[56] Quoting Wilferd Cantwell Smith, Naveeda Khan holds that the whole country, the society, and the self thus embarked on a "process of becoming," guided by efforts to render all that had already been established into ever more perfect forms, to be led by the question "what was to become of it."[57] To Pakistani citizens in 1947, this new beginning was what set them apart from all other Muslim majority states of the time because they were offering Islam "a political existence that otherwise it has not had for centuries. Yet once again, their claim was based not on what the nation had accomplished but, rather, on the spirit it embodied.[58] To be sure, this embrace of the not-yet-realized and the proclamation of Pakistan as a bold, inspiring vision was no inclusive process. Rather, it came with repeated closures to "illegitimate" forms of striving, which Naveeda Khan sees as culminating in the declaration of the Ahmadis as non-Muslims when the Pakistani state itself tested out its relationship with Islam.[59]

The ʿulama constituted only one group of political actors among many in the early decades of Pakistan's existence. Religio-political parties, most of them under the leadership of religious scholars, did not make significant inroads in West Pakistan until their unprecedented success in the 1970 national elections. The political purchase of this strong showing was further enhanced by the breakaway of Bangladesh, which meant that Pakistan became almost exclusively Muslim after losing the sizable Hindu and Buddhist minorities in its former eastern wing. As members of the National Assembly and coalition partners in provincial governments, the religio-political parties set in motion a process that is usually described as Islamization.[60] Complex politics in this regard under both the elected "secular" president and later prime minister Zulfiqar Ali Bhutto and the "Islamist" military ruler Zia ul-Haq cemented the central role which the ʿulama have since then enjoyed in Pakistani society. Despite his image as a "socialist," the 1973 constitution sponsored by Bhutto was the first to recognize Islam as Pakistan's state religion. The PPP leader shifted the country's economic and cultural orientation toward the Middle East and acted as a strong supporter for the popular Sindhi saint Lal Shahbaz Qalandar in order to cultivate his ties with rural pirs.[61] Under his watch, Pakistan's National Assembly voted in 1974 to declare the Ahmadis non-Muslims "for the purposes of the Constitution or law."[62] In 1976 the Ministry of Education implemented a decision by Pakistan's National Assembly to recognize degrees awarded by *dini madaris* (religious seminaries) as equivalent to bachelor's degrees obtained from the country's universities.[63] This process of opening new career paths for madrasa graduates by drawing them into the state bureaucracy accelerated under Zia ul-Haq despite occasional vocal protests by certain ʿulama who feared a state takeover of the religious sphere.[64] While the ruling general and state institutions dominated by his loyalists might have been driven by precisely such considerations of control, their measures empowered and emboldened the religious scholars both quantitatively and qualitatively beyond the confines of the bureaucracy. The percentage increase in madrasa graduates by far outstripped population growth in the 1970s and 1980s. While Pakistan between 1972 and 1981 experienced a population growth of about 29 percent, the number of madrasa graduates rose by 195 percent during this time period and by 85 percent between 1981 and 1984.[65] Additionally, the ʿulama have been largely successful in repelling attempts by the government to reform the madrasa curricula.[66] This surge in status and influence is still palpable. ʿUlama not affiliated with the state have continuously demonstrated their ability to challenge and outflank official organs like the Council of Islamic Ideology by insisting on implementing Islamic law according to their definition.[67]

In this context, then, the military rule from 1977 to 1988 with its emphasis on "Islamization" of the state was not so much a deviation and a clear break with previous Pakistani politics as a continuation of striving with a stronger emphasis on the ʿulama. After 1979, those religious scholars who later went on to found the SSP came to see Shiʿi Islam as an ideology that threatened to undo the very idea of Pakistan as a God-given (*khuda dad*) Islamic country.[68] In their view, imposing a final solution in the form of vilayat-i faqih was a real concern. Keeping Pakistan's Sunni horizon open by organizing its defenders was consequently understood by them as an effective way to counter this threat. That political parties were banned until the end of Zia ul-Haq's rule, leaving religious organizations as one of the few alternatives for mobilization, might have helped their efforts in this particular moment of Pakistan's history.[69] At the same time, however, the hostile relationship to Shiʿi Islam in general and Iran in particular was much more dialectical than these sectarian authors would be willing to acknowledge. Muhammad Qasim Zaman has pointed out similarities between the veneration of the Companions of the Prophet advocated by the Sipah-i Sahabah and Shiʿi attitudes toward their Imams. The group also attempted to substitute commemorations of the Companions' death dates for the powerful Shiʿi mourning ceremonies of Muharram.[70] Their effort to turn Pakistan into a Sunni state "seems, ironically, to be indebted above all to post-1979 Iran."[71]

PREREVOLUTIONARY SECTARIANISM: THE CASE OF IHSAN ILAHI ZAHIR

As has become apparent in the preceding chapters on pre-Partition India and Shiʿi activism, religious polemics and perceived sectarian grievances were long-standing phenomena in the subcontinent. In the wider context of Pakistan's history, the early years of Ayub Khan's military dictatorship from 1958 to 1962 seem to stand out as a period of calm. Andreas Rieck writes that a combination of martial law, strict censorship, and severe prison sentences provided "enough deterrence to prevent all incidents of sectarian violence until March 1961."[72] The 1970s also live on in Shiʿi memory as an era entirely different from the situation today. It was a time when Muhammad ʿAli Naqvi, an early leader and later important inspirational figure for the Imamia Student Organisation (ISO), could openly sell a calendar promoting the group's goals in front of King Edward Medical College in Lahore during the early summer of 1972. "Since the poison of sectarianism had not yet spread in the country during this time," many Sunni students and passersby bought the "beautiful" product, which made no attempt to hide its specific Shiʿi provenance: the calendar featured nothing less than a photo of Imam Husayn's tomb in Karbala, the logo of the ISO, and its slogan, "hayya ʿala khayr al-ʿamal" (Hasten to the best of works), which is part of the Shiʿi call to prayer (*adhan*).[73]

It was only one year later that Ihsan Ilahi Zahir, now back in Pakistan, released his first decidedly anti-Shiʿi publication, *al-Shiʿa wa-l-Sunna* (*Shiʿis and Sunnis*), which became an instant success and had been reprinted nineteen times by 1984.[74] His polemical activity went hand in hand with the development of a political persona. In 1972 Zahir joined the oppositional Tahrik-i Istiqlal (Independence Movement; TI). He first was a member of this centrist party's executive committee (*majlis-i ʿamal*) before rising to the position of general secretary.[75] Attaching himself to a moderate party which mostly catered to the educated middle-class looks like a surprise move on Zahir's part. A possible explanation is the even greater incompatibility of his religious outlook with either the Islamist Jamaʿat-i Islami, the Barelvi Jamʿiyyat-i ʿUlamaʾ-i Pakistan, or the Deobandi Jamʿiyyat al-ʿUlamaʾ-i Islam. But Zahir's animosity toward Zulfiqar Ali Bhutto outweighed even these considerations. The ʿalim later accused Bhutto and the PPP governor of the Punjab, Malik Ghulam Mustafa Khar, of torture in prison and the fabrication of bogus murder charges revolving around the death of a taxi driver.[76] The TI eventually united with the religious parties mentioned and some additional groups to contest Bhutto's PPP in the 1977 elections under the umbrella of the Pakistan National Alliance. The resulting election manifesto predominantly focused on the Islamization of Pakistan. Their demands included the banning of coeducation, obscenity, alcohol, financial speculation, and programs promoting family planning.[77] Zahir left the TI after Zia ul-Haq's coup in 1978, according to his own testimony, due to his disappointment with the political inexperience of the Tahrik's founder, the retired Air Marshal Asghar Khan, and the party's "naive" stance in the face of Zia ul-Haq's efforts to splinter the opposition.[78] In the years until his death, Zahir moved from reserved optimism about the general's motives, manifested by accepting his invitation to become a member of his ʿulama advisory council, to an increasingly hostile attitude toward the military dictator.[79] He took issues with Zia ul-Haq's repeated efforts to get a "Shariat Bill" passed, which was supposed to make the shariʿa the law of the land, and denounced a proposed extension of prerogatives of the Federal Shariat Court to areas like personal or fiscal law. Zahir dismissed these initiatives as thinly veiled initiatives to consolidate power.[80] His criticism also applied to those Deobandi ʿulama who supported the Shariat Bill in the hopes of pushing through a purely Hanafi version of Islamic law.[81] Even more abhorrent for Zahir was the potential damage the general could inflict on Islam with his "wrong" program of Islamization. In the same way that Bhutto had effectively acted as gravedigger for socialism in Pakistan by merely posing as a socialist, Zia ul-Haq could set a similar process in motion for Islam by pretending to be a committed Islamist.[82] Zahir already noticed signs that the common people were turning away from religion because they did not perceive any improvement in morals or the lowering of crime rates in an outwardly Islamized society.[83] In countering these dangers, Zahir did not join the left-leaning Movement for the Restoration of Democracy, an alliance of several parties; rather, he devoted himself to revamping the troubled Ahl-i Hadis organization, giving it more public visibility.[84] After taking over the position of general secretary and later chairman, Zahir embarked on a series of high-profile public speaking engagements across Pakistan and also initiated the purchase of a new property at 53 Lawrence Road in Lahore. Construction soon started for an ambitious religious center with a mosque, hospital, madrasa, and auditorium, but Zahir was killed before this grand project could be completed.[85]

Yet Zahir's active political life is strangely absent from his anti-Shiʿi polemics. None of his works, whether they were written before or after the Iranian Revolution, have any overtly political components. This choice puts him in stark contrast to ʿulama affiliated with the SSP, as I show below. In his 1982 book *al-Shiʿa wa-ahl al-bayt* (The Shiʿa and the members of Muhammad's household), for example, Zahir neither touched on the Iranian Revolution nor current politics. He mentioned as his main reason for writing the work the realization that the Shiʿis themselves were deeply ignorant about the true teachings of their sect (*fa-hum fi jahl kamil wa-ghafla ʿamiqa ʿan haqiqat madhhabihim*) and misled under the pretext of love for the members of Muhammad's household (*makhduʿin bi-ism hubb ahl bayt al-nabi*).[86] Explaining his motives for penning polemical works, Zahir never referred to current political events either. Rather, he located his own interest for clearly establishing and demarcating the boundaries of orthodoxy within the context of his upbringing in the Punjabi city of Sialkot. There he encountered (in his terminology) Ahmadis, Bahaʾis, Barelvis, Deobandis, Hanafis, Wahhabis, and Shiʿis. It was an atmosphere in which ʿulama affiliated with one of these various sects were always ready to plunge headlong into a religious debate (munazara). Since Zahir himself had a passion for public speaking, this particular environment encouraged him to explore the reason for the emergence of sects.[87] This deep interest and pondering of religious differences, he claimed, enabled him to discern the futility of all efforts at taqrib, rapprochement with the Shiʿis. Demonstrating the impossibility of unity as long as Shiʿis retained their allegiance to the tenets of their school was the main concern of his first anti-Shiʿi work:

> Away with this sort of unity [*wahda*] which is raised at the cost of Islam. To hell with the harmony [*ittihad*] which is built on aversion [*iʿrad*] from Muhammad the Prophet, his Companions, and his wives [. . .]. God [. . .] has taught us in His word [about a similar situation]. We believe that not a single letter of His word has been modified or changed, and not one word has been added and not a letter has been taken away from it. God has taught us in it that the unbelievers [kuffar] of Mecca also demanded from the reliable, trustworthy Messenger that he should do away with the division and dissension [*firqa wa-ikhtilaf*] of his call to worship God alone [. . .] and the denunciation [*ifdahuh*] of their goddesses and his rejection of them. He answered them with the command from God: "Say: 'O unbelievers, I serve not what you serve and you are not serving what I serve, nor am I serving what you have served, neither are you serving what I serve. To you your religion, and to me my religion.'"[88]

This emphasis on the proper Sunni belief in the integrity of the Qurʾan tied in for Zahir with a lack of respect for the divine book on the part of the Shiʿis, manifested in their alleged belief in its alteration (tahrif). The Pakistani Ahl-i Hadis scholar could point to important early Shiʿi Qurʾan commentators such as Furat b. Ibrahim al-Kufi (d. ca. 310/922), Saʿd b. ʿAbdallah al-Qummi (d. end of fourth/tenth century), or Muhammad b. Masʿud al-ʿAyyashi (d. ca. 320/932). These men all held that the names of the Imams had originally been mentioned in the Qurʾan. They also provided several alternate versions for individual verses. Other early writings reported the existence of separate revealed scriptures like the *Mushaf Fatima*, which was supposedly three times longer than the Qurʾan. Al-Kulayni (d. 329/940–41), whose collection *al-Kafi fi ʿilm al-din* is counted among the foundational works of the Shiʿi tradition, referred to a report of ʿAli who said that the Qurʾan had been revealed in three parts. The first part discussed the Imams and their enemies, the second part the exemplary deeds of the Prophet, and the last part religious commands and obligations.[89]

For Zahir, this tenet was worse than the Shiʿis' deification of their Imams or their machinations against Muslims, which had resulted, for example, in the fall of Baghdad to the Mongols in 1258 or the breaking away of Bangladesh due to actions of Pakistan's former Shiʿi military ruler Yahya Khan, who was in office from 1969–71.[90] Tahrif was the "real and fundamental disagreement" (*al-ikhtilaf al-haqiqi al-asasi*) between the Sunnis and the Shiʿis. A human being who did not believe that the Qurʾan recited today was exactly the one that Muhammad had propagated did not qualify as a Muslim.[91] Zahir's argumentation is very much in tune with other polemical writings in the twentieth century that identified tahrif as the "disagreement *par excellence*" at a time when among Shiʿi ʿulama no public voice could be found actively propagating this idea.[92] Rainer Brunner, for example, identifies Abu 'l-Qasim al-Khuʾi as the exponent of an "official" Shiʿi conception of tahrif that was prepared to disavow parts of the Shiʿi hadith corpus which claimed that ʿAli's copy of the Qurʾan was significantly more voluminous than today's Qurʾan. Al-Khuʾi was not willing, however, to also explicitly denounce the idea that the only true interpretation of the heavenly book rested with ʿAli.[93] Zahir repeatedly defended another anti-Shiʿi bestseller of the twentieth century, Muhibb al-Din al-Khatib's *al-Khutut al-ʿarida*, and also shared al-Khatib's argument that intimate knowledge of medieval Shiʿi texts was crucial for making sense of contemporary Shiʿism.[94] Like al-Khatib, Zahir was worried about Shiʿi attempts to seize the momentum of rapprochement in the wake of Mahmud Shaltut's fatwa, as mentioned in the last chapter. Zahir explained in the preface to his book *al-Shiʿa wa-l-tashayyuʿ: Firaq wa-tarikh* (The Shiʿa and Shiʿism: Sects and history) that the Iranian Revolution had added new urgency to this topic—a fact he had witnessed firsthand during a visit to the United States in September 1983. During his interactions with various mosque congregations, Zahir was bombarded with questions on the Shiʿis and their disagreements with the Sunnis. He was trying hard during these sessions to convince the brothers to situate Shiʿism where it belonged: far removed from proper Sunni Islam.[95] Yet he explicitly did not see the Iranian Revolution as a *political* threat to Sunnis in Pakistan and beyond. Commenting elsewhere on the Iran-Iraq War, for example, Zahir did not condone Iraq's attack as a necessary effort to contain the Iranian danger. Instead, he deplored this rupture in the unity of the Islamic world that promptly came to be exploited by the Soviet Union, which otherwise would have not managed to so easily prolong its occupation of Afghanistan.[96]

This attitude is also representative of how Zahir is remembered among fellow Salafis: as the author of anti-Shiʿi works ʿAbdallah b. ʿAbdallah al-Mawsili related the story that Khomeini himself sent a messenger to Zahir in order to express his approval of the latter's works on the Babis and Bahaʾis and to invite him to Tehran.[97] Zahir declined the offer, fearing for his safety. Instead, he inquired from the messenger why Khomeini had so far not taken any action to purge classical Shiʿi books from insults of the Companions (*sabb al-sahaba*). He did not, however, express any critique directed at the politics of Iran.[98] Also, Zahir's books reprinted after 1979 continued to feature passages that castigated the Shiʿis for their passivity, lack of practical piety, and nonrevolutionary outlook, so to speak. During the Occultation of the Twelfth Imam and the absence of the Prophet's mission (*risala*) on earth, the Shiʿis did not deem any prescribed rituals obligatory, Zahir wrote. Their ʿulama only demanded from the people "waiting and patience until the appearance of the mahdi who will never appear at all" (*fa-l-tawaqquf wa-l-intizar ila an yakhruj al-qaʾim alladhi lan yakhruj abad al-dahr*).[99] Due to their belief in the corruption of the Qurʾan, the Shiʿis did not feel bound by its commandments—for them religion did not extend beyond love for ʿAli and his descendants (*fa-laysa al-din ʿindahum illa hubban li-ʿAli wa-awladihi*). For this reason, they made up baseless reports (*riwayat batila*), mendacious stories (*qisas kadhiba*), and ridiculous fables (*asatir mudhika*) until there remained no difference between their Imams and divinity (*al-uluhiyya*).[100] But despite his alleged superhuman powers, it was under ʿAli's caliphate that the Jews managed to penetrate (*tasarrub*) the thoughts of the original Shiʿis and to increase the lies in the name of the ahl al-bayt.[101] The Twelfth Shiʿi Imam did not strike Zahir as a likely candidate to remedy the fact that none of the Imams after ʿAli wielded any palpable worldly power. Once the Mahdi returned equipped with ʿAli's legendary sword *Dhu ʾl-fiqar*, Zahir wrote, "I don't know what he will do with this weapon in a time of rockets and nuclear bombs."[102]

During his polemical preoccupation with the Shiʿis and others, Zahir adopted the posture of a discerning visionary who was called to a mission beyond the ugly sectarianism other groups were engaged in. In an interview, for instance, he referred to a newspaper article published in England that had used four portraits to illustrate Islam in South Asia. The piece featured a picture of Muhammad Iqbal as the visionary of Pakistan, of Muhammad Ali Jinnah as the realizer of this dream, of Jawaharlal Nehru as a conspirator with the British to bring about the recognition of the Ahmadis as Muslims—and of himself, Zahir, who had managed to undo the Ahmadi damage to Islam.[103] He even expressed skepticism about forming organizations because it was an all-too-human phenomenon that every *maulvi*, every group, and organization saw itself to be in the right.[104] Since it was the essential belief of the Ahl-i Hadis that the system of the madhhab, the school of law, had endowed mere human interpretations with divine authority, he could claim that his movement was not a *firqa* (sect) or a *jamaʿat* (party); rather, it advocated a system void of *firqah bandi*, of division into various sects. Pakistanis should leave behind them this sectarianism, which their rulers were always quick to take advantage of for their own goals.[105] They should assemble like the inhabitants of Medina during the time of the Prophet, debate, listen, and then make a decision about who was propagating the correct religion.[106] Zahir was at pains to argue that his goal was not to impose a certain version of Islam on his fellow countrymen. Such a view was utterly unrealistic anyway: he did not see a possibility of the Ahl-i Hadis coming to power politically in Pakistan before the Day of Judgment.[107] Instead, he emphasized, Islam was inherently averse to coercion and protected all forms of expression. In this context Zahir's remarks have a very Islamist flavor to them when he argues that Islam is not a madhhab, but a *din* that also guides people in this world. While claiming that parliamentary democracy was the system today which came closest to Islam's ideal, he nevertheless cautioned that a parliament had of course to operate within the boundaries established by religion, which had laid down complete rules (*ek mukammal dastur aur kamil zabitah*) for both spiritual and temporal affairs.[108]

Curiously, it may have been precisely this reluctance to boldly claim the single true interpretation of Islam for his group and to devise a political road map for the solution of the Shiʿi problem in Pakistan that inspired some of his allies to turn Zahir's death into a new beginning. After the funeral prayers in Medina, Zahir's corpse was brought to the Jannat al-Baqiʿ cemetery to be interred there. Some of his close companions uncovered his "dignified face." Suddenly, Zahir in his "unique God-given, thunderous voice" conveyed his last will (*akhiri vasiyyat*) to the Ahl-i Hadis, both assembled and absent.[109] Zahir demanded that rather than laying down their banners (*jhande*) in confronting the forces of falsehood (*batil quvvat*), they pledge their souls for this task. The shahada should be spread in Pakistan, and they should aim to give their last drop of blood while waging jihad and adopting the principles of unity (*ittihad*), organization (*tanzim*), and movement (*tahrik*).[110] This incident is not only interesting in that the dead Zahir gave his own blessing for a more organized, group-based sectarianism, which foreshadowed the Sipah-i Sahabah. It also demonstrates layers of South Asian veneration for the influence and charismatic powers (*baraka*) exerted by dead saints and Sufi masters (pirs) that are at odds with Wahhabi teachings and the crystallized opinion within the Ahl-i Hadis school.[111] The latter in particular went through a process of "disenchantment" that significantly altered previous positions. The biographical literature attributed miracle-working powers to early proponents of the school like Ghulam Rasul (d. 1871). Subsequent ʿulama were still credited with the capability of intercessory prayers (*qabuliyyat al-duʿaʾ*), but their scope became restricted in the twentieth century to cases that were not perceived to contradict everyday reality (*Alltagserfahrung*).[112] Finally, the fact that Zahir's posthumous testimony took place on Saudi soil points once again to the complicated relationship between a supposedly dominant center and its pliable periphery.

PREPARING FOR THE SUNNI ISLAMIC REVOLUTION: THE SIPAH-I SAHABAH-I PAKISTAN

None of these qualms about organizing and venturing into the political field as a decidedly sectarian force are present in the context of the Sipah-i Sahabah. As discussed earlier, the secondary literature portrays the organization as preoccupied with the danger of a Shiʿization of society on the level of the city and district of Jhang. These concerns are clearly reflected in one biography written by a close associate of Haqq Navaz Jhangvi, the founder of the SSP. This work related destructive Shiʿi propaganda efforts to a prominent family of Shiʿi landlords. They had converted from Sunni Islam a generation earlier because only their new sectarian home would serve them as a "safe haven for their luxurious life-styles and free-thinking" (*apni ʿayyashiyon aur azad fikriyon ki panah gah*).[113] Gradually, this elite conversion (so the argument goes) made its way through society, affecting first the peasants whom these landlords controlled and later members of other low-level professions like weavers or shoemakers. Consequently, Shiʿi customs such as mourning processions in Muharram and the public cursing of the sahaba became widespread, to the extent that all differences between Sunni and Shiʿi Islam were eradicated. Each time an upright Sunni scholar came to Jhang to preach proper creed and ritual and elaborated on the differences between the two sects, he would be labeled a troublemaker (*fitnah parvar*), narrow-minded sectarian (*firqah parast*), and an altogether unwelcome individual (*na pasandidah admi*). He would consequently be forced to leave the city. By contrast, Shiʿi preachers were in high demand.[114]

Like his more cosmopolitan colleague Ihsan Ilahi Zahir, the entirely Pakistan-educated Haqq Navaz Jhangvi had not turned to this Shiʿi danger immediately. Jhangvi was born in 1952 and grew up in a rural setting in a village about twenty-five miles northeast of Jhang. He received his religious training locally in Kabirvala, Multan, and, with a special focus on munazaras in Kot Addu. After a short stint at a small madrasa in Tobah Tek Singh, he was hired to teach the Qur'an in Jhang before taking over a permanent position in the city as the preacher of a mosque in August 1973.[115] Jhangvi, too, traveled the well-trodden polemical route of making a name for himself in anti-Ahmadi agitation before focusing increasingly on the Shiʿis.[116] He was a gifted orator around whom Sunni youth flocked like "honey bees around the bee-hive or moths around the candle," because he had found the philosopher's stone (*paras*) of stirring up emotions at religious gatherings: after leaving the venue of his speech, his followers reported, every participant was filled with love for the sahaba and hate for their enemies.[117] Other Sipah-i Sahabah members have compared listening to him to being in the midst of a battle (*maydan-i karzar*) where Jhangvi was pounding the enemy with lightning-like attacks (*bijli ki tarah*).[118] It is not surprising in this context that Haqq Navaz is credited with certain miracles as well: his *karama* (saintly charisma) enabled his supporters to slip through checkpoints, for example. During his funeral in Jhang, pouring rain was interpreted as the reaction of a lover being robbed of his beloved.[119]

Jhangvi could have surely continued on this path, calling for the drawing of boundaries between the sects by invoking South Asian stalwarts of anti-Shiʿi discourse like Shah Wali Allah Dihlavi or ʿAbd al-Shakur Lakhnavi.[120] Yet it was the Iranian Revolution that tipped the balance. Its aftermath entirely reshaped the thrust of Jhangvi's message and convinced him that a coordinated, organized response was needed to counter this assertive manifestation of Shiʿism.[121] A "frightening storm" (*khaufnak tufan*) of anti-Sunni literature swept the world. Authors in Pakistan and beyond could even quote passages from Khomeini's own works which—in their eyes—implicated him in the slander of the Companions, notwithstanding all of Iran's claims to work for Muslim unity. In particular, they pointed to pages in Khomeini's *Kashf al-asrar* (The revealing of the secrets), his first major political work, which had already been published in the early 1940s. Discussing why the names of the Imams were not mentioned in the Qur'an, Khomeini answered that they must have been removed by power-hungry people who corrupted the Qur'anic text. He also mentioned how Abu Bakr and ʿUmar had acted against the Qur'an.[122]

These statements by Shiʿi authors in pamphlets, books, and journals were now no longer simply outrageous because they slandered figures important to early Sunni history. Rather, these efforts had to be seen in the light of directly preparing the way for the Iranian system of government by undermining the support for the caliphate among the people. Ziya al-Rahman Faruqi, who became the third leader of the Sipah-i Sahabah after the assassination of Jhangvi's successor Israr al-Qasimi, remembered that Haqq Navaz called for an urgent meeting in the early 1980s. He had come across a work by the Shiʿi polemicist Ghulam Husayn Najafi (assassinated in 2005) that robbed him of sleep. Jhangvi situated this publication, which accused the second Caliph ʿUmar of having had sexual intercourse with the corpse of his deceased wife Umm Kulthum, within a new wave of *takfir* (declaration of unbelief) directed toward the sahaba and emerging from Iran.[123] Even the fact that Khomeini did not mention the first three Caliphs in his influential work on Islamic government, *Hukumat-i Islami,* was interpreted as a ploy to turn the simpleminded non-Shiʿis into a "tool" (*alah-i kar*) for his sinister goals of exporting the revolution.[124]

Such an evaluation also permeates statements by Abu Muʿawiya Aʿzam Tariq, a subsequent leader of the SSP. Tariq was born in March 1961 and did not come into contact with Shiʿism as a child because there were no Muharram processions in his home village near Multan. He studied first in local madrasas before switching in the late 1970s to Chiniot, where he focused on Arabic and munazaras against the Ahmadis. His local teacher recognized Tariq's passion for religious polemics and provided him with special training sessions, even taking him to nearby Rabvah, the Ahmadi center in Pakistan, for debates with Ahmadi scholars. In 1983 Tariq spent a year at the famous Jamiʿat al-ʿUlum al-Islamiyya in Banuri Town, Karachi, to complete his training in hadith. He met Haqq Navaz Jhangvi for the first time in Karachi in 1985 and joined the SSP a year later. In 1988, he was appointed general secretary for the Sindh chapter of the organization before assuming the same position within the nationwide structure of the SSP in 1991. Tariq became the head of the organization in 1997 and served in this function until his assassination near Islamabad in 2003.[125] Tariq put his opposition to the Shiʿis in the following terms:

> The biggest of all obstacles toward the dominance of Islam [*Islam ka ghalaba*] [. . .] are the Shiʿis because the caliphate is our ideal and our demand whereas for the Shiʿis it is evil [*zulm*] and a system of tyranny, unbelief, and apostasy [*jabr o kufr aur irtidad ka nizam*]. Today, even non-Muslim rulers praise the system of the *khilafat-i rashida,* but the Shiʿis denigrate it constantly. Putting an end to these filthy Shiʿi conspiracies [*napak sazish*] is, therefore, also a part of Islam's victory. [. . .] The Shiʿis have begun their efforts to change the system's design [*shakl o hay'at*] by denying Islam's fundamental belief in God's unicity [tauhid]. [. . .] They claim that the text of the Qur'an is corrupt. They want the Muslims to be cut off from it and claim that the twelve Imams are infallible [maʿsum] and have received revelations [. . .]. Similarly, after declaring the Companions of the Messenger—through whom Islam has been rendered victorious in the world—[. . .] unbelievers, they are busy day and night in cursing and reviling [*laʿnat o malama*] them.[126]

A pressing, worrisome sign for these sectarian Sunni ʿulama was the changing attitude of the Islamist Jamaʿat-i Islami (see chapter 4), which allegedly abandoned its once impeccable anti-Shiʿi heritage and embraced Khomeini as the flag bearer of the worldwide Islamic Revolution.[127] Maududi's critical disposition toward both the third Caliph ʿUthman for his indulgence in nepotism and Muʿawiya for having turned the caliphate into a purely worldly kingdom sounded suspiciously close to Shiʿi views of early Islamic history.[128] Thus inspired by the Iranian danger, Haqq Navaz attempted to build a broad anti-Shiʿi coalition, which originally included also Ahl-i Hadis and Barelvi scholars. These efforts quickly faltered, though, and he decided to go it alone;[129] he founded the Sipah-i Sahabah on 6 September 1985. Grounded in his concern about inroads the Shiʿis had already made in Jhang, his organization actively incorporated Shiʿi symbols and rituals and reframed them in acceptable, Sunni ways. This extended to the SSP flag, which presents the Companions, drawing on a saying of the Prophet, as stars that provide guidance in a way that clearly resembles the Shiʿi Imams.[130] Jhangvi also adopted a preaching style modeled on the outline of Shiʿi mourning sessions, which are commonly divided into a lengthy demonstration of the Imams' virtues (*fadaʾil*) before they proceed to an emotional account of their afflictions and deaths (*masaʿib*).[131] In an analogous instance of institutional isomorphism and mimicry, Jhangvi used to allocate three-quarters of a talk to extolling the high rank of the sahaba, while in the remainder of his time he devoted himself to Shiʿi denigrations of these elevated personalities.[132] More important, Jhangvi called for Pakistan to be imagined and restructured in a way that mirrored Iran by turning it into a "Sunni state." This vision gave the striving over the country's identity since its inception an entirely new spin. Jhangvi envisioned making slander of the Prophet's Companions a criminal offense, called for a ban on the public aspects of non-Sunni worship, and demanded modifications to the syllabi used in the country's schools so that they exclusively reflected the Sunni interpretation of Islamic history. He also promoted the idea of declaring the Shiʿis a non-Muslim minority.[133]

It was Haqq Navaz Jhangvi's successors, however, who elaborated more forcefully on the realization of this goal. While they might be labeled "peripheral ʿulama" in Pakistani society insofar as they did not hold teaching positions in any of the major Deobandi or Barelvi seminaries, their claims (and influence) did not reflect such a modest standing.[134] Instead, they attempted to shed any local connections with Jhang and vowed to turn the movement into a pan-Pakistani and even global organization. One way of reaching new audiences was the group's journal *Khilafat-i Rashida* (*The Rightly Guided Caliphate*), published since March 1990 in an attempt to "popularize the honor of the Companions and to openly announce the kufr of the Shiʿis."[135] These sectarian ʿulama increasingly used their representatives in Pakistan's

National Assembly to make their mission known and to gather support for a bill that would have punished *takfir* of the sahaba with the death penalty.[136] Under the leadership of Ziya al-Raman Faruqi from 1991 until his assassination 1997 in Lahore, the SSP set out to significantly increase its local chapters in Pakistan.[137] It established special suborganizations for students, advocates, and women and expanded internationally to places with a significant South Asian diaspora like the Gulf states, the United Kingdom, and Hong Kong.[138] From being merely an enemy of Shiʿi landlords, Haqq Navaz Jhangvi was turned into an ʿalim primarily concerned with the reestablishment of the caliphate on a worldwide scale.[139] In the next section, I examine the hermeneutic moves on which these SSP leaders embarked in order to muster decisive arguments for their reconstituted caliphate and ground it in the Islamic scholarly tradition.

LIFTING THE SAHABA, FUSING THE CALIPHATE

The ʿulama affiliated with the SSP claimed to belong to the first generation in Islamic history that was able to penetrate all the veils of deception intrinsic to Shiʿism. Ihsan Ilahi Zahir had still been forced to labor hard in order to establish the irrefutable argument of taqiyya (pious dissimulation) as one reason why the Shiʿis could never be trusted, even if they (outwardly) denied the corruption of the Qurʾan, for example.[140] For the scholars of the SSP, there was no longer any need to prove the true character of Shiʿism theoretically, since this was playing out in the open for the whole world to see.[141] Aʿzam Tariq pointed out a worldwide rise of publications against the Iranian Revolution that echoed these views, citing, among others, Manzur Nuʿmani for India, ʿAbdallah Muhammad Gharib for Lebanon, Dr. Musa al-Musawi for Iraq, and Haqq Navaz Jhangvi in Pakistan.[142] The SSP ʿulama could refer to authentic Shiʿi works that were made widely available in the subcontinent for the first time and no longer allowed the Shiʿis to pass as Muslims, something they had tried to do for fourteen hundred years.[143] The SSP devoted itself to extensively extracting and compiling quotes from these Shiʿi writings with the expectation that once "these books have reached the public sphere, the trick of taqiyya will surely become unsuccessful."[144] Aiming beyond Pakistan, these sectarian ʿulama argued that their organization had been the lonely global pioneer in fully comprehending the danger of the Iranian developments.[145] Steps taken in the neighboring country hardly qualified as merely abstract threats: Iran in their view systematically persecuted its Sunni minority. Within the first year after the revolution, twenty thousand Sunnis had been killed without any trial; they had simply been labeled as supporters of the deposed Shah.[146] Sunnis were not allowed to organize and had no representation in the army, the judiciary, or the Iranian Parliament despite allegedly constituting 40 percent of the Iranian population.[147] Even beyond Iran's borders the new regime was active in killing ʿulama in Pakistan. It helped Christian Armenia in its war against Azerbaijan, hatched conspiracies against Bahrain, and was bent on wresting the control over Mecca and Medina from the Saudis.[148] Pakistan's state institutions were all in the hands of the Shiʿis and staffed by bureaucrats eager to please Iran.[149] A man like Khomeini, who relied on bullets to remove his opponents, simply could not qualify as a propagator of a prophetic revolution (Muhammad Mustafa [. . .] *ke inqilab ka daʿi*) but must be seen in the same category as Genghis Khan, Hülägü, or Nimrod.[150] Taqrib and unity, then, were such outlandish terms that they did not even warrant the energy required to refute them as Ihsan Ilahi Zahir had devoted himself to doing.

To further demonstrate the seriousness of the slander by Shiʿi scholars and to make the case for the divinely sanctioned nature of the caliphate, SSP scholars elevated the Companions to unprecedented heights. I would argue that their exegetical strategies in this context are quite similar to those of modern Jihadist authors, who in their political reasoning focus on vague terms of the Islamic tradition in order to appropriate and fill them with their own particular meaning. They thus capitalized, for example, on the elusive writings of classical Sunni theoreticians of the state like ʿAli b. Muhammad al-Mawardi (d. 450/1058). These medieval thinkers operated with the crucial concept of the *ahl al-hall wa-l-ʿaqd* (the people of loosing and binding), who theoretically could depose a caliph who was acting against God's law. Yet al-Mawardi and others chose not to spell out the precise identity of this group because they "wanted to have their cake and eat it. There had to be a point where even a quasi-caliph (not to mention a mere king) forfeited his position, but it was best not to specify where and how, so as not to create an obligation to take action."[151]

The Sunni scholarly tradition in a similar fashion displays a comparable vagueness about the precise status and definition of the sahaba.[152] *Taʿdil* as a technical term in hadith criticism originally denoted that Muhammad's Companions should be seen as collectively free from falsehood in transmitting reports from the Prophet. The concept maintained a difference between this legal probity and more far-reaching concerns about the moral authority of the sahaba.[153] Medieval authors such as Ibn ʿAbd al-Barr (d. 463/1071)—possibly in order to counter Shiʿi arguments—expanded on this notion and granted a special status to this group. In attempting to construct a consensus, they awkwardly papered over "abundant evidence that the Prophet himself recognized some hierarchy among the *Ṣaḥāba*."[154] Consequently, there are important voices who either argued that Companions could lose their status due to errors, that only Companions very close to the Prophet could be considered just, or that they had to be weighed according to their involvement in the First Muslim Civil War between ʿAli and Muʿawiya.[155] Referring to legal debates over the proper punishment for insulting the Companions, Lutz Wiederhold commented that those found their way into legal manuals comparatively late, which "left a wider field for personal interpretations to the legists dealing with these issues."[156] Authors affiliated with the *salafiyya*, on the other hand, emphasized the preeminence of all Companions and specifically included Muʿawiya, whom the Prophet supposedly had recognized as one of his most trusted confidants.[157]

In the case of the SSP, the group's ʿulama utilized the imprecise concept of the sahaba and presented their highly syncretistic views as being perfectly in line with the Sunni mainstream, claiming that they only synthesized existing material and provided a fresh, compelling perspective suitable for the requirements of the present age (*ʿasri zaruraton ke mutabiq*).[158] Ziya al-Rahman Faruqi, for example, numbered the sahaba as 144,000, going beyond even the most extensive claims by Mamluk historians, in order to demonstrate the extent of the Prophet's success in teaching Islam.[159] He insisted—to the utter amazement of even his learned audiences, as he reports—that the sahaba were an essential part of the Qur'an: more than seven hundred verses directly referred to them, whereas there were only twenty-seven *aya*s about Jesus, nineteen about Moses, and nine about Abraham. When Faruqi discussed these views during a visit to Bangladesh, the "ʿulama who were seated [next to me] on the stage all got up and said: 'We have never before taught the Qur'an in such a way that in it God would declare the community of the sahaba to be accomplished (*kamyab*) in their position as a group.' They expressed their confusion about this issue."[160]

The fact that the Qur'an may be silent in listing veneration of the Companions as one of the fundamentals of religion (*usul-i din*) in the vein of the profession of faith (*kalimah-i tayyiba*), prayer, fasting, the hajj, and the alms tax, was no valid objection. Every time the profession of faith was affirmed, the "greatness" of the sahaba was simultaneously (and mysteriously) acknowledged (*sahabah-i kiram ki ʿazamat ka iqrar pushidah he*).[161] Faruqi compared this process to a marriage contract in which the husband only commits himself to providing for his wife's livelihood, although it is implied that he will also cover any additional needs (*bivi ki jumlah zaruriyat*) she may have. In the same vein, it was also obligatory for every Muslim to submit to the group through which tauhid and the *kalimah-i tayyiba* were transmitted.[162]

Faruqi did not stop, however, with (not uncontroversially) applying certain Qur'anic passages like "you are the best community" (Q3:110) in a matter-of-fact tone to the Companions.[163] The two influential commentators al-Tabari (d. 310/923) and Ibn Kathir (d. 774/1373), for example, both stated as their preference that this verse refers not to the Companions but to the Prophet's umma as a whole (as reflected in the Arabic: "kuntum khayra ummatin").[164] Faruqi also made the case that God himself felt obliged to defend the honor of the sahaba.[165] One striking example in this context is Faruqi's rereading of the story of Ibn Umm Maktum, which the Muslim exegetical tradition unanimously identified as the subject of the first verses of sura 80. In this Qur'anic passage God reprimands the Prophet for brushing off this blind Companion after the latter had interrupted a meeting between Muhammad and a group of visiting chiefs from his tribe Quraysh whom he hoped to win over to Islam. According to many commentators on the Qur'an, the Prophet thus adopted erroneous worldly criteria to allocate status and importance, in violation of God's diverging ranking of belief and unbelief.[166]

Yet what Faruqi saw as the real reason for God's intervention via a Qur'anic revelation was that Muhammad had shown disrespect to one of his Companions: "God could not bear the sight of a blind Companion being removed from the Prophet's gathering—and today Khomeini says that they all are kuffar (he shall be cursed countless times)."[167] A similar divine reaction was caused by the father of the first Caliph Abu Bakr: the former had criticized his son for spending his wealth on purchasing and setting free slaves who had converted to Islam. God also acted in order to absolve the Prophet's wife 'A'isha from rumors about adultery in the famous necklace episode.[168] By contrast, God did not come to the aid of Joseph or Mary when they were in similarly precarious situations of being falsely accused.[169] Faruqi concluded that if God was not willing to stay silent when the honor of the Companions was at stake, Sunni Muslims today had no right to do so either. If he, Faruqi, refrained from speaking out, this would mean going against God's own customs (*khuda ki sunnat par cal raha hun*):[170] "It is your obligation to pull out the tongue that will talk foolishly (lit. bark) about Abu Bakr, and to break the pen which will write such things about him [*to jo zaban-i siddiq ko bhaunkegi un ko khincna tumhara farz he, jo qalam likhega use torna tumhara farz he*]."[171]

The SSP built on the existing Pakistani blasphemy laws, which already made any defilement of "the sacred name of the Holy Prophet Mohammed" a crime punishable with death or imprisonment for life. Dating back to the colonial period, these laws were originally meant to protect the religious sensibilities of adherents of the various faiths of British India. Under Zia ul-Haq, legislation had been significantly revised and came to be primarily concerned with insults against Islam, targeting the Ahmadis in separate clauses.[172] Ziya al-Rahman Faruqi and Aʿzam Tariq pressed ahead in a different direction, demanding the death sentence for any insult to the Companions.[173] In order to back their positions up with quotations from the Islamic tradition, these proponents of the SSP utilized vague statements by prominent Sunni ʿulama that emphasized the necessity of punishment following a denigration of the sahaba. Yet these proof texts seldom spelled out the context of the insult, what was said, and with which particular motivation. Neither do these snippets reveal the definition of the sahaba their authors were operating with, which in turn rendered it relatively easy for SSP members to quote these texts while filling them with their own meaning. Faruqi relied on Ibn Taymiyya's (d. 728/1328) first major (and polemical) work *al-Sarim al-maslul ʿala shatim al-rasul* (The unsheathed sword against the vilifier of the messenger) for a clear-cut purpose.[174] He intended to demonstrate how the Umayyad Caliph ʿUmar b. ʿAbd al-ʿAziz (d. 101/720) ordered the severe flogging of a man who claimed that his hatred for ʿUthman had led him to insult the Third Caliph.[175] But the leader of the SSP was not interested in discussing Ibn Taymiyya's far more nuanced viewpoints about the sahaba, which led him, among other things, to clearly differentiate in merit even among the *rashidun*.[176] Similarly, Faruqi quoted Abu Hanifa (d. 150/767), the eponym of the Hanafi school of law, as stating that "someone who denies the Caliphate of Abu Bakr al-Siddiq is a kafir." Malik b. Anas's (d. 179/796) position was given as "anyone who declares the Companions to be unbelievers or misguided" has to be killed, whereas Ahmad Ibn Hanbal (d. 241/855) envisioned a "severe punishment" for any suggestion of vice, shame, or defect related to the Companions.[177] Pursuing this strategy, the SSP thus created a seemingly solid consensus, whereas in reality they reduced the complexity of the Islamic tradition and pushed it into an entirely new direction in the context of the nation-state. For example, Ibn Taymiyya mentions, shortly after the tradition which Faruqi extracted from him, a report quoted by Ahmad b. Hanbal on the authority of the famous transmitter ʿAsim al-Ahwal (d. ca. 142/759). Here a rather measured punishment is proposed. Al-Ahwal reported that he took it upon himself to lash a man ten times for insulting ʿUthman. When the offender repeated his action, he lashed him again ten times, up to a maximum of seventy lashes. For Abu Hanifa, on the other hand, even insulting the Prophet only meant, at the outset, that the offender had willingly excluded himself from the umma. Repentance and a return to Islam was called for. Only if these were not forthcoming would he advocate killing the person in question.[178]

Proceeding with elevating the status of the Companions within the field of practical politics, Faruqi emphasized that the mere actions of Muhammad had not been sufficient to set the Muslim community on its glorious early path. While the goal of a worldwide caliphate had to be the application of the Prophet's shariʿa, today's Muslims were obliged to look beyond an Islam that was only shaped by Qur'an and hadith. Rather, if their call for an Islamic state was not inspired by a deep understanding of the successful system of government put in place by the Rightly Guided Caliphs, it would prove impossible to implement Islam in a practical way.[179] Even Saudi Arabia fell short of this goal; it could only claim to be the single country worldwide that faithfully applied the divinely prescribed punishments mentioned in the Qur'an (*hudud*)—and little else.[180] What the *rashidun* clearly realized was that in their office they had a "special resemblance and connection" (*khass mushabahat aur munasabat*) with the Prophet.[181] Drawing on Shah Wali Allah's *Izalat al-khafa' ʿan khilafat al-khulafa'* (Removing the secrecy regarding the caliphate of the caliphs), Faruqi identified an exoteric (*zahir*) and an esoteric (*batin*) aspect of the caliphate. The first denoted rulership and the authority to give orders (*riyasat aur farmanrava'i*). The second qualified the office of the caliph as a "divine institution" (*iradah-i ilahiyya*) that was on par with prophethood in its aim of providing "reform and welfare for the world" (*ʿalam ki islah o falah*).[182] In making this far-reaching claim, however, Faruqi deliberately misconstrued Shah Wali Allah's approach. The latter had considered the realization of the *batin* and *zahir* aspects of the caliphate as the distinct prerogative of the immediate successors to the Prophet, for which he coined the term *al-khilafa al-khassa* (Extraordinary Caliphate). Only the four *rashidun*—and hence not Muʿawiya, whom Faruqi strove to include in his definition of the sahaba—fulfilled the necessary and related criteria that the Prophet had promised them paradise, singled them out for their trustworthiness and piety, and charged them in his lifetime with some of his duties. Shah Wali Allah recognized Muʿawiya as a rightful ruler within the conceptual framework of *al-khilafa al-ʿamma* which—while enforcing religion—lacks the tight connection with the Prophet that protects it from the temptations of property (*mal*) and following reprehensible inclinations (*hawa*).[183] The era of the Rightly Guided Caliphs thus constituted a "remnant" (*baqiyya*) of the prophetic era; the only difference was that now, instead of uttering explicit verbal statements (*tasrihan ba-zaban mi-farmud*), the Prophet instead provided guidance to the first four Caliphs in dreams.[184] This model of political rule, Shah Wali Allah held, ended with ʿAli, who "deflected the fire of prophethood, of which the flames shot up, in the opposite direction so that its flames vanished into *butun* (levels of esoteric meanings)."[185] Shah Wali Allah elsewhere pointed out that the esoteric aspects of the caliphate in the post-*rashidun* period are carried out by those

> who are concerned with the teaching of the prescriptions of Islamic Law [*al-sharaʾiʿ*], the Qurʾan, and the traditions relating to the Prophet [*sunan*], and with commanding right and forbidding wrong; [and] those who through their words obtain a victory for religion, either through disputation like the dialectical theologians [*al-mutakallimun*], or through sermons like the preachers of Islam, or through their close companionship [*bi-suhbatihim*] like the Sufi *shaykhs* and those who establish obligatory prayer or the hajj, or who guide the people on the path of the acquisition of doing good [*ihsan*], and those who desire devotion to God and asceticism [*zuhd*].[186]

In once again fusing the two aspects that the Islamic tradition in the subcontinent had historically separated, Faruqi tried to elevate the importance and significance of the office of the caliph. In advancing such a claim, however he drew quite close to Khomeini's own conception of vilayat-i faqih. This observation does not only uncover a further instance of local-transnational dialectics in Sunni-Shiʿi sectarianism in Pakistan. It also shows how tempting the Guardianship of the Jurisprudent as an alternative model of sovereignty really was. Sectarian religious scholars in Pakistan were drawn to it because it provided them with the tools to rethink Islam in entirely novel, politicized ways.

THE SHIʿI REACTION

Faced with these changing sectarian discourses, Shiʿi groups and authors in the aftermath of the Iranian Revolution were not inclined to ignore the increasing political connotations of polemics between the two sects. This meant on the extreme ends that Shiʿis too perpetrated acts of at times indiscriminate violence. Instead of mapping these acts of Shiʿi brutality and discussing its justification, however, in this last part of the chapter I focus on a different aspect of the shifting sectarian landscape. As I pointed out in the discussion of Sayyid ʿArif Husayn al-Husayni, responses to the challenges posed by the SSP could take many forms. In the 1980s and 1990s, two distinct Shiʿi strategies become visible. On the one hand, there is a continued call for a proper Islamic revolution, which was supposed to do away with the corrupt and rotten structures of the Pakistani state that had given rise to sectarianism in the first place. On the other hand, and by contrast, there were attempts to influence public opinion against the SSP. Shiʿi authors set out to rally the Pakistani public behind the idea that sectarianism was not so much directed against "heterodox" minorities like their own community as against the continuous existence of their God-given polity itself. What unites these two diverging approaches is that by placing contending visions of the political center stage, those Shiʿi ʿulama and activists who reacted to the sectarian discourses of the SSP found themselves deeply engaged in their own striving relationship with the idea of Pakistan.

Such efforts to recover the original promise of the country manifested themselves in the journal of the Imamia Students Organisation (ISO), which even after the death of al-Husayni openly spoke about the necessity of revolutionary change. In an article titled "Pakistan's Most Important Question and Its Solution," Taslim Riza Khan, the editor of the ISO's journal, *al-ʿArif*, dwelt on his country's global mission: "Pakistan came into existence so that Muslims can be free in a particular region and can, drawing on this independence [*khud mukhtari se*], implement an Islamic system. [Pakistan was supposed to enable Muslims] to build a model society [*misali muʿasharah*] in economic, political, societal, educational, and cultural terms so that the whole world in witnessing these blessings would embrace Islam and breathe with tranquility [*puri dunya Islam ki aghush men a kar sukun ka sans le*]."[187]

By contrast, the contribution continued, Pakistan's reality was dominated by corruption, foreign supremacy, imperialism, injustice, and an exploitation of Islam (*Islam ka istihsal*) for other goals. The country's social system, erected on British political models and infused with Western capitalism, was beyond repair.[188] The dividing wall (*divar*) between the people and the rulers, regardless of whether they were military dictators or elected presidents, stemmed from inherent flaws in the system's structure that logically necessitated such an outcome (*yeh masaʾil is nizam ka mantiqi natijah hen*).[189] Khan added that a new, alternative order could not be constructed in collaboration with the existing religious parties in Pakistan because they split the people along religious lines, thus perverting Islam's unifying power. Only an Islamic revolution could repair these fissures. It would bring to power people whose mind-set was above and beyond sectarianism (*firqah varanah soc se buland o bala*).[190] In order to smooth the way for this postsectarian utopia of Pakistan, *al-ʿArif*—like all Shiʿi publications—was at pains to play up the hidden hands of outside actors as the true culprits behind rising instances of sectarianism. The blame for violence and division was squarely placed on the shoulders of the United States, Iraq, and Saudi Arabia.[191] This was the case, for example, when on 2 May 1986 a bomb blast killed ISO Joint Central Secretary Rajah Iqbal and a former divisional leader in their student dorm at the Lahore Engineering University. *Rah-i ʿAmal* promptly identified the attack as the work of Iraqi operatives who had acted on the behest of the United States to derail efforts of spreading the Iranian Revolution.[192]

Despite the ISO's grand visions for Pakistan's Islamic transformation, members of the group displayed a keen awareness of the lack of unity even within their own Shiʿi camp. An article published on the first anniversary of Sayyid ʿArif Husayn al-Husayni's death implicated Pakistan's Shiʿis in his murder. In the same way that the Kufans had encouraged Husayn to rise against Yazid only to abandon his cause in the hour of need, so today's Shiʿis were guilty of entrusting al-Husayni with leadership without also taking a principled stance with him. This is a contentious argument to make, especially given that it has been used by Sunni scholars to argue that the Shiʿis themselves bear the actual responsibility for their Third Imam's death.[193] The article continued that instead of showing wholehearted support for Sayyid ʿArif Husayn al-Husayni, his coreligionists had entrapped him in useless debates about Shiʿi markers of identity, questioning him about his understanding of the phrase *Ya ʿAli madad* or whether he was opposed to ʿazadari.[194] After al-Husayni's death, the same people restricted themselves to praising him without applying any of the revolutionary lessons he had taught.

> Say, how will Islam benefit from this? If a student would [only] stand outside of his college and every day shout the slogan "My curriculum is great, my teachers are capable"—how will he pass the exams? Can we only become the army of the Imam [*imam ke sipahi*] through the Imam of the Age [*imam-i zamanah*] or by grieving for [the tragic events of] Karbala? I wish that we would realize how [through our own actions] gradually obstacles are set up which we should instead tear down and shatter. The first obstacle is that we [are content to] sit in waiting for the Mahdi until he comes and himself removes all these hindrances.[195]

Most Pakistani Shiʿi voices in the 1980s and 1990s did not share this maximalist response to sectarianism. Instead of calling for an outright overthrow of the existing structures, they chose to petition the state and to reclaim Pakistan as the inalienable fruit of joint Sunni-Shiʿi efforts. Tensions between the two communities were framed as a law-and-order problem and an impediment preventing Pakistan from realizing her true potential. Such a view is predominant in the massive 1,220-page compendium *Tahqiqi Dastavez* (The authentic document), published under a pseudonym in 1997 by a group of Shiʿi ʿulama in response to the SSP leader Ziya al-Rahman Faruqi's *Tarikhi*

Dastavez.[196] Rebutting his claims, the authors turned the tables on Faruqi by drawing on the Sunni hadith tradition. The book notices, for instance, that verbal slander among the Companions had occurred frequently in early Islamic history without resulting in either an intervention by the Prophet or a punishment of those involved. Building on these examples, the authors affirmed the universal Muslim consensus that insulting the Prophet should result in the death penalty, which—as they claimed—did not apply for slandering the Companions. Although the anonymous Shiʿi writers could adduce supporting evidence for their view from early and medieval authorities and quote modern South Asian Hanafi scholars, their exegesis nevertheless strikes the reader as just as one-sided and uncomplex as the treatment of the matter by the SSP.[197] In particular, they paid no attention to Sunni authors' attempts to synthesize views on the subject. For example, the Shafiʿi jurist Taqi al-Din al-Subki (d. 755/1355) had held that merely insulting a Companion in a worldly matter (*amr dunyawi*) would not put the offender beyond the pale, whereas *sabb al-sahaba* that included *takfir* "may be punished by the death penalty unless the blasphemer repents." Subki made it clear, however, that for him the *rafidi*s in their enmity toward Abu Bakr and ʿUmar clearly belonged to the second category.[198] The problem of reading certain views into the material also comes up in a quotation from Ibn Taymiyya's *Minhaj al-sunna al-nabawiyya* (The method of the prophetic precedent), where the Damascene scholar dismissed the "My Companions are like stars" hadith, favored by the SSP, as weak.[199] Yet the Shiʿi polemicists conveniently overlooked the context of Ibn Taymiyya's evaluation: his Shiʿi adversary al-ʿAllama al-Hilli (d. 726/1325) had used the stars hadith, which addressed all Companions as equal sources of guidance, to argue from Sunni sources against the preeminence of Abu Bakr and ʿUmar. Consequently, Ibn Taymiyya, was keen to extol the status of the first two Caliphs—a motivation he hardly shared with the Pakistani Shiʿi ʿulama, who seized the quote without any regard for its context.[200]

The main argument of the *Tahqiqi Dastavez*, however, is that sectarianism was responsible for making Pakistan forfeit its great potential to become "the example of an outstanding Islamic state."[201] The Sunni entity advocated by the SSP was unable to realize this calling and was doomed to fail due to the unbridgeable internal tensions among Deobandis, Barelvis, Ahl-i Hadis, and others.[202] Further, the SSP only posed as a religious group: it should in fact have been seen as a security problem that warranted the government's fist, not the negotiation table. The SSP was no more than a tiny and criminal splinter group within a larger Deobandi context that had always been opposed to the creation of Pakistan.[203] This argument, which contrasted Shiʿi sacrifices and leadership for the nation's creation with Deobandi hostility to the Muslim homeland, is echoed in many other writings of the time.[204]

Yet the authors of the *Tahqiqi Dastavez* maintained that not all hope was lost for Pakistan. The country's initial promise of constituting the true "reflection of Qur'anic teachings" and acting as the "interpreter of the Prophet's sunna" (*qur'ani taʿlimat ka a'inah dar aur sunnat-i nabavi ka tarjuman*) could still be grasped.[205] To do this, Pakistanis would need to reach back to the inclusive ʿulama convention of January 1951, to which the Deobandi ʿalim Ihtisham al-Haqq Thanavi had invited representatives from all Islamic sects. During their meeting in Karachi, the thirty-three assembled religious scholars had agreed on twenty-two principles of an Islamic state.[206] For the Shiʿis, clause 9 was particularly important, since it enshrined the right for each "established Islamic sect" to be bound by its particular interpretation of Islamic law.[207] The *Tahqiqi Dastavez* also quoted at length Ihtisham al-Haqq's remarks in the newspaper *Musavat*: "The terms 'minority' or 'majority' are purely political terms which are given weight in the collaboration over political rights or in order to decide political questions. If one uses, however, the criteria of minority or majority in the context of the religious rights of Islamic sects, this would mean giving rise to the gravest danger of internal dissent [*fitna*]." According to Ihtisham al-Haqq, every Islamic sect was only bound by its own interpretation of the Qur'an and the sunna according to its most respected and reliable books. Referring to the ʿulama convention, he expressed the shared agreement that "those people who widen the gulf of sectarianism in an unscholarly and unconstructive manner [*ghayr ʿilmi aur ghayr taʿmiri andaz men*] [. . .] do not only play with the fate of Pakistan but convey to other nations an image of Islam which shows that in the present age the experience of an Islamic system has failed."

To drive home this point about the necessity of closing ranks, the Shiʿi authors employed an extensive and highly political definition of tauhid. According to them, the "unicity of the Islamic nation" (*tauhid-i millat-i islamiyyah*) should be considered the "most fundamental basis" (*asl al-usul*) of all Islamic teachings. In the same way that Muslims were prohibited from associating any partner with God, they should also not endanger the unity of their community. Only by drawing on this "fountainhead of faith-power" (*imani taqat ka sarcashmah*) could the umma confront the world of unbelief and tyranny.[208]

Reaching back to Shiʿi voices of the 1980s and 1990s, then, this chapter and previous discussions of Pakistan's first decades and the colonial period have pointed to the historical depth of such discourses directed against sectarianism. This depth, I would contend, is vital if one wants to make sense of Shiʿi attitudes to sectarianism today. Covering such debates in contemporary Pakistan, Mashal Saif has observed that the particular "theo-political projects" advanced by her Shiʿi interlocutors during fieldwork in 2010 and 2011 ranged from the demand for a secular state to a "sectarianly unaligned Islamic state" and—referring to Javad Naqvi—the implementation of vilayat-i faqih. According to Saif, these diverging visions of the state are "all propelled by the same force—the spectre of violence."[209] Crucial for my argument, she also states that the ʿulama she interviewed all utilized specific aspects of Pakistani history to argue for their preferred polity. They either emphasized that Muhammad Ali Jinnah had envisioned a *Muslim*, not an Islamic state; stressed that Pakistan's raison d'être was to be precisely such an *Islamic* entity; or claimed that Muhammad Iqbal's conception of wilaya perfectly aligned with Khomeini's ideas.[210] These (diverging) positions are all bound up with repeated references to Pakistan's promise and potential as the "best of places"—an issue that Saif notes but does not comment on.[211] Bringing the notion of "striving" into play and situating these arguments within long-standing efforts by Shiʿi ʿulama and activists to reclaim their country, I argue, illuminates why even today Shiʿis "narrativise Pakistani history in a manner that legitimises and animates their particular theo-political projects."[212] More so than simply reacting to violence, they boldly insert themselves into the powerful tradition of reflecting on the uniqueness of Pakistan as a political idea.[213]

CONCLUSION

In this chapter I have argued that the Iranian Revolution constituted a crucial watershed for sectarian discourses in Pakistan. It brought to the fore new actors who superseded Ihsan Ilahi Zahir's influential, ʿaqida-focused polemics. Deobandi scholars relied on many of the arguments popularized by their Ahl-i Hadis coreligionists but framed the intellectual and physical struggle against the Shiʿis as contestations about the future character and ownership of the Pakistani state. By contrast, often-repeated arguments about the importance of local economic grievances or clear-cut Saudi Arabian (or Wahhabi) agendas are not reflected in the literature produced by ʿulama affiliated with the SSP. Drawing on Naveeda Khan's observation on Pakistan as a country suspended in a "striving" relationship with Islam, I contend that for the SSP the possible export of the Iranian model constituted a particular moment of threatening closure to this open-ended process of envisioning their country. In formulating their answer to Khomeini and the Islamic Revolution, they attempted to exclude the Shiʿis from the Muslim community and thus from partaking in the collective deliberations about Pakistan. The Shiʿis and their rival ideology were a major stain on the pure Muslim land which the ʿulama affiliated with the SSP hoped to bring about. In countering this danger, they drew on the vague and flexible concept of the sahaba. The religious scholars whom we have encountered in this chapter were inspired to reimagine the importance of the Companions as political actors, endowing them with an unprecedented status. In addition, by creatively reinterpreting the South Asian scholarly tradition they attempted to reclaim the caliphate as a divinely sanctioned office that resembled and transcended Khomeini's conceptions of vilayat-i faqih. SPP activists were tempted by the potentials of political sovereignty that went beyond a mere application of Islamic laws. Importantly, such a move should also be seen as part of an internal Sunni struggle. Maududi, for example, had envisioned the caliph as a purely political office, "as a tool to legitimise political rule."[214] Shiʿi ʿulama and activists responded to these SSP attacks by advancing alternative forms of envisioning Pakistan as a political utopia within reach. Some of them made the case for redoubled efforts to bring about an Islamic Revolution that would do away with all foreign-fabricated dissensions among the Muslims. The more mainstream reaction of the Shiʿi ʿulama, however, was to urge the Pakistani public to reach back to its ecumenical early years and to reclaim the squandered promise their polity had originally entailed.

CONCLUSION

South Asia, the Middle East, and Muslim Transnationalism

When the AISC president Navab Mir Fazl ʿAlikhan from Bigan Pali lashed out against Lucknow's ignorant ʿulama in 1928, he was riding the high tide of anticlericalism.[1] Confident that modernist landowners like himself were the new and enduring face of Shiʿi leadership, he would have had trouble to make sense of the main Shiʿi organization in contemporary Pakistan, founded exactly eighty years after his speech. Undoubtedly, the Majlis-i Vahdat-i Muslimin (Council of Unity of Muslims) would have surely impressed ʿAlikhan with its demonstrated street power. In 2012, it managed to assemble 250,000 participants in Karachi for a rally in protest over the "Shiʿi genocide" in Pakistan. Yet the upper echelons of the party, overwhelmingly composed of religious scholars, would have struck the landlord as utterly retrograde.[2] Similarly, ʿAlikhan's training in Persian as part of a traditional ashraf education would have enabled him to follow with ease the highly Iranianized Urdu in which Javad Naqvi addresses his audiences in today's Lahore. But because he was politically active during a time when both Atatürk and Reza Shah were held up as political role models for India's Shiʿis by the AISC, ʿAlikhan in all likelihood would have struggled to grasp the necessity, not to mention the wisdom, of putting clerics in charge of government and the state.[3]

These contrasts vividly underline some of the fundamental transformations that Shiʿi Islam in South Asia experienced over the last century. The ʿulama appear to have forcefully reclaimed lost ground, warding off all challenges mounted on their authority. The Shiʿi community strikes the observer as having shifted its gaze entirely away from the subcontinent, becoming more integrated than ever into the circuits of the Shiʿi transnational. Sectarian violence between Sunnis and Shiʿis has seemingly become the main fault line that enforces internal unity and pushes aside any conflicts between Shiʿis. This book, however, has mapped far less linear processes of how the three interrelated questions of religious authority, sectarianism, and transnational ties have evolved. Instead, I have shown the many different layers of how South Asian Muslims have been engaged in far-reaching attempts to redefine and relocate centers of authority in modern Islam. Shiʿi ʿulama and intellectuals in the late colonial period conceived of themselves not necessarily as a double minority within a Hindu-dominated India but as a spiritual elite vis-à-vis the Sunnis. Shiʿi barristers proclaimed that the All India Shiʿa Conference as a site of modernizing collective deliberation would relegate Lucknow's old-fashioned mujtahids to the qaum's periphery. Esoteric Shiʿi preachers after Partition challenged claims to orthodoxy made by reformist scholars in Pakistan. They pointed out that Khomeini and other leading clerical figures also belonged to their camp. In their view, the subcontinent was brimming with miracles of the Imams no less than the shrine cities of Iran and Iraq and was thus a pure Muslim land in its own right. Far from rejecting or passively accepting the towering role of the marajiʿ, Pakistan's Shiʿis rethought their own position as meditators and brokers of such extranational authority. In the same vein, the Iranian Revolution was first of all an impetus that provided an attractive discursive foil. Pakistani scholars strove to become associated with the Islamic Republic and the appeal of transnational Shiʿism. At the same time, they carefully controlled the import of messages emanating from Tehran to their own country. Crucially, these observations hold true for Sunni thinkers and ʿulama studied here as well. While for Shiʿis the whole-hearted embrace of Pakistan as a model Islamic state remained a stretch, the sectarian thinkers of the Sipah-i Sahabah did not face the same constraints. They alerted the public to the perceived political threat of Shiʿism, called for the establishment of a Sunni Islamic state, and made the case that they were committed to unearthing Pakistan's buried promise. In their speeches and books, these sectarian figures referred to debates that had surrounded the founding of a home for the Muslims of the Indian subcontinent in 1947. ʿUlama affiliated with the SSP held that through the implementation of their exclusivist program, Islam could finally come into its own in the modern world and thus provide a Deobandi-inspired model to be emulated on a global scale. This was a conception of Pakistan that held no space for Shiʿis due to its narrow and sectarian understanding of the "Land of the Pure."

Moving on from these findings, I reflect in this conclusion on two comprehensive issues. My first goal is to briefly compare the experiences of the Pakistani Shiʿi community with their Indian coreligionists after Partition. Second, I explore some of the implications of my approach for broader connections between South Asia and the Middle East. As far as India is concerned, the country's Shiʿis were more hesitant to build on the transnational potentials uncovered in chapter 1 and less enthusiastic about orienting themselves toward the shrine cities of Iran and Iraq, as chapters 2 and 3 discussed for Pakistan. In part this might be because the community inherited an extensive Shiʿi infrastructure of madrasas and associations. Sayyid ʿAli Naqi Naqvi, who has made frequent appearances in this volume, remained in India and exerted a commanding presence as a senior, Lucknow-based mujtahid. Leaving the pan-Shiʿi world of seminary scholarship in Arabic and Persian behind, in the last fifty years of his life he shifted his focus to addressing the pressing intellectual and social issues of his Indian followers. He tackled these concerns in accessible Urdu writings and quite frequently from the pulpit during majalis.[4] Sayyid ʿAli Naqi Naqvi strove to emphasize the continuous relevance of religion in the face of what he perceived as Westernizing and secularizing trends among Indian Muslims. He therefore encouraged his coreligionists to follow a model of "detached cooperation" with the political order "for the sake of general peace in society."[5] Such an India-centric approach is carried on by the prominent contemporary cleric Sayyid Kalb-i Sadiq, who descends from the famed *khandan-i ijtihad* and is a vice president of the All India Muslim Personal Law Board.[6] Renowned as a majalis preacher, he is involved with a wide range of charitable projects and puts a "comprehensive" notion of justice at the center stage of his outreach to Indian society as a whole. Muslims are supposed to strive for a socially just world in which the rights of all human beings irrespective of religion and gender are guaranteed.[7] Although he is a muqallid of ʿAli al-Sistani, Kalb-i Sadiq claims the right for independent thinking and to decide how to apply his marjiʿ's rules to the specific South Asian context.[8]

In general, however, Shiʿi Islam in India seems to be weighed down by its glorious past, which tends to drown out the present. The splendor of the Shiʿi Navabs is still on display in Lucknow, a city that is famous in scholarship and public perception for its "refinement" and nostalgic longing for a supposedly luxurious and harmonious but bygone area. Yet it is precisely this unique mythologization of Lucknow that brings the much bleaker present of crumbling Shiʿi madrasas and institutions in decline into even sharper relief.[9] After independence, the erstwhile patronage of leading Shiʿi notables such as the Navab of Rampur was no longer forthcoming. The Mahmudabads, while still hosting mourning ceremonies at their palace today, were engaged in their own struggle to reclaim their extensive landholdings that had been declared "enemy property" by the Indian state during the 1965 war.[10] Another major difference about Pakistan, beyond the diverging personal and material resources right after independence, is also the extent of sectarian conflict between Sunnis and Shiʿis. To be sure, India had its fair share of anti-Shiʿi polemics. These publications also saw an increase after the Iranian Revolution. Tensions resurface regularly in conjunction with Muharram or regarding the issue of tabarra.[11] Shiʿi activists in particular regularly attribute these to political juggling in UP, fueled by attempts of the nationalist Bharatiya Janata Party (BJP) to split the Muslim "vote bank." Scholars have voiced skepticism about explanations in this vein and have instead highlighted economic rivalries, most prominently in the real estate sector, as an aggravating factor. Also, intra-Shiʿi competition over authority within the community could quickly take on anti-Sunni, intersectarian overtones. Such processes can be observed in the push by certain factions for an alternative All India Shia Muslim Personal Law Board or in the context of debates regarding new forms of middle-class morality.[12] In the grand scheme of things, however, the dynamics involving citizenship are entirely different in twenty-first-century Pakistan and in India. Whereas the Iranian Cultural Center in Lahore, for example, is a heavily secured fortress, manned by a machine gun nest and guarded by the police and private contractors, in Delhi the visitor can simply walk into its sister institution.

Beyond rethinking the religious history of the subcontinent, the findings of this book also have important implications for the study of modern and contemporary Islam on a more transnational and even global scale. Disciplinary traditions and the modern nation-state system have obscured from our view the intimate and competitive relationship between the Middle East and Muslim South Asia. Muslim scholars in both regions, Sunnis and Shiʿis alike, can draw on a rich, often shared heritage of texts, institutions, and revered personalities. Despite obvious barriers in language, the two regions form a common discursive space for ideas and religious concepts. This does not mean that we necessarily see generic forms of global Islam emerging that are "valid in any cultural context" even "beyond the heterogeneity of societies and cultures."[13] Rather, local and especially national lenses remain crucially important in modifying and reshaping modern visions of Islam.[14] I emphasize, however, that these conceptualizations do not respond exclusively to local questions but are also formulated with an envisioned broader reach. To put it differently, transnational linkages and the forces of globalization have increasingly encouraged South Asian Muslims to "think big." The book has shown that Sunnis and Shiʿis from the subcontinent do not accept being relegated to the periphery (or semiperiphery, relative to more far-flung areas of the Muslim world, like Central Asia) of a global Islamic system.[15] Instead, they emphasize the historical contributions of Muslim thinkers from their region and strive to be recognized once again as a major center of religious authority and even hermeneutical hegemony.[16] These efforts might also be seen as an attempt to stem the fragmentation of religious authority and reorient the contemporary Islamic landscape. Many scholars describe the latter as an "ambiguous and ever-changing field" that attracts a growing number of participants.[17]

Similar dynamics of self-assertion are at play with many actors located in but not limited to South Asia. Chishti Sufis, for example, revere their former Shaykh Zauqi Shah (d. 1951) as the true spiritual founder of Pakistan, whereas Muhammad Ali Jinnah only qualified in their view as the "outward" facilitator of the state's inception. The Muslim homeland is thus understood as the teleological culmination of Chishti leadership, which stretches back as far as the eleventh-century Delhi Sultanate. For these mystics, Pakistan is supposed to "assume the vanguard of a global Islamic renaissance," a task which their Sufi brotherhood already prepares for by expanding on a transnational scale.[18] In a comparable vein, Tahir al-Qadri (b. 1951), head of the neo-Sufi organization Minhaj al-Qur'an, which is active in over fifty countries and has its headquarters in Lahore, lays claim to being not only a "global *mufti*" but also a "global Sufi master." In contrast to the Qatar-based jurist Yusuf al-Qaradawi, to whom the first label is most commonly applied, al-Qadri is fluent not only in Arabic but also in English and Urdu. His global ambitions to be perceived as an influential legal thinker came to the fore with his publication in 2010 of a "fatwa" against terrorism that numbered six hundred pages and was released in both English and Urdu versions.[19] A further case in point is the Indian ʿalim Abu 'l-Hasan ʿAli Nadvi (d. 1999), who was known for his close ties to the Middle East. These enabled him to become a visiting professor at Damascus University in 1956 on the invitation of Mustafa al-Sibaʿi (d. 1964), a Syrian Muslim Brother and dean of the freshly established Shariʿa Faculty.[20] Nadvi was also one of the founding members of the Saudi-sponsored Muslim World League (Rabitat al-ʿAlam al-Islami, RAI).[21] He later became marginalized in the League due to his outspoken support for Sufism and his emphasis on the important contributions by South Asian Muslims toward both the shaping of a global Islamic culture and the Islamic renaissance in the modern Arab world.[22] An especially sour point for RAI was Nadvi's staunch support for a major global proselytizing movement that originated in South Asia, the Tablighi Jamaʿat. This organization, which today boasts a global membership of around 10 million people, was perceived as a "serious threat" to attempts to spread Wahhabi interpretations of Islam.[23]

In light of these examples, I suggest a new research paradigm, one that pays attention to the *bidirectional* flows of religious thought between the Middle East and South Asia. In doing so, I draw inspiration from the robust debates in the field of new imperial history, which investigate the mutual influences between Britain and her colonies in the nineteenth and twentieth centuries. Most scholars today agree that imperial encounters and experiments in the colonies shaped perspectives on race, gender, and religion in the "mother country," too.[24] Differences of emphasis persist primarily about how to measure these impacts, especially given that British society itself was "diverse and pluralistic."[25] Such questions, however, have rarely been explored in the field of Islamic studies for the last two centuries. As I have shown throughout this book, conventional wisdom understands the Middle East as a center of scholarship and South Asia as its either reluctant or overly eager periphery. Until now, the reverse transfer of ideas from the Indian subcontinent to Arab countries, Turkey, or Iran has received only limited attention. We still do not know, for example, to what extent the Egyptian reformer Muhammad ʿAbduh (d. 1905) was familiar with and inspired by the writings of Sir Sayyid Ahmad Khan (d. 1898).[26] Groundbreaking works on the construction of Salafism as a modern movement by and large ignore the crucial impact of South Asia in the formation of these ideas during the course of the late nineteenth and twentieth centuries.[27] In his brilliant study on the Islamic University of Medina, Michael Farquhar mentions only in passing the role and influence of Ahl-i Hadis and other South Asian ʿulama teaching at the institution. Instead he concedes pride of place to Muslim Brothers and Salafi scholars from Egypt and Syria. Farquhar credits these men, not their South Asian peers, with steering the curriculum toward an engagement with topics they perceived as detrimental to Islam, such as secularism, socialism, or Zionism.[28] They were responsible for nothing less than an "expansion" of Wahhabism and for helping this school of thought overcome its parochial origins and initial Hanbali-centrism.[29] This lack of interest in the South Asian backstory to modern Salafism is surprising. It disregards the fact that traditionalist scholars in the Middle East in the first half of the twentieth century considered the Ahl-i Hadis and their rejection of the four Sunni schools of law one of the main threats to Islam's further existence.[30] ʿUlama in the Arab world were familiar with the writings of Siddiq Hasan Khan (d. 1889), for example. After marrying the female ruler of Bhopal, Shah Jahan Begum (d. 1901), he had turned this princely state into a powerhouse of Ahl-i Hadis scholarship and printing.[31] Lithographs of his numerous works in Arabic circulated widely in the Ottoman Empire.[32]

A notable exception to this general trend of downplaying the intellectual religious production of South Asia is the discussion of Maududi's influence on the Egyptian Muslim Brother Sayyid Qutb (d. 1966). The latter appropriated Maududi's views of Islam as a stable and comprehensive system (*nizam*), as well as the concept of God's sovereignty (*hakimiyya*) and human servitude.[33] Radicalizing his South Asian source of inspiration, Qutb merged formerly distinct concepts of jihad and revolution.[34] Leading figures of Islamist organizations in Egypt kept such a reading alive and explicitly referred to the founder of the Jamaʿat-i Islami, thus underlining his continuing importance in the Middle East.[35] But even in this comparably established and well-researched case of a substantial conceptual transfer, the "concrete course of the reception" remains unclear. Some scholars have advocated the importance of nine crucial writings by Maududi, circulating in Arabic editions among members of the Muslim Brotherhood in Cairo by 1951. Others, however, have underlined the salient intermediary role of Abu 'l-Hasan ʿAli Nadvi in making South Asian Islamist thought available to Egypt and the wider Arab world.[36] Beyond Maududi and in a different context, Stéphane Dudoignon has drawn our attention to the ways in which Persian-speaking Sunni ʿulama in the cities of Zahedan and Saravan in eastern Iran have established themselves as important "intermediaries between the Indian cradle of the School of Deoband and its new horizons in the Middle East and ex-Soviet Central Asia."[37]

Much work remains to be done to situate these pioneering studies within wider trends and to recover the importance of the subcontinent for modern Islamic thought. This book has shown the complex negotiations of closeness and distance among South Asian Sunnis and Shiʿis when facing the Middle East. Combined with their self-perception as being able to provide decisive answers for the most pressing religious questions in the region and beyond, this challenges us to rethink center-periphery relations in modern and contemporary Islam. Many fruitful avenues of further investigation suggest themselves. In the context of Shiʿi Islam, I find it rewarding to explore how scholarly works produced during Lucknow's zenith as a hauza in the late nineteenth and early twentieth centuries were received and commented on in Iran and Iraq. Current efforts by South Asian Shiʿi students and scholars in Qum to republish many of these writings should render such a task significantly more feasible.[38] Similarly, we currently do not have a clear grasp to what extent long-standing South Asian sectarian discourses have left their traces in current Middle Eastern debates. Pursuing these lines of inquiry, I propose, will significantly improve our understanding of how authoritative religious centers and conceptions of a pure Muslim land are made, unmade, and reconfigured in modern Islam.

GLOSSARY

adhan: Muslim call to prayer
ahadith: sing. of hadith
ahl al-bayt, ahl-i bayt: "people of the house" of the Prophet Muhammad, meaning his daughter Fatima and the Shiʿi Imams
Ahl-i Hadis: South Asian Muslim sect that aims at deriving the injunctions of Islam only from Qurʾan and *hadith*
ahl-i kitab: "people of the book," i.e., mostly Jews and Christians
ahl-i sunnat: Sunni Muslims
Akhbaris: Shiʿi scholars who favor a more literalist reading of the *ahadith* transmitted from the Imams than their Usuli rivals
aʿlam: the most learned Shiʿi jurisprudent of the age according to his followers
ʿalam: flag or banner used for the commemoration of Imam Husayn
ʿalim: sing. of *ʿulama*
Al-i Muhammad: family of the Prophet Muhammad; *ahl al-bayt*
anjuman: voluntary association
ʿaqida, pl. *ʿaqaʾid*: creed
ʿashuraʾ: the tenth day of the Muslim month of Muharram on which Imam Husayn was killed in the year 680
auqaf: pl. of *waqf*
aya: verse of the Qurʾan
ʿazadari: collective term for Shiʿi mourning ceremonies for the Imam Husayn and other members of the *ahl al-bayt*
Barelvis: followers of the school of thought of Ahmad Riza Khan of Bareilly
batin: the inner, esoteric aspects of religion, opposite to *zahir*
bhadralok: new class of "gentlefolk" who arose during the British colonial period in Bengal
bidʿa, pl. *bidaʿ*: unlawful innovation in Islamic law or practice
cadur: Iranian-style outer garment for Shiʿi women
Dar al-ʿUlum: "house of the sciences," a designation for many *dini madaris*
dars-i kharij: the highest cycle of learning at Shiʿi religious seminaries
Deobandis: followers of the school of thought of the Dar al-ʿUlum Deoband
din: religion
dini madaris: religious schools
fadila, pl. *fadaʾil*: virtues of the Imams
faqih, pl. *fuqahaʾ*: specialist in Islamic jurisprudence

faqir: mendicant Sufi
fatwa: a juristic responsa issued by a mufti
fiqh: Islamic jurisprudence
fiqh-i jaʿfariyya: Twelver Shiʿi religious jurisprudence, named after the Sixth Shiʿi Imam, Jaʿfar as-Sadiq
furuʿ, sing. *farʿ*: lit. "branches," the norms of law or religion, parallel to *usul*
ghayba: occultation, denoting the hiddenness of the Twelfth Shiʿi Imam
ghulat, sing. *ghali*: adherents of Shiʿi doctrines that are considered "extreme" by mainstream scholars, often pertaining to their supposedly "heretical doctrines" and "undue" veneration of the Imams
hadith, pl. *ahadith*: sayings and traditions attributed to the Prophet Muhammad or the Shiʿi Imams
hafiz: a Muslim who has memorized the entire Qurʾan
hajj: obligatory pilgrimage to Mecca
Hanafi: one of the four schools of law in Sunni jurisprudence
haram: religiously forbidden
hauza ʿilmiyya: Shiʿi religious seminary of the highest rank
hudud, sing. *hadd*: limited number of punishments mentioned in the Qurʾan
husayniyya: building that holds Shiʿi *majalis*
ijaza, pl. *ijazat*: license a religious scholar has obtained from his teacher to teach and transmit certain religious works
ijmaʿ: consensus of the *ʿulama*, one source of Islamic law
ijtihad: lit. "exerting oneself," technical term for the process of independent legal reasoning on the basis of reason and the principles of jurisprudence (*usul al-fiqh*)
ʿilm: (religious) knowledge
imama: imamate, i.e., the (cosmological) status and role of the Shiʿi Imams
imambargah/imambara: building used for Shiʿi *majalis*
ʿismat: status of sinlessness of the Shiʿi Imams
jalsa: "session"
julus: Shiʿi mourning procession
kafir, pl. *kuffar*: unbeliever
kalima: the Muslim profession of faith
khatib: preacher, orator
khawarij, sing. *khariji*: early and often violent Muslim sect refusing to acknowledge either ʿAli Ibn Abi Talib or Muʿawiya as Caliph
khilafa: caliphate
khums: lit. "one fifth," obligatory payment for Shiʿi Muslims that is handed over to the *marjiʿ al-taqlid* whom they follow, often via his *wakil*
kufr: unbelief
madhhab: can refer to both a school of law within Sunni Islam and religion more broadly
Mahdi: lit. "the rightly guided one," refers to the Hidden Imam who will eventually reveal himself in order to restore religion and bring about a reign of justice

madh-i sahaba: public and poetical praise of the virtues of the *sahaba*
madrasa: school in which the Islamic sciences are taught
majlis, pl. *majalis*: "session," a Shiʿi mourning gathering to commemorate the martyrdom of Imam Husayn and other members of the *ahl al-bayt*
marjiʿ al-taqlid: "source of emulation," the rank obtained by grand ayatollahs, who serve as the highest religious authority for Twelver Shiʿis
maslak: denotes in South Asia usually a particular group within Sunni Islam, such as Barelvis or Deobandis, but can also be used synonymously with *madhhab*
maʿsum: sinless; a quality ascribed to the Shiʿi Imams and the *ahl al-bayt*
matam: Shiʿi mourning ceremony of self-flagellation or other forms of (symbolically) injuring oneself
maulana, *maulvi*: honorary titles denoting Muslim religious scholars
millat: "people," "nation"; in Urdu also used to refer to one's religious denomination
minbar: pulpit in a mosque or also in a Shiʿi *majlis*
muballigh, pl. *muballighun*: preacher
mufti: Islamic jurisprudent who issues fatwas
muhajir: those Muslim residents of Pakistan who migrated to the country during the course of Partition in 1947 or later
mujaddid: the "renewer" of religion
mujtahid: a religious scholar who is qualified to pursue independent legal reasoning (*ijtihad*)
munazara, pl. *munazarat*: religious debate, often polemical and held in front of an audience
munazir: one who is trained to hold religious disputes
muqallid: a lay Shiʿi who is supposed to emulate a *marjiʿ al-taqlid*
muqassir: one who "belittles" the status of the Shiʿi Imams
murid: disciple or follower of a *pir*
mushkilkusha: lit. "Dispeller of Problems," Shiʿi title for ʿAli and other Imams
mushrik: polytheist
namaz: mandatory daily Muslim prayers
navab: denoted a viceroy or a governor of a province in the Mughal empire, title of several rulers of princely states, but also a general designation of rank
nubuwwa, *nubuvvat*: prophethood
pir: a Sufi saint and spiritual director for his followers
qasba: small, predominantly Muslim settlement in North India
qaum: "nation, people, sect, community"; term used by South Asian Shiʿis to refer to their coreligionists
qibla: direction of prayer toward the Kaʿba in Mecca
rafidi, pl. *rawafid*: derogatory term for the Shiʿis as "rejecters" because they do not accept the first three Caliphs as rightful rulers
raʾis: aristocratic title in British India, denoting a landlord
rashidun: the Rightly Guided first four Caliphs of Islam
rauzah khani: the art of leading Shiʿi *majalis*

risala: the prophetic mission
risala ʿamaliyya: legal compendium that a *marjiʿ al-taqlid* issues for the use of his *muqallids*
sadat: pl. of *sayyid*
sahaba (pl.): companions of the Prophet Muhammad
sajjada nashin: lit. "the one who sits on the prayer rug," a descendant of a Muslim saint who controls his shrine and its income
sayyid, pl. *sadat*: a descendant of the Prophet Muhammad
shahada: the Islamic profession of faith
shariʿa: the comprehensive Islamic religious law that covers both mundane aspects and questions of worship
shirk: polytheism
Sufi: a Muslim mystic and saint
sunna: exemplary conduct of the Prophet Muhammad
taʿalluqdar: holder of property rights over an area
tabarra: the verbal profession of disassociation from the "enemies of the *ahl al-bayt*"
tabligh: preaching; propagating one's religion; proselytizing
tafsir: commentary or exegesis of the Qurʾan
tahrif: "alteration," referring to the alleged Shiʿi belief that the text of the Qurʾan has been corrupted
takfir: pronouncing someone a *kafir*
taqiyya: pious dissimulation, legally permissible for Shiʿis to deny their religious identity when facing danger
taqlid: "emulation," following the instructions of a *mujtahid* in questions of religious law
taqrib: "rapprochement," efforts at bringing various Islamic sects and in particular Shiʿis and Sunnis closer together during the course of the twentieth century
taqsir: "degrading," belittling of the status of the Imams
tauhid: unicity of God
tawalla: the profession of loyalty to the *ahl al-bayt*, opposite of *tabarra*
taʿziya: an effigy representing the tomb of Imam Husayn
taʿziya dari: action of parading around *taʿziyas* during a procession
ʿulamaʾ, sing. *ʿalim*: religious scholars in Islam
umma: the worldwide community of all Muslims
usul al-din: principles of religion
usul al-fiqh: principles of (Islamic) jurisprudence
Usulis: Shiʿi scholars who subscribe to the rationalist application of principles of jurisprudence, opposed by the Akhbaris
vilayat-i faqih: "Guardianship of the Jurisprudent," doctrine of clerical leadership that is reflected in the Iranian political system
vilayat-i takvini: attribution of creational powers directly to the Shiʿi Imams
wakil, pl. *wukalaʾ*: representative of a Shiʿi grand ayatollah who collects religious taxes on his behalf

waqf, pl. *auqaf*: religious endowment
zahir: outward, exoteric aspects of religion, opposite to *batin*
zakat: obligatory alms tax
zakir: a popular preacher who holds sermons on the virtues and sufferings of the *ahl al-bayt* during Shiʿi *majalis*
ziyarat: pilgrimage to a Shiʿi shrine
zuljanah: a horse representing Imam Husayn's riding animal, an element of Shiʿi processions

NOTES

INTRODUCTION

1. In the following, I am solely concerned with the Twelver branch of Shiʿism. While Ismāʿīlīs form a substantial minority in Pakistan, particularly in the Northern Areas, their structures of religious authority (and hence their debates) are entirely different, given their reliance on a living, approachable Imām, the Āqā Khān. On the topic, see Holzwarth, *Die Ismailiten in Nordpakistan*; and Marsden, *Living Islam*. On the Bohra community, another smaller Shiʿi sect in the subcontinent, see Blank, *Mullahs on the Mainframe*.

2. For a more detailed discussion of these aspects of Shiʿi worship in South Asia and the concept of *taqiyya*, see chapters 1 and 2.

3. The seminary had been founded in the town of Deoband (located in the Sahāranpūr district of today's Indian state of Uttar Pradesh) in 1866. Modeled on European educational institutions, it combined a reformist orientation with a focus on the study of traditions related to the Prophet Muḥammad (hadith). While "orthodox" Ṣūfism (as defined by them) was taken very seriously by Deobandī scholars, they were highly critical of Shiʿi Islam. The Deobandīs accused the Shiʿis of compromising God's unicity (*tauḥīd*) and denying the humanity of the Prophet Muḥammad as well as the finality of his mission as the last Prophet (*khatm-i nubuvvat*). See Metcalf, *Islamic Revival in British India*.

4. Multānī, "Ahl-i Panjāb ke liye ʿibrat," 3–4. I explore the rise of Lucknow and its importance in the colonial period in chapter 1.

5. On the history of the school and the involvement of Multan's influential Gardezī family in its founding, see Sibṭayn Naqvī, "Iqtibās az diary," 37–38.

6. Kāẓimī, *Imāmiyyah dīnī madāris-i Pākistān*, 2, 533.

7. Robinson attributes the visibility largely to Shiʿi procession and mourning ceremonies. See Robinson, "Introduction: The Shiʿa in South Asia," 353.

8. Rieck, *The Shias of Pakistan*, ix. My figures, which differ from Rieck's, are based on the provisional data of the latest census, carried out in 2017. For details, see https://www.dawn.com/news/1353867.

9. Jones, *Shiʿa Islam in Colonial India*.

10. Illustrative examples are Pinault, *Notes from the Fortune-Telling Parrot*; Hegland, "Flagellation and Fundamentalism"; and Schubel, *Religious Performance in Contemporary Islam*.

11. See, for instance, Kamran, "Contextualizing Sectarian Militancy in Pakistan";

Abou Zahab, "The Politicization of the Shia Community in Pakistan"; Nasr, "The Rise of Sunni Militancy in Pakistan"; and Zaman, "Sectarianism in Pakistan."

12. Rieck, *The Shias of Pakistan.*

13. Naqvi, "The Controversy about the Shaykhiyya Tendency"; Rieck, *The Shias of Pakistan.*

14. Every Shiʿi believer who has not himself reached the level of independent legal interpretation (*ijtihād*) is expected to choose a marjiʿ al-taqlīd whose legal opinions he follows. See especially chapter 3 for a more detailed discussion of the concept. Technically speaking, *marjaʿ* (and, consequently, *marjaʿiyya* as denoting the concept of emulation) are defective transliterations from the Arabic but remain widely used in Western scholarship.

15. In particular, I engage with Khan, *Muslim Becoming*; Devji, *Muslim Zion*; and Dhulipala, *Creating a New Medina.*

16. One example of the contestation approach is Laurence Louër's study about exile politics in the Gulf between the two rival Shiʿi organizations al-Daʿwa and the so-called Shīrāziyyīn. In her work the emphasis is on the politics of rivalry but the substance of the conflict, the arguments employed, and the struggle over religious authority more broadly remains elusive (see Louër, *Transnational Shia Politics*). As far as models of wholesale adoption are concerned, Joseph Alagha has repeatedly made the case that the Lebanese group Hezbollah has since its inception "fully abided by the ideas and opinions of Imam Khomeini as communicated by Khamenei." See Alagha, "Hezbollah's Conception of the Islamic State" and *Hizbullah's Identity Construction*, 45–60. See also Formichi, "Shaping Shiʿa Identities in Contemporary Indonesia." For an example from South Asia and the argument that Hyderabad's Shiʿis defy pressures exerted by Iranian and Iraqi ʿulamā to reform their customs, see Ruffle, *Gender, Sainthood, and Everyday Practice*, 167–68.

17. With respect to related scholarly debates on the "indissoluble duality or dialectic" of the relationship between structure/system and individual agency in the field of culture, see Sewell, "The Concept(s) of Culture," 47.

18. In a different context, Dipesh Chakrabarty has argued that not even the logic of capitalism can have its way unchallenged while transforming relations of labor across the globe in postcolonial settings since "the universal, in that case, can only exist as a place holder, its place always usurped by a historical particular seeking to present itself as the universal" (see Chakrabarty, *Provincializing Europe*, 70). See also Said, *The World, the Text, and the Critic*, 226.

19. Østebø, *Localising Salafism*, 21–22. For another argument on the indigenization of transnational flows from the "metropolises," see Appadurai, "Disjuncture and Difference in the Global Cultural Economy," 295. Roschanak Shaery-Eisenlohr also advocates studying how "religious groups with transnational ties" position themselves in a particular local national setting "against the backdrop of a widely held view that national identifications and religious solidarities with transnational dimensions are separate and irreconcilable forces." She holds that "Hizbullah members selectively choose from the flow of the network those elements that prove useful for their agenda

in Lebanon." See Shaery-Eisenlohr, *Shi'ite Lebanon*, 195–213; and Shaery-Eisenlohr, "Imagining Shiʿite Iran," 17–35.

20. For some recent theoretical considerations of deliberate and selective "transfers" involving ideas and concepts from one national context to the other and the role of cultural brokers, see Paulmann, "Internationaler Vergleich und interkultureller Transfer"; Osterhammel, "Transfer und Migration von Ideen"; Werner and Zimmermann, "Vergleich, Transfer, Verflechtung"; and Middell, "Kulturtransfer und transnationale Geschichte."

21. It is important to point out that while Urdu is both Pakistan's national language and the language of Islamic (and Shiʿi) scholarship in the subcontinent, poetry, music, and popular preaching all can and frequently do happen in Sindhi, Punjabi, Seraiki, Gujrati, or Balti, among many other languages. All these expressions of Shiʿi Islam deserve far more attention in scholarship. For some background information on the local and regional languages mentioned, see Rahman, "Language Policy, Multilingualism and Language Vitality"; Ayres, *Speaking like a State*; and Magnusson, "The Baltistan Movement."

22. For an exploration of how "trans-imperial subjects" managed to inhabit several categories as culture brokers, see Rothman, "Genealogies of Mediation"; and Alavi, *Muslim Cosmopolitanism in the Age of Empire*, 12–13.

23. On such a strategy of elevating one's local standing through claims to influence abroad, see also Saunier, *Transnational History*, 90.

24. For a sophisticated discussion of how the concept of "spiritual capital" might be employed to study the inner dynamics of the Islamic University in Medina, see Farquhar, *Circuits of Faith*, 13.

25. Compare Rieck, *The Shias of Pakistan*.

26. For a critique of transnational history that merely assumes connections without attempting to map the sociocultural background, representative character, and impact of the voices discussed, see Wehler, "Transnationale Geschichte"; and Conrad, *What Is Global History?*, 68.

27. The same also applies of course to Sunni figures when they make an appearance in (chiefly) chapters 1, 4, and 5.

28. For an argument about the importance of connecting discussions of transfers to "identifiable actors and institutions," so that it "should be possible to study intentions, interests, and functions related to the transfers," see Osterhammel, "A 'Transnational' History of Society," 46–48.

29. Rothschild, "Arcs of Ideas," 221–22.

30. For a (slightly dated) account of Iran's internal complexity, see Buchta, *Who Rules Iran?*; and Moslem, *Factional Politics in Post-Khomeini Iran*.

31. For such a danger when comparing historical phenomena, see Kocka and Haupt, "Comparison and Beyond," 20. For a critique of how postcolonial scholarship has frequently operated with a flattened image of Europe that was readily equated with post-Enlightenment rationality, see Cooper, *Colonialism in Question*, 19–22.

32. For a critique of transnational history that focuses only on connections with-

out paying attention to underlying structures of power, thus conferring "agency on everyone who is involved in exchange and interaction," see Conrad, *What Is Global History?*, 70–71, 127.

33. For further reflections on the inherent problems of comparing "boundaries fluctuating in the wake of reciprocal movements between the units of comparison," see Juneja and Pernau, "Lost in Translation?," 105–29. For a perspective that tackles the "reflexivity deficit" of many comparisons in historical time, see also Werner and Ẓimmermann, "Beyond Comparison."

34. See Krämer and Schmidtke, "Introduction: Religious Authority and Religious Authorities"; and Zaman, *Modern Islamic Thought*, 32.

35. Zaman, *Religion and Politics*, 3.

36. Zaman, *The Ulama in Contemporary Islam*, 10.

37. This is not to say that ʿulamā cannot be Sufis and vice versa, but this topic cannot be discussed here at length. For some examples within a vast field of study that investigates the contested notions of religious authority in Islam, see Crone and Hinds, *God's Caliph*; Aigle, "Essai sur les autorités religieuses"; Berkey, "Popular Culture under the Mamluks"; Berkey, *Popular Preaching and Religious Authority*; Karamustafa, *God's Unruly Friends*; Griffel, *Apostasie und Toleranz im Islam*; and Gaborieau and Zeghal, "Autorités religieuses en islam."

38. See El Shamsy, "The Social Construction of Orthodoxy," 97.

39. Martin and Barzegar, "Formations of Orthodoxy," 185. See also Knysh, "'Orthodoxy' and 'Heresy' in Medieval Islam"; Fierro, "The Treatises against Innovations"; and Asad, "The Idea of an Anthropology of Islam."

40. In many national contexts, the ʿulamā have successfully met these challenges to their authority and influence. Thomas Pierret has argued for Baʿthist Syria that the country's ʿulamā managed to remain relevant by adopting a flexible political approach, sustaining close relationships with merchants, and conducting informal learning circles. See Pierret, *Religion and State in Syria*; Hatina, "The Clerics' Betrayal?"; and Zeghal, *Gardiens de l'Islam*.

41. For an overview, see Zaman, *The Ulama in Contemporary Islam*, 1–17. For attempts by the ʿulamā to develop new mechanisms for sustaining their religious authority by redefining the boundaries of the concept of consensus (*ijmāʿ*) or institutionalizing the dispensation of legal opinions (*fatāwa*, sing. fatwa), see Zaman, *Modern Islamic Thought*, 45–107.

42. Mervin, "Les Autorités religieuses," 71. See also Gleave, "Conceptions of Authority."

43. Madelung, "Authority in Twelver Shiism." See also Amanat, "From ijtihād to wilāyat-i faqīh."

44. Amirpur, "A Doctrine in the Making?," 218.

45. See Ende, "The Flagellations of Muharram"; and Amanat, "In between the Madrassa and the Marketplace."

46. Corboz, *Guardians of Shiʿism*, 201.

47. Mervin, "Les Autorités religieuses," 70–71. Even in the Islamic Republic of Iran,

the most senior grand ayatollahs are careful to display their distance from the workings of the state (Amirpur, "A Doctrine in the Making?," 221–26). For the cautious approaches by the leading Sources of Emulation Muḥsin al-Ḥakīm (d. 1970) and Abū 'l-Qāsim al-Khū'ī (d. 1992) to politics in the oppressive Iraqi setting, see Corboz, *Guardians of Shi'ism*, 124–31, 166–76.

48. Clarke, "Neo-Calligraphy."

49. Dispensation of charity, another fundamental role played by each marjiʿ, is beyond the scope of this book. See Corboz, *Guardians of Shi'ism*, 94–121. Sabrina Mervin has likened the role of the *wukalā'* to "tentacles stretching across the Shi'a worlds" (Mervin, "Introduction," 20). Yet, as can be seen on the subsequent pages, those "tentacles" may easily develop a life of their own.

50. This could also be the reason why Chibli Mallat prefers to speak of a "Shīʿī International" when referring to Najaf (see Mallat, *The Renewal of Islamic Law*). For reflections in the field of intellectual history on the relationship between the nation, transnational history, and global history, see Hill, "Conceptual Universalization."

51. Ismail, *Saudi Clerics and Shi'a Islam*, 211. For aspects of "minoritization" in the context of modern nation-states, see Mufti, *Enlightenment in the Colony*, 11–13.

52. Matthiesen, *The Other Saudis*, 16–18, 217.

53. Gaiser, "A Narrative Identity Approach," 69–70.

54. For such an argument, see Jones, *Shi'a Islam in Colonial India*, 20–29; and Alam, "The Enemy Within."

55. See Cook, "Weber and Islamic Sects."

56. See the bibliography for a list of the journals on which this book draws. The attention I pay to Shiʿi journals was also inspired by the argument that such publications are a primary representative of a lively public sphere. See Bashkin, "The Iraqi Afghanis and 'Abduhs," 169. For an attempt to mine Islamic journals for statistical purposes and combine these insights with a close scrutiny of the role of their editors and qualitative textual analysis, see Rock-Singer, "A Pious Public."

57. There is a growing and dynamic literature on female religious authority. For a study of the various ways urban women in Pakistan interpret and teach Islam, see Ahmad, *Transforming Faith*, 92–128. For the exploration of broader trends regarding the increasing visibility and impact of female Islamic religious authority in mosque and madrasa spaces of the Middle East, South Asia, Europe, and the United States, see Bano and Kalmbach, *Women, Leadership and Mosques*.

58. Pandey, *The Construction of Communalism*, 116–17.

59. On the Shiʿi Tūrī tribe, see Rieck, *The Shias of Pakistan*, 8, 298–307.

60. I am keenly (and painfully) aware that this necessary choice cements an unfortunate general trend in the literature that excludes East Pakistan from the picture by presenting an exclusively West Pakistan story. East Pakistan mostly makes an appearance in connection with the war of 1971. See Uddin, "In the Land of Eternal Eid," 12–13.

61. Bose, *Recasting the Region*, 187–236.

62. On the Northern Areas, see Rieck, "A Stronghold of Shi'a Orthodoxy."

63. In an observation that supports my argument, Michael Farquhar has drawn our

attention to several prominent graduates of the Islamic University of Medina, "who have at points in their careers used the positions of religious authority that they negotiated partly on the basis of capital accumulated in Medina in order to advance strident critiques of the Saudi political or religious establishments." See Farquhar, *Circuits of Faith*, 181.

CHAPTER ONE

1. He was a member of Lahore's most prominent Shiʿi family, which had not only managed to retain (and significantly enlarge) its wealth and influence by supporting the British in the Rebellion of 1857, but also distinguished itself as the most lavish supporter of Shiʿi causes in the Punjab (see Rieck, *The Shias of Pakistan*, 10–11). For some additional information about the Qizilbashes' close relations with the British, who praised them for their unquestionable "loyalty," see Conran et al., *Chiefs and Families of Note*, 253–59.

2. Mushirul Hasan describes these smaller, predominantly Muslim settlements as "involuntary heirs of the once-powerful Indo-Persian Culture, built on "pluralism and syncretism." This phenomenon extended in his view not only to Muslim-Hindu interaction but specifically also to a "Shia-tinged culture" that was reflected in poetry and mourning for Ḥusayn (see Hasan, *From Pluralism to Separatism*, 1–51). Justin Jones's study on Shiʿi Islam in colonial India instead has attempted to show "the deterioration of this alleged assimilationist culture of Lucknow and the nineteenth-century Muslim *qasbas* into a series of more rigid, compartmentalized equivalents" which reflected a "heightened consciousness of inner-Islamic sectarian difference" (see Jones, *Shi'a Islam in Colonial India*, 15–16). For a view that North Indian commercial *qaṣbas* as "Islamic gentry towns" developed something of a "corporate identity and self-organisation," see Bayly, *Rulers, Townsmen, and Bazaars*, 346–68. For a recent argument about how such settlements took part in broader debates on reform and community formation, see also Jones, "The Local Experiences of Reformist Islam." The only other exception to the pattern of AISC meetings organized in cities of substantial size was the convocation held in 1920 in a small town near Bijnūr (UP). See Mīrzā, *Rūʾidād-i ijlās-i sīzdahum-i All India Shīʿah Conference 2, 3, 4 April 1920.*

3. See Khan, "Local Nodes of a Transnational Network."

4. The following description is based on the account of the "reception committee" (*majlis-i istiqbāliyya*) for the 1940 meeting. See ʿAbbās, *Rūʾidād-i ijlās-i sīyum-i All India Shīʿah Conference munʿaqidah 29–30 September ō yīkum October 1940*, 25–27.

5. The electrification of rural areas of the Punjab had already begun in 1925 with the development of the Uhl River hydro-electrical project. See Narayan, *Indian Water Power Plants*, 95–96. The AISC had not always embraced electricity in such an enthusiastic fashion. In 1931, the twenty-third annual meeting in Montgomery had issued a note of protest to the UP government. The AISC lamented that hundreds of utility poles installed in Amroha and other places interfered with the established routes of Muḥarram processions and constituted an obstacle for their *taʿziyahs* (replicas of the

Imāms' tombs) and their *ʿalams* (standards). See ʿAlīkhān, *Rūʾidād-i ijlās-i bist ō sivūm-i All India Shīʿah Conference*, 4.

6. Kalb-i ʿAbbās, *Rūʾidād-i ijlās-i sīyum-i All India Shīʿah Conference*, 38–39.

7. During the previous meeting of the AISC in Patna the delegates had adopted the flag as the Shiʿis' "communal emblem" (*qaumī nishān*). See Kalb-i ʿAbbās, *Rūʾidād-i ijlās-i bist ō nahum-i All India Shīʿah Conference*, 3, 18.

8. For this number of Shiʿi associations affiliated with the AISC, see Kalb-i ʿAbbās, *Rūʾidād-i ijlās-i sīyum-i All India Shīʿah Conference*, 62–63.

9. See Rieck, *The Shias of Pakistan*, 350.

10. In contrast to previous sessions, the 1940s meeting does not include a detailed roster of conference attendees. For an earlier example, see the 1938 report which lists 316 attending members and 186 visitors. The list can be found in the section "Asmāʾ-i kharīdārān-i ticket dues," in Kalb-i ʿAbbās, *Rūʾidād-i ijlās-i bist ō nahum-i All India Shīʿah Conference*, 1–17. The 1924 annual meeting in Fayżābād sold nine hundred member tickets and four hundred visitor tickets. See ʿAlī, *Rūʾidād-i All India Shīʿah Conference bābat-i ijlās-i haftadum*, 251.

11. This designation marks him as an advocate who received his education not in England but in India. See Paul, *The Legal Profession in Colonial South India*, 82–101.

12. *Tabarrā* is the Persianized form of the Arabic *tabarruʾ*, deriving from the root b-r-ʾ, meaning "to be or to become quit of." In this context, it refers to the Shiʿi practice of disassociating themselves from the first three Caliphs of Islam. I discuss these sectarian tensions in Lucknow in more detail below.

13. Kalb-i ʿAbbās, *Rūʾidād-i ijlās-i sīyum-i All India Shīʿah Conference*, 28–29.

14. Afzal, *A History of the Muslim League*, 267–68.

15. Kalb-i ʿAbbās, *Rūʾidād-i ijlās-i sīyum-i All India Shīʿah Conference*, 52.

16. Justin Jones relied only on proceedings covering the years 1907, 1908, 1910, 1912, and 1914 (see Jones, *Shiʿa Islam in Colonial India*, 114–25, 252), whereas Andreas Rieck based his observations not on the proceedings themselves but instead on the book *Ṣaḥīfat al-millat maʿrūf bi-lakht-i jigar* (Lucknow: Niẓāmī Press, 1939) by Sayyid ʿAlī Naqī Ṣafī (1862–1937). Ṣafī was known as "The Community's Tongue" (*lisān al-qaum*) and produced in this work a history of the AISC in verse (*naẓm*). See Rieck, *The Shias of Pakistan*, 348–49.

17. Lucknow was the capital of the Shiʿi ruled princely state of Awadh from 1722 to 1856. See Llewellyn-Jones, *A Fatal Friendship*.

18. On the expanding positions of Lucknow's mujtahids and the founding of madrasas in the nineteenth and early twentieth centuries, see Jones, *Shiʿa Islam in Colonial India*, 32–66. Juan Cole credits one man's travel with the emergence of a class of professional Shiʿi clerics: Sayyid Dildār ʿAlī Naṣīrābādī (1753–1820). The scholar spent only eighteen months at the important Shiʿi shrine cities of Karbala and Najaf, yet this time period was sufficient to fundamentally rework his Akhbārī outlook, adopt an Uṣūlī stance, and to challenge the traditional religious elite of Awadh. Yet Cole's neat narrative, based only on one single unpublished, anonymous Persian biography, is problem-

atic. Cole simply suggests that Naṣīrābādī and his successors transferred a somehow stable and clear-cut conception of Uṣūlī thought from Iraq to India. We are not told, however, of existing intra-Uṣūlī debates, whether adjustments occurred in the Indian context, or at least which thinkers would feature prominently in such an Uṣūlī setting. See Cole, *Roots of North Indian Shīʿism.*

19. As I already mentioned in the introduction, this in no way is meant to suggest that other areas of the subcontinent like the Deccan, Sindh, Pakistan's Northern Areas (today officially known as the Gilgit-Baltistan autonomous territory), or Kargil have received sufficient attention so far. For a recent study on Kargil, see Gupta, "Experiments with Khomeini's Revolution in Kargil." Substantial work on Sufi-Shiʿi overlap, conflict, and interaction in both Pakistan and India is still a desideratum, as is further research on the relationship between Twelver and Ismāʿīlī Shiʿis in the subcontinent.

20. An exception is Andreas Rieck, who provides a helpful discussion of how Shiʿi actors have tried to extract explicit safeguards from the Muslim League. See Rieck, *The Shias of Pakistan,* 41–53. For a contribution that draws on some of my findings, see Jones, "'The Pakistan That Is Going to Be Sunnistan.'"

21. For such an argument about the fluid, developing character of sectarianism in the Lebanese context, see Weiss, *In the Shadow of Sectarianism,* 9.

22. Gilmartin, "A Magnificent Gift," 418.

23. Malik, "Muslim Anjumans and Communitarian Consciousness"; Khan, *The All India Muslim Educational Conference,* 211.

24. Most alumni of the Muslim College at Aligarh went into public service, with those practicing as lawyers before British courts forming the second largest category. See Lelyveld, *Aligarh's First Generation,* 321–22.

25. Gilmartin, "Rethinking the Public through the Lens of Sovereignty," 383–86.

26. See Pandey, *The Construction of Communalism,* 210, 241.

27. Minault, *The Khilafat Movement,* 75. For the participation of Shiʿi members of the Muslim League in the Khilāfat movement, which Andreas Rieck calls "somewhat artificial, although understandable given the political context." See Rieck, *The Shias of Pakistan,* 37.

28. Minault, *The Khilafat Movement,* 11. For the view that one of the major reasons for the later faltering of the Khilāfat movement (besides Atatürk's abolition of the office of the caliph altogether) was that it meant "entirely different things to different people," see ibid., 209–10.

29. See Zaman, *The Ulama in Contemporary Islam,* 32–37. See also Metcalf, *Husain Ahmad Madani,* 112–19; and Metcalf, "Maulana Husain Ahmad Madani and the Jamiʿat ʿUlama-i-Hind." The term *qaum* as used in Indian debates took on a wide variety of meanings that reached from linguistic and regional connotations to caste, religion, and the nation. An example of its contested character is provided in Muḥammad Iqbal's exchange with the Deobandi scholar Ḥusayn Aḥmad Madanī (d. 1957), which brought to light their diverging understandings of the term. See Sevea, *The Political Philosophy of Muhammad Iqbal,* 151–63.

30. In Nair's view the debates leading up to the passing of section 295A of the Indian penal code in 1927 "hearken to a more fluid and shifting politics of legislative pragmatism," finally enabling a negotiated consensus among lawmakers belonging to different religious communities. See Nair, "Beyond the 'Communal' 1920s," 318, 336–37.

31. Jones, *Shiʿa Islam in Colonial India*, 118.

32. For a discussion of the backstory of its founding, which had to do with especially Shiʿi landed families growing weary of Aligarh as "an attempt by a nascent clique of primarily Sunni activists and professionals to weaken the economic influence and cultural legitimacy of the region's Shiʿa communities," see ibid., 156–64.

33. The memorandum in question also contained the evaluation that the AISC "cannot be said to be fully representative of the Shia community; several prominent Shias, including Jinnah himself, owe allegiance to the Moslem League." It further advised that demands expressed by this organization should not be taken "very seriously." See IOC, Coll 117/E7, "Hag A, Pol. 5380/44," IOR L/PJ/8/693.

34. The All India Shīʿa Political Conference had been founded in December 1929 out of the consideration that resolutions passed by the AISC mother organization that were too overtly political might imperil the position of its many members who held government employment. See Ḥusayn, *Kashmakash-i ḥayāt*, 294; and ʿAlīkhān, *Rūʾidād-i ijlās-i bist ō sivum-i All India Shīʿah Conference*, 44.

35. Jones, "'The Pakistan That Is Going to Be Sunnistan,'" 360.

36. The barrister had played an important role in bringing the Muslim League more in line with the Congress by drafting a revised constitution in 1912 which defined the attainment of self-government for India as the Muslim League's goal. Vazīr Ḥasan is also credited with convincing Muhammad Ali Jinnah to join the League in 1913. Yet, the conflict in 1937 had to do with "venomous propaganda" formulated by Sunni opponents against Ḥasan's son Sayyid ʿAlī Ẓahīr, who competed in the provincial elections in the United Provinces. Ḥasan saw especially Jinnah's ally Chaudry Khaliquzzaman as implicated in these sectarian moves. See Rieck, *The Shias of Pakistan*, 35–36, 40; and *Muslims in India*, 2:206–8.

37. Vazīr Ḥasan had thus also succumbed to the temptation of Congress rhetoric, which worried Jinnah so much that, for example, in 1944 "indignantly refused to allow Gandhi to address the League's working committee, since both the Mahatma and he seem to have realized the effect of Congress's temptations upon even the highest officials of the Muslim League." See Devji, *Muslim Zion*, 146.

38. Zaidi, *Evolution of Muslim Political Thought in India*, 5:623–26.

39. For an argument that such instances of sectarianism and conflict within India's religious communities require more research, see Gilmartin, "The Historiography of India's Partition," 31. Compare how certain "cardboard-cutout caricature" depictions of religious communities survive in the media and in some scholarship: Eaton, "Rethinking Religious Divides," 305.

40. For an overview of intra-Muslim tensions, see Qasmi and Robb, "Introduction."

41. See Daechsel, *The Politics of Self-Expression*, 59.

42. See Hartung, *A System of Life.*

43. Minault, *The Khilafat Movement,* 45. See also Freitag, *Collective Action and Community,* 80–81.

44. See, for example, Ahmad, "The Shia-Sunni Dispute in Lucknow"; Freitag, *Collective Action and Community,* 249–79; Mushirul Hasan, "Traditional Rites and Contested Meanings"; Ilahi, "Sectarian Violence and the British Raj"; Dhulipala, "Rallying the Qaum"; Rieck, *The Shias of Pakistan,* 19–23. For a problematic account that confuses the causalities of the events, see Awan, *Political Islam in Colonial Punjab,* 90–91.

45. On this South Asian practice, see Ali, *Observations on the Mussulmauns of India,* 17–33.

46. Rizvi, *A Socio-Intellectual History of the Isnā ʿAsharī Shīʿīs,* 2:332.

47. Jones, *Shiʿa Islam in Colonial India,* 87.

48. See Freitag, *Collective Action and Community,* 264–70; Ilahi, "Sectarian Violence and the British Raj," 192; Cole, *Roots of North Indian Shiʿism,* 170–71.

49. Jones, *Shiʿa Islam in Colonial India,* 105. I discuss the implications of this argument in more depth below.

50. Ibid., 191. See also chapter 5.

51. See Allsopp and Ross, "Report of the Madh-e-Sahaba Committee."

52. The Majlis-i Aḥrār was founded in 1929 by former Punjabi Khilāfatists who combined socialist leanings with sympathy for the Deobandī school. By 1936, more than a thousand of its members had been arrested in Lucknow during the civil disobedience campaign there. See Awan, *Political Islam in Colonial India,* 10–16, 91. For their involvement in Lucknow, see Kamran, "Majlis-i-Ahrar-i-Islam," 478–79. For the Aḥrār's earlier activities during the Kashmir agitation, see also Gilmartin, *Empire and Islam,* 96–99.

53. There is some confusion in the secondary literature regarding this date. Jones takes 31 March, the day when the communique was issued, to be the day of the Prophet's birthday (Jones, *Shiʿa Islam in Colonial India,* 194), while Rieck identifies it as 3 May (Rieck, *The Shias of Pakistan,* 21). It is 2 May, however, that corresponds with the 12 Rabīʿ al-Awwal of the Islamic calendar, the Prophet's birthday.

54. Rieck, *The Shias of Pakistan,* 21. Jones is skeptical about the "split the Muslim" argument, since it would have required enormous "manipulative skill" on the part of the Congress Government. He suggests instead that Lucknow's tremendous growth in the 1920s and its transformation from a "provincial *taʿluqdari* [*sic*] backwater into a city of increased size, commercial and political importance" played a decisive role. See Jones, *Shiʿa Islam in Colonial India,* 199–204.

55. For discussion of numerical participation in the events, see IOC, Fortnightly reports, Punjab, July–August 1939, IOR L/PJ/5/242. See also Khan, *Why 14,000 Shias Went to Jail.*

56. For more information on him, see also IOC, Fortnightly Reports, United Provinces, Second Half of 1941, IOR/L/PJ/5/270, Sir Maurice Garnier Hallett, "Demi-official Letter No. U.P. 92, dated April 23, 1941."

57. See the file IOC, Madh-e Sahaba, MSS Eur IOR Pos 10773.

58. Jones, *Shi'a Islam in Colonial India*, 196–98. For an example of the participation of senior mujtahids, see Ḥasan, *Tazkirah-i ḥayāt-i Sarkār Nāṣir al-Millat*, 17.

59. Sayyid Rižā ʿAlī obtained his BA and LLB from Aligarh and started practicing law in Murādābād in 1908. In 1924, he presided over the Muslim League's Bombay Session. See *Muslims in India*, 2:114–16. For brief sketches covering the biographies of the most influential Shiʿi scholars under discussion, see Jones, *Shi'a Islam in Colonial India*, 245–47.

60. See NA, British Empire Report, No. 15 (14 April 1920), CAB/24/156.

61. See ʿAlī, *Aʿmāl nāmah*, 355–56. Sayyid Rižā ʿAlī propagated global Islamic brotherhood and emphasized that historically the only difference non-Muslim had ever managed to notice between Shiʿis and Sunnis was their diverging ways to offer prayer (ibid., 368).

62. Jones, *Shi'a Islam in Colonial India*, 180–82.

63. Ibid., 215.

64. Ibid., 232.

65. As an example of how the colonial analysis of the internal Shiʿi contestations was shaped, see the article entitled "'Greatest Sin—Sectarianism' Appeal to Leaders to Call of Agitation," written by ʿAbd al-Vaḥīd Khān, the joint secretary of the Provincial Muslim League, in the newspaper *Pioneer*. It is preserved in the file IOR, Madh-e Sahaba, MSS Eur IOR Pos 10773.

66. An additional argument is that colonial administrators lost touch with events on the ground from the 1920s onward due to the "strategy of establishing a headquarters near a telephone and remaining within it." See Freitag, *Collective Action and Community*, 79–80.

67. The first view is expressed by Rieck, *The Shias of Pakistan*, 25; the second by Jones, *Shi'a Islam in Colonial India*, 119.

68. Rieck, *The Shias of Pakistan*, 26.

69. Jones, *Shi'a Islam in Colonial India*, 119.

70. Rieck, *The Shias of Pakistan*, 27–28.

71. Jones, *Shi'a Islam in Colonial India*, 119.

72. Rieck, *The Shias of Pakistan*, 27–28.

73. Ibn-i Ḥasan was born in Lucknow in 1874 and received an *ijāza* of ijtihād before leaving the city for Iraq in 1909. He studied in Karbala and Najaf and also spent some time in Samarra, receiving several certificates from leading ayatollahs. The British chose him as one of the distributors for the Oudh Bequest. In 1917, Ibn-i Ḥasan decided to return to Lucknow due to the difficult situation in Iraq during World War I. See Ḥusayn, *Maṭlaʿ-i anvār*, 42–43. On the history of the Oudh Bequest, see also Nakash, *The Shiʿis of Iraq*, 212–28; and Jones, *Shi'a Islam in Colonial India*, 133–37.

74. His father, Sayyid Abū 'l-Qāsim Ḥā'irī (1833–1906), had come to Lahore on the insistence of Navāb Qizilbāsh. After studying with his father, Sayyid ʿAlī went to Iraq, where he completed his higher religious education with Mīrzā Muḥammad Ḥasan Shīrāzī while also attending the study circles of other leading ʿulamā. He completed the *tafsīr* initiated by his father, traveled all over India to speak, and is also said to have

had *muqallids* in Burma and East Africa. Unfortunately, his extensive library in Lahore was destroyed in a flood (see Ḥusayn, *Maṭlaʿ-i anvār*, 341–43). Sayyid ʿAlī Ḥāʾirī's descendants in Lahore told me in the summer of 2012 that the remnants of his library had supposedly been transferred to the Jāmiʿat al-Muntaẓar in Model Town, but I was not able to locate books formerly part of Ḥāʾirī's library there. In the course of my research I have come across references that point out the close relationship which Muhammad Iqbal enjoyed with several Shiʿi scholars, among them Sayyid ʿAlī Ḥāʾirī (see, for example, "Muṣāḥabah bā ḥażrat Āyatullāh Ḥājj Shaykh Muḥammad Ḥusayn Najafī Pākistānī," 157–58). Other Shiʿi interlocutors of Iqbal in Lahore were the Iranian emigré and *ʿālim* ʿAbd al-ʿAlāʾ al-Haravī al-Ṭihrānī (d. 1922) and Mīrzā ʿAbd al-Karīm Zanjāni (d. 1968), a Najafī scholar who traveled extensively in India and met with Iqbal in the late 1920s. To my knowledge, no study has been done on this topic in a Western language. Some useful information is provided in Akbar Ḥaydarī Kashmīrī, *Iqbāl aur ʿAllāmah Shaykh Zanjānī*, 63–107.

75. Sayyid Ḥashmat ʿAlī was born in 1858 and studied with Sayyid Abū 'l-Qasim Ḥāʾirī the *dars-i niẓāmī, tafsīr*, hadith, and fiqh before entering Lahore's Oriental College. Even though Hāʾirī wanted to see him proceed to Lucknow, Sayyid Ḥashmat preferred to obtain *ijāzas* from Deobandī scholars first. Thereafter, he made his way to Najaf via Karachi, Basra, and Karbala. He also studied for several months with Sayyid Muḥammad Ḥasan Shīrāzī in Samarra and spent a total of twelve years in Najaf, interrupted by a yearlong return to India. Sayyid Ḥashmat ʿAlī attained the rank of marjiʿiyya. Additionally, he went for a year to Istanbul in order to study the rational sciences (*maʿqūlāt*). Yet, in his native India it was not possible to live out his "scholarly disposition" (*ʿilmī mizāj*) and to devote himself entirely to research, instead demands were made on him to engage in *munāẓaras* and to work for *qaumī iṣlāḥ*—something to which he reluctantly agreed (see Ḥusayn, *Maṭlaʿ-i anvār*, 206–8).

76. Najm al-Ḥasan received several *ijāzas* from Iraqi jurists but seems to have spent only a limited amount of time in the Middle East and was mostly educated in Lucknow. He gained a reputation for modernizing religious education in the subcontinent, which led to an invitation by the Navāb of Rāmpūr to act as the director of education in this princely state. In particular, Najm al-Ḥasan's affiliation with the preaching-focused Madrasat al-Wāʿiẓīn was said to have contributed to the spread of his fame in India and beyond through the *muballigh*s sent out by the school (see ibid., 675–78).

77. ʿAlīkhān, *Rūʾidād-i ijlās-i pānzdahum-i All India Shīʿa Conference*, 38–39.

78. Ibid., 40. The resolutions passed during the Annual Meetings of the AISC in 1919 and 1920 do not address any objectionable or controversial issues. I would argue, however, that the conflict between the ʿulamā and the modernist AISC members ran deeper than a critique of one particular resolution, as I intend to show. See, for example, Sayyid Muḥsin Mīrzā, *Rūʾidād-i ijlās-i sīzdahum-i All India Shīʿah Conference*, 1–5.

79. Ibid., 42–43.

80. Ibid., 8.

81. See Ḥusayn, *Rūʾidād-i All India Shīʿah Conference bābat ijlās-i shānzdahum munʿaqidah 31 March ō yikum ō 2 April 1923*, 62. Later efforts (e.g., in 1925 and 1935) to bring about such a meeting were equally unsuccessful (see Ḥusayn, *Rūʾidād-i All India Shīʿah Conference bābat ijlās-i hīcdahum munʿaqidah 9 li-ghāyatah 12 March 1925*; Kalb-i ʿAbbās, *Rūʾidād-i ijlās-i bist ō shishum-i All India Shīʿah Conference munʿaqidah 26, 27, 28 October 1935*, 5). By 1935, some delegates had lost all faith in the prospects of reconciliation. They called on the AISC to finally give up trying to get the ʿulamā involved (ibid., 44).

82. He was born into a scholarly family in Bombay and studied with Lucknow's leading Shiʿi scholars before leaving the subcontinent for Iraq in 1909. After returning to Lucknow in 1913 or 1914, he taught at the Nāẓimiyya school and at the Madrasat al-Wāʿiẓīn. He became the latter's director in 1935 after the death of Sayyid Sibṭ-i Ḥasan (1878–1935), who was known as the *khaṭīb-i aʿẓam* (Greatest Orator) (see Ḥusayn, *Maṭlaʿ-i anvār*, 53–54). On Sibṭ-i Ḥasan and the Madrasat al-Wāʿiẓīn, see also Imāmiyyah Mission Lucknow, *Khaṭīb-i Āl-i Muḥammad*. Justin Jones has argued that Sibṭ-i Ḥasan "embodies perfectly some of the transformations taking place in the Shiʻa clergy, and the way in which religious authority was designated, through the early twentieth century. Although he was not a formal mujtahid, the fact that he was often declared as such by lay sources is evidence of the extent to which formal clerical authority, and skill as a public orator and narrator of majalis, were becoming increasingly mixed and conflated at the level of popular religion" (Jones, *Shiʻa Islam in Colonial India*, 83–84).

83. Cited in Arjomand, "Islam and Constitutionalism since the Nineteenth Century," 41. The committee of mujtahids was never formed, however, mostly because "the great majority of Shiʻite jurists selected by the Second Majles (1909–11) in several rounds considered it beneath their dignity to accept" (ibid., 44). See also Bayat, *Iran's First Revolution*, 174–83; and, for a discussion of how this idea was later picked up and modified in Iranian Shiʿi thought, Reza Hajatpour, *Iranische Geistlichkeit zwischen Utopie und Realismus*, 93–230.

84. ʿAlī, *Rūʾidād-i All India Shīʿah Conference bābat ijlās-i haftadum*, 253.

85. Ibid., 253–54. The Shiʿi scholars formulated their proposal in the aftermath of an initiative by "second rank" Sunni scholars who were affiliated with the Jamʿiyyat al-ʿUlamāʾ-i Hind. During the organization's meeting in December 1921, they had suggested electing an Amīr-i Hind who was to enforce the shariʿa and to create parallel Muslim institutions like a treasury, courts, and an administration of *auqāf*, thus establishing an *imperium in imperio*. See Hardy, *Partners in Freedom*, 32–35; and Robinson, *Separatism among Indian Muslims*, 329–30.

86. ʿAlī, *Rūʾidād-i All India Shīʿah Conference bābat ijlās-i haftadum*, 256–57.

87. Ibid., 256.

88. Ibid., 255. This specific attempt by the ʿulamā to recast their role in society as "experts" who are equally or even more relevant than "experts" in other fields, with religion being turned into a specialization, is by no means a strategy unique to South Asian Shiʿi ʿulamā. For a discussion of the issue in the broader context of modern

Islamic thought, see Zaman, *The Ulama in Contemporary Islam*, 98–99; and Zaman, *Modern Islamic Thought*, 105. See also Dhulipala, *Creating a New Medina*, 371–72.

89. ʿAlī, *Rūʾidād-i All India Shīʿah Conference bābat ijlās-i haftadum*, 257.

90. The AISC voted to approach the important Lucknow-based *mujtahids* Sayyid Āqā Ḥasan, Sayyid Najm al-Ḥasan, Sayyid Nāṣir Ḥusayn, Sayyid Bāqir Riżvī, Sayyid Sibṭ-i Ḥusayn (1867–1952; see Ḥusayn, *Maṭlaʿ-i anvār*, 259–61), Sayyid Ẓuhūr Ḥusayn (1864–1938; ibid., 295–96), Sayyid Aḥmad known as ʿAllāmah Hindī (1878–1947; ibid., 71–73, and more on him also below), Sayyid Muḥammad ʿAlī (1879–1942, ibid., 582–83), and Sayyid Abū ʾl-Ḥasan Riżvī (1846–1924; ibid., 54–57). They also suggested to include Sayyid Yūsuf Ḥusayn (1885–1933; ibid., 708) who had temporarily moved to the city of Meerut.

91. Ḥusayn, *Rūʾidād-i All India Shīʿah Conference bābat ijlās-i hīcdahum*. In this context the Supervisory Council decided that it had no basis to rule on the shariʿa compliance of female education, since its members had not been provided with the charter for an envisioned AISC girls school.

92. ʿAlī, *Rūʾidād-i All India Shīʿah Conference bābat ijlās-i haftadum*, 131–32. For an account of the 1924 events and the strained relationship with the ʿulamā that had led many of the latter to boycott the session in Fāyżābād, see also Ḥusayn, *Kashmakash-i ḥayāt*, 292–93.

93. This list demonstrates of course that the AISC was most of all a forum of the literate and wealthy Shiʿi elite (Ḥusayn, *Rūʾidād-i All India Shīʿah Conference bābat ijlās-i hīcdahum*, 92–93).

94. He had settled in Britain by the early 1920s and was involved in conveying the viewpoints of the Khilāfat movement to the British government, but seems to have returned to Bombay later (see M. Naeem Qureshi, *Pan-Islam in British Indian Politics*, 76–81). Rieck incorrectly lists him as the Bombay session's president, an office that was instead occupied by Navāb Sarfarāz Ḥusayn (see Rieck, *The Shias of Pakistan*, 28).

95. See Smith, *Modern Islām in India*, 21; and Ingram, "Crisis of the Public in Muslim India," 412–13.

96. Ḥusayn, *Rūʾidād-i All India Shīʿah Conference bābat ijlās-i hīcdahum*, 94–95.

97. The proceedings list ʿAllāmah Hindī, Sayyid Abū ʾl-Ḥasan, Sayyid Muḥammad ʿAlī and the ʿālim Sayyid Muḥammad, known as Mīran Ṣāhib (1895–1961; Ḥusayn, *Maṭlaʿ-i anvār*, 464–65). In attendance were also a preacher from Delhi, Sayyid Muhammad Dihlavī (1899–1971; ibid., 465–67), and the Punjab-based scholar Muḥammad Sibṭayn Sarsavī (1885–1947). Sarsavī especially would also make a fascinating object of further study. He was educated at a madrasa in Meerut and later obtained a *maulvī fāżil* degree from Punjab University. He served as a teacher for Arabic at various colleges and from 1916 published the journal *al-Burhān*, which remained in circulation for thirty-five years (ibid., 543–44). For more information on the *maulvī fāżil* degree, see note 108 below.

98. Ḥusayn, *Rūʾidād-i ijlās-i bist ō yikum-i All India Shīʿah Conference munʿaqidah 27, 28, 29 December 1928*, 28–29. For a discussion of how Iranian ʿulamā of the time

reacted to modernization initiatives by Reza Shah, see Akhavi, *Religion and Politics in Contemporary Iran*, 32–59; and Rajaee, *Islamism and Modernism*, 52–89.

99. See also Rieck, *The Shias of Pakistan*, 28.

100. Kalb-i ʿAbbās, *Rūʾidād-i ijlās-i bist ō nahum-i All India Shīʿah Conference bi-maqām-i Paṭnah munʿaqidah 29, 30, 31 December 1938*, 1–2.

101. Kalb-i ʿAbbās, *Rūʾidād-i ijlās-i bist ō haftum-i All India Shīʿah Conference bi-maqām-i Lakhnāuʾ munʿaqidah 25, 26, 27 December 1936*, 20.

102. Ḥasan, *Rūʾidād-i ijlās-i bist ō cahārum-i All India Shīʿah Conference bi-maqām-i Lāhōr munʿaqidah 24, 25, 26 March 1932*, 29.

103. Sayyid Kalb-i ʿAbbās was a lawyer from Rāʾe Barelī who was elected to the UP Legislative Council from 1937 to 1946. He was a member of the Central Working Committee of the AISC from 1914 until his death and served as honorary secretary general of the AISC since 1935. He was also involved with the All India Shīʿa Political Conference (see Jain, *Muslims in India*, 2:84).

104. This invocation of Sayyid Naṣīr Ḥusayn's authority underlines Justin Jones's finding that he was "revered as the single most influential Indian Shiʿa scholar since Dildar ʿAli and is widely referenced in much contemporaneous literature as the chosen *mujtahid* of most north Indian Shiʿa, and as having a transnational network of *muqallids*" (Jones, *Shiʿa Islam in Colonial India*, 245).

105. Players try to get their game pieces home first. Since it is possible to knock other pieces off the board and gambling might be involved, too, a game of Pachisi "is by no means a sedate affair." See Finkel, "Round and Round the Houses."

106. Kalb-i ʿAbbās, *Rūʾidād-i ijlās-i bist ō haftum-i All India Shīʿah Conference*, 40–41.

107. Ḥusayn, *Rūʾidād-i ijlās-i bist ō yikum-i All India Shīʿah Conference*, 30; Kalb-i ʿAbbās, *Rūʾidād-i ijlās-i bist ō shastum-i All India Shīʿah Conference bi-maqām-i Kānpūr munʿaqidah 26, 27, 28 December 1937*, 9.

108. The *maulvī fāżil* degree obtained by Jārcāvī denoted the highest level of Arabic studies and its examination encompassed rhetoric, literature, prosody, logic, philosophy, laws of inheritance, and composition. His second degree, the *munshī fāżil*, was its Persian equivalent with a stronger focus on literature (see Hussain, *History of University Oriental College Lahore*, 787–92). The Oriental College in Lahore had been the vision of the Hungarian-British Orientalist Wilhelm Gottlieb Leitner, who had suggested using Arabic, Sanskrit, or Persian as the basis for an education in the vernacular and in English in order to "teach English thought, English inventions, English science and art, and English civilisation." See Diamond, "The Orientalist-Literati Relationship in the Northwest"; and Perrill, "Punjab Orientalism." The Islamia College had been founded in 1907 by the Anjuman-i Ḥimāyat-i Islām as part of its efforts to establish educational institutions in order to counter the activities of both the American Presbyterian Church and the Arya Samaj (see Sevea, *The Political Philosophy of Muhammad Iqbal*, 22).

109. This school had been founded in response to Aligarh Trustees rejecting an ulti-

matum for joining the noncooperation movement against the British (see Minault, *The Khilafat Movement*, 118).

110. Later he initially did not migrate to Pakistan but instead chose to stay behind in Lucknow, working there as the principal of the Shīʿa College. Due to the shifting political landscape in India he felt forced to move in 1951 to Karachi, where he became the first lecturer in Shiʿi theology at Karachi University. See Jārcavī, *Jārcah. Savāniḥ-i ʿAllāmah Ibn-i Ḥasan Riżvī Sabzvārī*, 8–15; and Ḥusayn, *Maṭlaʿ-i anvār*, 43–46.

111. Ḥasan, *Rūʾidād-i ijlās-i bist ō cahārum-i All India Shīʿah Conference*, 14.

112. Ibid., 15.

113. Reforming women ranked high on the agenda of many Muslim reformists of the time due to the perceived female influence over their children and husbands and their social relations that extended well beyond the home. See Minault, *Secluded Scholars*, 63.

114. Ḥasan, *Rūʾidād-i ijlās-i bist ō cahārum-i All India Shīʿah Conference*, 18. For other initiatives aimed at reforming customs supported by Jārcavī, like a committee that was supposed to work toward changes within Shiʿi mourning sessions, see Kalb-i ʿAbbās, *Rūʾidād-i ijlās-i bist ō haftum-i All India Shīʿah Conference*, 8.

115. Jārcavī, *Falsafah-i Āl-i Muḥammad*, 102. I am quoting here from the 1999 imprint of this work because it is more readily available. The text is identical with that of the 1940 version from Lucknow.

116. Jārcavī, *Falsafah-i Āl-i Muḥammad*, 5–9.

117. Ibid., 53–62.

118. Ḥasan, *Rūʾidād-i ijlās-i bist ō cahārum-i All India Shīʿah Conference*, 18–19.

119. For such a view, see Jones, "Shiʿism, Humanity and Revolution," 423.

120. Ibid., 423–24.

121. See Kamran and Shahid, "Shariʿa, Shiʿas and Chishtiya Revivalism," 173–75. Jhang later in the twentieth century gained notoriety for Sunni-Shiʿi violence, as chapter 5 discusses at some length.

122. Mir, "Genre and Devotion in Punjabi Popular Narratives."

123. See, for example, ʿAlī, *Taṣḥīḥ al-ʿaqāʾid*, 12, and the anonymous *Shīʿah ō Sunnī ke munāẓare*, 5. On the complex internal Shiʿi debates over the centuries regarding the permissibility or even obligation to perform *taqiyya*, which "though widespread and well-known, by no means excluded other, often contrasting, forms of behaviour," see Kohlberg, "Some Imāmī-Shiʿi Views on Taqiyya." Egbert Meyer has also argued that *taqiyya* should be understood as a "mixture between elements of and virtue and situation ethics." See Meyer, "Anlaß und Anwendungsbereich der *taqiyya*," 262.

124. ʿĀrif Naqvī, *Taẕkirah-i ʿulamāʾ-i imāmiyyah-i Pākistān*, 329–30.

125. On the saint, see Zubayrī, *Taẕkirah-i auliyāʾ-i Jhang*, 109–11.

126. The comment on "exoteric affluence" strikes the reader as an elegant way to justify the fused role of pīr and large wealthy landowner many *sajjāda nashīns* occupied (and still occupy today) in the Punjab.

127. Ḥusayn, *Rūʾidād-i All India Shīʿah Conference bābat ijlās-i shānzdahum*, 26–27. For a more detailed discussion of Shiʿi Sufism, see chapter 3.

128. On the tensions between the pīrs and Sunni reformist ʿulamā, see Gilmartin, "Religious Leadership and the Pakistan Movement," 496.

129. Naqvī, *Shīʿōn̲ kī tāzah zindagī*, 11–12. On the Imamia mission, see also Jones, *Shi'a Islam in Colonial India*, 210–12.

130. Naqvī, *Shīʿōn̲ kī tāzah zindagī*, 10. The fact that the city's special character was stressed so explicitly in conjunction with the Sunni-Shiʿi trouble also calls into question the argument of Justin Jones that Lucknow during the first half of the twentieth century gained the status of an almost "holy city" for South Asia's Shiʿis (see Jones, *Shi'a Islam in Colonial India*, 122).

131. Ibid., 16.

132. See Kalb-i ʿAbbās, *Rūʾidād-i ijlās-i sīyum-i All India Shīʿah Conference*, 18.

133. Jones, *Shi'a Islam in Colonial India*, 152.

134. Ibid., 141, 226.

135. See, for example, Ḥasan, *Rūʾidād-i ijlās-i bist ō cahārum-i All India Shīʿah Conference*, 3.

136. ʿAlīkhān, *Rūʾidād-i ijlās-i bist ō sivum-i All India Shīʿah Conference*, 15.

137. For a discussion of how Abū 'l-Aʿlā Maudūdī conceived of Islam as a "well-arranged system, the basis of which had been determined as a number of firm principles," see Hartung, *A System of Life*, 83–155. See also Sivan, *Radical Islam*, 83–129.

138. See, for example, ʿAlī Khān, *ʿAzādārī māh-i muḥarram*; and Pānīpatī, *Miʿyār al-ḥaqīqat*.

139. Chatterji, *Bengal Divided*, 27.

140. ʿAllāmah Hindī, an epithet given to Sayyid Aḥmad Naqvī Lakhnavī, was born into Lucknow's famed *khāndān-i ijtihād* in 1878. He received his initial education at the Nāẓimiyya and was very active in *tablīgh* and *munāẓaras* in northern India before studying and taking up residence in Iraq. He returned to India during World War I but set out again for Iraq after the end of the war. Over the next decades he often traveled between the subcontinent and Iraq, where he was charged with, among other things, the restructuring of the Oudh Bequest. See Ḥusayn, *Maṭlaʿ-i anvār*, 71–73; and Fāẓilī and Lakhnavī, *Warāthat al-anbiyāʾ*, 19. More research on ʿAllāmah Hindī is required, especially in order to explain his support for the AISC and AISPC at a time when all other senior ʿulamā had cut their ties with the organization. See Ḥusayn, *Kashmakash-i ḥayāt*, 299; and Kalb-i ʿAbbās, *Rūʾidād-i ijlās-i bist ō haftum-i All India Shīʿah Conference*, 38–42.

141. Hindī, *Shīʿah aur khilāfat*, 4.

142. Ibid., 18–19.

143. Ibid., 26. See also Najmul Hasan, *Islam in the Light of Shiaism*, 48–71.

144. Jārcavī, *Falsafah-i Āl-i Muḥammad*, 58. It has to be noted that there exists a tension between these claims and Jārcavī's emphasis on social justice. For similar points about the spiritual kingdom of the Imāms, see also Ḥasan, *Shīʿōn̲ kī be naẓīr qurbāniyān̲*, 15. Sayyid Ẓafar Ḥasan was born in 1890 in Amroha, where he received his basic religious education. He continued his more advanced studies at the Nāẓimiyya in Lucknow before returning home to teach Arabic and Persian in local high

schools. In 1950, he migrated to Pakistan where he founded the Jāmiʿah-i Imāmiyyah (also known as Madrasat al-Wāʿiẓīn) in Karachi. He was a very prolific author and sought-after speaker and also ran his own publishing house (ʿĀrif Naqvī, *Tazkirah-i ʿulamā'-i imāmiyyah,* 147–48).

145. Lakhnavī, *Shahīd-i sālis,* 14.

146. Ḥasan, *Aṣl al-uṣūl,* 5. On the author, see Ḥusayn, *Maṭlaʿ-i anvār,* 277.

147. Ḥusayn, *Mauʿiẓat-i sajjādiyya,* 6. The author makes the case that his reading is backed up by al-Thaʿlabī's (d. 427/1035) *tafsīr,* which supposedly was a "respected commentary among the Sunnis." Both statements are problematic. For one, al-Thaʿlabī has met with a lot of skepticism from the Sunni side, especially for including Shiʿi and mystical material, which rendered him "too costly a burden on the Sunni camp. Ibn Taymīyah would see to it that the situation was corrected" (Saleh, *The Formation of the Classical Tafsīr Tradition,* 219). This was surely unfair treatment, since al-Thaʿlabī's goal in incorporating Shiʿi material had been nothing more than "robbing it of any Shīʿī significance and making it part of the Sunnī worldview" (ibid., 186). Yet it was an attitude that stuck. The first edition of al-Thaʿlabī's commentary was published in 2002 by a Shiʿi scholar in Beirut (ibid., 229). Additionally, Murtażā Ḥusayn's claim seems to originate from a misreading of the Arabic in al-Thaʿlabī's *tafsīr.* Instead of mentioning the supposed alternative reading, al-Thaʿlabī only provides a variant of the vocalization for the word *tanzīl* (sending down, revelation). The version *tanzīlan* (in lieu of *tanzīla*) could, according to al-Thaʿlabī, be traced back to Imām ʿAlī (see al-Thaʿlabī, *al-Kashf wa-l-bayān,* 8:121). Other Shiʿi publications also do not mention the possibility of *ʿAlī ṣirāṭun mustaqīmun.* Compare, for example, al-Thaʿlabī, *Ahl al-Bayt fi tafsīr al-Thaʿlabī,* 165.

148. Weiss, *In the Shadow of Sectarianism,* 26.

149. Ibid., 155–59, 185.

150. See chapter 5 for more information on Amritsarī.

151. See the following chapter for internal Shiʿi debates over the implications of this statement.

152. See Ḥaydar, "Lāhōr meṉ ḥaqīqat-i mazhab-i shīʿah kā zabardast muʿjizah." Amritsarī's view was rejected outright by the Shiʿi journal, which held that the miracle clearly favored ʿAlī, since no one else of the first four Caliphs was mentioned on the tree by name.

153. Minault, *The Khilafat Movement,* 94.

154. Ḥasan, *Shīʿōṉ kī be naẓīr qurbāniyāṉ,* 9–10.

155. Ibid., 17.

156. See Lalljee, *Shia Muslims' Case,* 17.

157. The work was written by Sayyid ʿAlī Ḥaydar (1885–1961), who was born into a family of scholars in Khajvā, located in the Saran district of Bihar. He was originally set on an engineering path but physical weakness put an end to his further college career. Instead, he helped his father with his publishing activities. In 1907, his uncle, who served as editor of the Shiʿi journal *al-Shams,* presented the youth to Lucknow's leading ʿulamā who developed an instant liking for him, because he "knew modern

sciences, was skilled with the pen, and intelligent." In 1910, Sayyid ʿAlī Ḥaydar moved to Lahore and obtained a *maulvī fāżil* degree in 1912. He continued his education at Lucknow, passing the *ṣadr al-afāżil* degree in 1336 (1917 or 1918) and then returned to Khajvā to assist his father with editorial work for the newspaper *Iṣlāḥ*. After a short stint in Patna he moved in 1921 back to the Sulṭān al-Madāris school on the invitation of Bāqir al-ʿUlūm. Ḥaydar stayed in Lucknow until 1928 before taking over all responsibilities for *Iṣlāḥ* (see Ḥusayn, *Maṭlaʿ-i anvār*, 354–56). On Sayyid ʿAlī Ḥaydar's political role, see also Rieck, *The Shias of Pakistan*, 48–52.

158. Ḥaydar, *Kitāb-i mustaṭāb-i hidāyat*, 10–13.

159. Ibid., 18.

160. See, for example, ibid., 20, 36–38, 74–75.

161. Ibid., 500–501.

162. See Hasan, "Traditional Rites and Contested Meanings," 549. See also Ilahi, "Sectarian Violence and the British Raj," 201.

163. See, as a recent example, Afzal, *A History of the All-India Muslim League*, 442.

164. IOC, File 462/38E Shias, IOR/L/I/1/880, 1942–43.

165. Jinnah was born into a Khōja Ismāʿīlī family but converted to Twelver Shiʿi Islam around 1904 when he was twenty-eight years old. See Wolpert, *Jinnah of Pakistan*, 18; and Khān, *Tashkīl-i Pākistān*, 279–83. For a review of the uneven quality of scholarship on Jinnah and the blind spots in the existing literature, see Robinson, "The Jinnah Story."

166. See Rieck, *The Shias of Pakistan*, 39; and, for the biographies of Cundrīgar and Iṣfahānī, ibid., 360. A critical biography of the Rājā of Maḥmūdābād is a major desideratum in the modern history of South Asia. Existing publications unfortunately merely read as hagiographies that are focused on the unmatchable personality of Amīr Aḥmad Khān, who is even compared with Jesus in the context of Jinnah's dependence on him: "And the response from the Raja Saheb belonged to the class of: 'Ask and it shall be given, Knock and it shall be opened and seek and ye shall find'" (Husain, *The Life and the Times*, xx).

167. See "Hasan Ispahani to the Maharajkumar of Mahmudabad." See also *The Case of Muslim India*.

168. "M. A. Jinnah to Syed Ali Zaheer, SHC (127)." In 1938, when the annual meeting of the AISC was held in conjunction with the meeting of the Muslim League in Patna, Jinnah made a short appearance on stage but ultimately did not speak. See Kalb-i ʿAbbās, *Rūʾidād-i ijlās-i bist ō nahum-i All India Shīʿah Conference*, 8.

169. Devji, *Muslim Zion*, 66. Compare also Rieck, *The Shias of Pakistan*, 41–53.

170. Dhulipala, *Creating a New Medina*, 206–17, 445–46.

171. Ibid., 11.

172. Ibid., 445.

173. Ibid., 353–57.

174. For his biography and an analysis of how he aimed at refuting the theory of united nationalism while conceptualizing Pakistan as the fountainhead for a return of Islam, see ibid., 357–76.

175. Binder, *Religion and Politics in Pakistan*, 29–30, 137–54.

176. See ʿUs̱mānī, *Khuṭbāt-i ʿUs̱mānī*, 134, 142.

177. See Shani, "Noah's Ark and the Ship of Faith"; and Sindawi, "Noah and Noah's Ark."

178. See al-Shaybānī, *The Islamic Law of Nations*, 22–57. On the *khawārij*, see Crone, *God's Rule*, 54–64.

179. Al-Shaybānī, *The Islamic Law of Nations*, 193–94.

180. ʿUs̱mānī, *Khuṭbāt-i ʿUs̱mānī*, 143–44. For a discussion of the punishment of the Thamūd, see Sinai, "Religious Poetry from the Quranic Milieu." Dhulipala has taken the *khawārij* analogy to mean the westernized ML leadership without exploring in more detail its specific anti-Shiʿi thrust and, surely even more pronounced, similar anti-Aḥmadī reasoning by the JUI. See Dhulipala, *Creating a New Medina*, 367–68. For ʿUs̱mānī, the Aḥmadīs were clearly apostates (*murtadd, mulḥid*). See, for example, ʿUs̱mānī, *Khuṭbāt-i ʿUs̱mānī*, 144; and Qasmi, *The Ahmadis and the Politics of Religious Exclusion*, 41–49.

181. See Rieck, *The Shias of Pakistan*, 51. On Ẓafar Aḥmad ʿUs̱mānī's biography and opposition to united nationalism, see Zaman, *The Ulama in Contemporary Islam*, 41–49.

182. Dhulipala, *Creating a New Medina*, 104.

183. Ibid., 446.

184. ʿUs̱mānī, *Khuṭbāt-i ʿUs̱mānī*, 212.

185. Gilmartin, "A Magnificent Gift," 426. For the Qurʾānic account, see Q 7:148–57, 20:83–98. Compare also Speyer, *Die biblischen Erzählungen im Qoran*, 323–33.

186. See Rieck, *The Shias of Pakistan*, 51.

187. Syed Pirzada, *Foundations of Pakistan*, 2:440–45. See also Jalal, *The Sole Spokesman*, 95–96.

188. Ibid., 172.

189. ʿUs̱mānī, *Khuṭbāt-i ʿUs̱mānī*, 86. These comments were published in the newspaper *al-Manshūr* on 16 November 1945.

190. For the broader history of the term, see Crone, *God's Rule*, 223–33.

191. See "Fazil Mooraj to M. A. Jinnah, SHC (606)."

192. See, for example, the pamphlet *Who Is Responsible for the Shia-Sunni Dispute?* by Sayyid Akbar ʿAlī, a member of the Central Standing Committee of the All India Shīʿa Political Conference, in the file IOC, 958; the Sunni-Shia controversy in Lucknow, 25 March 1939–2 April 1942, IOR/L/PJ/7/2587.

193. See Madanī, *Maktūbāt-i Shaykh al-Islām*, 3:171–72. Madanī in his argument drew on one of Sirhindī's letters. See Sirhindī, *Maktūbāt-i Imām-i Rabbānī*, 2:28–29. See chapter 3 for a more detailed discussion on the role of Aḥmad Sirhindī in the context of Sunni thought and his relations with the Shīʿis.

194. Madanī, *Maktūbāt-i Shaykh al-Islām*, 3:172–74.

195. Metcalf, *Husain Ahmad Madani*, 122–23.

196. See "Amir Haider Khan to Jinnah, QAD (126)."

197. Andreas Rieck mentions that Jinnah's statements concerning *auqāf* and *fiqh*

"have been quoted again and again by Shia organisations and journals in Pakistan during five decades to argue for their cause" (see Rieck, *The Shias of Pakistan*, 43–44).

198. See "Musalmānān-i Hind kī qaumī taʿmīr kā su'āl." According to Afzal, the "All-India Muslim League and the provincial Muslim Leagues had no direct control on the All-India Muslim Students Federation or provincial Muslim Students Federations but the League leaders on Jinnah's direction used to advise and guide the All-India Muslim Students Federation and its branches, where needed. Some leaders enrolled themselves as associate members and were formally elected presidents" (Afzal, *A History of the All-India Muslim League*, 328–29). Bashīr Aḥmad belonged to this group. After his education in Lahore and Oxford he was called to the bar and also taught as a professor of history at Lahore's Islamia College. He was a member of the council of the Anjuman-i Ḥimāyat-i Islām and involved with various other associations, served as president of the Punjab Muslim Students Federation in 1941–42, was a member of the Muslim League's Executive Committee from 1942 to 1947, and acted as secretary for the Reception Committee of the AIML session in Lahore 1940 (see Jamil, *The Muslim Year Book of India*, 27; Mirza, *The Punjab Muslim Students Federation*, 409–10). On the important role that the Punjab Muslim Students Federation played in popularizing the concept of Pakistan, see also Gilmartin, *Empire and Islam*, 207–11.

199. It is not entirely clear whether Aḥmad here refers to Iqbal, Muhammad Ali Jinnah, or perhaps to Choudhary Rahmat Ali, who had coined the term *Pakistan* as an acronym for its parts Punjab, Afghanistan, Kashmir, Sindh, and Balochistan in 1933 while he was a student at Cambridge.

200. For this argument on Jinnah, see Jones, "'The Pakistan That Is Going to Be Sunnistan,'" 369.

201. For a further discussion of Ḥamīd's *Atrāk aur musalmānān-i ʿālam*, see "Lāhōr kī qābil-i iʿtirāẓ kitab."

202. "Muslim League aur ham."

203. See "Proceedings All Parties Shia Conference." For some background on the All Parties Shīʿa Conference, see Rieck, *The Shias of Pakistan*, 49–52. See also Mitra, *Indian Annual Register* 2 (July–December 1945): 160–62.

204. See Rieck, *The Shias of Pakistan*, 50. Ghażanfar ʿAlī Khān had been a member of the ML since 1927. He served in several functions within the party, was from 1933 to 1937 a member of the Council of State, from 1937 to 1945 a member of the Punjab Legislative Assembly, and one of the five League members in the Interim Government of India (as minister of health) (see *Muslims in India*, 1:172–73). In the early 1930s, he had also served as president of the AISPC sessions 1931 in Montgomery and 1932 in Lucknow. See Zaidi, *Evolution of Muslim Political Thought in India*, 4:538–39, 580–82).

205. IOC, Coll 117/E7, "Proceedings of the All Parties Shia Conference, 13–16 October 1945," IOR L/PJ/8/693.

206. For his former affiliation with the Muslim League and his role in municipal politics in Bombay, see *Muslims in India*, 2:29. In 1946, Lalljee contested in the elections against Jinnah and, according to two authors, only lost because "a shrewd Jinnah

pulled a trump card out of his sleeve. Just a couple of days before the polling Syedna Mulla Tahir Saifuddin, the spiritual head of the Bohra community, issued a *fatwa* (religious edict) to vote and support Jinnah. It was a great setback to the hopes of Lalji. Jinnah emerged triumphant" (see Hasnain and Husain, *Shias and Shia Islam in India*, 162–63). Why a Bohra fatwa allegedly should have been the decisive factor for Jinnah's success requires further investigation, however. For the political maneuvering in Bombay ahead of the elections, see also Ḥusayn, *Kashmakash-i ḥayāt*, 324–28.

207. Lalljee, *Shia Muslims' Case*, 29; also IOC, Coll 117/E7, "Preliminary Statement RE: Shia Muslims Position," IOR L/PJ/8/693. Andreas Rieck has argued that "Congress tried to play the 'Shia card' again" by supposedly arranging for Lalljee to express his views before the Cabinet Mission (Rieck, *The Shias of Pakistan*, 52). Yet he seems to conflate with this evaluation the Parliamentary Delegation and the Cabinet Mission. The first was meant to "convey the general desire of the British people to see India speedily attaining her rightful position as an independent partner state in the Commonwealth" (Hodson, *The Great Divide*, 130). The second was announced by the British government on 19 February 1946 with much clearer goals: a team of three cabinet ministers was "to seek an agreement with the leaders of Indian opinion on the principles and procedures to be followed on the constitutional issue." The stated goal was that "Indians themselves would frame their constitutional future" (ibid., 133–60). While Lalljee met with the parliamentary delegation, he only sent two telegrams to the Cabinet Mission (see Lalljee, *Shia Muslims' Case*, 67–68, 71–72).

208. IOC, Coll 117/E 7, "Statement regarding the Shia Muslim position in India, made by the Anjuman Tanzimul Mominin to Parliamentary Delegation in Lucknow, February 1, 1946," IOR L/PJ/8/693.

209. Mirzā Jaʿfar Ḥusayn was born in 1899 into a *sharīf* family in Fayżābād, studied law at Lucknow University, and started to practice in 1925 as a lawyer. In the late 1920s, the Mahārājā of Maḥmūdābād offered him a position as his private secretary. After the latter's death in 1932, he once again took up law as a profession (see his autobiography: Ḥusayn, *Kashmakash-i ḥayāt*, 1–288). In 1932, Ḥusayn was elected general secretary of the All India Shīʿa Political Conference and remained affiliated with it until Partition (ibid., 294–96). He also served as editor of the Shiʿi journal *Moonlight*. In 1939, he criticized the AISPC for deciding to stay aloof from both the Congress and the League, since this would be "harmful" to the Shiʿi community (see Mitra, *Indian Annual Register* 2 [July–December 1939]: 355). For his praise of Congress leaders, see also Ḥusayn, *Kashmakash-i ḥayāt*, 339–60.

210. "Enclosure to No. 233 (Fazil Mooraj to M A Jinnah SHC (682)," 290–93. In forwarding this letter to Jinnah, Mūraj commented that people of the ilk of Mirzā Jaʿfar Ḥusayn "are selfish and want themselves fully provided for even at the sacrifice of others. Their bigotry in their religious beliefs can result in their own ruination. Inconsiderate publicity and such statement as made in Mirza Sahib's letter can cause a flare-up and breach between the two sections of Islam which can never be filled up." He also justified sending along the letter to Jinnah because he did not want it to "fall

into hands which may use it indiscreetly after I am gone." Jinnah replied that he "had nothing more to say" (ibid., 288–90).

211. Lalljee, *Shia Muslims' Case*, 11–12. This meeting on 5 July 1945 was attended by the *mujtahids* Sayyid Muḥammad Naṣīr (1895–1966; see Jones, *Shi'a Islam in Colonial India*, 245), Sayyid Muḥammad Sa'īd (1914–67; see Ḥusayn, *Maṭla'-i anvār*, 546–50), Sayyid 'Alī Naqī Naqvī and Sayyid Muḥammad (Mīran Ṣāḥib), along with several lower-ranking scholars who taught at religious schools in Lucknow.

212. Cited in Chatterji, *Bengal Divided*, 231.

213. See Jārcavī, *Jārcah*, 15. In his speech, 'Usmānī claimed that disregarding the viewpoint of the Muslim League meant ignoring the convictions of the entire Muslim qaum. See Shīrkūṭī, *Ḥayāt-i 'Usmānī*, 524–25.

214. See Rieck, *The Shias of Pakistan*, 52.

215. See Mahmudabad, "Some Memories," 419. The raja later moved to Iraq and finally settled in the United Kingdom (see Latham, "The Raja of Mahmudabad," 41–43).

216. Ḥusayn, *Maṭla'-i anvār*, 45.

217. See Rieck, *The Shias of Pakistan*, 46, 53.

218. Talbot, *Khizr Tiwana*, 129. For a discussion of this sudden collapse of the Unionist Party, attributed to discontent with wartime rationing, the death of Chhotu Ram on 9 January 1945, and the failure of the Simla Conference, see ibid., 133–40. See also Talbot, *Provincial Politics*, 82–103.

219. Jalal, *The Sole Spokesman*, 144–48; Gilmartin, "Religious Leadership and the Pakistan Movement," 497–98, 508–13; Talbot, *Punjab and the Raj*, 210–17. For a discussion of the dependency of the Unionist Party on landholding families and *sajjāda nashīns* and its difficulties in seeking to establish a "modern" party organization, see also Gilmartin, *Empire and Islam*, 108–45.

220. Ibid., 218–19.

221. See Nair, *Changing Homelands*, 179–218. Deconstructing a narrative of neat communal lines regarding such instances of carnage, Nair has also found reports on how "some people managed to stay sane, not unmoved by the events that threatened to destroy the closely-knit communities, amongst which they lived, but safe, alert, still caring for members of the 'other' religious community, perhaps with a new touch of self-consciousness" (ibid., 197). She also assigns much blame to British officials, who "were keenly aware of the possibilities of violence failing agreement and the decreasing powers they had over their almost-free subjects," yet chose to remain "silent spectators" (ibid., 214).

222. Minault, *The Khilafat Movement*, 201.

223. Jones, *Shi'a Islam in Colonial India*, 177, 227–28.

224. Robb, "Advising the Army of Allah," 149–51.

225. I am grateful to Faisal Devji for this suggestion.

226. Qureshi, *Pan-Islam in British Indian Politics*, xxv.

227. Ende, "Baqī' al-Gharqad." For a contemporaneous description of the cemetery's destruction, see Rutter, *The Holy Cities of Arabia*, 2:256–57. On the consolidation of

Saudi rule in the Ḥijāz and beyond, see Al-Rasheed, *A History of Saudi Arabia*, 39–71, as well as Haykel and Crawford, "Introduction."

228. Jārcavī, *Jārcah*, 11–12.

229. Jārcavī, *Falsafah-i Āl-i Muḥammad*, 70–78, 88.

230. Ibid., 105–6. It remains to be investigated whether these calls for a boycott by Shi'is and Barelvī groups had any palpable impact. According to British estimates compiled by Nate Hodson, the number of Indian pilgrims indeed decreased from approximately 19,000 (1926) and 27,000 (1927) to 14,000 (1928), 11,000 (1930), and 7,300 (1931). I am grateful to Nate for sharing his findings with me. For the economic importance of the annual pilgrimage in the pre-oil period, see also Miller, "Pilgrim's Progress," 189–228.

231. Ḥusayn, *Rū'idād-i ijlās-i bist ō yikum-i All India Shī'ah Conference*, 91–92.

232. Ḥusayn, *Rū'idād-i ijlās-i bist ō duvum-i All India Shī'ah Conference*, 201–5; Kalb-i 'Abbās, *Rū'idād-i ijlās-i bist ō shishum-i All India Shī'ah Conference*, 105–6. The proceedings list 3,658 written letters for 1928 and 4,729 for 1929, for example.

233. Riżvī, *Rū'idād-i ijlās-i bist ō panjum-i All India Shī'ah Conference*, 76.

234. Ibid., 78. For attempts in the modern era to promote a Shi'i-Barelvī alliance, see also chapter 5.

235. Riżvī, *Rū'idād-i ijlās-i bist ō panjum-i All India Shī'ah Conference*, 80.

236. Ibid., 78.

237. Ibid., 82–83.

238. Kalb-i 'Abbās, *Rū'idād-i ijlās-i siyum-i All India Shī'ah Conference*, 18.

239. See Ḥusayn, *Rū'idād-i ijlās-i bist ō yikum-i All India Shī'ah Conference*, 86–90.

240. See, for example, Ḥusayn, *Rū'idād-i ijlās-i bist ō yikum-i All India Shī'ah Conference*, 19; Kalb-i 'Abbās, *Rū'idād-i ijlās-i bist ō haftum-i All India Shī'ah Conference*, 142–43. This is not to say that the AISC was always uncritical of Iran. During its 1935 meeting, the organization passed a resolution to send a fact-finding mission to Iran. This delegation was supposed to explore the background of reports that the shrine of Imām Riżā in Mashhad had been fired upon and protesters arrested (see Kalb-i 'Abbās, *Rū'idād-i ijlās-i bist ō shishum-i All India Shī'ah Conference*, 9). On the Mashhad protests, which were partially directed against new laws that demanded the unveiling of women and prescribed brimmed hats for men and during which approximately one hundred people lost their lives, see Abrahamian, *Iran between Two Revolutions*, 152–53. See also Chehabi, "Dress Codes for Men in Turkey and Iran."

241. Kalb-i 'Abbās, *Rū'idād-i ijlās-i bist ō nahum-i All India Shī'ah Conference*, 17.

242. Ibid., 18. Sayyid Riżā 'Alī also mentioned that in comparison to other Muslim countries, the rules pertaining to female seclusion (*pardah*) in India were probably the strictest, which had extremely detrimental effects on girls' education in the country (ibid., 10–11).

243. Kalb-i 'Abbās, *Rū'idād-i ijlās-i bist ō haftum-i All India Shī'ah Conference*, 147.

244. This observation applies to influential Muslim scholars like Ḥusayn Aḥmad Madanī, too. For a discussion of the aftermath of Partition which also saw a significant

number of Muslims returning to India before stricter permits and in 1952 passports were required, see Zamindar, *The Long Partition*, 79–119.

245. Rieck, *Shias of Pakistan*, 53.

246. Binder, *Religion and Politics in Pakistan*, 98.

247. Rieck, *Shias of Pakistan*, 62.

248. Ibid., 64.

249. Ibid., 68. The Aḥmadīs regard themselves as Muslims, but their belief that Mirzā Ghulām Aḥmad (d. 1908), the founder of their community, was a prophet puts them at odds with the Muslim doctrine that Muhammad was the last Prophet sent by God.

250. Dhulipala, *Creating a New Medina*, 360–62.

CHAPTER TWO

1. See Baram, *Saddam Husayn and Islam*, 91. The crackdown on Shiʿi processions and organizations came in the wake of the 6 March 1975 Algiers accord between Iran and Iraq. The Iraqi regime used this breathing space to go against the Shiʿis with a mixture of carrot and stick. Even though, for example, *ʿāshūrāʾ* was declared a national holiday, the official calendar placed it on the ninth and not the tenth of Muḥarram "to the chagrin of the Shiʿi religious establishment. The reason for this was simple: the regime did everything it could to dissuade people from participating in the ceremonies and processions, which were often used for antiregime demonstrations" (see ibid., 124–25).

2. This school was founded in 1930 by Muftī Sayyid Khādim Ḥusayn (d. 1953) with support by the Ṭālpūr Mīrs of the princely state of Khairpur, who donated 150 acres of agricultural land as a source of *waqf* income for the school. See Kāẓimī, *Imāmiyyah dīnī madāris-i*, 390–92. No further study exists on the Shiʿi leanings of the Mīr dynasty. For a description of how seriously the ruler and the court took Muḥarram, see Langley, *Narrative of a Residence*, 2:177–84. Muftī Sayyid Khādim Ḥusayn, a native of Derah Ismāʿīl Khān, had graduated from Rampur, the Sulṭān al-Madāris, and the Madrasat al-Wāʿiẓīn in Lucknow. Thereafter he was sent to Khayrpūr in order to propagate Shiʿi Islam in the area. See Ḥusayn, *Maṭlaʿi anvār*, 213.

3. There is some disagreement about his exact date of birth. While Naqvī gives it as 1 August 1945, the author of the biographical account on which the following anecdote is based, Naẓr-i ʿAbbās Ḥaydarī, principal of the Madrasat al-Imām al-Ḥusayn in the district of Jhang, states that al-Sābiqī was born on 1 August 1946. Even more confusingly, he provides the supposedly matching *hijrī* date of 8 Dhū 'l-ḥujja 1365, which corresponds to 3 November 1946. See ʿĀrif Naqvī, *Taẕkirah-i ʿulamāʾ-i imāmiyyah*, 290; al-Sābiqī, *Rusūm al-shīʿa*, 5–7.

4. See Eliash, "Ḥasan al-ʿAskarī."

5. I was only able to identify the first of the two. Sayyid Āghā ʿAlī Ḥusayn Qummī was born in 1952 in the Punjabi city of Bhakkar. He studied in both Najaf and Qum and retained his close connection with al-Sābiqī later in life. When he founded the

school Jāmiʿah-i Āl ʿImrān in 1978, al-Sābiqī taught there for a while as head teacher (see ʿĀrif Naqvī, *Tazkirah-i ʿulamāʾ-i imāmiyyah,* 179). Additionally, Qummī wrote a note of introduction for al-Sābiqī's *Rusūm al-Shīʿa.*

6. Al-Sābiqī, *Rusūm al-shīʿa,* 8–9.

7. The importance of the shrine, located in a city that has a predominantly Sunni population, was underlined recently by two bomb attacks carried out in February 2006 and June 2007. On the historical development of the shrine, see Jiyad, "Samarra: Shiʿi Heritage and Culture"; and Northedge, "The Shrine in Its Historical Context."

8. For such a portrayal of reform, see Abou Zahab, "'Yeh matam kayse ruk jae?,'" 108.

9. Al-Sābiqī, *Qawāʿid al-sharīʿa,* 13–14.

10. See Amanat, "In between the Madrassa and the Marketplace," 123.

11. Green, *Bombay Islam,* 241–42.

12. Ibid., 22–23.

13. Jones, *Shiʿa Islam in Colonial India,* 110–13.

14. Rieck, *The Shias of Pakistan,* 171, 176. As I argue below, I do not regard this classification as helpful. These "populists" held very elitist religious views on their own.

15. Naqvi, "The Controversy about the Shaykhiyya Tendency," 136–37. It has to be noted, though, that also within the academic study of Shiʿism there is an ongoing debate between those who side with the idea of rational, sober origins of Shiʿi Islam and those who emphasize its essentially esoteric character. Hossein Modarressi is a representative for the first position. He singles out Qum as a place of learning where early moderate scholars were trying hard to keep a "flow of extremist literature that was spreading fast" at bay. Even though Shiʿi Imāms like Jaʿfar al-Ṣādiq and ʿAlī al-Riḍā condemned the *ghulāt* as infidels and the *mufawwiḍa* as polytheists, "populist authors who tended to put together and offer whatever report in their judgment could strengthen the faith of the people in the Imāms although the authors themselves could never guarantee the authenticity of many reports or many of the sources they quoted" managed to insert their inauthentic material into the authoritative Shiʿi hadith collections (see Modarressi Tabataba'i, *Crisis and Consolidation in the Formative Period of Shiʿite Islam,* 34–47). Mohammad Ali Amir-Moezzi, on the other hand, has made the case for "esoteric nonrational Imamism" as being the "original tradition" of Shiʿi Islam that was gradually pushed aside by a "turn toward rationalization and attempts at rapprochement with 'orthodox' positions." See Amir-Moezzi, *The Divine Guide in Early Shiʿism,* 18–19).

16. Mervin, *Un réformisme chiite,* 252 (my translation from the French). For another example of a work that exclusively discusses reformist authors and credits them with the development of an "homogenising version of Islam" and an "enlightened cross-sectarian commitment to Islam" focused on tauḥīd, see Machlis, *Shiʿi Sectarianism in the Middle East.*

17. ʿĀrif Naqvī, *Tazkirah-i ʿulamāʾ-i imāmiyyah,* 290.

18. Rieck, *The Shias of Pakistan,* 129, 133.

19. Rahnema, *Superstition as Ideology,* 240.

20. Ibid., xi.

21. Ibid., 21.

22. For Sharīʿatī's intellectual formation, compare also Rahnema, *An Islamic Utopian.*

23. Rahnema, *Superstition as Ideology,* 19.

24. See Gesink, *Islamic Reform and Conservatism,* 4. For comparable observations on the "historiographical hegemony" that certain Sikh reformists enjoy in the existing literature, see Oberoi, *The Construction of Religious Boundaries,* 30–35.

25. Ali Usman Qasmi has made the argument that a focus on "orthodox" Islam can cut both ways. It not only entails relegating all expressions of the faith that do not live up to this bar to the realm of "folk Islam" but also presupposes "the existence of a normative or orthodox Islam constituting a pattern of perfection which seems to be an unchanging essence." See Qasmi, *Questioning the Authority of the Past,* 13.

26. Jones, *Shiʿa Islam in Colonial India,* 238.

27. Sabrina Mervin has observed that Lebanese Shiʿi ʿulamā starting to contribute articles to the journal *al-ʿIrfān* led to a radical shift in the way knowledge was transmitted as well as a "nouveau rapport pédagogique avec leur ouailles." See Mervin, *Un réformisme chiite,* 193.

28. Verkaaik, "Reforming Mysticism," 114.

29. Ewing, *Arguing Sainthood,* 102.

30. Reetz, *Islam in the Public Sphere,* 90–91. See also Gilmartin, *Empire and Islam,* 59–61.

31. Al-Sābiqī, *Rusūm al-shīʿa,* 19–20.

32. Al-Zamān Naqvī Bukhārī, *Ṭarīq al-muntaẓirīn,* 16.

33. Jones, *Shia Islam in Colonial India,* 63–64.

34. Rieck, *The Shias of Pakistan,* 133.

35. Veer, *Imperial Encounters,* 23. On the changing nature of Sunni-Shiʿi sectarianism in Pakistan, see also chapter 5.

36. Ende, "The Flagellations of Muḥarram," 31, 37. Dietrich Reetz has pointed out a similar "dilemma" faced by reformist and revivalist groups who were setting themselves apart from the "orthodox, uninformed, and unreformed ʿulamāʾ of their time." While going against the latter and calling for their "improvement" to better meet the manifold challenges of the time, "the authority of the ʿulamā could not be challenged" (Reetz, *Islam in the Public Sphere,* 111).

37. For such a view, see Mervin, *Un réformisme chiite,* 119–20. The same might apply to scholarly characterizations of the Barelvīs as well. Dietrich Reetz, for example, classified them as not being among "those who followed strict monism in their doctrinal teachings" (Reetz, *Islam in the Public Sphere,* 5).

38. This chapter does not attempt to be an exhaustive survey of both reformist and traditionalist Shiʿi thought in Pakistan. I have selected influential scholars from both camps in order to show their diversity. Especially the fascinating topic of contemporary majālis preachers in Pakistan and a careful analysis of the vast amount of audiovisual material produced by this group surely warrants much more scholarly attention.

An interesting example is the *ẕākir* Ghażanfar ʿAbbās Tunsavī who has often been described to me in Pakistan as the quintessential *ghālī* preacher. See his website, http://www.allamaghazanfar.com, for his videos.

39. Naqvi, "The Controversy about the Shaykhiyya Tendency," 135–49. A historical precedent for the rise of new rituals connected with (a much smaller-scale) migration would be the introduction of Iranian-style passion plays in South Lebanon during the course of the twentieth century. See Mervin, *Un réformisme chiite*, 245–46.

40. Hermann, "Political Quietism in Contemporary Shīʿism," 279. Unfortunately, Denis Hermann's latest book on the topic could not be consulted any more for this study. See Hermann, *Le shaykhisme à la période qajare.*

41. Amir-Moezzi, "An Absence Filled with Presences," 41–43. Among other things, Uṣūlī writings produced in Awadh charged al-Aḥsāʾī with heresy for his division of God's knowledge into an essential and an active kind and attacked his Muʿtazilī-inspired negative theology with respect to God's attributes (Cole, *Roots of North Indian Shīʿism*, 185–89). Denis MacEoin has argued that although the charges laid against al-Aḥsāʾī included such matters as his views on the resurrection and the ascension of the Prophet (*miʿrāj*), "the real reason for disquiet lay in the fact that the Shaykh had taken rather too far certain possibilities inherent in the Uṣūlī position itself. In departing from the strict Akhbārī position of reliance on texts, the Uṣūlīs had to rely not only on deductive reasoning but also on non-rational modes of understanding in religious matters." Al-Aḥsāʾī, McEoin holds, simply went too far in stressing *kashf* (intuitive revelation) in this context. See MacEoin, "Orthodoxy and Heterodoxy in Nineteenth-Century Shiʿism," 327.

42. Amir-Moezzi, "An Absence Filled with Presences," 42.

43. Bayat, *Mysticism and Dissent*, 55–56, 75–77. In particular, the concept of the "fourth pillar" came under attack from a rival Shaykhī school that formed in Tabriz. This branch accused Karīm Khān of inventing the concept and distorting the teachings of Aḥsāʾī and the master's first successor, Sayyid Kāẓim Rashtī (d. 1844) (see ibid., 68).

44. Naqvi, "The Controversy," 140. Naqvi identifies Hyderabad in the Deccan as another center of Shaykhī thought. For an endorsement of Naqvi's portrayal of Lucknow, see ʿĀrifī, *Shīʿīyān-i Pākistān*, 141–42. Sayyid ʿAlī Naqī Naqvī remarked on the other hand in 1937 that the Shaykhīs had only a very marginal influence in North India. See Naqvī, *Bāb ō maẕhab-i Bahāʾī*, 128–29.

45. Reformist authors hold that the competing Shaykhī centers in Kerman and Kuwait (which took over from Tabriz) have been actively trying to obtain a foothold in Pakistan, allegedly at the behest of the "imperialists" (see Aʿvān, *Mard-i ʿilm maydān-i ʿamal meṉ*, 52). The reformist-minded author Muḥammad Ḥusayn Zaydī Barsatī makes the rather charged claim that Bashīr Anṣārī, a leading traditionalist scholar whom I discuss in more depth below, was introduced to Shaykhism while traveling as a spy for the British to Iraq during World War II (see Barsatī, *Pākistān meṉ shaykhiyyat*, 25).

46. Cole, *Roots of North Indian Shīʿism*, 189.

47. Rieck, "The Struggle for Equal Rights," 272–73.

48. See Naqi, *Azadari*, 483. See also Jones, *Shi'a Islam in Colonial India*, 237.

49. Rieck, "A Stronghold," 390.

50. Large parts of the present-day state were known as the "United Provinces" under British rule from 1902 until independence.

51. I have based these two lists on Andreas Rieck's discussion of the development of internal Shiʿi debates, as well as on various instances in both the reformist and traditionalist literature where the two camps are placed in opposition against each other. See Rieck, *The Shias of Pakistan*, 129–33, 171–80; and, for example, Ḍōgar, *Muḥammad Ḥusayn Ḍhakkō se 150 su'āl*, 41.

52. Jones, *Socio-Religious Reform Movements*, 120.

53. Ibid., 121.

54. In addition to the quotes from *Asad* given below, see also, for example, "Ghaur kijīye" and "Daur-i ḥāżir ke dīnī taqāże." See also Rieck, *The Shias of Pakistan*, 81–85.

55. The journal's editor was Sayyid Akhtar Ḥusayn (d. 1987), who wrote under the pen name Shā'iq Anbālavī. He later became the first general secretary of the Taḥrīk-i Nifāẕ-i Fiqh-i Jaʿfariyya (TNFJ). See Salayc, *Vafayāt-i nāmvarān-i Pākistān*, 387. For more information on the TNFJ, see also chapter 4.

56. See "Hamāre qaumī idāre 2." The journal *Asad* continued its series over the next months, introducing to its readers other schools and organizations like the Jāmiʿat al-Muntaẓar in Lahore (2 June 1959), the Jāmiʿah-i ʿIlmiyyah-i Bāb al-Najaf in Jāṛā (10 September 1959) or the Madrasat al-Wāʿiẓīn in Karachi (2 October 1959). For more information on the history and leadership of the APSC and the ITHS, see Rieck, "The Struggle for Equal Rights," 271–76; and Rieck, *The Shias of Pakistan*, 58–66.

57. See "Hamāre qaumī idāre 6."

58. His father was an Ahl-i Ḥadīs̱ scholar called Sulṭān ʿAlī. Muḥammad Ismāʿīl went to Deoband, where he studied with Anvār Shāh Kashmīrī (d. 1933) and Iʿjāz ʿAlī. He later became a preacher in Ṭōbah Ṭek Singh's biggest Deobandī madrasa. It was during his tenure there that he converted to Shiʿi Islam, allegedly after meeting an adherent of the Imāmī faith and intensive personal research (*bā taḥqīq ō justujūyī*). As a consequence of his conversion, his family cut all ties with him (see ʿĀrif Naqvī, *Taẕkirah-i ʿulamā'-i imāmiyyah*, 260–61).

59. Rieck, *The Shias of Pakistan*, 124–25. Debates over the status of sayyids among Pakistani Shiʿis would be a fascinating topic to explore in more depth. Juan Cole has identified a "pattern of early settlement, imperial land grants, and later adoption of Shīʿism" among Sayyids in Mughal North India (see Cole, *Roots of North Indian Shīʿism*, 72–84). For the arguments that the failure of land-reforms in Pakistan "has perpetuated Syed power in rural and tribal Pakistan longer than in India," see Wright, "The Changing Role of the Sādāt," 656–58. See also Buehler, "Trends of Ashrāfization in India."

60. He was born in 1920 in the village of Jāṛā, not far away from Derah Ismāʿīl Khān. Ḥusayn Bakhsh Jāṛā received his foundational education at Chowk 38 at the hands of Sayyid Muḥammad Bāqir Naqvī, Sayyid Yār Shāh Najafī, and Mufti Jaʿfar Ḥusayn. After studying the rational sciences (*durūs-i maʿqūl*) at a Sunni madrasa in Gūj-

rānvālah, he passed his *fāżil* degree in Arabic at Punjab University in 1945. Jāṛā taught at various schools afterward, most notably from 1951 onward at the Dār al-ʿUlūm Muḥammadiyya in Sargōdhā, before leaving for Najaf to pursue higher studies inter alia with the grand ayatollahs Sayyid Abū ʾl-Qāsim al-Khūʾī and Sayyid ʿAbdullāh Shīrāzī (d. 1984). Jāṛā returned to Pakistan in 1954 and opened a madrasa called Jāmiʿah-i ʿIlmiyyah-i Bāb al-Najaf in his native village while also teaching elsewhere in Pakistan, inter alia at the Jāmiʿat al-Muntaẓar in Lahore. See ʿĀrif Naqvī, *Tazkirah-i ʿulamāʾ-i imāmiyyah*, 83–85.

61. Jāṛā, *Lumʿat al-anwār*, 29–30.

62. Rieck, *The Shias of Pakistan*, 127–31.

63. On this feature of Shiʿism, see also Mervin, "Transnational Intellectual Debates."

64. Rieck, "A Stronghold," 292–94. It was only after the Iranian Revolution that Qum and Mashhad fully replaced the Iraqi centers of learning.

65. For a list of his teachers, see ʿĀrif Naqvī, *Tazkirah-i ʿulamāʾ-i imāmiyyah*, 295; http://www.sibtain.com/en/Biography.aspx.

66. On the Dār al-ʿUlūm Muḥammadiyya, see Kāẓimī, *Imāmiyyah dīnī madāris-i Pākistān*, 185–87.

67. Aʿvān, *Mard-i ʿilm maydān-i ʿamal meṉ*, 66–67. See also Rieck, *The Shias of Pakistan*, 130, for additional examples of Ḍhakkō's critique.

68. For vivid descriptions of various processions in the subcontinent, see Pinault, *Horse of Karbala*, 87–132.

69. Al-Najafī Ḍhakkō, *Iṣlāḥ al-rusūm*, 175–76. See also Naqvi, "The Controversy," 141.

70. Al-Najafī Ḍhakkō, *Iṣlāḥ al-rusūm*, 16.

71. Ibid., 35–36.

72. Ibid., 38–39, 138–46.

73. Ibid., 40–41.

74. Al-Najafī Ḍhakkō, *Uṣūl al-sharīʿa*, 19. This book has been reprinted at least seven times since it was published for the first time in 1967. See also Rieck, *The Shias of Pakistan*, 131–32.

75. Al-Najafī Ḍhakkō, *Uṣūl al-sharīʿa*, 58.

76. Aʿvān, *Mard-i ʿilm*, 68–69, 177. Ḍhakkō himself claims that his views have not changed over the last fifty years. This feat qualified him, according to a professor of psychology he was acquainted with, to be labeled a "servant (or man) of truth" (*bandah-i ḥaqq*). Interview with Muḥammad Ḥusayn al-Najafī Ḍhakkō, Jāmiʿat al-Muntaẓar, Lahore, 18 July 2012.

77. For a discussion of this work, see Fyzee, "The Creed of Ibn Bābawayhi."

78. Rieck, *The Shias of Pakistan*, 131.

79. Al-Najafī Ḍhakkō, *Iṣlāḥ al-rusūm*, 49–50.

80. See al-Najafī Ḍhakkō, *Aḥsān al-fawāʾid*, 149–52; al-Najafī Ḍhakkō, *Uṣūl al-sharīʿa*, 29–30; al-Najafī Ḍhakkō, *Iṣlāḥ al-rusūm*, 72–73.

81. Interview with Muḥammad Ḥusayn al-Najafī Ḍhakkō, 18 July 2012.

82. Peskes, *Muḥammad B. ʿAbdalwahhāb (1703–92) im Widerstreit*, 21–27. See also Crawford, *Ibn ʿAbd al-Wahhab*, 57–58.

83. See al-Muẓaffar, *al-ʿAqāʾid al-imāmiyya*, 14–15. Muḥammad b. Mahdī al-Khāliṣī by contrast focused in his discussion of tauḥīd on the fact that the whole creation pointed toward its maker (see al-Khāliṣī, *Iḥyāʾ al-sharīʿa*, 38–40).

84. For an overview of the different variations this label took on, see Sanyal, *Devotional Islam and Politics*, 240–55. See also Riexinger, *Ṣanāʾullāh Amritsarī (1868–1948) und die Ahl-i-Ḥadīs*, 138–41, 523–36.

85. Rieck, *The Shias of Pakistan*, 129. Ḍhakkō repeatedly denied that there was anything related to the Wahhābī school of thought in his books, since their interpretation of Islam was diametrically opposed to Shiʿism. If anyone understood his words in this way, this only showed that they were ignorant of the "original *madhhab* of the Āl-i Muḥammad" (see Ḍōgar, *Muḥammad Ḥusayn Ḍhakkō se 150 suʾāl*, 17).

86. Al-Najafī Ḍhakkō, *Iṣlāḥ al-rusūm*, 86–87.

87. Al-Najafī Ḍhakkō, *Uṣūl al-sharīʿa*, 387. In comparison with this earlier work, dating to 1967, Ḍhakkō's positions further crystallized toward an even less sectarian approach in *Iṣlāḥ al-rusūm*, published initially in 1995. In *Uṣūl al-sharīʿa* he still affirmed that the Infallibles (*maʿṣūmīn*, meaning the *ahl al-bayt* and the Imāms) obtained their knowledge from a wide range of sources. These included *ilhām* (non-Prophetic inspiration), the Holy Spirit (*rūḥ al-qudus*), the service of *jinns* and non-Qurʾānic scripture like the mysterious *Muṣḥaf-i Fāṭimah* (The [divine] book of Fāṭimah) and the *Kitāb-i jafr* (The book of divination). For more information on the role of these two books in the Shiʿi tradition, see Brunner, *Die Schia und die Koranfälschung*, 5; Momen, *An Introduction to Shiʿi Islam*, 150.

88. Al-Najafī Ḍhakkō, *Iṣlāḥ al-rusūm*, 80–82.

89. Al-Najafī Ḍhakkō, *Uṣūl al-sharīʿa*, 76–80.

90. Ḍōgar, *Muḥammad Ḥusayn Ḍhakkō se 150 suʾāl*, 70.

91. Al-Najafī Ḍhakkō, *Uṣūl al-sharīʿa*, 144–49.

92. Al-Najafī Ḍhakkō, *Iṣlāḥ al-rusūm*, 95.

93. Ibid., 90–91.

94. See Ḍōgar, *Muḥammad Ḥusayn Ḍhakkō se 150 suʾāl*, 21.

95. Ibid., 53.

96. Al-Najafī Ḍhakkō, *Uṣūl al-sharīʿa*, 192–98, 230.

97. Ibid., 85–86; al-Najafī Ḍhakkō, *Iṣlāḥ al-rusūm*, 158.

98. Al-Najafī Ḍhakkō, *Uṣūl al-sharīʿa*, 96.

99. Ḍōgar, *Muḥammad Ḥusayn Ḍhakkō se 150 suʾāl*, 20.

100. Al-Najafī Ḍhakkō, *Iṣlāḥ al-rusūm*, 98.

101. Ibid., 33–34. The claim that Shiʿi law is traditionally opposed to *maṣlaḥa*, while factually accurate, has been rather difficult to uphold since the Islamic Republic of Iran came into being. The new state has from its early days based many ordinances (like edicts to limit private ownership of agricultural land or laws on taxation) on this principle, despite the protest of senior clerics like Ayatollah Ibrāhīm Jannātī, who rejected

maṣlaḥa because it "could be interpreted as an admission that Islamic legislation suffers from deficiencies, and it establishes the possibility that different opinions may be represented at the same time and that conflicts may break out between them." *Maṣlaḥa* officially took center stage with the formation of the Assessment Council shortly before Khomeini's death in 1988. See Schirazi, *The Constitution of Iran*, 233–44.

102. Al-Najafī Ḍhakkō, *Iṣlāḥ al-rusūm*, 98.

103. Ibid., 109–13.

104. Al-Najafī Ḍhakkō, *Uṣūl al-sharīʿa*, 231–32. In explaining this fine distinction, Ḍhakkō never addressed the question of the effectiveness of the Imāms' intervention and whether they had a sort of coercing power over God (see Ḍōgar, *Muḥammad Ḥusayn Ḍhakkō se 150 suʾāl*, 31).

105. Al-Najafī Ḍhakkō, *Iṣlāḥ al-rusūm*, 122–23.

106. Ibid., 135–36.

107. Ibid., 105–6.

108. Ibid., 107–9.

109. Like al-Ṣadūq, for example, Ḍhakkō affirmed that he of course stood with the meaning of the third shahāda, since ʿAlī was without any doubt the *walī* of God and the rightful Caliph after the Prophet's death. See Takim, "From Bidʿa to Sunna," 166, 171.

110. On al-Khāliṣī, see Ende, "Success and Failure of a Shiite Modernist."

111. Takim, "From Bidʿa to Sunna," 175.

112. On Muḥsin al-Ḥakīm, see the next chapter. Sayyid ʿAbdullāh b. Muḥammad Ṭāhir Ṭāhirī Shīrāzī was born in 1891, studied in Najaf, and taught in Mashhad. Due to his opposition to the Shah, he was put in jail and later left for Iraq. He was one of the leading marājiʿ in Najaf after the death of Muḥsin al-Ḥakīm and opened three religious schools there (see Momen, *An Introduction to Shiʿi Islam*, 321).

113. Al-Najafī Ḍhakkō, *Iṣlāḥ al-rusūm*, 118–19.

114. Ende, "Bidʿa or Sirr al-Īmān?," 213. See also al-Muqarram, *Sirr al-īmān*, 57–58.

115. For more information on these towering *marājiʿ*, compare chapter 3.

116. Ende, "Bidʿa or Sirr al-Īmān?," 215.

117. "Muṣāḥabah bā ḥażrat-i Āyatullāh Ḥājj Shaykh Muḥammad Ḥusayn Najafī," 170–71. The title of Ḍhakkō's polemical work was *Tajalliyāt-i ṣadāqat bā-javāb Aftāb-i hidāyat*. For more information on the anti-Shiʿi discourse of the SSP, see chapter 5.

118. "Muṣāḥabah bā ḥażrat-i Āyatullāh Ḥājj Shaykh Muḥammad Ḥusayn Najafī," 170. See also Rieck, *The Shias of Pakistan*, 308–9.

119. Al-Najafī Ḍhakkō, *Iṣlāḥ al-rusūm*, 167–70.

120. Ibid., 146–47. Ḍhakkō claimed for himself the intellectual prowess necessary to stem this antischolarly tide. See al-Najafī Ḍhakkō, *Uṣūl al-sharīʿa*, 57.

121. Al-Najafī Ḍhakkō, *Iṣlāḥ al-rusūm*, 152. For a more detailed discussion of the goals of Ḥusayn, who deliberately only chose a small band of followers so that no one could accuse him of striving for rulership but rather wanted to be overcome by Yazīd in order to ultimately destroy *yazīdiyyat*, see al-Najafī Ḍhakkō, *Saʿādat al-dārayn*, 172–78.

122. See Jones, "Shiʿism, Humanity and Revolution," 423–24.

123. Al-Najafī Ḍhakkō, *Iṣlāḥ al-rusūm*, 142–43; al-Najafī Ḍhakkō, *Uṣūl al-sharīʿa*, 54.

124. Ḍhakkō here seems to echo arguments made by Muḥammad b. al-Ḥasan al-Ṭūsī (d. 459 or 460/1066–7), who advocated taqlīd in the uṣūl. In his view, one could not expect the "ignorant" (*jāhil*) layperson to grasp the reality of divine retribution, which was a prerequisite for being motivated to seek further knowledge about the uṣūl. Al-Ṭūsī's position was rejected, however, by the overwhelming majority of later scholars. They held that for the common believer all that was necessary was "knowledge of the general sense" (*al-dalīl al-ijmālī*), which could be attained with very little study. For a discussion, see Clarke, "The Shīʿī Construction of Taqlīd," 44–48.

125. Al-Najafī Ḍhakkō, *Uṣūl al-sharīʿa*, 20–21.

126. Al-Najafī Ḍhakkō, *Iṣlāḥ al-rusūm*, 136–37.

127. Aʿvān, *Mard-i ʿilm*, 11–12.

128. Ibid., 14–15.

129. Ruffle, *Gender, Sainthood, and Everyday Practice*, 153–54. *Rawḍat al-shuhadāʾ* itself was produced in the context of the (Sunni) Timurid Court, which had nevertheless marked a pinnacle of "imāmophilia." This mindset made it difficult "even for strictly Sunni orders like the Naqshbandiyya to distinguish between an 'approved' version of love for the imams and the disapproved hatred and cursing of the first three caliphs as well as ʿĀisha." See Anzali, "Safavid Shiʿism," 182; and Melvin-Koushki, "The Quest for a Universal Science," 69–71.

130. Aʿvān, *Mard-i ʿilm*, 16. On the water issue, see Zamir, "ʿAlī Naqvī and His Thought," 222; Jones, "Shiʿism, Humanity and Revolution," 430.

131. See Rieck, *The Shias of Pakistan*, 131–33; al-Najafī Ḍhakkō, *Uṣūl al-sharīʿa*, 424–30.

132. Interview with Muḥammad Ḥusayn al-Najafī Ḍhakkō, Jāmiʿat al-Muntaẓar, Lahore, 18 July 2012. Ḍhakkō stated that after receiving *ijāzas* in Najaf, he stopped doing taqlīd of Muḥsin al-Ḥakīm and started to devise his own rulings (see Ḍōgar, *Muḥammad Ḥusayn Ḍhakkō se 150 suʾāl*, 14).

133. Ibid., 17.

134. Ibid., 41. On the trope of the fraudulent wandering beggar-ascetic, also known as *qalandar*, see Ewing, *Arguing Sainthood*, 201–52.

135. "Muṣāḥabah bā ḥażrat-i Āyatullāh Ḥājj Shaykh Muḥammad Ḥusayn Najafī Pākistānī," 135. Usually, the *suṭūḥ* stages take four to five years to complete. See Khalid Sindawi, "Ḥawza Instruction," 841.

136. Aʿvān, *Mard-i ʿilm*, 25.

137. Ibid., 91–92. Ḍhakkō's traditionalist opponents accused him of regularly backing out at the last minute from arranged munāẓaras. This behavior in their view only added to the suspicion revolving around Ḍhakkō's *ʿaqāʾid*. See "Tabṣirah-i māhnāmah-i al-S̱aqalayn Multān." See also Rieck, *The Shias of Pakistan*, 76.

138. For an Iranian example of a decidedly nonpolitical reformist approach that went further than Ḍhakkō in its rationalizing outlook, see Richard, "Sharīʿat Sangalajī."

139. See Shigri, "Who Is? [*sic*] Agha Syed Ali Sharfuddin Mousvi Baltistani." Unfortunately, there are no truly reliable sources to establish the exact dates of Sayyid Sharaf al-Dīn's education and travels. Even accounts written by his supporters differ tremendously, with some claiming that he spent fifteen years in Iran alone, while others write that his education in both Iran and Iraq lasted twelve years (compare Roundovi, "Ali Sharfuddin Moosavi Baltistani"). Mūsavī is not mentioned in any of the relevant biographical dictionaries for Shiʿis in Pakistan (compare Ḥusayn, *Maṭlaʿ-i anvār*; Naqvī, *Taẕkirah-i ʿulamāʾ-i imāmiyyah*; ʿĀrif Naqvī, *Taẕkirah-i ʿulamāʾ-i imāmiyyah-i Pākistān [shamālī ʿalāqah jāt]*). My efforts to meet with Sayyid Sharaf al-Dīn Mūsavī in Karachi were met with his refusal. At least I had the chance to explore the bookshop of his Dār al-Thaqāfa al-Islāmiyya in Karachi's Nāẓimābād quarter and purchase many of his writings there.

140. See chapters 4 and 5 for more information on this group. ʿAlī Sharaf al-Dīn Mūsavī is inter alia mentioned as a member of the ISO's Advisory Council in "Report-i ijlās-i majlis-i- ʿāmilah," *Rāh-i ʿAmal* 46, 36.

141. Mūsavī ʿAlīābādī, *Miṡālī ʿazādārī*, 20.

142. Mūsavī ʿAlīābādī, *Intikhāb-i maṣāʾib*, 5–6.

143. Ibid., 8. See also Mūsavī ʿAlīābādī, *Tafsīr-i siyāsī*, 21–22; Mūsavī ʿAlīābādī, "Imām Ḥusayn ʿalayhi al-salām," 31–32.

144. Mūsavī ʿAlīābādī, *Tafsīr-i siyāsī*, 96, 155.

145. Mūsavī ʿAlīābādī, *Asrār-i qiyām-i Imām Ḥusayn*, 274–75.

146. Mūsavī ʿAlīābādī, *Tafsīr-i siyāsī*, 155.

147. Ibid., 134–41, 148–50. In the Shiʿi hadith corpus, Ḥusayn b. ʿAlī indeed figures as a personality with whom forbidding wrong and righteous rebellion are associated (see Cook, *Commanding Right and Forbidding Wrong*, 259–60). It is interesting to note that Mūsavī with his presentation is more in line with the classical Shiʿi scholarly tradition which emphasized inter alia the conditions of efficacy and the avoidance of mortal danger for commanding right and forbidding wrong (ibid., 276–81). Politicized Shiʿi scholars in the twentieth century like Khomeini, Kāẓim Sharīʿatmadārī (d. 1986), or Murtażā Muṭahharī (d. 1979), however, differed from Mūsavī and adopted a principle of relative weight (*ahammiyya*) with regard to the danger condition. They argued that there might be certain wrongs (like endangering the Qurʾān or Islam as a whole) which overrode the obligation to avoid harm (ibid., 534–39).

148. Mūsavī ʿAlīābādī, *Miṡālī ʿazādārī*, 40, 74–79.

149. Ibid., 112–15; Mūsavī ʿAlīābādī, *Dār al-Thaqāfa al-Islāmiyya*, 3.

150. Mūsavī ʿAlīābādī, *ʿAqāʾid ō rusūmāt-i shīʿah*, 105–10. This line of thought also echoes some of the statements by Sayyid ʿĀrif Ḥusayn al-Ḥusaynī, as chapter 4 discusses in more detail.

151. Ibid., 37–38.

152. Ibid., 60–62. It is interesting to note that Mūsavī chose a rather complimentary term for those Shiʿis he saw as misguided. One might speculate that he intended to avoid alienating them right away while at the same time emphasizing their "excessive" veneration for ʿAlī.

153. Ibid., 76–78.
154. Ibid., 98–102.
155. Ibid., 117–18.
156. Ibid., 86–87.
157. Mūsavī ʿAlīābādī, *Mis̱ālī ʿazādārī*, 40.
158. Ibid., 53.
159. Mūsavī ʿAlīābādī, *Madāris-i dīnī aur ḥauzāt-i ʿilmiyyah*, 18–19.
160. Mūsavī ʿAlīābādī, *Mis̱ālī ʿazādārī*, 60–61.
161. Mūsavī ʿAlīābādī, *Madāris-i dīnī aur ḥauzāt-i ʿilmiyyah*, 14–16.
162. Mūsavī ʿAlīābādī, *Mis̱ālī ʿazādārī*, 16–17, 43–44.
163. Mūsavī ʿAlīābādī, *Madāris-i dīnī aur ḥauzāt-i ʿilmiyyah*, 9.
164. Mūsavī ʿAlīābādī, *Mis̱ālī ʿazādārī*, 5.
165. For a discussion of how Khamenei's fatwa did not constitute a game changer in the context of Shiʿi populations in Kargil, a region located in the Indian part of Kashmir, see Gupta, "Experiments with Khomeini's Revolution in Kargil," 393–96.
166. During my fieldwork in Pakistan, Iran, and Iraq, I have tried my best to get hold of as many refutations of Ḍhakkō's writings as possible. I was not able, however, to consult the following works: Sayyid Żamīr al-Ḥasan Riżvī Najafī, *Maʿālim al-sharīʿa fī 'l-naqd wa-l-tabṣira ʿalā ʿaqāʾid al-shīʿa* (Aḥmadpūr Siyāl: Jāmiʿat al-Ghadīr); Sayyid Muḥammad ʿĀrif Naqvī, *Kāshif al-ḥaqāʾiq fī jawāb tafwīḍ Aḥsan al-fawāʾid* (Jhang: Dār al-ʿUlūm Ḥusayniyya); Mīrzā Yūsuf Ḥusayn, *Ḥaqāʾiq al-ʿaqāʾid* (Mīānwālī); Ḥasnayn al-Sābiqī, *Jawāhir al-asrār fī manāqib al-nabī wa-l-āʾimma al-athār* (Talah Gang: Maktabah-i Ḥamadānī); and Muhammad ʿĀrif Naqvī, *Asrār al-sharīʿa fī ʿaqāʾid ithnā ʿashariyya* (Jhang). For a listing of these publications, see Rieck, *The Shias of Pakistan*, 398–99.
167. Shiftah, *Tāʾyīd-i ḥaqq*, 11. Shiftah was born in 1924 in Jaunpūr (UP), where he received his education at the Madrasah-i Nāṣiriyya up to the degrees of *fāżil* and *tāj al-afāżil*. He also spent a short time at the Madrasah-i Nāẓimiyya in Lucknow and completed his *dars-i niẓāmī* there. Shiftah later obtained master's degrees in Persian, Arabic, Islamic studies, and Urdu. The last three were awarded by the University of Karachi after his emigration to Pakistan in 1951. Shiftah taught in government colleges in both Karachi and Sargōdhā. Sayyid Ḥusayn ʿĀrif Naqvī and Murtażā Ḥusayn both accuse him of doing propaganda work for the Shaykhīs in Pakistan (see ʿĀrif Naqvī, *Taẕkirah-i ʿulamāʾ-i imāmiyyah*, 179–81).
168. Letter by Żamīr al-Ḥasan Riżvī, reproduced in Aʿvān, *Mard-i ʿilm*, 97, 249–50.
169. Naqvi, "The Controversy," 142.
170. Rieck, *The Shias of Pakistan*, 132–33.
171. For more information on the *mubāhala* precedent par excellence, namely the confrontation between the Prophet and the Christians of Najrān, which is also crucial for grounding the Shiʿi concept of the ahl al-bayt in a Qurʾānic verse (Q33:33), see Strothmann, "Die Mubāhala in Tradition und Liturgie"; and Schmucker, "Die christliche Minderheit von Nağrān."
172. ʿĀbidī, *Ṭamāncah bar rukhsār*, 8–9, 77.

173. A'vān, *Mard-i 'ilm*, 171–73.

174. Mūsavī 'Alīābādī, *Dār al-Thaqāfa al-Islāmiyya*, 2.

175. Bashīr Anṣārī extolled the uniqueness of this school with its focus on preaching and proselytizing in the Shi'i world. According to him, the Madrasat al-Wā'iẓīn even attracted mujtahids from Najaf and Qum who attended the same classes with him. See Anṣārī, *Maqām-i ahl-i bayt*, lām.

176. For his role, see Rieck, *The Shias of Pakistan*, 58. According to Rieck, Anṣārī "was most of all interested in the *Shi'a Majlis-i 'Ulamā-i Pākistān* (SMUP) [. . .] which he envisioned as a 'supervisor' of the APSC—following the example of the *Shī'a Majlis-i 'Ulamā'* and the AISC in Lucknow."

177. 'Ārif Naqvī, *Tazkirah-i 'ulamā'-i imāmiyyah*, 276–79. The Shi'i community remembers in particular one debate held in 1934 during which a Deobandī 'ālim called Maḥbūb 'Ālam conceded his defeat in writing while his colleagues Maulānā 'Abd al-'Azīz and Maulānā Amīr Allāh Khān reportedly converted to Shi'i Islam. As a result, Anṣārī earned the title "*fātiḥ-i Ṭiksilā*" (Conqueror of Texila), referring to the location of the munāẓara. Bashīr Anṣārī himself estimated that his missionary activities over forty years had converted more than a hundred thousand people to Shi'i Islam (see Anṣārī, *Maqām-i ahl-i bayt*, ṭā).

178. Rieck, *The Shias of Pakistan*, 180.

179. Anṣārī, *Ḥaqā'iq al-wasā'iṭ*, 10–11.

180. Ibid., 13. For similar views, see also Ismā'īl, *Kalimah-i vilāyat*, 41; al-Zamān Naqvī Bukhārī, *Afkār al-muntaẓirīn*, 15, 37.

181. Anṣārī, *Ḥaqā'iq al-wasā'iṭ*, 88.

182. Ibid., 57. See also Sarḥadī, *Ṣirāt al-īmān*, 15, 38.

183. Anṣārī, *Ḥaqā'iq al-wasā'iṭ*, 14.

184. See al-Sābiqī, *Qawā'id al-sharī'a*, 402–7; al-Zamān, *Afkār al-muntaẓirīn*, 142–52.

185. Anṣārī, *Ḥaqā'iq al-wasā'iṭ*, 16.

186. 'Abidī was born in Khairpur in 1950 and died in a car accident near Karachi on 22 January 1998. See "Allama Abidi, Wife Laid to Rest." After graduating with a master's in political science from the University of Karachi, he quickly made a name for himself as a sought-after preacher from the 1970s onward, filling the void after the death of the legendary *ẓākir* Rashīd Turābī in 1973 (Caman, *Merī yādgār mulāqāteṉ*, 268–86). 'Ābidī served as a member of the Council of Islamic Ideology between 1990 and 1996 and also appeared on Pakistani Television (see Ḥaydar, *Islāmī naẓariyātī council*, 770–72; Naqvī, "Khaṭīb-i shām-i gharībān").

187. For the account, see Ṭabarī, Watt, and McDonald, *Muḥammad at Mecca*, 63–64.

188. 'Ābidī, *Ṭamāncah bar rukhsār*, 80–81. See also for another expression of this idea, Shiftah, *Tā'yīd-i ḥaqq*, 93. For 'Alī's military campaigns and credentials on the battlefield, see Haider, *Shi'i Islam*, 58.

189. Anṣārī, *Ḥaqā'iq al-wasā'iṭ*, 20.

190. Ibid., 118–21.

191. See Schmidtke, *The Theology of al-'Allāma al-Ḥillī*, 162–63.

192. Carney, "The Theos Agnostos," 11–12.

193. Ibid., 16.

194. Eschraghi, *Frühe Šaiḫī- und Bābī-Theologie*, 53–54.

195. Corbin, "L'École shaykhie," 207.

196. Eschraghi, *Frühe Šaiḫī- und Bābī-Theologie*, 85.

197. ʿĀbidī, *Ṭamāncah bar rukhsār*, 62–63.

198. See Carney, "The Theos Agnostos," 26–29; Eschraghi, *Frühe Šaiḫī- und Bābī-Theologie*, 43–44.

199. Anṣārī, *Ḥaqāʾiq al-wasāʾiṭ*, 22. See also al-Zamān al-Naqvī al-Bukhārī, *Afkār al-muntaẓirīn*, 281–83.

200. Anṣārī, *Ḥaqāʾiq al-wasāʾiṭ*, 54.

201. Ḍōgar, *Ṣaḥīfah-i ḥaqāʾiq*, 1:46.

202. Ibid., 49–50.

203. On the role of al-Khiḍr in Islamic thought, see Franke, *Begegnung mit Khidr*.

204. Ḍōgar, *Ṣaḥīfah-i ḥaqāʾiq*, 62–63.

205. Anṣārī, *Ḥaqāʾiq al-wasāʾiṭ*, 55. For Aḥmad al-Aḥsāʾī's and Karīm Khān's critiques of those scholars who are limited to legalistic understandings of religion, see Bayat, *Mysticism and Dissent*, 49, 74–75.

206. Ibid., 78. Anṣārī showed some understanding for the reformist ʿulamā, since they had chosen a course of caution in the face of the many hadiths denouncing the *ghulāt* (ibid., 122).

207. Ibid., 102.

208. ʿĀbidī, *Ṭamāncah bar rukhsār*, 164–65. For such an argument regarding the involvement of Shiʿi ʿulamā in the deaths of the important Shiʿi scholars Muḥammad b. Makkī (734–86/1333–84), known as *al-shahīd al-awwal* (the First Martyr), and Zayn al-Dīn b. ʿAlī al-ʿĀmilī (911–65 or 966 / 1506–57, 1506–58, or 1558–59), known as *al-shahīd al-thānī* (the Second Martyr), see al-Sābiqī, *Qawāʿid al-sharīʿa*, 6–8.

209. Anṣārī, *Ḥaqāʾiq al-wasāʾiṭ*, 17.

210. Al-Mūsawī was born in 1930 and died sometime during the 1990s. His grandfather Ayatollah al-Sayyid Abū 'l-Ḥasan al-Mūsawī al-Iṣfahānī (d. 1946) was one of the few supporters of the Lebanese reformist Muḥsin al-Amīn. He received an *ijāza* at the age of twenty-one from Kāshif al-Ghiṭā and in Paris completed a doctoral degree on Islamic philosophy. Later he became a university teacher in Tehran and was also a member of the Iranian Parliament. The SAVAK made an attempt on his life in 1968, which led al-Mūsawī to leave Iran. He reportedly taught until the revolution in Halle/Saale (Germany), at Harvard, in Tripoli (Libya), and Los Angeles and ran for office in the Iranian presidential elections of 1980. Al-Mūsawī has argued that Shiʿi Islam had been deformed through political power, especially under the Buyids when deviations such as the divine designation of ʿAlī as Caliph, the lifting of the concept of the imāmate into the rank of *uṣūl-i dīn*, *taqiyya*, or the belief in the infallibility (*iṣma*) of the Imāms came to be propagated. He called for a purging of Shiʿi hadith that was hostile toward the first three Caliphs and rejected the third shahāda as well as self-flagellation during Muḥarram. Julian Siddon has thus argued that al-Mūsawī advocated the most

radical approach toward Shiʿi reform in the twentieth century. His ideas were often identical with Sunni polemics against the Imāmīs, which meant that his suggested reforms would have led to the "inevitable destruction of the Shīʿa." See Siddons, *"Die Korrektur der Irrtümer,"* 11–28, 32–33, 36–37, 51–52, 128, 237. See also Brunner, "A Shiite Cleric's Criticism of Shiism."

211. I am not aware of any academic study that would discuss his thought. For a list of his works and some biographical data, see http://www.borqei.com/.

212. Ḍhakkō repeatedly stated that while studying in Najaf he and other Pakistani students only visited al-Khāliṣī "three or four times" in al-Kāẓimiyya, raising with him some controversial questions (*baʿẓ-i ikhtilāfī masāʾil*) (see Ḍhakkō, *Uṣūl al-sharīʿa*, 267). See also al-Sābiqī, *Khāliṣiyyatnāmah*, 5. For a more detailed discussion of al-Khāliṣī's thought and his reception in Pakistan, see Fuchs, "Failing Transnationally."

213. Al-Sābiqī, *Rusūm al-shīʿa*, 42–44.

214. Anṣārī, *Ḥaqāʾiq al-wasāʾiṭ*, 17.

215. Ibid., 141.

216. Ibid., 267. A famous prophetic hadith refers to ʿAlī as the "gate to the city of knowledge," with the Prophet being the city itself.

217. See Qasmi, *The Ahmadis and the Politics of Religious Exclusion*, 185–220; and chapter 5 of this book.

218. Anṣārī, *Ḥaqāʾiq al-wasāʾiṭ*, 184.

219. ʿĀbidī, *Ṭamāncah bar rukhsār*, 15–16.

220. Shiftah, *Tāʾyīd-i ḥaqq*, 10. Henry Corbin reaches a similar conclusion when relating the Shaykhī school to the Shiʿi heritage more broadly. He writes that it required a "certain hâte maladroite" if one wanted to accuse the Shaykhīs of *ghuluww*. Instead, he credited them with the desire to "maintenir intégralement la tradition. Cette volonté ne mérite pas que l'on porte un jugement dépréciatif sur une école qui continue de faire partie intégrante du shîʿisme" (Corbin, "L'École shaykhie," 211).

221. The verse reads as follows in Arberry's translation: "When it is said to them, 'Do not corruption in the land,' they say, 'We are only ones that put things right [*muṣliḥūn*].'" See ʿĀbidī, *Ṭamāncah bar rukhsār*, 57.

222. Sachedina, *The Just Ruler*, 128.

223. Al-Sābiqī, *Rusūm al-shīʿa*, 19–21. See chapter 3 for more information on the senior jurists and the Pakistani debate regarding the authority of the marājiʿ (Sources of Emulation) and their *wakīls*.

224. Ibid., 39–40.

225. Shiftah, *Tāʾyīd-i ḥaqq*, 36–37.

226. Al-Sābiqī, *Qawāʿid al-sharīʿa*, 12.

227. Ibid., cover page and al-Sābiqī, *Rusūm al-shīʿa*, 20. For such a portrayal of al-Iḥqāqī, see also "Āyatullāh al-ʿuẓmā Mīrzā Ḥasan al-Ḥāʾirī al-Iḥqāqī."

228. On the networks of both branches and their leading scholars since the nineteenth century, see Matthiesen, "Mysticism, Migration and Clerical Networks," 389–92, 399. Al-Sābiqī mentions that he acted as *wakīl* for Iḥqāqī and also translated his writings into Urdu (see al-Sābiqī, *Khāliṣiyyatnāmah*, 2). Similar to the lack of schol-

arly work on the early and mid-twentieth-century transmission of Shaykhī ideas between the Middle East and South Asia, there is also no study that would discuss such networks after the establishment of Pakistan. The remaining Shaykhī center in present-day Islamabad is connected to the Iḥqāqī branch in Kuwait, as becomes obvious from pictures of al-Iḥqāqī included in their publications. Andreas Rieck refers to some involvement of—and indeed rivalry between—both the Tabrizi and the Kermani branches in Pakistan without, however, providing a deeper exploration of these connections (see Rieck, *The Shias of Pakistan*, 175–77).

229. Khumaynī, *Vilāyat-i faqīh*, 67–68. It is interesting to speculate as to why Khomeini had only provided such a short, uncontextualized discussion of creational guardianship. Ali Rahnema argued that the Iranian leader tried to stay clear of this field of Shiʿi beliefs, since it had no immediate implication for his political project: "As a Shiʿi jurist, Khomeyni seems obliged to touch on the Divine-based spiritual authority of the Imams and separate it from the material responsibility of establishing government in the absence of the Hidden Imam. As a Shiʿi political theorist interested in the conceptualization and realization of an Islamic government, Khomeyni saw no reason to evoke or rely on *velayat-e takvini* or creational guardianship, as it was inapplicable to the here and the now" (see Rahnema, *Superstition as Ideology*, 103).

230. Al-Sābiqī, *Qawāʿid al-sharīʿa*, 12.

231. ʿĀbidī, *Ṭamāncah bar rukhsār*, 73–74. Compare also ibid., 97–98, for an example of how Qur'ānic verses speaking about the Prophet are extended to the Imāms.

232. See Schmidtke, *The Theology of al-ʿAllāma al-Ḥillī*, 142–43. For this discussion in the work of al-Shaykh al-Mufīd, see also McDermott, *The Theology of al-Shaikh al-Mufīd*, 107.

233. Shiftah, *Tā'yīd-i ḥaqq*, 45–46.

234. On his unique method of "letting the Book speak for itself" (*istinṭāq*), which is also known as "*tafsīr* of the Qur'ān by the Qur'ān," see Medoff, "Ijtihad and Renewal in Qur'anic Hermeneutics."

235. Al-Sābiqī, *Qawāʿid al-sharīʿa*, 189–203.

236. Ḍōgar, *Ṣaḥīfah-i ḥaqā'iq*, 46.

237. Steigerwald, *La pensée philosophique et théologique de Shahrastānī*, 53–56. See also Gaiser, "Satan's Seven Specious Arguments." On the development of the Ashʿarī school, see Nagel, *Die Festung des Glaubens*.

238. Angelika Hartmann, "Ismâʿîlitische Theologie bei sunnitischen 'Ulamâ' des Mittelalters?," 199–200. See also van Ess, *Das Eine und das Andere*, 860–900.

239. Al-Sābiqī, *Qawāʿid al-sharīʿa*, 75. See also al-Shahrastānī, *al-Milal wa-l-niḥal*, 2:352.

240. Al-Sābiqī, *Qawāʿid al-sharīʿa*, 72–73. See also al-Shahrastānī, *al-Milal wa-l-niḥal*, 2:345.

241. See Steigerwald, *La pensée philosophique et théologique de Shahrastānī*, 196–225.

242. Al-Sābiqī, *Qawāʿid al-sharīʿa*, 77.

243. Ibid., 92–93. See also al-Ghazālī, *Maʿārij al-quds*, 109.

244. Al-Sābiqī, *Qawāʿid al-sharīʿa,* 222–24. On al-Baghawī, see Robson, "al-Baghawī." On the Qāḍī ʿIyād, see Gómez-Rivas, "Qāḍī ʿIyāḍ (d. 544/1149)."

245. For a call to unity issued by Bashīr Anṣārī, see Anṣārī, "Islām dushman quvattōn ke ittiḥād ke pīsh naẓr."

246. Ismāʿīl, *Kalimah-i vilāyat,* 7.

247. Rieck, *The Shias of Pakistan,* 177.

248. Ismāʿīl, *Futūḥāt-i shīʿah,* 6.

249. Dakake, *The Charismatic Community,* 7.

250. Corbin, "Rûzbehân Baqlî Shîrâzî (522/1128–606/1209)," 9–10.

251. Cornell, *Realm of the Saint,* xvii–xx.

252. Buehler, "Aḥmad Sirhindī," 123.

253. See Friedmann, *Shaykh Aḥmad Sirhindī,* 51–52.

254. Ibid., 53.

255. See Ismāʿīl, *Kalimah-i vilāyat,* 21–23; Sirhindī, *Maktūbāt-i Imām-i Rabbānī,* 2:584–85. See also Friedmann, *Shaykh Aḥmad Sirhindī,* 35–36.

256. Haar, *Follower and Heir of the Prophet,* 87–88.

257. For reverse efforts of blurring Sufi-Shiʿi distinctions in eighteenth- and nineteenth-century Iran from a Sufi perspective by turning the Mahdi into the Sufi pole and arguing that due "to the Perfect Man, the Imam's *vilāyat* is not in occultation but accessible in the person of the Perfect Shiʿa," see Oliver Scharbrodt, "The *Quṭb* as Special Representative of the Hidden Imam," 40–49. Richard Gramlich, on the other hand, found that those Iranian dervishes that he interacted with only used the pronunciation *wilāya* and did not make a conceptual distinction between *wilāya* and *walāya.* See Gramlich, *Die schiitischen Derwischorden Persiens,* 158. For a recent treatment of efforts by Sufi orders under the Safavids to redefine the (Sunni) Sufi past and to show that the mystical path was fully rooted in the teachings of the Imāms, culminating in the argument that a true Shiʿi is a Sufi, see also Anzali, "Safavid Shiʿism," 133–85.

258. Ismāʿīl, *Kalimah-i vilāyat,* 20. For a conception of Ḥusayn as forming the center of unity, and an argument about an intimate connection between Ḥusayn and Pakistan, since both would stand for the affirmation that there was no God besides God, see ʿĀbidī, "Ḥażrat Imām Ḥusayn ʿalayhi al-salām."

259. Ḍōgar, *Ṣaḥīfah-i ḥaqāʾiq,* 1:197. For a similar accusation leveled against Ḍhakkō for allegedly conspiring with the SSP, compare ʿĀbidī, *Ṭamāncah bar rukhsār,* 165. For a detailed discussion of the SSP discourse, see also chapter 5.

260. Al-Sābiqī, *Rusūm al-shīʿa,* 32.

261. Ibid., 33. For the resemblances (and differences) between Barelvī and Shiʿi teachings, see Sanyal, *Devotional Islam and Politics,* 208–16.

262. On Thānavī's role within the Deobandī school, see Zaman, *Ashraf ʿAli Thanawi.*

263. Al-Sābiqī, *Rusūm al-shīʿa,* 36.

264. ʿĀbidī, *Ṭamāncah bar rukhsār,* 29.

265. Al-Sābiqī, *Rusūm al-shīʿa*, 31.

266. Abbas, "A few words." S. G. Abbas is introduced as "Professor of English, Former Principal Sirajuddaoulah Gov. College Karachi," who was tasked by Jaʿfar al-Zamān with reviewing and proofreading *The Last Great Reformer*, which al-Zamān had originally written in English shortly before his death.

267. This can be gathered from the fact that al-Zamān's younger brother Sayyid Ṭālib Ḥusayn Shāh Naqvī continues this function and receives more than two hundred visitors every night (see ʿĀrifī, *Shīʿīyān-i Pākistān*, 182–83). ʿĀrifī mentions several other Shiʿi pīrs located all over Pakistan, like Pīr Sayyid Bāvā Ṣadā-yi Ḥusayn in Lahore, Sayyid Anvar Shāh Miyān̲ from the Shiʿi section of the Tūrī tribe, Sayyid Miyān̲ and Pīr Sayyid Maḥmūd Muʿallim (both located in Khyber Pakhtunkhwa), Pīr Sayyid ʿAlamdār Shāh in Attock, and Pīr Sayyid Ṣādiq ʿAlī Shāh in Jacobābād. According to ʿĀrifī, all of these figures are engaged in writing special prayers and producing talismans (*taʿvīẕ*) for their followers (ibid., 184–85).

268. Besides the preface by S. G. Abbas, the book also includes an additional introduction written by two followers who are introduced as Professor Zulfiqar Husain Khan and Professor Faqir Shamim Ijaz (see Jafar-uz-Zaman Naqvi, *The Last Great Reformer*, i, vii). Al-Zamān's website is www.jamanshah.com.

269. In his analysis there is some overlap with the notion of an "objectification" of Islam among modernist thinkers as described by Dale Eickelman and James Piscatori. Such authors treat religion as a "self-contained system that its believers can describe, characterize, and distinguish from other belief systems." See Eickelman and Piscatori, *Muslim Politics*, 38.

270. Al-Zamān Naqvī Bukhārī, *Afkār al-muntaẓirīn*, 5–6.

271. Ibid., 7.

272. Ibid., 19.

273. Al-Zamān Naqvī Bukhārī, *Ṭarīq al-muntaẓirīn*, 24.

274. Jafar-uz-Zaman Naqvi, *The Last Great Reformer*, 122–24.

275. Ibid., 60.

276. Al-Zamān Naqvī Bukhārī, *Afkār al-muntaẓirīn*, 36.

277. Al-Zamān Naqvī Bukhārī, *Ṭarīq al-muntaẓirīn*, 5.

278. Ibid., 125.

279. Ibid., 125–29.

280. Jafar-uz-Zaman Naqvi, *The Last Great Reformer*, 254–55.

281. This invocation does not have any specific currency among the usual Shiʿi prayers. Personal communication from Sajjad Rizvi, 7 October 2014.

282. This sentence is rendered in the Urdu translation of the text as "*is vaqt nah merā kōʾī maẕhab he, aur nah kōʾī ʿaqīdah he.*" See Sayyid Muḥammad Jaʿfar al-Zamān Naqvī Bukhārī, *Mauʿūd al-rusul*, 330.

283. Jafar-uz-Zaman Naqvi, *The Last Great Reformer*, 256–57.

284. Ibid., 258.

285. Al-Zamān Naqvī Bukhārī, *Ṭarīq al-muntaẓirīn*, 33–34.

286. Sachedina, *Islamic Messianism,* 143–48.

287. Amir-Moezzi, "Contribution à la typologie des rencontres avec l'Imâm caché," 132–34.

288. Aigle, "Le symbolisme religieux šīʿite dans l'éloge funèbre de l'Imām Khomeyni," 76.

289. Braswell, "Civil Religion in Contemporary Iran," 227–29.

290. Rahnema, *Superstition as Ideology,* 110–11.

291. Ourghi, "'Ein Licht umgab mich . . . ,'" 163–80. See also Rahnema, *Superstition as Ideology,* 70–85.

292. Ibid., 86.

293. Ourghi, *Schiitischer Messianismus,* 243, 252–53.

CHAPTER THREE

1. A *ḥusayniyya* denotes a building in which Shiʿi mourning sessions (majālis) are held. While such majālis take place year-round, their frequency and intensity sharply increase during the first ten days of the Muslim month of Muḥarram in the run-up to the commemoration of the Battle of Karbala on 10 Muḥarram 61 (10 October 680) during which Ḥusayn was killed.

2. The school was founded as Madrasat al-Wāʿiẓīn—Jāmiʿah-i Imāmiyyah in 1955 and became fully operational in 1958 (see Kāẓimī, *Imāmiyyah dīnī madāris-i Pākistān,* 432–33).

3. Interview with Dr. ʿAqīl Mūsā, 23 July 2012, Karachi.

4. Conversation in the office of Shaykh ʿAlī al-Najafī, Najaf, Iraq, 16 January 2013.

5. See Jones, *Shiʿa Islam in Colonial India,* 39–44; Cole, *Roots of North Indian Shīʿism,* 65.

6. ʿĀrifī, *Shīʿīyān-i Pākistān,* 141–44.

7. Cole, *Roots of North Indian Shīʿism,* 65.

8. Sibṭayn Naqvī, "Iqtibās az diary," 37–40.

9. Interview with Muḥammad Ḥusayn Akbar, principal of Idārah-i Minhāj al-Ḥusayn, Lahore, 15 July 2012. For his madrasa, see http://www.minhaj-ul-hussain.org/. This fact was also corroborated by Muḥammad Ḥasan Sharīfī, director of the Kitābkhānah-i ʿAllāmah Iqbāl Lāhūrī, Qum, 23 August 2012. On the efforts of founding new schools in Pakistan, see Rieck, *The Shias of Pakistan,* 78–86.

10. See Mottahedeh, "Traditional Shiʿite Education in Qom," 454; Sindawi, "Ḥawza Instruction and Its Role in Shaping Modern Shīʿite Identity," 841–42. For an overview of the texts used in ḥauza education, see Fischer, *Iran,* 247–51.

11. Interview with Sayyid Ghulām Jābir Muḥammad and Sayyid Ḥusayn Zaydī, Al-Mustafa Open University, Qum, 29 August 2012. The claim by Muḥammad Ḥusayn Najafī Ḍhakkō to act as a marjiʿ does not seem to be widely shared. See "Muṣāḥabah bā ḥażrat-i Āyatullāh Ḥājj Shaykh Muḥammad Ḥusayn Najafī."

12. The most influential among these four towering jurists is doubtlessly the Iranian-born Sayyid ʿAlī al-Sīstānī (b. 1930). Besides him, there are also Muḥammad

Isḥāq al-Fayyāḍ (b. 1930 in Afghanistan's Ghaznī province) and Sayyid Muḥammad Saʿīd al-Ḥakīm (b. 1936 in Najaf). For further information on the current dynamics in Najaf in general and among the leading four grand ayatollahs in particular, see also Norton, "Al-Najaf"; Mervin, Tabbaa, and Bonnier, *Najaf*, 109–34.

13. ʿĀrif Naqvī, *Taẕkirah-i ʿulamā'-i imāmiyyah*, 60–61.

14. Ḥusayn al-Najafī, *Satabqā al-Najaf rā'idat ḥauzāt al-ʿalam.*

15. Interview with Grand Ayatollah Bashīr Ḥusayn Najafī, Najaf, Iraq, 22 January 2013.

16. Cole, *North Indian Shīʿism*, 124. It has to be said that Cole's depiction of Akhbārī legal and religious thought in the context of North India strikes the reader as somewhat one-sided and generalized. Robert Gleave, for example, has drawn our attention to the internal diversity of the Akhbārī school, which also had room for complex discussions of theology, relying on rational argumentation and philosophical reasoning. See Gleave, *Scripturalist Islam*, 138–39. Additionally, Gleave has called into question the egalitarian aspect of the school, arguing that Akhbārī ʿulamā were equally concerned with upholding their religious authority because even in their focus on texts available to the whole community "complex hermeneutic procedures" where still required when the texts were silent, contradictory or ambiguous (ibid., 302–3). Compare also Stewart, "The Genesis of the Akhbārī Revival."

17. Cole, *North Indian Shīʿism*, 284.

18. Ibid., 215.

19. Jones, *Shi'a Islam in Colonial India*, 20.

20. Ibid., 142. For a discussion of the competition between various sects and their affiliated organizations in the context of colonial Mumbai, see Green, *Bombay Islam*, 24–48.

21. Jones, *Shi'a Islam in Colonial India*, 179.

22. Ibid., 227–28.

23. For a pioneering and detailed study on the organizational aspects of al-Ḥakīm's *marjiʿiyya*, which involved his sons and representatives and also saw the founding of the World Ahl al-Bayt Islamic League in London (as well as later political activism of family members in Iraq and Iran), see Corboz, *Guardians of Shiʿism*, 21–47, 123–64.

24. Rieck, *The Shias of Pakistan*, 172.

25. Abū 'l-Qāsim al-Khū'ī was born in 1899 in Iran. In the early 1910s his family migrated to Najaf, where al-Khū'ī received his education. While twelve senior ʿulamā backed al-Khū'ī after the death of al-Ḥakīm as the new universal marjiʿ, his position never became absolute due to the presence of many other senior scholars at the time (as also discussed below). Elvire Corboz has also carefully studied al-Khū'ī and his family's leadership structures, in particular the philanthropic and at times political activist Al-Khoei Foundation which served the promotion and institutionalization of the marjiʿ's authority even after his death (Corboz, *Guardians of Shiʿism*, 100–118, 177–88).

26. Nasr, "The Iranian Revolution and Changes in Islamism," 239. On the competi-

tion of al-Khūʾī and Khomeini in Najaf, which included an escalating battle over who would pay higher stipends to students, see Corboz, *Guardians of Shiʿism*, 96.

27. Keddie, "Shīʿism and Change," 400.

28. Pinault, *Notes from the Fortune-Telling Parrot*, 79.

29. See Marsden, *Living Islam*, 9; Khan, *Muslim Becoming*, 145–70.

30. See Heern, "Thou Shalt Emulate the Most Knowledgeable," 336, and the discussion below.

31. Amanat, "In between the Madrassa and the Marketplace," 100.

32. For such an account, see Akbar, *Pākistān ke dīnī masālik*, 225–26. Akbar, a former activist and president of the Imamia Students Organisation (ISO) and now the head of a think tank in Islamabad, provides an account which portrays Pakistan as being perfectly in line with an essentialist version of the marjiʿiyya while not acknowledging any local variations during the course of the twentieth century.

33. See below for more biographical details.

34. This opinion was often voiced during my interviews, including by the London-based mujtahid Ḥasan Riżā Ghadīrī (interview in his residence, London, 20 June 2012). See also for a detailed discussion of the school's origins and its development, Kāẓimī, *Dīnī Madāris*, 237–72.

35. Andreas Rieck in his book only refers to *Payām-i ʿAmal* twenty-six times, to *al-Muntaẓar* sixteen times, and to *al-Ḥujjat* four times.

36. See Asadī, *al-Imām al-Ḥakīm*, 279–81. Elvire Corboz also emphasizes the general importance al-Ḥakīm attached to his representatives. He sent these wakīls even to villages in his native Iraq, whereas his predecessors had only dispatched them to the country's urban centers (Corboz, *Guardians of Shiʿism*, 25).

37. Burūjirdī was born in 1875 in central Iran. After studying in Isfahan and Najaf and teaching for thirty-four years in his native Burūjird, he assumed the leadership of the ḥauza in Qum in 1944. His tenure witnessed the expansion of mosques, schools, and libraries and significantly increased the population of students and teachers in the city (Rāzī, *Ganjīnah-i dānishmandān*, 1:344–56). On Burūjirdī's religious leadership, see also Mottahedeh, *The Mantle of the Prophet*, 236–41. We know of two prominent scholars whom Burūjirdī sent to Pakistan as his representatives. Akhtar ʿAbbās (d. 1999), known in Pakistan as Shaykh al-Jāmiʿa, came to Lahore in 1954 to take over as principal of the Jāmiʿat al-Muntaẓar (see ʿĀrif Naqvī, *Taẕkirah-i ʿulamāʾ-i imāmiyyah*, 31–32). Even earlier, Burūjirdī had ordered Muḥammad Sharīʿat to install himself in Karachi in 1952 (ibid., 313).

38. Clarke, "The Shīʿī Construction of Taqlīd," 41–43. For a detailed discussion of how the Shiʿi community came to terms with the traumatic absence of an Imām in their midst, see Modarressi Tabataba'i, *Crisis and Consolidation*, 53–99.

39. Clarke, "The Shīʿī Construction of Taqlīd," 48–49.

40. For the Akhbārīs, however, certainty (*al-ʿilm* or *al-yaqīn*) played a central role in their "stratified epistemology" (Gleave, *Scripturalist Islam*, 61–101).

41. For arguments that the Lebanese ʿālim Sayyid Muḥammad Ḥusayn Faḍlallāh (d. 2010) was so attuned to the latest technological developments and ahead of his

time that his legal opinions could be followed for many years after his death, see Clarke, "After the Ayatollah," 153–86.

42. Clarke, "The Shīʿī Construction of Taqlīd," 53–54.

43. Moussavi, "The Institutionalization of Marjaʿ-i Taqlīd," 280. Devin Stewart has challenged this notion, arguing that "the condition of *aʿlamīyah* is not a recent phenomenon that has arisen in the last few centuries in Twelver Shiite law, but rather a standard feature of Shiite legal theory found in the works of jurisprudence from the early eleventh century until the present" (Stewart, *Islamic Legal Orthodoxy*, 230). It seems to me, however, that there does not need to be a contradiction between Stewart's argument about premodern jurists defending *aʿlamiyya* and the nineteenth century providing the material conditions for putting this idea into practice on a global level.

44. Moussavi, "The Institutionalization of Marjaʿ-i Taqlīd," 286–87.

45. Heern, "Thou Shalt Emulate the Most Knowledgeable Living Cleric," 325.

46. Moussavi, "The Institutionalization of Marjaʿ-i Taqlīd," 290. Khums (the fifth) is payable for Shiʿis on (1) booty, (2) objects obtained from the sea, (3) treasure, (4) mineral resources, (5) gainful earnings, (6) lawful earnings that have become mixed up with unlawful income, and (7) land transferred from a Muslim to a protected non-Muslim (*dhimmī*). Shiʿis are supposed to pay this to their Imām, who is the proprietor of the whole earth, or, during the Occultation, to a just mujtahid who acts as representative of the Twelfth Imām. According to the standard Shiʿi interpretation, half of this amount received by the mujtahid is to be used for activities related to the propagation of the faith (including expenses for students, schools, etc.), while the second half is to be distributed among needy sayyids (Sachedina, "Al-Khums: The Fifth in the Imāmī Shīʿī Legal System," 237–45). Juan Cole suggests that Sayyid Muḥammad Ḥasan Najafī appointed Anṣārī in order to "formalize the selection of the new source for emulation, and to make that selection the prerogative of the preceding holder of the post." See Cole, "Imami Jurisprudence and the Role of the Ulama," 41.

47. Litvak, *Shiʿi Scholars and Patrons*, 108.

48. Heern, "Thou Shalt Emulate the Most Knowledgeable Living Cleric," 327–34.

49. Litvak, *Shiʿi Scholars and Patrons*, 72–73.

50. Ibid., 74–75.

51. Moussavi, "The Institutionalization of Marjaʿ-i Taqlīd," 295.

52. Mallat, *The Renewal of Islamic Law*, 48.

53. Moussavi, "The Institutionalization of Marjaʿ-i Taqlīd," 296–97.

54. Aziz, "Baqir al-Sadr's Quest for the Marjaʿiya," 145. For attempts (and the ultimate failure) by the Iranian state to equate the office of *rahbar* (Leader of the Revolution) with the position of universal marjiʿ, see also Gieling, "The Marjaʿiya in Iran."

55. Corboz, *Guardians of Shiʿism*, 25–31; Lambton, "A Reconsideration of the Position of the Marja' Al-Taqlid," 119.

56. Litvak, *Shiʿi Scholars and Patrons*, 8–9; Amanat, "In between the Madrassa and the Marketplace," 118–23. On the competition between Najaf and Qum (and between Persian- and Arabic-speaking Shiʿis), see Stewart, "The Portrayal of an Academic Rivalry."

57. Mallat, *The Renewal of Islamic Law*, 57–58. On the *ahl al-khibra*, who are also known as *ahl al-tamyīz* (The People of Discernment), see Gleave, "Conceptions of Authority in Iraqi Shi'ism," 67–70. See also Walbridge, *The Thread of Mu'awiya*, 24–42.

58. Akbar, *Pākistān ke dīnī masālik*, 317. See also Shāh Kāẓimī, "Ahl-i tashayyuʿ kī ek imtiyāzī khuṣūṣiyyat," 22.

59. Sayyid Muḥammad Bāqir spent ten years in Najaf. He is credited with emphasizing the study of Arabic and Arabic poetry in his role as headmaster of the Madrasat Sulṭān al-Madāris. He mostly wrote fiqh works in Arabic and is buried in Karbala. His network of *muqallids* supposedly extended to both Africa and Europe (see Ḥusayn, *Maṭlaʿ-i anvār*, 494–99).

60. See ʿĀrif Naqvī, *Taẕkirah-i ʿulamāʾ-i imāmiyyah*, 135–36; Ḥusayn, *Maṭlaʿ-i anvār*, 716–17. Mashhadī was also very active in the agitations of the 1970s against the Aḥmadīs.

61. Mashhadī, "Shīʿōn̠ ke tanazzul ke asbāb. Qisṭ-i 12," 5; Mashhadī, "Shīʿōn̠ ke tanazzul ke asbāb. Qisṭ-i 11," 8.

62. Mashhadī, "Ek khaṭāʾ aur us kī javāb," 28.

63. Mashhadī, "Shīʿōn̠ ke tanazzul ke asbāb. Qisṭ-i 15," 14. Mashhadī's reasoning here bears some similarity to that of Murtażā Anṣārī, who required that junior mujtahids must follow a single supreme marjiʿ (*marjiʿ al-taqlīd al-muṭlaq*). The supreme mujtahid was dependent on this support because only this way would the ʿulamā form a unified front (see Heern, "Thou Shalt Emulate the Most Knowledgeable Living Cleric," 338).

64. Born into a Shiʿi scholarly family in Kashmīr, he studied with his father, Sayyid Mahdī Shāh Riżvī (d. 1896), and proceeded to Lucknow where his intellect reportedly even astonished the senior teachers. He was in Lucknow during the rebellion against the British. When as a consequence he felt that "the space for scholarship was tightening" (*ʿilmī fażā tang makhṣūṣ hōne lagī*) in the city, he traveled around 1867 with his maternal uncle to Iraq's "exalted thresholds" (*ʿatabāt-i ʿāliyāt*) and studied with the major scholars of the time. When the leading Ayatollah Mīrzā Muḥammad Ḥasan b. Maḥmūd Shīrāzī (1815–95) was asked about whether in his view Kashmīrī qualified as an "absolute mujtahid" (*mujtahid-i muṭlaq*), Shīrāzī answered that there was no doubt about this. Kashmīrī settled in Karbala where he engaged in teaching and also led the congregational prayer each Friday (see Kashmīrī, *Dānishnāmah-i Shīʿīyān-i Kashmīr*, 247–51). On the role Shīrāzī played in the Iranian Tobacco Protest, see Keddie, *Religion and Rebellion in Iran*, 65–109.

65. For more biographical details on Sayyid Muḥammad Bāqir, see Ḥusayn, *Maṭlaʿ-i anvār*, 494–99.

66. Mashhadī, "Shīʿōn̠ ke tanazzul ke asbāb. Qisṭ-i 15," 15.

67. Mashhadī, "Shīʿōn̠ ke tanazzul ke asbāb. Qisṭ-i 16," 30. See also Mashhadī, "Ek aham tavajjuh dahānī."

68. Mashhadī, "Shīʿōn̠ ke tanazzul ke asbāb. Qisṭ-i 18," 8.

69. Andreas Rieck seems to echo some of Mashhadī's criticism, claiming that both organizations "were mainly financed by big landlords and wealthy traders, with

ʿulamāʾ, advocates, and some professional agitators trying to mobilize the Shiite rank-and-file to stand up for their rights with conventions and oratory meetings, while at the same time singing the praise of their sponsors" (see Rieck, "The Struggle for Equal Rights as a Minority," 274). Both the APSC and the ITHS "did occupy themselves with numerous minor Shia demands and grievances, including purely local problems and conflicts, but the main issues taken up by these organisations were principal questions regarding the status of the Shia minority in the country. The ITHS attached special importance to constitutional safeguards, to 'adequate representation' of Shias in various departments and institutions of the state, and the demand for separate religious instruction in schools and colleges. The APSC was much less apprehensive for 'Shia rights' at the time of its foundation, but gradually it had to adopt a more assertive communalist approach, too, in a bid to catch up with the popular appeal of the ITHS" (see Rieck, *The Shias of Pakistan*, 66–67).

70. Mashhadī, "Shīʿōn̲ ke tanazzul ke asbāb. Qisṭ-i 21," 22; Mashhadī, "Shīʿōn̲ ke tanazzul ke asbāb. Qisṭ-i 23," 15.

71. Mashhadī, "Shīʿōn̲ ke tanazzul ke asbāb. Qisṭ-i 17," 6.

72. "Al-Istiftāʾ," 8. See also Mashhadī, "Shīʿōn̲ ke tanazzul ke asbāb. Qisṭ-i 27," 31.

73. On him, see Algar, "Behbahānī, Moḥammad."

74. Al-Ḥakīm, "Telegraph," 5.

75. For the original announcement, see "Aham khūshkhabarī."

76. Asadī, *al-Imām al-Ḥakīm*, 281. Gulāb ʿAlī Shāh was a teacher of many reformist minded scholars in Pakistan, such as Shaykh Akhtar ʿAbbās, Muḥammad Ḥusayn al-Najafī Ḍhakkō, or Ṣafdar Ḥusayn Najafī. He attracted criticism from more traditionalist scholars for emphasizing the human nature of the Imāms and prophets (see ʿĀrif Naqvī, *Taẕkirah-i ʿulamāʾ-i imāmiyyah*, 240–43).

77. Sayyid Muḥsin is listed for Karachi, Ghulām Mahdī for Sindh (see ʿĀrif Naqvī, *Taẕkirah-i ʿulamāʾ-i imāmiyyah*, 210–11), Nāṣir Ḥusayn and Muḥammad Ḥusayn for Punjab and Ṣafdar Ḥusayn Najafī for Lahore. Ṣafdar Ḥusayn Mashhadī is credited with a particularly strong following in Rawalpindi. See Shāh Riżvī, "Shīʿīyān-i Pākistān kā ʿajīb takhayyul," 4.

78. Mashhadī, "Shīʿōn̲ ke tanazzul ke asbāb. Qisṭ-i 12," 5.

79. Zamān ʿAlavī, "ʿUlamāʾ kā maqām."

80. *Hāẕā* [*sic*] *āp par vājib he ke ayse faqīh ō mujtahid ke pāband banen̲ jis ke ẕarīʿe āp aʿlam kī taqlīd par qāʾim ō bar qarār rah sakten̲* [*sic*]. See Shāh Riżvī, "Taqlīd ke maʿne," 15.

81. See "ʿUlamāʾ-i Najaf-i Ashraf kā Lāhōr men̲ vurūd-i masʿūd" and Shāh Riżvī, "Shīʿīyān-i Pākistān kā ʿajīb takhayyul," 2.

82. Ibid.

83. Ibid., 3.

84. Since *al-Ḥujjat* does not provide any names, it is difficult to identify those groups and individuals who were criticized for pressing ahead with a certain candidate (the exception being the journal *al-Muntaẓar*; see below). In a rare instance in which a specific name was mentioned, in this case a certain Yūsuf Bīrjandī Khurāsānī,

who was criticized for doubting the credentials of well-established mujtahids without having himself reached this rank, the culprit seems to have resided outside of Pakistan. See "Jamāʿat-i ʿulamāʾ-i Baghdād kā maktūb."

85. Mashhadī, "Marājiʿ al-taqlīd," 20.

86. Zamān ʿAlavī, "Taqlīd aur aʿlamiyyat," 20.

87. Mashhadī, "Taqlīd-i aʿlam ō sharāʾiṭ-i taqlīd," 27. For Shiʿi political activism during the 1950s and 1960s in Pakistan, which mostly revolved around attempts to secure special Shiʿi rights and safeguards vis-à-vis the state, see Rieck, "The Struggle for Equal Rights," 268–83, and *The Shias of Pakistan*, 66–78, 114–24. See also chapter 4. For an earlier critique of ʿulamā who rendered themselves subservient to *anjuman* leaders, compare Mashhadī, "Shīʿōn̲ ke tanazzul ke asbāb. Qisṭ-i 29," 12.

88. Shāh Riżvī, "Niyābat-i Imām ʿalayhi al-salām," 47. The journal does not elaborate any further, however, as to how the "most righteous" could and should be identified.

89. Mashhadī, "Marājiʿ al-taqlīd," 21.

90. See, for example, Shāh Riżvī, "Mashhūr marājiʿ al-taqlīd," 28–29, for a list of the eight leading marājiʿ of the time. A list published in August 1971 lists five of them as being particularly well-known in Pakistan. See "Shīʿah-i dīnī ō ʿilmī marākiz," 5.

91. Zaidi, *Issues in Pakistan's Economy*, 91–97.

92. For a detailed discussion of leftist rhetoric during the 1960s in Pakistan, see Iqtidar, *Secularizing Islamists?*, 55–97.

93. See Uddin, "In the Land of Eternal Eid," 165, 238.

94. Talbot, *Pakistan*, 101.

95. Quoted in Syed, *The Discourse and Politics of Zulfikar Ali Bhutto*, 66–67.

96. Despite all fiery rhetoric, "the whole nationalization episode appears to have been marked by a good deal of caution." See Gustafson, "Economic Reforms under the Bhutto Regime," 241–44.

97. Ali, *Communism in Pakistan*, 193. Ali points out, however, that Bhutto often initiated these measures without taking into account the view of trade unions. Additionally, strikes during the early 1970s were frequently broken up by administrative and coercive means. At the end of the day, Bhutto failed both to regard political opposition as legitimate or to transform the PPP into an institutionalized party. See Milam, *Bangladesh and Pakistan*, 48.

98. Jaffrelot, *The Pakistan Paradox*, 230–31.

99. Pirzada, *The Politics of the Jamiat Ulema-i-Islam Pakistan*, 32–33.

100. For Muḥsin al-Ḥakīm's opposition to communism and his fatwa of February 1960 that forbade membership in the Iraqi Communist Party, see also Corboz, *Guardians of Shiʿism*, 126–27.

101. Al-Ḥakīm, "Cih dilāvar ast duzdī kih be kaf cirāgh dārad," 72.

102. Shāh Naqvī, "Naql-i khaṭṭ."

103. See Ḥusayn Shāh "Khaṭṭ," 4; and Mashhadī, "Masʾalah-i taqlīd se ʿadam wāqafiyyat," 11.

104. Shāh Riżvī, "Nāmah ō javāb-i nāmah," 34.

105. Jones, *Shi'a Islam in Colonial India*, 247.

106. Zamir, *ʿAlī Naqvī and His Thought*, 42–43.

107. Ibid., 54, 58.

108. Ibid., 87.

109. Jones, "Shiʿism, Humanity and Revolution," 433.

110. Zamir, *ʿAlī Naqvī and His Thought*, 21. See also Hyder, *Reliving Karbala*, 102.

111. It would be a fascinating, if daunting, endeavor to compare the literary output of the two sister-missions, given that one senior missionary of the Pakistani Imamia Mission, Mirzā Aḥmad ʿAlī, alone was credited with having written over six hundred pamphlets (see Ghażanfar Riżvī, "Nā-qābil-i farāmūsh," 17–18).

112. This changed only in 1968, when Naqvī answered legal questions in the January and March issues of *Payām-i ʿAmal*.

113. Al-Hamadānī, "Aʿlam-i zamān," 16–17.

114. See, for example, Ḥakīm, "Tashrīḥ al-masāʾil (January 1964)," 26; and Ḥakīm, "Tashrīḥ al-masāʾil (July 1963)," 23–24.

115. "Sālānah Report Imāmiyyah Mission Pakistan," 13.

116. See, for example, *Payām-i ʿAmal* 15, no. 8 (October 1971). Here the letter features prominently on the first page of the journal.

117. Jaʿfar, "Payām-i ʿAmal meṉ kā payghām," 8.

118. Ḥusayn Najafī, "Islām kā markaz-i rūḥānī," 20. Sayyid Ṣafdar Ḥusayn Najafī inter alia translated Khomeini's *Tawḍīḥ al-Masāʾil* and his *Ḥukūmat-i Islāmī* into Urdu (see ʿĀrif Naqvī, *Taẕkirah-i ʿulamāʾ-i imāmiyyah*, 136–39).

119. Al-Shāhrūdī, "Masāʾil-i sharʿiyyah."

120. Al-Khūʾī, "Istiftāʾ."

121. *Payām-i ʿAmal* 17, nos. 1–2 (March 1973).

122. Shāh Kāẓimī, "Ahl-i tashayyuʿ kī ek imtiyāzī khuṣūṣiyyat," 25.

123. "Rithāʾ-i Muḥsin al-Ḥakīm."

124. Zaydī had earned a *maulvī fāżil* degree at the age of eighteen from the Madrasah-i Manṣibiyya in Meruṭh and later acted as preacher (*khaṭīb*) for twenty-two years in Barelī before migrating to Pakistan. In Lahore, he became a preacher at the main Shiʿi mosque of the predominantly Shiʿi Islāmpūrah neighborhood (ʿĀrif Naqvī, *Taẕkirah-i ʿulamāʾ-i imāmiyyah*, 280–81).

125. Jaʿfar, "Taẕkirah-i mashāhīr-i shīʿah. Qiṣt-i duvum," 23.

126. Jaʿfar, "Dō fiqhī suʾālōṉ ke javāb," 31–32; Jaʿfar, "Masāʾil-i sharʿiyyah aur un ke javābāt."

127. Jaʿfar, "Rasūl-i Khudā kī kitnī bīṭiyāṉ thī?," 25–26.

128. See, for example, al-Ḥakīm, "Bāb al-masāʾil. Taqlīd," al-Hamadānī, "Fasādāt-i Muḥarram," and *al-Muntaẓar* 8, nos. 4–5 (20 April and 5 May 1966): 7.

129. See Jaʿfarī and Karāravī, "Kahne kī bāteṉ (June 1966)," 5; "Press Branch mutawajjah hō!," 23.

130. Alī Shāh, "Jān gudāz sānihah."

131. See chapter 4 for more biographical information on Sayyid Murtażā Ḥusayn. An English version of his biography of Muḥsin al-Ḥakīm was published in 1973. See Ḥusayn, *Hayat-e-Hakeem*; ʿĀrif Naqvī, *Tazkirah-i ʿulamāʾ-i imāmiyyah*, 347–49.

132. For a detailed account of the background to the war and its various offensives, see Bajwa, *From Kutch to Tashkent.*

133. Ḥusayn, "Āyatullāh al-Ḥakīm kī riḥlat," 15.

134. Ibid. For the letter sent by Muḥsin al-Ḥakīm, see Sarrāj, *al-Imām Muḥsin al-Ḥakīm.*

135. For a discussion of Sunni-Shiʿi tensions during this time, see Rieck, *The Shias of Pakistan*, 109–14. A brief English account of the events in 1963 can be found at http://www.shaheedfoundation.org/tragic.asp?Id=13.

136. Ḥusayn, "Āyatullāh al-Ḥakīm kī riḥlat," 15.

137. Jāṛā, "Tauẓīḥāt (20 May 1965)," 20.

138. See, for example, al-Ḥakīm, "Bāb al-masāʾil (20 March 1966)," 18.

139. Jāṛā, "Tauẓīḥāt (20 June 1965)," 12.

140. For some observations on his role as a teacher in Qum, see Fischer, *Iran*, 62–66.

141. ʿAbbās, "Tazkirah-i jamīl," 4–5.

142. Ibid., 8.

143. Ibid., 8–9.

144. Ibid., 11.

145. *Al-Muntaẓar*'s readers had already been informed in May 1966 that Akhtar ʿAbbās had taken over this new position at the Dār al-Tablīgh (see *al-Muntaẓar* 8, no. 6: 1).

146. Abbās, "Tazkirah-i jamīl," 11–12.

147. Ibid., 12.

148. Jaʿfarī and Karāravī, "Marjiʿ-i vaqt kā iʿlān," 15.

149. He was known to the community as the "Greatest Preacher" (*khaṭīb-i aʿẓam*) and also established an important library in Karachi (see ʿĀrif Naqvī, *Tazkirah-i ʿulamāʾ-i imāmiyyah*, 254–56). For his political activities, compare also Rieck, "The Struggle for Equal Rights as a Minority," 277–81; Rieck, *The Shias of Pakistan*, 114–24; and chapter 4 of this book.

150. Jaʿfarī and Karāravī, "Marjiʿ-i vaqt kā iʿlān," 16.

151. "Marjiʿ-i vaqt kā ʿamaliyyah-i tauẓīḥ al-masāʾil."

152. Jaʿfar and Karāravī, "Taʿyīn-i marjiʿ-i vaqt aur ahl-i khibrah," 16.

153. ʿAlī, "Masʾalah-i aʿlamiyyat," 37.

154. "Dār al-Tablīgh-i Islāmī-yi Qum meṉ mujāhid-i Islām kī āmad," 68.

155. Jaʿfarī and Karāravī, "Numāʾyandigān-i sarkār-i Āyatullāh al-ʿuẓmā Aqāʾ-i Sharīʿatmadār," 27.

156. *Āshnāʾī bā faʿālīyathā-yi Dār al-Tablīgh-i Islāmī*, 28. See also Shāh Kāẓimī, "Ahl-i tashayyuʿ kī ek imtiyāzī khuṣūṣiyyat," 22.

157. Fischer, *Iran*, 91. In a different institutional context and for the argument that the support of the Al-Khoei Foundation in 1992 might have contributed to the rise of ʿAlī al-Sīstānī, see also Corboz, *Guardians of Shiʿism*, 66–70.

CHAPTER FOUR

1. Qamar Zaydī, *Pānc hafte Āyatullāh Khumaynī ke Īrān men̲*, 24–26. For a similar account of the country's complete transformation within a matter of weeks from a police state where pork and alcohol were freely available, see Malik, "Īrān se wāpasī par Maulānā Ṣafdar Ḥusayn Najafī se ek interview."

2. See Qamar Zaydī, *Rahbar-i mā Khumaynī*. The most influential of his travel companions, and the one to whom Qamar Zaydī referred frequently, was Ibn-i Ḥasan Najafī, who was born in Lucknow in 1928. After receiving his advanced religious education in Najaf, Ibn-i Ḥasan was first employed in the educational bureaucracy of the princely state of Hyderabad/Deccan before moving to Pakistan in 1953. Besides being a prolific writer, he was involved with various educational activities for which the Pakistani government bestowed on him the Sitārah-i Imtiyāz, Pakistan's third highest civilian award, in 1980 (see ʿĀrif Naqvī, *Taẕkirah-i ʿulamāʾ-i imāmiyyah*, 11–12). Ibn-i Ḥasan, for his part, praised Qamar Zaydī as a true ʿālim who in his travelogue combined *ʿaql* (intellect) with trustworthiness (Qamar Zaydī, *Pānc hafte*, 6).

3. Qamar Zaydī, *Pānc hafte*, 29, 31–32, 50.

4. Ibid., 32.

5. Ibid., 56.

6. Ibid., 26–27.

7. Ibid., 12–13.

8. See Ḥasan, *Inqilāb-i Īrān*, 8.

9. Ibid., 21.

10. Ibid., 340.

11. Qamar Zaydī, *Pānc hafte*, 47.

12. Ibid., 16–17. On this phenomenon of televised confessions, see also the exhaustive study Abrahamian, *Tortured Confessions*. Abrahamian has termed these televised confessions "propaganda by self-denunciation" because the accused had to formulate the charges which the state had leveled against them in their own words. The inmates attested to their own "religious deviation" or "ideological contamination" and described themselves as "fifth column" or workers of the "counterrevolution." Recantation shows, termed "conversations" or "round table discussions," were aired during prime time and often filmed in the auditorium of the infamous Evin prison, with inmates serving as the audience (ibid., 142–44).

13. Nasr, "The Iranian Revolution and Changes in Islamism," 334.

14. Quoted in Ḥusayn, *Āyatullāh Khumaynī Qum se Qum tak*, 527–28.

15. Ibid., 530.

16. Ibid., 535.

17. Nasr, *The Vanguard of the Islamic Revolution*, 189–95.

18. See Vatanka, *Iran and Pakistan*, 179–85. Vatanka provides a detailed exploration of Pakistani-Iranian ties since Partition throughout the book.

19. See, for example, Hammad, "Khomeini and the Iranian Revolution in the Egyptian Press"; Hatina "Debating the 'Awakening Shia'"; Menashri, *The Iranian Revolution and the Muslim World*; Esposito, *The Iranian Revolution*; Kramer, *Shiʿism, Resis-*

tance, and Revolution; and Zonis and Brumberg, *Khomeini, the Islamic Republic of Iran, and the Arab World.*

20. Ahmed, "Shi'i Political Activism in Pakistan," 64. For similar statements, see Roy, "The Impact of the Iranian Revolution on the Middle East," 35–36; Syed, "The Sunni-Shia Conflict in Pakistan," 255.

21. Mervin, "Introduction," 17.

22. Louër, *Transnational Shia Politics*, 155–56.

23. Ibid., 296.

24. Shaery-Eisenlohr, *Shiʿite Lebanon*, 195.

25. Ibid., 207.

26. Abou Zahab, "The Politicization of the Shia Community in Pakistan," 100–101.

27. See more on the Qurʾānic and historical implications of this name below.

28. Qamar Zaydī, *Pānc hafte*, 21.

29. Ibid., 62.

30. Muntaẓirī, together with Mahdī Hāshimī, the brother of his son-in-law, at that time also coordinated the help for "resistance movements" that took shelter in Iran. See Louër, *Transnational Shia Politics*, 179; Buchta, "Die Inquisition der Islamischen Republik Iran," 71–72. Muntaẓirī was later designated Khomeini's successor, only to fall from grace in 1989, shortly before Khomeini's death, due to his increasing criticism of authoritarian tendencies in the Islamic Republic (see Akhavi, "The Thought and Role of Ayatollah Hossein'ali Montazeri," 650–51). Under house arrest until his death in 2009, he later became an important internal critic of the "absolute rule of the jurisprudent" without, however, giving up the idea of a political role for the ʿulamā. For a discussion of the transformation of his thought as well as of its internal contradictions, see Hajatpour, "Reflections and Legal Analysis of the Relationship between 'Religious Government and Human Rights.'"

31. Qamar Zaydī, *Pānc hafte*, 63.

32. Ibid., 64.

33. Ibid., 75.

34. Ibid., 77.

35. Ibid., 79.

36. See, for example, in the context of Lebanon, Norton, *Amal and the Shiʿa*, 13–36.

37. ʿĀrifī, "Shīʿīyān-i Pākistān" (2003), 209.

38. Abou Zahab, "The Politicization," 97. For a similar view, see Ahmed, "The Shiʿis of Pakistan," 280–81.

39. Abou Zahab, "The Regional Dimension of Sectarian Conflicts in Pakistan," 116.

40. On his biography, see ʿĀrif Naqvī, *Tazkirah-i ʿulamāʾ-i imāmiyyah*, 254–56. A prolific writer and gifted orator, Dihlavī was referred to as the greatest preacher (*khāṭib-i aʿẓam*) in the Shiʿi community.

41. For a discussion of Shiʿi demands during the years from 1947 until 1954 for separate religious education and the modification of syllabi used in the country's schools, see Rieck, *The Shias of Pakistan*, 75–78.

42. Rieck, "The Struggle for Equal Rights as a Minority," 278–80.

43. These rights were conceded gradually by the government of Zulfiqar Ali Bhutto, only to be abolished again under Zia ul-Haq in 1978 (see ibid., 282–83).

44. Ibid., 283.

45. See, for example, ʿĀrifī, *Junbish-i islāmī-yi Pākistān*, 120.

46. See Rieck, "A Stronghold of Shiʿa Orthodoxy," 402.

47. Rieck, *The Shias of Pakistan*, 180.

48. Compare the previous chapter on the topic of taqlīd.

49. Abou Zahab, "The Regional Dimension," 116.

50. See "Āyatullāh al-ʿuẓma Āghā-yi Rūḥ Allāh Khumaynī kā interview."

51. See "Īrān kā ʿaẓīm islāmī inqilāb aur ISO."

52. See "Press Release: Imāmiyyah Organisation Pākistān."

53. Sayyid Murtażā Ḥusayn was born in 1923 in Lucknow. He graduated with a *ṣadr al-afāżil* degree from the city's Sulṭān al-Madāris seminary and obtained degrees in Urdu, Literature, and Administrative Sciences from Punjab University as well as from the University of Lucknow and the University of Allahabad. After migrating to Pakistan in 1950, he taught at both secular and religious institutions and was involved in the founding of various madrasas. Besides publishing on Shiʿi history and literature, he wrote important biographical works on Shiʿi scholars of the subcontinent and the Middle East (see ʿĀrif Naqvī, *Tażkirah-i ʿulamā'-i imāmiyyah*, 347–49). Ṣafdar Ḥusayn Najafī was born in 1933 in the Punjabi city of ʿAlīpūr. He received his initial religious training at various madrasas in the Punjab, after which he lived in Najaf from 1951 to 1956. From 1968 until his death in 1989 he was the head of Pakistan's most important Shiʿi religious seminary, the Jāmiʿat al-Muntaẓar in Lahore. In addition to his own writings, he was a prolific translator of, among other things, Khomeini's *Tawḍīḥ al-masā'il* and *Ḥukūmat-i Islāmī* (see ibid., 136–39).

54. "Pākistān se ek wafd Āyatullāh Khumaynī ke ḥuẓūr."

55. Jones, "Shiʿism, Humanity and Revolution," 428.

56. Hyder, *Reliving Karbala*, 91.

57. For a sophisticated discussion of the magnitude of the strikes and Iran's economic position in 1978, see Kurzman, *The Unthinkable Revolution*, 77–104.

58. Ḥusayn, *Inqilāb-i Islāmī-yi Īrān*, 86–88.

59. Devji, *The Impossible Indian*, 87, 99.

60. Khomeini and Algar, *Islam and Revolution*, 242–45.

61. Devji, *The Impossible Indian*, 6.

62. Ibid., 8. Even though Ḥusayn wrote his book before the outbreak of the Iran-Iraq War, it would be an interesting project to compare Gandhi's view on violence with the way the Islamic Republic honored her martyrs and justified the use of the infamous "human waves" tactics in attacking Iraqi positions (see Hiro, *The Longest War*, 86–113).

63. Baqer Moin, *Khomeini*, 176.

64. Devji, *The Impossible Indian*, 140.

65. Ḥusayn Najafī, *Mabādiyāt-i ḥukūmat-i islāmī*, 13–15.

66. Ibid., 32.

67. Ḥusayn Najafī, *Mabādiyāt*, 45–46. On Sayyid Quṭb's interpretation, see Wild, "Political Interpretations of the Qur'ān," 283. See also Abu Rabi', *Intellectual Origins of Islamic Resurgence*, 166–219.

68. See Khumaynī, *Vilāyat-i faqīh*, 58–64; Ḥusayn Najafī, *Mabādiyāt*, 32.

69. Arjomand, "Ideological Revolution in Shi'ism," 192.

70. Ṣafdar Ḥusayn Najafī mentioned that the deliberations of the Assembly of Experts were still ongoing. This means he must have written the book between 18 August 1979, when the assembly convened, and 15 November, when it completed its deliberations (see Ṣafdar Ḥusayn Najafī, *Mabādiyāt*, 60).

71. The official preliminary draft of the constitution, published on 14 June 1979, had granted limited individual rights and freedoms, and, most importantly, had not specified that Iran would follow the model of *vilāyat-i faqīh*. See Schirazi, *The Constitution of Iran*, 22–24.

72. Ṣafdar Ḥusayn Najafī, *Mabādiyāt*, 60. For a detailed account of the shrewd political maneuvering that scrapped the original plan of a constituent assembly in favor of a much less representative Assembly of Experts and the subsequent skillful electoral engineering, which meant that fifty-five of its seventy-two delegates were clerics who followed the "line of the Imam," see Schirazi, *The Constitution of Iran*, 27–38.

73. Ibid., 33.

74. Ḥusayn Najafī, *Mabādiyāt*, 61.

75. Ibid., 62.

76. See 'Abbās, "Himmat afzā'ī aur naṣīḥat."

77. Ḥusayn Najafī, *Mabādiyāt*, 63.

78. Ibid., 65. On the hurdles of sending an Iranian mujtahid to the Jāmi'at al-Muntaẓar, see also Rieck, *The Shias of Pakistan*, 216.

79. For a detailed discussion, including some dissenting Deobandī voices, see Zaman, *Modern Islamic Thought in a Radical Age*, 75–107.

80. I am indebted to Faisal Devji for this thought.

81. Landau-Tasseron, "The 'Cyclical Reform,'" 84.

82. Ibid., 95–96.

83. Alvi, *Perspectives on Mughal India*, 91–93.

84. Ibid., 96–97.

85. Friedmann, *Prophecy Continuous*, 105–9.

86. Hartung, *A System of Life*, 79–81.

87. Interestingly, the idea of a mujaddid must have gained some limited currency in Shi'i circles as well. Ḥusayn Najafī can rely on a handy list of mujaddids that was compiled by Muḥammad Hāshim b. Muḥammad 'Alī Khurasānī (d. 1933) and ranges from Imām Muḥammad Bāqir to the combative 'ālim Mīrzā Muḥammad Ḥasan Shīrāzī. Ḥusayn Najafī of course ignores Khurasānī's inclusion of rulers in a separate list of mujaddids but relies exclusively on the aforementioned 'ulamā and simply adds Khomeini to the existing canon (see Khurasānī, *Muntakhab al-tawārīkh*, 90–98).

88. Ḥusayn Najafī, *Mabādiyāt*, 41.

89. On Muṭahharī and his thought, see Hajatpour, *Iranische Geistlichkeit zwischen Utopie und Realismus*, 179–202.

90. In his view, the idea of a mujaddid entered Shiʿi thought via Shaykh Bahāʾī (d. 1621), who wrote that Sunni scholars held the Shiʿi traditionist al-Kulaynī (d. 941) in such high regard that they labeled him the renewer of the Shiʿi school of law (see Muṭahharī, "Ẓuhūr-i mujaddid-i dīn dar har ṣad sāl"). I am grateful to Hossein Modarressi for drawing my attention to this reference.

91. Ferdows, "Women and the Iranian Revolution," 290–92. See also Kashani-Sabet, *Conceiving Citizens*, 197; and Nashat, "Women in the Ideology of the Islamic Republic," 208–9.

92. For a reprint of Khomeini's speech on the occasion of Women's Day on 24 April 1981, see Khumaynī, "ʿAuratōn̲ kā din."

93. Nashat, "Women in the Ideology of the Islamic Republic," 212.

94. Poya, *Women, Work and Islamism*, 80.

95. Jāmiʿat al-Zahrāʾ developed out of the Maktab-i Tauḥīd school, which was opened in 1974 in Qum by the female scholar Zuhrah Ṣifātī (born 1948). In the mid-1990s, however, Iran's Supreme Leader, Sayyid Ali Khamenei, ordered the simplification of the curriculum. This move once again "demoted *Jāmiʿat al-Zahrāʾ* to an institution that prepares women for *tablīgh* (Islamic propagation) rather than scholarship." See Künkler and Fazaeli, "The Life of Two *Mujtahidahs*." See also Fazaeli and Künkler, "Training Female Ulama in Jamʿiat al-Zahra"; Rutner, "Religious Authority, Gendered Recognition, and Instrumentalization"; and, for a thorough discussion of the diverging views on women in postrevolutionary Iran, Mir-Hosseini, *Islam and Gender*.

96. Ḥusayn Najafī, "ʿAurat aur pardah," 7.

97. Ibid., 8–9. Such a position was obviously embarrassing for the ISO. A later article in their journal, not written by an ʿālim, suggested that women were indeed not restricted to their houses and were also allowed to drive cars as long as all stipulations of Islam were kept (see Gill, "Ḥaqīqat men̲ khurāfāt khō gayī").

98. The term *jaʿfarī* relates to the sixth Shiʿi Imām, Jaʿfar al-Ṣādiq (d. 148/765). *Jaʿfarī* became increasingly used during the twentieth century in the context of energetic efforts to recast Shiʿism as a fifth school of law (madhhab) along with the four established Sunni schools, culminating in an interview (and later fatwa) given by the Shaykh al-Azhar Maḥmūd Shaltūt in 1959. Shaltūt even declared that Muslims were free to attach themselves to any of the five schools (see Brunner, *Islamic Ecumenism in the 20th Century*, 289–93). Muftī Jaʿfar Ḥusayn was born in Gūjrānvālā in 1916 and studied in both Lucknow and Najaf before embarking on a teaching career in Pakistan. In 1949 he was chosen as a member of the Board of Islamic Education, and he served two terms under Ayub Khan on the Council of Islamic Ideology (see ʿĀrif Naqvī, *Taẕkirah-i ʿulamāʾ-i imāmiyyah*, 70–72).

99. Zaman, "Sectarianism," 396.

100. See Balūc, "Islāmābād Convention," 5.

101. See Haydar, "The Politicization of the Shias," 81; and Tirmazi, *Profiles of Intelligence*, 272. Vali Nasr is the only author to point out that revolutionary Iran exerted significant pressure on Pakistan (see Nasr, "Iranian Revolution," 88).

102. The slogan is a vivid example of the richness of Urdu, which can draw on words of both Arabic and Persian origin: "Ek hī qā'id, ek hī rahbar, Muftī Jaʿfar, Muftī Jaʿfar" (Only one leader [*qā'id*, Arabic], only one leader [*rahbar*, Persian], Mufi Jaʿfar, Muftī Jaʿfar). See Balūc "Islāmābād Convention," 6.

103. See "Daurān-i julūs-i ʿazā namāz kā program"; "Majālis aur ʿazādārī."

104. "Daurān-i julūs-i ʿazā namāz kā program," 6–7.

105. Kāẓimī, *Muftī Jaʿfar Ḥusayn*, 23.

106. Ibid., 28.

107. See Rieck, *The Shias of Pakistan*, 216–17.

108. See Khurramābādī and Ṭālishīyān, *Khāṭirāt-i Āyatullāh Ṭāhirī Khurramābādī*, 48–50. See also Jaʿfarī, "Sālānah Convention 1983 kī report," 9–10.

109. Bukhārī, "Ḥajj ke ʿaẓīm siyāsī maqāṣid." For another example among many (in this case defending Iran from Western criticism), see Sabzvārī, "Islāmī inqilāb-i Īrān," 4.

110. Naqvī, "Āyatullāh Khumaynī—aye mere qā'id"; Ḥusayn, "Inqilāb-i Īrān aur javānān-i Pākistān."

111. Khān, "ʿĀlamī ḥālāt aur āj kā Muslim," 8.

112. Ibid., 11. On the slogan "The road to Jerusalem goes through Karbala" and the importance of Jerusalem in the Iranian propaganda, see Grube, "Jerusalem in the Visual Propaganda."

113. Bukhārī, "Āyatullāh Ḥasan Ṭāhirī kā ikhrāj."

114. "Hamārī sargarmiyāṉ," 12.

115. See Rieck, *The Shias of Pakistan*, 220–21.

116. Ahmed, "Political Activism," 66.

117. This is of course a rather problematic term and reflects first of all Iranian views on the "extreme" (*ifrāṭī*) forms of traditional Shiʿi ritual in Pakistan. See Nuʿaymīyān, "Bāztāb-i inqilāb dar Pākistān."

118. Unfortunately, Abou Zahab only provides some examples of how Iranian slogans in the vein of "Kull yaum ʿāshūrā', kull arḍ Karbalā" (Every day is *ʿāshūrā'*, every piece of land is Karbala) were gaining prominence at Shiʿi gatherings. See Abou Zahab, "The Politicization," 108–9.

119. Nuṣūḥīyān, *Shīʿīyān-i Pākistān va Inqilāb-i Islāmī-yi Īrān.*

120. None of his biographers discusses whether his sayyid pedigree facilitated his career. His family traces their lineage back to a grandchild of al-Ḥusayn (d. 680), Ḥusayn al-Aṣghar, son of Zayn al-ʿĀbidīn (d. 713).

121. Khān, *Zindagīnāmah-i ʿAllāmah Shahīd ʿĀrif Ḥusayn al-Ḥusaynī*, 155. Al-Ḥusaynī refers to him as his main teacher (see al-Ḥusaynī, *Guftār-i ṣidq*, 107–8).

122. On his life and influence in the Iraqi context and beyond, see Mallat, *The Renewal of Islamic Law.*

123. Taslīm Rizā Khān singles him out as the only Pakistani student to do so (see Khān, *Safīr-i nūr*, 41). See also Ṣādiqī, "ʿAllāmah Sayyid ʿĀrif Ḥusayn Ḥusaynī," 84.

124. For the former view, see Zaman, "Sectarianism," 695; for the latter, Abou Zahab, "The Politicization," 105.

125. Khān, *Safīr-i nūr,* 43. *Rāh-i ʿAmal* later reproduced a new letter from Khomeini in which he declared al-Ḥusaynī to be his wakīl (see "Vikālatnāmah-i Imām Khumaynī").

126. ʿĀrif Naqvī, *Taẕkirah-i ʿulamāʾ-i imāmiyyah,* 156.

127. Abou Zahab, "The Politicization," 106.

128. Khān, *Zindagīnāmah-i ʿAllāmah Shahīd ʿĀrif Ḥusayn al-Ḥusaynī,* 27.

129. Ibid., 28.

130. Rieck, *The Shias of Pakistan,* 220.

131. Andreas Rieck mainly discusses the rise of al-Ḥusaynī to the leadership and his confrontational relationship with the government. See ibid., 219–30.

132. See al-Ḥusaynī, *Mīs̱āq-i khūn,* 165. There are no written works by al-Ḥusaynī referenced in ʿĀrif Naqvī, *Taẕkirah-i ʿulamāʾ-i imāmiyyah.* The bibliographical collection of Shiʿi Urdu texts by the same author likewise only lists a couple of short pamphlets on the life of Sayyid ʿĀrif Ḥusayn al-Ḥusaynī. See ʿĀrif Naqvī, *Barr-i ṣaghīr ke imāmiyyah muṣannifīn,* 1:484, 2:453, 2:512.

133. Besides *Mīs̱āq-i khūn,* I draw on al-Ḥusaynī, *Guftār-i ṣidq;* al-Ḥusaynī, *Sukhan-i ʿishq;* al-Ḥusaynī, *Uslūb-i siyāsat;* and al-Tirmiẕī, *Naqīb-i vaḥdat.*

134. See, for example, al-Ḥusaynī, *Mīs̱āq-i khūn,* 65–72, 110–18, 142–48.

135. Khān, *Safīr-i nūr;* Khān, *Zindagīnāmah-i ʿAllāmah Shahīd ʿĀrif Ḥusayn al-Ḥusaynī.* The al-ʿĀrif Academy does not seem to be active beyond compiling al-Ḥusaynī's speeches.

136. See *Riżākār* 49, no. 25 (1 July 1985), for various articles and extensive discussion of this agreement.

137. Naqvi, "The Controversy," 147; al-Ḥusaynī, *Mīs̱āq-i khūn,* 206–7.

138. See, for example, al-Ḥusaynī, *Mīs̱āq-i khūn,* 199.

139. For a sample of his extensive traveling schedule in 1986, see ʿĀrif Naqvī, *Taẕkirah-i ʿulamāʾ-i imāmiyyah,* 159–60.

140. "ISO Pākistān kā universityōṉ meṉ maqām ō kirdār," 18.

141. The prisoners were finally released in late April 1986. See Aṣghar, "Asīrān-i Kwiṭah kī rahāʾī."

142. Zaman, "Sectarianism in Pakistan," 696.

143. Rieck, *The Shias of Pakistan,* 230. Whereas Rieck holds that the murder was carried out by circles tied to Zia ul-Haq, others have blamed Iraq and Saudi Arabia (Khān, *Zindagīnāmah-i ʿAllāmah Shahīd ʿĀrif Ḥusayn al-Ḥusaynī,* 91–93).

144. Buchta, *Die iranische Schia und die islamische Einheit,* 64–77.

145. See al-Tirmiẕī, *Naqīb-i vaḥdat,* 39–41. For more information regarding Ẓahīr's anti-Shiʿi polemics, see chapter 5.

146. Khān, *Zindagīnāmah-i ʿAllāmah Shahīd ʿĀrif Ḥusayn al-Ḥusaynī,* 102.

147. See, for example, al-Ḥusaynī, *Uslūb-i siyāsat,* 27.

148. See Brunner, *Islamic Ecumenism,* 237. This saying is missing in all major Sunni hadith collections but is widely cited in authoritative Shiʿi sources.

149. Al-Ḥusaynī, *Uslūb-i siyāsat*, 25; al-Ḥusaynī, *Guftār-i ṣidq*, 30–31, 81. See also Lodhi, "Pakistan's Shia Movement," 813.

150. Al-Ḥusaynī, *Guftār-i ṣidq*, 52; al-Ḥusaynī, *Uslūb-i siyāsat*, 33. On these early proponents of intra-Islamic ecumenism, see Brunner, *Islamic Ecumenism*, 34–36, 284–337.

151. Khān, *Zindagīnāmah-i ʿAllāmah Shahīd ʿĀrif Ḥusayn al-Ḥusaynī*, 110.

152. Al-Tirmiẕī, *Naqīb-i vaḥdat*, 80.

153. Al-Ḥusaynī, *Uslūb-i siyāsat*, 80.

154. Ibid., 60.

155. Buchta, *Die iranische Schia*, 101.

156. Al-Tirmiẕī, *Naqīb-i vaḥdat*, 19.

157. Amirpur, "A Doctrine in the Making?," 229–30; Buchta, "Tehran's Ecumenical Society," 334–35. See also Calder, "Accommodation and Revolution," 53–54.

158. Al-Ḥusaynī, *Guftār-i ṣidq*, 73, 120–22.

159. Khān, *Zindagīnāmah-i ʿAllāmah Shahīd ʿĀrif Ḥusayn al-Ḥusaynī*, 169. For a more realistic assessment of the Iranian involvement in Afghanistan, see Khalilzad, "The Iranian Revolution and the Afghan Resistance"; Rieck, "Irans Politik im Afghanistankonflikt."

160. *Khān, Zindagīnāmah-i ʿAllāmah Shahīd ʿĀrif Ḥusayn al-Ḥusaynī*, 156, 171.

161. Ibid., 158.

162. Al-Ḥusaynī, *Sukhan-i ʿishq*, 71.

163. Al-Ḥusaynī, *Mīs̱āq-i khūn*, 39.

164. Khān, *Zindagīnāmah-i ʿAllāmah Shahīd ʿĀrif Ḥusayn al-Ḥusaynī*, 123, 129.

165. Lodhi, "Pakistan's Shiʿa Movement," 810–11.

166. Al-Ḥusaynī, *Uslūb-i siyāsat*, 127–18.

167. See Roy, "The Impact of the Iranian Revolution," 35.

168. Abou Zahab, "The Regional Dimensions of Sectarian Conflicts," 116.

169. Al-Ḥusaynī, *Guftār-i ṣidq*, 34, 43, 49, 191, 237, 247.

170. Ibid., 39–40, 110.

171. "Awakening" in this context is contrasted with the "traditional" view, which regarded political activism as running counter to the pious acceptance of what God provided (*taqwā*) (see Khān, *Zindagīnāmah-i ʿAllāmah Shahīd ʿĀrif Ḥusayn al-Ḥusaynī*, 32–33).

172. ʿĀrif Naqvī, *Taẕkirah-i ʿulamāʾ-i imāmiyyah*, 158–59.

173. Khān, *Zindagīnāmah-i ʿAllāmah Shahīd ʿĀrif Ḥusayn al-Ḥusaynī*, 103.

174. Ibid., 172.

175. Ibid., 146.

176. Ibid., 107; al-Ḥusaynī, *Guftār-i ṣidq*, 138.

177. Al-Ḥusaynī, *Uslūb-i siyāsat*, 64–65.

178. Ibid., and al-Ḥusaynī, *Guftār-i ṣidq*, 137.

179. Al-Ḥusaynī, *Uslūb-i siyāsat*, 63–64. See also Lodhi, "Pakistan's Shiʿa Movement," 808.

180. Al-Ḥusaynī, *Guftār-i ṣidq*, 81–82; al-Tirmiẕī, *Naqīb-i vaḥdat*, 86–87. Chapter 2 above challenges such a reading of the traditionalists' messages and motivations.

181. Al-Ḥusaynī, *Guftār-i ṣidq*, 61; Khān, *Zindagīnāmah-i ʿAllāmah Shahīd ʿĀrif Ḥusayn al-Ḥusaynī*, 147.

182. Al-Ḥusaynī, *Mīs̱āq-i khūn*, 191.

183. Al-Ḥusaynī, *Uslūb-i siyāsat*, 69.

184. Al-Tirmiẕi, *Naqīb-i vaḥdat*, 89.

185. Syed Rizwan Zamir, *ʿAlī Naqvī and His Thought*, 181.

186. Al-Ḥusaynī, *Guftār-i ṣidq*, 127.

187. Khān, *Zindagīnāmah-i ʿAllāmah Shahīd ʿĀrif Ḥusayn al-Ḥusaynī*, 132.

188. Ibid., 128.

189. Menashri, *Post-Revolutionary Politics in Iran*, 187–88.

190. Ramazani, "Iran's Export of the Revolution," 73–75.

191. With the exception of a *Burgfrieden* policy between 1983 and 1987 (see Buchta, *Die iranische Schia*, 84–85).

192. See Rieck, *The Shias of Pakistan*, 223–24.

193. Khān, *Zindagīnāmah-i ʿAllāmah Shahīd ʿĀrif Ḥusayn al-Ḥusaynī*, 120, 171.

194. Al-Ḥusaynī, *Guftār-i ṣidq*, 200.

195. Ibid., 73; Khān, *Zindagīnāmah-i ʿAllāmah Shahīd ʿĀrif Ḥusayn al-Ḥusaynī*, 169, 191. On the International Islamic University, established in 1980, see Malik, "Islamic Mission and Call."

196. Al-Ḥusaynī, *Guftār-i ṣidq*, 196–97. For a discussion of tensions between Iran and Saudi Arabia in this regard, see Harrop, "Pakistan and Revolutionary Iran," 120.

197. Al-Ḥusaynī, *Uslūb-i siyāsat*, 327–29.

198. For the debate among Islamist and jihadi groups regarding the question as to whether the United States or local oppressive rulers (the "near enemy") should be targeted first, see Gerges, *The Far Enemy*.

199. Khān, *Zindagīnāmah-i ʿAllāmah Shahīd ʿĀrif Ḥusayn al-Ḥusaynī*, 122.

200. Al-Ḥusaynī, *Guftār-i ṣidq*, 50; al-Ḥusaynī, *Uslūb-i siyāsat*, 136, 318.

201. Al-Ḥusaynī, *Guftār-i ṣidq*, 149.

202. Buchta, *Die Iranische Schia*, 84–85. This changed with the horrific events of 31 July 1987, when several hundred people, most of them Iranian pilgrims, were killed during the hajj. See Matthiesen, *The Other Saudis*, 131.

203. Harrop, "Pakistan and Revolutionary Iran," 125.

204. Rieck, *The Shias of Pakistan*, 226. See also the coverage in *Riżākār* 50, nos. 2–3 (16 January 1986).

205. See his main website, www.islamimarkaz.com.

206. Javād Naqvī, "Vārid-i daurān-i nuqraʾī-yī ṣudūr-i inqilāb."

207. Even though the Iranian influence seems to be obvious, I have no further information as to the nature and origin of Naqvī's funds. He himself mentioned a group of "four believers from Lahore" who pooled their resources to establish the seminary (see the video recording Javād Naqvī, "Jāmiʿat al-ʿUrwa al-Wuthqā kā taʿlīmī niẓām,"

min. 14:20). Mashal Saif, who questioned Shiʿi ʿulamā in Lahore about this issue, received very direct comments pointing to Iran. I am thankful to Mashal for sharing her field notes with me.

208. Hourani, *Arabic Thought in the Liberal Age*, 122–29.

209. See Moussavi, "The Establishment of the Position of Marjʿiyyt-i [*sic*] Taqlid," 39–40. Scholars have described him as "the most conservative senior *mujtahid* of Najaf" and mentioned that his work was held in high esteem among Shiʿi ʿulamā. It was commented on by Khomeini, al-Khūʾī, Sayyid Muḥammad Riżā Gulpāyagānī (d. 1993), and Muḥammad ʿAlī Arākī (d. 1994). See Martin, *Iran between Islamic Nationalism and Secularism*; and Mervin, "La quête du savoir à Naǧaf," 179. More research on Yazdī and his legal reasoning seems to be required, however, before we can establish a connection between Sayyid Javād Naqvī and the Najaf-based marjiʿ.

210. Video recording, Javād Naqvī, "Tisrā yaum-i taʾsīs-i ḥauzah-i Jāmiʿat al-ʿUrwa al-Wuthqā," min. 23:30.

211. See Kalbe Ali, "New Shia Party Emerging"; Rieck, *The Shias of Pakistan*, 311–26.

212. See Louër, *Transnational Shia Politics*, 188–94.

213. See the video recording Javād Naqvī, "Īrān men̲ makhmalī inqilāb kī nākāmī." For more information on the Iranian Green Movement, which emerged after the presidential election in June 2009 with the removal of Mahmoud Ahmadinejad from office as one of its key demands, see Reisinezhad, "The Iranian Green Movement."

214. Video recording, Javād Naqvī, "Inqilāb-i Islāmī: Siyāsī tajziyah baʿd az intikhābāt-i Īrān 2013."

215. Mostyn, "Ali Akbar Hashemi Rafsanjani Obituary."

216. Video recording, Javād Naqvī, "Inqilāb-i Islāmī: Siyāsī tajziyah baʿd az intikhābāt-i Īrān 2013," min. 22:43.

217. Ibid., min. 44:00.

218. Jawad Naqvi, *The System of Wilayat*, 141–42.

219. Video recording, Javād Naqvī, "Intiẓār al-Faraj az naẓar-i Qurʾān," min. 57:15.

220. Jawad Naqvi, *The System of Wilayat*, 35.

221. Ibid., 94. See also the video recording Javād Naqvī, "ʿAṣr-i ḥāżir aur ṭulabāʾ kī z̲imahdāriyān̲," min. 38:33.

222. Naqvī, "Jāmiʿat al-ʿUrwa al-Wuthqā kā taʿlīmī niẓām," min. 01:20:30.

223. Video recording Javād Naqvī, "Barsī ʿAllāmah Muftī Jaʿfar Ḥusayn," min. 55:53.

224. Ibid., min. 01:09:15.

225. Ibid., min. 01:13:07.

226. Jawad Naqvi, *The System of Wilayat*, 106.

227. Javād Naqvī, "Jāmiʿat al-ʿUrwa al-Wuthqā kā taʿlīmī niẓām," min. 01:05:50; Javād Naqvī, "Barsī ʿAllāmah Muftī Jaʿfar Ḥusayn," min. 01:34:14.

228. Javād Naqvī, "Vārid-i daurān-i nuqraʾī-yī ṣudūr-i inqilāb."

229. This statement by Naqvī is factually incorrect. Even though the foreign minister ʿAlī Akbar Vilāyatī propagated a fundamental change of course after Khomeini's death and parallel structures like the Office for Islamic Liberation Movements (OLIM),

intended to support militant Islamists abroad, were established, the Iranian Foreign Ministry (with Vilāyatī at its head since 1981) was never dissolved after the Iranian Revolution. The Iranian Parliament in 1985 also passed a law that specified the duties of the ministry, such as providing "the necessities for the defense of the just struggles of the *mustaazafans* [the downtrodden], especially the Moslems (struggling) against oppressors in every corner of the globe" (see Fürtig, *Islamische Weltauffassung und aussenpolitische Konzeptionen*, 112–27). On OLIM, see Schwerin, *The Dissident Mullah*, 90–105.

230. Javād Naqvī, "Vārid-i daurān-i nuqra'ī-yī ṣudūr-i inqilāb."

231. Video recording, Javād Naqvī, "Imām Khumaynī kā payghām bīdārī millat-i Pākistān ke nām," min. 57:13.

232. Ibid., min. 51:20.

233. Video recording, Javād Naqvī, "Jāmiʿat al-ʿUrwa al-Wuthqā kā taʿlīmī niẓām," min. 01:17:55.

234. Video recording, Javād Naqvī, "ʿAṣr-i ḥāżir aur ṭulabā' kī ẕimahdāriyāṉ," min. 55:13.

235. Video recording, Javād Naqvī, "Jāmiʿat al-ʿUrwa al-Wuthqā kā taʿlīmī niẓām," min. 58:30. See also the video recording Javād Naqvī, "Parcam-i āzādī ke nīce kisht-i ghulāmī," mins. 22:40, 32:20, and 01:04:54.

236. For a similar argument as far as the limited Saudi control over their "export" of the Wahhābī message is concerned, see Farquhar, *Circuits of Faith*, 183–84.

CHAPTER FIVE

1. The Saudi king Saʿūd b. ʿAbd al-ʿAzīz Āl Saʿūd (d. 1969) announced his plan to establish the university in May 1961. One of the immediate reasons for its founding was to provide a home to neo-*salafī* immigrant scholars from other parts of the Arab world. In the long run, however, the goal was a renewal of the propagation of Islam (*daʿwa*) on an international level, to shore up the domestic legitimacy of the regime vis-à-vis the Wahhābī religious establishment, and to compete with the regional influence of Nasser's Egypt. See Schulze, *Islamischer Internationalismus im 20. Jahrhundert*, 156–60; Farquhar, *Circuits of Faith*, 67–85.

2. See Zahrānī, *al-Shaykh Iḥsān Ilāhī Ẓahīr*, 86–87.

3. See Farquhar, "The Islamic University of Medina since 1961," 21–40. On Ibn Bāz's career, see al-Atawneh, *Wahhābī Islam Facing the Challenges of Modernity*, 31–33.

4. Jāved, "ʿAllāmah Iḥsān Ilāhī Ẓahīr kā ākharī interview," 601–2. This interview was originally printed in the *Moon Digest*, January 1987.

5. Zahrānī, *al-Shaykh Iḥsān Ilāhī Ẓahīr*, 86–87.

6. Haykel "Al-Qaʿida and Shiism," 191.

7. Translations into Urdu and English were usually released shortly thereafter. Ẓahīr clearly and repeatedly stated that he penned his monographs in Arabic (he still wrote many op-eds and journal articles in Urdu; see, for example, Jāved, "ʿAllāmah Iḥsān Ilāhī Ẓahīr kā ākharī interview," 601). Yet the secondary literature shows a certain confusion about these politics of language: Mumtaz Ahmad, Vali Nasr, Mariam Abou Zahab,

and Amélie Blom all hold that the Saudis later financed "translations" into Arabic. See Ahmad, "Revivalism, Islamization, Sectarianism," 111; Nasr, "The Rise of Sunni Militancy in Pakistan," 160; Abou Zahab, "The Politicization of the Shia Community," 104; Blom, "Les Partis Islamistes," 109.

8. Abou Zahab, "Salafism in Pakistan," 131.

9. Haykel calls a study of Ẓahīr's work a "major desideratum" (see Haykel, "Al-Qaeda and Shiism," 201n23).

10. Ẓahīr first studied at the Ahl-i Ḥadīṣ–affiliated Jāmiʿah-i Muḥammadiyya before transferring to Fayṣalābād's Jāmiʿah-i Salafiyya. One of his teachers there, Ḥāfiẓ Muḥammad Gūndlavī, later became his father-in-law and also took over the chair for hadith from Nāṣir al-Dīn al-Albānī at the Islamic University in Medina. After completing his religious education in Pakistan, Ẓahīr also went on to obtain various master's degrees in Arabic, Persian, and Urdu from Punjab University. See Riexinger, *Ṣanāʾullāh Amritsarī*, 567–69; Zahrānī, *al-Shaykh Iḥsān Ilāhī Ẓahīr*, 84–85.

11. Riexinger, *Ṣanāʾullāh Amritsarī*, 525–26.

12. This organization was originally called Anjuman-i Sipāh-i Ṣaḥābah (its acronym, ASS, was a rather unfortunate choice), but for the sake of simplicity I refer to it exclusively by its later name.

13. See, for example, Khaled Ahmed's statement that "with the funding came the Arab [*sic*] agenda" (Ahmed, *Sectarian War*, 107). See also Kamran, "Contextualizing Sectarian Militancy in Pakistan," 73; Shehabi, "The Role of Religious Ideology," 188–89; Toor, *The State of Islam*, 160–61; and Rehman, *Karachi in Turmoil*, 53–54. For a statement about the "growing influence of anti-Shia Wahhabism in Pakistan," see also Sakurai, "Women's Empowerment and Iranian-Style Seminaries," 49.

14. Ian Talbot, for example, writes that madrasas "funded from Saudi Arabia taught a mixture of Wahhabism and Deobandism," without, however, providing any reference for such a claim. See Talbot, *Pakistan*, 131; Nasr, "International Politics, Domestic Imperatives, and Identity Mobilization," 88.

15. Nasr, "Sunni Militancy," 150.

16. See Murphy, *The Making of Terrorism in Pakistan*, 131. In making his bold argument this author only draws on available secondary literature.

17. The origin of the phenomenon of Shiʿi landholders still requires more research. One argument is that the British apparently "made no difference between Sunnis and Shias when strengthening the landed aristocracy in the Punjab." Consequently, the Shiʿis had more reason to remain loyal to the Raj, since the British provided "full religious freedom for the first time" (see Rieck, *The Shias of Pakistan*, 9). See also chapter 1 for some reflections on the religious landscape of the Punjab during the late colonial period.

18. Makdisi, *The Culture of Sectarianism*, 166.

19. See Hashemi and Postel, "Introduction: The Sectarianization Thesis," 4–5.

20. Nasr, "Rise of Sunni Militancy," 142. Nasr's source, an article in the Pakistani magazine *The Herald*, is just as vague: "An investigation recently conducted by a secret

agency has discovered that 1,700 of the 2,463 registered religious madrassas in the Punjab are recipients of foreign aid. No less than 750 madrassas are believed to be involved in activities fanning sectarian tension, and some are even training militants and carrying out terrorist activities" (see Khan, "The Fanatics Strike Back," 54).

21. Rieck, *The Shias of Pakistan*, 231–32.

22. Brunner, *Islamic Ecumenism in the 20th Century*, 336. Alix Philippon has made similar remarks about religious polemics exchanged between Barelvīs and Deobandīs. In her view, such literature "est répétitive, les mêmes arguments étant inlassablement réitérés d'un texte à l'autre. [. . .] La polémique n'a guère changé depuis son avènement aux XIXème siècle" (see Philippon, *Soufisme et politique au Pakistan*, 131–32). Additionally, Sabrina Mervin has described sectarian debates between Sunnis and Shiʿis in the Arab world as "fastidieux et, surtout, très répétitif" (see Mervin, *Un réformisme chiite*, 299).

23. Laurent Bonnefoy has pointed out comparable dynamics in Yemen, where the major Salafī figure Muqbil al-Wādiʿī was very careful to appear as an "endogenous and legitimate" actor and not as a Saudi "Trojan horse" (see Bonnefoy, "Salafism in Yemen"). It has to be emphasized that conceptualizing Saudi Arabia's domestic religious scene as monolithic and unified carries its own risk of a myopic perspective on the Kingdom. See Al-Rasheed, *Contesting the Saudi State*; and Lacroix, *Awakening Islam*, 249–62.

24. For a discussion of the influence of Salafī-inspired thought in Iraq, see Steinberg, "Jihadi Salafism and the Shiʿis," 108–11; Haykel "Al-Qaʿida and Shiism," 185–88. For internal tactical debates among Salafī thinkers in Iraq on the strategic benefits of attacking the Shiʿis, see Wagemakers, *A Quietist Jihadi*, 88–93. For the contemporary Syrian case, see Qureshi, "Middle-East's Sectarian Balance Shifts." For sectarian discourses in Syria before the uprising, see Pierret, "Karbala in the Umayyad Mosque." For a discussion of the context in Jordan, see Wagemakers, "Anti-Shiʿism without the Shiʿa."

25. Brown and Rassler, *Fountainhead of Jihad*, 60–63.

26. For a discussion of Islamist views of the state, see Euben and Zaman, *Princeton Readings in Islamist Thought*, 12.

27. Zaman, *The Ulama in Contemporary Islam*, 107.

28. Hallaq, *Sharīʿa*, 488–89.

29. Mallat, *The Renewal of Islamic Law*, 89–96.

30. See "Newspaper Editorials on Hazara Killings."

31. Akbar and Farhan, "22 Killed in Explosion"; Rieck, *The Shias of Pakistan*, 298–307.

32. "Gunmen Kill Three Lawyers."

33. Haider, "Murtaza Haider Is Dead."

34. On 23 April 2014 Pakistan's interior minister, Chaudhry Nisar Ali Khan, informed the country's upper house, the Senate, that in the five-year period from 2009 to 2014, 2,090 people had been killed in instances of sectarian violence. See Ghauri, "Sectarian Violence."

35. "At Least 20 Shias Pulled off Bus."

36. Rieck, *The Shias of Pakistan*, 260–61.

37. Ibid., 252.

38. Devji, *Muslim Zion*, 8–9.

39. Ibid.

40. Matthiesen, *Sectarian Gulf*, ix.

41. Ibid., xiv.

42. Abou Zahab, "The Sunni-Shia Conflict in Jhang (Pakistan)," 136. Tahir Kamran has also argued that intra-Shiʿi rivalries between leading families of the Sayyid *birādarī* fanned the flames of sectarianism since 1951 because the two feuding sections attempted each to build alliances with Sunni pīrs and ʿulamā. It is unclear to me how this "ploy" should have led to "Shiʿa–Sunni differences being considerably whipped up in the run-up to the electoral contest" since the strategies under discussion strike me more as efforts to form coalitions that cut across any particular sectarian affiliation (see Kamran, "Contextualizing Sectarian Militancy," 65). Kamran undoubtedly provides fascinating details about the deliberate manufacturing of controversies during the 1969 *Bāb-i ʿUmar* incident. Yet the oral disclosure of the "secret" political motives of those involved to him in 2006, thirty-seven years after the event, remains methodologically questionable as an argument (ibid., 69–70).

43. See Arif, *Economic and Social Impacts of Remittances*, 13; Pew Research Center, "Changing Patterns of Global Migration."

44. For a sophisticated discussion, see Zaman, *The Ulama in Contemporary Islam*, 126–27.

45. G. M. Arif, *Impacts of Remittances*, 79–91.

46. Kamran, "Contextualizing Sectarian Militancy," 76. No scholarly work exists that looks into religious change and Saudi "conversion" efforts among guest workers of Pakistani nationality (personal communication, Bernard Haykel, 14 March 2014).

47. Lefebvre, *Kinship, Honour and Money*, 213.

48. Ahmad, "Explanation Is Not the Point."

49. See, for example, Lefebvre, *Kinship, Honour and Money*. Given the fact that Pakistani migrants are predominantly "unskilled" or "skilled" workers who mostly live in segregated communities and do not mingle with Gulf Arabs, it would be interesting to explore to what extent the Saudis and other Gulf states cared about the religious orientation of this group and how the interaction with the broader society in these different locales played out.

50. See Nasr, "Rise of Sunni Militancy," 167–68; Kamran "Contextualizing Sectarian Militancy," 57, 76; Ahmad "Violence in Pakistan," 117–18; Irfani, "Pakistan's Sectarian Violence," 161.

51. See Pirzada, *The Politics of the Jamiat Ulema-i-Islam Pakistan*.

52. For a fascinating discussion of how Justices Munir and Kiyani claimed for themselves an "original understanding" of Islam that entitled them to expose the "ignorance" of the ʿulamā involved in the anti-Aḥmadī agitation of 1952–53, see Qasmi, *The Ahmadis and the Politics of Religious Exclusion*, 119–64. Envisioning Pakistan was not

necessarily restricted to religiously infused projects. For communist and progressive imaginations of the new state, see Ali, *Communism in Pakistan*, 13, 110–12.

53. Devji, *Muslim Zion*, 96.

54. Ibid., 104.

55. See Siddique, *Pakistan's Experience with Formal Law*, 43.

56. Khan, *Muslim Becoming*, 7.

57. Ibid., 8–9.

58. Smith made these observations during a visit to West Pakistan in 1948. See Smith, *Islam in Modern History*, 217.

59. Khan, *Muslim Becoming*, 91–119. See also Zaman, *The Ulama in Contemporary Islam*, 114.

60. For an excellent summary of these developments during the 1970s with further references to the relevant secondary literature, see Qasmi, *The Ahmadis and the Politics of Religious Exclusion*, 167–73.

61. Talbot, *Pakistan. A New History*, 98; Shaikh, *Making Sense of Pakistan*, 95–96.

62. In contrast to Shaikh (see *Making Sense of Pakistan*), who holds that Bhutto was also eager to strip the Aḥmadīs of their status as Muslims, Ali Usman Qasmi points out that Bhutto wanted to avoid the impression of yielding to ʿulamā pressure too quickly, perhaps hoping that by referring the process to parliament, "this would slow down the course of the agitations and provide some room for a compromised situation [*sic*]." See Qasmi, *The Ahmadis and the Politics of Religious Exclusion*, 177.

63. Malik, *Colonialization of Islam*, 128–30.

64. For a critique by Muftī Muḥammad Yūsuf Ludhiānavī, a leading scholar affiliated with the Jāmiʿat al-ʿUlūm al-Islāmiyya madrasa in Karachi, who feared that the religious schools might thus stray from their "purely religious mission" and be subordinated to Western sciences, see Zaman, *The Ulama in Contemporary Islam*, 78–81.

65. See Malik, *Colonialization of Islam*, 230–32.

66. Ibid., 133–40.

67. I am grateful to Mashal Saif for raising with me these points, which are discussed in her PhD dissertation. See Saif, "The 'Ulama' and the State."

68. Similar to Khan, Max Weiss has also emphasized the importance of processes in the development of sectarianism. He holds that sectarian politics, personal status law, and religious culture may simultaneously produce new modes of identification and restrict the prospects for national as well as non- or trans-sectarian political identities. See Weiss, *In the Shadow of Sectarianism*, 9–15.

69. Ahmad, "Revivalism, Islamization, Sectarianism," 116. It has also been suggested that Zia ul-Haq deliberately supported sectarian Sunni groups in order to render widespread Shiʿi support for the PPP that spearheaded the demand for the return to democracy, into a liability for the party. See Nasr, "International Politics, Domestic Imperatives, and Identity Mobilization," 86.

70. Zaman, "Sectarianism in Pakistan," 702–3.

71. Zaman, *The Ulama in Contemporary Islam*, 123.

72. See Rieck, *The Shias of Pakistan*, 103–4. During the 1950s, the Deobandī organi-

zation Tanẓīm Ahl-i Sunnat was at the forefront of anti-Shiʿi propaganda. It organized attacks on Shiʿi ʿazādārī processions and called on the Shiʿis to give up their madhhab or otherwise to leave Pakistan for Iran. See ibid., 88–100.

73. See Khān, *Safīr-i inqilāb*, 37–38.

74. Sajjād, "ʿAllāmah Iḥsān Ilāhī Ẓahīr shahīd," 25–26. Ẓahīr stated in July 1982 that more than one hundred thousand authorized and unauthorized copies had been printed in Arabic alone. See Ẓahīr, *al-Shīʿa wa-ahl al-bayt*, 7.

75. Ibid., 23.

76. According to his version of the events in question, Ẓahīr had been traveling with fellow Ahl-i Ḥadīs̱ members when their taxi driver dozed off, steered the car into a canal, and died as a result of the accident. Khar, according to Ẓahīr, seized on this event, claiming that the driver had been a PPP member. See Jāved, "ʿAllāmah Iḥsān Ilāhī Ẓahīr se khuṣūṣī interview," 363–64.

77. See Weinbaum, "The March 1977 Elections in Pakistan," 606–9.

78. Jāved, "Ẓahīr kā ākharī interview," 608–9. Asghar Khan has, on his part, accused the other parties of the Pakistan National Alliance of not being "really interested in democracy." The TI decided to leave the alliance after Zia's coup because his former fellow campaigners against Bhutto were "lacking political realism" and "have played a role that has provided adventurers with an opportunity to capture power and rob the people of their rights." See Khan, *Generals in Politics*, 134.

79. Jāved, "Ẓahīr se khuṣūṣī interview," 368.

80. Ibid., 371. For some more background on the domestic dynamics in mid-1980s Pakistan, see Kennedy, "Islamization and Legal Reform in Pakistan."

81. Ḍaskavī, *ʿAllāmah Iḥsān Ilāhī Ẓahīr*, 82–85.

82. Jāved, "Ẓahīr se khuṣūṣī interview," 372.

83. Ḍaskavī, *ʿAllāmah Iḥsān Ilāhī Ẓahīr*, 73.

84. On the Movement for the Restoration of Democracy, see Nasr, *Islamic Leviathan*, 148–50.

85. Sajjād, *ʿAllāmah Iḥsān Ilāhī Ẓahīr shahīd*, 23. Ẓahīr denied the receipt of any Saudi funds for this and other projects beyond the royalties for his books. He claimed that his only regular salary consisted of the fifty thousand rupees he received annually as the imām of the Ahl-i Ḥadīs̱ mosque in Lahore. If money had been his concern, he suggested, it would have been more lucrative for him to simply stay on at the Islamic University in Medina. See Jāved, "ʿAllāmah Iḥsān Ilāhī Ẓahīr," 611.

86. See Ẓahīr, *al-Shīʿa wa-ahl al-bayt*, 7–8.

87. Jāved, "ʿAllāmah Iḥsān Ilāhī Ẓahīr," 604.

88. Ẓahīr, *al-Shīʿa wa-l-sunna*, 5–6. The verses are taken from sura 109, al-Kāfirūn (The Unbelievers).

89. Other early authorities tried to counter the idea of taḥrīf, however: Muḥammad b. ʿAlī Ibn Bābawayh al-Qummī (d. 381/991–92) stated that whoever claimed there was another Qurʾān beyond the one contained between the book covers was a liar. Similarly, Abū Jaʿfar Muḥammad b. Ḥasan al-Ṭūsī (d. 460/1066–67) rejected all Shiʿi hadiths that pointed to a change of the text, because all of these reports were based on

one (unreliable) single chain of transmission (*akhbār āḥād*). For a detailed discussion of the topic, see Brunner, *Die Schia und die Koranfälschung*, 4–8. For the view that only seven Shiʿi scholars from the fourth/tenth century to the present have subscribed to the belief in taḥrīf, see Modarressi, "Early Debates on the Integrity of the Qur'ān."

90. Ẓahīr, *al-Shīʿa wa-l-sunna*, 8. On Yahya Khan's rule, see Ziring, "Militarism in Pakistan."

91. Ẓahīr, *al-Shīʿa wa-l-sunna*, 70. See also Zahrānī, *al-Shaykh Iḥsān Ilāhī Ẓahīr*, 449–50. Ẓahīr differs in his argumentation from Ṣanā'ullāh Amritsarī (d. 1948), who, while clearly rejecting the Shiʿis, refrained from a final verdict as to whether they were unbelievers. He conceded that the Shiʿis also carried out the mandatory prayers but held that their denunciation of the ṣaḥāba amounted to an act of kufr. Amritsarī's more ambivalent attitude also came to the fore (as discussed in chapter 1) in the context of his efforts to calm sectarian tensions in Lahore. Instead of taqrīb or taḥrīf, however, Amritsarī was primarily interested in the question of ranking the four Rightly Guided Caliphs. He restricted their equality (*Gleichrangigkeit*) to their piety whereas he portrayed Abū Bakr, ʿUmar, and ʿUthmān in their political achievements as superior to ʿAlī (see Riexinger, *Ṣanā'ullāh Amritsarī*, 261–68).

92. Brunner situates the focus on taḥrīf in the backlash to efforts to foster inner-Islamic ecumenism in the 1950s (Brunner, *Die Schia und die Koranfälschung*, 71).

93. Ibid., 92.

94. See, for example, Ẓahīr, *al-Shīʿa wa-l-Sunna*, 5, 13, 20. The full title of al-Khaṭīb's work is *al-Khuṭūt al-ʿarīḍa lil-usus allatī qāma ʿalayhā dīn al-shīʿa al-imāmiyya al-ithnā ʿashariyya* (The broad lines of the foundations on which the religion of the Imāmi Twelver Shīʿīs is based). The first Arabic edition was published in 1961. On al-Khaṭīb's Salafi background and his role as editor of al-Azhar's journal *Majallat al-Azhar*, see Brunner, *Islamic Ecumenism*, 255–65. In Werner Ende's view, Ẓahīr's breadth of knowledge of both medieval and modern Shiʿism is quite unique, since "the majority of contemporary Sunni polemicists look somewhat amateurish in their attempts to corroborate their judgments on Shiʿism by quoting Shiʿi sources." See Ende, "Sunni Polemical Writings on the Shiʿa," 226–27.

95. Ẓahīr, *al-Shīʿa wa-l-tashayyuʿ*, 6–7.

96. Ḍaskavī, *ʿAllāmah Iḥsān Ilāhī Ẓahīr*, 63.

97. The name might by a pseudonym. Zahrānī writes that he met with the author of the work *Ḥattā lā nankhadiʿ* (So that we may not be deceived) in the year 1419 (1998 or 1999) in Kuwait.

98. Zahrānī, *al-Shaykh Iḥsān Ilāhī Ẓahīr*, 56–57. As I show below, other anti-Shiʿi writers after the Iranian Revolution always pointed to the same passages in an early work by Khomeini that were perceived as an insult to the Companions.

99. Ẓahīr, *al-Shīʿa wa-l-Sunna*, 23.

100. Ibid., 104.

101. Ẓahīr, *al-Shīʿa wa-l-tashayyuʿ*, 71. The originating of Shiʿism as a Jewish plot hatched by the mysterious ʿAbdallāh b. Saba' is a standard trope of anti-Shiʿi polemics. In Twelver Shiʿi heresiography, Ibn Saba' functions as the founder of "extremist

Shiʿism" (*al-shīʿa al-ghāliya*). See Halm, *Die Islamische Gnosis*, 33–42; Anthony, *The Caliph and the Heretic*, 139–60.

102. Ẓahīr, *al-Shīʿa wa-l-Sunna*, 79. See also Zahrānī, *al-Shaykh Iḥsān Ilāhī Ẓahīr*, 512.

103. Jāved, "ʿAllāmah Iḥsān Ilāhī Ẓahīr," 607.

104. Ẓahīr, "Firqah vāriyyat kā khatmah," 288.

105. Ḍaskavī, *ʿAllāmah Iḥsān Ilāhī Ẓahīr*, 76.

106. Ibid., 292–94.

107. Jāved, "ʿAllāmah Iḥsān Ilāhī Ẓahīr," 605–6.

108. See Ẓahīr, "Niẓām-i ḥukūmat kaysā hōnā cāhiye?," 466–71.

109. The Urdu original is as follows: "jab shahīd qāʾid ke wajīh cehrah se kafan haṭāyā giyā tō shahīd zabān-i ḥāl se apnī khudādād garajdār āvāz se har ahl-i ḥadīs̱ ke nām yeh payghām de rahe the." See Hazaravī and Isḥāq, "ʿAllāmah shahīd kā akharī payghām," 89. The accuracy of this whole account was vouched for by two members of the Ahl-i Ḥadīs̱, Fażl al-Raḥmān Hazaravī and Ḥāfiẓ Muḥammad Isḥāq, who were both based at the Islamic University of Medina at that time.

110. Ibid.

111. Peskes, *Muḥammad B. ʿAbdalwahhāb (1703–92) im Widerstreit*, 23–34.

112. Riexinger, *S̱anāʾullāh Amritsarī*, 249–50. Similarly, David Cook has observed that in martyr accounts of the jihad in Afghanistan we often encounter classical topoi like the lack of decomposition of the martyr's body, visions of the martyr in paradise, or his continued influence in the world helping out his fellow warriors. Cook sees a strong topical relationship to Sufi martyrologies and holds that "the complete cult of relics of the martyrs has been resurrected by radical Muslims." See Cook, *Martyrdom in Islam*, 160–61.

113. Balākōṭī, *Amīr-i ʿazīmat*, 20. See also Kamran, "Contextualizing Sectarian Militancy," 63–64.

114. Balākōṭī, *Amīr-i ʿazīmat*, 21–22.

115. Ibid., 15–18.

116. Ḥaqq Navāz was arrested for the first time on 30 May 1974 after he had delivered a very emotional speech against the Aḥmadīs (ibid., 29–30).

117. Ibid., 36.

118. See Qāsim, *Ḥayāt-i Aʿẓam Ṭāriq*, 60. Especially the metaphor of the candle and the moth is a longstanding Sufi image which usually denotes the desire of the mystic to become annihilated in God. See, for example, Attar, *The Conference of the Birds*, 100, 141, 167.

119. See Qāsim, *Ḥayāt-i Aʿẓam Ṭāriq*, 74.

120. Ibid., 45–46. Justin Jones regards ʿAbd al-Shakūr's polemics in late colonial Lucknow as a turning point because "his conversion of classical scholarship into more accessible, vernacular confutation, whether spoken or written, set the bedrock for many of the arguments that have become the staple of Shiʿa-Sunni polemics in South Asia today." See Jones, *Shiʿa Islam in Colonial India*, 70–71.

121. I do not share Tahir Kamran's view about the importance of local concerns like

the Bāb-i ʿUmar incident in 1969 since this is not reflected in the writings of leading members of the Sipāh-i Ṣaḥābah (see Kamran, "Contextualizing Sectarian Militancy," 75).

122. See Brunner, *Die Schia und die Koranfälschung*, 103–5. For examples of how these passages from Khomeini's work were used in polemical texts in Pakistan, see Qāsim, *Ḥayāt-i Aʿẓam Ṭāriq*, 118; Fārūqī, *Khumaynīizm aur Islām*, 140–41; Fārūqī, *Sitāre cānd ke Islām men̲ ṣaḥābah-i kirām kī āʾīnī hays̱iyyat*, 114.

123. Fārūqī, *Fārūqī shahīd kā payghām*, 11–12. The quote is from Ghulām Ḥusayn Najafī. See Najafī, *Qaul-i maqbūl*, 432 (*us ke murdah se hambistarī kartā rahā*). For Najafī's biography, see ʿĀrif Naqvī, *Taẕkirah-i ʿulamāʾ-i imāmiyyah*, 195–96.

124. See Fārūqī, *Khumaynīizm aur Islām*, 16–18; Shujāʿābādī, *ʿAllāmah Żiyā al-Raḥmān Fārūqī shahīd*, 55–57. For similar evaluations of the unprecedented character of Shiʿi propaganda, now freely distributed by Iranian embassies and cultural institutions in India, see Nuʿmānī, *Īrānī inqilāb*, 19.

125. Ṭāriq's family had migrated from the district of Ludhīanah in today's Indian Punjab. They ran into resistance in their new village near Multan for propagating a form of Islam that was deemed "Wahhābī" by the local population. Ṭāriq reports that his grandfather, father, and uncle were later addressed as *maulvī*—despite the lack of any formal religious training—due to their initiative in building a mosque and a madrasa in the village. See Qāsim, *Ḥayāt-i Aʿẓam Ṭāriq*, 26–76.

126. Ṭāriq, "Sipāh-i Ṣaḥābah kā mission kyā he?," 471–72.

127. The author quoted from an op-ed Maudūdī had written in June 1945. In this piece, Maudūdī had accused the Shiʿis of not being required to carry out ritual obligations during the *ghayba*. Fārūqī interpreted this position as the Jamāʿat's original stance (Fārūqī, *Khumaynīizm aur Islām*, 14). More research is required to pursue this internal Sunni debate further and to review the various publications that lumped together Khomeini and Maudūdī like the anonymous work *Dō bhāʾī: Abū ʾl-Aʿlā Maudūdī aur Imām Khumaynī sansanī khīz inkishāfāt* (Two brothers: Sensational revelations about Abū ʾl-ʿĀlā Maudūdī and Imām Khomeini).

128. Zaman, "South Asian Islam," 68–69.

129. Ḥaqq Navāz blamed the Barelvīs for leaving the Taḥaffuẓ-i Nāmūs-i Ṣahābah Committee (Committee for Defending the Honor of the Companions) in the face of pressures that declared this institution to be "Wahhābī" (Balākōṭī, *Amīr-i ʿazīmat*, 36).

130. Zaman, "Sectarianism in Pakistan," 702–3.

131. For the "mimetic processes" of organizations modeling themselves on other organizations, see DiMaggio and Powell, "The Iron Cage Revisited," 151. Homi Bhabha likens mimicry to "camouflage, not a harmonization or repression of difference, but a form of resemblance that differs/defends presence by displaying it in part, metonymically." See Bhabha, "Of Mimicry and Man," 131. For a detailed description of the various elements of a Shiʿi mourning session in Hyderabad/Deccan (India) and the transition from the *faḍāʾil* to the *maṣāʾib*, see Howarth, *The Twelver Shīʿa*, 64–68.

132. Fārūqī, *Fārūqī shahīd kā payghām*, 15.

133. For a list of his demands, see Balākōṭī, *Amīr-i ʿazīmat*, 56, 69.

134. Zaman, *The Ulama in Contemporary Islam*, 133.

135. Fārūqī, *Fārūqī shahīd kā payghām*, 9.

136. Ibid., 14; Qāsim, *Ḥayāt-i Aʿẓam Ṭāriq*, 121–23.

137. Fārūqī was born in 1953 into a Deobandī immigrant family and early on embarked on a scholarly path. In 1968 he studied the *Gulistān* with Yūsuf Ludhīanvī in the Jāmīʿah-i Rāshidiyya in Sāhivāl. After some time in Multan, he spent three years at the Dār al-ʿUlūm in Kabīrvālā, where he encountered Ḥaqq Navāz Jhangvī, who was one year his senior. Fārūqī was arrested for the first time in 1973 for an anti-Bhutto speech and also imprisoned in 1974 for organizing an anti-Aḥmadī demonstration after Friday prayers during which the slogan "khatm-i nubuvvat zindahbād, mīrzāʾiyyat murdahbād" (Long live the movement for the finality of Muḥammad's Prophethood, death to the Aḥmadī religion) was shouted. Fārūqī began to cooperate with Ḥaqq Navāz Jhangvī in 1978 and joined the SSP in 1986 when he delivered a fiercely anti-Iranian speech at the Difāʿ-i Ṣaḥābah Conference (Defending the Companions of the Prophet Conference) in Jhang. See Shujāʿābādī, *ʿAllāmah Żiyā al-Raḥmān Fārūqī shahīd*, 24–59.

138. Ibid., 16–17. For the voice of the first leader of the women's chapter of the Sipāh-i Ṣaḥābah, see Żiyā, *Ghāzī shaykh Ḥaqq Navāz shahīd.*

139. Fārūqī, *Khilāfat ō ḥukūmat*, 20.

140. Ẓahīr, *al-Shīʿa wa-l-sunna*, 141–42.

141. Fārūqī, *Khilāfat ke ʿālamī naṣb al-ʿayn kī daʿvat*, 154–55. See also Fārūqī, *Tārīkhī dastāvez*, 18.

142. Qāsim, *Ḥayāt-i Aʿẓam Ṭāriq*, 118–19. On Gharīb (a pseudonym for Muḥammad Surūr), see Haykel, "Al-Qa'ida and Shiism," 187; for al-Mūsawī, see Brunner, "A Shiite Cleric's Criticism of Shiism"; Siddons, *"Die Korrektur der Irrtümer."* See also chapter 2.

143. Fārūqī, *Khumaynīizm aur Islām*, 101. Fārūqī relied here primarily on Nuʿmānī's *Īrānī inqilāb* for this argument. The issue of wrongfully passing as Muslims echoes similar arguments that were part of Pakistan's Supreme Court ruling in 1993. The court found the Aḥmadīs guilty of infringing on a protected trademark. See Khan, *Muslim Becoming*, 114–15, and Qasmi, *The Ahmadis and the Politics of Religious Exclusion in Pakistan*, 221–26.

144. Fārūqī, *Tārīkhī dastāvez*, 14. In this book, Fārūqī made a point of excerpting the original pages from 232 Shiʿi works.

145. Qāsim, *Ḥayāt-i Aʿẓam Ṭāriq*, 189. For the claim that the SSP managed to open the eyes of prominent Sunni ʿulamā who were originally inclined to coexistence with the Shiʿis as Muslims during a meeting with Prime Minister Nawaz Sharif on 28 September 1991 as well as during later sessions of the Committee for the Eradication of Sectarianism, see Fārūqī, *Tārīkhī dastāvez*, 30–32.

146. Fārūqī, *Khumaynīizm aur Islām*, 88.

147. Qāsim, *Ḥayāt-i Aʿẓam Ṭāriq*, 278–79. The percentage of Sunnis in Iran might be closer to somewhere between 5 and 10 percent of the population. For a fascinating study of the opposition of Iranian Sunni ʿulamā to the Iranian Revolution and the way the most remote area of Iranian Balochistan has been turned into a springboard

for Deobandī outreach to Central Asia and the Middle East, see Dudoignon, "Sunnis and Shiites in Iran since 1979."

148. Ṭāriq, "Īrān ne ʿālam-i Islāmi kō kyā diyā?," 158–59. See also Shujāʿābādī, *ʿAllāmah Żiyā al-Raḥmān Fārūqī shahīd*, 62.

149. See, for example, Balākōṭī, *Amīr-i ʿazīmat*, 82–88; Muḥammad Aʿẓam Ṭāriq, "'Ṭālibān' ḥukūmat kā kirdār," 144. For some further examples that were supposed to underline Shiʿi domination in Pakistan, see Fuchs, "The Long Shadow of the State."

150. Ṭāriq, "Īrān ne ʿālam-i Islāmi kō kyā diyā?," 158–59.

151. See Crone and Hinds, *God's Caliph*, 230. For examples of contemporary jihādī appropriations of the term, see Fuchs, "Do Excellent Surgeons Make Miserable Exegetes?," 204, 230–31.

152. On the Shiʿi side, the doctrine of *takfir al-ṣaḥāba*, accusing the Companions of collective unbelief due to their failure of recognize ʿAlī's imāmate, is associated with Hishām b. al-Ḥakam (d. 183/799). Only a few "good Companions" who had remained loyal to ʿAlī were exempted by Shiʿi authors. See Kohlberg, "Some Imāmī Shīʿī Views on the Ṣaḥāba," 148–50. This is not to say that Shiʿi authors did not also at times discuss more nuanced and complex conceptions of the ṣaḥāba. See Kohlberg, "The Attitude of Imāmī Shīʿīs," 123–24.

153. See Khalek, "Medieval Biographical Literature," 274–75, 281–83; Osman, "ʿAdālat al-Ṣaḥāba," 275–77. See also Juynboll, *Muslim Tradition*, 190–206; Lucas, *Constructive Critics*, 222–85.

154. Khalek, "Medieval Biographical Literature," 286–90.

155. See Jabali, *The Companions of the Prophet*, 2. Amr Osman, on the other hand, has argued that Ibn al-Ṣalāḥ (d. 643/1245) provided a thorough discussion "that would settle all disagreements on the subject once and for all." According to Ibn al-Ṣalāḥ, all Companions shared a common characteristic: "Their integrity and reliability were not matters of question or scrutiny, for they were secured in the Qur'ān, the Sunna, and the consensus of 'those whose consensus matters.' Because it was the guarantee that religion was properly transmitted, he [Ibn al-Ṣalāḥ] argues, God must have made possible this consensus on the necessity of accrediting (*taʿdīl*) all the Companions, including those who took part in the schisms." See Osman, "ʿAdālat al-Ṣaḥāba," 290–91.

156. See Wiederhold, "Blasphemy against the Prophet Muḥammad and His Companions," 49.

157. See Ende, *Arabische Nation und islamische Geschichte*, 91–96.

158. Fārūqī, *Ṣaḥābah-i kirām*, 64.

159. While Ibn Ḥajar al-ʿAsqalānī (d. 852/1449) counted more than 100,000 Companions at the time of the Prophet's death, the traditionist Abu Zurʿa al-Rāzī (d. 264/878) had claimed much earlier that there were 114,000 of them. Yet, the most comprehensive attempt to collect their biographies (*al-Iṣāba* by Ibn Ḥajar) only lists 11,000 (see Jabali, *The Companions of the Prophet*, 2). Even in this context Nancy Khalek has stressed Ibn Ḥajar's "sheer exhaustiveness." The Mamlūk scholar "included biographical entries for people who claimed to have *ṣubḥa* but may not have actually been Companions, as well as children who were too young to be considered Compan-

ions but may be considered *tābiʿīs*" (see Khalek, "Medieval Biographical Literature," 290). Especially early Muslim jurists adopted at times rather strict definitions in the vein that only someone who had been with the Prophet for a substantial amount of time qualified as a Companion. Yet, restricting the number of the Companions in such a way was seen as a problem by the collectors of hadith because many transmitters "would be excluded and the status of their *ḥadīth* consequently downgraded from *al-musnad* to *al-mursal*. And since the majority of the traditionists classified the *mursal ḥadīth* as weak, this meant that they could not be used as an authoritative source (*ḥujja*) of law" (see Jabali, *The Companions of the Prophet*, 47–50).

160. Fārūqī, "Rufaqā'-i payghambar," 356.

161. Fārūqī, *Ṣaḥābah-i kirām*, 42–43.

162. Ibid., 43.

163. Ibid., 44.

164. Jabali, *The Companions*, 72. See also Osman, "ʿAdālat al-Ṣaḥāba," 284n53.

165. For further examples of revisionist Qur'ānic exegesis by the SSP and its successor organizations, see Fuchs, "The Long Shadow of the State."

166. For an in-depth discussion of al-Qurṭūbī's (d. 671/1272) treatment of the passage, see Tannous, "Frowning in Cordoba." For a similar approach within the Deobandī tradition, see Thānavī, *Tafsīr bayān al-Qur'ān*, 12:76–78.

167. Fārūqī, "Rufaqā'-i payghambar," 358–59.

168. Ibid., 367–72. When the Medinese caravan returned from a raid on the Banū al-Muṣṭaliq and stopped in the desert, ʿĀ'isha used this opportunity to answer the call of nature and lost her necklace. Because of her frantic search for the precious item she returned late to the camp and found that the whole troop, including the camel with her litter on top, had already departed. A latecomer spotted her by chance and brought her to Medina, where immediately rumors began to swirl about inappropriate conduct between the warrior and the Prophet's wife. See Ibn Hishām and Ibn Isḥāq, *The Life of Muhammad*, 493–99.

169. Fārūqī, "Rufaqā'-i payghambar," 374–75. The Urdu text is as follows: "khudā tō nā bīne [*sic*] ṣaḥābī kō nabī kī maḥfil se uṭhā hū'ā nahīṉ dekh saktā . . . Aur āj Khumaynī kah keh ye sāre kāfir the . . . (laʿnat be shumār)."

170. Ibid., 359.

171. Ibid., 363.

172. For a detailed discussion of these laws and the view that they should be seen as part of a larger pattern of "subjugation of legislation to political expediency," see Siddique and Hayat, "Unholy Speech and Holy Laws."

173. See Qāsim, *Ḥayāt-i Aʿẓam Ṭāriq*, 285; Zaman, "Sectarianism in Pakistan," 702.

174. For the background of this work, see Laoust, "La Biographie d'Ibn Taimīya," 118.

175. Fārūqī, *Ṣaḥābah-i kirām*, 112. The quotation can be found in Ibn Taymiyya, *al-Ṣārim al-maslūl*, 569.

176. See Laoust, *Essai sur les doctrines sociales et politiques*, 204–25.

177. Fārūqī, *Ṣaḥābah-i kirām*, 112–13.

178. See Andræ, *Die Person Muhammeds*, 264.

179. Fārūqī, *Khilāfat ō ḥukūmat,* 25–26.

180. Ibid., 32.

181. Ibid., 46.

182. Ibid. Fārūqī only gives the title of Shāh Walī Allāh's book as *Izālat al-khulafā'.*

183. Ahmad, "An Eighteenth-Century Theory of the Caliphate," 140. For a discussion of additional criteria, see al-Ghazali, *The Socio-Political Thought of Shāh Walī Allāh,* 93–96.

184. Muḥaddis̱ Dihlavī, *Izālat al-khafā',* 25. See also Baljon, *Religion and Thought,* 122.

185. Quoted ibid., 124. While Shāh Walī Allāh still counted ʿAlī as a proper *khalīfah-i khāṣṣ,* who was as close to the Prophet as Abū Bakr, he found him lacking in his ability to establish authority throughout the Islamic empire (ibid., 123–24). For a dissenting view that ʿAlī is not included in the category of the Extraordinary Caliphate, see Bhat, "Shah Wali Allah's Political Theory," 251–54.

186. See Muḥaddis̱ Dihlavī, *Fuyūḍ al-ḥaramayn,* 83–84. See also Ghazi, "State and Politics," 364.

187. The name of the journal was changed in the aftermath of Sayyid ʿĀrif Ḥusayn al-Ḥusaynī's death from its previous title *Rāh-i ʿAmal.* See Khān, "Pākistān kā aham mas'alah," 41.

188. Ibid.

189. Ibid., 42. For such a view, see also the video recording Javād Naqvī, "Parcam-i āzādī," min. 35:58.

190. Khān, "Pākistān kā aham mas'alah," 42.

191. For some examples among many, see "CIA, Żiyā-yi ḥukūmat, ghaddārān-i millat," Riżā Naqvī, "Ceh July aur tanẓīm," 5; ʿAbbās Naqvī, "Aṭok shahr, rūz-i ʿāshūrā' aur saʿūdī agent," 31.

192. "Sāniḥah-i ʿaẓīm," 3. This event itself was interpreted by the ISO as propelling them from mere theoretical considerations of the consequences of martyrdom to a deeper, practical understanding of Khomeini's teachings. See Riżā Naqvī, "Payghām-i yaum-i ta'sīs," 11.

193. For such a line of reasoning, see Fārūqī, "Ahl-i bayt kōn heṉ?," 268.

194. See chapter 2 for more background on debates over these expressions of Shiʿi identity.

195. Kāẓimī, "Shahīd qā'id ke qātil kōn?," 3. Interestingly, earlier issues of *Rāh-i ʿAmal* report a decision by the group's Executive Committee in April 1987 to dissolve the ISO's Advisory Board, which had consisted of ʿulamā and community leaders. Instead, the ISO decided to submit directly to the leadership of Sayyid ʿArif Ḥusayn al-Ḥusaynī. In this context, the Executive Committee stated that from now on "nothing should be published by the ISO which contravenes Islamic ideologies (*islāmī naẓariyyāt*), the statutes of the *tanẓīm,* the fundamental principles (*bunyādī uṣūlōṉ*) and the institution of Guardianship of the Jurisprudent (*idārah-i vilāyat-i faqīh*)." See "Report-i ijlās-i majlis-i ʿāmilah," 14. This curious statement begs of course the question how unified the ISO actually was with regard to *vilāyat-i faqīh.*

196. Javādī, *Vazīr-i Aʿẓam, vuzarā-yi aʿlā*. Sajjad Rivzi has suggested that the work was produced by a collective, which resorted to a pseudonym in order to protect the individual authors (private communication, 21 April 2014).

197. Javādī, *Taḥqīqī dastāvez*, 86–92.

198. See Wiederhold, "Blasphemy against the Prophet Muḥammad," 63.

199. Javādī, *Taḥqīqī dastāvez*, 116–17. Early Shiʿi authors such as ʿAlī b. Aḥmad al-Kūfī (d. 352/963) and al-Sharīf al-Murtaḍā (d. 436/1044) dismissed the hadith as spurious because it would not make sense for the Prophet (who addressed his Companions when he supposedly uttered it) to urge the Companions to adopt their own conduct as an example of guidance. Additionally, the hadith could not apply to a group that was known to have sinners who disobeyed the Prophet and ʿAlī in its midst (see Kohlberg, "Some Imāmī Shīʿī views on the Ṣaḥāba," 158).

200. See Ibn Taymiyya, *Minhāj al-sunna al-nabawiyya*, 4:238–39. On al-Ḥillī, see Laoust, "La critique du sunnisme."

201. Javādī, *Taḥqīqī dastāvez*, 3.

202. Ibid., 111.

203. Ibid., 142. For a detailed discussion about the colonial debates over Pakistan, compare also chapter 1.

204. See, for example, "Sunnī State ke nām par deobandī riyāsat ke qiyām"; Mushtāq, *Ayṭam bam kā dūsrā nām*, 15, 20–23.

205. Javādī, *Taḥqīqī dastāvez*, 41.

206. Binder, *Religion and Politics in Pakistan*, 213–16; Rieck, *The Shias of Pakistan*, 69.

207. Javādī, *Taḥqīqī dastāvez*, 111. Needless to say, this formulation deliberately excluded the Aḥmadīs.

208. Javādī, *Taḥqīqī dastāvez*, 40.

209. Saif, "Notes from the Margins," 89–90.

210. Ibid., 74, 80, 86. The contest over claiming Muhammad Iqbal also manifests itself in the lines of poetry provided at the beginning of the chapter. Both Sunni and Shiʿi sectarian groups quote this particular verse for their various divergent goals. For the entire poem, see Iqbāl, *Żarb-i Kalīm*, 41. On the issue of Iqbal's elusiveness and multilevel appropriation, compare also Khan, *Muslim Becoming*, 59.

211. Saif, "Notes from the Margins," 74, 77, 87.

212. Ibid., 68.

213. Devji, *Muslim Zion*, 137–38.

214. Hartung, *A System of Life*, 107.

CONCLUSION

1. See chapter 1.

2. On the background of its founding, see Rieck, *The Shias of Pakistan*, 311–13.

3. See chapter 4.

4. Zamir, *ʿAlī Naqvī and His Thought*, 21.

5. Ibid., 136, 274.

6. For an account of the origins and inner workings of the All India Muslim Personal Law Board, see Jones, "'Signs of Churning.'"

7. Sikand, "An Islamic Critique of Patriarchy," 644–46.

8. Ibid., 648.

9. Jones, "Urban Mythologies and Urbane Islam," 4.

10. Mahmudabad, "Enemy Property Bill."

11. Jones, *Shi'a Islam in Colonia India*, 232–33.

12. Jones, "'Signs of Churning,'" 197–98; Susewind, "The 'Wazirganj Terror Attack,'" 7–13.

13. Roy, *Globalized Islam*, 21–26.

14. Green, *Terrains of Exchange*, 7–16.

15. In Immanuel Wallerstein's world-systems theory, which aims at explaining the rise and stability of modern capitalism, political, military, and economic might is concentrated in core states, which are engaged in unequal exchanges with peripheral states. In between, Wallerstein locates a semiperiphery which fulfills an important political function: "The existence of the third category means precisely that the upper stratum is not faced with the *unified* opposition of all the others because the *middle* stratum is both exploited and exploiter." See Wallerstein, "The Rise and Future Demise of the World Capitalist System," 18–23, and *Capitalist Agriculture*, 347–48. Interesting for our discussion might be the observation that semi-peripheral states are viewed by theorists as potentially disruptive actors that have the ability to transform a system. See Worth, "Whatever Happened to the Semi-Periphery?," 15–18.

16. For the earlier "supremely confident," even "arrogant" Mughal self-view about being the center of the Islamic world, see Moin, "Margins of Anxiety," 263–64.

17. See Kersten and Olsson, "Introduction: Alternative Islamic Discourses," 10–12.

18. Rozehnal, *Islamic Sufism Unbound*, 89–127.

19. See Philippon, "Le charisme comme ressource émotionnelle du mouvement social?" On al-Qaraḍāwī, see Gräf and Skovgaard-Petersen, *Global Mufti*.

20. On al-Sibāʿī, see Hatina, "An Earlier Sunnī Version of Khomeini's Rule of the Jurist."

21. For details on this organization, see Schulze, *Islamischer Internationalismus im 20. Jahrhundert*.

22. For a comprehensive study on Nadvī, see Hartung, *Viele Wege und ein Ziel*. For Nadvī's transnational activities, see especially ibid., 401–51.

23. Ibid., 433. On the global reach of the Tablīghī Jamāʿat and the special attention it paid to the Middle East, see Gaborieau, "The Transformation of the Tablīghī Jamāʿat." For a comparative study of the Deobandī Tablīghī Jamāʿat and the rival Barelvī organization Daʿvat-i Islāmī, see Gugler, *Mission Medina*. Gugler pays particular attention to the inner workings of both organizations.

24. For a maximalist version of this argument, see Hall, *Civilising Subjects*. Hall argues that English missionaries and abolitionists of the early nineteenth century initially advocated the substantial equality of Europeans and non-Europeans. Due to violent upheavals against the colonial state, however, such perspectives gave way after the

1860s to an emphasis on unbridgeable racial differences. This, in turn, influenced the domestic self-fashioning of the English as belonging to a distinctly superior race. For a rather isolated attempt at dismissing the claim that Britain's colonies had any palpable impact on the wider British public beyond a small upper and upper-middle class fixated on the empire, compare Porter, *The Absent-Minded Imperialists.*

25. See Thompson, *The Empire Strikes Back?*, 4–5; Potter, "Empire, Cultures and Identities." Given this problem, Steven Howe has thus suggested that the issue needs to be approached in the plural (new imperial histories) rather than in the singular. See Howe, "Introduction: New Imperial Histories."

26. See Troll, *Sayyid Ahmad Khan.*

27. Lauzière, *The Making of Salafism.*

28. Farquhar, *Circuits of Faith*, 136.

29. Ibid., 146–50, 191.

30. See Sarḥān, *Rasāʾil al-Imām Muḥammad Zāhid al-Kautharī.*

31. For more details, see Preckel, "Islamische Bildungsnetzwerke und Gelehrtenkultur im Indien des 19. Jahrhunderts."

32. Alavi, *Muslim Cosmopolitanism*, 298–302.

33. See Hartung, *A System of Life*, 196–205. For an exploration of how Maudūdī, in turn, was influenced by the wider South Asian Islamic milieu of his time, see also Zaman, "The Sovereignty of God in Modern Islamic Thought."

34. Hartung, *A System of Life*, 212.

35. Ibid., 219–23.

36. Ibid., 194–95.

37. Dudoignon, "Sunnis and Shiites in Iran since 1979."

38. For the website of the Indian Sub-Continental Literal Revival Centre (this is what the Markaz-i Iḥyāʾ-i Ās̱ār-i Barr-i Ṣaghīr calls itself in English), see www.maablib.org.

BIBLIOGRAPHY

INTERVIEWS BY THE AUTHOR

The following are listed in chronological order.

Sajjād ʿAlī Astūrī and Dr. Zāhid ʿAlī Zāhidī, Karachi, 5 September 2011
Sayyid ʿAlī Ḥasan Naqvī, Karachi, 6 September 2011
ʿAbbās Kumaylī, Karachi, 6 September 2011
Hādī ʿAskarī, Karachi, 6 September 2011
Dr. Muḥammad Ḥasan Riżvī, Karachi, 7 September 2011
Ṣāqib Akbar, Islamabad, 12 October 2011 and 1 August 2012
Sayyid Niṣār ʿAlī al-Ḥusaynī al-Tirmiẕī, Lahore, 5 November 2011
Sayyid Żamīr Akhtar Naqvī, Karachi, 18 November 2011
Ḥasan Riżā Ghadīrī, London, 20 June 2012
Muḥammad Ḥusayn Akbar, Lahore, 15 July 2012
Muḥammad Ḥusayn Najafī Ḍhakkō, Lahore, 18 July 2012
Dr. Zāhid ʿAlī Zāhidī, Karachi, 21 July 2012
Dr. ʿAqīl Mūsā, Karachi, 23 July 2012
Murtażā Pūyā, Islamabad, 1 August 2012
Shaykh Aḥmad Nūrī, Skardu, 2 August 2012
Muḥammad Ḥasan Jaʿfarī, Skardu, 3 August 2012
Fiżā ʿĀbidī, Skardu, 8 August 2012
Irshād Nāṣir, Lahore, 12 August 2012
Zuhayr al-Muṣtafā, Lahore, 13 August 2012
Students of the Jāmiʿat al-ʿUrwa al-Wuthqā, Lahore, 18 August 2012
Muḥammad Baqīr, Qum, 22 August 2012
Muḥammad Ḥasan Sharīfī and Niyāz ʿAlī Ḥijāzī, Qum, 23 August 2012
Sayyid Ṣaghīr ʿAbbās, Qum, 26 August 2012
Ghulām Jābir Muḥammad and Sayyid Ḥusayn Zaydī, Qum, 29 August 2012
Grand Ayatollah Bashīr Ḥusayn al-Najafī, Najaf, 22 January 2013

PRIVATE PAPERS, MANUSCRIPTS AND OFFICIAL RECORDS IN THE INDIA OFFICE COLLECTION (IOC), BRITISH LIBRARY

The following are listed in ascending order according to their file number.

File 462/38E Shias, IOR/L/I/1/880
Ahmed, Sir Syed Sultan, IOR/L/I/1/1265
Fortnightly Reports, Punjab, 1937, IOR/L/PJ/5/238
Fortnightly Reports, Punjab, July–December 1938, IOR/L/PJ/5/240

Fortnightly Reports, Punjab, January–June 1939, IOR/L/PJ/5/241
Fortnightly Reports, Punjab, July–August 1939, IOR L/PJ/5/242
Fortnightly Reports, United Provinces, January–June 1938 (1938), IOR/L/PJ/5/265
Fortnightly Reports, United Provinces, July–December 1938 (1938), IOR/L/PJ/5/266
Fortnightly Reports, United Provinces, January–June 1939, IOR/L/PJ/5/267
Fortnightly Reports, United Provinces, Second Half of 1939 (August–December 1939), IOR/L/PJ/5/268
Fortnightly Reports, United Provinces, 1940, IOR/L/PJ/5/269
Fortnightly Reports, United Provinces, Second Half of 1941, IOR/L/PJ/5/270
Fortnightly Reports, United Provinces, 1942, IOR/L/PJ/5/271
Fortnightly Reports, United Provinces, 1943, IOR/L/PJ/5/272
Husain, Nazir (7/23/1927): An Unprecedented Mass Meeting of the Muhammadans of Multan, IOR/L/PJ/6/1941, File 1689
2392; Appointment of Mr Justice Allsop and Mr H. Ross to the Madh-e-Sahaba Committee (22 May 1937–4 February 1938), IOR/L/PJ/7/1263
1958; The Sunni-Shia Controversy in Lucknow, 25 March 1939–2 April 1942 IOR/L/PJ/7/2587
Coll 117/E7; Muslim Organisations in India, including All-India Momin Conference, All-Indian Muslim Majlis and All Parties Shia Conference, and their aims and objects (March 1942–January 1947), IOR L/PJ/8/693
Coll 23/95 Kurram Affairs: including Assessment Report of Kurram Valley (15 September 1938–4 October 1949), IOR/L/PS/12/3259
E-UP-26: Petition of the Shia Mohamedans of Jaunpur (5/26/1928), IOR/Q/13/1/14, item 1
E-UP-870: Saiyyed Ali Mohammad, Lucknow (11/28/1928), IOR/Q/13/1/15, item 25 Memorandum to the Indian Statutory Commission
E-UP-894: Syed Abdul Ghaffar Rizavi, Zamindar, Lucknow (1928), IOR/Q/13/1/15, item 29
Madh-e Sahaba, MSS Eur IOR Pos 10773. India Office Records and Private Papers, MSS Eur IOR Pos 10773

OFFICIAL PUBLICATIONS AND ORGANIZATIONAL PROCEEDINGS

The following are listed in chronological order.

Government Gazette of the United Provinces.
Sayyid Muḥsin Mīrzā, ed. *Rū'idād-i ijlās-i sīzdahum-i All India Shī'ah Conference 2, 3, 4 April 1920 bi-maqām-i Iḥāṭah Ḍāk Banglah Qaṣbah Nagīnah żila'-i Bijnūr.* Lucknow: Fakhr al-Maṭābi', 1920.
Yasīn 'Alīkhān, ed. *Rū'idād-i ijlās-i pānzdahum-i All India Shī'ah Conference mun'aqidah 27, 28, 29 December 1921 bi-maqām-i Multān khiṭṭah-i Panjāb.* Lucknow: Ādabī Press, 1922.
Sayyid Maqbūl Ḥusayn, ed. *Rū'idād-i All India Shī'ah Conference bābat ijlās-i shānzdahum mun'aqidah 31 March ō yikum ō 2 April 1923 bi-maqām-i Jhang Maghīyānah (Panjāb).* Lucknow: Niẓāmī Press, 1923.

Mīr Vājid ʿAlī, ed. *Rūʾidād-i All India Shīʿah Conference bābat ijlās-i haftadum munʿaqidah 21 li-ghāyatah 23 March 1924 bi-maqām-i Fayżābād (Awadh)*. Rāʾe Barīlī: Istibṣār Press, 1924.
Mirzā ʿĀbid Ḥusayn, ed. *Rūʾidād-i All India Shīʿah Conference bābat ijlās-i hīcdahum munʿaqidah 9 li-ghāyatah 12 March 1925 bi-maqām-i Bombay*. Lucknow: Niẓāmī Press, 1925.
Mirzā ʿĀbid Ḥusayn, ed. *Rūʾidād-i ijlās-i nūzdahum-i All India Shīʿah Conference munʿaqidah 26, 27, 28 December 1926 bi-maqām-i Paṭnah*. Lucknow: Niẓāmī Press, 1927.
Mirzā ʿĀbid Ḥusayn, ed. *Rūʾidād-i ijlās-i bistum-i All India Shīʿah Conference munʿaqidah 7, 8, 9 April 1928 bi-maqām-i Calcutta*. Lucknow: Sarfarāz Qaumī Press, 1928.
Mirzā ʿĀbid Ḥusayn, ed. *Rūʾidād-i ijlās-i bist ō yikum-i All India Shīʿah Conference munʿaqidah*. 1929.
Mirzā ʿĀbid Ḥusayn, ed. *Rūʾidād-i ijlās-i bist ō duvum-i All India Shīʿah Conference bi-maqām-i Allāhābād munʿaqidah 27, 28, 29 December 1929*. Lucknow: Sarfarāz Qaumī Press, 1930.
Navāb Mirzā Aḥmad Muḥsin ʿAlīkhān, ed. *Rūʾidād-i ijlās-i bist ō sivum-i All India Shīʿah Conference bi-maqām-i Montgomery Panjāb munʿaqidah 4 li-ghāyatah 6 April 1931*. Lucknow: Sarfarāz Qaumī Press, 1931.
Sayyid Muʿjiz Ḥasan, ed. *Rūʾidād-i ijlās-i bist ō cahārum-i All India Shīʿah Conference bi- maqām-i Lāhōr munʿaqidah 24, 25, 26 March 1932*. Lucknow: Sarfarāz Qaumī Press, 1932.
Sayyid Ḥasan ʿAbbās Riżvī, ed. *Rūʾidād-i ijlās-i bist ō panjum-i All India Shīʿah Conference (Dar al-ṣalṭanat Dihlī) munʿaqidah 14, 15, 16 March 1933*. Lucknow: Sarfarāz Qaumī Press, 1933.
Sayyid Kalb-i ʿAbbās, *Rūʾidād-i ijlās-i bist ō shishum-i All India Shīʿah Conference munʿaqidah 26, 27, 28 October 1935 bi-maqām-i Rāʾe Barelī*. Lucknow: Sarfarāz Qaumī Press, 1935.
Sayyid Kalb-i ʿAbbās, ed. *Rūʾidād-i ijlās-i bist ō haftum-i All India Shīʿah Conference bi-maqām-i Lakhnāuʾ munʿaqidah 25, 26, 27 December 1936*. Lucknow: Sarfarāz Qaumī Press, 1937.
Sayyid Kalb-i ʿAbbās, ed. *Rūʾidād-i ijlās-i bist ō shastum-i All India Shīʿah Conference bi-maqām-i Kānpūr munʿaqidah 26, 27, 28 December 1937*. Lucknow: Sarfarāz Qaumī Press, 1938.
Sayyid Kalb-i ʿAbbās, ed. *Rūʾidād-i ijlās-i bist ō nahum-i All India Shīʿah Conference bi-maqām-i Patnah munʿaqidah 29, 30, 31 December 1938*. Lucknow: Sarfarāz Qaumī Press, 1939.
Sayyid Kalb-i ʿAbbās, ed. *Rūʾidād-i ijlās-i sīyum-i All India Shīʿah Conference munʿaqidah 29–30 September ō yikum October 1940 bi-maqām-i qaṣbah-i Dōkōhā Sādāt żilaʿ-i Jālandhar (Panjāb)*. Lucknow: Sarfarāz Qaumī Press, 1941.

NEWSPAPERS AND JOURNALS

Asad (Lahore)
al-ʿĀrif (Lahore)
al-Ḥujjat (Peshawar)
al-Muballigh (Sargodha)
al-Muntaẓar (Lahore)
Dawn (Karachi)
Express Tribune (Karachi)
Ḥauzah (Qum)
The Herald (Karachi)
Iṣlāḥ (Khajvā)
Payām-i ʿAmal (Lahore)
Rāh-i ʿAmal (Lahore)
Riżākār (Lahore)
Sarfarāz (Lucknow)
Ẕūlfiqār (Peshawar)

VIDEO RECORDINGS

The video recordings are listed in chronological order.

Sayyid Javād Naqvī. *Īrān meṉ makhmalī inqilāb kī nākāmī*, 2009. http://www.islamimarkaz.com/video/2009others/election.wmv.

———. *Fake and Zionist Paid Maraje—kuch nām nihād marājiʿ ke libās meṉ*, 29 April 2012. http://www.youtube.com/watch?v=kDLDO1upbN8&feature=plcp.

———. *Jāmiʿat al-ʿUrwa al-Wuthqā kā taʿlīmī niẓām*, 2012. http://www.islamimarkaz.com/video/2012Others/UrwatWuthqaTalimiNizam.wmv.

———. *Imām Khumaynī kā payghām bīdārī millat-i Pākistān ke nām*, August 2013. http://www.islamimarkaz.com/video/2013Ramazan/BarsiShaheedHussani/Day 26.wmv.

———. *Inqilāb-i Islāmī: Siyāsī tajziyah baʿd az intikhābāt-i Īrān 2013*, 18 June 2013. http://www.islamimarkaz.com/video/2013Others/18062013-HalateHazraAfterElectionsSituatlion/18062013-HalateHazraAfterElectionsSituatlion.wmv.

———. *Intiẓār al-Faraj az naẓar-i Qurʾān*, 24 June 2013. http://www.islamimarkaz.com/video/2013others/24062013-15Shaban/24062013-5Shaban.wmv.

———. *Tisrā yaum-i tāʾsīs-i ḥauzah-i Jāmiʿat al-ʿUrwa al-Wuthqā*, 26 May 2013. http://www.islamimarkaz.com/video/2013Others/26052013-Jashan-e-Molud-e-Kaba_3rd_Yom-e-Tases/26052013-Jashan-e-Molud-e-Kaba_3rd_Yom-e-Tases.wmv.

———. *Barsī ʿAllāmah Muftī Jaʿfar Ḥusayn*, 28 August 2016. http://islamimarkaz.com/imi/view_lecture.aspx?id=2188.

———. *Jashn-i inqilāb-i islāmī*, 11 February 2017. http://islamimarkaz.com/imi/view_lecture.aspx?id=2241.

———. *ʿAṣr-i ḥāżir aur ṭulabāʾ kī ẕimahdāriyāṉ*, 25 February 2017. http://islamimarkaz.com/imi/view_lecture.aspx?id=2246.

———. *Parcam-i āzādī ke nīce kisht-i ghulāmī*, 23 March 2017. http://islamimarkaz.com/imi/view_lecture.aspx?id=2248.

SECONDARY SOURCES

ʿAbbās, Akhtar. "Taẕkirah-i jamīl-i Āyatullāh al-ʿuẓma al-ḥājj Sayyid Muḥammad Kāẓim Sharīʿatmadārī." *al-Muntaẓar* 12, no. 10 (1970): 4–14.

ʿAbbās, Sayyid ʿAlī, and Muḥammad Ashraf Khān. *Mubāḥasah mutʿalliqah ahl-i bayt.* Amritsar: Manager Akhbār-i Ahl-i Ḥadis̤, 1919.
ʿAbbās, Sayyid Żiyāʾ. "Himmat afzāʾī aur naṣīḥat." *Rāh-i ʿAmal,* no. 9 (1979): 15.
ʿAbbās Naqvī, Sayyid Rashīd. "Aṭok shahr, rūz-i ʿāshūrāʾ aur saʿūdī agent." *Rāh-i ʿAmal,* no. 55–56 (1987): 31, 54.
ʿAbd al-Salām, Muḥammad. *Muḥarram al-ḥarām kī bidʿaten̲.* Hyderabad, 1917.
ʿĀbidī, Sayyid ʿIrfān Ḥaydar. "Ḥażrat Imām Ḥusayn ʿalayhi al-salām ummat-i muslimah ke liye mukammal namūnah-i ittiḥād hen̲." *Z̤ūlfiqār* 13, no. 22 (1984): 6.
———. *Khaṭīb-i shām-i gharībān. Majmuʿah-i taqārīr.* Multan: Mohsin Naqvi Academy, 2002.
———. *Al-Majālis al-ʿirfān [sic]. Sharīʿat ō shīʿat.* Karachi: Maḥfūẓ Book Agency, 2000.
———. *Ṭamāncah bar rukhsār-i munkar-i vilāyat-i ʿAlī.* Lahore: Idārah-i Nidā-yi Shīʿah, 2009.
Abisaab, Rula Jurdi. "Lebanese Shiʿites and the Marjaʿiyya: Polemic in the Late Twentieth Century." *British Journal of Middle Eastern Studies* 36, no. 2 (2009): 215–39.
Abou Zahab, Mariam. "Between Pakistan and Qom: Shiʿi Women's Madrasas and New Transnational Networks." In *The Madrasa in Asia: Political Activism and Transnational Linkages,* edited by Farish A. Noor, Yoginder Sikand, and Martin van Bruinessen, 123–40. Amsterdam: Amsterdam University Press, 2008.
———. "'It's Just a Sunni-Shiite Thing.' Sectarianism and Talibanism in the FATA (Federally Administered Tribal Areas) of Pakistan." In *The Dynamics of Sunni-Shia Relationships: Doctrine, Transnationalism, Intellectuals and the Media,* edited by Brigitte Maréchal and Sami Zemni, 179–92. London: Hurst, 2012.
———. "The Politicization of the Shia Community in Pakistan in the 1970s and 1980s." In *The Other Shiites: From the Mediterranean to Central Asia,* edited by Alessandro Monsutti, Silvia Naef, and Farian Sabahi, 97–112. Bern: Peter Lang, 2007.
———. "The Regional Dimension of Sectarian Conflicts in Pakistan." In *Pakistan: Nationalism without a Nation,* edited by Christophe Jaffrelot, 115–28. London: Zed Books, 2002.
———. "Salafism in Pakistan: The Ahl-i Hadith Movement." In *Global Salafism: Islam's New Religious Movement,* edited by Roel Meijer, 126–42. New York: Columbia University Press, 2009.
———. "The SSP: Herald of Militant Sunni Islam in Pakistan." In *Armed Militias of South Asia: Fundamentalists, Maoists and Separatists,* edited by Laurent Gayer and Christophe Jaffrelot, 159–76. New York: Columbia University Press, 2009.
———. "The Sunni-Shia Conflict in Jhang (Pakistan)." In *Lived Islam in South Asia: Adaptation, Accommodation and Conflict,* edited by Imtiaz Ahmad and Helmut Reifeld, 135–48. Delhi: Social Science, 2004.
———. "'Yeh matam kayse ruk jae?' ('How Could This Matam Ever Cease?'):

Muharram Processions in the Pakistani Punjab." In *South Asian Religions on Display: Religious Processions in South Asia and in the Diaspora*, edited by Knut A. Jacobsen, 104–14. London: Routledge, 2008.

Abrahamian, Ervand. *Iran between Two Revolutions*. Princeton, NJ: Princeton University Press, 1982.

———. *Tortured Confessions: Prisons and Public Recantations in Modern Iran*. Berkeley: University of California Press, 1999.

Abu-Rabiʿ, Ibrahim M. *Intellectual Origins of Islamic Resurgence in the Modern Arab World*. Albany: State University of New York Press, 1996.

Adelkhah, Fariba, and Keiko Sakurai. "Introduction: The Moral Economy of the Madrasa." In *The Moral Economy of the Madrasa: Islam and Education Today*, edited by Keiko Sakurai and Fariba Adelkhah, 1–10. Abingdon: Routledge, 2011.

Afzal, M. Rafique. *A History of the All-India Muslim League, 1906–1947*. Karachi: Oxford University Press, 2014.

Aghaie, Kamran Scot. *The Martyrs of Karbala: Shi'i Symbols and Rituals in Modern Iran*. Seattle: University of Washington Press, 2004.

"Aham khūshkhabarī: Imamia Mission Pakistan kī iʿānat-i sahm-i Imām se bhī kī jā saktī he." *Payām-i ʿAmal* 9, no. 2 (1965): 34.

Ahmad, Attiya. "Explanation Is Not the Point: Domestic Work, Islamic Dawa and Becoming Muslim in Kuwait." *Asia Pacific Journal of Anthropology* 11, nos. 3–4 (2010): 293–310.

Ahmad, Aziz. "An Eighteenth-Century Theory of the Caliphate." *Studia Islamica* 28 (1968): 135–44.

———. *Islamic Modernism in India and Pakistan*. London: Oxford University Press, 1967.

Ahmad, Imtiaz. "The Shia-Sunni Dispute in Lucknow, 1905–1980." In *Islamic Society and Culture: Essays in Honour of Professor Aziz Ahmad*, edited by Milton Israel and N. K. Wagle, 335–50. New Delhi: Manohar, 1983.

Aḥmad, Maḥbūb. *Al-Kitāb al-majīd fi wujūb al-taqlīd*. Amritsar: Muḥammad ʿAbd al-Aḥad, 1909.

Ahmad, Mumtaz. "Revivalism, Islamization, Sectarianism, and Violence in Pakistan." In *Pakistan, 1997*, edited by Craig Baxter and Charles H. Kennedy, 101–21. Boulder: Westview Press, 1998.

Ahmad, Sadaf. *Transforming Faith: The Story of Al-Huda and Islamic Revivalism among Urban Pakistani Women*. Syracuse, NY: Syracuse University Press, 2009.

Aḥmad, Sayyid Khayrāt. *ʿAqāʾid al-shīʿa*. Lucknow: Sayyid Sulṭān Aḥmad, 1918.

———. *Nūr-i imān*. Lahore: Kutubkhānah-i Iṣnāʾʿasharī, 1976.

Ahmed, Khaled. *Sectarian War: Pakistan's Sunni-Shia Violence and Its Links to the Middle East*. Karachi: Oxford University Press, 2011.

Ahmed, Mumtaz. "Shiʿi Political Activism in Pakistan." *Studies in Contemporary Islam* 5, nos. 1–2 (2003): 57–71.

Ahmed, Munir D. "The Shiʿis of Pakistan." In *Shiʿism, Resistance, and Revolution*, edited by Martin Kramer, 275–87. Boulder: Westview Press, 1987.

Aigle, Denise. "Essai sur les autorités religieuses dans l'islam médiéval oriental." In *Les autorités religieuses entre charismes et hiérarchie: Approches comparatives*, edited by Denise Aigle, 17–40. Turnhout: Brepols, 2011.
———. "Le symbolisme religieux šīʿite dans l'éloge funèbre de l'Imām Khomeyni à l'occasion de la prière de Kumayl." *Arabica* 41 (1994): 59–83.
Akbar, Ali, and Hassan Farhan. "22 Killed in Explosion outside Imambargah in Parachinar Market." *Dawn*, 31 March 2017.
Akbar, Muḥammad Ḥusayn. *Istiʿmār-i shaykhiyyat ke rūp meṉ*. Gujrāt: Kitābkhānah-i Ḥusayniyyah, 1984.
Akbar, Ṣāqib. *Callō phir Īrān kō calte heṉ*. Islāmābād: al-Baṣīra, 2009.
———. *Pākistān ke dīnī masālik*. Islāmābād: al-Baṣīra, 2010.
Akhavi, Shahrough. *Religion and Politics in Contemporary Iran: Clergy-State Relations in the Pahlavī Period*. Albany: State University of New York Press, 1980.
———. "The Thought and Role of Ayatollah Hossein'ali Montazeri in the Politics of Post-1979 Iran." *Iranian Studies* 41, no. 5 (2008): 646–66.
Alagha, Joseph. "Hezbollah's Conception of the Islamic State." In *The Shiʿa Worlds and Iran*, edited by Sabrina Mervin, 89–114. London: Saqi, 2010.
———. *Hizbullah's Identity Construction*. Amsterdam: Amsterdam University Press, 2011.
———. "Ideological Tensions between Hizbullah and Jihadi Salafism: Mutual Perceptions and Mutual Fears." In *The Dynamics of Sunni-Shia Relationships: Doctrine, Transnationalism, Intellectuals and the Media*, edited by Brigitte Maréchal and Sami Zemni, 61–82. London: Hurst, 2012.
———. *The Shifts in Hizbullah's Ideology: Religious Ideology, Political Ideology and Political Program*. Amsterdam: Amsterdam University Press, 2006.
Alam, Arshad. "The Enemy within: Madrasas and Muslim Identity in North India." *Modern Asian Studies* 42, nos. 2–3 (2008): 605–27.
———. *Inside a Madrasa: Knowledge, Power, and Islamic Identity in India*. London: Routledge, 2011.
Alavi, Seema. *Muslim Cosmopolitanism in the Age of Empire*. Cambridge, MA: Harvard University Press, 2015.
Algar, Hamid. "Behbahānī, Moḥammad." In *Encylopaedia Iranica*, vol. 4: *Bayju–Carpets*, edited by Ehsan Yarshater, 96–97. London: Routledge and Kegan Paul, 1990.
ʿAlī, Ḥashmat. *Ghāyat al-marām fī żarūrat al-imām*. Lahore: Kutubkhānah-i Is̱nāʾʿasharī, n.d.
———. "Mas'alah-i aʿlamiyyat." *al-Muntaẓar* 12, nos. 19–20 (1970): 35–37.
Ali, Kamran Asdar. *Communism in Pakistan: Politics and Class Activism, 1947–1982*. London: I. B. Tauris, 2015.
Ali, Meer Hassan. *Observations on the Mussulmauns of India: Descriptive of their Manners, Customs, Habits and Religious Opinions Made during a Twelve Year Residence in Their Immediate Society*. London: Humphrey Milford, 1917.

ʿAlī, Sayyid ʿAbīd. *Fażīlatnāmah-i taʿzīyah.* Bahrayc, 1909.
ʿAlī, Sayyid Ḥamza. *Ḥaqq kī kasōṭī yaʿnī muʿtabar aur āsān ẕarāʾiʿ se maṣnūʿī aur ḥaqīqī pīshvāyān-i Islam kī jānc.* Delhi: Delhi Printing Works, 1916.
———. *Taṣḥīḥ al-ʿaqāʾid.* Amroha: Sayyid Aḥmad Ḥusayn, 1919.
ʿAlī, Sayyid Riżā. *Aʿmāl nāmah yaʿnī Sir Sayyid Riżā ʿAlī ke TS, BA, MLL ke savāniḥ-i ḥayāt khūd mauṣūf ke qalam se.* Delhi: Hindustānī, 1943.
ʿAlī Khān, Aḥmad. *ʿAzādārī māh-i muḥarram.* Lucknow: Maṭbaʿ-i Isnā ʿĀsharī, 1905.
ʿAlī Shāh, Sayyid Ṣādiq. "Jān gudāz sāniḥah." *al-Muntaẓar* 12, nos. 8–9 (1970): 4–5.
"Allama Abidi, Wife Laid to Rest." *Dawn,* 24 January 1998.
Al-Rasheed, Madawi. *A History of Saudi Arabia.* Cambridge: Cambridge University Press, 2002.
Alvi, Sajida Sultana. *Perspectives on Mughal India: Rulers, Historians, ʿulamāʾ and Sufis.* Karachi: Oxford University Press, 2012.
Amanat, Abbas. *Apocalyptic Islam and Iranian Shiʿism.* London: I. B. Tauris, 2009.
———. "From ijtihād to wilāyat-i faqīh: The Evolution of the Shiite Legal Authority to Political Power." In *Shariʿa: Islamic Law in the Contemporary Context,* edited by Abbas Amanat and Frank Griffel, 120–36. Stanford, CA: Stanford University Press, 2007.
———. "In Between the Madrassa and the Marketplace: The Designation of Clerical Leadership in Modern Shiʿism." In *Authority and Political Culture in Shiʿism,* edited by Said Amir Arjomand, 98–132. Albany: State University of New York Press, 1988.
———. "Messianic Aspirations in Contemporary Iran." In *Apocalyptic Islam and Iranian Shiʿism,* 221–51. London: I. B. Tauris, 2009.
al-Amīn, Ḥasan. *Dāʾirat al-maʿārif al-islāmiyya al-shīʿiyya.* Beirut: Dār al-Taʿārruf lil-Maṭbūʿāt, 1990.
———. *Min balad ilā balad: Riḥlāt fi al-sharq wa-l-gharb.* Beirut: Dār al-Turāth al-Islāmī, 1974.
"Amir Haider Khan to Jinnah, QAD (126)." In *Quaid-i-Azam Mohammad Ali Jinnah Papers. Pakistan: The Goal Defined, 1 January–31 August 1940,* edited by Zawwar Husain Zaidi, 238–40. Islamabad: Quaid-i-Azam Papers Project, National Archives of Pakistan, 2007.
Amir-Moezzi, Mohammad Ali. "An Absence Filled with Presences: Shaykhiyya Hermeneutics of the Occultation." In *The Twelver Shia in Modern Times: Religious Culture and Political History,* edited by Rainer Brunner and Werner Ende, 38–57. Leiden: Brill, 2001.
———. "Contribution à la typologie des rencontres avec l'Imâm caché (Aspects de l'Imâmologie duodécimaine II)." *Journal Asiatique* 284, no. 1 (1996): 109–35.
———. *The Divine Guide in Early Shiʿism: The Sources of Esotericism in Islam.* Albany: State University of New York Press, 1994.
———. "Vision d'Imams en mystique duodécimaine moderne et contemporaine (Aspects de l'imamologie duodécimaine VIII)." In *Autour du regard: Mélanges Gimaret,* edited by Éric Chaumont, 97–124. Paris: Peeters, 2003.

Amirpur, Katajun. "A Doctrine in the Making? Velayat-e Faqih in Post-Revolutionary Iran." In *Speaking for Islam: Religious Authorities in Muslim Societies*, edited by Gudrun Krämer and Sabine Schmidtke, 218–40. Leiden: Brill, 2006.

———. *Die Entpolitisierung des Islam: 'Abdolkarīm Sorūšs Denken und Wirkung in der islamischen Republik Iran.* Würzburg: Ergon, 2003.

Amrūhī, Sayyid Muḥammad Rizā Naqvī. *Al-Taqiyya fi-l-Islām.* Murādābād: Sayyid Aḥmad Ḥusayn, 1919.

Andræ, Tor. *Die Person Muhammeds in Lehre und Glauben seiner Gemeinde.* Stockholm: P. A. Norstedt, 1917.

Anṣārī, Muḥammad Bashīr. *Ḥaqā'iq al-wasā'iṭ ya'nī ma'rifat-i Muḥammad ō Āl-i Muḥammad bi-javāb-i Uṣūl al-sharī'a.* 2 vols. Gujrāt: Baqīat Allāh, 2013.

———. "Islām dushman quvattōn ke ittiḥād ke pīsh naẓar ō 'ālam-i Islām kā ittiḥād nāguzīr he." *Ẕūlfiqār* 11, nos. 20–21 (1982): 1.

———. *Maqām-i ahl-i bayt.* Lahore: Imāmiyyah Kutub Khānah.

Ansari, Sarah F. D. *Sufi Saints and State Power: The Pirs of Sind, 1843–1947.* Cambridge: Cambridge University Press, 1992.

Anthony, Sean W. *The Caliph and the Heretic: Ibn Saba' and the Origins of Shī'ism.* Leiden: Brill, 2012.

———. "The Legend of Abdallāh ibn Saba' and the Date of Umm al-Kitāb." *Journal of the Royal Asiatic Society* 21 (2011): 1–30.

Anzali, Ata. "Safavid Shi'ism, the Eclipse of Sufism and the Emergence of 'Irfān." PhD diss., Rice University, 2012.

Appadurai, Arjun. "Disjuncture and Difference in the Global Cultural Economy." *Theory, Culture and Society* 7 (1990): 295–310.

Arberry, A. J., trans. *Al-Qur'ān al-Karīm: Holy Qur'an.* Qum: Ansariyan, 2003.

Arif, G. M. *Economic and Social Impacts of Remittances on Households: The Case of Pakistani Migrants Working in Saudi Arabia.* Geneva: International Organization for Migration, 2010.

Arif, K. M. *Working with Zia: Pakistan's Power Politics, 1977–1988.* Karachi: Oxford University Press, 1995.

'Ārifī, Muḥammad Akram. *Junbish-i islāmī-yi Pākistān: Barrasī-yi 'avāmil-i nākāmī dar ījād-i niẓām-i islāmī.* Qum: Būstān-i Kitāb, 2003.

———. "Shī'īyān-i Pākistān." *Faṣlnāmah-i takhaṣṣuṣī-yi Shī'ahshināsī* 1, nos. 3–4 (2003): 197–211.

———. *Shī'īyān-i Pākistān.* Qum: Intishārāt-i Mu'assasah-i Shī'ahshināsī, 2006 or 2007.

'Ārif Naqvī, Sayyid Ḥusayn. *Barr-i ṣaghīr ke imāmiyyah muṣannifīn kī maṭbū'ah taṣānīf aur tarājim.* Islamabad: Markaz-i Taḥqīqāt-i Fārsī-yi Irān va Pākistān, 1997.

———. *Kitābiyyāt 'alayh-i imāmiyyah dar Pākistān.* Islamabad: Dār al-Tablīgh-i Imāmiyyah, 1999.

———. *Taẕkirah-i 'ulamā'-i imāmiyyah-i Pākistān.* Mashhad: Bunyād-i Pažūhishā-yi Islāmī-yi Āstān-i Quds-i Rażavī, 1991.

———. *Taẕkirah-i ʿulamāʾ-i imāmiyyah-i Pākistān (shamālī ʿalāqah jāt).* Islamabad: Imāmiyyah Dār al-Tablīgh, 1994.
Arjomand, Said Amir. "Ideological Revolution in Shiʿism." In *Authority and Political Culture in Shiʿism*, edited by Said Amir Arjomand, 178–209. Albany: State University of New York Press, 1988.
———. "Islam and Constitutionalism since the Nineteenth Century: The Significance and Peculiarities of Iran." In *Constitutional Politics in the Middle East: With Special Reference to Turkey, Iraq, Iran, and Afghanistan*, edited by Said Amir Arjomand, 33–63. Oxford: Hart, 2008.
———. "The Shiʿite Hierocracy and the State in Pre-modern Iran: 1785–1890." *European Journal of Sociology* 22, no. 1 (1981): 40–78.
Asad, Talal. "The Idea of an Anthropology of Islam." *Qui Parle* 17, no. 2 (2009): 1–30.
Asadī, Muḥammad al-Shaykh Hādī. *Al-Imām al-Ḥakīm: ʿArḍ tārīkhī li-daurihi al-siyāsī wa-l-thaqāfī.* Baghdad: Muʾassasat Afāq lil-Dirāsāt wa-l-Abḥāth al-ʿIrāqī, 2007.
Aṣghar, Mulāzim-i Ḥusayn. "Asīrān-i Kwiṭah kī rahāʾī." *Riżākār* 50, no. 17 (1986): 3.
Asghar Khan, Mohammad. *Generals in Politics: Pakistan 1958–1982.* New Delhi: Vikas, 1983.
Āshnāʾī bā faʿālīyathā-yi Dār al-Tablīgh-i Islāmī. Qum: Dār al-Tablīgh-i Islāmī, n.d.
Al-Atawneh, Muhammad K. *Wahhabi Islam Facing the Challenges of Modernity: Dar al-Ifta in the Modern Saudi State.* Leiden: Brill, 2010.
"At Least 20 Shias Pulled off Bus, Shot Dead in Northern Pakistan." *Dawn*, 12 August 2012. https://www.dawn.com/news/742618/several-forced-off-buses-killed-in-northern-pakistan.
Attar, Farid ud-Din. *The Conference of the Birds.* London: Penguin, 1984.
Aʿvān, Ṭāhir ʿAbbās. *Mard-i ʿilm maydān-i ʿamal meṉ yaʿnī sarkār ʿallāmah āyatullāh al-shaykh Muḥammad Ḥusayn al-Najafī ke savāniḥ aur ʿilmī ō ʿamalī kārnāme ō dīgar ḥālāt.* Liya: Jāmiʿat Walī al-Aṣr, 2005.
———. *Tabṣirat al-maghmūm ʿalā ajwibat Iṣlāḥ al-rusūm.* Sargōdhā: Maktabat al-Sibṭayn, 2009.
Awan, Samina. *Political Islam in Colonial Punjab: Majlis-i Ahrar 1929–1949.* Karachi: Oxford University Press, 2010.
"Āyatullāh al-ʿuẓma Āghā-yi Rūḥ Allāh Khumaynī kā interview." *Rāh-i ʿAmal*, no. 3 (1978): 2–5.
"Āyatullāh al-ʿuẓmā Mīrzā Ḥasan al-Ḥāʾirī al-Iḥqāqī madda ẓillahu kī jānib se cand važāḥateṉ." *Ẕūlfiqār* 19, no. 16 (1990): 7.
Ayres, Alyssa. *Speaking like a State: Language and Nationalism in Pakistan.* Cambridge: Cambridge University Press, 2009.
Aziz, Talib. "Baqir al-Sadr's Quest for the Marjaʿiya (sic)." In *The Most Learned of the Shiʿa: The Institution of the Marjaʿ Taqlid*, edited by Linda S. Walbridge, 140–48. New York: Oxford University Press, 2001.
Bajwa, Farooq Naseem. *From Kutch to Tashkent: The Indo-Pakistan War of 1965.* London: Hurst, 2013.

Balākōṭī, Muḥammad Ilyās. *Amīr-i ʿazīmat. Ḥażrat Maulānā Ḥaqq Navāz Jhangvī shahīd.* Jhang: Jāmiʿah-i ʿUs̱māniyyah.

Baljon, J. M. *Religion and Thought of Shāh Walī Allāh Dihlawī, 1703–1762.* Leiden: Brill, 1986.

Balūc, Iqbāl Ḥusayn. "Islamabad Convention." *Rāh-i ʿAmal,* nos. 13–14 (1980): 5–9.

Bangash, ʿAbd al-Wahhāb. *Sharīʿatnāmah. Inqilāb-i Islāmī Īrān meṉ Āqā-yi Sharīʿatmadār kā kirdār.* Lahore: Āyatullāh Sharīʿatmadār Komiṭī, 1982.

Baram, Amatzia. *Saddam Husayn and Islam, 1968–2003: Baʿthi Iraq from Secularism to Faith.* Baltimore: Woodrow Wilson Center Press, 2014.

Barsatī, Sayyid Muḥammad Ḥusayn Zaydī. *Pākistān meṉ shaykhiyyat kā shīʿiyyat aur shīʿah-i ʿulamāʾ se ṭakrāʾū.* Ciniūṭ: Idārāh-i Nashr ō Ishāʿat-i Ḥaqāʾiq-i Islām.

Bashkin, Orit. "The Iraqi Afghanis and ʿAbduhs: Debate over Reform among Shiʿite and Sunni ʿUlamaʾ in Interwar Iraq." In *Guardians of Faith in Modern Times: ʿUlamaʾ in the Middle East,* edited by Meir Hatina, 141–70. Leiden: Brill, 2009.

Baxter, Craig. "The People's Party vs. the Punjab 'Feudalists.'" *Journal of Asian and African Studies* 8, nos. 3–4 (1973): 166–89.

Bayat, Mangol. *Iran's First Revolution: Shiʿism and the Constitutional Revolution of 1905–1909.* New York: Oxford University Press, 1991.

———. "Mahmud Taleqani and the Iranian Revolution." In *Shiʿism, Resistance, and Revolution,* edited by Martin Kramer, 67–94. Boulder: Westview Press, 1987.

———. *Mysticism and Dissent: Socioreligious Thought in Qajar Iran.* Syracuse: Syracuse University Press, 1982.

Bayly, C. A. *Rulers, Townsmen, and Bazaars: North Indian Society in the Age of British Expansion, 1770–1870.* Cambridge: Cambridge University Press, 1983.

Berkey, Jonathan Porter. "Popular Culture under the Mamluks: A Historiographical Survey." *Mamlūk Studies* 9 (2005): 133–46.

———. *Popular Preaching and Religious Authority in the Medieval Islamic Near East.* Seattle: University of Washington Press, 2001.

Bhabha, Homi K. *The Location of Culture.* London: Routledge, 2004.

———. "Of Mimicry and Man: The Ambivalence of Colonial Discourse." *October* 28 (1984): 125–33.

Bhat, Abdur Rashid. "Shah Wali Allah's Political Theory in General." In *Shah Waliullah (1703–1762): His Religious and Political Thought,* edited by Muhammad Ikram Chaghatai, 243–66. Lahore: Sang-e-Meel, 2005.

Bindemann, Rolf. *Religion und Politik bei den schiʿitischen Hazâra in Afghanistan, Iran und Pakistan.* Berlin: Das Arabische Buch, 1987.

Binder, Leonard. *Religion and Politics in Pakistan.* Berkeley: University of California Press, 1963.

Bin Sayeed, Khalid. "Pakistan in 1983: Internal Stresses More Serious Than External Problems." *Asian Survey* 24, no. 2 (1984): 219–28.

Blank, Jonah. *Mullahs on the Mainframe: Islam and Modernity among the Daudi Bohras.* Chicago: University of Chicago Press, 2001.

Blom, Amélie. "Les Partis Islamistes à la recherche d'un second souffle." In *Le*

Pakistan, carrefour de tensions régionales, edited by Christophe Jaffrelot, 99–115. Paris: Editions Complexe, 1999.
Boivin, Michel. *Le soufisme antinomien dans le sous-continent indien: La'l Shahbâz Qalandar et son héritage, XIIIe–XXe siècle*. Paris: Cerf, 2012.
———. "Representations and Symbols in Muharram and Other Rituals: Fragments of Shiite Worlds from Bombay to Karachi." In *The Other Shiites: From the Mediterranean to Central Asia*, edited by Alessandro Monsutti, Silvia Naef, and Farian Sabahi, 149–72. Bern: Peter Lang, 2007.
Bonnefoy, Laurent. "Salafism in Yemen: A 'Saudisation'?" In *Kingdom without Borders: Saudi Political, Religious and Media Frontiers*, edited by Madawi Al-Rasheed, 245–62. New York: Columbia University Press, 2008.
———. *Salafism in Yemen: Transnationalism and Religious Identity*. London: Hurst & Co., 2011.
Bonnell, Victoria E., and Lynn Hunt. "Introduction." In *Beyond the Cultural Turn: New Directions in the Study of Society and Culture*, edited by Victoria E. Bonnell, Lynn Hunt, and Richard Biernacki, 1–34. Berkeley: University of California Press, 1999.
Bose, Neilesh. *Recasting the Region: Language, Culture, and Islam in Colonial Bengal*. New Delhi: Oxford University Press, 2014.
Braswell, George W., Jr. "Civil Religion in Contemporary Iran." *Journal of Church and State* 21, no. 2 (1979): 223–46.
Brown, Jonathan. *The Canonization of al-Bukhārī and Muslim: The Formation and Function of the Sunnī Ḥadīth Canon*. Leiden: Brill, 2007.
Brown, Vahid, and Don Rassler. *Fountainhead of Jihad: The Haqqani Nexus, 1973–2012*. New York: Columbia University Press, 2012.
Brunner, Rainer. *Annäherung und Distanz: Schia, Azhar und die islamische Ökumene im 20. Jahrhundert*. Berlin: Schwarz, 1996.
———. *Islamic Ecumenism in the 20th Century: The Azhar and Shiism between Rapprochement and Restraint*. Leiden: Brill, 2004.
———. *Die Schia und die Koranfälschung*. Würzburg: Ergon, 2001.
———. "A Shiite Cleric's Criticism of Shiism: Mūsā al-Mūsawī." In *The Twelver Shia in Modern Times: Religious Culture and Political History*, edited by Rainer Brunner and Werner Ende, 178–87. Leiden: Brill, 2001.
Buchta, Wilfried. "Die Inquisition der Islamischen Republik Iran: Einige Anmerkungen zum Sondergerichtshof der Geistlichkeit." In *Islamstudien ohne Ende: Festschrift für Werner Ende zum 65. Geburtstag*, edited by Rainer Brunner, Monika Gronke, Jens Peter Laut, and Ulrich Rebstock, 69–78. Würzburg: Ergon, 2002.
———. *Die iranische Schia und die islamische Einheit: 1979–1996*. Hamburg: Deutsches Orient-Institut, 1997.
———. "Tehran's Ecumenical Society (Majmaʿ al-Taqrīb): A Veritable Ecumenical Revival or a Trojan Horse of Iran?" In *The Twelver Shia in Modern Times:*

Religious Culture and Political History, edited by Rainer Brunner and Werner Ende, 333–53. Leiden: Brill, 2001.

———. *Who Rules Iran? The Structure of Power in the Islamic Republic.* Washington: Washington Institute for Near East Policy, 2000.

Buehler, Arthur F. "Aḥmad Sirhindī: A 21st-Century Update." *Der Islam* 86 (2011): 122–41.

———. "Trends of Ashrāfization in India." In *Sayyids and Sharifs in Muslim Societies: The Living Links to the Prophet*, edited by Kazuo Morimoto, 231–46. London: Routledge, 2012.

Bukhārī, Ghulām Shabbīr. "Āyatullāh Ḥasan Ṭāhirī kā ikhrāj." *Rāh-i ʿAmal*, no. 32 (1984): 1–2.

———. "Ḥajj ke ʿaẓīm siyāsī maqāṣid se anjān apnā iḥtisāb kareṉ." *Rāh-i ʿAmal*, no. 28 (1983): 1.

Calder, Norman. "Accommodation and Revolution in Imami Shiʿi Jurisprudence: Khumayni and the Classical Tradition." In *Shiʿism, State and Government*, edited by Paul Luft and Colin Turner, 39–58. London: Routledge, 2008.

———. "The Limits of Islamic Orthodoxy." In *Intellectual Traditions in Islam*, edited by Farhad Daftary, 66–86. London: I. B. Tauris, 2000.

Caman, Amīr Ḥusayn. *Merī yādgār mulāqāteṉ: Miḥrāb ō minbar kī nāmvar shakhṣīyāt se mulāqāt va marāsim kī un kahī aur dilcasp ḥikāyāt.* Islamabad: Print Media, 2000.

Carney, ʿAbd al-Hakeem. "The Theos Agnostos: Ismaili and Shaykhi Perspectives." *Journal for Islamic Studies* 23 (2003): 3–35.

Carroll, Lucy. "Nizam-i-islam: Process and Conflicts in Pakistan's Programme of Islamisation, with Special Reference to the Position of Women." *Journal of Commonwealth and Comparative Politics* 20, no. 1 (1982): 57–95.

Chakrabarty, Dipesh. *Provincializing Europe: Postcolonial Thought and Historical Difference.* Princeton, NJ: Princeton University Press, 2008.

Chatterji, Joya. *Bengal Divided: Hindu Communalism and Partition, 1932–1947.* Cambridge: Cambridge University Press, 1994.

———. "Partition Studies: Prospects and Pitfalls." *Journal of South Asian Studies* 73, no. 2 (2014): 309–12.

Chehabi, H. E. "Religion and Politics in Iran: How Theocratic Is the Islamic Republic?" *Daedalus* 120, no. 3 (1991): 69–91.

Chehabi, H. E., and Rula Jurdi Abisaab. *Distant Relations: Iran and Lebanon in the Last 500 Years.* Oxford: I. B. Tauris, 2006.

Chehabi, Houchang. "Dress Codes for Men in Turkey and Iran." In *Men of Order: Authoritarian Modernization under Ataturk and Reza Shah*, edited by Touraj Atabaki and Erik Jan Zürcher, 209–37. London: I. B. Tauris, 2004.

Chibber, Vivek. *Postcolonial Theory and the Specter of Capital.* London: Verso, 2013.

Chubin, Shahram. *Iran and Its Neighbours: The Impact of the Gulf War.* London, 1987.

"CIA, Żiyā-yi ḥukūmat, ghaddārān-i millat: Quetta kō Karbalā kis ne banāya." *Rāh-i ʿAmal*, no. 41 (1985): 5.
Clarke, L. "The Shīʿī Construction of Taqlīd." *Journal of Islamic Studies* 12, no. 1 (2001): 40–64.
Clarke, Morgan. "After the Ayatollah: Routinisation and Succession in the Marjaʿiyya of Sayyid Muhammad Husayn Fadlallah." *Die Welt des Islams* 56, no. 2 (2016): 153–86.
———. "Neo-Calligraphy: Religious Authority and Media Technology in Contemporary Shiite Islam." *Comparative Studies in Society and History* 52, no. 2 (2010): 351–83.
Cole, Juan Ricardo. "Imami Jurisprudence and the Role of the Ulama: Murtaza Ansari on Emulating the Supreme Exemplar." In *Religion and Politics in Iran: Shiʿism from Quietism to Revolution*, edited by Nikki R. Keddie, 33–46. New Haven, CT: Yale University Press, 1983.
———. *Roots of North Indian Shīʿism in Iran and Iraq: Religion and State in Awadh, 1722–1859*. Berkeley: University of California Press, 1988.
———. *Sacred Space and Holy War: The Politics, Culture and History of Shiʿite Islam*. London: I. B. Tauris, 2002.
Conrad, Sebastian. *What Is Global History?* Princeton, NJ: Princeton University Press, 2016.
Conran, W. L., H. D. Craik, Lepel Henry Griffin, and Charles Francis Massy. *Chiefs and Families of Note in the Punjab*. Delhi: Low Price, 2010.
Cook, David. *Martyrdom in Islam*. Cambridge: Cambridge University Press, 2007.
Cook, Michael. *Commanding Right and Forbidding Wrong in Islamic Thought*. Cambridge: Cambridge University Press, 2000.
———. "Weber and Islamic Sects." In *Max Weber and Islam*, edited by Toby E. Huff and Wolfgang Schluchter, 273–80. New Brunswick, NJ: Transaction, 1999.
Cooke, Miriam, and Bruce B. Lawrence. "Introduction." In *Muslim Networks from Hajj to Hip Hop*, edited by Miriam Cooke and Bruce B. Lawrence, 1–28. Chapel Hill: University of North Carolina Press, 2005.
Cooper, Frederick. *Colonialism in Question: Theory, Knowledge, History*. Berkeley: University of California Press, 2010.
Corbin, Henry. "L'École shaykhie." In *En Islam iranien: Aspects spirituels et philosophiques*, 4:205–300. Paris: Gallimard, 1972.
———. "Rûzbehân Baqlî Shîrâzî (522/1128–606/1209) et le soufisme des fidèles d'amour." In *En Islam iranien: Aspects spirituels et philosophiques*, 3:9–147. Paris: Gallimard, 1972.
———. "Shiite Thought." In *History of Islamic Philosophy*, edited by Henry Corbin, Liadain Sherrard, and Philip Sherrard, 319–63. London: Kegan Paul International, 1993.
Corboz, Elvire. *Guardians of Shiʿism: Sacred Authority and Transnational Family Networks*. Edinburgh: Edinburgh University Press, 2015.

Cornell, Vincent J. *Realm of the Saint: Power and Authority in Moroccan Sufism.* Austin: University of Texas Press, 1998.
Crawford, Michael. *Ibn ʿAbd al-Wahhab.* London: Oneworld, 2014.
Crone, Patricia. *God's Rule: Government and Islam.* New York: Columbia University Press, 2004.
Crone, Patricia, and Martin Hinds. *God's Caliph: Religious Authority in the First Centuries of Islam.* Cambridge: Cambridge University Press, 1986.
Dabashi, Hamid. *Theology of Discontent: The Ideological Foundations of the Islamic Revolution in Iran.* New York: New York University Press, 1993.
Daechsel, Markus. "Being Middle Class in Late Colonial Punjab." In *Punjab Reconsidered: History, Culture, and Practice,* edited by Anshu Malhotra and Farina Mir, 320–55. New Delhi: Oxford University Press, 2012.
———. *The Politics of Self-Expression: The Urdu Middle-Class Milieu in Mid-Twentieth Century India and Pakistan.* London: Routledge, 2006.
Daftary, Farhad. *The Ismāʿīlīs: Their History and Doctrines.* Cambridge: Cambridge University Press, 2007.
Dakake, Maria Massi. *The Charismatic Community: Shiʿite Identity in Early Islam.* Albany: State University of New York Press, 2007.
"Dār al-Tablīgh-i Islāmī-yi Qum men̲ mujāhid-i Islām kī āmad." *al-Muntaẓar* 13, nos. 9–10 (1971): 68–70.
Ḍaskavī, Jāved Jamāl. *ʿAllāmah Iḥsān Ilāhī Ẓahīr.* Lahore: Jang, 1990.
"Daurān-i julūs-i ʿazā namāz kā program." *Rāh-i ʿAmal,* no. 11 (1980): 10.
"Daur-i ḥāżir ke dīnī taqāże." *Payām-i ʿAmal* 5, no. 10 (1961): 4.
Deeb, Lara. *An Enchanted Modern: Gender and Public Piety in Shiʿi Lebanon.* Princeton, NJ: Princeton University Press, 2006.
Devji, Faisal. "Apologetic Modernity." *Modern Intellectual History* 4, no. 1 (2007): 61–76.
———. "The Equivocal History of a Muslim Reformation." In *Islamic Reform in South Asia,* edited by Filippo Osella and Caroline Osella, 3–25. Cambridge: Cambridge University Press, 2013.
———. *The Impossible Indian: Gandhi and the Temptation of Violence.* London: Hurst, 2012.
———. *Muslim Zion: Pakistan as a Political Idea.* Cambridge, MA: Harvard University Press, 2014.
Dhulipala, Venkat. *Creating a New Medina: State Power, Islam and the Quest for Pakistan in Late Colonial India.* New Delhi: Cambridge University Press, 2015.
———. "A Nation State Insufficiently Imagined? Debating Pakistan in Late Colonial North India." *Indian Economic and Social History Review* 48, no. 3 (2011): 377–405.
———. "Rallying the Qaum: The Muslim League in the United Provinces, 1937–1939." *Modern Asian Studies* 44, no. 3 (2010): 603–40.
———. *Towards a New Medina: Jinnah, the Deobandi Ulama, and the Quest for Pakistan in Late Colonial India.* Occasional Papers 59, 26 July 2013.

Diamond, Jeffrey M. "The Orientalist-Literati Relationship in the Northwest: G. W. Leitner, Muhammad Hussain Azad and the Rhetoric of Neo-Orientalism in Colonial Lahore." *South Asia Research* 31, no. 1 (2011): 25–43.

DiMaggio, Paul J., and Walter W. Powell. "The Iron Cage Revisited: Institutional Isomorphism and Collective Rationality in Organizational Fields." *American Sociological Review* 48, no. 2 (1983): 147–60.

Dittmer, Kerrin. *Die indischen Muslime und die Hindi-Urdu-Kontroverse in den United Provinces.* Wiesbaden: O. Harrassowitz, 1972.

Dō bhāʾī: Abū ʾl-Aʿlā Maudūdī aur Imām Khumaynī sansanī khīz inkishāfāt. Karachi: ʿĀlamī-yi Majlis-i Taḥaffuẓ-i Islām.

Ḍōgar, Ṣafdar Ḥusayn. *Muḥammad Ḥusayn Ḍhakkō se 150 suʾāl.* Lahore: al-Qāʾim, 1987.

———. *Ṣaḥīfah-i ḥaqāʾiq dar javāb-i ʿaqāʾid-i bāṭilah ō afkār-i muntashirah. Janāb Sharaf al-Dīn Mūsavī ṣāḥib kī ṭaraf se shīʿīyān-i ḥaydar karrār par lagāʾye giye ittihāmāt kā mudallal aur bā ḥavālah javāb.* Vol. 1. Mianwala: Sharīkat al-Ḥusayn, 2004.

———. *Ṣaḥīfah-i ḥaqāʾiq (jild-i duvum).* Vol. 2. Mianwala: Sharīkat al-Ḥusayn, 2006.

Doostdar, Alireza Mohammadi. "Fantasies of Reason: Science, Superstition, and the Supernatural in Iran." PhD diss., Harvard University, 2012.

D'Souza, Diane. "Devotional Practices among Shia Women in South Asia." In *Lived Islam in South Asia: Adaptation, Accommodation and Conflict,* edited by Imtiaz Ahmad and Helmut Reifeld, 187–206. Delhi: Social Science, 2004.

Dudoignon, Stéphane A. "Sunnis and Shiites in Iran since 1979: Confrontations, Exchanges, Convergences." In *The Dynamics of Sunni-Shia Relationships: Doctrine, Transnationalism, Intellectuals and the Media,* edited by Brigitte Maréchal and Sami Zemni, 141–62. London: Hurst, 2012.

Eaton, Richard M. "Rethinking Religious Divides." *Journal of South Asian Studies* 73, no. 2 (2014): 305–8.

Eickelman, Dale F., and James Piscatori. *Muslim Politics.* Princeton, NJ: Princeton University Press, 2004.

———. "Social Theory in the Study of Muslim Societies." In *Muslim Travellers: Pilgrimage, Migration, and the Religious Imagination,* edited by Dale F. Eickelman and James P. Piscatori, 3–25. London: Routledge, 1990.

Eliash, J. "Ḥasan al-ʿAskarī." In *Encyclopaedia of Islam,* 2nd ed., edited by P. Bearman, Th. Bianquis, C. E. Bosworth, E. van Donzel, and W. P. Heinrichs. http://dx.doi.org/10.1163/1573-3912_islam_SIM_2762. Posted 2012.

"Enclosure to No. 233 (Fazil Mooraj to M A Jinnah SHC [682] 29 October 1945), Mirza Mohammad Jafer Husain to Fazil Mooraj SHC (684)." In *Quaid-i-Azam Mohammad Ali Jinnah Papers: The Verdict for Pakistan, 1 August 1945–31 March 1946,* edited by Zawwar Husain Zaidi, 290–93. Islamabad: Quaid-i-Azam Papers Project National Archives of Pakistan, 2005.

Ende, Werner. *Arabische Nation und islamische Geschichte: Die Umayyaden im Urteil arabischer Autoren des 20. Jahrhunderts.* Wiesbaden: F. Steiner, 1977.

———. "Baqīʿ al-Gharqad." In *Encyclopaedia of Islam*, 3rd ed., edited by Kate Fleet, Gudrun Krämer, Denis Matridge, John Nawas, and Everett Rowson. http://dx.doi.org/10.1163/1573-3912_ei3_COM_23494. Posted 2010.
———. "Bidʿa or Sirr al-Īmān? Modern Shiʿi Controversies over the Third Shahāda in the Adhān." In *Le Shīʿisme Imāmite quarante ans après: Hommage à Etan Kohlberg*, edited by Mohammad Ali Amir-Moezzi, Meir M. Bar-Asher, and Simon Hopkins, 203–17. Turnhout: Brepols, 2009.
———. "The Flagellations of Muharram and the Shiʿite ʿUlamāʾ." *Der Islam* 55 (1978): 19–37.
———. "From Revolt to Resignation: The Life of Shaykh Muḥsin Sharāra." In *Humanism, Culture, and Language in the Near East: Studies in Honor of Georg Krotkoff*, edited by Georg Krotkoff, Asma Afsaruddin, and A. H. Mathias Zahniser. Winona Lake: Eisenbrauns, 1997.
———. "Success and Failure of a Shiite Modernist: Muhammad ibn Muhammad Mahdi al-Khalisi (1890–1963)." In *The Other Shiites: From the Mediterranean to Central Asia*, edited by Alessandro Monsutti, Silvia Naef, and Farian Sabahi, 230–44. Bern: Peter Lang, 2007.
———. "Sunni Polemical Writings on the Shiʿa and the Iranian Revolution." In *The Iranian Revolution and the Muslim World*, edited by David Menashri, 219–32. Boulder: Westview Press, 1990.
Ernst, Carl W. *Rūzbihān Baqlī: Mysticism and the Rhetoric of Sainthood in Persian Sufism*. Richmond, UK: Curzon, 1996.
Eschraghi, Armin. *Frühe Šaiḫī- und Bābī-Theologie: Die Darlegung der Beweise für Muḥammads besonderes Prophetentum (ar-Risāla fī iṯbāt an-nubūwa al-ḫāṣṣa)*. Leiden: Brill, 2004.
Euben, Roxanne Leslie, and Muhammad Qasim Zaman. *Princeton Readings in Islamist Thought: Texts and Contexts from al-Banna to Bin Laden*. Princeton, NJ: Princeton University Press, 2009.
Ewing, Katherine Pratt. *Arguing Sainthood: Modernity, Psychoanalysis, and Islam*. Durham, NC: Duke University Press, 1997.
Farquhar, Michael. *Circuits of Faith: Migration, Education, and the Wahhabi Mission*. Stanford, CA: Stanford University Press, 2016.
———. "The Islamic University of Medina since 1961: The Politics of Religious Mission and the Making of a Modern Salafi Pedagogy." In *Shaping Global Islamic Discourses: The Role of Al-Azhar, Al-Medina, and Al-Mustafa*, edited by Masooda Bano and Keiko Sakurai, 21–40. Edinburgh: Edinburgh University Press, 2015.
Fārūqī, Muḥammad Khālid. *Īrān men̲ islāmī inqilāb ke qāʾid Āyatullāh Khumaynī*. Karachi: al-Ikhwān, 1979.
Fārūqī, Żiyā al-Raḥmān. "Ahl-i bay kōn hen̲?" In *Javāhirāt-i Fārūqī shahīd*, edited by Qārī Shabbīr Ḥaydar Fārūqī Jalālpūrī, 268–90. Multan: Idārat Ishāʿat al-Maʿārif, 2001.
———. *Fārūqī shahīd kā payghām sipāh-i ṣaḥābah ke nām*. Samundari: Fārūqī Shahīd Academy, n.d.

———. *Khilāfat ke ʿālamī naṣb al-ʿayn kī daʿvat al-maʿrūf Khilāfat world order.* Fayṣalābād: Idārah-i Ishāʿat al-Maʿārif, 2003.
———. *Khilāfat ō ḥukūmat.* Fayṣalābād: Idārah-i Ishāʿat al-Maʿārif, 1995.
———. *Khumaynīizm aur Islām.* Fayṣalābād: Ishāʿat al-Maʿārif, 1984.
———. "Payghambar-i inqilāb (alif)." In *Javāhirāt-i Fārūqī shahīd,* edited by Qārī Shabbīr Ḥaydar Fārūqī Jalālpūrī, 381–98. Multan: Idārat Ishāʿat al-Maʿārif, 2001.
———. "Rufaqāʾ-i payghambar." In *Javāhirāt-i Fārūqī shahīd,* edited by Qārī Shabbīr Ḥaydar Fārūqī Jalālpūrī. Multan: Idārat Ishāʿat al-Maʿārif, 2001.
———. *Sitāre cānd ke Islām meṉ ṣaḥābah-i kirām kī āʾīnī haysiyyat.* Fayṣalābād: Idārah Ishāʿat al-Maʿārif, 1994.
———. *Tārīkhī dastāvez.* Jhang: Shuʿbah-i Nashr ō Ishāʿat-i Sipāh-i Ṣaḥābah (Pākistān), 1995.
Fazaeli, Roja, and Mirjam Künkler. "Training Female ulama in Jamʿiat al-Zahra—New Opportunities for Old Role Models?" In *Knowledge and Authority in Shiʿi Islam: Clerics and the Hawza System in the Middle East,* vol. 1, edited by Robert Gleave. London: I. B. Tauris, forthcoming.
"Fazil Mooraj to M. A. Jinnah, SHC (606)." In *Quaid-i-Azam Mohammad Ali Jinnah Papers: The Verdict for Pakistan, 1 August 1945–31 March 1946,* edited by Zawwar Husain Zaidi, 138–39. Islamabad: Quaid-i-Azam Papers Project, National Archives of Pakistan, 2005.
Ferdows, Adele K. "Women and the Iranian Revolution." *International Journal of Middle East Studies* 15, no. 2 (1983): 283–98.
Fierro, Maribel. "The Treatises against Innovations (kutub al-bidaʿ)." *Der Islam* 69, no. 2 (1992): 204–46.
Finke, Roger, and Christopher P. Scheitle. "Understanding Schisms: Theoretical Explanations for Their Origins." In *Sacred Schisms: How Religions Divide,* edited by James R. Lewis and Sarah M. Lewis, 11–34. Cambridge: Cambridge University Press, 2009.
Finkel, Irving L. "Round and Round the Houses: The Game of Pachisi." In *Asian Games: The Art of Contest,* edited by Irving L. Finkel and Colin Mackenzie, 46–57. New York: Asia Society, 2004.
Fischer, Michael M. J. *Iran: From Religious Dispute to Revolution.* Cambridge, MA: Harvard University Press, 1980.
Formichi, Chiara. "Shaping Shiʿa Identities in Contemporary Indonesia between Local Tradition and Foreign Orthodoxy." *Die Welt des Islams* 54, no. 2 (2014): 212–36.
Franke, Patrick. *Begegnung mit Khidr: Quellenstudien zum Imaginären im traditionellen Islam.* Beirut: Franz Steiner, 2000.
Freitag, Sandria B. *Collective Action and Community: Public Arenas and the Emergence of Communalism in North India.* Berkeley: University of California Press, 1989.
Freitag, Ulrike, and Achim von Oppen. "Introduction: 'Translocality': An Approach

to Connection and Transfer in Area Studies." In *Translocality: The Study of Globalising Processes from a Southern Perspective*, edited by Ulrike Freitag and Achim von Oppen, 1–21. Leiden: Brill, 2010.

Friedmann, Yohanan. *Prophecy Continuous: Aspects of Ahmadi Religious Thought and Its Medieval Background.* Berkeley: University of California Press, 1989.

———. *Shaykh Aḥmad Sirhindī: An Outline of His Thought and a Study of His Image in the Eyes of Posterity.* New Delhi: Oxford University Press, 2000.

Fuchs, Simon Wolfgang. "Do Excellent Surgeons Make Miserable Exegetes? Negotiating the Sunni Tradition in the Ǧihādī Camps." *Welt des Islams* 53, no. 2 (2013): 192–237.

———. "Failing Transnationally: Local Intersections of Science, Medicine, and Sectarianism in Modernist Shiʿi Writings." *Modern Asian Studies* 48, no. 2 (2014): 433–67.

———. "The Long Shadow of the State: The Iranian Revolution, Saudi Influence, and the Shifting Arguments of Anti-Shiʿi Sectarianism in Pakistan." In *Pan-Islamic Connections: Transnational Networks between South Asia and the Gulf*, edited by Christophe Jaffrelot and Laurence Louër, 217–32 and 290–300. London: Hurst, 2017.

———. *Proper Signposts for the Camp: The Reception of Classical Authorities in the Ǧihādī Manual al-ʿUmda fī Iʿdād al-ʿUdda.* Würzburg: Ergon, 2011.

Fürtig, Henner. *Islamische Weltauffassung und aussenpolitische Konzeptionen der iranischen Staatsführung seit dem Tod Ajatollah Khomeinis.* Berlin: Das Arabische Buch, 1998.

Fyzee, Asif Ali Asghar. "The Creed of Ibn Bābawayhi." *Journal of Bombay University* 12 (1943): 70–86.

Gaborieau, Marc. "The Transformation of Tablīghī Jamāʿat into a Transnational Movement." In *Travellers in Faith: Studies of the Tablīghī Jamāʿat as a Transnational Islamic Movement for Faith Renewal*, edited by Muhammad Khalid Masud, 121–38. Boston: Brill, 2000.

Gaborieau, Marc, and Malika Zeghal. "Autorités religieuses en islam." *Archives de sciences sociales des religions* 49, no. 125 (2004): 5–21.

Gaiser, Adam R. "A Narrative Identity Approach to Islamic Sectarianism." In *Sectarianization: Mapping the New Politics of the Middle East*, edited by Nader Hashemi and Danny Postel, 61–76. London: Hurst, 2017.

———. "Satan's Seven Specious Arguments: Al-Shahrastānī's Kitāb al-Milal wa-l-niḥal in an Ismaʿili Context." *Journal of Islamic Studies* 19, no. 2 (2008): 178–95.

Gerges, Fawaz A. *The Far Enemy: Why Jihad Went Global.* Cambridge: Cambridge University Press, 2009.

Gesink, Indira Falk. *Islamic Reform and Conservatism: Al-Azhar and the Evolution of Modern Sunni Islam.* London: Tauris Academic Studies, 2010.

Ghauri, Irfan. "Sectarian Violence: Over 2,000 People Killed in 5 Years, Interior Ministry Tells Senate." *Express Tribune*, 23 April 2014.

"Ghaur kijīye." *Payām-i ʿAmal* 3, no. 2 (1959): 4.
al-Ghazālī, Abū Ḥāmid Muḥammad b. Muḥammad. *Maʿārij al-quds fī madārij maʿrifat al-nafs.* Cairo: al-Maktaba al-Tijāriyya al-Kubrā, 1963.
Ghazali, Muhammad. *The Socio-Political Thought of Shāh Walī Allāh.* Islamabad: International Institute of Islamic Thought, 2001.
Ghażanfar Riżvī, ʿAlī. "Nā-qābil-i farāmūsh." *Payām-i ʿAmal* 7, no. 1 (1963): 17–18.
Ghazi, Mahmood A. "State and Politics in the Philosophy of Shah Waliy Allah." *Islamic Studies* 23, no. 4 (1984): 353–71.
Ghūlām-i Ḥusayn, Sayyid. *Intiṣār-i islām. Ibṭāl-i shubahāt ō auhām men̲ bar ṭabq-i uṣūl-i jadīdah-i Europe America.* Lahore: Gulzār Muḥammadī Steam Press, 1917.
Gill, Maqṣūd Ḥusayn. "Ḥaqīqat men̲ khurāfāt khō gayī." *Rāh-i ʿAmal*, no. 23 (1982): 17.
Gilmartin, David. "*Biraderi* and Bureaucracy: The Politics of Muslim Kinship Solidarity in Twentieth Century Punjab." *International Journal of Punjab Studies* 1, no. 1 (1994): 1–29.
———. *Empire and Islam: Punjab and the Making of Pakistan.* Berkeley and Los Angeles: University of California Press, 1988.
———. "Environmental History, Biradari, and the Making of Pakistani Punjab." In *Punjab Reconsidered: History, Culture, and Practice,* edited by Anshu Malhotra and Farina Mir, 289–319. New Delhi: Oxford University Press, 2012.
———. "The Historiography of India's Partition: Between Civilization and Modernity." *Journal of South Asian Studies* 74, no. 1 (2015): 23–41.
———. "A Magnificent Gift: Muslim Nationalism and the Election Process in Colonial Punjab." *Comparative Studies in Society and History* 40, no. 3 (1998): 415–36.
———. "A Networked Civilization?" In *Muslim Networks from Hajj to Hip Hop,* edited by Miriam Cooke and Bruce B. Lawrence, 51–68. Chapel Hill: University of North Carolina Press, 2005.
———. "Religious Leadership and the Pakistan Movement in the Punjab." *Modern Asian Studies* 13, no. 3 (1979): 485–517.
———. "Rethinking the Public through the Lens of Sovereignty." *South Asia: Journal of South Asian Studies* 38, no. 3 (2015): 371–86.
Gleave, Robert. "Conceptions of Authority in Iraqi Shiʿism: Baqir al-Hakim, Ha'iri and Sistani on Ijtihad, Taqlid and Marjaʿiyya." *Theory, Culture and Society* 24, no. 2 (2007): 59–78.
———. "Political Aspects of Modern Shiʿi Legal Discussions: Khumayni and Khuʾi on ijtihād and qadaʾ." *Mediterranean Politics* 7, no. 3 (2002): 96–116.
———. *Scripturalist Islam: The History and Doctrines of the Akhbārī Shīʿī School.* Leiden: Brill, 2007.
Gómez-Rivas, Camilo. "Qāḍī ʿIyāḍ (d. 544/1149)." In *Islamic Legal Thought: A Compendium of Muslim Jurists,* edited by David Powers, Susan Spectorsky, and Oussama Arabi, 323–38. Leiden: Brill, 2013.
Gramlich, Richard. *Die schiitischen Derwischorden Persiens.* Wiesbaden: Steiner, 1976.

Green, Nile. *Bombay Islam: The Religious Economy of the West Indian Ocean, 1840–1915.* Cambridge: Cambridge University Press, 2011.

———. *Terrains of Exchange: Religious Economies of Global Islam.* London: Hurst, 2014.

Griffel, Frank. *Apostasie und Toleranz im Islam: Die Entwicklung zu al-Ġazālīs Urteil gegen die Philosophie und die Reaktionen der Philosophen.* Leiden: Brill, 2000.

Grube, Chistiana J. "Jerusalem in the Visual Propaganda of Post-Revolutionary Iran." In *Jerusalem: Idea and Reality*, edited by Suleiman Ali Mourad and Tamar Mayer, 168–97. Milton Park, UK: Routledge, 2008.

Gugler, Thomas K. *Mission Medina: Daʿwat-e Islāmī und Tablīġī Ǧamāʿat.* Würzburg: Ergon, 2011.

"Gunmen Kill Three Lawyers in Karachi." *Dawn*, 25 January 2012. https://www.dawn.com/news/690723/gunmen-kill-three-lawyers-in-karachi.

Gupta, Radhika. "Experiments with Khomeini's Revolution in Kargil: Contemporary Shiʿa Networks between India and West Asia." *Modern Asian Studies* 40, no. 2 (2014): 370–98.

Gustafson, W. Eric. "Economic Reforms under the Bhutto Regime." *Journal of Asian and Africa Studies* 8, nos. 3–4 (1973): 241–58.

Haar, J. G. J. ter. *Follower and Heir of the Prophet: Shaykh Aḥmad Sirhindī (1564–1624) as Mystic.* Leiden: Het Oosters Instituut, 1992.

Habib, Meherafroze Mirza. *A Georgian Saga: From the Caucasus to the Indus.* Karachi: Oxford University Press, 2005.

Haddad, Fanar. *Sectarianism in Iraq: Antagonistic Visions of Unity.* London: Hurst, 2011.

Hādī, Sayyid Muḥammad. *Itmām al-ḥujjat.* Jaunpūr: Kāẓim Ḥusayn Khān, 1917.

Ḥafīẓ Allāh, Ḥāfiẓ. "Siyālkūṭ meṉ shahīd-i millat ḥażrat ʿAllāmah Iḥsān Ilāhī Ẓahīr kā ākharī yādgār khiṭāb." In *ʿAllāmah shahīd-i millat number, al-maʿrūf maqālāt-i ʿAllāmah Iḥsān Ilāhī Ẓahīr*, edited by ʿAbd al-Raḥmān Munīr Rājūvālvī, 91–104. Lahore: Ahl-i Ḥadīs̱ Dār al-Ishāʿat, 1988.

Haider, Murtaza. "Murtaza Haider Is Dead, Does Anyone Care?" *Dawn*, 20 February 2013.

Haider, Najam Iftikhar. *The Origins of the Shīʿa: Identity, Ritual, and Sacred Space in Eighth-Century Kūfa.* Cambridge: Cambridge University Press, 2011.

———. *Shiʿi Islam: An Introduction.* Cambridge: Cambridge University Press, 2014.

Ḥāʾirī, Sayyid ʿAlī. *Al-Burhān.* Lahore: Khvājah Book Agency, 1924 or 1925.

———. *Al-Hudā.* Lahore: Khvājah Book Agency, 1924 or 1925.

———. *Al-Liwāʾ li-ahl al-wilāʾ.* Lahore: Khvājah Book Agency, 1924 or 1925.

———. *Malfūẓāt al-Ḥāʾirī (yaʿnī jō taqrīr keh ʿalījanāb ṣadr al-mufassirīn ẓahīr al-millat wa-l-dīn ḥujjat al-Islām wa-l-muslimīn qiblah ō kaʿbah Abū Turāb sarkār sharīʿatmadār ʿAllāmah al-Sayyid ʿAlī al-Ḥāʾirī ṣāḥib mujtahid-i Panjāb Lahōr madd ẓillahu ne bi-javāb-i suʾalāt-i ek fāẓil sunnat jamāʿat ke cand mutavātir ṣuḥbatōṉ meṉ irshād farmāʾī).* Lahore: Shiah Young Men Society, 1916.

———. *Maṣīḥ mauʿūd*. Lahore: Khvājah Book Agency, 1926.
Hajatpour, Reza. *Iranische Geistlichkeit zwischen Utopie und Realismus*. Wiesbaden: Reichert, 2002.
———. "Reflections and Legal Analysis of the Relationship between 'Religious Government and Human Rights' from the Perspective of Grand Ayatullāh Muntaẓirī." *Die Welt des Islams* 51, nos. 3–4 (2011): 382–408.
al-Ḥakīm, Muḥammad Mahdī. "Cih dilāvar ast duzdī kih be kaf cirāgh dārad." *al-Ḥujjat* 11, no. 7 (1971): 71–72.
al-Ḥakīm, Muḥsin. "Bāb al-masāʾil: Taqlīd." *al-Muntaẓar* 7, no. 23 (1966): 24.
———. "Bāb al-masāʾil (20 March 1966)." *al-Muntaẓar* 8, no. 2 (1966): 18–19.
———. "Tashrīḥ al-masāʾil (July 1963)." *Payām-i ʿAmal* 5, no. 7 (1963): 23–24.
———. "Tashrīḥ al-masāʾil (January 1964)." *Payām-i ʿAmal* 7, no. 11 (1964): 26.
———. "Telegraph." *al-Ḥujjat* 2, no. 10 (1962): 4–5.
"Hamāre qaumī idāre 2." *Asad*, 10 May 1959, 2.
"Hamāre qaumī idāre 6." *Asad*, 10 June 1960, 2.
"Hamārī sargarmiyān̲." *Rāh-i ʿAmal*, no. 28 (1983): 10–13.
Hall, Catherine. *Civilising Subjects: Metropole and Colony in the English Imagination, 1830–1867*. Cambridge: Polity, 2002.
Hallaq, Wael B. *Sharīʿa: Theory, Practice, Transformations*. Cambridge: Cambridge University Press, 2009.
Halm, Heinz. *Die islamische Gnosis*. Zurich: Artemis, 1982.
al-Hamadānī, Zawār al-Ḥusayn. "Aʿlam-i zamān—Āqāʾ-i Sayyid Muḥsin Ḥakīm." *Payām-i ʿAmal* 5, no. 11 (1962): 11–18.
———. "Fasādāt-i Muḥarram." *al-Muntaẓar* 4, no. 11 (1963): 26.
Hammad, Hanan. "Khomeini and the Iranian Revolution in the Egyptian Press: From Fascination to Condemnation." *Radical History Review* 105 (2009): 39–57.
Haq, Farhat. "Women, Islam and the State in Pakistan." *Muslim World* 136, no. 2 (1996): 158–75.
Hardy, Peter. *Partners in Freedom—and True Muslims: The Political Thought of Some Muslim Scholars in British India, 1912–1947*. Lund: Studentlitteratur, 1971.
Harrop, W. Scott. "Pakistan and Revolutionary Iran: Adjusting to Necessity." *Journal of South Asian and Middle Eastern Studies* 13, nos. 1–2 (1989): 110–27.
Hartmann, Angelika. "Ismâʿîlitische Theologie bei sunnitischen 'Ulamâ' des Mittelalters?" In *"Ihr alle aber seid Brüder": Festschrift für A. Th. Khoury zum 60. Geburtstag*, edited by Ludwig Hagemann and Ernst Pulsfort, 190–206. Würzburg: Echter, 1990.
Hartung, Jan-Peter. *A System of Life: Mawdūdī and the Ideologisation of Islam*. London: Hurst & Co., 2013.
———. *Viele Wege und ein Ziel: Leben und Wirken von Sayyid Abū l-Ḥasan ʿAlī al-Ḥasanī Nadwī (1914–1999)*. Würzburg: Ergon, 2004.
Ḥasan, Mirzā Aḥmad. *Taẕkirah-i ḥayāt-i sarkār Nāṣir al-Millat*. Lucknow: Niẓāmī Press, 1943.

Hasan, Mushirul. *From Pluralism to Separatism: Qasbas in Colonial Awadh*. New Delhi: Oxford University Press, 2004.
———. "Traditional Rites and Contested Meanings: Sectarian Strife in Colonial Lucknow." *Economic and Political Weekly* 31, no. 9 (1996): 543–50.
Ḥasan, Sayyid Nasīm. *Istikhlāf*. Amroha: Sayyid Aḥmad Ḥusayn, 1919.
Ḥasan, Sayyid Shafīq. *Aṣl al-uṣūl dar bayān-i ḥaqīqat-i tavallā ō tabarrā*. N.p., 1918.
Ḥasan, Sayyid Sibṭ-i. *Inqilāb-i Irān*. Karachi: Maktabah-i Dānyāl, 1980.
Ḥasan, Sayyid Ẓafar. *Shīʿōn̲ kī be naẓīr qurbāniyān̲ al-maʿrūf bih sarfurūshān-i millat*. Murādābād: Shahmīm Book Depot, 1939.
Hasan, Syed Najmul. *Islam in the Light of Shiaism, Being a Translation of The Shariatul Islam (Part I)*. Lucknow: Darul Tasneef, Mowayyedul-Ulum Association, 1924.
———. *The Prophetship and the Caliphate—Being a Translation of Alnubuwwat-wa-Al-Khilafat: Translated by L. A. Haidari, General Secretary, Muwayyed-ul-Ulum Association, Madrasat-ul-Waizeen, Lucknow*. Lucknow: Darul Tasaneef, 1924.
"Hasan Ispahani to the Maharajkumar of Mahmudabad (Enclosure to No. 148), 25 September 1945." In *Quaid-i-Azam Mohammad Ali Jinnah Papers: Consolidating the Muslim League for Final Struggle, 1 August 1944–31 July 1945*, edited by Zawwar Husain Zaidi, 169–70. Islamabad: Quaid-i-Azam Papers Project, National Archives of Pakistan, 2005.
Hashemi, Nader, and Danny Postel. "Introduction: The Sectarianization Thesis." In *Sectarianization: Mapping the New Politics of the Middle East*, edited by Nader Hashemi and Danny Postel, 1–21. London: Hurst, 2017.
Hāshim, ʿAbd al-Hādī Muḥammad. *Al-Mujaddid al-Najafī fī talīdihi wa-ṭārifihi*. Najaf: Muʾassasat al-Anwār al-Najafiyya, 2011.
Hasnain, Nadeem, and Sheikh Abrar Husain. *Shias and Shia Islam in India*. Delhi: Harnam, 1988.
Hatina, Meir. "An Earlier Sunnī Version of Khomeini's Rule of the Jurist: Muṣṭafā al-Sibāʿī on ʿUlamāʾ and Politics." *Arabica* 57 (2010): 455–76.
———. "Debating the 'Awakening Shia': Sunni Perceptions of the Iranian Revolution." In *The Sunna and Shiʿa in History: Division and Ecumenism in the Muslim Middle East*, edited by Ofra Bengio and Meir Litvak, 203–22. New York: Palgrave Macmillan, 2014.
———. "The Clerics' Betrayal? Islamists, 'Ulama' and the Polity." In *Guardians of Faith in Modern Times: 'Ulama' in the Middle East*, edited by Meir Hatina, 247–64. Leiden: Brill, 2009.
Haydar, Afak. "The Politicization of the Shias and the Development of the Tehrik-e-Nifaz-e-Fiqh-e-Jafaria in Pakistan." In *Pakistan, 1992*, edited by Charles H. Kennedy, 75–94. Boulder: Westview Press, 1992.
Ḥaydar, Ghulām. *Intibāh al-Shīʿah bi-aqvāl al-aʾimma al-murḍiyya*. Multan, 1938.

Ḥaydar, Sayyid Afżal. *Islāmī naẓariyātī council: irtiqā'-ī safar aur kārkardagī.* Islamabad: Dūst, 2006.
Ḥaydar, Sayyid ʿAlamdār. "ʿAllāmah Ḥasan Turābī mahnāmah Qaumī Jā'iza kā interview." In *Shahīd-i rāh-i vaḥdat: ʿAllāmah Ḥasan Turābī shahīd,* edited by Ḥasan Murtażā, 144–61. Karachi: Idārah-i Taḥaffuẓ-i Āsār-i Shuhadā'-i Islām (Pākistān), 2007.
Ḥaydar, Sayyid ʿAlī. *Kitāb-i mustaṭāb-i hidāyat ma'āb musamme bih Jauhar-i Qur'ān.* Kajhvā: Iṣlāḥ Machine Press, 1938.
———. "Lāhōr men̲ ḥaqīqat-i maẕhab-i shīʿah kā zabardast muʿjizah." *Iṣlāḥ* 9, no. 32 (1932): 2–6.
Ḥaydarī, Aṣghar. *Āyatullāh Sharīʿatmadārī bih rivāyat-i asnād.* Tehran: Intishārāt-i Markaz-i Asnād-i Inqilāb-i Islāmī, 2010.
Haykel, Bernard. "Al-Qaʿida and Shiism." In *Fault Lines in Global Jihad: Organizational, Strategic and Ideological Fissures,* edited by Assaf Moghadam and Brian Fishman, 184–202. Milton Park: Routledge, 2011.
Haykel, Bernard, and Michael Crawford. "Introduction." In *The Expansion of Wahhabi Power in Arabia, 1798–1932: British Documentary Records,* vol. 1: *1798–1848,* edited by Anita L. P. Burdett, ix–xxvii. Cambridge: Cambridge University Press, 2013.
Hazaravī, Fażl al-Raḥmān, and Ḥāfiẓ Muḥammad Isḥāq. "ʿAllāmah shahīd kā akharī payghām." In *ʿAllāmah shahīd-i millat number, al-maʿrūf maqālāt-i ʿAllāmah Iḥsān Ilāhī Ẓahīr,* edited by ʿAbd al-Raḥmān Munīr Rājūvālvī, 89. Lahore: Ahl-i Ḥadīs̱ Dār al-Ishāʿat, 1988.
Heern, Zackery Mirza. "Thou Shalt Emulate the Most Knowledgeable Living Cleric: Redefinition of Islamic Law and Authority in Usuli Shiʿism." *Journal of Shiʿa Islamic Studies* 7, no. 3 (2014): 321–44.
Hefner, Robert W. "Introduction: The Culture, Politics, and Future of Muslim Education." In *Schooling Islam: The Culture and Politics of Modern Muslim Education,* edited by Robert W. Hefner and Muhammad Qasim Zaman. Princeton, NJ: Princeton University Press, 2007.
Hegland, Mary Elaine. "A Mixed Blessing: The Majales—Shiʿa Women's Rituals of Mourning in Northwest Pakistan." In *Mixed Blessings: Gender and Religious Fundamentalism Cross Culturally,* edited by Judy Brink and Joan P. Mencher, 179–208. New York: Routledge, 1997.
———. "Flagellation and Fundamentalism: (Trans)Forming Meaning, Identity, and Gender through Pakistan Women's Rituals of Mourning." *American Ethnologist* 25, no. 2 (1998): 240–66.
Hermann, Denis. *Le shaykhisme à la période qajare: Histoire sociale et doctrinale d'une école chiite.* Turnhout: Brepols, 2017.
———. "Political Quietism in Contemporary Shīʿism: A Study of the Siyāsat-i mudun of the Shaykhī Kirmānī Master ʿAbd al-Riḍā Khān Ibrāhīmī." *Studia Islamica,* no. 109 (2014): 274–302.
Hill, Christopher L. "Conceptual Universalization in the Transnational Nineteenth

Century." In *Global Intellectual History*, edited by Samuel Moyn and Andrew Sartori, 134–58. New York: Columbia University Press, 2009.
Hindī, ʿAllāmah. *Shīʿah aur khilāfat*. Lucknow: Sarfarāz Qaumī Press, 1939.
Hiro, Dilip. *The Longest War: The Iran-Iraq Military Conflict*. London: Grafton Books, 1989.
Hodson, H. V. *The Great Divide. Britain—India—Pakistan*. London: Hotchinson, 1969.
———. *The Great Divide: Britain-India-Pakistan with an Epilogue Written in 1985 Which Sums Up the Events since Partition*. Karachi: Oxford University Press, 1985.
Hollister, John Norman. *The Shiʿa of India*. London: Luzac, 1953.
———. "The Shiite Community in India Today." *Muslim World* 36, no. 4 (1946): 319–30.
Holzwarth, Wolfgang. *Die Ismailiten in Nordpakistan: Zur Entwicklung einer religiösen Minderheit im Kontext neuer Aussenbeziehungen*. Berlin: Das Arabische Buch, 1994.
Horkheimer, Max, and Theodor W. Adorno. *Dialektik der Aufklärung: Philosophische Fragmente*. Frankfurt am Main: Fischer, 1988.
Hourani, Albert. *Arabic Thought in the Liberal Age, 1798–1939*. Oxford: Oxford University Press, 1962.
Howarth, Toby M. *The Twelver Shīʿa as a Muslim Minority in India: Pulpit of Tears*. London: Routledge, 2011.
Howe, Stephen. "Introduction: New Imperial Histories." In *The New Imperial Histories Reader*, edited by Stephen Howe, 1–20. London: Routledge, 2010.
Hull, Matthew. "Uncivil Politics and the Appropriation of Planning in Islamabad." In *Beyond Crisis: Re-Evaluating Pakistan*, edited by Naveeda Khan, 452–81. London: Routledge, 2010.
Humphreys, Stephen. *Muʿawiya ibn Abi Sufyan: The Saviour of the Caliphate*. Oxford: Oneworld, 2006.
Husain, Syed Ishtiaq. *The Life and the Times of Raja Saheb of Mahmudabad*. Karachi: Mehboob Academy, 1990.
Husain, Syed Kamil. *Social Institutions of Shia Muslims (An Anthropological Analysis)*. New Delhi: Classical, 1998.
Ḥusayn, Mirzā Jaʿfar. *Kashmakash-i ḥayāt*. Lucknow: Mirzā Jaʿfar Ḥusayn, 1984.
Ḥusayn, Murtażā. *Mauʿiẓat-i sajjādiyya maʿrūf bih ṣirāṭ-i mustaqīm*. Jaunpūr: Aṣghar Ḥusayn Khān Minjur, 1918.
Ḥusayn, Ṣaghīr. "Inqilāb-i Īrān aur javānān-i Pākistān." *Rāh-i ʿAmal*, no. 6 (1979): 3.
Ḥusayn, Sayyid Murtażā. "Āyatullāh al-Ḥakīm kī riḥlat." *al-Muntaẓar* 5, no. 20 (1970): 7–20.
———. *Āyatullāh Khumaynī Qum se Qum tak*. Lahore: Imāmiyyah, 1979.
———. *Hayat-e-Hakeem: Life of Aqae Syed Mohsin al-Hakeem (A.R.)*. Karachi: Peermahomed Ebrahim Trust, 1973.
———. *Inqilāb-i islāmī-yi Īrān: Maʿrakah-i Mashhad aur Āyatullāh Shīrāzī*. Lahore: Imāmiyyah, 1981.

———. *Maṭlaʿ-i anvār: Taẕkirah-i shīʿah afāẓil ō ʿulamāʾ-i kibār-i barr-i ṣaghīr pāk ō hind*. Karachi: Khorasan Islamic Research Center, 1981.
Ḥusayn, Sayyid Sajjād. *Dalīl al-mutaḥayyirīn radd-i khilāfat-i shaykhayn*. Delhi: Maṭbaʿa Yūsufī, 1906.
———. *Pākizah khayāl*. Delhi: Maṭbaʿa Yūsufī, 1906.
Ḥusayn, Sayyid Taḥavvur. *Risālah-i mutʿa*. Lucknow: Sarfarāz Qaumī Press, 1930.
Ḥusayn al-Najafī, Bashīr. *Satabqā al-Najaf rāʾidat ḥauzāt al-ʿālam*. Najaf: Muʾassasat al-Anwār al-Najafiyya, 2012.
Ḥusayn Najafī, Sayyid Ṣafdar. "ʿAurat aur pardah." *Rāh-i ʿAmal*, no. 10 (1980): 7–9.
———. "Islām kā markaz-i rūḥānī-yi Najaf-i Ashraf." *Payām-i ʿAmal* 15, no. 6 (1971): 6–9, 20.
———. *Mabādiyāt-i ḥukūmat-i Islāmī: Naẓariyātī aur ʿamalī pahlūʾon̲ se*. Lahore: Imāmiyyah, 1981.
Ḥusayn Riżvī, Muḥammad Akbar. *Madrasat al-Wāʿiẓīn kā āwāz*. Lucknow, 1928 (?).
Ḥusayn Shāh, Sayyid Mumtāz. "Khaṭṭ." *al-Ḥujjat* 17, no. 7 (1977): 4–5.
al-Ḥusaynī, Sayyid ʿArif Ḥusayn. *Guftār-i ṣidq: Maʿārif-i Qurʾān ō taʿlīmāt-i ahl-i bayt ʿalayhim al-salām par mushtammil shahīd-i maẓlūm Sayyid ʿArif Ḥusayn al-Ḥusaynī ke khiṭābāt*. Edited by al-ʿĀrif Academy Lahore. Lahore: al-ʿĀrif Academy Lahore, 1996.
———. *Mīs̱āq-i khūn: Avāʾil-i qiyādat aur ḥauzah-i ʿilmiyyah ke mutaʿalliq shahīd qāʾid ke khiṭābāt*. Edited by al-ʿĀrif Academy Lahore. Lahore: al-ʿĀrif Academy Lahore, 1997.
———. *Sukhan-i ʿishq: Majālis-i ʿazāʾ-i sayyid al-shuhadāʾ*. Edited by al-ʿĀrif Academy Lahore. Lahore: al-ʿĀrif Academy Lahore, 1996.
———. *Uslūb-i siyāsat: Islām-i Muḥammad ke ijrāʾ aur ʿālamī umūr par qāʾid-i shahīd ke khiṭābāt*. Edited by Malik Javād. Lahore: al-ʿĀrif Academy Lahore, 2007.
Hussain, Syed Sultan Mahmood. *History of University Oriental College Lahore, 1870–2000*. Lahore: Izharsons, 2007.
el-Husseini, Rola. "Resistance, Jihad, and Martyrdom in Contemporary Lebanese Shiʿa Discourse." *Middle East Journal* 62 (2008): 399–414.
Hyder, Syed Akbar. *Reliving Karbala: Martyrdom in South Asian Memory*. New York: Oxford University Press, 2006.
Ibn Hishām, ʿAbd al-Malik, Muḥammad Ibn Isḥāq, and Alfred Guillaume. *The Life of Muhammad: A Translation [from Ibn Hishām's Adaptation] of Isḥāq's Sīrat Rasūl Allāh*. Karachi: Oxford University Press, 1967.
Ibn Taymiyya, Taqī al-Dīn Aḥmad b. ʿAbd al-Ḥalīm. *Minhāj al-sunna al-nabawiyya fī naqḍ kalām al-shīʿa wa-l-qadariyya*. Cairo: al-Maṭbaʿa al-Kubrā al-Amīriyya, 1904.
———. *Al-Ṣārim al-maslūl ʿalā shātim al-rasūl*. Ṭanṭā: Maktabat Tāj, 1960.
Ilahi, Shereen. "Sectarian Violence and the British Raj: The Muharram Riots of Lucknow." *India Review* 6, no. 3 (2007): 184–208.
Ingram, Brannon. "Crisis of the Public in Muslim India: Critiquing 'Custom' at Aligarh and Deoband." *South Asia: Journal of South Asian Studies* 38, no. 3 (2015): 403–18.

Intizar Husain, and Frances W. Pritchett. *Basti*. New York: New York Review of Books, 2012.
Iqtidar, Humeira. *Secularizing Islamists? Jama'at-e-Islami and Jama'at-ud-Da'wa in Urban Pakistan*. Chicago: University of Chicago Press, 2011.
"Īrān kā ʿaẓīm islāmī inqilāb aur ISO." *Rāh-i ʿAmal*, no. 11 (1980): 11–13.
Irfani, Suroosh. "Pakistan's Sectarian Violence: Between the 'Arabist Shift' and Indo-Persian Culture." In *Religious Radicalism and Security in South Asia*, edited by Satu P. Limaye, Mohan Malik, and Robert Wirsing, 147–69. Honolulu: Asia-Pacific Center for Security Studies, 2004.
Ismāʿīl, Muḥammad. *Barāhīn-i mātam*. Fayṣalābād: Muballigh-i Aʿẓam Academy, n.d.
———. *Futūḥāt-i shīʿah*. Edited by Nāṣir Ḥusayn Najafī. Jauharābād: Muballigh-i Aʿẓam Academy.
———. *Kalimah-i vilāyat*. Lyallpur: Idārah-i Dars-i Āl-i Muḥammad, 1977.
Ismail, Raihan. *Saudi Clerics and Shi'a Islam*. New York: Oxford University Press, 2016.
"ISO Pākistān kā universityōn̲ men̲ maqām ō kirdār." *Rāh-i ʿAmal*, no. 35 (1984): 18–20.
Ispahani, M. A. H. *The Case of Muslim India*. New York: Allendale Press, 1946.
"al-Istiftāʾ." *al-Ḥujjat* 10, no. 10 (1970): 8.
Jabali, Fuad. *The Companions of the Prophet: A Study of Geographical Distribution and Political Alignments*. Leiden: Brill, 2003.
Jaʿfar, Ḥusayn. *Sīrat Amīr al-Muʾminīn*. Lahore: Imāmiyyah Kutub Khānah, 1973.
Jaʿfar, Sayyid Muḥammad. "Dō fiqhī suʾālōn̲ ke javāb." *Payām-i ʿAmal* 14, no. 9 (1970): 31–33.
———. "Masāʾil-i sharʿiyyah aur un ke javābāt (August 1971)." *Payām-i ʿAmal* 15, no. 6 (1971): 19–20.
———. "Payām-i ʿAmal men̲ ʿamal kā payghām." *Payām-i ʿAmal* 14, no. 8 (1970): 7–8.
———. "Rasūl-i Khudā kī kitnī bīṭiyān̲ thī?" *Payām-i ʿAmal* 15, no. 7 (1971): 25–26.
———. "Taẕkirah-i mashāhīr-i shīʿah: Qiṣt-i duvum." *Payām-i ʿAmal* 14, nos. 3–4 (1970): 23–27.
Jaʿfarī, A. H., and ʿAyn Gha Karāravī. "Kahne kī bāten̲ (June 1966)." *al-Muntaẓar* 8, no. 7 (1966): 4–5.
———. "Marjiʿ-i vaqt kā iʿlān." *al-Muntaẓar* 12, no. 10 (1970): 15–18.
———. "Numāʾyandigān-i sarkār-i Āyatullāh al-ʿuẓmā Aqāʾ-i Sharīʿatmadār madda ẓillahu kā Pākistān men̲ vurūd-i suʿūd." *al-Muntaẓar* 13, nos. 9–10 (1971): 10–65.
———. "Taʿyīn-i marjiʿ-i vaqt aur ahl-i khibrah." *al-Muntaẓar* 12, nos. 19–20 (1970): 16–23.
Jaʿfarī, Sayyid Aḥmad Shāh Gardezī. *Taẕkirah-i sādāt-i gardeziyyah jaʿfariyyah*. Pūnch, 1929.
Jaʿfarī, Sayyid Khurram. "Sālānah Convention 1983 kī report ō taṣwīrī jhalkiyān̲." *Rāh-i ʿAmal*, no. 26 (1983): 9–15.
Jaffrelot, Christophe. *A History of Pakistan and Its Origins*. London: Anthem, 2002.
———. *Le syndrome pakistanais*. Paris: Fayard, 2013.

———. *The Pakistan Paradox: Instability and Resilience.* Oxford: Oxford University Press, 2016.

Jahanbakhsh, Forough. *Islam, Democracy and Religious Modernism in Iran, 1953–2000: From Bāzargān to Soroush.* Leiden: Brill, 2001.

Jalal, Ayesha. *The Sole Spokesman: Jinnah, the Muslim League and the Demand for Pakistan.* Cambridge: Cambridge University Press, 1985.

———. *The State of Martial Rule: The Origins of Pakistan's Political Economy of Defence.* Cambridge: Cambridge University Press, 1990.

Jalalzai, Musa Khan. *The Sunni-Shia Conflict in Pakistan.* Lahore: Book Traders, 1998.

"Jamāʿat-i ʿulamāʾ-i Baghdād kā maktūb." *al-Ḥujjat* 11, no. 10 (1970): 20–22.

Jāmiʿat al-Muntaẓar. *Ḥauzah ʿilmiyya Jāmiʿat al-Muntaẓar: Munfarad ō mumtāz markaz-i ʿilm ō hidāyat.* Lahore, 2012.

Jāṛā, Ḥusayn Bakhsh. *Lumʿat al-anwār fī ʿaqāʾid al-abrār.* Daryā Khān: Maktabat Anwār al-Najaf, 1992.

———. "Taużīḥāt (20 May 1965)." *al-Muntaẓar* 7, no. 5 (1965): 20.

———. "Taużīḥāt (20 June 1965)." *al-Muntaẓar* 7, no. 9 (1965): 12.

Jārcavī, Ibn-i Ḥasan. *Falsafah-i Āl-i Muḥammad.* Lucknow: Niẓāmī Press, 1940.

———. *Falsafah-i Āl-i Muḥammad.* Karachi: Raḥmat Allāh Book Agency, 1999.

Jārcavī, Sayyid Lāʾiq al-Ḥasan Riżvī Sabzvārī. *Jārcah: Savānih-i ʿAllāmah Ibn-i Ḥasan Riżvī Sabzvārī Jārcavī.* Lahore: Lāʾiq al-Ḥasan Riżvī Sabzvārī Jārcavī, 1981.

Javādī, Abū Muṣʿab. *Vazīr-i Aʿẓam, vuzarā-yi aʿlā, Qaumī Assembly, Senat, Ṣūbāʾī Assemblyōn ke arākīn, ʿadliyah, intiẓāmiyah ko pish kī jāne vālī tahqīqī dastāvez.* Rawalpindi: Markaz-i Muṭālaʿāt-i Islāmī-yi Pākistān, 1997.

Javād Naqvī, Sayyid. "Vārid-i dūrān-i nuqraʾī-yī ṣudūr-i inqilāb shudahʾīm." *Fars News Agency,* 5 September 2013. http://www.farsnews.com/newstext.php?nn=8807250070.

Jāved, Maḥbūb. "ʿAllāmah Iḥsān Ilāhī Ẓahīr se khuṣūṣ interview." In *ʿAllāmah shahīd-i millat number, al-maʿrūf maqālāt-i ʿAllāmah Iḥsān Ilāhī Ẓahīr,* edited by ʿAbd al-Raḥmān Munīr Rājūvālvī, 352–73. Lahore: Ahl-i Ḥadīs̱ Dār al-Ishāʿat, 1988.

Jawad Naqvi, Syed. *The System of Wilayat.* Qum: Matab, 2008.

Jiyad, Sajad. "Samarra: Shiʿi Heritage and Culture." In *The Shiʿa of Samarra: The Heritage and Politics of a Community in Iraq,* edited by Imranali Panjwani and Charles Tripp, 25–48. London: I. B. Tauris, 2012.

Jones, Justin. "The Local Experiences of Reformist Islam in a 'Muslim' Town in Colonial India: The Case of Amroha." *Modern Asian Studies* 43, no. 4 (2009): 871–908.

———. "'The Pakistan That Is Going to Be Sunnistan': Indian Shiʿa Responses to the Pakistan Movement." In *Muslims against the Muslim League: Critiques of the Idea of Pakistan,* edited by Ali Usman Qasmi and Megan Eaton Robb, 350–80. Cambridge: Cambridge University Press, 2017.

———. "Sectarianism and Identity Politics among the Shiʿa Muslims of Lucknow in Late-Colonial India." MPhil, Cambridge University, 2003.
———. *Shiʿa Islam in Colonial India: Religion, Community and Sectarianism.* Cambridge: Cambridge University Press, 2011.
———. "Shiʿism, Humanity and Revolution in Twentieth-Century India: Selfhood and Politics in the Husainology of ʿAli Naqi Naqvi." *Journal of the Royal Asiatic Society* 24, no. 3 (2014): 415–34.
———. "'Signs of Churning': Muslim Personal Law and Public Contestation in Twenty-First Century India." *Modern Asian Studies* 44, no. 1 (2010): 175–200.
———. "Urban Mythologies and Urbane Islam: Refining the Past and Present in Colonial-Era Lucknow." *South Asia Multidisciplinary Journal*, no. 11 (2015): 1–20.
Jones, Kenneth W. *Socio-Religious Reform Movements in British India.* Cambridge: Cambridge University Press, 1989.
Juneja, Monica, and Margrit Pernau. "Lost in Translation? Transcending Boundaries in Comparative History." In *Comparative History and the Quest for Transnationality: Central European Approaches and New Perspectives*, edited by Jürgen Kocka and Heinz-Gerhard Haupt, 105–29. New York: Berghahn Books, 2009.
Juynboll, G. H. A. *Muslim Tradition: Studies in Chronology, Provenance, and Authorship of Early Ḥadīth.* Cambridge: Cambridge University Press, 1983.
Kalbe Ali. "New Shia Party Emerging." *Dawn*, 23 April 2012.
Kamran, Tahir. "Contextualizing Sectarian Militancy in Pakistan: A Case Study of Jhang." *Journal of Islamic Studies* 20, no. 1 (2009): 55–85.
———. "Majlis-i-Ahrar-i-Islam: Religion, Socialism and Agitation in Action." *South Asian History and Culture* 4, no. 4 (2013): 465–82.
Kamran, Tahir, and Amir Khan Shahid. "Shariʿa, Shiʿas and Chishtiya Revivalism: Contextualising the Growth of Sectarianism in the Tradition of the Sialvi Saints of Punjab." In *The Shiʿa in Modern South Asia: Religion, History and Politics*, edited by Justin Jones and Ali Usman Qasmi, 159–78. New Delhi: Cambridge University Press, 2015.
Kandiyoti, Deniz. "Islam, Modernity and the Politics of Gender." In *Islam and Modernity*, edited by Muhammad Khalid Masud, Armando Salvatore, and Martin van Bruinessen, 91–124. Edinburgh: Edinburgh University Press, 2009.
Karamustafa, Ahmet T. *God's Unruly Friends: Dervish Groups in the Islamic Later Middle Period, 1200–1550.* Salt Lake City: University of Utah Press, 1994.
Kashani-Sabet, Firoozeh. *Conceiving Citizens: Women and the Politics of Motherhood in Iran.* Oxford: Oxford University Press, 2011.
Kashmīrī, Akbar Ḥaydarī. *Iqbāl aur ʿAllāmah Shaykh Zanjānī: Maʿ Vaḥī ō ilhām aur burhān-i imāmat.* Srīnagar: Akbar Ḥaydar Kashmīrī, 2006.
Kashmīrī, Sayyid Muḥsin Ḥusayn. *Dānishnāmah-i Shīʿīyān-i Kashmīr.* Karachi: Markaz-i Iḥyāʾ-i Āṣār-i Barr-i Ṣaghīr, 2011.
Kāẓim, Sayyid Amīr. *Iḥqāq al-ḥaqq li-ibṭāl al-bāṭil bi-radd al-ibṭāl uṣūl al-shīʿa bi-l-dalāʾil al-ʿaqīla.* Nakinah: Riyāẓ Fayẓ Press.

Kāẓim, Shaykh Muḥammad. *Tanqīd al-Taqlīd*. Jaunpūr: Kāẓimī Press, 1914.
Kāẓimī, Ghażanfar. *Muftī Ja'far Ḥusayn marḥūm (1914–1983): Ayām-i raftah par mukhtaṣar naẓar*. N.p., 1983.
Kāẓimī, Muqaddas. "Shahīd qā'id ke qātil kōn?" *Rāh-i 'Amal*, no. 63 (1989): 3–4.
Kāẓimī, Sayyid Muḥammad Ṣaqalayn. "Muqaddamah." In *Imāmiyyah dīnī madāris-i Pākistān*, edited by Sayyid Muḥammad Ṣaqalayn Kāẓimī. Lahore: Wifāq al-Madāris al-Shī'a Pākistān, 2004.
Keddie, Nikki R. *Religion and Rebellion in Iran: The Tobacco Protest of 1891–1892*. London: Frank Cass, 1966.
———. *The Shi'a of Pakistan: Reflections and Problems for Further Research*. Los Angeles: G. E. Grunebaum Center for Near Eastern Studies, 1993.
———. "Shī'ism and Change: Secularism and Myth." In *Shī'ite Heritage: Essays on Classical and Modern Traditions*, edited by Lynda Clarke, 389–406. Binghamton: Global, 2001.
Kennedy, Charles H. "Islamization and Legal Reform in Pakistan, 1979–1989." *Pacific Affairs* 63, no. 1 (1990): 62–77.
Kerr, Ian J. "The Railway Workshops of Lahore and their Employees: 1863–1930." In *Punjab in Perspective: Proceedings of the Research Committee on Punjab Conference 1987*, edited by Surjit S. Dulai and Arthur Wesley Helweg, 67–77. East Lansing: Asian Studies Center, Michigan State University, 1987.
Kerr, Malcolm H. *Islamic Reform: The Political and Legal Theories of Muhammad Abduh and Rashid Rida*. Berkeley: University of California Press, 1966.
Kersten, Carool, and Susanne Olsson. "Introduction: Alternative Islamic Discourses and Religious Authority." In *Alternative Islamic Discourses and Religious Authority*, edited by Carool Kersten and Susanne Olsson, 1–15. Farnham: Ashgate, 2013.
Khalek, Nancy. "Medieval Biographical Literature and the Companions of Muḥammad." *Der Islam* 91, no. 2 (2014): 272–94.
Khalilzad, Zalmay. "The Iranian Revolution and the Afghan Resistance." In *Shi'ism, Resistance, and Revolution*, edited by Martin Kramer, 257–73. Boulder: Westview Press, 1987.
al-Khāliṣī, Muḥammad. *Iḥyā' al-sharī'a fī madhhab al-shī'a (qism al-'aqā'id)*. Tehran: Al-Shaykh Hāshim al-Dabbāgh, 1998.
Khan, Abdul Rashid. *The All India Muslim Educational Conference: Its Contribution to the Cultural Development of Indian Muslims, 1886–1947*. Karachi: Oxford University Press, 2001.
Khān, Aḥmad Riżā. "'Ālamī ḥālāt aur āj kā Muslim." *Rāh-i 'Amal*, no. 32 (1984): 8–11.
Khan, Hasan Ali. *Constructing Islam on the Indus: The Material History of the Suhrawardi Sufi Order, 1200–1500 AD*. Cambridge: Cambridge University Press, 2016.
Khan, Mirza Sajjad Ali. *Why 14,000 Shias Went to Jail? U.P. Congress Government*

and Justice—"Fundamental Rights of People Overthrown"—Severe Repression of the Shia Minority. Lucknow: Tanzeem-ul-Momineen, 1939.
Khan, Muhammad Amir Ahmad. "Local Nodes of a Transnational Network: A Case Study of a Shi'i Family in Awadh, 1900–1950." In *The Shi'a in Modern South Asia: Religion, History and Politics*, edited by Justin Jones and Ali Usman Qasmi, 57–79. New Delhi: Cambridge University Press, 2015.
Khān, Muḥammad Gulshīr. *Khōlā khāṭṭ Muḥibbān-i Ḥusayn ʿalayhi al-salām ke nām.* Dīūlghaṭ, 1916.
Khān, Muḥammad Vaṣī. *Tashkīl-i Pākistān meṉ shīʿān-i ʿAlī kā kirdār.* Karachi: Mirzā ʿAlī Saʿīd, 1982.
Khan, Naveeda. "Mosque Construction or the Violence of the Ordinary." In *Beyond Crisis: Re-Evaluating Pakistan*, edited by Naveeda Khan, 482–518. London: Routledge, 2010.
———. *Muslim Becoming: Aspiration and Skepticism in Pakistan.* Durham, NC: Duke University Press, 2012.
———. "Of Children and Jinns: An Enquiry into an Unexpected Friendship during Uncertain Times." In *Islam and Society in Pakistan: Anthropological Perspectives*, edited by Magnus Marsden, 1–33. Karachi: Oxford University Press, 2010.
Khan, Sarfraz, and Hafeez-ur-Rehman Chaudry. "Major Consequences of the Sectarian Militancy in Jhang, Pakistan." *Academic Research International* 1, no. 3 (2011): 73–81.
Khān, Taslīm Riżā. "Pākistān kā aham masʾalah aur us ki ḥall." *al-ʿĀrif* 2, no. 2 (1991): 41–42.
———. *Safīr-i inqilāb shahīd Doctor Muḥammad ʿAlī Naqvī.* Lahore: Al-ʿĀrif, 2013.
———. *Safīr-i nūr.* Lahore: al-ʿĀrif Academy Lahore, 1998.
———. *Zindagīnāmah-i ʿAllāmah Shahīd ʿĀrif Ḥusayn al-Ḥusaynī az vilādat tā shahādat.* Qum: Muʾassasah-i Shahīd al-Ḥusaynī, 1990.
Khan, Zaigham. "The Fanatics Strike Back." *The Herald*, October 1996, 52–57.
Khaṭīb, Muḥibb al-Dīn. *Al-Khuṭūṭ al-ʿarīḍa lil-usus allatī qāma ʿalayhā dīn al-shīʿa al-imāmiyya al-ithnā ʿashariyya.* Cairo: al-Maṭbaʿa al-Salafiyya, 1968.
Khomeini, Ruhollah, and Hamid Algar. *Islam and Revolution: Writings and Declarations of Imam Khomeini.* Berkeley: Mizan Press, 1981.
al-Khūʾī, Sayyid Abū ʾl-Qāsim. "Istiftāʾ." *Payām-i ʿAmal* 15, no. 7 (1971): 39.
Khumaynī, Rūḥallāh al-Mūsavī. "ʿAuratōṉ kā din." *Rāh-i ʿAmal*, no. 18 (1981): 7.
———. *Vilāyat-i faqīh (ḥukūmat-i islāmī).* Tehran: Amīr Kabīr, 1978.
Khurasānī, Muḥammad Hāshim b. Muḥammad. *Muntakhab al-tawārīkh.* Tehran: Muḥammad Ḥasan ʿAlamī, 1960.
Khurramābādī, Ḥasan Ṭāhirī, and Muḥammad Riżā Aḥmadī Ṭālishiyyān. *Khāṭirāt-i Āyatullāh Ṭāhirī Khurramābādī.* Tehran: Markaz-i Asnād-i Inqilāb-i Islāmī, 1998 or 1999.
Klemm, Verena. "Orthodoxie versus Heterodoxie? Europäisch-christliche Konzepte und Begrifflichkeiten in den Schia-Studien." In *Orient—Orientalistik—*

Orientalismus: Geschichte und Aktualität einer Debatte, edited by Burkhard Schnepel, 71–92. Bielefeld: transcript, 2010.
Knysh, Alexander. "'Irfan' Revisited: Khomeini and the Legacy of Islamic Mystical Philosophy." *Middle East Journal* 46, no. 4 (1992): 631–53.
———. "'Orthodoxy' and 'Heresy' in Medieval Islam: An Essay in Reassessment." *Muslim World* 83, no. 1 (1993): 48–67.
Kocka, Jürgen, and Heinz-Gerhard Haupt. "Comparison and Beyond: Traditions, Scope, and Perspectives of Comparative History." In *Comparative History and the Quest for Transnationality: Central European Approaches and New Perspectives*, edited by Jürgen Kocka and Heinz-Gerhard Haupt, 1–30. New York: Berghahn Books, 2009.
Kohlberg, Etan. "The Attitude of Imāmī Shīʿīs to the Companions of the Prophet." DPhil diss., University of Oxford, 1971.
———. "The Evolution of the Shīʿa." *Jerusalem Quarterly* 27 (1983): 109–26.
———. "Imam and Community in the Pre-Ghayba Period." In *Authority and Political Culture in Shiʿism*, edited by Said Amir Arjomand, 25–53. Albany: State University of New York Press, 1988.
———. "Some Imāmī-Shīʿī Views on *taqiyya*." *Journal of the American Oriental Society* 95 (1975): 395–402.
———. "Some Imāmī Shīʿī Views on the Ṣaḥāba." *Jerusalem Studies in Arabic and Islam* 5 (1984): 143–75.
Krämer, Gudrun, and Sabine Schmidtke. "Introduction: Religious Authority and Religious Authorities in Muslim Societies. A Critical Overview." In *Speaking for Islam: Religious Authorities in Muslim Societies*, edited by Gudrun Krämer and Sabine Schmidtke, 1–14. Leiden: Brill, 2006.
Kugle, Scott Alan. "Framed, Blamed and Renamed: The Recasting of Islamic Jurisprudence in Colonial South Asia." *Modern Asian Studies* 35, no. 2 (2001): 257–313.
Kumar, Anand, and Frank Welz. "Culture in the World-System: An Interview with Immanuel Wallerstein." *Social Identities: Journal for the Study of Race, Nation and Culture* 7, no. 2 (2001): 221–31.
Künkler, Mirjam, and Roja Fazaeli. "The Life of Two Mujtahidahs: Female Religious Authority in Twentieth-Century Iran." In *Women, Leadership and Mosques: Changes in Contemporary Islamic Authority*, edited by Masooda Bano and Hilary Kalmbach, 127–60. Leiden: Brill, 2012.
Kurzman, Charles. *The Unthinkable Revolution in Iran*. Cambridge, MA: Harvard University Press, 2004.
Lacroix, Stéphane. *Awakening Islam: The Politics of Religious Dissent in Contemporary Saudi Arabia*. Cambridge, MA: Harvard University Press, 2011.
Lahidji, Abdol Karim. "Constitutionalism and Clerical Authority." In *Authority and Political Culture in Shiʿism*, edited by Said Amir Arjomand, 133–58. Albany: State University of New York Press, 1988.
"Lāhōr kī qābil-i iʿtirāẓ kitāb." *Sarfarāz*, 29 November 1942, 4.

Lakhnavī, Mirzā Muḥammad Hādī ʿAzīz. *Shahīd-i s̱ālis̱*. Lucknow: Munshī Naval Kishūr, 1916.

Lalljee, Hooseinbhoy Abdoolabhoy. *Shia Muslims' Case*. Bombay: Jawahir P. Press, 1946.

Lambton, Ann K. S. "A Reconsideration of the Position of the Marja' Al-Taqlid and the Religious Institution." *Studia Islamica* 20 (1964): 115–35.

Landau-Tasseron, Ella. "The 'Cyclical Reform': A Study of the Mujaddid Tradition." *Studia Islamica*, no. 70 (1989): 79–117.

Langley, Edward Archer. *Narrative of a Residence at the Court of Meer Ali Moorad; with Wild Sports in the Valley of the Indus*. London: Hurst and Blackett, 1860.

Laoust, Henri. "La biographie d'Ibn Taimīya d'après Ibn Kaṯīr." *Bulletin d'Études Orientales* 9 (1942–43): 115–62.

———. "La critique du sunnisme dans la doctrine d'al-Ḥillī." *Revue des Études Islamique*, no. 34 (1966): 35–60.

———. *Essai sur les doctrines sociales et politiques de Takī-d-Dīn Ahmad b. Taimīya*. Cairo: Impr. de l'Institut français d'archéologie orientale, 1939.

Latham, J. D. "The Raja of Mahmudabad (1914–1973)." *Bulletin of the British Society for Middle Eastern Studies* 1, no. 1 (1974): 41–43.

Lauzière, Henri. *The Making of Salafism: Islamic Reform in the Twentieth Century*. New York: Columbia University Press, 2016.

Lefebvre, Alain. *Kinship, Honour and Money in Rural Pakistan: Subsistence Economy and the Effects of International Migration*. Richmond, UK: Curzon, 1999.

Leichtman, Mara A. "Migration, War, and the Making of a Transnational Lebanese Shiʿi Community in Senegal." *International Journal of Middle East Studies* 42 (2010): 269–90.

Lelyveld, David. *Aligarh's First Generation: Muslim Solidarity in British India*. Princeton, NJ: Princeton University Press, 1978.

Litvak, Meir. "'More Harmful Than the Jews': Anti-Shiʿi Polemics in Modern Radical Sunni Discourse." In *Le Shīʿisme Imāmite quarante ans après: Hommage à Etan Kohlberg*, edited by Mohammad Ali Amir-Moezzi, Meir M. Bar-Asher, and Simon Hopkins. Turnhout: Brepols, 2009.

———. *Shiʿi Scholars and Patrons of Nineteenth-Century Iraq: The 'Ulama' of Najaf and Karbala'*. Cambridge: Cambridge University Press, 1998.

Llewellyn-Jones, Rosie. *A Fatal Friendship: The Nawabs, the British, and the City of Lucknow*. Delhi: Oxford University Press, 1985.

Lodhi, Maleeha. "Pakistan's Shia Movement: An Interview with Arif Hussaini." *Third World Quarterly* 10, no. 2 (1988): 806–17.

Louër, Laurence. *Transnational Shia Politics: Religious and Political Networks in the Gulf*. London: Hurst, 2008.

Lucas, Scott C. *Constructive Critics, Ḥadīth Literature, and the Articulation of Sunnī Islam: The Legacy of the Generation of Ibn Saʿd, Ibn Maʿīn, and Ibn Ḥanbal*. Leiden: Brill, 2004.

MacEoin, Denis. "Orthodoxy and Heterodoxy in Nineteenth-Century Shiʿism: The Cases of Shaykhism and Babism." *Journal of the American Oriental Society* 110, no. 2 (1990): 323–29.

———. *The Sources for Early Bābī Doctrine and History: A Survey*. Leiden: Brill, 1992.

Machlis, Elisheva. "The Cross-Sectarian Call for Islam: A Sample of Shiʿa Reformist Thought." *Journal of Shiʿa Islamic Studies* 2, no. 2 (2009): 195–219.

———. *Shiʿi Sectarianism in the Middle East: Modernisation and the Quest for Islamic Universalism*. London: I. B. Tauris, 2014.

Madanī, Sayyid Ḥusayn Aḥmad. *Maktūbāt-i Shaykh al-Islām*. Edited by Najm al-Dīn Iṣlāḥī. Deoband: Maktabah-i Dīniyyah, 1952–64.

———. *Naqsh-i ḥayāt: Khūdnavisht-i savāniḥ-i ḥażrat Maulānā Sayyid Ḥusayn Aḥmad ṣāhib Madanī*. Karachi: Farzand-i Tauḥīd, 1973.

Madelung, Wilferd. "Authority in Twelver Shiism in the Absence of the Imam." In *Religious Schools and Sects in Medieval Islam*, edited by Wilferd Madelung, 163–72. London: Variorum Reprints, 1985.

———. *The Succession to Muḥammad: A Study of the Early Caliphate*. Cambridge: Cambridge University Press, 1997.

Magnusson, Jan. "The Baltistan Movement and the Power of Pop Ghazals." *Asian Ethnology* 70, no. 1 (2011): 33–57.

Mahmudabad, Ali Khan. "Enemy Property Bill: 'Vilifying Son for Sins of Father.'" *News18*, 17 March 2017.

"M. A. Jinnah to Syed Ali Zaheer, SHC (127)." In *Quaid-i-Azam Mohammad Ali Jinnah Papers: Consolidating the Muslim League for Final Struggle, 1 August 1944–31 July 1945*, edited by Zawwar Husain Zaidi, 108–9. Islamabad: Quaid-i-Azam Papers Project, National Archives of Pakistan, 2005.

Makdisi, Ussama Samir. *The Culture of Sectarianism: Community, History, and Violence in Nineteenth-Century Ottoman Lebanon*. Berkeley: University of California Press, 2000.

Malik, Iʿjāz Ḥusayn. "Īrān se wāpasī par Maulānā Ṣafdar Ḥusayn Najafī se ek interview." *Rāh-i ʿAmal*, no. 8 (1979): 11–12.

Malik, Ikram Ali. "Muslim Anjumans and Communitarian Consciousness." In *Five Punjabi Centuries: Polity, Economy, Society, and Culture, c. 1500–1990. Essays for J. S. Grewal*, edited by Indu Banga, 112–25. New Delhi: Manohar, 1997.

Malik, Jamal. *Colonialization of Islam: Dissolution of Traditional Institutions in Pakistan*. New Delhi: Manohar, 1996.

———. "Introduction." In *Madrasas in South Asia: Teaching Terror?*, edited by Jamal Malik, 1–22. London: Routledge, 2008.

———. "Islamic Mission and Call: The Case of the International Islamic University, Islamabad." *Islam and Christian-Muslim Relations* 9, no. 1 (1998): 121–44.

———. *Islamische Gelehrtenkultur in Nordindien: Entwicklungsgeschichte und Tendenzen am Beispiel von Lucknow*. Leiden: Brill, 1997.

Mallat, Chibli. *The Renewal of Islamic Law: Muhammad Baqer as-Sadr, Najaf and the Shi'i International.* Cambridge: Cambridge University Press, 1995.

Mansergh, Nicholas, E. W. R. Lumby, and Penderel Moon. *The Transfer of Power 1942–7.* London: HMSO, 1970–83.

Maréchal, Brigitte, and Sami Zemni. "Conclusion: Analyzing Contemporary Sunnite-Shiite Relationships." In *The Dynamics of Sunni-Shia Relationships: Doctrine, Transnationalism, Intellectuals and the Media,* edited by Brigitte Maréchal and Sami Zemni, 215–41. London: Hurst, 2012.

"Marjiʿ-i vaqt kā ʿamaliyyah-i tauẓīḥ al-masāʾil." *al-Muntaẓar* 12, no. 10 (1970): 25.

Marsden, Magnus. *Living Islam: Muslim Religious Experience in Pakistan's North-West Frontier.* Cambridge: Cambridge University Press, 2005.

Martin, Richard C., and Abbas Barzegar. "Formations of Orthodoxy: Authority, Power, and Networks in Muslim Societies." In *Rethinking Islamic Studies: From Orientalism to Cosmopolitanism,* edited by Carl W. Ernst and Richard C. Martin, 179–202. Columbia: University of South Carolina Press, 2010.

Martin, Vanessa. *Iran between Islamic Nationalism and Secularism: The Constitutional Revolution of 1906.* London: I. B. Tauris, 2013.

Mashhadī, Ṣafdar Ḥusayn. "Ek aham tavajjuh dahānī." *al-Ḥujjat* 10, no. 10 (1970): 27–30.

———. "Ek khaṭāʾ aur us kī javāb." *al-Ḥujjat* 12, no. 3 (1971): 28–33.

———. "Marājiʿ al-taqlīd." *al-Ḥujjat* 10, no. 11 (1970): 19–22.

———. "Masʾalah-i taqlīd se ʿadam wāqafiyyat aur us ke nuqṣānāt." *al-Ḥujjat* 17, no. 9 (1977): 11–19.

———. "Shīʿōn̲ ke tanazzul ke asbāb: Qisṭ-i 10." *al-Ḥujjat* 2, no. 5 (1962): 10–12.

———. "Shīʿōn̲ ke tanazzul ke asbāb: Qisṭ-i 11." *al-Ḥujjat* 2, no. 6 (1962): 7–8.

———. "Shīʿōn̲ ke tanazzul ke asbāb: Qisṭ-i 12." *al-Ḥujjat* 2, no. 7 (1962): 5–7.

———. "Shīʿōn̲ ke tanazzul ke asbāb: Qisṭ-i 15." *al-Ḥujjat* 2, no. 10 (1962): 13–17.

———. "Shīʿōn̲ ke tanazzul ke asbāb: Qisṭ-i 16." *al-Ḥujjat* 2, no. 11 (1963): 29–30.

———. "Shīʿōn̲ ke tanazzul ke asbāb: Qisṭ-i 17." *al-Ḥujjat* 2, no. 12 (1963): 6–7.

———. "Shīʿōn̲ ke tanazzul ke asbāb: Qisṭ-i 18." *al-Ḥujjat* 3, no. 2 (1963): 8–9.

———. "Shīʿōn̲ ke tanazzul ke asbāb: Qisṭ-i 21." *al-Ḥujjat* 3, no. 5 (1963): 20–23.

———. "Shīʿōn̲ ke tanazzul ke asbāb: Qisṭ-i 23." *al-Ḥujjat* 3, no. 8 (1963): 12–15.

———. "Shīʿōn̲ ke tanazzul ke asbāb: Qisṭ-i 27." *al-Ḥujjat* 4, no. 2 (1964): 30–32.

———. "Shīʿōn̲ ke tanazzul ke asbāb: Qisṭ-i 29." *al-Ḥujjat* 4, no. 4 (1964): 12–13.

———. "Taqlīd-i aʿlam ō sharāʾiṭ-i taqlīd." *al-Ḥujjat* 10, no. 11 (1970): 26–27.

Masud, Muhammad Khalid. "Islamic Modernism." In *Islam and Modernity,* edited by Muhammad Khalid Masud, Armando Salvatore, and Martin van Bruinessen, 237–60. Edinburgh: Edinburgh University Press, 2009.

Masud, Muhammad Khalid, and Armando Salvatore. "Western Scholars of Islam on the Issue of Modernity." In *Islam and Modernity,* edited by Muhammad Khalid Masud, Armando Salvatore, and Martin van Bruinessen, 36–53. Edinburgh: Edinburgh University Press, 2009.

Matthiesen, Toby. "Mysticism, Migration and Clerical Networks: Ahmad al-Ahsa'i and the Shaykhis of al-Ahsa, Kuwait and Basra." *Journal of Muslim Minority Affairs* 34, no. 4 (2014): 386–409.

———. *The Other Saudis: Shiism, Dissent and Sectarianism.* New York: Cambridge University Press, 2015.

———. *Sectarian Gulf: Bahrain, Saudi Arabia, and the Arab Spring That Wasn't.* Stanford, CA: Stanford University Press, 2013.

McDermott, Martin J. *The Theology of al-Shaikh al-Mufid (d. 413/1022).* Beirut: Dar el-Machreq éditeurs, 1978.

Medoff, Louis Abraham. "Ijtihad and Renewal in Qur'anic Hermeneutics: An Analysis of Muḥammad Ḥusayn Ṭabāṭabā'ī's al-Mīzān fī Tafsīr al-Qur'ān." PhD diss., University of California, Berkeley, 2007.

Melvin-Koushki, Matthew S. "The Quest for a Universal Science: The Occult Philosophy of Ṣā'in al-Dīn Turka Iṣfahānī (1369–1432) and Intellectual Millenarianism in Early Timurid Iran." PhD diss., Yale University, 2012.

Menashri, David. *Post-Revolutionary Politics in Iran: Religion, Society, and Power.* London: Frank Cass, 2001.

Mervin, Sabrina. "Les autorités religieuses dans le chiisme duodécimain contemporain." *Archives de sciences sociales des religions* 49, no. 125 (2004): 63–77.

———. "The Clerics of Jabal 'Amil and the Reform of Religious Teaching in Najaf since the Beginning of the 20th Century." In *The Twelver Shia in Modern Times: Religious Culture and Political History,* edited by Rainer Brunner and Werner Ende, 79–86. Leiden: Brill, 2001.

———. "Introduction." In *The Shi'a Worlds and Iran,* edited by Sabrina Mervin, 9–23. London: Saqi, 2010.

———. "On Sunnite-Shiite Doctrinal and Contemporary Geopolitical Tensions." In *The Dynamics of Sunni-Shia Relationships: Doctrine, Transnationalism, Intellectuals and the Media,* edited by Brigitte Maréchal and Sami Zemni, 11–24. London: Hurst, 2012.

———. "La quête du savoir à Naǧaf: Les études religieuses chez les chi'ites imâmites de la fin du XIXe siècle à 1960." *Studia Islamica* 81 (1995): 165–85.

———. *Un réformisme chiite: Ulémas et lettrés du Ǧabal 'Āmil, actuel Liban-Sud, de la fin de l'Empire ottoman à l'indépendance du Liban.* Paris: Karthala, 2000.

———. "Transnational Intellectual Debates." In *The Shi'a Worlds and Iran,* edited by Sabrina Mervin, 321–46. London: Saqi, 2010.

Mervin, Sabrina, Yasser Tabbaa, and Erick Bonnier. *Najaf: The Gate of Wisdom. History, Heritage and Significance of the Holy City of the Shi'a.* Paris: Unesco, 2014.

Metcalf, Barbara D. *Husain Ahmad Madani: The Jihad for Islam and India's Freedom.* Oxford: Oneworld, 2009.

———. *Islamic Revival in British India: Deoband, 1860–1900.* Princeton, NJ: Princeton University Press, 1982.

———. "Maulana Husain Ahmad Madani and the Jami'at 'Ulama-i-Hind: Against Pakistan, against the Muslim League." In *Muslims against the Muslim League: Critiques of the Idea of Pakistan,* edited by Ali Usman Qasmi and Megan Eaton Robb, 35–64. New York: Cambridge University Press, 2017.
———. "The Pilgrimage Remembered: South Asian Accounts of the Hajj." In *Muslim Travellers: Pilgrimage, Migration, and the Religious Imagination,* edited by Dale F. Eickelman and James P. Piscatori, 85–107. London: Routledge, 1990.
Meyer, Egbert. "Anlaß und Anwendungsbereich der *taqiyya.*" *Der Islam* 57, no. 2 (1980): 246–80.
———. "Tendenzen der Schiaforschung: Corbins Auffassung von der Schia." *Zeitschrift der Deutschen Morgenländischen Gesellschaft,* suppl. 3, no. 1 (1977).
Middell, Matthias. "Kulturtransfer und transnationale Geschichte." In *Dimensionen der Kultur- und Gesellschaftsgeschichte: Festschrift für Hannes Siegrist zum 60. Geburtstag,* edited by Matthias Middell, 49–69. Leipzig: Leipziger Universitätsverlag, 2007.
Milam, William B. *Bangladesh and Pakistan: Flirting with Failure in South Asia.* New York: Columbia University Press, 2011.
Miller, Michael Barry. "Pilgrim's Progress: The Business of the Hajj." *Past and Present,* no. 191 (2006): 189–228.
Millward, William G. "Aspects of Modernism in Shīʿa Islam." *Studia Islamica* 37 (1973): 111–28.
Minault, Gail. *The Khilafat Movement: Religious Symbolism and Political Mobilization in India.* New York: Columbia University Press, 1982.
———. *Secluded Scholars: Women's Education and Muslim Social Reform in Colonial India.* Delhi: Oxford University Press, 1998.
Mir, Amir. *The True Face of Jehadis.* Lahore: Mashal Books, 2004.
Mir, Farina. "Genre and Devotion in Punjabi Popular Narratives: Rethinking Cultural and Religious Syncretism." In *Punjab Reconsidered: History, Culture, and Practice,* edited by Anshu Malhotra, and Farina Mir, 221–60. New Delhi: Oxford University Press, 2012.
Mir-Hosseini, Ziba. *Islam and Gender: The Religious Debate in Contemporary Iran.* Princeton, NJ: Princeton University Press, 1999.
Mitra, Nripendra Nath. *The Indian Annual Register: An Annual Digest of Public Affairs of India,* vol. 1: *January–June 1940.* Calcutta: Annual Register Office, 1940.
Modarressi, Hossein. *Crisis and Consolidation in the Formative Period of Shiʿite Islam: Abū Jaʿfar ibn Qiba al-Rāzī and His Contribution to Imāmite Shīʿite Thought.* Princeton, NJ: Darwin Press, 1993.
———. "Early Debates on the Integrity of the Qur'an: A Brief Survey." *Studia Islamica* 77 (1993): 5–39.
———. "Review: The Just Ruler or the Guardian Jurist: An Attempt to Link Two Different Shi'ite Concepts." *Journal of the American Oriental Society* 111, no. 3 (1991): 549–62.

Moin, A. Afzar. "Margins of Anxiety and Centres of Confidence." *South Asian History and Culture* 5, no. 2 (2014): 262–65.
Moin, Baqer. *Khomeini: Life of the Ayatollah.* New York: St. Martin's, 2000.
Momen, Moojan. *An Introduction to Shiʿi Islam: The History and Doctrines of Twelver Shiʿism.* New Haven, CT: Yale University Press, 1985.
Moslem, Mehdi. *Factional Politics in Post-Khomeini Iran.* Syracuse: Syracuse University Press, 2002.
Mostyn, Trevor. "Ali Akbar Hashemi Rafsanjani Obituary." *The Guardian,* 8 January 2017.
Mottahedeh, Roy P. *Loyalty and Leadership in an Early Islamic Society.* Princeton, NJ: Princeton University Press, 1980.
———. *The Mantle of the Prophet: Religion and Politics in Iran.* New York: Oneworld, 2014.
———. "Traditional Shiʿite Education in Qom." In *Philosophers on Education: Historical Perspectives,* edited by Amélie Oksenberg Rorty, 451–57. London: Routledge, 1998.
Moussavi, Ahmad Kazemi. "The Establishment of the Position of Marjaʿiyyt-i [*sic*] Taqlid in the Twelver-Shiʿi Community." *Iranian Studies* 18, no. 1 (1985): 35–51.
———. "The Institutionalization of Marjaʿ-i Taqlīd in the Nineteenth Century Shīʿite Community." *Muslim World* 83, nos. 3–4 (1994): 279–99.
Mufti, Aamir. *Enlightenment in the Colony: The Jewish Question and the Crisis of Postcolonial Culture.* Princeton, NJ: Princeton University Press, 2007.
Muḥaddis̱ Dihlavī, Shāh Walī Allāh. *Fuyūḍ al-ḥaramayn maʿ urdū tarjumah saʿādat-i kaunayn.* Ḥaydarābād: Shah Wali Allah Academy, 2007.
———. *Izālat al-khafāʾ ʿan khilāfat al-khulafāʾ.* Lahore: Suhayl Academy, 1976.
Muḥī al-Dīn, Sayyid Aḥmad. *Shamshīr-i Ḥusayn.* Madrās: Bashīr Khān, 1930 (?).
Mulsow, Martin, and Andreas Mahler. "Einleitung." In *Die Cambridge School der politischen Ideengeschichte,* edited by Martin Mulsow and Andreas Mahler, 7–20. Berlin: Suhrkamp, 2010.
Multānī, Sayyid Muḥammad ʿĀrif. "Ahl-i Panjāb ke liye ʿibrat." *Sarfarāz,* 1 November 1929, 3–4.
al-Muqarram, ʿAbd al-Razzāq al-Mūsawī. *Sirr al-īmān: Al-Shahāda al-thālitha fī ʾl-adhān.* Dār al-Firdaus, 1986.
Murphy, Eamon. *The Making of Terrorism in Pakistan: Historical and Social Roots of Extremism.* New York: Routledge, 2013.
Murtażā, Ḥasan. "Qaṭrah se gohr hone tak: Shahīd ʿAllāmah Muḥammad Ḥasan Turābī." In *Shahīd-i rāh-i vaḥdat: ʿAllāmah Ḥasan Turābī shahīd,* edited by Ḥasan Murtażā, 48–93. Karachi: Idārah-i Taḥaffuẓ-i Ās̱ār-i Shuhadāʾ-i Islām (Pākistān), 2007.
"Muṣāḥabah bā hażrat Āyatullāh Ḥājj Shaykh Muḥammad Ḥusayn Najafī Pākistānī." *Ḥauzah* 123 (2004): 126–81.
"Musalmānān-i Hind kī qaumī taʿmīr kā suʾāl." *Sarfarāz,* 5 December 1942, 2.

Mūsavī ʿAlīābādī, Sayyid ʿAlī Sharaf al-Dīn. *ʿAqāʾid ō rusūmāt-i shīʿah*. Karachi: Dār al-Thaqāfa al-Islāmiyya Pākistān, 2004.

———. *Asrār-i qiyām-i Imām Ḥusayn aur hamārī ẕimahdārīyāṉ*. Karachi: Dār al-Thaqāfa al-Islāmiyya Pākistān, 1999.

———. *Dār al-Thaqāfa al-Islāmiyya se ʿUrwa al-Wuthqā*. Karachi: Dār al-Thaqāfa al-Islāmiyya Pākistān, 2013.

———. "Imām Ḥusayn ʿalayhi al-salām aur iṣlāḥ-i muʿāsharah." *Rāh-i ʿAmal*, nos. 33–34 (1984): 31–35.

———. *Intikhāb-i maṣāʾib: Tarjīḥāt, tarmīmāt*. Karachi: Dār al-Thaqāfa al-Islāmiyya Pākistān, 2000.

———. *Madāris-i dīnī aur ḥauzāt-i ʿilmiyya par nagārshāt*. Karachi: Dār al-Thaqāfa al-Islāmiyya Pākistān, 2003.

———. *Miṡālī ʿazādārī kayse manāʾyeṉ?* Karachi: Dār al-Thaqāfa al-Islāmiyya Pākistān, 1996.

———. *Tafsīr-i siyāsī-yi qiyām-i Imām Ḥusayn*. Karachi: Dār al-Thaqāfa al-Islāmiyya Pākistān, 1996.

Mushtāq, ʿAbd al-Karīm. *Ayṭam bam kā dūsrā nām Anjuman-i Sipāh-i Ṣaḥābah-i Pākistān: Fitnah-i nāṣibiyyat ō khārijiyyat*. Karachi: Maktabat al-Difāʿ, 1997.

"Muslim League aur ham." *Sarfarāz*, 12 December 1942, 2–3.

Muslims in India: A Biographical Dictionary, vol. 1: *(A–J)*. Lahore: Vanguard Books, 1985.

Muslims in India: A Biographical Dictionary, vol. 2: *(K–Z)*. Lahore: Vanguard Books, 1985.

Muṭahharī, Murtażā. "Ẓuhūr-i mujaddid-i dīn dar har ṣad sāl." http://www.mortezamotahari.com/fa/questionview.html?QuestionID=62435. Posted 13 February 2012.

al-Muẓaffar, Muḥammad Riḍā. *Al-ʿAqāʾid al-imāmiyya*. Cairo: Maktabat al-Najāh, 1961.

Nagel, Tilman. *Die Festung des Glaubens: Triumph und Scheitern des islamischen Rationalismus im 11. Jh.* Munich: Beck, 1988.

Nair, Neeti. "Beyond the 'Communal' 1920s: The Problem of Intention, Legislative Pragmatism, and the Making of Section 295A of the Indian Penal Code." *Indian Economic and Social History Review* 50, no. 3 (2013): 317–40.

———. *Changing Homelands: Hindu Politics and the Partition of India*. Cambridge, MA: Harvard University Press, 2011.

Najafī, Ghulām Ḥusayn. *Qaul-i maqbūl fī ithbāt waḥdat bint al-rasūl*. Lahore: Idārah-i Tablīgh-i Islāmī, 1982.

al-Najafī Ḍhakkō, Muḥammad Ḥusayn. *Aḥsān al-fawāʾid fī sharḥ al-ʿaqāʾid*. Sargōdhā: Maktabat al-Sibṭayn, 1965.

———. *Iṣlāḥ al-rusūm al-ẓāhira bi-kalām al-ʿitra al-ṭāhira al-maʿrūf bih aṣlī islām aur rasmī islām*. Sargōdhā: Maktabat al-Sibṭayn, 2009.

———. *Saʿādat al-dārayn fī maqtal al-Ḥusayn*. Islamabad: Islamic Book Center, 2009.

———. *Uṣūl al-sharīʿa fī ʿaqāʾid al-shīʿa.* Sargōdhā: Maktabat al-Sibṭayn, 2006.
Najm Āfindī. *Shāʿir-i ahl-i bayt jail meṉ.* Lucknow: Sarfarāz Qaumī Press, 1939.
Nakash, Yitzhak. *Reaching for Power: The Shiʿa in the Modern Arab World.* Princeton, NJ: Princeton University Press, 2006.
———. *The Shiʿis of Iraq.* Princeton, NJ: Princeton University Press, 1994.
Naqi, Maulana Syed Ali. *Azadari: A Historical Review of Institution [sic] of Azadari for Imam Husain (A.S.). Translation of "Aza-i-Husaini par Tarikhi Tabsera."* Karachi: Peermahomed Trust, 1974.
Naqvi, Syed Hussain Arif. "The Controversy about the Shaykhiyya Tendency among Shia 'Ulamā' in Pakistan." In *The Twelver Shia in Modern Times: Religious Culture and Political History*, edited by Rainer Brunner and Werner Ende, 135–49. Leiden: Brill, 2001.
Naqvī, Ṣāqib. "Āyatullāh Khumaynī—aye mere qāʾid." *Rāh-i ʿAmal*, no. 4 (1978): 6.
Naqvī, Sayyid ʿAlī Naqī. *Bāb ō mazhab-i bahāʾī.* Lucknow: Imāmīyya Mission, 1934.
———. "Muqaddamah-i kitāb." In *Khaṭīb-i Āl-i Muḥammad: Ḥażrat malik al-nāṭiqīn, shams al-ʿulamāʾ Maulānā Sayyid Sibṭ-i Ḥasan ṣāḥib qiblah aʿlā Allāh maqāmahu*, edited by Imāmiyyah Mission Lucknow. Lucknow: The Pioneer, 1935.
———. *Radd al-mughālaṭa.* Lucknow: Sayyid Ḥamīd Ḥusayn, 1917.
———. *Shahīd-i insāniyyat.* Lucknow: Sarfarāz Qaumī Press, 1940.
———. *Shīʿōṉ kī tāzah zindagī.* Lucknow: Imāmīyyah Mission, 1939.
Naqvī, Sayyid Muḥsin. "Khaṭīb-i shām-i gharībān—naqīb-i ṣubḥ-i qalam." In *Khaṭīb-i shām-i gharībān: Majmuʿah-i taqārīr*, 9–14. Multan: Mohsin Naqvi Academy, 2002.
Naqvi, Syed Muhammad Jafar-uz-Zaman. *The Last Great Reformer of the World as Highlighted by Prophets.* Karachi: Al-Qaim Welfare Trust, 2003.
Narayan, Shiv. *Indian Water Power Plants: A Companion Volume to Hydro-Electrical Installations of India.* Poona: Poona Electrical Supply Company, 1937.
Nashat, Guity. "Women in the Ideology of the Islamic Republic." In *Women and Revolution in Iran*, edited by Guity Nashat, 195–216. Boulder: Westview Press, 1983.
Nasr, Seyyed Vali Reza. "International Politics, Domestic Imperatives, and Identity Mobilization: Sectarianism in Pakistan, 1979–1998." In *Sectarianization: Mapping the New Politics of the Middle East*, edited by Nader Hashemi and Danny Postel, 77–100. London: Hurst, 2017.
———. "The Iranian Revolution and Changes in Islamism in Pakistan, India, and Afghanistan." In *Iran and the Surrounding World: Interactions in Culture and Cultural Politics*, edited by Nikki R. Keddie and Rudolph P. Matthee, 327–52. Seattle: University of Washington Press, 2002.
———. "Islam, the State and the Rise of Sectarian Militancy." In *Pakistan: Nationalism without a Nation*, edited by Christophe Jaffrelot, 88–114. London: Zed Books, 2002.
———. *Islamic Leviathan: Islam and the Making of State Power.* Oxford: Oxford University Press, 2001.

———. "The Rise of Sunni Militancy in Pakistan: The Changing Role of Islamism and the Ulama in Society and Politics." *Modern Asian Studies* 36, no. 3 (2000): 139–80.

———. *The Shia Revival: How Conflicts within Islam Will Shape the Future.* New York: Norton, 2006.

———. *The Vanguard of the Islamic Revolution: The Jamaʿat-i Islami of Pakistan.* Berkeley: University of California Press, 1994.

Naẕr-i ʿAlī, Munshī. *Ḥadīs̤-i S̤aqalayn aur maẕhab-i shīʿah.* Qadiyān: Yaʿqūb ʿAlī Turāb, 1905.

Nelson, Matthew J. "Embracing the Ummah: Student Politics beyond State Power in Pakistan." *Modern Asian Studies* 45, no. 3 (2011): 565–96.

Netton, Ian Richard. *Allāh Transcendent: Studies in the Structure and Semiotics of Islamic Philosophy, Theology, and Cosmology.* London: Routledge, 1989.

Newman, Andrew J. *The Formative Period of Twelver Shīʿism: Ḥadīth as Discourse between Qum and Baghdad.* Richmond, UK: Curzon, 2000.

Newman, Karl J., Heinz Pankalla, and Robert Krumbein-Neumann. *Pakistan unter Ayub Khan, Bhutto und Zia-ul-Haq.* Munich: Weltforum Verlag, 1986.

"Newspaper Editorials on Hazara Killings." *Hazara News Pakistan,* 16 April 2012. http://hazaranewspakistan.wordpress.com/2012/04/16/newspaper-editorials-on-hazara-killings/.

Nomani, Mohammad Manzoor. *Khomeini, Iranian Revolution and the Shiʿite Faith.* London: Al-Furqān Book Depot, 1988.

Noor, Farish A., Yoginder Sikand, and Martin van Bruinessen. "Introduction: Behind the Walls. Re-appraising the Role and Importance of Madrasas in the World Today." In *The Madrasa in Asia: Political Activism and Transnational Linkages,* edited by Farish A. Noor, Yoginder Sikand, and Martin van Bruinessen, 9–30. Amsterdam: Amsterdam University Press, 2008.

Northedge, Alistair. "The Shrine in Its Historical Context." In *The Shiʿa of Samarra: The Heritage and Politics of a Community in Iraq,* edited by Imranali Panjwani and Charles Tripp, 49–66. London: I. B. Tauris, 2012.

Norton, August Richard. *Amal and the Shiʿa: Struggle for the Soul of Lebanon.* Austin: University of Texas Press, 1987.

———. "Al-Najaf: Its Resurgence as a Religious and University Center." *Middle East Policy* 18, no. 1 (2011): 132–45.

Nuʿaymīyān, Ẕabīḥallāh. "Bāztāb-i Inqilāb-i Islāmī dar Pākistān." *Māhnāmah-i Zamānah,* nos. 45–46 (2006): 50–57.

Nuʿmānī, Muḥammad Manẓūr. *Īrānī inqilāb, Imām Khumaynī, aur shīʿat.* Karachi: Ḥajjī ʿĀrifīn Academy, 1987.

Nuṣūḥīyān, Mahdī. "Shīʿīyān-i Pākistān va Inqilāb-i Islāmī Irān." 18 May 2018. http://basirat.ir/fa/news.

Oberoi, Harjot. *The Construction of Religious Boundaries: Culture, Identity and Diversity in the Sikh Tradition.* Delhi: Oxford University Press, 1995.

Osella, Filippo, and Caroline Osella. "Introduction." In *Islamic Reform in South Asia,* edited by Filippo Osella, and Caroline Osella, x–xxviii. Cambridge: Cambridge University Press, 2013.

Osman, Amr. "ʿAdālat al-Ṣaḥāba: The Construction of a Religious Doctrine." *Arabica* 60 (2013): 272–305.

Østebø, Terje. *Localising Salafism: Religious Change among Oromo Muslims in Bale, Ethiopia.* Leiden: Brill, 2012.

Osterhammel, Jürgen. "Transfer und Migration von Ideen: China und der Westen im 19. und 20. Jahrhundert." In *Das Eigene und das Fremde: Festschrift für Urs Bitterli*, edited by Urs Bitterli, Urs Faes, and Béatrice Ziegler, 97–115. Zurich: NZZ, 2000.

———. "A 'Transnational' History of Society: Continuity or New Departure?" In *Comparative History and the Quest for Transnationality: Central European Approaches and New Perspectives*, edited by Jürgen Kocka and Heinz-Gerhard Haupt, 39–51. New York: Berghahn Books, 2009.

Ourghi, Mariella. "'Ein Licht umgab mich . . .': Die eschatologischen Visionen des iranischen Präsidenten Maḥmūd Aḥmadīnežād." *Die Welt des Islams* 49, no. 2 (2009): 163–80.

———. *Schiitischer Messianismus und Mahdī-Glaube in der Neuzeit.* Würzburg: Ergon, 2008.

"Pākistān se ek wafd Āyatullāh Khumaynī ke ḥuẓūr." *Rāh-i ʿAmal*, no. 6 (1979): 16–17.

Pandey, Gyanendra. *The Construction of Communalism in Colonial North India.* New Delhi: Oxford University Press, 2006.

Pānīpatī, Ghulām al-Ḥasnayn. *Miʿyār al-ḥaqīqat al-maʿrūf bi kashf al-ḥaqīqat, ḥiṣṣah-i duvum.* Lahore: Al-Burhān, 1914.

Paul, John Jeya. *The Legal Profession in Colonial South India.* Bombay: Oxford University Press, 1991.

Paulmann, Johannes. "Internationaler Vergleich und interkultureller Transfer: Zwei Forschungsansätze zur europäischen Geschichte des 18. bis 20. Jahrhunderts." *Historische Zeitschrift* 267, no. 3 (1998): 649–85.

Pernau, Margrit. *Transnationale Geschichte.* Göttingen: Vandenhoeck & Ruprecht, 2011.

Perrill, Jeffrey Price. "Punjab Orientalism: The Anjuman-i-Punjab and Punjab University, 1865–1888." PhD diss., University of Missouri, 1976.

Peskes, Esther. *Muḥammad B. ʿAbdalwahhāb (1703–92) im Widerstreit: Untersuchungen zur Rekonstruktion der Frühgeschichte der Wahhābīya.* Stuttgart: Steiner, 1993.

Pew Research Center. "Changing Patterns of Global Migration and Remittances." 15 June 2015. http://www.pewsocialtrends.org/files/2013/12/global-migration-final_12-2013.pdf.

Philippon, Alix. "Le charisme comme ressource émotionnelle du mouvement social? Dispositifs de sensibilisation dans une néo-confrérie pakistanaise." *Critique internationale* 66, no. 1 (2015): 105–24.

———. *Soufisme et politique au Pakistan: Le mouvement barelwi à l'heure de la guerre contre le terrorisme.* Paris: Karthala, 2011.
———. "Sunnis against Sunnis. The Politicization of Doctrinal Fractures in Pakistan." *Muslim World* 101 (2011): 347–68.
Pierret, Thomas. "Karbala in the Umayyad Mosque: Sunnite Panic at the 'Shiitization' of Syria in the 2000s." In *The Dynamics of Sunni-Shia Relationships: Doctrine, Transnationalism, Intellectuals and the Media,* edited by Brigitte Maréchal and Sami Zemni, 99–115. London: Hurst, 2012.
———. *Religion and State in Syria: The Sunni Ulama from Coup to Revolution.* Cambridge: Cambridge University Press, 2013.
Pinault, David. *Horse of Karbala: Muslim Devotional Life in India.* New York: St. Martin's, 2000.
———. *Notes from the Fortune-Telling Parrot: Islam and the Struggle for Religious Pluralism in Pakistan.* London: Equinox, 2008.
———. "The Shi'a as a Minority Community in Pakistan and India." *Studies in Contemporary Islam* 5, nos. 1–2 (2003): 49–56.
———. *The Shiites: Ritual and Popular Piety in a Muslim Community.* London: I. B. Tauris, 1992.
Pirzada, Sayyid A. S. *The Politics of the Jamiat Ulema-i-Islam Pakistan: 1971–1977.* Karachi: Oxford University Press, 2000.
Porter, Bernard. *The Absent-Minded Imperialists: Empire, Society, and Culture in Britain.* Oxford: Oxford University Press, 2004.
Potter, Simon J. "Empire, Cultures and Identities in Nineteenth- and Twentieth-Century Britain." *History Compass* 5, no. 1 (2007): 51–71.
Powell, Avril A. "Maulānā Raḥmat Allāh Kairānawī and Muslim-Christian Controversy in India in the Mid-19th Century." *Journal of the Royal Asiatic Society of Great Britain and Ireland* 1 (1976): 42–63.
Poya, Maryam. *Women, Work and Islamism: Ideology and Resistance in Iran.* London: Zed Books, 1999.
Preckel, Claudia. "Islamische Bildungsnetzwerke und Gelehrtenkultur im Indien des 19. Jahrhunderts: Muḥammad Ṣiddīq Ḥasan Ḫān (st. 1890) und die Entstehung der Ahl-e ḥadīṯ Bewegung in Bhopal." PhD diss., Ruhr Universität Bochum, 2005.
"Press Branch mutawajjah hō!" *al-Muntaẓar* 8, no. 13 (1966): 20–23.
"Press Release: Imāmiyyah Organisation Pākistān." *Rāh-i ʿAmal,* no. 5 (1978): 25.
"Proceedings All Parties Shia Conference, 13th, 14th, 15th and 16th October 1945." *Moonlight,* 27 October 1945, 17–20.
Qamar Zaydī, Sayyid Muḥammad ʿAbbās. *Pānc hafte Āyatullāh Khumaynī ke Īrān meṉ.* Karachi: Maktabah-i Miʿrāj-i Adab, 1979.
———. *Rahbar-i mā Khumaynī. Junbish-i Islāmī-yi Īrān.* Karachi: Maktabah-i Miʿrāj-i Adab, 1979.
Qāsim, Ḥāfiẓ Muḥammad Nadīm. *Ḥayāt-i Aʿẓam Ṭāriq: Sānī-yi general-i Sipāh-i Ṣaḥābah (rażī Allāh ʿanhum), ghāzī-yi Islām, muḥāfiẓ-i nāmūs-i ṣaḥābah ḥażrat*

Maulānā Muḥammad Aʿẓam Ṭāriq (madda ẓillahu al-ʿāle) ke mufaṣṣil ḥālat-i zindagī. Fayṣalābād, 1998.
Qāsimī, Nadīm. *Javāhirāt-i Ḥaydarī*. Lahore: Maktabah al-Ṣaḥāba, 2010.
Qasmi, Ali Usman. *The Ahmadis and the Politics of Religious Exclusion in Pakistan*. London: Anthem Press, 2014.
———. "God's Kingdom on Earth? Politics of Islam in Pakistan, 1947–1969." *Modern Asian Studies* 44, no. 6 (2010): 1197–1253.
———. *Questioning the Authority of the Past: The Ahl al-Qur'an Movements in the Punjab*. Karachi: Oxford University Press, 2011.
Qasmi, Ali Usman, and Megan Eaton Robb. "Introduction." In *Muslims against the Muslim League: Critiques of the Idea of Pakistan*, edited by Ali Usman Qasmi and Megan Eaton Robb, 1–33. New York: Cambridge University Press, 2017.
Quddūsī, ʿUmār Fārūqī. *Khuṭbāt-i shahīd-i Islām, imām al-ʿaṣr ʿAllāmah Iḥsān Ilāhī Ẓahīr*. Lahore: Maktabah-i Qudūsiyyah, 2001.
Qureshi, Jawad Anwar. "Middle-East's Sectarian Balance Shifts as Syrian Uprising Enters Its Fourth Year." Martin Marty Center for the Public Understanding of Religion, University of Chicago Divinity School, 15 June 2015. http://divinity.uchicago.edu/sightings/middle-east%E2%80%99s-sectarian-balance-shifts-syrian-uprising-enters-its-fourth-year-%E2%80%94-jawad.
Qureshi, M. Naeem. *Pan-Islam in British Indian Politics: The Politics of the Khilafat Movement, 1918–1924*. Karachi: Oxford University Press, 2009.
Qureshi, Saleem. "The Politics of the Shia Minority in Pakistan: Context and Developments." In *Religious and Ethnic Minority Politics in South Asia*, edited by Dhirendra Kumar Vajpeyi and Yogendra K. Malik, 109–38. New Delhi: Manohar, 1989.
al-Rāḍī, Muḥammad b. al-Ḥusayn Sharīf. *Nahj al-balāgha: Majmūʿah-i kāmil, khuṭbahhā nāmahhā va ḥikmathā (mavāʿiẓ-i qiṣār)*. Qum: Mashriqayn-i Qum, 2002.
Radice, Hugo. "Halfway to Paradise? Making Sense of the Semi-Periphery." In *Globalization and the "New" Semi-Peripheries*, edited by Owen Worth and Phoebe V. Moore, 25–39. Houndmills: Palgrave Macmillan, 2009.
Raḥānī, ʿAbd al-Ḥamīd. "Bhāʾī Iḥsān kī yād meṇ." In *ʿAllāmah shahīd-i millat number, al-maʿrūf maqālāt-i ʿAllāmah Iḥsān Ilāhī Ẓahīr*, edited by ʿAbd al-Raḥmān Munīr Rājūvālvī, 323–34. Lahore: Ahl-i Ḥadīs̱ Dār al-Ishāʿat, 1988.
Rahman, Fazlur. *Selected Letters of Shaikh Aḥmad Sirhindī*. Karachi: Iqbal Academy, 1968.
Rahman, M. Raisur. "Beyond Centre-Periphery: Qasbahs and Muslim Life in South Asia." *South Asian History and Culture* 5, no. 2 (2014): 163–78.
Rahman, Tariq. "Language Policy, Multilingualism and Language Vitality in Pakistan." In *Lesser-Known Languages of South Asia: Status and Policies, Case Studies, and Applications of Information Technology*, edited by Anju Saxena and Lars Borin, 73–104. Berlin: Mouton de Gruyter, 2006.

Rahnema, Ali. *An Islamic Utopian: A Political Biography of Ali Shari'ati*. London: I. B. Tauris, 1998.
———. *Superstition as Ideology in Iranian Politics: From Majlesi to Ahmadinejad*. New York: Cambridge University Press, 2011.
Rajaee, Farhang. *Islamism and Modernism: The Changing Discourse in Iran*. Austin: University of Texas Press, 2007.
Raja of Mahmudabad. "Some Memories." In *India's Partition: Process, Strategy, and Mobilization*, edited by Mushirul Hasan, 408–19. Delhi: Oxford University Press, 1993.
Ramazani, Ruhollah. "Iran's Export of the Revolution: Politics, Ends, and Means." In *The Iranian Revolution: Its Global Impact*, edited by John L. Esposito, 68–86. Miami: Florida International University Press, 1990.
Rao, Ursula. *Kommunalismus in Indien: Eine Darstellung der wissenschaftlichen Diskussion über Hindu-Muslim-Konflikte*. Halle (Saale): Institut für Indologie und Südasienwissenschaften der Martin-Luther-Universität Halle-Wittenberg, 2003.
Rasheed, Madawi. *Contesting the Saudi State: Islamic Voices from a New Generation*. Cambridge: Cambridge University Press, 2007.
Rāzī, Muḥammad Sharīf. *Ganjīnah-i dānishmandān*. Tehran: Kitābfurūshī-yi Islāmiyyah, 1973.
Reetz, Dietrich. "'Alternate' Globalities? On the Cultures and Formats of Transnational Muslim Networks from South Asia." In *Translocality: The Study of Globalising Processes from a Southern Perspective*, edited by Ulrike Freitag and Achim von Oppen, 293–334. Leiden: Brill, 2010.
———. "Change and Stagnation in Islamic Education: The Dar al-ʿUlum of Deoband after the Split in 1982." In *The Madrasa in Asia: Political Activism and Transnational Linkages*, edited by Farish A. Noor, Yoginder Sikand, and Martin van Bruinessen, 71–104. Amsterdam: Amsterdam University Press, 2008.
———. *Islam in the Public Sphere: Religious Groups in India, 1900–1947*. New Delhi: Oxford University Press, 2006.
———. "Migrants, Mujahidin, Madrassa Students: The Diversity of Transnational Islam in Pakistan." In *Transnational Islam in South and Southeast Asia: Movements, Networks, and Conflict Dynamics*, edited by Peter Mandaville, 53–77. Seattle: National Bureau of Asian Research, 2009.
Rehman, Zia Ur. *Karachi in Turmoil*. Islamabad: Narratives, 2013.
Reichmuth, Stefan. "The Interplay of Local Developments and Transnational Relations in the Islamic World: Perceptions and Perspectives." In *Muslim Culture in Russia and Central Asia from the 18th to the Early 20th Centuries*, vol. 2: *Inter-Regional and Inter-Ethnic Relations*, edited by Anke von Kügelgen, Michael Kemper, and Allen J. Frank, 5–38. Berlin: Schwarz, 1998.
———. "'Netzwerk' und 'Weltsystem': Konzepte zur neuzeitlichen 'Islamischen Welt' und ihrer Transformation." In *Die islamische Welt als Netzwerk:*

Möglichkeiten und Grenzen des Netzwerkansatzes im islamischen Kontext, edited by Roman Loimeier, 53–86. Würzburg: Ergon, 2000.
Reisinezhad, Arash. "The Iranian Green Movement: Fragmented Collective Action and Fragile Collective Identity." *Iranian Studies* 48, no. 2 (2015): 193–222.
"Report-i ijlās-i majlis-i ʿāmilah." *Rāh-i ʿAmal*, no. 53 (1987): 13–17.
"Report-i ijlās-i majlis-i ʿāmilah-i Imamia Students Organisation Pakistan." *Rāh-i ʿAmal*, no. 46 (1986): 31–38.
Ricci, Ronit. *Islam Translated: Literature, Conversion, and the Arabic Cosmopolis of South and Southeast Asia*. Chicago: University of Chicago Press, 2011.
Richard, Yann. "Sharīʿat Sangalajī: A Reformist Theologian of the Riḍā Shāh Period." In *Authority and Political Culture in Shiʿism*, edited by Said Amir Arjomand, 159–77. Albany: State University of New York Press, 1988.
Rieck, Andreas. "A Stronghold of Shiʿa Orthodoxy in Northern Pakistan." In *Islamstudien ohne Ende: Festschrift für Werner Ende zum 65. Geburtstag*, edited by Rainer Brunner, Monika Gronke, Jens Peter Laut, and Ulrich Rebstock, 383–409. Würzburg: Ergon, 2002.
———. "Irans Politik im Afghanistankonflikt seit 1992." In *Afghanistan in Geschichte und Gegenwart: Beiträge zur Afghanistanforschung*, edited by Conrad J. Schetter and Almut Wieland-Karimi, 109–28. Frankfurt: IKO, 1999.
———. "From Mountain Refuge to 'Model Area': Transformation of Shiʿi Communities in Northern Pakistan." In *Perspectives on History and Change in the Karakorum, Hindukush, and Himalaya*, edited by Irmtraud Stellrecht and Matthias Winiger, 215–31. Cologne: Köppe, 1997.
———. *The Shiʿas of Pakistan: An Assertive and Beleaguered Minority*. London: Hurst, 2015.
———. "The Struggle for Equal Rights as a Minority: Shia Communal Organizations in Pakistan, 1948–1968." In *The Twelver Shia in Modern Times: Religious Culture and Political History*, edited by Rainer Brunner and Werner Ende, 268–83. Leiden: Brill, 2001.
Riexinger, Martin. *Ṣanāʾullāh Amritsarī (1868–1948) und die Ahl-i-Ḥadīs im Punjab unter britischer Herrschaft*. Würzburg: Ergon, 2004.
"Rithāʾ-i Muḥsin al-Ḥakīm." *Payām-i ʿAmal* 15, no. 9 (1971): 6.
Riyāż, Sayyid Riyāż ʿAlī. *Islām aur uske shāriʿ muqaddas kī baʿż-i khuṣūṣiyyāt*. Benares, 1923.
Rižā Naqvī, ʿAlī. "Ceh July aur tanẓīm." *Rāh-i ʿAmal*, no. 47 (1986): 5–6.
———. "Payghām-i yaum-i taʾsīs." *Rāh-i ʿAmal* 46 (1986): 11, 30.
Rizvi, Sajjad. "Faith Deployed for a New Shiʿi Polity in India: The Theology of Sayyid Dildar ʿAli Nasirabadi." *Journal of the Royal Asiatic Society* 24, no. 3 (2014): 363–80.
Rizvi, Sayyid Athar Abbas. *A Socio-Intellectual History of the Isnā ʿAsharī Shīʿīs in India*, vol. 2: *16th to 19th Century*. Canberra: Maʿrifat, 1986.
Robb, Megan Eaton. "Advising the Army of Allah: Ashraf Ali Thanawi's Critique of the Muslim League." In *Muslims against the Muslim League. Critiques of the Idea*

of Pakistan, edited by Ali Usman Qasmi and Megan Eaton Robb, 142–68. New York: Cambridge University Press, 2017.

Robinson, Francis. "Introduction: The Shi'a in South Asia." *Journal of the Royal Asiatic Society* 24, no. 3 (2014): 353–61.

———. "Islamic Reform and Modernities in South Asia." In *Islamic Reform in South Asia*, edited by Filippo Osella and Caroline Osella, 26–50. Cambridge: Cambridge University Press, 2013.

———. *Separatism among Indian Muslims: The Politics of the United Provinces' Muslims, 1860–1923*. London: Cambridge University Press, 1974.

———. "Strategies of Authority in Muslim South Asia in the Nineteenth and Twentieth Centuries." *Modern Asian Studies* 47, no. 1 (2013): 1–21.

———. "The Jinnah Story." In *M. A. Jinnah: Views and Reviews*, edited by M. R. Kazimi, 80–90. Karachi: Oxford University Press, 2005.

———. *The 'Ulama of Farangi Mahall and Islamic Culture in South Asia*. London: C. Hurst, 2001.

Robson, J. "al-Bag͟hawī." *Encyclopaedia of Islam*, 2nd ed. Edited by P. Bearman, T. Bianquis, C. E. Bosworth, E. van Donzel, and W. P. Heinrichs. BrillOnline Reference Works. Accessed 4 August 2018. http://dx.doi.org/10.1163/1573-3912_islam_SIM_1024.

Rock-Singer, Aaron. "A Pious Public: Islamic Magazines and Revival in Egypt, 1976–1981." *British Journal of Middle Eastern Studies* 42, no. 4 (2015): 427–46.

Rose, Sonya O. "Cultural Analysis and Moral Discourses. Episodes, Continuities, and Transformations." In *Beyond the Cultural Turn: New Directions in the Study of Society and Culture*, edited by Victoria E. Bonnell, Lynn Hunt, and Richard Biernacki, 217–38. Berkeley: University of California Press, 1999.

Rosiny, Stephan. "The Tragedy of Fāṭima al-Zahrā' in the Debate of Two Shiite Theologians in Lebanon." In *The Twelver Shia in Modern Times: Religious Culture and Political History*, edited by Rainer Brunner and Werner Ende, 207–19. Leiden: Brill, 2001.

———. "The Twelver Shia Online: Challenges for Its Religious Authority." In *The Other Shiites: From the Mediterranean to Central Asia*, edited by Alessandro Monsutti, Silvia Naef, and Farian Sabahi, 245–62. Bern: Peter Lang, 2007.

Rothmann, E. Natalie. "Genealogies of Mediation: 'Culture Broker' and Imperial Governmentality." In *Anthrohistory: Unsettling Knowledge, Questioning Discipline*, edited by Edward Murphy, 67–79. Ann Arbor: University of Michigan Press, 2011.

Rothschild, Emma. "Arcs of Ideas: International History and Intellectual History." In *Transnationale Geschichte: Themen, Tendenzen und Theorien*, edited by Gunilla-Friederike Budde, Sebastian Conrad, and Oliver Janz, 217–26. Göttingen: Vandenhoeck & Ruprecht, 2006.

Roundovi, Hassan Musanna. "Ali Sharfuddin Moosavi Baltistani: A Short Biography." 10 December 2014. http://www.scribd.com/doc/186488454/Allama-Ali-Sharfuddin-Baltistani-A-Short-Biography.

Roy, Olivier. *Globalized Islam: The Search for a New Ummah.* New York: Columbia University Press, 2004.

———. "L'impact de la révolution iranienne au Moyen-Orient." In *Les mondes chiites et l'Iran,* edited by Sabrina Mervin, 29–42. Paris: Karthala, 2007.

———. *The Failure of Political Islam.* Cambridge, MA: Harvard University Press, 1994.

———. "The Impact of the Iranian Revolution on the Middle East." In *The Shiʿa Worlds and Iran,* edited by Sabrina Mervin, 29–44. London: Saqi, 2010.

Rozehnal, Robert Thomas. *Islamic Sufism Unbound: Politics and Piety in Twenty-First Century Pakistan.* New York: Palgrave Macmillan, 2007.

Rubin, Uri. "Traditions in Transformation: The Ark of the Covenant and the Golden Calf in Biblical and Islamic Historiography." *Oriens* 36 (2001): 196–214.

Ruffle, Karen G. *Gender, Sainthood, and Everyday Practice in South Asian Shiʿism.* Chapel Hill: University of North Carolina Press, 2011.

Rūḥānī, Ḥamīd. *Nahżat-i Imām Khumaynī.* Tehran: Markaz-i Asnād-i Inqilāb-i Islāmī, 2003.

Rutner, Maryam. "Religious Authority, Gendered Recognition, and Instrumentalization of Nusrat Amin in Life and after Death." *Journal of Middle East Women's Studies* 11, no. 1 (2015): 24–41.

Rutter, Eldon. *The Holy Cities of Arabia.* London: G. P. Putnam's Sons, 1928.

al-Sābiqī, Muḥammad Ḥasnayn. *Khāliṣiyyatnāmah.* Multān: Markaz-i Tablīghāt-i Islāmī Shīʿah, 1987.

———. *Qawāʿid al-sharīʿa fī ʿaqāʾid al-shīʿa bi-jawāb uṣūl al-sharīʿa fī ʿaqāʾid al-shīʿa.* Multan: Madrasat Jāmiʿat al-Thaqalayn, 1989.

———. *Rusūm al-shīʿa fī mīzān al-sharīʿa.* Multan: Idārat Jāmiʿat al-Thaqalayn, 2000.

Sabzvārī, Ghulām Shabbīr. "Islāmī inqilāb-i Īrān aur ẕarāʾiʿ-i iblāgh." *Rāh-i ʿAmal,* no. 19 (1981): 4–5.

Sachedina, Abdulaziz. "Al-Khums: The Fifth in the Imāmī Shīʿī Legal System." *Journal of Near Eastern Studies* 39, no. 4 (1980): 275–89.

———. *Islamic Messianism: The Idea of Mahdī* [sic] *in Twelver Shīʿism.* Albany: State University of New York Press, 1981.

———. *The Just Ruler (al-sulṭān al-ʿādil) in Shīʿite Islam: The Comprehensive Authority of the Jurist in Imamite Jurisprudence.* New York: Oxford University Press, 1988.

Ṣādīqī, Sayyid Ghulām Ḥusayn. "ʿAllāma Sayyid ʿArif Ḥusayn Ḥusaynī." In *Sitāragān-i ḥaram: Akhtarān-i ḥarīm-i maʿṣūmah,* edited by Gurūhī āz nivīsandigān-i māhānah-i kauṡar, 81–96. Qum: Zāʾir, 2004.

Sadri, Mahmoud. "Sacral Defense of Secularism: The Political Theologies of Sorush, Shabestari, and Kadivar." *International Journal of Politics, Culture and Society* 15, no. 2 (2001): 257–70.

Said, Edward W. *The World, the Text, and the Critic.* Cambridge, MA: Harvard University Press, 1983.

Saif, Mashal. “Notes from the Margins: Shi‘a Political Theology in Contemporary Pakistan.” *Journal of Shi‘a Islamic Studies* 7, no. 1 (2014): 65–97.

———. “The ‘Ulama’ and the State: Negotiating Tradition, Authority and Sovereignty in Contemporary Pakistan.” PhD diss., Duke University, 2014.

Sajjād, Miyāṉ Muḥammad Yūsuf. “‘Allāmah Iḥsān Ilāhī Ẓahīr Shahīd.” In *‘Allāmah shahīd-i millat number, al-ma‘rūf maqālāt-i ‘Allāmah Iḥsān Ilāhī Ẓahīr*, edited by ‘Abd al-Raḥmān Munīr Rājūvālvī, 17–41. Lahore: Ahl-i Ḥadīs̱ Dār al-Ishā‘at, 1988.

Sajjad, Mohammad. *Muslim Politics in Bihar: Changing Contours*. New Delhi: Routledge, 2014.

Sakurai, Keiko. “Women’s Empowerment and Iranian-Style Seminaries in Iran and Pakistan.” In *The Moral Economy of the Madrasa: Islam and Education Today*, edited by Keiko Sakurai and Fariba Adelkhah, 32–58. Abingdon: Routledge, 2011.

“Sālānah Report Imāmiyyah Mission Pakistan: 1 April 1960 tā 31 March 1961.” *Payām-i ‘Amal* 5, no. 3 (1961): 13–23.

Salayc, Muḥammad Munīr Aḥmad. *Vafayāt-i nāmvarān-i Pākistān (14 August 1947 se 31 December 2004 tak vafāt pāne vālī aham Pākistānī shakhṣīyāt kā mukhtaṣar ta‘āruf aur mustanad tārīkh-i vafāt)*. Lahore: Urdu Science Board, 2006.

Saleh, Walid A. *The Formation of the Classical Tafsīr Tradition: The Qur’ān Commentary of al-Tha‘labī (d. 427/1035)*. Boston: Brill, 2004.

Salvatore, Armando. “Qaraḍāwī’s Maṣlaḥa—From Ideologue of the Islamic Awakening to Sponsor of Transnational Public Islam.” In *Global Mufti: The Phenomenon of Yūsuf al-Qaraḍāwī*, edited by Bettina Gräf and Jakob Skovgaard-Petersen, 239–50. London: Hurst & Co., 2009.

———. “The Reform Project in the Emerging Public Spheres.” In *Islam and Modernity*, edited by Muhammad Khalid Masud, Armando Salvatore, and Martin van Bruinessen, 185–205. Edinburgh: Edinburgh University Press, 2009.

———. “Tradition and Modernity within Islamic Civilisation and the West.” In *Islam and Modernity*, edited by Muhammad Khalid Masud, Armando Salvatore, and Martin van Bruinessen, 3–35. Edinburgh: Edinburgh University Press, 2009.

“Sāniḥah-i ‘aẓīm.” *Rāh-i ‘Amal*, no. 46 (1986): 3–5.

Sankari, Jamal. *Fadlallah: The Making of a Radical Shi‘ite leader*. London: Saqi, 2005.

Sanyal, Usha. “Ahl-i Sunnat Madrasas: The Madrasa Manzar-i Islam, Bareilly, and Jamia Ashrafiyya, Mubarakpur.” In *Madrasas in South Asia: Teaching Terror?*, edited by Jamal Malik, 23–44. London, New York: Routledge, 2008.

———. *Devotional Islam and Politics in British India: Ahmed Riza Khan Barelwi and His Movement, 1870–1920*. Delhi: Oxford University Press, 1996.

Sarḥadī, Mubīn. *Ṣirāṭ al-Īmān bi-ḍau’ al-ḥadīth wa-l-qur’ān: Ma‘ārif-i īmāniyyah ke bāre meṉ ek rūḥ parvar pishkash*. Cakkarkoṭ Bālā, Kohāṭ: Jāmi‘ah-i ‘Alaviyyah, 1984.

Sarḥān, Saʿūd ibn Ṣāliḥ. *Rasāʾil al-Imām Muḥammad Zāhid al-Kautharī ilā al-ʿAllāma Muḥammad Yūsuf al-Bannūrī, fī-l-sanawāt min 1358 H ḥattā 1371 H.* ʿAmmān: Dār al-Fatḥ li-l-Dirāsāt wa-l-Nashr, 2013.

Sarrāj, ʿAdnān Ibrāhīm. *Al-Imām Muḥsin al-Ḥakīm, 1889–1970: Dirāsat tārīkhiyya tabḥathu sīratahu wa-mawāqifahu wa-ārāʾahu al-siyāsiyya wa-l-iṣlāḥiyya wa-atharahā ʿalā al-mujtamaʿ wa-l-daula fī-l-ʿIrāq.* Beirut: Dār al-Zahrāʾ, 1993.

Saskia, Gieling. "The Marjaʿiya in Iran and the Nomination of Khamanei in December 1994." *Middle Eastern Studies* 33, no. 4 (1997): 777–87.

Saunier, Pierre-Yves. *Transnational History.* New York: Palgrave Macmillan, 2013.

Sayf, Qāżī Muḥammad Aslam. *Armaghān-i Ẓahīr.* Gujrānvālah: Ahl-i Ḥadīs̱, 1990.

Scharbrodt, Oliver. "The Quṭb as Special Representative of the Hidden Imam: The Conflation of Shiʿi and Sufi Vilāyat in the Niʿmatullāhī Order." In *Shiʿi Trends and Dynamics in Modern Times (XVIIIth–XXth Centuries): Courants et dynamiques chiites à l'époque moderne (XVIIIe–XXe siècles),* edited by Denis Hermann, and Sabrina Mervin, 33–49. Würzburg: Ergon, 2010.

Schimmel, Annemarie. "Ein Frauenbildungsroman auf Sindi: Mirzā Qalīch Bēg's Zīnat." *Der Islam: Zeitschrift für Geschichte und Kultur des Islamischen Orients* 39 (1964): 210–25.

Schirazi, Asghar. *The Constitution of Iran: Politics and the State in the Islamic Republic.* London: I. B. Tauris, 1997.

Schmidtke, Sabine. "Al-ʿAllāma al-Ḥillī and Shiʿite Muʿtazilite Theology." *Spektrum Iran* 7 (1994): 10.

———. *The Theology of al-ʿAllāma al-Hillī (d. 726/1325).* Berlin: K. Schwarz, 1991.

Schmucker, Werner. "Die christliche Minderheit von Nağrān und die Problematik ihrer Beziehungen zum frühen Islam." *Bonner Orientalistische Studien,* no. 27 (1975): 183–236.

Schubel, Vernon J. *Religious Performance in Contemporary Islam: Shiʿi Devotional Rituals in South Asia.* Columbia: University of South Carolina Press, 1993.

Schulze, Reinhard. *Islamischer Internationalismus im 20. Jahrhundert: Untersuchungen zur Geschichte der Islamischen Weltliga.* Leiden: Brill, 1990.

Schwerin, Ulrich von. *The Dissident Mullah: Ayatollah Montazeri and the Struggle for Reform in Revolutionary Iran.* London: I. B. Tauris, 2015.

Sedghi, Hamideh. *Women and Politics in Iran: Veiling, Unveiling, and Reveiling.* Cambridge: Cambridge University Press, 2007.

Sevea, Iqbal Singh. *The Political Philosophy of Muhammad Iqbal: Islam and Nationalism in Late Colonial India.* Cambridge: Cambridge University Press, 2012.

Sewell, William H., Jr. "The Concept(s) of Culture." In *Beyond the Cultural Turn: New Directions in the Study of Society and Culture,* edited by Victoria E. Bonnell, Lynn Hunt, and Richard Biernacki, 35–61. Berkeley: University of California Press, 1999.

Shaery-Eisenlohr, Roschanack. "Imagining Shiʿite Iran: Transnationalism and

Religious Authenticity in the Muslim World." *Iranian Studies* 40, no. 1 (2007): 17–35.
———. *Shi'ite Lebanon: Transnational Religion and the Making of National Identities.* New York: Columbia University Press, 2008.
Shafqat, Saeed. "Political Culture in Pakistan: A Case of Disharmony between Democratic Creed and Autocratic Reality." In *Contemporary Issues in Pakistan Studies,* edited by Saeed Shafqat, 61–74. Lahore: Azad, 1998.
Shāh Kāẓimī, Sayyid Ḥasan ʿAlī. "Ahl-i tashayyuʿ kī ek imtiyāzī khuṣūṣiyyat." *Payām-i ʿAmal* 20, no. 4 (1976): 22–25.
Shāh Naqvī, Sayyid Aḥmad ʿAlī. "Naql-i khaṭṭ." *al-Ḥujjat* 12, no. 10 (1972): 2.
al-Shahrastānī, Abī al-Fatḥ Muḥammad b. ʿAbd al-Karīm b. Abī Bakr Aḥmad. *Al-Milal wa-l-niḥal.* Beirut: Dār al-Maʿrifa, 1990.
Shāh Riżvī, Sayyid Maḥmūd. "Mashhūr marājiʿ al-taqlīd." *al-Ḥujjat* 10, no. 11 (1970): 28–30.
———. "Nāmah ō javāb-i nāmah." *al-Ḥujjat* 2, no. 6 (1962): 33–34.
———. "Niyābat-i Imām ʿalayhi al-salām." *al-Ḥujjat* 10, no. 12 (1970): 45–47.
———. "Shīʿīyān-i Pākistān kā ʿajīb takhayyul." *al-Ḥujjat* 8, no. 2 (1967): 2–4.
———. "Taqlīd ke maʿne." *al-Ḥujjat* 10, no. 10 (1970): 14–16.
al-Shāhrūdī, al-Sayyid Maḥmūd al-Ḥusaynī. "Masāʾil-i sharʿiyyah." *Payām-i ʿAmal* 15, no. 6 (1971): 21.
Shaikh, Farzana. *Making Sense of Pakistan.* New York: Columbia University Press, 2009.
El Shamsy, Ahmed. "The Social Construction of Orthodoxy." In *The Cambridge Companion to Classical Islamic Theology,* edited by Tim Winter, 97–117. Cambridge: Cambridge University Press, 2009.
Shani, Raya Y. "Noah's Ark and the Ship of Faith in Persian Painting: From the Fourteenth to the Sixteenth Century." *Jerusalem Journal of Arabic and Islamic Studies* 27 (2002): 127–203.
al-Shaybānī, Muḥammad ibn al-Ḥasan. *The Islamic Law of Nations: Shaybānī's Siyar.* Baltimore: Johns Hopkins University Press, 1966.
Shehabi, Saeed. "The Role of Religious Ideology in the Expansionist Policies of Saudi Arabia." In *Kingdom without Borders: Saudi Political, Religious and Media Frontiers,* edited by Madawi Al-Rasheed, 183–98. New York: Columbia University Press, 2008.
"Shīʿah-i dīnī ō ʿilmī marākiz." *al-Ḥujjat* 11, no. 10 (1971): 5–7.
Shīʿah ō Sunnī ke munāẓare sanah 1328 h par taḥqīqī naẓar. Lucknow: Nūr al-Maṭābiʿ, 1910.
Shiftah, ʿAlī Ḥasnayn. *Tāʾyīd-i ḥaqq ō tardīd-i bāṭil.* Sargōdhā: Sayyid Akbar Ḥusayn Zaydī, 1978.
Shigri, Safdar Abbas. "Who Is? [*sic*] Agha Syed Ali Sharfuddin Mousvi Baltistani." 16 June 2015. http://aghaalisharfuddinbaltistani.blogspot.com/search/label/WHO%20IS%20AGHA%20SYED%20ALI%20SHARFUDDIN%20%20BALTISTANI.

Shīrkhānī, ʿAlī, and ʿAbbās Zāriʿ. *Taḥavvulāt-i ḥauzah-i ʿilmīyyah-i Qum: Pas az pīrūzī-yi inqilāb-i Islāmī.* Tehran: Intishārāt-i Markaz-i Asnād-i Inqilāb-i Islāmī, 2005.

Shīrkūṭī, Muḥammad Anvār al-Ḥasan. *Ḥayāt-i ʿUs̱mānī.* Karachi: Maktabah-i Dār al-ʿUlūm, 1985.

Shujāʿābādī, Ṣanāʾullāh Saʿd. *ʿAllāmah Żiyā al-Raḥmān Fārūqī shahīd: ḥayāt ō khidmāt.* Karachi: Al-Ḥasnayn, 2002.

Sibṭayn Naqvī, Sayyid Muḥammad. "Iqtibās az diary." In *Imāmiyyah dīnī madāris-i Pākistān,* edited by Sayyid Muḥammad S̱aqalayn Kāẓimī, 36–62. Lahore: Wifāq al-Madāris al-Shīʿa Pākistān, 2004.

Siddique, Osama. *Pakistan's Experience with Formal Law: An Alien Justice.* Cambridge: Cambridge University Press, 2013.

Siddique, Osama, and Zahra Hayat. "Unholy Speech and Holy Laws in Pakistan—Controversial Origins, Design Defects, and Free Speech Implications." *Minnesota Journal of International Law* 17, no. 2 (2008): 303–85.

Siddons, Julian. *"Die Korrektur der Irrtümer": Mūsā al-Mūsawīs Versuch, die schiitische Glaubenslehre zu reformieren.* Würzburg: Ergon, 2005.

Siegel, Evan. "The Politics of Shahīd-i Jāwīd." In *The Twelver Shia in Modern Times: Religious Culture and Political History,* edited by Rainer Brunner and Werner Ende, 150–77. Leiden: Brill, 2001.

Sikand, Yoginder. "An Islamic Critique of Patriarchy: Mawlana Sayyed Kalbe Sadiq's Approach to Gender Relations." In *The Blackwell Companion to Contemporary Islamic Thought,* edited by Ibrahim M. Abu-Rabiʿ, 644–56. Malden, MA: Blackwell, 2006.

———. "Voices for Reform in the Indian Madrasas." In *The Madrasa in Asia: Political Activism and Transnational Linkages,* edited by Farish A. Noor, Yoginder Sikand, and Martin van Bruinessen, 31–69. Amsterdam: Amsterdam University Press, 2008.

Sinai, Nicolai. "Religious Poetry from the Quranic Milieu: Umayya b. Abī l-Ṣalt on the Fate of the Thamūd." *Bulletin of the School of Oriental and African Studies* 74, no. 3 (2011): 397–416.

Sindawi, Khalid. "Ḥawza Instruction and Its Role in Shaping Modern Shīʿite Identity: The Ḥawzas of al-Najaf and Qumm as a Case Study." *Middle Eastern Studies* 43, no. 6 (2007): 831–56.

———. "Noah and Noah's Ark as the Primordial Model of Shīʿism in Shīʿite Literature." *Quaderni di Studi Arabi,* n.s., no. 1 (2006): 29–48.

Sirhindī, Aḥmad. *Maktūbāt-i Imām-i Rabbānī: Az irshādāt ʿalayh ghaus̱-i rabbānī ḥażrat mujaddid-i alf-i s̱ānī murattabah mūridān-i khāṣṣ al-khāṣṣ ḥażrat ʿirfān bayān.* Lucknow: Munshī Naval Kishōr, 1900.

———. *Maktūbāt-i Imām-i Rabbānī Ḥażrat Mujaddid-i Alf-i S̱ānī.* Istanbul: Işik Kitâbevi, 1977.

Sivan, Emmanuel. *Radical Islam: Medieval Theology and Modern Politics.* New Haven, CT: Yale University Press, 1990.

Skovgaard-Petersen, Jakob. "Yūsuf al-Qaraḍāwī and al-Azhar." In *Global Mufti: The Phenomenon of Yūsuf al-Qaraḍāwī*, edited by Bettina Gräf and Jakob Skovgaard-Petersen, 27–54. London: Hurst, 2009.
Smith, Wilferd Cantwell. *Islam in Modern History*. Princeton, NJ: Princeton University Press, 1957.
———. *Modern Islām in India. A Social Analysis*. London: Victor Gollancz, 1946.
Sökefeld, Martin. "Selves and Others: Representing Multiplicities of Difference in Gilgit and the Northern Areas of Pakistan." In *Islam and Society in Pakistan: Anthropological Perspectives*, edited by Magnus Marsden, 235–58. Karachi: Oxford University Press, 2010.
Speyer, Heinrich. *Die biblischen Erzählungen im Qoran*. Hildesheim: Georg Olms Verlagsbuchhandlung, 1961.
Stark, Ulrike. *An Empire of Books: The Naval Kishore Press and the Diffusion of the Printed Word in Colonial India*. Ranikhet: Permanent Black, 2007.
Steigerwald, Diane. *La pensée philosophique et théologique de Shahrastānī, (m. 548/1153)*. Sainte-Foy: Presses de l'Université Laval, 1997.
Steinberg, Guido. "Jihadi Salafism and the Shi'is." In *Global Salafism: Islam's New Religious Movement*, edited by Roel Meijer, 107–25. New York: Columbia University Press, 2009.
Stewart, Devin J. *Islamic Legal Orthodoxy: Twelver Shiite Responses to the Sunni Legal System*. Salt Lake City: University of Utah Press, 1998.
———. "The Genesis of the Akhbārī Revival." In *Safavid Iran and Her Neighbors*, edited by Michel M. Mazzaoui, 169–93. Salt Lake City: University of Utah Press, 2003.
———. "The Portrayal of an Academic Rivalry: Najaf and Qum in the Writings and Speeches of Khomeini, 1964–78." In *The Most Learned of the Shiʿa: The Institution of the Marjaʿ Taqlid*, edited by Linda S. Walbridge, 216–29. New York: Oxford University Press, 2001.
Stowasser, Barbara Freyer. "Yūsuf al-Qaraḍāwī on Women." In *Global Mufti: The Phenomenon of Yūsuf al-Qaraḍāwī*, edited by Bettina Gräf and Jakob Skovgaard-Petersen, 181–211. London: Hurst, 2009.
Strothmann, Rudolf. "Die Mubāhala in Tradition und Liturgie." *Der Islam*, no. 33 (1958): 5–29.
"Sunnī State ke nām par deobandī riyāsat ke qiyām kī sāzish." *Riżākār* 54, no. 10 (1990): 2.
Susewind, Raphael. "The 'Wazirganj Terror Attack': Sectarian Conflict and the Middle Classes." *South Asia Multidisciplinary Journal* 11 (2015): 1–17.
Syed, Anwar H. "The Sunni-Shia Conflict in Pakistan." In *Pakistan: Founder's Aspirations and Today's Realities*, edited by Hafeez Malik, 244–62. Karachi: Oxford University Press, 2001.
Syed, Anwar Hussain. *The Discourse and Politics of Zulfikar Ali Bhutto*. New York: St. Martin's, 1992.
Szanto, Edith. "Sayyida Zaynab in the State of Exception: Shiʿi Sainthood as a

'Qualified Life' in Contemporary Syria." *International Journal of Middle East Studies* 44, no. 2 (2012): 285–99.
Ṭabarī, W. Montgomery Watt, and M. V. McDonald. *Muḥammad at Mecca.* Albany: State University of New York Press, 1988.
"Tabṣirah-i māhnāmah-i al-Ṣaqalayn Multān: Ikhtilāfī ʿaqāʾid par munāẓarah." *Ẕūlfiqār* 21, no. 56 (1991): 4.
Takim, Liyakat A. "From Bidʿa to Sunna: The Wilāya of ʿAlī in the Shīʿī Adhān." *Journal of the American Oriental Society* 120, no. 2 (2000): 166–77.
Talbot, Ian. *Khizr Tiwana, the Punjab Unionist Party and the Partition of India.* Richmond, UK: Curzon, 1996.
———. *Pakistan: A Modern History.* London: Hurst, 1998.
———. *Pakistan: A New History.* London: Hurst, 2015.
———. *Provincial Politics and the Pakistan Movement: The Growth of the Muslim League in North-West and North-East India, 1937–1947.* Karachi: Oxford University Press, 1988.
———. *Punjab and the Raj, 1849–1947.* New Delhi: Manohar, 1988.
———. "The Punjabization of Pakistan: Myth or Reality?" In *Pakistan: Nationalism without a Nation,* edited by Christophe Jaffrelot, 51–62. London: Zed Books, 2002.
———. "Understanding Religious Violence in Contemporary Pakistan: Themes and Theories." In *Religion, Violence, and Political Mobilisation in South Asia,* edited by Ravinder Kaur, 145–64. New Delhi: Sage, 2005.
Talib, Mohammad. "Construction and Reconstruction of the World in the Tablīghī Ideology." In *Travellers in Faith: Studies of the Tablīghī Jamāʿat as a Transnational Islamic Movement for Faith Renewal,* edited by Muhammad Khalid Masud, 59–78. Boston: Brill, 2000.
Tannous, Jack. *Frowning in Cordoba (and Copying, Too).* Unpublished ms., 2005.
Ṭāriq, Abū Muʿāwiya Muḥammad Aʿẓam. "Īrān ke tamām-i manṣūbe khāk meṉ mil giye heṉ." In *Jaẕbāt-i asīr-i nāmūs-i ṣaḥābah al-maʿrūf payghāmāt-i jail,* edited by Muḥammad Sājid, 216–20. Karachi: Idārat al-Āthār, 2002.
———. "Īrān ne ʿālam-i Islāmi kō kyā diyā?" In *Jaẕbāt-i asīr-i nāmūs-i ṣaḥābah al-maʿrūf payghāmāt-i jail,* edited by Muḥammad Sājid, 158–59. Karachi: Idārat al-Āthār, 2002.
———. "Mister Khāminaʾī ṣāḥib!" In *Jaẕbāt-i asīr-i nāmūs-i ṣaḥābah al-maʿrūf payghāmāt-i jail,* edited by Muḥammad Sājid, 154–57. Karachi: Idārat al-Āthār, 2002.
———. "Najāt kā dār ō madār aʿmāl-i ṣāliḥa par mubannī he." In *Jaẕbāt-i asīr-i nāmūs-i ṣaḥābah al-maʿrūf payghāmāt-i jail,* edited by Muḥammad Sājid, 230–53. Karachi: Idārat al-Āthār, 2002.
———. "Sipāh-i Ṣaḥāba kā mission kyā he?" In *Khuṭbāt-i Jarnayl al-maʿrūf khuṭbāt-i jail,* edited by Abū Usāmah Ḥakīm Ẓiyā al-Raḥmān Nāṣir Sardārpūrī. Jhang: Sipāh-i Ṣaḥābah-i Pākistān, 2001.
———. "Ṣirf meṉ hī wājib al-qatl kyōṉ? 10 May 98 kō rūznāmah 'Avṣāf' meṉ shāʾeʿ

hōnīvālā mażmūn." In *Jazbāt-i asīr-i nāmūs-i ṣaḥābah al-maʿrūf payghāmāt-i jail,* edited by Muḥammad Sājid, 73. Karachi: Idārat al-Āthār, 2002.

———. "'Ṭālibān' ḥukūmat kā kirdār hamāre liye mashʿal-i rāh he." In *Jazbāt-i asīr-i nāmūs-i ṣaḥābah al-maʿrūf payghāmāt-i jail,* edited by Muḥammad Sājid, 144–48. Karachi: Idārat al-Āthār, 2002.

———. "Tārīkh-i Islām gavāh he ke ākharī fatḥ ḥaqq kī hōtī he." In *Jazbāt-i asīr-i nāmūs-i ṣaḥābah al-maʿrūf payghāmāt-i jail,* edited by Muḥammad Sājid, 104–9. Karachi: Idārat al-Āthār, 2002.

———. "Usāmah bin Lādin kā mission har musalmān ka mission he." In *Jazbāt-i asīr-i nāmūs-i ṣaḥābah al-maʿrūf payghāmāt-i jail,* edited by Muḥammad Sājid, 122–28. Karachi: Idārat al-Āthār, 2002.

Tayob, Abdelkader I. "Ṭabarī on the Companions of the Prophet: Moral and Political Contours in Islamic Historical Writing." *Journal of the American Oriental Society* 119, no. 2 (1999): 203–10.

al-Thaʿlabī, Aḥmad b. Muḥammad. *Ahl al-bayt fī tafsīr al-Thaʿlabī: Mā ruwiya ʿanhum wa-mā ruwiya fīhim.* Edited by ʿĀdil Kaʿbī. Qum: Dalīl-i Mā. N.p., 2002 or 2003.

———. *Al-Kashf wa-l-bayān: al-maʿrūf tafsīr al-Thaʿlabī.* Edited by Abū Muḥammad b. ʿĀshūr and Naẓīr al-Sāʿidī. Beirut: Dār Iḥyāʾ al-Turāth al-ʿArabī, 2002.

Thānavī, ʿAshraf ʿAlī. *Tafsīr Bayān al-Qurʾān.* Lahore: Maktabat al-Ḥasan, 1978.

Ther, Philipp. "Comparisons, Cultural Transfers, and the Study of Networks: Toward a Transnational History of Europe." In *Comparative History and the Quest for Transnationality: Central European Approaches and New Perspectives,* edited by Jürgen Kocka and Heinz-Gerhard Haupt, 204–25. New York: Berghahn, 2009.

Thompson, Andrew S. *The Empire Strikes Back? The Impact of Imperialism on Britain from the Mid-Nineteenth Century.* Harlow: Pearson Longman, 2005.

Tirmazi, Syed A. I. *Profiles of Intelligence.* Lahore, 1995.

al-Tirmiẕī, Sayyid Niṣār ʿAlī al-Ḥusaynī. *Naqīb-i vaḥdat ʿAllāmah Sayyid ʿArif Ḥusayn al-Ḥusaynī.* Islāmābād: al-Baṣīra, 2011.

Toor, Saadia. *The State of Islam: Culture and Cold War Politics in Pakistan.* London: Pluto, 2011.

Troll, Christian W. *Sayyid Ahmad Khan: A Reinterpretation of Muslim Theology.* New Delhi: Vikas, 1978.

Tschacher, Torsten. "Can 'Om' Be an Islamic term? Translations, Encounters, and Islamic Discourse in Vernacular South Asia." *South Asian History and Culture* 5, no. 2 (2014): 195–211.

Uddin, Layli. "In the Land of Eternal Eid: Maulana Bhashani and the Political Mobilisation of Peasants and Lower-Class Urban Workers in East Pakistan, c. 1930–1971." PhD diss., Royal Holloway, University of London, 2015.

"ʿUlamāʾ-i Najaf-i Ashraf kā Lāhōr meṉ vurūd-i masʿūd." *Payām-i ʿAmal* 10, no. 3 (1966): 25–26.

ʿUṣmānī, Shabbīr Aḥmad. *Hamārā Pākistān: Khuṭbah-i ṣadārat-i ṣubah-i Panjāb-i*

ʿUlamāʾ-i Islām-i Conference Lahore. Munʿaqadah 25, 26, 27 January 1946. Hayderabad (Deccan): Nafis Academy, 1946.
———. *Khuṭbāt-i ʿUs̱mānī: Shaykh al-Islām ʿAllāmah Shabbīr Aḥmad ʿUs̱mānī ke millī, siyāsī aur naẓariyyah-i Pākistān se mutaʿalliq ʿālimānah khuṭbāt, maktūbāt aur makāmalāt kā mukammal majmūʿah.* Edited by Muḥammad Anvār al-Ḥasan Shīrkōṭī. Lahore: Naẕr Sanz, 1972.
van Bruinessen, Martin. "Sufism, 'Popular' Islam and the Encounter with Modernity." In *Islam and Modernity,* edited by Muhammad Khalid Masud, Armando Salvatore, and Martin van Bruinessen, 125–57. Edinburgh: Edinburgh University Press, 2009.
van Ess, Josef. *Das Eine und das Andere: Beobachtungen an islamischen häresiographischen Texten.* Berlin: Walter de Gruyter, 2011.
Vatanka, Alex. *Iran and Pakistan: Security, Diplomacy and American Influence.* London: I. B. Tauris, 2015.
Veer, Peter van der. *Imperial Encounters: Religion and Modernity in India and Britain.* Princeton, NJ: Princeton University Press, 2001.
Verkaaik, Oskar. "Reforming Mysticism: Sindhi Separatist Intellectuals in Pakistan." In *Islam and Society in Pakistan: Anthropological Perspectives,* edited by Magnus Marsden, 111–31. Karachi: Oxford University Press, 2010.
"Vikālatnāmah-i Imām Khumaynī barāʾ-yi qāʾid-i millat-i jaʿfariyyah al-Sayyid ʿĀrif Ḥusayn al-Ḥusaynī." *Rāh-i ʿAmal,* no. 35 (1984): i.
Vikør, Knut S. *Sufi and Scholar on the Desert Edge: Muḥammad b. ʿAlī al-Sanūsī and His Brotherhood.* London: Hurst, 1995.
Visser, Reidar. "The Territorial Aspect of Sectarianism in Iraq: The Case of Anbar." In *The Dynamics of Sunni-Shia Relationships: Doctrine, Transnationalism, Intellectuals and the Media,* edited by Brigitte Maréchal and Sami Zemni, 83–99. London: Hurst, 2012.
Wagemakers, Joas. *A Quietist Jihadi: The Ideology and Influence of Abu Muhammad al-Maqdisi.* Cambridge: Cambridge University Press, 2012.
———. "Anti-Shiʿism without the Shiʿa: Salafi Sectarianism in Jordan." *Maydan,* 17 October 2016. http://www.themaydan.com/2016/10/anti-shiism-without-the-shia-salafi-sectarianism-in-jordan/.
Walbridge, Linda S. "The Counterreformation—Becoming a Marjaʿ in the Modern World." In *The Most Learned of the Shiʿa: The Institution of the Marjaʿ Taqlid,* edited by Linda S. Walbridge, 230–46. New York: Oxford University Press, 2001.
———. *The Thread of Muʿawiya: The Making of a Marjaʿ Taqlid.* Bloomington, IN: Ramsay Press, 2014.
Wallerstein, Immanuel Maurice. *Capitalist Agriculture and the Origins of the European World-Economy in the Sixteenth Century.* New York: Academic Press, 1974.
———. "The Rise and Future Demise of the World Capitalist System: Concepts for Comparative Analysis." In *The Capitalist World-Economy: Essays,* edited by

Immanuel Maurice Wallerstein, 1–36. Cambridge: Cambridge University Press, 1979.
Ward, Stuart. "Echoes of Empire." *History Workshop Journal* 62 (2006): 264–78.
Waseem, Mohammad. "Political Sources of Islamic Militancy in Pakistan." In *The Deadly Embrace: Religion, Politics, and Violence in India and Pakistan, 1947–2002*, edited by Ian Talbot, 145–63. Karachi: Oxford University Press, 2007.
Wehler, Hans-Ulrich. "Transnationale Geschichte—der neue Königsweg historischer Forschung?" In *Transnationale Geschichte: Themen, Tendenzen und Theorien*, edited by Gunilla-Friederike Budde, Sebastian Conrad, and Oliver Janz, 161–74. Göttingen: Vandenhoeck & Ruprecht, 2006.
Weinbaum, Martin. "The March 1977 Elections in Pakistan: Where Everyone Lost." *Asia Survey* 17, no. 7 (1977): 599–618.
Weiss, Max. *In the Shadow of Sectarianism: Law, Shiʿism, and the Making of Modern Lebanon*. Cambridge, MA: Harvard University Press, 2010.
Werner, Michael, and Bénédicte Zimmermann. "Vergleich, Transfer, Verflechtung: Der Ansatz der Histoire croisée und die Herausforderung des Transnationalen." *Geschichte und Gesellschaft* 28 (2002): 607–36.
———. "Beyond Comparison: Histoire Croisée and the Challenge of Reflexivity." *History and Theory* 45, no. 1 (2006): 30–50.
Wiederhold, Lutz. "Blasphemy against the Prophet Muḥammad and His Companions (*Sabb al-Rasūl, Sabb al-Ṣaḥābah*): The Introduction of the Topic into Shāfiʿī Legal Literature and Its Relevance for Legal Practice under Mamluk Rule." *Journal of Semitic Studies* 42, no. 1 (1997): 39–70.
Wild, Stefan. "Political Interpretations of the Qurʾān." In *The Cambridge Companion to the Qurʾān*, edited by Jane Dammen McAuliffe, 273–90. Cambridge: Cambridge University Press, 2006.
Winkelmann, Mareike Jule. "'Inside and Outside' in a Girls' Madrasa in New Delhi." In *The Madrasa in Asia: Political Activism and Transnational Linkages*, edited by Farish A. Noor, Yoginder Sikand, and Martin van Bruinessen, 105–22. Amsterdam: Amsterdam University Press, 2008.
———. *"From behind the Curtain": A Study of a Girls' Madrasa in India*. Amsterdam: Amsterdam University Press, 2005.
Wolpert, Stanley A. *Jinnah of Pakistan*. New York: Oxford University Press, 1984.
Worth, Owen. "Whatever Happened to the Semi-Periphery?" In *Globalization and the "New" Semi-Peripheries*, edited by Owen Worth and Phoebe V. Moore, 9–24. Houndmills: Palgrave Macmillan, 2009.
Wright, Theodore P., Jr. "The Changing Role of the Sādāt in India and Pakistan." *Oriente Moderno*, n.s., 18, no. 2 (1999): 649–59.
Yamane, So. "The Rise of New Madrasas and the Decline of Tribal Leadership within the Federal [*sic*] Administrated Tribal Areas (FATA), Pakistan." In *The Moral Economy of the Madrasa: Islam and Education Today*, edited by Keiko Sakurai and Fariba Adelkhah, 11–31. Abingdon: Routledge, 2011.

Yavār Ḥusayn, Muḥammad. *Żarūriyyat-i ʿashrah-i muḥarram*. Gōpāmaʾō: Ḥabīb al-Raḥmān ʿUs̱mānī, 1920.
Zafarulmulk. *Official Vagaries in Lucknow*. New Delhi, 1945.
Zaheer, Ehsan Elahi. *The Shiʿites and the Sunna*. Lahore: Idara Tarjuman-al-Sunnah, 1984.
Ẓahīr, Iḥsān Ilāhī. "Firqah vāriyyat kā khatmah." In *Khuṭbāt-i shahīd-i Islām, imām al-ʿaṣr ʿAllāmah Iḥsān Ilāhī Ẓahīr*, 285–303. Lahore: Maktabah-i Qudūsiyyah, 2001.
——— . "Mudīr-i tarjumān kā namāyandah-i jang kō interview." In *ʿAllāmah shahīd-i millat number, al-maʿrūf maqālāt-i ʿAllāmah Iḥsān Ilāhī Ẓahīr*, edited by ʿAbd al-Raḥmān Munīr Rājūvālvī, 461–65. Lahore: Ahl-i Ḥadīs̱ Dār al-Ishāʿat, 1988.
——— . "Niẓām-i ḥukūmat kaysā hōnā cāhiye." In *ʿAllāmah shahīd-i millat number, al-maʿrūf maqālāt-i ʿAllāmah Iḥsān Ilāhī Ẓahīr*, edited by ʿAbd al-Raḥmān Munīr Rājūvālvī, 466–72. Lahore: Ahl-i Ḥadīs̱ Dār al-Ishāʿat, 1988.
——— . *Al-Shīʿa wa-ahl al-bayt*. Lahore: Idārat Tarjumān al-Sunna, 1983.
——— . *Al-Shīʿa wa-l-Sunna*. Cairo: Dār al-Anṣār, 1979.
——— . *Al-Shīʿa wa-l-tashayyuʿ. Firaq wa-tārīkh*. Lahore: Idārat Tarjumān al-Sunna, 1984.
——— . "Vāqiʿah-i Karbalā." In *ʿAllāmah shahīd-i millat number, al-maʿrūf maqālāt-i ʿAllāmah Iḥsān Ilāhī Ẓahīr*, edited by ʿAbd al-Raḥmān Munīr Rājūvālvī, 166–92. Lahore: Ahl-i Ḥadīs̱ Dār al-Ishāʿat, 1988.
Zahrānī, ʿAlī ibn Mūsā. *Al-Shaykh Iḥsān Ilāhī Ẓahīr: Manhajuhu wa-juhūduhu fī taqrīr al-ʿaqīda wa-l-radd ʿalā al-firaq al-mukhālifa*. al-Riyāḍ: Dār al-Muslim, 2004.
Zaidi, S. A. *Issues in Pakistan's Economy*. Oxford: Oxford University Press, 1999.
Zaman, Muhammad Qasim. *Ashraf ʿAli Thanawi: Islam in Modern South Asia*. Oxford: Oneworld, 2008.
——— . "Consensus and Religious Authority in Modern Islam: The Discourses of the ʿUlama." In *Speaking for Islam: Religious Authorities in Muslim Societies*, edited by Gudrun Krämer and Sabine Schmidtke, 153–80. Leiden: Brill, 2006.
——— . *Modern Islamic Thought in a Radical Age: Religious Authority and Internal Criticism*. Cambridge: Cambridge University Press, 2012.
——— . *Religion and Politics under the Early ʿAbbāsids: The Emergence of the Proto-Sunnī Elite*. Leiden: Brill, 1997.
——— . "Review Essay: Modernity and Religious Change in South Asian Islam." *Journal of the Royal Asiatic Society* 14, no. 3 (2004): 253–63.
——— . "Sectarianism in Pakistan: The Radicalization of Shiʿi and Sunni Identities." *Modern Asian Studies* 32, no. 3 (1998): 689–716.
——— . "South Asian Islam and the Idea of the Caliphate." In *Demystifying the Caliphate: Historical Memory and Contemporary Contexts*, edited by Madawi Al-Rasheed, Carool Kersten, and Marat Shterin, 57–79. London: Hurst & Co., 2013.
——— . "The Sovereignty of God in Modern Islamic Thought." *Journal of the Royal Asiatic Society* 25, no. 3 (2015): 389–418.

———. "The Ulama and Contestations on Religious Authority." In *Islam and Modernity*, edited by Muhammad Khalid Masud, Armando Salvatore, and Martin van Bruinessen, 206–36. Edinburgh: Edinburgh University Press, 2009.
———. *The Ulama in Contemporary Islam: Custodians of Change*. Princeton, NJ: Princeton University Press, 2002.
———. "Tradition and Authority in Deobandi Madrasas of South Asia." In *Schooling Islam: The Culture and Politics of Modern Muslim Education*, edited by Robert W. Hefner and Muhammad Qasim Zaman, 61–86. Princeton, NJ: Princeton University Press, 2007.
al-Zamān, Naqvī Bukhārī, and Sayyid Muḥammad Jaʿfar. *Afkār al-muntaẓirīn*. Jaman Shāh: Al-Muntaẓirīn Research Center, 2003.
———. *Mauʿūd al-rusul yaʿnī dunyā kā ākhirī muṣliḥ-i aʿẓam (ʿajalla Allāh farjahu al-sharīf) farmūdāt-i anbiyāʾ kī rūshnī meṉ*. Karachi: al-Qāʾim Welfare Trust, 2008.
———. *Ṭarīq al-muntaẓirīn dar farāʾiż-i mūʾminīn*. Karachi: al-Qāʾim Welfare Trust.
Zamān ʿAlavī, Muḥammad. "ʿUlamāʾ kā maqām." *al-Ḥujjat* 7, no. 7 (1967): 39–40.
———. "Taqlīd aur aʿlamiyyat." *al-Ḥujjat* 10, no. 10 (1970): 17–20.
Zamindar, Vazira Fazila-Yacoobali. *The Long Partition and the Making of Modern South Asia: Refugees, Boundaries, Histories*. New York: Columbia University Press, 2007.
Zamir, Syed Rizwan. "ʿAlī Naqvī and His Thought." PhD diss., University of Virginia, 2011.
Zeghal, Malika. *Gardiens de l'Islam: Les oulémas d'Al Azhar dans l'Egypte contemporaine*. Paris: Presses de la Fondation Nationale des Sciences Politiques, 1996.
Ziring, Lawrence. "Militarism in Pakistan: The Yahya Khan Interregnum." *Asian Affairs* 1, no. 6 (1974): 402–20.
Żiyā, Miṣbāḥ. *Ghāzī shaykh Ḥaqq Navāz shahīd Miyānvālī jail se ākharī mulāqāt par vaṣiyyat nāmah: Ek mujāhid kī mujāhidānah bāteṉ*. Fayṣalābād: Bukhārī Academy, 2001.
———. *Ḥażrat Imām Mahdī: Ahl-i Islām aur ahl-i tashayyuʿ ke mutażad naẓariyyāt kā ḥaqīqī tajziyyah*. Fayṣalābād: Idārah-i Ishāʿat Al-Maʿārif, 2000.
———. *Maulānā Żiyā al-Raḥmān Fārūqī shahīd ke ʿilmī taqārīr*. Edited by Ṣanāʾullāh Saʿd. Lahore: Al-Hādī, 2010.
Zonis, Marvin, and Daniel Brumberg. *Khomeini, the Islamic Republic of Iran, and the Arab World*. Cambridge: Center for Middle Eastern Studies, 1987.
Zubaida, Sami. "Political Modernity." In *Islam and Modernity*, edited by Muhammad Khalid Masud, Armando Salvatore, and Martin van Bruinessen, 57–90. Edinburgh: Edinburgh University Press, 2009.
Zubayrī, Bilāl. *Taẕkirah-i auliyāʾ-i Jhang*. Lahore: Takhlīq Markaz, 1968.

INDEX

ʿAbbas, Akhtar, 62, 115
ʿAbd al-Shakur Lakhnavi, 22, 266n120
ʿAbduh, Muhammad, 141, 191
ʿAbidi, Sayyid ʿIrfan Haydar, 53, 80, 85, 234n186
Abraham, 175
Abu Bakr (First Caliph), 22, 170, 176, 177, 182, 265n91, 271n185
Abu Hanifa, 177
Abu ʾl-Hasan, Sayyid, 27, 211n82
Adam, 82
adhan, 69, 90, 163
Afghani, Jamal al-Din al-, 141, 147
Afghanistan, 142, 155, 166
ahl al-bayt, 37, 38, 64, 74, 76, 141, 144, 167; and Islamic law, 69; virtues of, 31, 96, 167
ahl al-khibra, 100, 117
Ahl-i Hadis, 24, 70, 140, 156, 158, 164, 165, 168, 182, 191; and sectarianism, 15, 36, 156, 167, 172, 184; and Wahhabis, 153, 154
ahl-i hall o ʿaqd, 41, 174
ahl-i ridda, 66
Ahmad, Attiya, 159
Ahmad, Bashir, 43, 219n198
Ahmadinejad, Mahmud, 93
Ahmadis, 132, 152, 153, 167, 171, 177, 218n180, 223n249; declaration as non-Muslims of, 51, 83, 161, 164
Ahrar. *See* Majlis-i Ahrar
Ahsaʾi, Shaykh Ahmad al-, 60, 79, 81, 87
Ahwal, ʿAsim al-, 177
ʿAʾisha, 176, 270n168
Akhbaris, 97, 205–6n18, 241n16
Alagha, Joseph, 200n16
aʿlamiyya, 100, 104, 105, 115, 147, 243n43
ʿAli, Sayyid Hashmat, 26, 30, 61, 210n75
ʿAli, Sayyid Riza, 24, 26, 30, 49, 209n59, 209n61
ʿAli b. Abi Talib, 68, 74, 89, 93, 120, 165, 167; authority of, 24, 35, 36, 53, 66, 69, 75, 88, 130, 147, 216n147; and caliphate, 24, 35, 106, 167, 235n210, 265n91, 271n185; and exegesis of Qurʾan, 83, 166; as God's appointee, 24, 35, 36, 42, 43, 69, 230n109, 269n152; shrine of, 83, 98; wars of, 80, 175
Aligarh, 31, 206n24, 207n32
ʿAlikhan, Navab Mir Fazl, 29, 186
ʿAllama al-Hilli al-, 85, 86, 182
Amin, Muhsin al-, 55, 72
ʿAllamah Hindi, 35, 50, 215n140
All India Muslim Personal Law Board, 188
All India Muslim Students Federation, 38, 219n198
All India Shiʿa Conference (AISC), 12, 22, 25, 33, 37; annual meeting of, 16, 17; and communalism, 20, 21, 30; and modern education, 29, 187; and *mujtahids* of Lucknow, 12, 21, 26, 27, 28, 29, 30, 32, 50, 186, 187; and Pakistan, 17, 43; paramilitary force of, 49; proceedings of, 10, 18, 25, 205n16; as progressive center of Shiʿi Islam, 25, 31, 34, 37, 50; and sectarianism, 21, 34; and Supervisory Council, 27, 28, 212n90, 212n91; and *taqlid*, 29, 30; trans-

national concerns of, 47, 48, 49, 50, 222n240
All India Shiʿa Political Conference, 21, 44, 207n34
All Pakistan Shiʿa Conference, 63, 77, 106
All Parties Shiʿa Conference, 44
Allsop Committee, 22
Al Saʿud, ʿAbd al-ʿAziz b. ʿAbd al-Rahman, 48, 154, 259n1
Amritsar, 40, 47
Amritsari, Sana'ullah, 36, 154, 265n91
Amroha, 35
Anjuman-i Himayat-i Islam, 43, 213n108
Anjuman-i Tahaffuz-i Ma'asir-i Mutabarrakah, 48
Ansari, Muhammad Bashir, 61, 66, 77, 84, 226n45; and God's transcendence, 79; and Shaykhism, 79, 81; success as polemicist, 234n186; and supernatural abilities of Imams, 79, 80, 81; view of ʿulama of, 82, 83
Ansari, Murtaza, 102, 103, 104, 244n63
Ansari, Shaykh Murtada al-, 93
al-ʿAqa'id al-imamiyya (al-Muzaffar), 67
ʿaqida, 66, 75, 76, 83, 84, 86, 87, 89, 110, 156, 184
al-ʿaql al-awwal, 68, 81, 86, 87
Arabian Peninsula, 19
Arabic, 10, 36, 92, 125, 152, 190; scholarship in, 56, 73, 95, 96, 97, 125, 148, 188, 191; study of, 31, 37, 122, 171, 213n108; terms in Urdu, 200n14, 205n12, 254n102; and translation, 5, 192, 216n147, 259n7
Ardabili, Muqaddas, 130
Al-ʿArif (journal), 180–81
Al-ʿArif Academy, 138
Armenia, 174
Arya Samaj, 38
Asad (journal), 62
Ashʿarism, 86
ʿashura, 69, 74, 76, 144
ʿAskari, Hasan al- (Eleventh Shiʿi Imam), 54
Asl al-usul (Shafiq Hasan), 35
Assembly of Experts, 131
Atatürk, Mustafa Kemal, 43, 47, 49, 186
auqaf, 43, 127
Avicenna, 87
Awadh, 23, 61
ayatucracy, 120
ʿAyyashi, Muhammad b. Masʿud al-, 165
Azad, Abu Kalam, 36, 37
ʿazadari, 64, 77, 89, 90, 141, 144, 181; freedom to perform, 127, 139; reform of, 72, 74, 75
Azerbaijan, 115, 174
Al-Azhar, 56, 253n98
ʿAzzam, ʿAbdullah, 155

Bab al-ʿUlum Madrasa (Multan), 2, 115
Baghawi, Husayn b. Masʿud, 87
Baghdad, 132, 165
Bahawalpur, 54
Bahrain, 122, 125, 136, 174
Baku, 24
Bangladesh, 11, 125, 161, 165, 175
Baqir, Sayyid Muhammad, 104, 105, 244n59
Baraghani, Muhammad-Taqi, 60
barah vafat, 23
Barelvi, Ahmad Riza Khan, 57, 71
Barelvis, 57, 70, 89, 164, 172, 182, 225n37
BBC, 126, 147
bhadralok, 12, 35
Bhashani, ʿAbd al-Hamid Khan, 109
Bhopal, 191
Bhutto, Zulfiqar Ali, 101, 109, 121, 161, 163, 164, 246n97, 263n62
bidʿa/bidaʿ, 69, 70, 133, 154
bidari, 143
Bigan Pali, 29
Bihar al-anwar (al-Majlisi), 56
Bihbahani, Muhammad, 107

Bihisht-i Zahra' cemetery, 121
Bin Baz, ʿAbd al-ʿAziz, 153
Black Friday massacre, 129
Blasphemy Laws (of Pakistan), 176
Bollywood, 64
Bombay, 29, 38, 42, 44, 55, 104, 108, 219–20n206
British colonial government, 18, 129, 154, 167, 180, 191; Pakistan's break with, 160; and Shiʿi Islam, 22, 24, 25, 33, 36, 42, 59, 64, 106
British India, 10, 177
British Parliamentary Delegation, 44
Brown, Vahid, 155
Brunner, Rainer, 155, 166
Bukhari, Sayyid Jaʿfar al-Zaman Naqvi, 58
Bukhari, Shah Ismaʿil, 33
Bulbula, Mirza Muhammad Rahim, 24
Burma, 61
Burqaʾi, Abu 'l-Fazl b. Riza al-, 83
Burujirdi, Sayyid Husayn, 70, 98, 101, 111, 115, 242n37
Buyid dynasty, 70

Cairo, 132, 191
Calcutta, 16, 45
caliphate, 20, 24, 36, 41, 47, 82, 132, 167, 172; and Shiʿis, 35, 74; SSP conception of, 15, 156, 170, 171, 173, 174, 177, 178, 179, 185
Center for Research Libraries, 101
Chakrabarty, Dipesh, 200n18
Chamberlain, Neville, 45
Chatterji, Joya, 35
Chiniot, 33
Chishti Sufis, 190
Christianity, 29, 38, 74, 98, 113, 132, 143, 149, 233n171
Churchill, Winston, 45, 148
citizenship, 109, 120, 131, 157, 160, 189
clothing restrictions, 133, 134, 135
Cole, Juan, 61, 97
colonialism, 27
commanding right and forbidding wrong, 74, 179, 232n147
communalism, 12, 19, 20, 21, 221n221
communism, 75, 110
Companions of the Prophet. See *sahaba*
Congress. *See* Indian National Congress
Constituent Assembly of India, 46
Constitutional Revolution, 27
conversion (to Shiʿi Islam), 32, 33, 38, 77, 169
Council of Islamic Ideology, 80, 162
Cundrigar, Ismaʿil Ibrahim, 38

Damascus University, 190
Dar al-Tabligh-i Islami, 115, 117, 118
Dar al-ʿUlum Muhammadiyya, 63, 64
Dars-i Al-i Muhammad, 87
dars-i kharij, 96, 136
daʿwa, 159
Deccan, 61, 226n44
Delhi, 31, 48, 189
Delhi Sultanate, 190
Deoband(is), 12, 37, 63, 70, 164, 172, 182, 192; and Pakistan movement, 12, 20, 40, 51, 183; and politics, 163, 164; and sectarianism, 4, 15, 22, 89, 90, 145, 154, 155, 158, 184, 187; seminary of, 2, 37, 199n3; and *taqlid*, 131, 132; and outreach to Shiʿis, 51, 70, 140, 183
Devji, Faisal, 39, 158
Dhakko, Muhammad Husayn al-Najafi, 6, 53, 62, 64, 70, 77, 94, 138, 229n87; attacks on, 72, 76, 82, 83, 84, 89, 90, 229n85; conception of Shiʿi identity of, 68, 69; and al-Khalisi, 83, 236n212; reformist ideas of, 66, 67, 68, 69, 71, 72; and self-view, 72, 73
dhu 'l-fiqar, 16, 167
Dhulipala, Venkat, 39
Dihlavi, Muhammad Baqi bi'llah, 88

Dihlavi, Sayyid Muhammad, 115, 126, 127
Dogar, Safdar Husayn, 82, 86, 89
Dokoha, 16
Dudoignon, Stéphane, 192

East India Company, 59
East Pakistan, 109, 203n60
economic exchanges, 55
Egypt, 49, 56, 130, 191, 192
emulation. See *taqlid*
Ende, Werner, 70, 265n94
Europe, 29, 37, 56, 199n3, 201n31, 273n24
Ewing, Katherine, 57

Fahd b. ʿAbd al-ʿAziz Al Saʿud (Crown Prince), 153
Farangi Mahall, 61
Farangi Mahalli, Muhammad Husayn Mubin Hanafi, 87
Farquhar, Michael, 191
Faruqi, Ziya al-Rahman, 170, 268n137; and conception of *sahaba*, 175, 176, 177, 178; and global ambitions, 173, 178; and honor of *sahaba*, 176, 177; and Shah Wali Allah, 178,179; Shiʿi reaction to, 181, 182
Fatima (daughter of Muhammad), 48, 133
Faysalabad, 87
Fayzabad, 26, 28
Fazl al-Rahman, Maulana, 140
Federal Shariat Court, 163
female education, 31
fiqh, 12, 41, 42, 43, 97, 102
First Intellect. See *al-ʿaql al-awwal*
First Muslim Civil War, 175
Fischer, Michael, 118
fitra, 68
Friedman, Yohanan, 88

Gandhi, Mahatma, 20, 31, 35, 128, 129, 130, 151, 207n37, 251n62
Gharib, ʿAbdallah Muhammad, 173
Ghazali, Abu Hamid Muhammad b. Muhammad al-, 87
Germany, 44, 80
Gesink, Indira Falk, 56
Ghulam Ahmad, Mirza, 132
Ghulam Rasul, 168
ghulat, 7, 224n15
Gilgit and Baltistan, 10, 123, 127, 157, 206n19
gnostic knowledge, 82
Golden Calf, 41
government (of Pakistan), 10, 139, 141, 161,182; and Islamization, 120, 140, 161; and sectarian bias, 44, 51, 126; Shiʿi confrontation with, 126, 127, 134, 135, 136, 140, 142, 145, 146
grand ayatollahs, 3, 13, 58, 64, 70, 84, 96, 97, 104
Green, Nile, 55
Green Movement, 148
Gulf States, 122, 158, 159, 173

Haʾiri, Sayyid ʿAli, 26, 61, 209–10n74
hajj, 48, 136, 179; restrictions for Shiʿis, 145; Iranian demonstrations during, 146; Shiʿi boycott of, 222n230; as venue for Muslim unity, 49, 140
Hakim, Sayyid Mahdi al-, 110, 112, 117
Hakim, Sayyid Muhammad ʿAli al-, 107
Hakim, Sayyid Muhsin al-, 13, 64, 70, 98, 101; as global *marjiʿ*, 13, 98, 99, 101, 109, 111, 113; and Imamia Mission, 107, 111; influence in Pakistan of, 98, 109, 110; interest in Pakistan of, 113, 131; legal opinions of, 70, 107, 111, 112, 113; as the most learned, 105, 106, 113; representatives of, 105, 106, 107, 242n36; succession to, 108, 112, 113, 114
halal, 69, 79
Hallaq, Wael, 156
Hanafi school, 12, 42, 43, 44, 49, 164, 177, 182
haqiqa muhammadiyya, 81

Haqq, Sayyid Nazir al-, 41
Haqqani, Jalal al-Din, 155
haram, 69, 79, 110
Hasan, Sayyid Aqa, 24
Hasan, Sayyid Vazir, 21, 207n36
Hasan b. ʿAli (second Imam), 88
Hauza (journal), 73
hauza, 96, 97, 99, 115, 136, 137, 150, 192
Haykel, Bernard, 153
Hazarahs, 157
Hejaz, 48, 49
Hejaz Conference, 48
Hezbollah, 122, 149, 200n16, 200n19
Hidden Imam, 27, 90; contact with, 13, 54, 58, 64, 92, 93; deputyship of, 105, 106, 108, 142, 237n229; as shared Sunni-Shiʿi figure, 90, 91, 94; and reform, 133; return of, 58, 76, 91, 133, 167; ʿulama as representative of, 91, 99, 102, 105, 119, 130, 148; waiting for, 181
Hinduism, 29
Hindus, 17, 20, 64, 98, 187; "extremism" of, 43; in Bengal, 45, 161; in Punjab, 47
Hitler, Adolf, 44, 45
Hong Kong, 173
hudud, 84, 178
Al-Hujjat (journal), 100, 105, 106, 107, 108, 110, 112, 113, 114, 245n84
Hukumat-i Islami (Khomeini), 85, 171
Husayn, Jaʿfar, 44, 220n209
Husayn, Mirza Yusuf, 61
Husayn, Mufti Jaʿfar, 62, 149, 253n98; authority of, 135; and Iran, 134, 135, 136; local approach of, 134, 136, 145, 151
Husayn, Navab Sarfaraz, 16
Husayn, Sayyid Nasir, 24, 30, 213n104
Husayn, Sayyid Tajir, 17
Husayn b. ʿAli (Third Shiʿi Imam), 48, 73, 82, 111; criticism of, 148; and Khomeini, 128; martyrdom of, 22, 72, 83, 181; and reformist reading of mission of, 64, 71, 73, 74, 111, 144; shrine of, 48, 80, 93, 163; and Sufism, 88; universal conceptualization of, 32, 64, 70, 71, 133, 144
Husayni, Sayyid ʿArif al-, 14, 53, 135, 137, 138, 181, 223n1, 254n120; as admirer of Khomeini and Iran, 137, 140, 142, 150; and authority of the ʿulama, 140, 143; enemies of, 139, 141, 143, 145; and Imam Husayn, 143, 144; and Islamic revolution, 142, 143, 144, 145; leader of TNFJ, 123, 127, 138; and Muslim unity, 140, 179; political activism of, 140, 143, 145; and *taqlid*, 143; and *vilayat-i faqih*, 95, 146; as *wakil* of Khomeini, 138, 143, 150
Hyderabad (Deccan), 37
Hyderabad (Sindh), 80

Ibn ʿAbd al-Barr, 174
Ibn ʿAbd al-Wahhab, 66
Ibn Hanbal, Ahmad, 177
Ibn-i Hasan, Sayyid, 26, 28, 209n73
Ibn Kathir, Ismaʿil b. ʿUmar, 176
Ibn Saʿud. *See* Al Saʿud, ʿAbd al-ʿAziz b. ʿAbd al-Rahman
Ibn Taymiyya, 66, 177, 182
Ibn Umm Maktum, 176
ʿid al-adha, 105
ʿid al-fitr, 105
Idarah-i Minhaj al-Husayn, 101
Idarah-i Tahaffuz-i Huquq-i Shiʿa (ITHS), 63, 106
Ihqaqi, Mirza Hasan al-Haʾiri al-, 85
Ihsan (newspaper), 51
Ihyaʾ al-shariʿa (al-Khalisi), 83
ijaza, 57, 84
ijmaʿ, 35, 93, 177, 182
ijtihad, 2, 25, 35, 96, 98, 131, 132, 144; Shiʿi theory of, 102, 106; traditionalist critique of, 82, 83
ilham, 67, 229n87
ʿilm-i ghayb, 67, 85
imambara, 23, 42, 113

Imamia Mission, 33, 100, 107, 110, 111, 112, 117
Imamia Organisation (IO), 128
Imamia Students Organisation (ISO), 73, 127, 128; and political activism, 134, 135, 136, 137; and revolutionary change, 180, 181, 271n195; and sectarianism, 162, 163
Imamiyyah Kutubkhanah, 147
Imam Khomeini Library, 95
Imam Riza (shrine of, in Mashhad), 47, 136
Imams (Shiʿis), 8, 16, 60, 90, 149; authority of, 28, 35, 68, 69, 75, 80, 87, 88, 89, 106, 130, 167; cosmological position of, 69, 82, 83, 85, 90, 148; creation of, out of light, 67, 75, 79, 81, 85; graves of, 1, 12, 48, 71; humanity of, 59, 82, 84; infallibility of, 84, 85, 86, 171; as intermediaries between God and humans, 58, 79, 81; knowledge of, 67, 68, 85; and Pakistan, 13, 39, 40; in Qur'an, 165, 170; sayings of, 69, 73, 75, 141; Shiʿi veneration of, 37, 51, 66, 68, 121; and SSP, 22, 162, 171, 172; supernatural abilities of, 54, 79, 80, 81, 82, 139, 187; ʿulama as deputies of, 111, 142, 149
imperialism, 141, 143, 180
impetus (concept of), 4
India, 101, 188
Indian National Congress, 20, 21, 22, 23, 36, 42, 45, 129, 207n36, 220n207, 220n209
Institute of Islamic Preaching, 13. *See also* Dar al-Tabligh-i Islami
institutional isomorphism, 172
International Islamic University (Islamabad), 145
Iqbal, Muhammad, 131, 152, 167, 184, 210n74, 272n210
Iqbal, Raja, 181
Iran, 2, 27, 49, 56, 91, 115, 189, 249n12; autonomization from, 112, 148, 155; as center of learning, 5, 47, 50, 56, 60, 95, 123; centrality of, 5, 6, 14, 112, 115, 142; critique of, 91, 99, 120, 122, 149; domestic situation of, 133, 134, 148; and leadership of ʿulama, 4, 27, 75; relations with Pakistan, 19, 97, 121, 122, 123, 124, 150; as role model, 15, 43, 47, 49, 76, 120, 123, 140, 142; Sunni minority of, 140, 173, 174, 268n147; and superpowers, 141, 145. *See also* Iranian Revolution
Iranian Revolution, 2, 3, 5, 7, 93, 155; consequences of, for Pakistan, 14, 122, 127, 187; export of, 6, 14, 135, 139, 140, 149; global impact of, 121, 122, 137, 181, 189; and implications for religious authority, 9, 101, 124, 187; localization of, 128, 129, 133, 136, 137, 139, 140, 141, 142, 143, 144, 145, 146, 155; perception of Islamization of, 120, 121; and politicization of scholars, 73, 121, 127, 137; and reformist discourses, 60, 73; and sectarianism, 15, 19, 52, 156, 164, 166, 170, 173, 179, 184; stages of reception in Pakistan, 123, 124, 126, 127, 128, 136, 181; and *taqrib*, 122, 140; and women, 144, 145. See also *vilayat-i faqih*
Iran-Iraq War, 121, 122, 133, 134, 136, 139, 146, 149, 166
Iraq, 19, 31, 35, 50, 53, 70, 105, 114; leading scholars of, 60, 61, 63, 75, 96, 99, 105; political situation in, 117, 126, 137, 223n1; religious education in, 5, 12, 31, 83, 96, 97; and sectarianism, 173, 180, 181; sources from, 2, 6, 10; ties with Pakistan, 35, 47, 123
Isfahani, Mirza Hashim, 29, 212n94
Isfahani, Mirza Abu 'l-Hasan, 38
Isfahani, Sayyid Abu 'l-Hasan, 104, 105
Ismaʿilis, 81, 86, 87, 199n1, 206n19
islah, 31, 133, 144, 178
Islah al-Rusum (Dhakko), 53, 89

Islamabad, 10, 77, 134, 135, 139, 145, 146, 147, 158, 171
Islamabad Agreement, 135, 136, 139
Islamia College (Lahore), 31, 35, 213n108
Islamic modernism, 29
Islamic Republic (of Iran), 4, 125, 130, 131, 142, 146, 148, 156, 187, 202n47, 229n101
Islamic Revolution, 120, 122, 134, 155; in Pakistan, 15, 137, 140, 142, 150, 179, 180, 184, 185; Sunni version of, 169, 172. *See also* Iranian Revolution
Islamic scholarly tradition, 4, 5, 7, 8, 38, 173, 174, 185
Islamic Socialism, 109
Islamic studies (field of), 7, 191
Islamic University of Medina, 152, 153, 191, 203–4n63, 259n1
Islamists, 8, 70, 144, 163, 168, 171, 192; Shiʿi Islamists, 21, 35, 130; and the state, 156, 161, 164
Ismaʿil, Muhammad, 61, 66, 87; family background of, 227n58; and polemical debates, 87; and Sufism, 88, 89; and *taqrib*, 87
Israel, 119
istikbar-i jahani, 145

Jaʿfari, Sayfullah, 62
Jaʿfari Court, 36
jahiliyya, 132
Jalandhar, 16, 97
Jamaʿat-i Islami, 21, 121, 163, 171, 172, 191
Jaman Shah, 90
Jamiʿah-i Imamiyya, 95, 215–16n144
Jamia Millia, 31
Jamiʿat al-Kauthar, 77
Jamiʿat al-Muntazar, 97, 101, 112, 114, 115, 136, 209–10n74
Jamʿiat al-ʿUlum al-Islamiyya (Banuri Town), 171
Jamiʿat al-ʿUrwa al-Wuthqa, 124, 147, 150
Jamiʿat al-Zahraʾ, 134, 253n95
Jamʿiyyat al-ʿUlamaʾ-i Hind, 22, 23, 39, 211n85
Jamʿiyyat al-ʿUlamaʾ-i Islam, 39, 41, 51, 140, 163
Jamʿiyyat al-ʿUlamaʾ-i Pakistan, 163
Jamkaran, 93
Jang (newspaper), 140
Jannat al-Baqiʿ cemetery, 12, 48, 168
Jara, Husayn Bakhsh, 62, 63, 114, 227–28n60
Jarcavi, Sayyid Ibn-i Hasan, 31, 32, 35, 46, 48, 128, 213n108, 214n110
Jauhar-i Qurʾan (Haydar), 37, 216n157
Jerusalem, 136
Jesus, 175
Jews, 74, 129, 167
Jhang, 32, 33, 158, 159, 169, 170, 172
Jhangvi, Haqq Navaz, 154, 155, 171, 172; anti-Ahmadi agitations of, 169; charisma of, 170; and declaration of Shiʿis as non-Muslims, 172; education of, 168; and Iranian Revolution, 170, 171, 173; and Shiʿi symbols, 172
Jhansath, 26
Jihad (newspaper), 135
Jinnah, Muhammad Ali, 38, 40, 42, 43, 45, 217n165; and Pakistan, 160, 167, 184
Jones, Justin, 24, 34, 47, 55, 56, 98, 204n2, 205n16, 211n82, 213n104, 215n130
Jones, Kenneth, 62

Kaʿba, 142
Al-Kafi fi ʿilm al-din (al-Kulayni), 67, 165
Kalb-i ʿAbbas, Sayyid, 30, 213n103
Kalb-i Sadiq, Sayyid, 188
kalimah, 42, 175, 176
Kamran, Tahir, 32, 262n42
Karachi, 10, 95, 108, 119, 121, 125, 126, 145, 171, 183, 186
Karbala, 13, 53, 72, 73, 74, 93; earth from, 80; and Gandhi, 128; global implica-

tions of, 144, 181; liberation of, 136; and shrine of Husayn, 163
Kashf al-asrar (Khomeini), 170
Kashif al-Ghita, Muhammad Husayn, 84
Kashifi, Kamal al-Din Husayn b. ʿAli al-Waʿiz, 72
Kashmir, 113, 143
Kashmiri, Sayyid Aqa Murtaza, 105, 244n64
Kayhan International, 135
Keddie, Nikki R., 99
Kenya, 125
Khairpur, 53
Khalisi, Muhammad b. Muhammad Mahdi al-, 70, 83, 85
Khamenei, Ali, 76, 142, 146, 148, 150, 156
Khan, Amir Haydar, 26, 34, 42, 43, 49
Khan, Asghar, 163, 264n78
Khan, Ayub, 101, 109, 113, 127, 162
Khan, Muhammad Amir Ahmad, 26, 38, 39, 46, 51
Khan, Navab Muzaffar ʿAli Khan, 26
Khan, Naveeda, 99, 160, 161, 184
Khan, Raja Ghazanfar ʿAli, 44, 219n204
Khan, Sayyid Ahmad, 29, 191
Khan, Siddiq Hasan, 191
Khan, Taslim Riza, 180
Khan, Yahya, 101, 165, 166
khandan-i ijtihad, 31, 35, 111, 188
Khandaq, 80
Khar, Malik Ghulam Mustafa, 163
Kharijites, 40, 74
Khatami, Muhammad, 148
Khatib, Muhibb al-Din al-, 166
khatm al-nubuwwat, 83
Khatun, Hidayat, 37
Khaybar, 89
Al-Khidr, 82
khilafa. See caliphate
Khilafat-i Rashida (journal), 172
Khilafat movement, 18, 20, 24, 47, 48, 98, 154
al-Khutut al-ʿarida (al-Khatib), 166
King Edwards Medical College, 163
Khomeini, Ruhallah, 74, 85, 119, 136; appropriation of, by traditionalists, 84, 93, 187; authority of, in Pakistan, 6, 13, 14, 73, 99, 112, 119, 123, 124, 127, 128, 137, 140; and enemies of Revolution, 145, 186; influence of, on Sunnis, 15, 147, 156, 172, 176, 179, 185, 267n127; as leader of Islamic Republic, 119, 130, 131, 149, 156, 184; as leader of worldwide movement, 133, 139, 141, 142; as *marjiʿ*, 105, 112, 117, 143; as *mujaddid*, 132, 133; and nonviolence, 128, 129, 130; outreach of, to Sunnis, 140, 166, 172; and "slander" of *sahaba*, 170, 171, 172, 176; ties with Pakistan, 120, 125, 127, 136, 137, 138, 150, 184; views of, on women, 133, 134; and *vilayat-i takvini*, 85, 149, 237n229
Khuʾi, Abu ʾl-Qasim al-, 70, 84, 99, 109, 112, 166, 241n25
khums, 63, 72, 82, 83, 99, 102, 106, 107, 110, 111, 115
Khurramabadi, Hasan Tahiri, 136
Khushab, 114
Kirmani, Muhammad Karim Khan, 60
Kufa, 74, 93, 137, 181
Kufi, Furat b. Ibrahim al-, 165
kuffar, 36, 42, 67, 74, 165, 176
kufr, 75, 80, 88, 140, 172
Kulayni, Muhammad b. Yaʿqub al-, 67, 165, 253n90
Kurram Agency, 137, 157
Kuwait, 122, 136, 159, 226n45, 236–37n228

labor migration, 158, 159
Lahore, 16, 17, 47, 61, 114, 124, 138, 189, 190; as center of Shiʿi learning, 10, 26, 97, 112, 147; education in, 31, 34, 163, 164, 181, 190; and Iranian Revolution, 14, 124, 128, 141, 146, 147, 151, 186, 213n108; journals published in, 62, 101,

110, 138; libraries of, 101; prominent families of, 204n1, 209–10n74; and sectarianism, 36, 43, 153, 163, 173
Lahore Resolution, 17, 42
Lalljee, Hooseinbhoy, 37, 44, 219–20n206
Landau-Tasseron, Ella, 132
The Last Great Reformer of the World (Ja'far al-Zaman), 90
League of Nations, 31
Lebanon, 36, 55, 70, 122, 126, 136, 138, 141, 149, 151, 154, 173
Le Monde, 128
Lenin, Vladimir, 32, 75
Liaqatabad, 145
Libya, 125
Louër, Laurence, 122, 148, 200n16
Lucknow, 16, 22, 30, 31, 101, 104, 110, 118; as center of Shi'ism in subcontinent, 2, 18, 28, 32, 33, 50, 60, 96, 97, 128, 192; Iranian critique of, 96; *mujtahids* of, 12, 18, 21, 25, 26, 27, 28, 50, 106, 111, 186, 187, 205–6n18; and sectarianism, 12, 17, 21, 22, 23, 24, 34, 42, 44, 45, 266n120; and Shaykhism, 60, 61; as symbol of refinement, 188, 189
Ludhiana, 16
al-Lu'lu' wa-l-marjan fi adab ahl al-minbar (al-Tabarsi), 72
Lum'at al-Anwar fi 'aqa'id al-abrar (Jara), 63

Madani, Asadullah, 137
Madani, Sayyid Husayn Ahmad, 42, 206n29
madhhab, 36, 71, 72, 76, 139, 141, 154, 164, 167, 168
madh-i sahaba, 22, 23, 42, 49
Madras, 29, 61
Madrasah-i Nasiriyya, 26
Madrasah-i Nazimiyya, 2, 77
Madrasat Sultan al-Madaris (Khairpur), 53, 223n2
Madrasat Sultan al-Madaris (Sargodha), 77, 101
Madrasat al-Wa'izin, 77, 234n175
mahdi. See Hidden Imam
Mahdi, Sayyid Muhammad, 25, 26
Mahmudabad family, 16, 26, 31, 42, 46, 48, 188, 217n166
majalis, 48, 55, 89, 91, 106, 112, 143, 188, 225–26n38; reform of, 63, 64, 70, 71, 72, 74
Majlisi, Muhammad Baqir al-, 56, 79
Majlis-i Ahrar, 22, 23, 42, 208n52
Majlis-i Mutahhidah 'Amal, 70, 71
Majlis-i Vahdat-i Muslimin, 147, 148, 186
Makdisi, Ussama, 154
Maktubat-i Imam-i Rabbani (Sirhindi), 88
malang, 73
Malik b. Anas, 177
Al-Manshur (journal), 40
maraji' al-taqlid, 3, 4, 8, 112, 148, 200n14, 203n49, 240–41n12; appropriation of, by traditionalists, 84, 85, 86, 90; authority in Pakistan of, 73, 98, 112; emergence of, 104, 108; factors of influence of, 100, 118; and most learned, 104, 105, 106, 243n46; transnational influence of, 98, 99, 102, 112, 114. *See also* grand ayatollahs; *mujtahids*
Marsden, Magnus, 99
martyr(s), 32, 71, 129, 135, 136, 144, 235n208, 251n62, 266n112, 271n92
Marx, Karl, 32, 109
Mary (mother of Jesus), 176
Mashhad, 9, 47, 48, 73, 120, 123, 136, 222n240, 228n64
Mashhadi, Mirza Safdar Husayn, 100, 104, 117; and local authority, 107, 108, 110; and Muhsin al-Hakim, 105, 106, 107, 108, 109, 110; and scholarly hierarchy, 105, 106, 244n63
mashi'a, 81
maslaha, 69, 229–30n101

maʿsumin. *See* Imams
matam, 75, 80
Matthiesen, Toby, 158
Maududi, Abu 'l-Aʿla, 21, 121, 132, 172, 185, 191, 192, 267n127
Mawardi, ʿAli b. Muhammad al-, 174
Mawsili, ʿAbdallah b. ʿAbdallah al-, 166
Mecca, 77, 80, 145, 146, 165, 174
Medina, 12, 48, 145, 152, 153, 168, 174, 191, 203–4n63, 270n168
Mehrabad, 121
Mervin, Sabrina, 55, 122, 123
Middle East, 19, 58, 97, 121, 155, 187, 192; negotiations of authority with, 4, 5, 98, 113, 118, 189; Pakistan's ties to, 3, 12, 159, 161; as religious center, 50, 93, 96, 191; and travel of ideas, 7, 50, 190
al-Milal wa-l-nihal (al-Shahrastani), 86
Minault, Gail, 47
Minhaj al-Qur'an, 190
Minhaj al-sunna al-nabawiyya (Ibn Tamiyya), 182
Ministry of Foreign Affairs (Iran), 149–50, 258–59n229
Mir, Farina, 32
al-Mizan fi tafsir al-Qur'an (Tabataba'i), 86
modernists, 12, 13, 28, 48, 49, 67, 83, 160, 239n269; critique of ʿulama of, 8, 18, 23, 25, 29, 50, 186
Mongols, 165
moon sightings, 105, 107
Moses, 82, 175
Movement for the Implementation of Jaʿfari Law. *See* Tahrik-i Nifaz-i Fiqh-i Jaʿfariyyah
Movement for the Restoration of Democracy, 164
Muʿawiya b. Abi Sufyan, 74, 120, 172, 175, 178
mubahala, 77, 233n171
Mughals, 132, 160
muhajirs, 61, 76, 155
Muhammad, Tufayl, 121
Muhammad (Muslim Prophet), 7, 73, 75, 85, 90, 109, 153, 178, 199n3; birthday of, 23, 89; and blasphemy, 176, 177; custom of, 57, 69, 77, 179, 183; finality of prophethood of, 83; mission of, 16, 82, 167, 168; offspring of, 79, 133; opposition to, 77, 165, 182; and "pure" Islam, 43, 140; sayings of, 7, 44, 45, 73, 172, 174; succession to, 106, 132, 178; supernatural disposition of, 68, 79, 80, 85, 86, 89; veneration of, 23, 84, 89; and violence, 31, 35; wives of, 23, 37, 176, 270n168. See also *sahaba*
Muharram, 39, 51, 89, 95, 138, 145, 189; Shiʿi processions of, 22, 135, 138, 162, 169, 171
mujaddid, 14, 123, 130, 132, 143, 151, 252n87
mujtahid(s), 17, 29, 85, 89; of the age, 106, 107, 108, 111; hierarchy of, 97, 98, 103, 105, 106, 107, 117; of Iran and Iraq, 48, 61, 83, 98, 105; of Lucknow, 12, 18, 21, 24, 25, 26, 27, 28, 30, 33, 50, 187, 188; and religious authority, 30, 32, 55, 102, 104, 108; in subcontinent, 58, 72, 89, 96, 97, 98, 105, 111, 136; Sunni lack of, 131
mujtahida(s), 134
Mukherjee, Shyama Prasad, 45
Multan, 1, 2, 10, 26, 48, 54, 63, 96, 115, 169, 171
Multani, Sayyid Muhammad ʿArif, 1, 2
munazara, 73, 77, 86, 87, 164, 169, 171
Al-Muntazar (journal), 101, 113, 114, 115, 117
Muntaziri, Husayn ʿAli, 125, 250n30
Muraj, Fazil, 42, 44, 220–21n210
murids, 46, 109
Murtada, Sharif al-, 86

Musa, ʿAqil, 95, 118
Musavi, Sayyid Hamid ʿAli, 139
Musavi ʿAliabadi, Sayyid ʿAli Sharaf al-Din, 73, 87, 89, 94, 232n139; attacks on, 77; and Iranian Revolution, 138, 140; and political conception of Karbala, 73, 74; and Shiʿi reform, 74, 75, 76; and *ʿulama*, 76, 77
Musawi, Musa al-, 83, 173, 235n210
Mushaf Fatima, 165, 229n87
mushkilkusha, 79, 80
The Muslim (newspaper), 142
Muslim Brotherhood, 130, 191
Muslim League, 12, 17, 21, 23, 38; and sectarianism, 38, 40, 42, 43, 44, 45, 51; vision of Pakistan of, 18, 39, 42, 46
Muslim World League, 190
Mussolini, Benito, 45
Mutahhari, Murtaza, 72, 133
mutashabihat, 72
Muʿtazili(s), 86, 226n41
Muzaffar, Muhammad Rida al-, 67
Muzaffargarh, 54
Muzaffarnagar, 26

Nadvi, Abu 'l-Hasan ʿAli, 190, 191
Nair, Neeti, 20, 221n221
Najaf, 1, 2, 9, 13, 24, 53, 63, 97, 136, 137; as a center of learning, 83, 107, 112, 117; increased accessibility of, 102, 203n50; religious education in, 73, 150, 123. See also *mujtahids*
Najafi, Bashir Husayn al-, 96, 97
Najafi, Ghulam Husayn, 170
Najafi, Sayyid Muhammad Hasan, 102
Najafi, Sayyid Muhammad Yar Shah, 62, 115
Najafi, Sayyid Murtaza Husayn, 113, 128, 129, 130, 131, 151, 216n147, 251n53
Najafi, Sayyid Safdar Husayn, 112, 128, 130, 131, 144, 147, 151, 251n53; and *dars-i kharij* in Pakistan, 136; and Khomeini as *mujaddid*, 132, 133; views of, on *pardah*, 133, 134
Najafi, Sayyid Shihab al-Din Marʿashi, 84
Najafi, Sayyid Talib Husayn Shah Naqvi, 90
Najafi, Shaykh ʿAli, 96
Najd, 48
Najm al-Hasan, 26, 210n76
Naqshbandi-Mujaddidi teachings, 88
Naqvi, Sayyid ʿAli Naqi, 32, 33, 50, 61, 85, 128; influence of reformist thought of, 71, 72, 100, 101, 110, 133; legal opinions of, 58; and modernity, 111; portrayal of Husayn, 111, 133, 144; shift toward Urdu, 111, 137, 188
Naqvi, Sayyid Gulab ʿAli Shah, 62, 245n76
Naqvi, Sayyid Husayn ʿArif, 56, 60, 233n167
Naqvi, Sayyid Javad, 14, 124, 186, 257–58n207; and Hezbollah, 149; and Iran, 147, 148, 149, 150, 155; and Jamiʿat al-ʿUrwa al-Wuthqa, 147, 150; and political activism, 147, 148, 149; visibility of, in Pakistan, 146, 147; and *wilaya*, 124, 145, 148, 149, 184
Naqvi, Sayyid Muhammad ʿAli, 162
Naroval, 51
nasibi, 77
Nasir, Muhammad, 24
Nasirabadi, Sayyid Dildar ʿAli, 50, 96, 205–6n18
National Awami Party (NAP), 109
nationalism, 20
Nazimiyya seminary (Lucknow), 2, 77
Nehru, Jawaharlal, 167
New Imperial History, 190
Noah's Ark, 40
Non-Cooperation movement, 42, 129
nonviolence, 14, 123, 128, 129, 130
Northern Areas. *See* Gilgit and Baltistan

nubuwwa, 60, 82
Nuʿmani, Manzur, 173

Objectives Resolution, 40
Occultation (of the Twelfth Imam), 8, 58, 84, 91, 93, 102, 148, 167
Operation Gibraltar, 113
Oriental College (Lahore), 31, 213n108
Oriental College (Rampur), 31
orthodoxy: conceptions of in Islam, 8, 85, 164, 187, 225n25
Østebø, Terje, 4
Ottoman sultan, 20

Pachisi, 30, 213n105
Pahlavi, Muhammad Reza Shah, 111, 120, 121, 127, 128, 129, 130, 133, 136, 137, 138, 151
Pahlavi, Reza Shah, 43, 47, 49, 186
Pakistan, 5, 10, 51, 109, 131; envisioning of, 3, 4, 14, 17, 18, 39, 41, 44, 46, 160, 161, 180, 184, 187; as Islamic state, 40, 41, 51, 144, 180, 183, 187; and Islamization, 83, 120, 127, 145, 146, 150, 161, 162, 163; movement for, 12, 18, 19, 38, 42; problems of, 89, 123, 124, 131, 173, 174, 180; and Shiʿi education, 2, 60, 61, 96, 97, 114, 115; Shiʿi community of, 3, 14, 58, 60, 74, 75, 95, 96, 101, 123, 126, 127, 142, 145, 149, 150, 157, 158, 165, 166, 179, 180, 181, 182; as a Sunni state, 15, 43, 44, 45, 51, 156, 171, 172. *See also* Iranian Revolution; sectarianism; Shiʿism
Pakistan Civil Secretariat, 135
Pakistan National Alliance, 163
Pakistan People's Party (PPP), 109, 121, 161, 163, 246n97, 263n69
Palestine, 143
Pan-Islam, 48, 98, 147
Parachinar, 137, 138
pardah, 134, 222n242
Paris, 127, 128
Pars (newspaper), 135
Partition, 19, 47, 51, 60, 62, 154; and new nation-states, 4, 22, 51, 52, 126, 127, 160, 187; and Shiʿi institutions, 60, 61, 96; and Shiʿi religious authority, 18, 60, 62, 63, 96, 187
Pashto, 139, 140
passive resistance, 32
Patna, 26, 28
Payam-i ʿAmal (journal), 101, 110, 111, 112, 113, 117
periphery, 1, 2, 4, 9, 97, 98, 100, 187, 273n15; potentials of, 13, 169, 189, 191
Persian, 5, 10, 48, 50, 73, 95, 96, 107, 111, 125, 138, 186, 188
Persian Gulf, 158, 159
Peshawar, 10, 100, 105, 139, 145
philosophy, 31, 74, 145
piety, 32, 33, 104, 106, 117, 124, 125, 159, 167, 178, 265n91
Pinault, David, 99
Pir of Golrah Sharif, 46
popular customs, 54, 59, 61, 64, 66, 70, 76, 89, 214n114
Popular Islamic Army, 139
popular preachers. See *zakirs*
Pune, 44
Punjab, 1, 2, 10, 16, 28, 46, 61, 90, 96, 159, 163, 204n5; local religious authority in, 114, 147; and Partition, 46, 47, 51; and reformism, 12, 18, 22, 61, 62, 76; sectarian situation of, 32, 43, 44, 45, 89, 158, 163; spiritual landscape of, 32, 33, 93, 94
Punjab Muslim Students Federation, 43
Punjab Shiʿa Political Conference, 44
public sphere, 22, 98, 173, 203n56

Qadi ʿIyad, 87
Qadri, Tahir al-, 190
Qalandar, Lal Shabaz, 161
Qaradawi, Yusuf al-, 190
qasba, 16, 17, 204n2

Qasimi, Israr al-, 170
Qatar, 190
qaum, 20, 41, 150, 206n29. *See also* Shiʿi *qaum*
qiyas, 69, 132
Qizilbash, Navab Muzaffar ʿAli Khan, 46
Qizilbash, Navab Nisar ʿAlikhan, 16, 204n1
Quetta, 10, 139, 157
Qum, 83, 93, 97, 107, 115, 116, 117, 125, 137, 192; offices of *marajiʿ* in, 9, 13, 101, 107, 115; religious education in, 73, 95, 104, 123, 124, 138, 147, 150
Qummi, Saʿd b. ʿAbdallah al-, 165
Qummi, Sayyid Aqa ʿAli Husayn, 54, 223–24n5
Qurʾan, 8, 41, 54, 82, 89, 139, 147, 178; as comprehensive guidance, 71, 72, 75, 143, 144, 183; exegesis of, 36, 37, 75, 86, 111, 130, 134, 166, 169, 179, 183; integrity of, 38, 165; and *sahaba*, 6, 15, 175, 176; and Shiʿi Imams, 74, 83, 165, 166, 167, 170. See also *tahrif*
Qurʾan and Ahl al-Bayt Conference, 141
Qurʾan and Sunna Conference, 141
Quraysh, 176
Qureshi, M. Naeem, 47
Qutb, Sayyid, 130, 191

Rabvah, 171
Radio Pakistan, 105
Rafsanjani, Ali Akbar Hashemi, 148
Rah-i ʿAmal (journal), 73, 127, 139, 181
Rahnema, Ali, 56
Ramadan, 69, 90, 105, 141
Rampur, 25, 31, 37, 188
Rapprochement between Sunnis and Shiʿis. See *taqrib*
rashidun, 41, 42, 147, 177, 178, 179
Rashti, Sayyid Kazim, 81, 87
Rassler, Don, 155
Rawalpindi, 47, 110, 127
Rawdat al-Shuhadaʾ (al-Kashifi), 72
Reetz, Dietrich, 57
reformist discourses, 55, 56. *See also* Shiʿi reformists
religious authority, 54, 186, 189, 190, 205n57; centering on most learned *mujtahid*, 5, 13, 102, 104, 105, 106, 118, 243n43; construction of, 99, 100, 101, 104, 117; contestations over, 19, 25, 50; definition of, 7, 8, 9; local aspects of, 5, 12, 50, 98, 99, 100, 107, 108, 112, 114, 117, 124; mystical conceptions of, 6, 32, 33, 88; redefinition of, by traditionalists, 13, 54, 58, 82, 83, 84, 91; and Shiʿi Imams, 58, 68, 79, 82, 87, 89, 130, 144, 149; Shiʿi transformation of, 2, 25, 60; and Shiʿi ʿulama, 18, 24, 25, 26, 54, 55, 71, 99, 104, 130, 148, 186; transnational aspects of, 3, 5, 8, 9, 14, 15, 76, 96, 113, 117, 123, 150, 187. See also *mujtahids*; Shʿi reformists; Shiʿi traditionalists; Shiʿi *ʿulama*; *vilayat-i takvini*
religious polemics, 155, 261n22
remittances, 159
representative, of a *marjiʿ*. See *wakil*
response (concept of), 4
Revolutionary Council, 131
Rieck, Andreas, 6, 55, 56, 114, 127
Rightly Guided Caliphs. See *rashidun*
risala ʿamaliyya, 103, 107, 111, 117, 118
Risalah dar radd-i rawafiz (Sirhinid), 89
Risalat al-iʿtiqadat (al-Saduq), 66
Rizakar (journal), 135, 138
Rizakaran-i Jannat al-Baqiʿ, 49
Rizvi, Muhammad Baqir, 24
Rizvi, Sayyid Zamir al-Hasan, 61
Robinson, Francis, 2
Ruhani, Hasan, 148
al-rukn al-rabiʿ, 60, 85, 226n43
Russians, 115, 119, 129

sabb al-sahaba, 140, 166, 167, 182
Sabiqi, Muhammad Hasnayn al-, 55, 56, 57, 58, 88, 89, 90, 236n228; and

esoteric knowledge, 84, 86, 87; in Samarra, 53, 54, 55
Sabzavari, ʿAbd al-Aʿla Musavi, 84
Sadaqat (journal), 63
Sadiq, Jaʿfar al- (Sixth Shiʿi Imam), 67, 82, 253n98
Sadr, Muhammad Baqir al-, 84, 104, 137
Sadr, Musa al-, 138
Saduq, Ibn Babawayh al-, 66, 69
Safavids, 56, 70
sahaba, 6, 35, 42, 43, 162, 165, 170, 176, 182; definition of, 174, 175, 176, 177, 178; insulting of, 166, 169, 170, 171, 173, 177, 178, 269n152; and Islamic tradition, 174, 175, 269–70n159. *See also* Sipah-i Sahabah-i Pakistan
Sahla Mosque, 93
Saif, Mashal, 184
Salafis, 4, 5, 6, 8, 75, 153, 155, 166, 175, 191
Samarra, 53, 54, 58
Sarfaraz (journal), 16, 43
Sargodha, 63, 64, 77, 96, 101
Al-Sarim al-maslul ʿala shatim al-rasul (Ibn Taymiyya), 177
Satan, 41, 128, 129, 141
satyagraha, 128
Saudi Arabia, 5, 15, 122, 145, 146, 152, 153, 155, 178, 180, 184
SAVAK, 129
Sayyid Muhammad (Miran Sahib), 48, 49
sayyids, 32
Schaery-Eisenlohr, Roschanack, 122, 200n19
sectarianism, 2, 3, 7, 19, 36, 59, 94, 113, 114, 154, 155, 189; in colonial period, 17, 18, 21, 22, 25, 34, 39, 43, 50, 51, 56; definition of, 9, 10, 157, 158; economic explanations of, 154, 158, 159, 160, 184; and Ihsan Ilahi Zahir, 15, 152, 153, 162, 163, 164, 165, 166, 167, 168, 169; importance of ideas for, 158; outside origins of, 141, 145, 180; and Saudi Arabia, 15, 153, 154, 184; political explanation for, 15, 160, 161, 162, 183; and Shiʿis, 56, 139, 141, 149, 157, 179, 180, 181, 182, 183, 184, 186; and SSP, 169–79. *See also* Iranian Revolution; Sipah-i Sahabah-i Pakistan
sectarianization, 36, 154
Seraiki, 201n21
Shad, Muhammad Husayn, 135
Shafiʿis, 86, 132, 182
Shah, Pir Sayyid Muhammad Ghaus, 33
Shah, Sayyid Gulab ʿAli, 107
Shah, Zauqi, 190
shahada (third), 70, 77, 80, 81
Shahid (newspaper), 135
Shahid, Amir, 32
Shahid-i insaniyyat (Sayyid ʿAli Naqi Naqvi), 32, 71, 133, 144
Shah of Iran. *See* Pahlavi, Muhammad Reza Shah
Shahrastani, Muhammad b. ʿAbd al-Karim, 86, 87
Shahrudi, Sayyid Mahmud al-Husayni, 112
Shahrudi, Sayyid Muhammad, 64
Shaʾiq, Sayyid Akhtar Husayn, 44
Shaltut, Mahmud, 141, 166, 253n98
shariʿa, 9, 51, 57, 69, 84, 113, 131, 132, 156, 163, 178; and AISC, 25, 26, 27, 28, 30; and *mujtahid* of the age, 105, 106
Shariat Bill, 140, 163, 164
Shariaʿti, ʿAli, 56
Shariʿatmadari, Sayyid Muhammad Kazim, 13, 84, 110, 112; as leading *marjiʿ*, 115, 116, 117, 118
Shaybani, Muhammad b. al-Hasan al-, 40
Shaykhism, 60, 85; critique of, 84, 102, 226n41, 226n45, 236n220; esoteric aspects of, 61, 81, 85, 93, 94; in Pakistan, 61, 72, 79, 87, 139, 237n228
Shiʿa Mutalabat Committees, 126, 127
Shiʿah-i Haydar-i karrar, 74

Al-Shiʿa wa-ahl al-bayt (Zahir), 164
Al-Shiʿa wa-l-sunna (Zahir), 163
Al-Shiʿa wa-l-tashayyuʿ: Firaq wa-tarikh (Zahir), 166
Shiftah, ʿAli Hasnayn, 61, 85, 86, 233n167
Shiʿi cosmology, 5, 13, 81, 86
Shiʿi identity, 4, 36, 44, 45, 47, 68
Shiʿi mourning sessions. See *majalis*
Shiʿi *mujtahids*. See *mujtahids*
Shiʿi pilgrimage to shrines of Imams. See *ziyarat*
Shiʿi *qaum*, 27, 28, 31, 35, 37, 62, 139
Shiʿi reformists, 4, 5, 6, 7, 52, 54, 58, 137, 138, 187; attachment of, to Punjab, 12, 61, 62; and attacks on customs, 63, 107; influence of, 57, 58, 59, 60; and Iranian Revolution, 138, 139, 143, 148, 187; opposition to, 54, 56, 73, 74, 75, 76, 77, 83; and sectarianism, 13, 52, 59. *See also* Dhakko, Muhammad Husayn al-Najafi; Musavi ʿAliabadi, Sayyid ʿAli Sharaf al-Din
Shiʿi rights, 20, 45, 134, 244–45n69, 266n87
Shiʿi rituals, 2, 73, 74, 126, 137, 144, 149, 151, 172; "superstitious" character of, 12, 13, 59, 63, 64, 94
Shiʿism: as religious system, 34, 35, 36, 54, 55; popular forms of, 58, 59, 148, 149; spiritual/esoteric aspects of, 35, 50, 59, 60, 74, 82, 83, 224n15; transnational aspects of, 3, 4, 5, 6, 8, 9, 13, 19, 47, 48, 49, 96, 100, 113, 114, 118, 135, 186. *See also* Iranian Revolution; *marajiʿ al-taqlid*; *mujtahids*; religious authority; Shiʿi reformists; Shiʿi traditionalists; *taqlid*; *zakirs*
Shiʿi traditionalists, 5, 52, 55, 56, 58, 76, 139, 151; influence of, 57, 59; and attacks on reformists, 76, 77, 83; transcendent vision of God of, 13, 58, 77, 81, 86, 94; conceptions of Imams of, 69, 80, 81, 84, 85, 86; migration of, to Pakistan, 61, 62; and religious authority, 82, 84; and Sufism, 84, 88, 148, 239n267; and *taqrib*, 89, 90, 91, 92, 93, 94. *See also* Ansari, Muhammad Bashir; Sabiqi, Muhammad Hasnayn al-; Shiftah, ʿAli Hasnayn
Shiʿi *ʿulama*, 5, 8, 12, 45, 51, 60, 61, 76, 98, 166; authority of, 18, 54, 55, 70, 71, 72, 76, 100, 127, 130, 131, 143, 149, 186; conflicts of, with modernists, 18, 24, 26, 27, 28, 29, 30; hierarchy of, 82, 83, 91, 93, 94, 106; and Iranian Revolution, 6, 14, 129; local spaces of authority of, 5, 13, 14, 50, 96, 99, 107, 112, 117, 118, 186; political role of, 4, 123, 126, 127, 135, 148, 160; and progressive views, 22, 31, 32, 225n36; and reform, 12, 13, 54, 58, 64, 72, 225n27; and sectarianism, 181, 182, 183; skills of, 124, 125, 187; and *taqlid*, 18, 58, 108, 117; and transnational connections, 47, 50, 63, 123, 124, 128. See also *marajiʿ al-taqlid*; *mujtahids*; Shiʿi reformists; Shiʿi traditionalists
Shirazi, Sayyid ʿAbdullah, 70, 230n112
Shirazi, Sayyid Bashir Husayn, 54
shirk, 66, 68, 75, 141, 154
shrine cities (of Iran and Iraq), 3, 5, 50, 53, 64, 96, 97, 108, 110, 114, 118, 187, 188
Sialkot, 164
Sibaʿi, Mustafa al-, 190
Sibt-i Hasan, Sayyid, 120
Sikhs, 17, 47, 119, 132, 225n24
Sindh, 10, 31, 57, 61, 113, 114, 161, 171
Sindhi, 201n21
Sipah-i Sahabah-i Pakistan (SSP), 15, 22, 70, 89, 94, 154, 157, 168, 169, 170; and caliphate, 178, 179, 185; conception of *sahaba*, 174, 175, 184; and Iranian Revolution, 156, 162, 179, 185; and politics, 156, 182, 171, 172, 173, 184, 187; and Shiʿis, 172, 173, 174. *See*

also Faruqi, Ziya al-Rahman; Jhangvi, Haqq Navaz; Tariq, Abu Muʿawiya Aʿzam
Sirhindi, Shaykh Ahmad, 42, 88, 132
Sistani, Sayyid ʿAli al-, 188, 240n12
Skardu, 147
Smith, Wilferd Cantwell, 160
socialism, 31, 101, 109, 110, 115, 161, 164, 191, 208n52
social justice, 32, 109, 215n144
South Asian Muslims, 187, 189, 190
sovereignty, 21, 129, 132, 156, 179, 185, 191
Soviet Union, 133, 142, 166
spiritual capital, 5, 201n24
Stalin, Joseph, 45, 75
Subki, Taqi al-Din, 182
Sufi-Shiʿi synthesis, 4, 13, 84, 87, 88, 89, 94, 238n257
Sufism, 5, 8, 32, 55, 57, 133, 149, 190, 202n37; esoteric aspects of, 33, 168, 179, 266n112, 266n118; and politics, 109, 161; and religious authority, 33, 87, 88, 89
Suhravardi, Sir Hasan, 38
Sunni Islam, 1, 2, 4, 8, 9, 18, 22, 34, 35, 38, 69, 131, 166; conversion from, 32, 169; and Iran, 140, 192; and politics, 19, 21, 43, 51, 131, 174; and *sahaba*, 22, 23, 170, 174, 175, 182; and shared aspects with Shiʿism, 6, 47, 51, 84, 133, 141, 144, 149, 231n129. *See also* sectarianism; *taqrib*; unity
syncretism, 32, 175, 204n2
Syria, 190, 191, 202n40

Tabari, Abu Jaʿfar Muhammad al-, 176
Tabarra Agitation, 17, 21, 23, 33, 42, 49
Tabatabaʾi, Muhammad Husayn, 86
tabligh, 76, 106. *See also* Dar al-Tabligh-i Islami
Tablighi Jamaʿat, 190, 273n23
Tabrisi, Abu ʿAli al-Fadl al-, 130
Tabriz, 85, 115
taʿdil, 174, 269n155
Tahqiqi Dastavez, 181, 182, 183
tahrif, 15, 138, 165, 166, 171, 264–65n89
Tahrik-i Istiqlal, 163
Tahrik-i Nifaz-i Fiqh-i Jaʿfariyya (TNFJ), 14, 123, 134, 135, 137, 138, 141, 142, 144, 149, 158
takfir, 60, 88, 170, 173, 182, 269n152
Tanzim al-Muʾminin, 24, 44
taqiyya, 1, 33, 38, 92, 173, 214n123
taqlid, 13, 18, 35, 85, 96, 108, 143; limits of, 29, 30, 71, 90, 101; Shiʿi logic of, 58, 99, 102, 103, 107, 108, 117, 118, 124, 147, 200n14, 231n124; and Sunnis, 57, 131, 132. See also *marajiʿ al-taqlid*
taqrib, 13, 36, 59, 151, 165, 166, 174; and Iranian Revolution, 140, 141; and reformists, 70, 73; and traditionalists, 87, 90, 94
tarawih, 69, 141
Tarikhi Dastavez (Faruqi), 182
Tariq, Abu Muʿawiya Aʿzam, 171, 172, 173, 177, 267n125
tauhid, 58, 60, 66, 67, 68, 75, 77, 79, 94, 171, 176, 183
tawalla, 35
Taxila, 80
taʿzir, 84
taʿziya, 22, 45, 71
Tehran, 48, 107, 120, 121, 166, 187
Tehran University, 148
terrorism, 150, 190
Thaʿlabi, Abu Ishaq Ahmad b. Muhammad al-, 216n147
Thanavi, Ashraf ʿAli, 40, 47, 89, 90
Thanavi, Ihtisham al-Haqq, 51, 183
Tivanah, Malik Khizr Hayat, 46
Tobah Tek Singh, 169
Tolstoy, Leo, 32
transnational history, 6, 7
Turkey, 47, 49, 191
Tusi, Muhammad b. al-Hasan al-, 93, 130, 231n124

ʿulama, 3, 5, 6, 20, 27, 168, 169, 177, 178; authority of, 26, 91, 202n40, 202n41, 211n85, 211n88; definition of, 7, 8; and nation-state, 8, 15, 156, 161, 263n62; and Pakistan, 39, 40, 41, 51, 52, 160, 161, 162; and sectarianism, 7, 15, 154, 183; and transnational connections, 6, 137, 191, 192. *See also* Shiʿi ʿulama; Sipah-i Sahabah-i Pakistan; Zahir, Ihsan Ilahi
Ul-Haq, Zia, 14, 121, 136, 139, 162, 177; and Iran, 122, 136; and Islamization, 120, 127, 161, 163, 164; and Shiʿi activism, 134, 135, 145, 146, 151
ʿulum-i jadidah, 31
ʿUmar (Second Caliph), 22, 69, 140, 170, 182, 265n91
ʿUmar b. ʿAbd al-ʿAziz (Umayyad caliph), 177
umma, 140, 141, 144, 150, 176, 178
Umm Kulthum (wife of Caliph ʿUmar), 170
Unionist Party, 46, 47
United Kingdom, 80, 129, 167, 173
united nationalism, 20
United Nations, 93
United States, 80, 129, 133, 142, 145, 166, 180, 181
unity (among Muslims), 36, 37, 42, 59, 69, 74, 87, 89, 139, 140, 141, 165; among Shiʿis, 27, 38, 76, 106, 181. See also *taqrib*
Urdu, 2, 5, 10, 13, 47, 138, 139, 186, 201n21; Iranian outreach in, 115, 118, 128; lack of skills in, 76, 125, 152, 155; local scholarship in, 111, 153, 188; translation into, 5, 13, 66, 95, 111, 113, 118, 128, 190
ʿUsmani, Maulana Zafar Ahmad, 40
ʿUsmani, Shabbir Ahmad, 40, 41, 46, 51
usul al-din, 71, 72, 86
Usulis, 61, 102, 205–6n18
ʿUthman (Third Caliph), 22, 172, 177
Uttar Pradesh, 61

Verkaaik, Oskar, 57
Vihari, 54
vilayat-i faqih, 14, 73, 99, 122, 123, 132, 156, 179; and Sayyid ʿArif Husayn al-Husayni, 95, 142, 150; and Sayyid Javad Naqvi, 124, 146, 147, 148, 149, 184; and SSP, 162, 179, 185
vilayat-i takvini, 68, 75, 79, 82, 85, 148

Wahhabis, 49, 74, 75, 89, 145, 146, 184, 190, 191; and Ahl-i Hadis, 153, 154, 168; as designation in South Asia, 48, 67, 76, 77
wahy, 67, 86
wakil, 9, 58, 84, 106, 138, 150, 203n49
walaya, 87, 88, 89, 94, 238n257
wali, 36, 69, 230n109
Wali Allah Dihlavi, Shah, 132, 178–79, 271n185
wasi, 36
West Pakistan, 109, 161, 203n60
Wiederhold, Lutz, 175
wilaya, 82, 88, 89, 94, 146, 147, 148, 149, 184, 238n257
women, 32, 37, 57, 107, 111, 119, 129, 159, 173; and Iranian Revolution, 133, 134, 144
World War I, 1
World War II, 115

Ya ʿAli madad, 69, 80, 181
Yazdi, Ibrahim, 121
Yazdi, Muhammad Misbah, 93
Yazid b. Muʿawiya, 48, 71, 74, 128, 134, 181, 230n121

Zahab, Mariam Abou, 122, 123, 126, 127, 137, 138, 254n118
Zahedan, 119, 192
Zahir, Ihsan Ilahi, 5, 15, 140, 157, 168, 169, 173; closeness of, to Saudi Arabia, 152, 153, 168, 260n10, 264n85; political persona of, 163, 164; and Shiʿism, 163, 164, 165, 166, 167, 174, 184, 259–60n7

Zahir, Sayyid ʿAli, 39
zakat, 63, 72, 83, 134
zakirs, 17, 22, 59, 62, 106, 187; control of, over *majalis*, 143, 148, 151; economic interests of, 63, 64
Zaman, Muhammad Qasim, 139, 156, 162
Zaman, Sayyid Jaʿfar al-, 58, 90, 91, 92, 93, 94
zanjir, 144
zann, 102
Zaydi, Sayyid Muhammad Jaʿfar, 112, 113, 247n124
Zaydi, Sayyid Muhammad Qamar, 119, 120, 121, 124, 125, 126, 249n2
Zaynab (granddaughter of Muhammad), 133
ziyarat, 53, 70
Zuljanah, 64, 71
zulm, 120, 171
Zurarah b. Aʿyan, 82

ISLAMIC CIVILIZATION AND MUSLIM NETWORKS

Simon Wolfgang Fuchs, *In a Pure Muslim Land: Shiʿism between Pakistan and the Middle East* (2019).

Gary R. Bunt, *Hashtag Islam: How Cyber-Islamic Environments Are Transforming Religious Authority* (2018).

Ahmad Dallal, *Islam without Europe: Traditions of Reform in Eighteenth-Century Islamic Thought* (2018).

Irfan Ahmad, *Religion as Critique: Islamic Critical Thinking from Mecca to the Marketplace* (2017).

Scott Kugle, *When Sun Meets Moon: Gender, Eros, and Ecstasy in Urdu Poetry* (2016).

Kishwar Rizvi, *The Transnational Mosque: Architecture, Historical Memory, and the Contemporary Middle East* (2015).

Ebrahim Moosa, *What Is a Madrasa?* (2015).

Bruce Lawrence, *Who Is Allah?* (2015).

Edward E. Curtis IV, *The Call of Bilal: Islam in the African Diaspora* (2014).

Sahar Amer, *What Is Veiling?* (2014).

Rudolph T. Ware III, *The Walking Qur'an: Islamic Education, Embodied Knowledge, and History in West Africa* (2014).

Saʿdiyya Shaikh, *Sufi Narratives of Intimacy: Ibn ʿArabī, Gender, and Sexuality* (2012).

Karen G. Ruffle, *Gender, Sainthood, and Everyday Practice in South Asian Shiʿism* (2011).

Jonah Steinberg, *Ismaʿili Modern: Globalization and Identity in a Muslim Community* (2011).

Iftikhar Dadi, *Modernism and the Art of Muslim South Asia* (2010).

Gary R. Bunt, *iMuslims: Rewiring the House of Islam* (2009).

Fatemeh Keshavarz, *Jasmine and Stars: Reading More Than "Lolita" in Tehran* (2007).

Scott Kugle, *Sufis and Saints' Bodies: Mysticism, Corporeality, and Sacred Power in Islam* (2007).

Roxani Eleni Margariti, *Aden and the Indian Ocean Trade: 150 Years in the Life of a Medieval Arabian Port* (2007).

Sufia M. Uddin, *Constructing Bangladesh: Religion, Ethnicity, and Language in an Islamic Nation* (2006).

Omid Safi, *The Politics of Knowledge in Premodern Islam: Negotiating Ideology and Religious Inquiry* (2006).

Ebrahim Moosa, *Ghazālī and the Poetics of Imagination* (2005).

miriam cooke and Bruce B. Lawrence, eds., *Muslim Networks from Hajj to Hip Hop* (2005).

Carl W. Ernst, *Following Muhammad: Rethinking Islam in the Contemporary World* (2003).

MIX
Paper from
responsible sources
FSC® C013483
FSC
www.fsc.org